GREAT ATHLETES

GOLF & TENNIS

GREAT ATHLETES

GOLF & TENNIS

Edited by
The Editors of Salem Press

Special Consultant
Rafer Johnson

SALEM PRESS
Pasadena, California   Hackensack, New Jersey

Editor in Chief: Dawn P. Dawson

Editorial Director: Christina J. Moose	*Photo Editor:* Cynthia Breslin Beres
Managing Editor: R. Kent Rasmussen	*Acquisitions Editor:* Mark Rehn
Manuscript Editor: Christopher Rager	*Page Design and Layout:* James Hutson
Research Supervisor: Jeffry Jensen	*Additional Layout:* Frank Montaño and Mary Overell
Production Editor: Andrea Miller	*Editorial Assistant:* Brett Weisberg

Cover photos: © Photogolfer/Dreamstime.com; Kevin Lamarque/Reuters/Landov

Library of Congress Cataloging-in-Publication Data
Great athletes / edited by The Editors of Salem Press ; special consultant Rafer Johnson.
    p. cm.
Includes bibliographical references and index.
ISBN 978-1-58765-473-2 (set : alk. paper) — ISBN 978-1-58765-480-0 (golf, tennis : alk. paper)
1. Athletes—Biography—Dictionaries. I. Johnson, Rafer, 1935-   II. Salem Press.
GV697.A1G68 2009
796.0922—dc22
[B]
                                                                                                2009021905

First Printing

PRINTED IN THE UNITED STATES OF AMERICA

Contents

Publisher's Note

Great Athletes: Golf and Tennis is part of Salem Press's greatly expanded and redesigned *Great Athletes* series, which also includes self-contained volumes on baseball, basketball, boxing and soccer, football, Olympic sports, and racing and individual sports. The full 13-volume series presents articles on the lives, sports careers, and unique achievements of 1,470 outstanding competitors and champions in the world of sports. These athletes—many of whom have achieved world renown—represent more than 75 different nations and territories and more than 80 different sports. Their stories are told in succinct, 1,000-word-long profiles accessible in tone and style to readers in grades 7 and up.

The 13 *Great Athletes* volumes, which include a cumulative index volume, are built on the work of three earlier Salem Press publications designed for middle and high school readers—the 20 slender volumes of *The Twentieth Century: Great Athletes* (1992), their 3-volume supplement (1994), and the 8 stouter volumes of *Great Athletes, Revised* (2002). This new 13-volume edition retains articles on every athlete covered in those earlier editions and adds more than 415 entirely new articles—a 40 percent increase—to bring the overall total to 1,470 articles.

The present volume increases the numbers of articles on golfers from 47 to 73 and those on tennis players from 57 to 73, for a combined increase of nearly 40 percent. The content of other articles has been reviewed and updated as necessary, with many articles substantially revised, expanded, or replaced, and the bibliographical citations for virtually all articles have been undated. Information in every article is current up to at least the beginning of Spring, 2009.

Criteria for Inclusion

Within the pages of *Great Athletes: Golf and Tennis*, readers will see articles on virtually all the legends they expect to find: from Willie Anderson and Tommy Armour to Tiger Woods and Mickey Wright in golf and from Andre Agassi and Arthur Ashe to Serena and Venus Williams in tennis. The golf section in this volume also includes the legendary Babe Didrikson Zaharias, who was also a standout in basketball, softball, and track and field.

In selecting new names to add to *Great Athletes: Golf and Tennis*, first consideration was given to athletes whose extraordinary achievements have made their names household words in North America. These names include such established undeniable golfing stars as Ernie Els, Phil Mickelson, and Vijay Singh and such famous tennis players as Roger Federer and Pam Shriver. Consideration was next given to athletes who during the early twenty-first century appeared destined for future greatness, such as golfers Pádraig Harrington, Lorena Ochoa, and Michelle Wie and tennis players Ana Ivanovic, Rafael Nadal, and Maria Sharapova.

Organization

Each article covers the life and career of a single golfer or tennis player. Articles are arranged alphabetically within separate sections on golf and tennis. Every article is accompanied by at least one boxed table, summarizing the career statistics, honors and awards, records, and other milestones that set apart each great player. Most articles are also accompanied by photographs of their subjects. Every article also lists up-to-date bibliographical notes under the heading "Additional Sources." These sections list from three to five readily available books and articles containing information pertinent to the athlete and sport covered in the article. Appendixes at the end of the volume contain additional sources in published books and Web sites.

Averaging three pages in length, each article is written in clear language and presented in a uniform, easily readable format. All articles are divided into four subheaded sections that cover the athlete's life and achievements chronologically.

- *Early Life* presents such basic biographical information as vital dates, parentage, siblings, and early education. It also sketches the social milieu in which the athlete grew up and discusses other formative experiences.

- *The Road to Excellence* picks up where the athlete's earliest serious involvement in sports began. This section describes experiences and influences that shaped the subject's athletic prowess and propelled the athlete toward greatness in golf or tennis. These sections also often discuss obstacles—such as poverty, discrimination, and physical disabilities—that many great athletes have had to overcome.

- *The Emerging Champion* traces the subject's advance from the threshold of golf or tennis stardom to higher levels of achievement. This section explains the characteristics and circumstances that combined to make the athlete among the best in the world in his or her sport.

- *Continuing the Story* tracks the athlete's subsequent career, examining how the athlete may have set new goals and had achievements that inspired others. This section also offers insights into the athlete's life away from sports. Readers will also learn about the innovations and contributions that athletes have made to their sports and, in many cases, to society at large.

- *Summary* recapitulates the subject's story, paying special attention to honors that the subject has won and to the human qualities that have made the athlete special in the world of sports.

Appendixes

At the back of this volume, readers will find 8 appendixes, most of which are entirely new to this edition. The appendixes are arranged under these two headings:

- *Resources* includes a bibliography of recently published books on golf and tennis, a detailed, categorized listing of sites on the World Wide Web that provide golf and tennis information, a Glossary defining most of the specialized terms used in essays and 2 Time Lines that list all golfers and tennis players covered in essays in order of their birth dates.

- *All-Time Great Players* includes lists of members in the World Golf Hall of Fame and the International Tennis Hall of Fame and *Tennis* magazine's list of the 40 greatest players.

The *Cumulative Indexes* volume, which accompanies the full *Great Athletes* series, includes every appendix found in this and other volumes on specific sports, *plus* additional appendixes containing information that pertains to all sports. These appendixes include a general bibliography, a comprehensive Web site list, a Time Line integrating the names of all 1,470 athletes in *Great Athletes*, 2 lists of the greatest athletes of the twentieth century, 3 multisport halls of fame, and 10 different athlete-of-the-year awards.

Indexes

Following the Appendixes in *Great Athletes: Golf and Tennis*, readers will find indexes listing athletes by their names and countries. Because some athletes have competed in more than one sport, readers may wish also to consult the *Cumulative Indexes* volume. Its sport, country, and name indexes list all the athletes covered in the full *Great Athletes* series.

Acknowledgments

Once again, Salem Press takes great pleasure in thanking the 383 scholars and experts who wrote and updated the articles making *Great Athletes* possible. Their names can be found at the ends of the articles they have written and in the list of contributors that follows the "Introduction." We also take immense pleasure in again thanking our special consultant, Rafer Johnson, for bringing his unique insights to this project. As an Olympic champion and world record-holder in track and field's demanding decathlon, he has experienced an extraordinarily broad range of physical and mental challenges at the highest levels of competition. Moreover, he has a lifetime of experience working with, and closely observing, athletes at every level—from five-year-old soccer players to Olympic and professional champions. He truly understands what constitutes athletic greatness and what is required to achieve it. For this reason, readers will not want to overlook his "Introduction."

Acronyms Used in Articles

Salem's general practice is to use acronyms only after they have been explained within each essay. Because of the frequency with which many terms appear in *Great Athletes: Golf and Tennis,* that practice is partly suspended for the acronyms listed here:

ATP Association of Tennis Professionals

ESPN Entertainment and Sports Programming Network

LPGA Ladies Professional Golf Association

PGA Professional Golfers' Association

WTA Women's Tennis Association

Introduction

Five decades after reaching my own pinnacle of success in sports, I still get a thrill watching other athletes perform. I have competed with and against some of the greatest athletes in the world, watched others up close and from a distance, and read about still others. I admire the accomplishments of all of them, for I know something of what it takes to achieve greatness in sports, and I especially admire those who inspire others.

This revised edition of *Great Athletes* provides a wonderful opportunity for young readers to learn about the finest athletes of the modern era of sports. Reading the stories of the men and women in these pages carries me back to my own youth, when I first began playing games and became interested in sports heroes. Almost all sports interested me, but I gravitated to baseball, basketball, football, and track and field. Eventually, I dedicated most of my young adult years to track and field's decathlon, which I loved because its ten events allowed me to use many different skills.

Throughout those years, one thing remained constant: I wanted to *win*. To do that meant being the best that I could be. I wondered what I could learn from the lives of great athletes. From an early age I enjoyed reading about sports champions and wondered how they did as well as they did. What traits and talents did the greatest of them have? I gradually came to understand that the essence of greatness in sports lies in competition. In fact, the very word *athlete* itself goes back to a Greek word for "competitor." Being competitive is the single most important attribute any athlete can have, but other traits are important, too. Readers may gain insights into the athletes covered in these volumes by considering the ten events of the decathlon as symbols of ten traits that contribute to athletic greatness. All champions have at least a few of these traits; truly great champions have most of them.

Speed and Quickness

Decathlon events are spread over two days, with five events staged on each day. The first event is always the 100-meter dash—one of the most glamorous events in track and field. Men and women—such as Usain Bolt and Florence Griffith-Joyner—who capture its world records are considered the fastest humans on earth. In a race that lasts only a few seconds, speed is everything, and there is no room for mistakes.

Appropriately, speed is the first of the three standards of athletic excellence expressed in the Olympic motto, *Citius, altius, fortius* (faster, higher, stronger). Its importance in racing sports such as cycling, rowing, running, speed skating, swimming, and the triathlon is obvious: Athletes who reach the finish line soonest win; those who arrive later lose. Speed is also important in every sport that requires moving around a lot, such as baseball, basketball, boxing, football, handball, soccer, tennis, volleyball, water polo, and virtually all the events of track and field. The best athletes in these sports are usually fast.

Athletes who lack speed generally make up for it in other kinds of quickness. For example, while running speed has helped make some football quarterbacks—such as Vince Young—great, some quarterbacks who are slow afoot have achieved greatness with other forms of quickness. Joe Namath is an example. Although he was embarrassingly slow on his feet, he read opposing teams' defenses so fast that he could make lightning-quick decisions and release his passes faster than almost any other quarterback who played the game.

As important as speed is, there are a few sports in which it means little. Billiards, bowling, and golf, for example, all permit competitors to take considerable time responding to opponents' moves. Even so, speed can be important where one may least expect it. For example, major chess competitions are clocked, and making moves too slowly can cost players games.

Courage

The decathlon's second event, the long jump, represents one of the purest contests in sports: Competitors simply run up to a mark and jump as far as they can. Each jumper gets several tries, and only the best marks matter. While it sounds simple, it involves critical little things that can go wrong and ruin one's chance of winning. When the great Jesse Owens jumped in the 1936 Olympics in Berlin, for example, he missed his takeoff mark so many times that he risked disqualification. What saved him was the encouragement of a rival German jumper, who advised him to start his jump from well behind the regular takeoff mark. It takes courage to overcome the fear of making mistakes and concentrate on jumping. It also takes courage to overcome the fear of injury.

A great athlete may have abundant courage but rarely need to call upon it. However, most truly great athletes eventually face moments when they would fail if their courage abandoned them. In fact, courage is often what separates being good from being great. True courage should not be confused with the absence of fear, for it is the ability to overcome fear, including the very natural fears of injury and pain. A wonderful example is gymnast Kerri Strug's amazing spirit in the 1996 Olympics. Ignoring the pain of torn ligaments and a serious ankle sprain, she helped the U.S. women win a team gold medal by performing her final vault at great personal risk.

Some sports challenge athletes with real and persistent threats of serious injuries and even death. Among the most dangerous are alpine skiing, auto racing, boxing, football, horse racing, mountaineering, and rodeo—all of which have killed and disabled many fine athletes. No one can achieve greatness in such sports without exceptional courage.

Consider also the courage required to step up to bat against a baseball pitcher who throws hardballs mere inches away from your head at speeds of more than ninety miles an hour. Or, imagine preparing to dive from atop a 10-meter platform, resting only on your toes, with your heels projecting over the edge, knowing that your head will pass within inches of the rock-hard edge of the platform. Greg Louganis once cut his head open on such a dive. After he had his scalp stitched up, he returned to continue diving into a pool of water colored pink by his own blood. He won the competition.

Another kind of courage is needed to perform in the face of adversity that may have nothing to do with sport itself. The best known example of that kind of courage is the immortal Jackie Robinson, who broke the color line in baseball in 1947. As the first African American player in the modern major leagues, Jackie faced criticism, verbal harassment, and even physical abuse almost everywhere he played. He not only persevered but also had a career that would have been regarded as exceptional even if his color had never been an issue.

Strength

The shot put, the decathlon's third event, requires many special traits, but the most obvious is strength. The metal ball male shot putters heave weighs 16 pounds—more than an average bowling ball. Agility, balance, and speed are all important to the event, but together they can accomplish nothing without great strength. Strength is also the third standard expressed in the Olympic motto, *Citius, altius, fortius.*

Strength is especially valuable in sports that put competitors in direct physical contact with each other—sports such as basketball, boxing, football, and wrestling. Whenever athletes push and pull against each other, the stronger generally prevail. Strength is also crucial in sports requiring lifting, pulling, pushing, paddling, or propelling objects, or controlling vehicles or animals. Such sports include auto racing, baseball and softball, bodybuilding and weightlifting, canoeing and kayaking, golf, horse racing, rowing, and all track and field throwing events.

One sport in which the role of strength has never been underestimated is wrestling. One of the most impressive demonstrations of strength in the sport occurred at the 2000 Olympic Games at Sydney when Rulon Gardner, in a performance of a lifetime, defeated former Olympic champion Aleksandr Karelin in the super-heavyweight class of Greco-Roman wrestling.

Visualization

Visualization is the ability to see what one needs to do before actually doing it. Perhaps no sport better exemplifies its importance than the high jump—the decathlon's fourth event. In contrast to the long jump and throwing events—in which competitors strive to maximize distance in every effort, the high jump (like the pole vault) sets a bar at a fixed height that competitors must clear. Before jumping, they take time to study the bar and visualize what they must do to clear it. If the bar is set at 7 feet, a jump of 6 feet 11¾ inches fails; a jump of 8 feet succeeds, but counts only for 7 feet. To conserve strength for later jumps, jumpers must carefully calculate how much effort to exert at each height, and to do this, they must be able to visualize.

Great baseball and softball batters also visualize well. Before pitches even reach the plate, batters see the balls coming and visualize their bats hitting them. Likewise, great golfers see their balls landing on the greens before they even swing. Soccer players, such as Ronaldo, see the balls going into the goal before they even kick them. Billiard players, such as Jeanette Lee, see all the balls moving on the table before they even touch the cue balls. Bowlers, like Lisa Wagner, see the pins tumbling down before they release their balls.

Visualization is especially important to shooters, such as Lones Wigger, and archers, such as Denise Parker and Jay Barrs, who know exactly what their targets look like, as well as the spots from where they will fire, before they even take aim. In contrast to most other sports, they can practice in conditions almost identical to those in which they compete. However, the athletes against whom they compete have the same advantage, so the edge usually goes to those who visualize better.

Players in games such as basketball, hockey, soccer, and water polo fire upon fixed targets from constantly changing positions—often in the face of opponents doing everything they can to make them miss. Nevertheless, visualization is important to them as well. In basketball, players are said to be in a "groove," or a "zone," when they visualize shots so well they seem unable to miss. Kobe Bryant and Lisa Leslie are among the greatest visualizers in their sport, just as Babe Ruth, Hank Aaron, and Albert Pujols have been great at visualizing home runs in baseball. In tennis, I always admired Arthur Ashe's knack for planning matches in his mind, then systematically dismantling his opponents.

At another level, boxer Muhammad Ali was great at visualizing his entire future. Big, strong, and quick and able to move with the best of them, he had it all. I had the great pleasure of touring college campuses with him after we both won gold medals at the Rome Olympics in 1960. Muhammad (then known as Cassius Clay) had visualized his Olympic victory before it happened, and when I first knew him he was already reciting poetry and predicting what the future held for him. He saw it all in advance and called every move—something he became famous for later, when he taunted opponents by predicting the rounds in which he would knock them out.

Determination and Resilience

The final event of the first day of decathlon competition is the 400-meter run. Almost exactly a quarter mile, this race stands at the point that divides sprints from middle-distances. Should runners go all out, as in a sprint, or pace themselves, as middle-distance runners do? Coming as it does, as the last event of the exhausting first day of decathlon competition, the 400-meter race tests the mettle of decathletes by extracting one last great effort from them before they can rest up for the next day's grueling events. How they choose to run the race has to do with how determined they are to win the entire decathlon.

Every great athlete who wants to be a champion must have the determination to do whatever it takes to achieve that goal. Even so, determination alone is not enough. This was proven dramatically when basketball's Michael Jordan—whom journalists later voted the greatest athlete of the twentieth century—quit basketball in 1994 to fulfill his lifelong dream to play professional baseball. Despite working hard, he spent a frustrating season and a half in the minor leagues and merely proved two things: that determination alone cannot guarantee success, and that baseball is a more difficult sport than many people had realized.

Resilience, an extension of determination, is the ability to overcome adversity, or apparently hopeless situations, and to bounce back from outright defeat. Some might argue that no one can be greater than an athlete who never loses; however, athletes who continually win are never required to change what they do or do any soul searching. By contrast, athletes who lose must examine themselves closely and consider making changes. I have always felt that true greatness in sports is exemplified by the ability to come back from defeat, as heavyweight boxer Floyd Patterson did after losing his world title to Ingemar Johansson in a humiliating 3-round knockout in 1959. Only those athletes who face adversity and defeat can prove they have resilience.

Among athletes who have impressed me the most with their determination and resilience is speed skater Eric Heiden, who was not only the first American to win world speed-skating championships, but the first speed skater ever to win all five events in the Winter Olympics. Another amazingly determined athlete is Jim Abbott, who refused to allow the fact that he was born with only one hand stop him from becoming a Major League Baseball pitcher—one who even pitched a no-hit game. Who could not admire Bo Jackson? An all-star in both professional football and Major League Baseball, he suffered what appeared to be a career-ending football injury. After undergoing hip-joint replacement surgery, he defied all logic by returning to play several more seasons of baseball. Cyclist Lance Armstrong also falls into this category. He won multiple Tour de France championships after recovering from cancer.

Execution

Day two of the decathlon opens with the technically challenging 110-meter high hurdles. A brutally demanding event, it requires speed, leaping ability, and perfect timing. In short, it is an event that requires careful execution—the ability to perform precisely when it matters. Sports differ greatly in the precision of execution they demand. Getting off great throws in the discus, shot put, and javelin, for example, requires superb execution, but the direction in which the objects go is not critical. By contrast, archers, shooters, and golfers must hit precise targets. Some sports not only demand that execution be precise but also that it be repeated. A baseball pitcher who throws two perfect strikes fails if the opposing batter hits the third pitch over the fence. Likewise, a quarterback who leads his team down the field with five consecutive perfect passes fails if his next pass is intercepted.

Consider the differences between the kind of execution demanded by diving and pole vaulting. Divers lose points if their toes are not straight the moment they enter the water. By contrast, pole vaulters can land any way they want, so long as they clear the bar. Moreover, a diver gets only one chance on each dive, while pole vaulters get three chances at each height they attempt—and they can even skip certain heights to save energy for later jumps at greater heights. On the other hand, a diver who executes a dive badly will merely get a poor score, while a pole vaulter who misses too many jumps will get no score at all—which is exactly what happened to decathlete Dan O'Brien in the 1992 U.S. Olympic Trials. Although Dan was the world's top decathlete at that time, his failure to clear a height in the pole vault kept him off the Olympic team. (To his credit, he came back to win a gold medal in 1996.)

Figure skating and gymnastics are other sports that measure execution with a microscope. In gymnastics, the standard of perfection is a score of ten—which was first achieved in the Olympics by Nadia Comăneci in 1976. However, scores in those sports are not based on objective measures but on the evaluations of judges, whose own standards can and do change. By contrast, archery, shooting, and bowling are unusual in being sports that offer objective standards of perfection. In bowling, that standard is the 300 points awarded to players who bowl all strikes.

Among all athletes noted for their execution, one in particular stands out in my estimation: golf's Tiger Woods. After Tiger had played professionally for only a few years, he established himself as one of the greatest golfers ever. He has beaten the best that golf has had to offer by record margins in major competitions, and wherever he plays, he is the favorite to win. Most impressive is his seeming ability to do whatever he needs to win, regardless of the situation. Few athletes in any sport, or in any era, have come close to matching Tiger's versatile and consistent execution.

Focus

After the high hurdles, the decathlon's discus event is a comparative relief. Nevertheless, it presents its own special demands, one of which is focus—the ability to maintain uninterrupted concentration. Like shot putters, discus throwers work within a tiny circle, within which they must concentrate all their attention and all their energy into throwing the heavy disk as far as they can.

Not surprisingly, one of the greatest discus throwers in history, Al Oerter, was also one of the greatest examples of focus in sports. His four gold medals between 1956 and 1968 made him the first track and field athlete in Olympic history to win any event four times in a row. In addition to beating out the best discus throwers in the world four consecutive times, he improved his own performance at each Olympiad and even won with a serious rib injury in 1964. Eight years after retiring from competition, he returned at age forty to throw the discus farther than ever and earn a spot as an alternate on the 1980 U.S. Olympic team.

Important in all sports, focus is especially important in those in which a single lapse in concentration may result in instant defeat. In boxing, a knockout can suddenly end a bout. Focus may be even more crucial in wrestling. Wrestlers grapple each other continuously, probing for openings that will allow them to pin their opponents. Few sports match wrestling in nonstop intensity; a single split-second lapse on the part of a wrestler can spell disaster. Great wrestlers, such as Cael Sanderson and Aleksandr Karelin, must therefore rank among the most focused athletes in history.

Balance and Coordination

Of all the decathlon events, the most difficult to perform is the pole vault. Think of what it entails: Holding long skinny poles, vaulters run at full speed down a narrow path toward a pit; then, without breaking stride, push the tips of their poles into a tiny slot, propel their bodies upward, and use the poles to flip themselves over bars more than two or three times their height above the ground, finally to drop down on the opposite side. Success in the pole vault demands many traits, but the most important are balance and coordination. Vaulters use their hands, feet, and bodies, all at the same time, and do everything at breakneck speed, with almost no margin for error. There are no uncoordinated champion pole vaulters.

Despite its difficulty, pole vaulting is an event in which some decathletes have performed especially well—perhaps because they, as a group, have versatile skills. I have long taken pride in the fact that my close friend, college teammate, and Olympic rival, C. K. Yang, once set a world record in the pole vault during a decathlon. C. K.'s record was all the more impressive because he achieved it midway through the second day of an intense competition. Imagine what balance and coordination he must have had to propel his body over the record-breaking height after having subjected it to the wear and tear of seven other events.

I cannot think of any athlete, in any sport, who demonstrated more versatility in coordination and balance than Michael Jordan, who could seemingly score from any spot on the floor, at any time, and under any conditions. Not only did he always have

his offensive game together, he was also one of the greatest defensive players in the game. Moreover, his mere presence brought balance to his entire team.

Preparation

The ninth event of the decathlon is the javelin—a throwing event that goes back to ancient times. A more difficult event than it may appear to be, it requires more than its share of special preparation. This may be why we rarely see athletes who compete in both the javelin and other events, though the versatile Babe Didrikson Zaharias was an exception.

Along with determination—to which it is closely allied—preparation is a vital trait of great athletes, especially in modern competition. It is no longer possible for even the greatest natural athletes to win against top competition without extensive preparation, which means practice, training for strength and stamina, proper diet and rest, and studying opponents diligently. Football players, especially quarterbacks and defensive backs, spend hours before every game studying films of opponents.

I was fortunate to grow up with an athlete who exemplifies preparation: my younger brother, Jimmy Johnson, who would become defensive back for the San Francisco 49ers for seventeen years and later be elected to the Pro Football Hall of Fame. Every week, Jimmy had to face a completely different set of pass receivers, but he was always ready because he studied their moves and trained himself to run backward fast enough to keep offenses in front of him so he could see every move they made. Coach Tom Landry of the Dallas Cowboys once told me that he always had the Cowboys attack on the side opposite from Jimmy.

Another exceptionally well prepared athlete was Magic Johnson, the great Lakers basketball guard, who played every position on the floor in more than one game. During his rookie season he had one of the greatest performances in playoff history during the NBA Finals. When a health problem prevented the Lakers' great center, Kareem Abdul-Jabbar, from playing in the sixth game against Philadelphia, Magic stunned everyone by filling in for him at center and scoring 44 points. He went on to become one of the great point guards in basketball history because he always knew where every player on the court should be at every moment.

Stamina

If there is one event that most decathletes dread, it is the grueling 1,500-meter race that concludes the two-day competition. While C. K. Yang once set a world-record in the pole vault during a decathlon, no decathlete has ever come close to anything even resembling a world-class mark in the 1,500 meters. On the other hand, it is probable that no world-class middle-distance runner has ever run a 1,500-meter race immediately after competing in nine other events. To win a decathlon, the trick is not to come in first in this final race, but simply to survive it. For decathletes, it is not so much a race as a test of stamina.

When I competed in the decathlon in the Rome Olympics of 1960, I had to go head-to-head against my friend C. K. Yang through nine events, all the while knowing that the gold medal would be decided in the last event—the 1,500 meters. C. K. was one of the toughest and most durable athletes I have ever known, and I realized I could not beat him in that race. However, after the javelin, I led by enough points so that all I had to do was stay close to him. I managed to do it and win the gold medal, but running that race was not an experience I would care to repeat.

Stamina is not really a skill, but a measure of the strength to withstand or overcome exhaustion. Rare is the sport that does not demand some stamina. Stamina can be measured in a single performance—such as a long-distance race—in a tournament, or in the course of a long season.

The classic models of stamina are marathon runners, whose 26-plus-mile race keeps them moving continuously for more than two hours. Soccer is one of the most demanding of stamina among team sports. Its players move almost constantly and may run as far as 5 miles in a 90-minute game that allows few substitutions. Basketball players run nearly as much as soccer players, but their games are shorter and allow more substitutions and rest periods. However, the sport can be even more tiring than soccer because its teams play more frequently and play more games overall. Baseball players provide yet another contrast. They spend a great deal of time during their games sitting on the bench, and when they are on the field, players other than the pitcher and catcher rarely need to exert themselves more than a few seconds at a time. However, their season has the most games of all, and their constant travel is draining. All these sports and others demand great stamina from their players, and their greatest players are usually those who hold up the best.

To most people, chess seems like a physically undemanding game. However, its greatest players must be in top physical condition to withstand the unrelenting mental pressure of tournament and match competitions, which can last for weeks. Bobby Fisher, one of the game's greatest—and most eccentric—champions, exercised heavily when he competed in order to stay in shape. Even sprinters who spend only 10 or 11 seconds on the track in each race, need stamina. In order to reach the finals of major competitions, they must endure the physical and mental strains of several days of preliminary heats.

In reducing what makes athletes great to just ten traits, I realize that I have oversimplified things, but that matters little, as my purpose here is merely to introduce readers to what makes the athletes in these volumes great. Within these pages you will find stories exemplifying many other traits, and that is good, as among the things that make athletes endlessly fascinating are their diversity and complexity.

Rafer Johnson

Contributors

Randy L. Abbott
University of Evansville

Tony Abbott
Trumbull, Connecticut

Michael Adams
*City College of New York
Graduate Center*

Patrick Adcock
Henderson State University

Amy Adelstein
Toluca Lake, California

Richard Adler
University of Michigan, Dearborn

Paul C. Alexander II
Southern Illinois University

Elizabeth Jeanne Alford
*Southern Illinois University,
Carbondale*

Eleanor B. Amico
Whitewater, Wisconsin

Ronald L. Ammons
University of Findlay

Earl Andresen
University of Texas, Arlington

David L. Andrews
*University of Illinois, Urbana-
Champaign*

Frank Ardolino
University of Hawaii

Vikki M. Armstrong
Fayetteville State University

Bryan Aubrey
Maharishi International University

Patti Auer
United States Gymnastics Federation

Philip Bader
Pasadena, California

Sylvia P. Baeza
Applied Ballet Theater

Amanda J. Bahr-Evola
*Southern Illinois University,
Edwardsville*

Alan Bairner
Loughborough University

JoAnn Balingit
University of Delaware

Susan J. Bandy
United States International University

Jessie F. Banks
University of Southern Colorado

Linda Bannister
Loyola Marymount University

C. Robert Barnett
Marshall University

David Barratt
Montreat College

Maryanne Barsotti
Warren, Michigan

Bijan Bayne
*Association for Professional Basketball
Research*

Barbara C. Beattie
Sarasota, Florida

Suzanne M. Beaudet
University of Maine, Presque Isle

Joseph Beerman
*Borough of Manhattan Community
College, CUNY*

Keith J. Bell
Western Carolina University

Stephen T. Bell
Independent Scholar

Alvin K. Benson
Utah Valley University

Chuck Berg
University of Kansas

S. Carol Berg
College of St. Benedict

Milton Berman
University of Rochester

Terry D. Bilhartz
Sam Houston State University

Cynthia A. Bily
Adrian College

Nicholas Birns
New School University

Joe Blankenbaker
Georgia Southern University

Carol Blassingame
Texas A&M University

Elaine M. Blinde
*Southern Illinois University,
Carbondale*

Harold R. Blythe, Jr.
Eastern Kentucky University

Jo-Ellen Lipman Boon
Independent Scholar

Trevor D. Bopp
Texas A&M University

Stephen Borelli
USA Today

John Boyd
Appalachian State University

Marlene Bradford
Texas A&M University

Michael R. Bradley
Motlow College

Carmi Brandis
Fort Collins, Colorado

Kevin L. Brennan
Ouachita Baptist University

Matt Brillinger
Carleton University

John A. Britton
Francis Marion University

Norbert Brockman
St. Mary's University of San Antonio

Howard Bromberg
University of Michigan Law School

Valerie Brooke
Riverside Community College

Dana D. Brooks
West Virginia University

Alan Brown
Livingston University

Valerie Brown
*Northwest Kansas Educational
    Service Center*

Thomas W. Buchanan
Ancilla Domini College

Fred Buchstein
John Carroll University

David Buehrer
Valdosta State University

Cathy M. Buell
San Jose State University

Michael H. Burchett
Limestone College

Edmund J. Campion
University of Tennessee, Knoxville

Peter Carino
Indiana State University

Lewis H. Carlson
Western Michigan University

Russell N. Carney
Missouri State University

Bob Carroll
*Professional Football Researchers
    Association*

Culley C. Carson
University of North Carolina

Craig Causer
Pompton Lakes, New Jersey

David Chapman
*North American Society of
    Sports Historians*

Paul J. Chara, Jr.
Northwestern College

Frederick B. Chary
Indiana University Northwest

Jerry E. Clark
Creighton University

Rhonda L. Clements
Hofstra University

Douglas Clouatre
MidPlains Community College

Kathryn A. Cochran
University of Kansas

Susan Coleman
West Texas A&M University

Caroline Collins
Quincy University

Brett Conway
Namseoul University

Carol Cooper
University of Northern Iowa

Richard Hauer Costa
Texas A&M University

Michael Coulter
Grove City College

David A. Crain
South Dakota State University

Louise Crain
South Dakota State University

Scott A. G. M. Crawford
Eastern Illinois University

Lee B. Croft
Arizona State University

Ronald L. Crosbie
Marshall University

Thomas S. Cross
Texas A&M University

Brian Culp
Indiana University

Michael D. Cummings, Jr.
Madonna University

Joanna Davenport
Auburn University

Kathy Davis
North Carolina State University

Mary Virginia Davis
California State University, Sacramento

Buck Dawson
International Swimming Hall of Fame

Dawn P. Dawson
Pasadena, California

Margaret Debicki
Los Angeles, California

Bill Delaney
San Diego, California

Paul Dellinger
Wytheville, Virginia

Andy DeRoche
Front Range Community College

James I. Deutsch
Smithsonian Institution

Contributors

Joseph Dewey
University of Pittsburgh, Johnstown

M. Casey Diana
Arizona State University

Randy J. Dietz
South Carolina State University

Jonathan E. Dinneen
VeriSign, Inc.

Marcia B. Dinneen
Bridgewater State College

Dennis M. Docheff
Whitworth College

Cecilia Donohue
Madonna University

Pamela D. Doughty
Texas A&M University

Thomas Drucker
University of Wisconsin, Whitewater

Jill Dupont
University of Chicago

William G. Durick
Blue Valley School District

W. P. Edelstein
Los Angeles, California

Bruce L. Edwards
Bowling Green State University

William U. Eiland
University of Georgia

Henry A. Eisenhart
University of Oklahoma

Kenneth Ellingwood
Los Angeles, California

Julie Elliott
Indiana University South Bend

Mark R. Ellis
University of Nebraska, Kearney

Robert P. Ellis
Northboro, Massachusetts

Don Emmons
Glendale News-Press

Robert T. Epling
*North American Society of
Sports Historians*

Thomas L. Erskine
Salisbury University

Steven G. Estes
California State University, Fullerton

Don Evans
The College of New Jersey

Jack Ewing
Boise, Idaho

Kevin Eyster
Madonna University

Norman B. Ferris
Middle Tennessee State University

John W. Fiero
University of Southwestern Louisiana

Paul Finkelman
Brooklyn Law School

Paul Finnicum
Arkansas State University

Jane Brodsky Fitzpatrick
*Graduate Center, City University
of New York*

Michael J. Fratzke
Indiana Wesleyan University

Tom Frazier
Cumberland College

A. Bruce Frederick
*International Gymnastics Hall of Fame
and Museum*

Daniel J. Fuller
Kent State University

Jean C. Fulton
Maharishi International University

Carter Gaddis
Tampa Tribune

Thomas R. Garrett
Society for American Baseball Research

Jan Giel
Drexel University

Daniel R. Gilbert
Moravian College

Duane A. Gill
Mississippi State University

Vincent F. A. Golphin
The Writing Company

Bruce Gordon
Auburn University, Montgomery

Margaret Bozenna Goscilo
University of Pittsburgh

John Gould
Independent Scholar

Karen Gould
Austin, Texas

Lewis L. Gould
University of Texas, Austin

Larry Gragg
University of Missouri, Rolla

Lloyd J. Graybar
Eastern Kentucky University

Wanda Green
University of Northern Iowa

William C. Griffin
Appalachian State University

Irwin Halfond
McKendree College

Jan Hall
Columbus, Ohio

Roger D. Hardaway
*Northwestern Oklahoma State
University*

William Harper
Purdue University

Robert Harrison
University of Arkansas Community College

P. Graham Hatcher
Shelton State Community College

Karen Hayslett-McCall
University of Texas, Dallas

Leslie Heaphy
Kent State University, Stark

Bernadette Zbicki Heiney
Lock Haven University of Pennsylvania

Timothy C. Hemmis
Edinboro University of Pennsylvania

Steve Hewitt
University of Birmingham

Carol L. Higy
Methodist College

Randall W. Hines
Susquehanna University

Joseph W. Hinton
Portland, Oregon

Arthur D. Hlavaty
Yonkers, New York

Carl W. Hoagstrom
Ohio Northern University

William H. Hoffman
Fort Meyers, Florida

Kimberley M. Holloway
King College

John R. Holmes
Franciscan University of Steubenville

Joseph Horrigan
Pro Football Hall of Fame

William L. Howard
Chicago State University

Shane L. Hudson
Texas A&M University

Mary Hurd
East Tennessee State University

Raymond Pierre Hylton
Virginia Union University

Shirley Ito
Amateur Athletic Foundation of Los Angeles

Frederick Ivor-Campbell
North American Society of Sports Historians

Shakuntala Jayaswal
University of New Haven

Doresa A. Jennings
Shorter College

Albert C. Jensen
Central Florida Community College

Jeffry Jensen
Altadena, California

Bruce E. Johansen
University of Nebraska, Omaha

Lloyd Johnson
Campbell University

Mary Johnson
University of South Florida

Alexander Jordan
Boston University

David Kasserman
Rowan University

Robert B. Kebric
University of Louisville

Rodney D. Keller
Ricks College

Barbara J. Kelly
University of Delaware

Kimberley H. Kidd
East Tennessee State University
King College

Leigh Husband Kimmel
Indianapolis, Indiana

Tom Kinder
Bridgewater College

Joe King
Alameda Journal

Jane Kirkpatrick
Auburn University, Montgomery

Paul M. Klenowski
Thiel College

Darlene A. Kluka
University of Alabama, Birmingham

Lynne Klyse
California State University, Sacramento

Bill Knight
Western Illinois University

Francis M. Kozub
College at Brockport, State University of New York

Lynn C. Kronzek
University of Judaism

Shawn Ladda
Manhattan College

P. Huston Ladner
University of Mississippi

Philip E. Lampe
University of the Incarnate Word

Tom Lansford
University of Southern Mississippi

Eugene Larson
Los Angeles Pierce College

Rustin Larson
Maharishi International University

Kevin R. Lasley
Eastern Illinois University

Mary Lou LeCompte
University of Texas, Austin

Denyse Lemaire
Rowan University

Contributors

Victor Lindsey
East Central University

Alar Lipping
Northern Kentucky University

Janet Long
Pasadena, California

M. Philip Lucas
Cornell College

Leonard K. Lucenko
Montclair State College

R. C. Lutz
Madison Advisors

Robert McClenaghan
Pasadena, California

Arthur F. McClure
Central Missouri State University

Roxanne McDonald
New London, New Hampshire

Alan McDougall
University of Guelph

Mary McElroy
Kansas State University

Thomas D. McGrath
Baylor University

Marcia J. Mackey
Central Michigan University

Michelle C. K. McKowen
New York, New York

John McNamara
Beltsville, Maryland

Joe McPherson
East Tennessee State University

Paul Madden
Hardin Simmons University

Mark J. Madigan
University of Vermont

Philip Magnier
Maharishi International University

H. R. Mahood
Memphis State University

Barry Mann
Atlanta, Georgia

Nancy Farm Mannikko
*Centers for Disease Control &
Prevention*

Robert R. Mathisen
Western Baptist College

Russell Medbery
Colby-Sawyer College

Joella H. Mehrhof
Emporia State University

Julia M. Meyers
Duquesne University

Ken Millen-Penn
Fairmont State College

Glenn A. Miller
Texas A&M University

Lauren Mitchell
St. Louis, Missouri

Christian H. Moe
*Southern Illinois University,
Carbondale*

Mario Morelli
Western Illinois University

Caitlin Moriarity
Brisbane, California

Elizabeth C. E. Morrish
State University of New York, Oneonta

Todd Moye
Atlanta, Georgia

Tinker D. Murray
Southwest Texas State University

Alex Mwakikoti
University of Texas, Arlington

Alice Myers
Bard College at Simon's Rock

Michael V. Namorato
University of Mississippi

Jerome L. Neapolitan
Tennessee Technological University

Alicia Neumann
San Francisco, California

Caryn E. Neumann
Miami University of Ohio, Middletown

Mark A. Newman
University of Virginia

Betsy L. Nichols
Reynoldsburg, Ohio

James W. Oberly
University of Wisconsin, Eau Claire

George O'Brien
Georgetown University

Wendy Cobb Orrison
Washington and Lee University

Sheril A. Palermo
Cupertino, California

R. K. L. Panjabi
Memorial University of Newfoundland

Robert J. Paradowski
Rochester Institute of Technology

Thomas R. Park
Florida State University

Robert Passaro
Tucson, Arizona

Cheryl Pawlowski
University of Northern Colorado

Leslie A. Pearl
San Diego, California

Judy C. Peel
*University of North Carolina,
Wilmington*

Martha E. Pemberton
Galesville, Wisconsin

William E. Pemberton
University of Wisconsin, La Crosse

Lori A. Petersen
Minot, North Dakota

Nis Petersen
Jersey City State College

Douglas A. Phillips
Sierra Vista, Arizona

Debra L. Picker
Long Beach, California

Betty L. Plummer
Dillard University

Bill Plummer III
*Amateur Softball Association
of America*

Michael Polley
Columbia College

Francis Poole
University of Delaware

Jon R. Poole
*Virginia Polytechnic Institute and State
University*

David L. Porter
William Penn University

John G. Powell
Greenville, South Carolina

Victoria Price
Lamar University

Maureen J. Puffer-Rothenberg
Valdosta State University

Christopher Rager
San Dimas, California

Steven J. Ramold
Eastern Michigan University

C. Mervyn Rasmussen
Renton, Washington

John David Rausch, Jr.
West Texas A&M University

Abe C. Ravitz
*California State University,
Dominguez Hills*

Nancy Raymond
International Gymnast Magazine

Shirley H. M. Reekie
San Jose State University

Christel Reges
Grand Valley State University

Victoria Reynolds
Mandeville High School

Betty Richardson
*Southern Illinois University,
Edwardsville*

Alice C. Richer
Spaulding Rehabilitation Center

David R. Rider
Bloomsburg University

Robert B. Ridinger
Northern Illinois University

Edward A. Riedinger
Ohio State University Libraries

Edward J. Rielly
Saint Joseph's College of Maine

Jan Rintala
Northern Illinois University

Thurman W. Robins
Texas Southern University

Vicki K. Robinson
*State University of New York,
Farmingdale*

Mark Rogers
University of Chicago

Wynn Rogers
San Dimas, California

Carl F. Rothfuss
Central Michigan University

William B. Roy
United States Air Force Academy

A. K. Ruffin
George Washington University

Todd Runestad
American Ski Association

J. Edmund Rush
Boise, Idaho

Michael Salmon
*Amateur Athletic Foundation of
Los Angeles*

Rebecca J. Sankner
*Southern Illinois University,
Carbondale*

Timothy M. Sawicki
Canisius College

Ronald C. Sawyer
*State University of New York,
Binghamton*

Ann M. Scanlon
*State University of New York, College at
Cortland*

Daniel C. Scavone
University of Southern Indiana

Elizabeth D. Schafer
Loachapoka, Alabama

Lamia Nuseibeh Scherzinger
Indiana University

Walter R. Schneider
Central Michigan University

J. Christopher Schnell
Southeast Missouri State University

Kathleen Schongar
The May School

Stephen Schwartz
Buffalo State College

Deborah Service
Los Angeles, California

Chrissa Shamberger
Ohio State University

Contributors

Tom Shieber
Mt. Wilson, California

Theodore Shields
Surfside Beach, South Carolina

Peter W. Shoun
East Tennessee State University

R. Baird Shuman
University of Illinois, Urbana-Champaign

Thomas J. Sienkewicz
Monmouth College

Richard Slapsys
University of Massachusetts, Lowell

Elizabeth Ferry Slocum
Pasadena, California

John Slocum
Pasadena, California

Gary Scott Smith
Grove City College

Harold L. Smith
University of Houston, Victoria

Ira Smolensky
Monmouth College

A. J. Sobczak
Santa Barbara, California

Ray Sobczak
Salem, Wisconsin

Mark Stanbrough
Emporia State University

Alison Stankrauff
Indiana University South Bend

Michael Stellefson
Texas A&M University

Glenn Ellen Starr Stilling
Appalachian State University

Gerald H. Strauss
Bloomsburg University

Deborah Stroman
University of North Carolina

James Sullivan
California State University, Los Angeles

Cynthia J. W. Svoboda
Bridgewater State College

William R. Swanson
South Carolina State College

J. K. Sweeney
South Dakota State University

Charles A. Sweet, Jr.
Eastern Kentucky University

Glenn L. Swygart
Tennessee Temple University

James Tackach
Roger Williams University

Felicia Friendly Thomas
California State Polytechnic University, Pomona

Jennifer L. Titanski
Lock Haven University of Pennsylvania

Evelyn Toft
Fort Hays State University

Alecia C. Townsend Beckie
New York, New York

Anh Tran
Wichita State University

Marcella Bush Trevino
Texas A&M University, Kingsville

Kathleen Tritschler
Guilford College

Brad Tufts
Bucknell University

Karen M. Turner
Temple University

Sara Vidar
Los Angeles, California

Hal J. Walker
University of Connecticut

Spencer Weber Waller
Loyola University Chicago

Annita Marie Ward
Salem-Teikyo University

Shawncey Webb
Taylor University

Chuck Weis
American Canoe Association

Michael J. Welch
Guilford College

Paula D. Welch
University of Florida

Allen Wells
Bowdoin College

Winifred Whelan
St. Bonaventure University

Nan White
Maharishi International University

Nicholas White
Maharishi International University

Rita S. Wiggs
Methodist College

Ryan K. Williams
University of Illinois, Springfield

Brook Wilson
Independent Scholar

John Wilson
Wheaton, Illinois

Rusty Wilson
Ohio State University

Wayne Wilson
Amateur Athletic Foundation of Los Angeles

John D. Windhausen
St. Anselm College

Michael Witkoski
University of South Carolina

Philip Wong
Pasadena, California

Greg Woo
Independent Scholar

Sheri Woodburn
Cupertino, California

Jerry Jaye Wright
Pennsylvania State University, Altoona

Scott Wright
University of St. Thomas

Lisa A. Wroble
Redford Township District Library

Frank Wu
University of Wisconsin, Madison

Brooke K. Zibel
University of North Texas

Golf

Willie Anderson

Born: October 21, 1879
  North Berwick, Scotland
Died: October 25, 1910
  Philadelphia, Pennsylvania
Also known as: William Law Anderson (full
  name)

Early Life

William Law Anderson was born in North Berwick,
Scotland, in 1879. His father, Tom Anderson, was
the head professional at the North Berwick Golf
Club, one of the most famous in Scotland. Willie developed an interest in golf at an early age and participated in tournaments among the local caddies
even before he was a teenager. Not much is known
about Willie's early development. Although
slightly built, he was strong and showed golfing talent as soon as he began playing. He was
friendly and well liked, but on occasion he
displayed spells of temper and introversion.

The Road to Excellence

Although Scotland was the center of the golf
world during the nineteenth century, Willie
decided to try his luck in the United States.
His friend Frank Slazenger, the owner of a
sporting goods company, influenced Willie's
decision. Slazenger found a place for Willie
as the professional at a club in Rhode Island.
Willie showed remarkable enterprise in coming to the United States and taking this job;
he was only fourteen years old.

To understand Willie's rise to the top, it is
important to grasp that golf at the turn of
the twentieth century differed greatly from
golf of the present day. Golfers in Willie's
time used a gutta-percha ball that did not go
very far and was difficult to control. Golf
courses tended to have a large amount of
rough, and golfers did not have the clubs
needed to get out of trouble spots such as
sand traps. Thus, accuracy counted for much
more than distance. A player who could
keep the ball straight and in play had a commanding edge over his competitors.

Willie's slight physique was perfect for the style
of play prominent in the early days of modern golf.
His constant practice and naturally smooth swing
made him one of the straightest hitters of his time.
His skill was so great that he almost won the 1897
U.S. Open when he was seventeen years old. He
lost when another golfer, Joe Lloyd, scored a three
on the final hole, in those days a remarkable score.

An obstacle confronted Willie on his progress
toward the top. In his time, professional golfers
were not highly paid and respected athletes as
they are today. People in polite society viewed them
as ruffians not entitled to courteous treatment.
They had the social status of servants and were not
allowed to enter the dining rooms of the club-

Willie Anderson. (Courtesy of United States Golf Association)

Major Championship Victories

1901, 1903-05   U.S. Open

Other Notable Victories

1902, 1904, 1908-09   Western Open

houses at which they played. Most golf professionals accepted these terms, socializing among themselves. Willie was different. He bitterly resented condescending treatment and sometimes protested against it. The lack of respect to which he was subjected led him to drink heavily, a problem that plagued him later in life.

The Emerging Champion

By 1901, Willie was ready for the top. In the U.S. Open that year at Myopia, New York, the course was extremely difficult. It had been specially lengthened for the tournament, and the greens were exceptionally fast. Under these conditions, a short putt of two or three feet could run off the green entirely. Many of the top English and Scottish golfers came to try their hand.

After four rounds, Willie was tied for the lead with Alex Smith, a golfer who became Willie's greatest rival. In a playoff, Willie defeated Smith 85 to 86. These scores seem high by the standards of golfers using late twentieth century equipment, but were significant achievements in the early part of the twentieth century. Some experts who saw him play rated Willie as among the best the game has ever known.

A new problem soon threatened his seemingly impregnable position. Coburn Haskell, an American golfer, invented a new rubber ball that was more accurate and traveled farther than the gutta-percha ball. Distance, not Willie's strong point, was much more important, and the new ball required different techniques. Players schooled in the old way who wanted to remain at the top needed to revamp their games.

Continuing the Story

Willie had the necessary determination and skill to meet this challenge. Fortunately for him, the 1903 U.S. Open was held at the Balustrol Club in Springfield, New Jersey, one of the many places he had

served as a professional. He used his superior knowledge of the course to great effect and emerged as the winner. His victory made him the first person to win two U.S. Opens.

Over the next few years, Willie was at the height of his form. He won two more U.S. Opens, in 1904 and 1905. His victory in the 1905 U.S. Open was especially satisfying; he held his lead in the last round against his old rival, Alex Smith. He also became the first golfer to win the U.S. Open four times. At the time of his fourth win, Willie was only twenty-five, and he seemed assured of a dominant place in golf for many years to come. He faced one more obstacle, however, and this he could not overcome. His years of heavy drinking had taken a toll, and he was under a doctor's care.

In 1906, he again was locked in a tight duel with Smith for the U.S. Open title. This time he faltered in the last round, and Smith won the tournament. Willie never again finished near the top in the U.S. Open. Willie's problems increased. Golfers in his time earned very little money and had to go on grueling exhibition tours in order to earn a living. The pace of these tours proved exhausting for Willie. In one such exhibition, held near Pittsburgh, Willie and Gil Nichols, another professional, defeated two amateurs in a close match. Afterward, Willie was exhausted, and he died two days later, on October 25, 1910, in Whitemarsh Township, Pennsylvania.

Summary

Golf in the days of Willie Anderson's short life was not a big-time sport. Golfers had only rudimentary equipment and, by late-twentieth-century stan-

Records and Milestones

First player to dominate golf in America

Only golfer to have won the U.S. Open using both rubber-cored and gutta-percha types of balls

Four U.S. Open victories

Placed second in the U.S. Open once, third once, fourth twice, and fifth three times

Honors and Awards

1940   Inducted into PGA Hall of Fame

1975   Inducted into World Golf Hall of Fame

dards, scores were high. Nevertheless, some golfers of that era were undisputedly great players and Willie ranked among the best. He became a leading golfer at an early age, principally because of his unmatched accuracy. He dominated play in the United States for several years and his record of four U.S. Open wins ensured his place among golf's all-time greats.

Bill Delaney

Additional Sources

Frost, Mark. *The Greatest Game Ever Played: Harry Vardon, Francis Ouimet, and the Birth of Modern Golf.* New York: Hyperion, 2002.

Grimsley, Will. *Golf: Its History, People, and Events.* Englewood Cliffs, N.J.: Prentice-Hall, 1966.

McCord, Robert. *The Golf Book of Days: Fascinating Facts and Stories for Every Day of the Year.* Secaucus, N.J.: Citadel Press, 2002.

Tommy Armour

Born: September 24, 1895
    Edinburgh, Scotland
Died: September 11, 1968
    Larchmont, New York
Also known as: Thomas Dickson Armour (full
    name); Silver Scot

Early Life

Thomas Dickson Armour was born in Edinburgh, Scotland, on September 24, 1895. He developed an interest in golf from an early age and practiced at the famous Braid Hills Course in his native city. Golf ran in the family; his brother Alexander, nick-named "Landy," like Tommy, dreamed of becoming a professional golfer.

Tommy's devotion to golf far exceeded that of most talented young players. He took playing lessons from Harry Vardon, the greatest golfer of the early twentieth century, even though the expense of these lessons proved a heavy burden on the impecunious young man. From Vardon, Tommy learned the value of shot placement. Vardon was a master of planning his play so that he had as many easy shots as possible. Rather than simply driving at the green without thought, Vardon carefully considered the layout of each hole. Tommy absorbed Vardon's technique and became known as one of golf's best strategists. Tommy also had an unusually fine touch with irons—generally used on the fairway. He seemed set for an outstanding career in golf when disaster struck.

The Road to Excellence

By the time Tommy was a college freshman, he had already developed into an outstanding amateur player. The inception of his college years coincided with the onset of World War I, however, and Tommy enlisted in the famous Black Watch Regiment of the British Army. During his army career, he demonstrated the dexterity with his hands that was later to characterize his golf play. He set a record for assembling engine parts, a daunting task requiring great manual skill. His adeptness was matched by bravery, and he finished the war as a major.

Tommy's battle experiences almost killed him and affected him the remainder of his life. During fighting in Belgium, he suffered a severe head wound and was gassed. He lost his sight for six months and was permanently blinded in one eye. One of his lungs was gas-burned, and his bones were in large part shattered. He man-

Tommy Armour. (Library of Congress)

aged to recover most of his strength in an English military hospital, but his golf career seemed to be at an end before it had really begun.

Tommy refused to give up. During his lonely months in the hospital, he dreamed of winning major golf tournaments and achieving worldwide recognition. He resolved to let nothing stand in his way, and after release from the hospital, he returned to the game determined to succeed. His hands had not been damaged in the war, to his good fortune.

The Emerging Champion
Tommy's determination and courage enabled him to achieve exactly what he had dreamed while in convalescence. At the end of the war, he resumed his position as an outstanding amateur. After high finishes in the British amateur championships, he decided, in the early 1920's, to turn professional.

Tommy's professional triumphs often displayed the courage he had shown while in the armed service. During the 1920's and 1930's, golfers did not have the equipment needed to break par with regularity. On a difficult course, a round in the low 70's was considered outstanding, and most tournaments were won with scores well above par. Play tended to be erratic; a danger to be avoided was a very poor round, in the high 70's or worse, which ruined one's chances.

Tommy played at his best when under pressure. Unlike many of his rivals, his finishing rounds were often his best. His earliest major triumph, the 1927 U.S. Open, demonstrated this pattern. After three rounds of play, Tommy was well behind Harry Cooper, a small but highly proficient golfer. "Lighthorse Harry" collapsed in the last round and had a disastrously high score. Tommy kept on an even keel and won the tournament with his steady play.

Tommy faced another severe test in the finals of the 1930 Professional Golfers' Association (PGA)

Milestones
Took second place in the 1919 Irish Open
Turned professional in 1924

Honors and Awards
1940 Inducted into PGA Hall of Fame
1976 Inducted into World Golf Hall of Fame

Major Championship Victories
1927 U.S. Open
1930 PGA Championship
1931 British Open

Other Notable Victories
1920	French Amateur
1922	Walker Cup
1926	Ryder Cup
1927	National Open
1927, 1930, 1934	Canadian Open
1929	Western Open

tournament. The event was match play rather than a medal tournament. Instead of scoring by rounds, with the winner having the lowest total shots, entrants were paired in matches until only two were left in the finals. Tommy's opponent in the 1930's finals was Gene Sarazen, one of the greatest golfers of all time and a golfer who, like Tommy, produced his best play under pressure. On this occasion, however, Sarazen proved unequal to the pace. Tommy's ability to play at his peak when challenged again gained him a major championship. Tommy once more reached the finals of the PGA tournament in 1935, but Johnny Revolta defeated him for the title.

Continuing the Story
Perhaps Tommy's greatest achievement in golf was his victory in the 1931 British Open, which was played at Carnoustie in Scotland, an exceptionally difficult course. Before the 1930's, no one had ever broken 70 on this course in a tournament. To make matters even worse, there were unusually heavy winds that year. Tommy found himself in a poor position at the start of the last round. His first three rounds had put him well over par, and his third round was a poor 77. The Argentine golfer José Jurado, a favorite of the Duke of Windsor, seemed to have victory well in hand. Tommy lost confidence in his putting and chipping and felt near collapse. In the final round, Tommy lived up to his reputation of delivering in the "clutch." He felt his nervous condition inwardly but it failed to affect his play. He turned in his best round of the tournament, a 71, and overtook Jurado to win the event.

Tommy continued to play professionally during

the 1930's. After retirement as an active player, he became one of golf's most noted teachers. His 1953 book *How to Play Your Best Golf All the Time* is considered a classic of golf instruction. He died on September 11, 1968.

Summary

Tommy Armour began his career primed for golf success. He had outstanding manual dexterity and was ardently devoted to the game. He learned strategy from Harry Vardon, one of golf's masters. World War I appeared to end his chances for success when he received severe and disabling wounds that nearly ended his life. His determination and courage enabled him to recover, and he became one of the best golfers of the 1920's and 1930's.

Bill Delaney

Additional Sources

Armour, Tommy. *Classic Golf Tips.* Orlando, Fla.: Tribune, 1994.

_____. *How to Play Your Best Golf All the Time.* Rev. ed. New York: Simon and Schuster, 1995.

Grimsley, Will. *Golf: Its History, People, and Events.* Englewood Cliffs, N.J.: Prentice-Hall, 1966.

Wade, Don. *Talking on Tour: The Best Anecdotes from Golf's Master Storyteller.* Lincolnwood, Ill.: Mc-Graw-Hill/Contemporary, 2003.

Seve Ballesteros

Born: April 9, 1957
　　　　Pedreña, Spain
Also known as: Severiano Ballesteros (full name)

Early Life

Severiano Ballesteros was born in Pedreña, Spain, on April 9, 1957. Golf was a part of his heritage. Several of his older brothers were professional golfers, and an uncle, Ramon Sota, was one of the most famous Spanish golfers. Although Seve's father, a dairy farmer, was not a professional athlete, he had been a famous oarsman in his youth.

Seve found a convenient place to develop his golfing talent. His home was next door to the Real

Pedreña golf course, which had been built in 1929 on orders from King Alfonso XIII. From an early age, Seve was determined to become a topflight golfer. The stories his uncle Ramon told him about international competition entranced him. His uncle had competed in The Masters in the United States, and Seve wished to equal—and, if possible, to better—his uncle's achievements.

The Road to Excellence

Seve soon demonstrated that he had remarkable ability. At the age of twelve, he won the caddies' tournament at the Real Pedreña club, and the local golfers already marked him as a coming champion. Natural ability is never enough in itself, however. Seve soon showed that he had the necessary determination to develop his talent through countless hours of grueling practice. Seve estimated that, throughout his teen years, he hit about one thousand golf balls a day.

Seve continued to have the advantage of his uncle's expert tutoring. Because of his constant practice, he was able to develop a stroke of unusual rhythm and accuracy. Having supreme confidence in his swing, Seve exhibited a powerful, seemingly wild swing. In fact, his slashing style was under much more control than most spectators appreciated. His drives were among the longest of any touring professional.

Other characteristics of Seve's game were apparent in his teens. At the Real Pedreña, he made an extraordinarily close survey of the layout of each hole, a practice he was to continue as he extended his activity to other courses. Because of his knowledge of the course, he was able to get out of trouble in a way that few other golfers could match. A situation that ruined a hole for most golfers, for example, a ball placed behind trees, was an easy shot for Seve.

Still another feature of Seve's play was his remarkable short game. His chipping and putting were exceptional, even by professional standards. A typical hole for Seve might feature an enormously long drive that placed him in trou-

Spaniard Seve Ballesteros. (Ralph W. Miller Golf Library)

9

ble. A spectacular recovery shot often got him on the green, after which he often putted for a birdie, or one stroke below par. With his combination of talent and determination, not surprisingly, Seve decided to devote his complete attention to golf at the age of fifteen.

The Emerging Champion

By the age of nineteen, Seve had become an international star. In that year, he entered thirty-four tournaments and won more than $100,000. His most exciting achievement, however, was not in a tournament he won.

In the 1976 British Open, held at the Royal Birkdale Club, one of the world's most difficult courses, Seve led the tournament for three rounds. The course was famous for its unusually thick rough and its fiendishly positioned traps. Seve's ability with trouble shots served him well, and he was able to drive with his customary power, knowing that he had little to fear. Once near the green, his outstanding chipping and pitching distanced him even further from the competition.

Although on the last day the American professional Johnny Miller pulled away from Seve to win the tournament, his second-place finish was an outstanding achievement for a nineteen-year-old. He had, among other things, outplayed the great Jack Nicklaus.

Major Championship Victories

1979, 1984, 1988	British Open
1980, 1983	The Masters

Other Notable Victories

1976, 1980, 1986	Dutch Open
1976, 1983, 1986, 1988	Lancome Trophy
1977, 1982, 1985, 1987	French Open
1978	Greater Greensboro Open
1978, 1981, 1988	Scandinavian Enterprise Open
1981-82, 1984-85	Suntory World Match Play
1981, 1985	Spanish Open
1983, 1985-86	Irish Open
1983, 1988	Westchester Classic
1991	Volvo PGA Championship
	Toyota World Match Play
1994	Benson and Hedges International Open (England)
	Mercedes German Masters
1995	Peugot Spanish Open

Seve quickly proved that his high finish at the British Open was no fluke. He won the 1976 Lancome Trophy in Paris, this time besting Arnold Palmer. In the next few years, Seve established himself as one of the highest-earning European professionals.

Continuing the Story

A great golfer is not measured by native ability or near-wins. The real criterion of greatness is wins in golf's majors: the United States Open, the Professional Golfers' Association (PGA) Championship, the British Open, and The Masters. Seve met this rigid test.

The 1979 British Open was held at the Royal Lytham and St. Anne's Course near the Irish Sea. The fierce winds that often pummel this course make golfing unusually challenging. Once more, Seve relied on his troubleshooting ability and short game. He won the tournament with relative ease and was the only contestant whose four-round total was below par. He was only twenty-two years old, the youngest winner of the British Open in nearly a century.

In 1980, Seve proved he could win against the best players in the United States. In that year, he won The Masters, becoming the youngest player ever to do so. He won again in 1983, narrowly missing further victories in 1986 and 1987. However, an ongoing dispute with Deane

---

Records and Milestones

Youngest golfer to win the European Tour's Vardon Trophy (1976)

In all, won more than fifty tournaments worldwide

Made eight Ryder Cup appearances

First player to surpass $1 million in 1986

Leading money winner on the European Tour

Tied for second place in the 1976 British Open as a nineteen-year-old

European Tour scoring leader six times

Honors and Awards

1976-78, 1986, 1988, 1991	European Tour Order of Merit
1985, 1987, 1995, 1997	Ryder Cup Team (captain in 1997)
1988	Ritz Club Golfer of the Year
1997	Inducted into World Golf Hall of Fame
	Captain, European team, Ryder Cup
2000	Selected European Player of the Century
	Selected Spanish Sportsman of the Century

Beman and the U.S. PGA meant he played comparatively little golf in the United States during the 1980's.

Seve continued his triumphs in Europe during that decade, becoming universally recognized as among the top two or three players in the world. He won three British Opens; his 1984 win at St. Andrews was considered by many to be his greatest moment. His 1988 win was his last major championship victory.

In 1988, Seve married Carmen Botin, the twenty-three-year-old daughter of one of Spain's wealthiest families, having met her in England in 1981. They had three children together but divorced in 2004.

Seve's Ryder Cup playing record was exceptional. He was among the first Europeans to be chosen when the Great Britain team widened itself to include European players in 1979, and he brought the tournament to Spain in 1997 at the Valderrama course. From 1979 to 1997, he only missed the tournament once, in 1981, when in dispute with the European PGA Tour. In 1983, he gained 3½ points out of 5 and was even better in 1991. In 1987, he was paired with fellow Spaniard José María Olazábal, a historically successful partnership lasting through 1993. In 1997, he was appointed captain, and the Europeans won on the final hole of the final match.

With victories in the Volvo PGA Championship in 1991 and several others in the European Tour, Seve remained one of the world's premier golfers. However, his game began to deteriorate in 1992, reviving briefly in 1994. In 1999, Seve was inducted into the World Golf Hall of Fame.

Without a major-tournament win since the 1995 Ryder Cup Championship and the Spanish Open, Seve's best years seemed behind him. However, he had another brief revival when he defeated Colin Montgomerie to lead Europe to victory in the inaugural 2000 Seve Ballesteros Cup, which pits European Tour professionals against those of England and Ireland. As nonplaying captain, he led the Europeans to three further victories. He finally retired in 2007.

In November, 2008, Seve underwent brain surgery. Doctors hoped for a full recovery, and in early 2009, his chemotherapy treatments produced promising results.

Summary

Seve Ballesteros marched to the top in golf, seemingly without difficulty. He inspired a whole generation of Spanish players, including Olazábel and Sergio Garcia, and became a role model for them. He probably did as much for the European PGA Tour as any other player, and his influence on the Ryder Cup was tremendous. He was a charismatic figure, especially popular in the United Kingdom and his native country.

Bill Delaney, updated by David Barratt

Additional Sources

Ballesteros, Severiano. *Seve: The Autobiography*. New York: Yellow Jersey Press, 2007.

Ballesteros, Severiano, with John Andrisani. *Natural Golf*. New York: Atheneum, 1988.

Ballesteros, Severiano, and Dudley Doust. *Seve, the Young Champion*. Norwalk, Conn.: Golf Digest/Tennis, 1982.

Green, Robert. *Seve: Golf's Flawed Genius*. London: Robson Books, 2006.

St. John, Lauren. *Seve: Ryder Cup Hero*. Nashville, Tenn.: Rutledge Hill Press, 1997.

Tait, Alistair. *Seve: A Biography of Severiano Ballesteros*. London: Virgin Books, 2005.

Patty Berg

Born: February 13, 1918
    Minneapolis, Minnesota
Died: September 10, 2006
    Fort Myers, Florida
Also known as: Patricia Jane Berg

Early Life
Patricia Jane Berg was born on February 13, 1918, in Minneapolis, Minnesota. Her father Herman was a grain broker in Minneapolis and her mother Therese was a housewife. Patty was a freckle-faced tomboy who played sports at an early age on a vacant lot near her home. She was star quarterback on a boys' football team, the 50th Street Tigers, which was unbeaten during her tenure. As a young girl in South Minneapolis, Patty excelled in many sports. She set an elementary school track record. In speed skating, she finished third in the nation in the midget class. She later won several track events at Washburn High School.

The Road to Excellence
When Patty was fourteen, her parents decided that she should no longer play football with boys. Realizing that Patty excelled at sports and loved to play, her father shortened one of his golf clubs to fit Patty and gave her four of his other clubs. Patty began playing in 1932, after the family joined the Interlachen Country Club. Her father became her first teacher, and her golf game improved rapidly under his guidance. Within one year, she qualified for the state championships. Her early success was attributable to her dedication and hard work.

At the age of fifteen, Patty entered her first major competition, the 1933 Minneapolis city championship. She shot a score of 122, qualified for the final round, and lost the first match the next morning. The loss did not discourage Patty, however. She returned to the practice tee, determined to play better. In the following year, she returned to play in the city tournament. She was 40 strokes better than her 1933 qualifying score and won the title. This was the turning point in her career.

In 1935, at the age of seventeen, Patty won the first of three state championship titles in Minnesota. During the same year, she reached the finals of the United States Women's Amateur tournament, which was held at her home course of Interlachen. She was defeated by the five-time champion, Glenna Collet Vare, a well-known and more experienced golfer. Patty's performance increased attendance by fifteen thousand as people came to watch a young local player. This public support continued throughout her career; she was always well-liked by the press and the gallery.

In 1937, Patty's early success continued. She again reached the finals of the United States Women's Amateur tournament, losing to Estelle Lawson Page in a close match. After graduating from Washburn High School, Patty enrolled in the University of Minnesota in 1938. She continued to play ama-

Patty Berg. (Hulton Archive/Getty Images)

Milestones

Won forty-four professional titles between 1948 and 1962

LPGA money leader three times in four years (1954, 1956-57)

U.S. Women's Amateur runner-up (1935, 1937)

LPGA President from 1948 to 1952

National Golf Foundation honorary consultant (1983)

Voted Class A membership in the LPGA Teaching Division (1978)

First woman to receive the Humanitarian Sports Award from the United Cerebral Palsy Association (1978)

Honors and Awards

1938-47	*Golf* magazine Golfer of the Decade
1938, 1943, 1955	Associated Press Female Athlete of the Year
1951	Inducted into LPGA Hall of Fame
1953, 1955-56	LPGA Vare Trophy
1955-57	*Golf Digest* Performance Average Award
1955, 1957	*Golf Digest* Mickey Wright Award for Tournament Victories
1959	GWAA Richardson Award
1963	Bob Jones Award
1974	Inducted into World Golf Hall of Fame
1975	GWAA Ben Hogan Award
	Joe Graffis Award
1978	Inducted into PGA Hall of Fame
	Metropolitan New York Golf Writers Gold Tee Award
1980	Inducted into Sudafed International Women's Sports Hall of Fame
1981	*Golf Digest*-LPGA Founders Cup Award
	Herb Graffis Award
1982	Charlie Bartlett award
1986	Old Tom Morris Award
1987	U.S. Sports Academy Female Contributor to Sport Award
1988	Honored among *Golf* magazine's 100 Heroes of Golf

teur golf and once led her sorority to a softball victory by hitting a home run every time she came to bat.

The Emerging Champion

By the late 1930's, Patty had proven herself as an accomplished golfer. She had defeated the women golf stars of the 1930's: Joyce Wethered, Vare, Virginia Van Wie, Alexa Stirling, Marion Orcutt Creus, Helen Hicks, and Dorothy Campbell Hurd. In 1938, she won ten of the thirteen tournaments in which she played. For this accomplishment, Patty was named the Associated Press female athlete of the year. The following year proved to be difficult for

Patty. She missed most of the 1939 season because of an appendectomy. Late that year, en route to an exhibition match, she was in a car accident in which she crashed through the windshield and broke her leg. She stayed in the hospital for six months, and it took another six months of rehabilitation before she could return to the golf course.

In 1940, she became a professional with the Wilson Sporting Goods Company of Chicago. By this time, she had already won forty-one tournaments, including every major tournament at the local, state, and national level. Patty became one of the first women to become a professional athlete. During this time, there were no professional sports for women, and there was no professional golf tour. Often the women earned only a one-hundred-dollar war bond for victory. During the war, Patty served in the Marines. After the war, she returned to professional competition. She won the Western Women's Open title in 1941, 1943, and 1948, and the first U.S. Women's Open in 1946—a tournament in which both amateurs and professionals compete—the only time it was contested as match play.

Continuing the Story

Patty's dominance continued as she won the Titleholders Championship in 1953, 1955, and 1957. She was named female athlete of the year in three different decades.

In 1948, she joined with fellow golfers Betty Jameson and Mildred "Babe" Didrikson Zaharias to establish a women's professional golf tour and the organization to promote professional golf for women, the Ladies Professional Golf Association (LPGA). From 1948 to 1952, Patty served as the first LPGA president. Initially, there were few professional tournaments for women golfers, and very little prize money was offered. Patty's leadership and talent, however, enabled the LPGA to grow during the 1950's and 1960's.

During her best years of competition, Patty aver-

Major Championship Victories

1937-39, 1948, 1953, 1955, 1957	Titleholders Championship
1938	U.S. Women's Amateur
1941, 1943, 1948, 1951, 1955, 1957-58	Western Open
1946	U.S. Women's Open

Other Notable Victories

1936-40	Helen Lee Doherty Championship
1938	Western Amateur
	Western Derby
1938-39	Trans-Mississippi Championship
1943, 1945, 1953, 1955, 1957	All-American Open
1946-47	Northern California Open
1950	Eastern Open
1953-55, 1957	World Championship
1958	American Women's Open
1960	American Open

aged 75.5 strokes per round. By 1962, she had won more than forty professional tournaments and twice won six tournaments in a single year. In the first decade of the existence of the LPGA, she won thirty-nine tournaments. She earned more than $200,000 in prize money during her professional career. She continued to compete in tournaments until 1981, winning an estimated eighty-three professional career tournaments. In 1974, Patty became one of the thirteen charter members of the PGA/World Golf Hall of Fame.

After she retired from competition, Patty suffered from chronic injuries and illnesses. She had cancer surgery in 1971, major hip surgery in 1980, and back surgery in 1989. She continued, however, to represent Wilson Sporting Goods, traveling around the United States performing "The Patty Berg Golf Show." In 2006, Patty died of complications from Alzheimer's disease.

Summary

Patty Berg was considered by many to be the finest woman golfer in history. According to Jim Murray of the *Los Angeles Times*, she was "probably the greatest fairway wood player, man or woman or boy, ever to pull a spoon out of bag and rifle it to a pin." She pioneered women's golf in the United States and, through her hard work and dedication, contributed immeasurably to the sport.

Susan J. Bandy

Additional Sources

Barkow, Al. *Best of Golf: Best Golfers, Courses, Moments and More.* Lincolnwood, Ill.: Publications International, 2002.

Markel, Robert, Susan Waggoner, and Marcella Smith, eds. *The Women's Sports Encyclopedia.* New York: Henry Holt, 1997.

"Patty Berg." *Sports Illustrated* 105, no. 11 (September 18, 2006): 22.

Sherrow, Victoria, ed. *Encyclopedia of Women and Sports.* Santa Barbara, Calif.: ABC-Clio, 1996.

Julius Boros

Born: March 3, 1920
 Fairfield, Connecticut
Died: May 28, 1994
 Fort Lauderdale, Florida
Also known as: Julius Nicholas Boros (full name);
 Big Jules; Big Julie; Jay; Moose

Early Life

Julius Nicholas Boros was born on March 3, 1920, in the town of Fairfield, Connecticut. Julius's parents, hardworking people of Hungarian ancestry, raised Julius and his five brothers and sisters on a salary of twenty dollars a week. Therefore, the children were expected to help with the household chores. From the moment Julius began to walk, he had a golf club in his hands. The family home happened to be located adjacent to the Greenfield Hills golf course, and young Julius often followed his older brothers, Francis and Lance, over the fence and onto the golf course to play as many shots as possible before the greenskeeper ran them off. Golf became such a passion with Julius that he was often delinquent with his chores. He was on the course so much that it became a job. Julius became the smallest caddy at the country club in Fairfield.

The Road to Excellence

Upon entering high school, Julius stood 4 feet 11 inches and weighed 103 pounds. The golf team was a sensible activity for such a small lad, but Julius showcased his fine athletic ability by boxing and starring on the basketball team. Following public school, he entered Bridgeport University and completed a degree in accounting. The Sherman Construction Company of Hartford hired him to maintain company accounts. As it happened, Roger Sherman, the company owner, also owned the Rockledge Country Club. He enjoyed the easy manner and relaxed golf swing of

his accountant so much that Julius spent each work day by completing the company accounts in the morning and playing the company's golf course in the afternoon.

Sherman thought Julius had the skill and attitude to play golf on the professional tour. The boss was ready to finance Julius when World War II broke out. Julius enlisted in the Army and spent the next four years at the U.S. Army base in Biloxi, Mississippi. Just like Mr. Sherman, the base commander enjoyed playing golf, particularly with a quality player such as Private Boros.

Julius Boros, who was one of the founders of the Senior PGA Tour.
(Ralph W. Miller Golf Library)

Julius never had a formal golf lesson. During his accounting days in Connecticut, he had the opportunity to play golf with Tommy Armour. On one occasion, the legendary Scotsman tried to give Julius a lesson, but the younger Julius hit the ball so poorly that he asked that the lesson stop. His natural ability and the daily round with friends prepared him for the highest levels of competition. "Big Julie," as he was known to his peers on the Professional Golfers' Association (PGA) tour, had grown in skill and stature. Near 6 feet and 200 pounds, he began to gain tournament experience. His confidence received a great boost when he shot 64 at the Mid Pines golf course in North Carolina to beat Ben Hogan and Sam Snead. He was playing at a level competitive with the best golfers in the world.

The Emerging Champion

During the era in which Julius played, players caravanned between tournament sites to limit expenses. Ted Kroll, Doug Ford, and Bob Toski were common riders in Julius's Cadillac. They learned that Julius made quick, definitive decisions—a trait that allowed Julius to compete at a high level over a long period of time. He approached each shot with an uncluttered mind. Other golfers spent too much time analyzing a situation to the point of distraction. Julius made up his mind and was ready to perform. Whereas most players were found on the practice ground preparing for a tournament, "Big Julie" was fishing at one of the water hazards found on the golf course. He had a relaxed approach to golf and life.

In 1951, tragedy struck the Boros family. Julius's wife died of a cerebral hemorrhage two days after giving birth to their son. Julius stopped playing golf. A period of adjustment was needed before he

Major Championship Victories

1952, 1963	U.S. Open
1968	PGA Championship
1971, 1977	PGA Seniors Championship

Other Notable Victories

1952, 1955	World Championship
1959, 1963, 1965, 1967	Ryder Cup Team
1960, 1963	Colonial National
1963, 1967	Buick Open
1964	Greater Greensboro Open
1967	Citrus Open
	Florida Citrus Open Invitational
	Phoenix Open
1968	Westchester Classic
1979	Legends of Golf

could return to the game. When he did, it was a very quiet man who walked the golf course. At the U.S. Open that same year, he let his performance do the talking with a fourth-place finish behind Ben Hogan.

After the emotionally painful year of 1951, Julius rebounded triumphantly in 1952, his third year on tour. He played the last thirty-six holes of the U.S. Open so well that no other golfer could better his score. A few weeks later, he made an improbable birdie from a sand bunker on the sixteenth hole of the last round and won the world championship at Tam O'Shanter in Chicago. Julius had won thirty-seven thousand dollars for the year, making him the leading money winner and player of the year.

Continuing the Story

Julius did not reveal emotions where golf was concerned, but he had a special regard for the feelings of others. During the 1955 Western Open in Chicago, his caddy mistakenly lifted the golf ball, costing Julius a two-stroke penalty and several hundred dollars. The caddy was emotionally shaken and tournament officials planned to suspend the boy from his duties. However, Julius kept the boy as his caddy and, following the conclusion of the tournament, called the boy's parents to praise their son.

Though Julius had many health problems, he did not complain. Arthritis, bursitis, gout, back

Milestones

Leading money winner (1952, 1955)

Took third place at the Masters in 1963

Honors and Awards

1952, 1963	PGA Player of the Year
1974	Inducted into PGA Hall of Fame
1982	Inducted into World Golf Hall of Fame

trouble, and a hip operation plagued him during his career. At one tournament, he had to have a spinal correction performed by an osteopath in the early morning, then shot a final-round 68 in the afternoon. One of the club employees at the 1972 PGA Championship was assigned to follow Julius with a chair so he could sit between shots. On another occasion, while driving to a tournament, Julius had his travel buddy, George Bayer, stop the car every few miles so Julius could get out and walk until his back felt better.

Not expecting sympathy, Julius did not offer any when sickness was used as an excuse for bad play. At the 1963 U.S. Open in Brookline, Massachusetts, Julius scored two birdies and a par in the last three holes to tie Arnold Palmer and Jacky Cupit for the lead. He won the eighteen-hole playoff the following day. Palmer had taken a 7 on the eleventh hole and later remarked how sick he had been the night before the playoff. Julius informed Arnold that he would have been sick too after playing a hole like Palmer played the eleventh.

Summary

Julius Boros could never have been accused of contributing to the problem of slow play on the golf course. His quick style and relaxed swing were legendary on the PGA Tour. He stated that golf was a game to be played for enjoyment. Julius won twenty-two tournaments as a professional and his two U.S. Open victories put him in elite company. In 1994, Julius died of a heart attack, on a golf course, doing what he loved.

Thomas S. Cross

Additional Sources

Boros, Julius, and Lealand Gustavson. *Swing Easy, Hit Hard: Tips from a Master of the Classic Golf Swing.* Rev. ed. New York: Lyons & Burford, 2001.

Hickok, Ralph. *A Who's Who of Sports Champions.* Boston: Houghton Mifflin, 1995.

Porter, David L., ed. *Biographical Dictionary of American Sports: Outdoor Sports.* Westport, Conn.: Greenwood Press, 1988.

Pat Bradley

Born: March 24, 1951
   Westford, Massachusetts
Also known as: Patricia Ellen Bradley (full name)

Early Life

Patricia Ellen Bradley was born in Westford, Massachusetts, on March 24, 1951. Her parents encouraged Pat and her five brothers to learn to golf. Pat started playing golf when she was eight years old. Skiing also became one of her interests; her skill in skiing enabled her to become a ski instructor. Eventually, however, she decided to concentrate solely on golf and became a proficient amateur player.

The Road to Excellence

As a young amateur player, Pat competed in the New England area. She won the New Hampshire Amateur tournament in 1967 and 1969. She decided to attend college at Florida International University and continued her development as a golfer there. As a member of the school golf team, she was named a first team all-American in 1970, and in 1971, she was the Florida women's collegiate champion. She continued her successful amateur career by winning the Massachusetts Amateur in 1972, and the New England Amateur in 1972 and 1973.

Pat's success as an amateur encouraged her to join the Ladies Professional Golf Association (LPGA) Tour in 1974. In 1975, Pat won her first tournament as a professional, the Colgate Far East Open. In the years that followed, Pat successfully competed with Kathy Whitworth, Joanne Garner, Nancy Lopez, Amy Alcott, Sandra Haynie, Sandra Palmer, Hollis Stacy, Jan Stephenson, Donna Caponi, Beth Daniel, and the many other outstanding women golfers on the LPGA Tour. From 1976 to 1986, she finished among the top players on the LPGA money list each year and was considered to be one of the most consistent players on the tour.

The Emerging Champion

The year 1986 was a storybook one for Pat. She won three of the four major championships on the LPGA Tour—the Nabisco Dinah Shore, the LPGA Championship, and the Du Maurier Classic—a feat achieved by only two previous players in LPGA Tour history, Mickey Wright, in 1961, and Babe Didrikson Zaharias, in 1950. In the fourth major tournament, the U.S. Women's Open Championship, Pat finished only three strokes behind the winner, Jane Geddes. Pat also won two other tour events in 1986, earned a then-record-setting yearly total of $492,021, and was named LPGA player of the year.

However, the year exacted a toll from Pat. The stress of her position as the dominant player on the LPGA Tour caused Pat to compete to the utmost of her ability and tired her both physically and mentally. As she charged into the 1987 season, she was determined to keep up the pace she had set in 1986. She won the Standard Register Turquoise Classic in March, but two weeks later, at the Kyocera Inamori Golf Classic in San Diego, she began to feel tired. She took a week off the tour, and when she began playing again, she noticed that her shots were often falling short.

Pat believed that she was suffering from fatigue and blamed her swing. She worked harder at practice and consulted her coach, Gail Davis, to analyze her swing. Her style of play changed, from a steely deliberation to a hurried pace. She made adjustments to compensate for tremors in her hands. Despite her hard work and stoic effort, her game continued to deteriorate during 1987. In April, 1988, her older brother Tom persuaded her to see a doctor. She was diagnosed as having hyperthyroidism, a condition in which the thyroid gland begins to work too hard and makes the body run too fast. The stress of competition and her own drive to maintain the pace she had set were thought to have

---

Honors and Awards

1986, 1991	LPGA Player of the Year and leading money winner
	LPGA Vare Trophy
1991	LPGA Hall of Fame
2000	Honored as one of the LPGA's top 50 players
2001	Received Patty Berg Award

brought about the condition. Under the direction of Dr. Ronald F. Garvey, Pat underwent treatment to regulate her thyroid and return her metabolism to normal.

Continuing the Story

In 1989, Pat was able to return to championship form, and she pursued membership in the LPGA Hall of Fame. She needed eight more tournament victories in order to reach the total of thirty tour wins required for admission to the hall of fame. Pat won one tournament in 1989, and added three more victories in 1990. In 1991, she won four tournaments to reach the magic number of thirty victories and became a member of the LPGA Hall of Fame.

Pat's accomplishments in 1991 made her the leading money winner on the tour, and she was again named LPGA player of the year. Her mother, Kathleen, thoroughly enjoyed the pleasure of ringing the bell on the family's back porch for each of Pat's victories, as she had done over the years. Pat was the recipient of the Golf Writers Association of America's Ben Hogan Award for her comeback after suffering from Graves Disease. In 1995, she won the inaugural Healthsouth tournament and became only the second LPGA professional to break the $5 million mark in career earnings.

Having participated in three Solheim Cup Tournaments, helping the U.S. team defeat Europe in 1990 and 1996, Pat was named the Solheim Cup team captain in 2000. Europe defeated the United States 14½ to 11½, and Pat was criticized for showing poor sportsmanship when she insisted that Annika Sorenstam replay a perfectly placed shot that was inadvertently taken out of turn.

In 2001, Pat was the recipient of the Patty Berg Award. After retiring from the LPGA, Pat joined the Women's Senior Golf Tour. Her strongest tournament finish was in 2005, when she combined with Patty Sheehan to tie for first in the BJ's Charity Championship. In 2006, Pat was inducted as an inaugural member of Florida International University's Athletic Hall of Fame.

Summary

Pat Bradley's ability to hit long shots and play skillfully in the wind gained her respect as a veteran player on the LPGA Tour. Her experience with hyperthyroidism taught her not to let goals and ex-

pectations create stress, which can endanger mental well-being and physical health. Pat ranks among the best women golfers in the history of the LPGA.

Ray Sobczak

Additional Sources

Allis, Peter. *The Who's Who of Golf.* Englewood Cliffs, N.J.: Prentice-Hall, 1983.

Garrity, J. "Hitting the Hall." *Sports Illustrated* 76, no. 4 (February 3, 1992): 26-29.

Golf Magazine's Encyclopedia of Golf: The Complete Reference. New York: HarperCollins, 1993.

McCord, Robert. *The Golf Book of Days: Fascinating Facts and Stories for Every Day of the Year.* Secaucus, N.J.: Citadel Press, 2002.

Sherman, Adam. *Golf's Book of Firsts.* North Dighton, Mass.: JG Press, 2004.

Major Championship Victories

1980, 1985-86	du Maurier Classic
1981	U.S. Women's Open
1986	LPGA Championship
	Nabisco Dinah Shore
1990, 1996	Solheim Cup

Other Notable Victories

1975	Colgate Far East Open
1976	Girl Talk Classic
1977	Bankers Trust Classic
1978	Hoosier Classic
	J.C. Penney Classic (with Lon Hinkle)
	Lady Keystone Open
1978, 1991	Rail Charity Classic
1980	Greater Baltimore Classic
	Peter Jackson Classic
1981	Women's Kemper Open
1983	Chrysler-Plymouth Charity Classic
	Columbia Savings Classic
	Mazda Classic of Deer Creek
	Mazda Japan Classic
1985	LPGA Pro-Am
	Rochester International
1986	Nestlé World Championship of Women's Golf
	S&H Golf Classic
1987, 1990	Standard Register Turquoise Classic
1989	Al Star-Centinela Hospital Classic
	J.C. Penney Classic (with Bill Glasson)
1990	Corning Classic
	Oldsmobile Classic
1991	Centel Classic
	MBS Classic
	Safeco Classic
1992	J.C. Penney Skins Game
1995	Healthsouth Inaugural

Donna Caponi

Born: January 29, 1945
     Detroit, Michigan
Also known as: Donna Caponi-Byrnes (full
    name); Donna Caponi Young; the Watusi Kid;
    Boogie D

Early Life

Donna Caponi was born January 29, 1945, in Detroit, Michigan, one of three daughters of Harry
Caponi and his wife Dolly. The Caponi family
moved to Los Angeles, California, in 1949, so

Donna Caponi at the 1983 U.S. Women's Open. (AP/Wide
World Photos)

Harry Caponi, a professional golfer, could work as
an instructor at a course in Burbank. As children,
Donna and her younger sister Janet began picking
up golf balls at the driving range where their father
was head professional; both girls became interested in the game. By the age of six, with patient instruction from Harry, Donna had begun playing
golf. At the age of eleven, she captured the 1956
Los Angeles junior title. She attended Granada
Hills High School, where she was not allowed to
compete on the golf team because of her gender.
She practiced constantly and, after graduation, was ready to take the next step in her
golfing career.

The Road to Excellence

In 1964, Donna first qualified for the women's
pro tour. However, as a young, vivacious woman
just nineteen years of age, she did not dedi-
cate herself fully to her sport in her first year
as a professional. She stayed up late dancing
and acquired the nickname "The Watusi Kid."
The following year, she settled down enough
to begin touring with the Ladies Professional
Golf Association (LPGA). Between 1965 and
1968, she entered 119 events and—thanks to
her accurate, consistent drives—made the cut
into the finals 118 times. Though she showed
promise by finishing in the top ten ten times,
championships eluded her.
    Donna's first professional win, at the 1969
U.S. Women's Open in Pensacola, Florida,
came in dramatic fashion. She had to birdie
the final hole for a 1-stroke victory. The following year, she repeated as U.S. Women's
Open champion, becoming only the second
woman, after Mickey Wright in 1958 and 1959,
to win the 72-hole event in consecutive years;
the feat has since been equaled by five other
women golfers. In her second U.S. Women's
Open victory, Donna also tied Wright's record of 287 strokes. With two victories, three
second-places, one third-place, and fifteen
top-ten finishes, she ranked third in earnings
in 1969.

The Emerging Champion

After 1970, Donna went into a brief slump. Though still ranked high in earnings—she was fifth in 1971—she failed to win major tournaments. She experimented with her appearance: her hair color went from brunet to blond. Still a night owl who loved to dance, she dated celebrities such as Los Angeles Rams quarterback Roman Gabriel and big-league pitcher George Culver. In 1971, she met Ken Young, a divorcé with three children who owned a country-club pro shop and who later became a golf-tournament planner. The two were married, and, afterward, Donna played professionally as Donna Caponi Young.

In 1973, Donna's game began to pick up with a victory in the Bluegrass Invitational. By 1975, she had hit her stride again, reeling off wins in Burdine's Invitational and the Lady Tara Classic.

Between 1976 and 1981, Donna was one of the most dominating players on the LPGA Tour and ranked in the top five in earnings for five of those six years. She captured titles in such events as the 1976 Peter Jackson Classic (later the Du Maurier Classic, a major championship), the 1978 Sarah

Coventry, and the 1979 LPGA Championship. In 1980 and 1981, she took five titles each year, including the 1980 LPGA National Pro-Am, the 1980 Colgate-Dinah Shore Winner's Circle (later the Kraft Nabisco Championship), the 1981 LPGA Desert Inn Pro-Am, and the 1981 LPGA Championship. For Donna's performance in 1981 the Golf Writers Association of America named her female player of the year.

Continuing the Story

In 1980, Donna divorced her husband and played under her maiden name. She began to diet, and her weight dropped from 180 to 130 pounds. She had an operation to correct a deviated septum, which reshaped her nose. The personal changes did not aid her golf game. From the beginning of the 1980's her decline was as swift as her rise to the top had been in the previous decade. Between 1982 and 1988, when she left full-time competition, she did not win any events, though she placed second or third six times. She continued to enter occasional events until 1992, when she retired permanently. She had won twenty-four tournaments, including four majors, while pocketing nearly $1.4 million in prize money.

After quitting the LPGA tour, Donna was in high demand both as an on-air golf analyst and as an instructor. Her bubbly personality made her a natural on such television outlets as ESPN, NBC, CBS, TBS, and the Golf Channel. As a PGA professional at Mission Hills Country Club in Rancho Mirage, California, she specialized in teaching a wide range of corporate clients.

In 2000, Donna was honored during the LPGA's fiftieth anniversary as a top player and teacher. The following year, she was inducted into both the LPGA and the World Golf Halls of Fame. In 2005, she served as an assistant captain for the victorious American team at the Solheim Cup event, a compe-

LPGA Victories

1969	Lincoln-Mercury Open
1969-70	U.S. Open
1970, 1973	Bluegrass Invitational
1975	Burdine's Invitational
	Lady Tara Classic
1976	Peter Jackson Classic (Canadian Women's Open)
	Portland Classic
	The Carlton
	LPGA/Japan Mizuno Classic
1978	The Sarah Coventry
	Houston Exchange Clubs Classic
1979, 1981	LPGA Championship
1980	LPGA National Pro-Am
	Colgate-Dinah Shore (Kraft Nabisco Championship)
	Corning Classic
	United Virginia Bank Classic
	ERA Real Estate Classic
1981	LPGA Desert Inn Pro-Am
	American Defender/WRAL Golf Classic
	WUI Classic
	Boston Five Classic

tition between American and European golfers. In 2006, she married for the second time, to corporate attorney Edward "Ted" Byrnes, and became known as Donna Caponi-Byrnes.

Summary

One of the best—and best-liked—players during more than twenty-five seasons on the LPGA Tour, Donna Caponi was the second golfer to win the U.S. Open in consecutive years. A top money-winner for more than a decade, she won twenty-four tournaments, including four major events. An inductee into two prestigious halls of fame, she continued to win friends and influence golfers as a respected television analyst and instructor.

Jack Ewing

Additional Sources

Cherney, Ron, and Michael Arkush. *My Greatest Shot: The Top Players Share Their Defining Golf Moments.* New York: Collins Living History, 2004.

McCord, Robert. *The Golf Book of Days: Fascinating Facts and Stories for Every Day.* Champaign, Ill.: Sports, 2002.

Sherman, Adam. *Golf's Book of Firsts.* New York: Courage Books, 2002.

JoAnne Carner

Born: April 4, 1939
    Kirkland, Washington
Also known as: JoAnne Gunderson (birth name);
    JoAnne Gunderson Carner (full name);
    Big Mamma; the Great Gundy; Miss Slugs;
    Hot Pepper

Early Life

JoAnne Carner, one of the finest players in the history of women's golf, was born in 1939, in Kirkland, Washington. JoAnne had strawberry-blond hair, a strong physique, and innate athletic talent. At an early age, she became accustomed to winning at sports. While she was in high school, she played on her school's undefeated tennis team; she had picked up a tennis racket for the first time ever only two weeks before the opening match.

JoAnne began playing golf at the age of ten. One day, her older brother, Bill, teased her, saying she would never make a good golfer because she held

JoAnne Carner drops to the green after sinking a putt on the 17th hole, 1976. (AP/Wide World Photos)

irons with a baseball grip and because she stepped into the ball. Before too long, however, JoAnne was outdriving Bill; consequently, he gave up the sport.

Even as a youngster, JoAnne displayed exceptionally good sportsmanship. She competed for the fun of the game, never minding the outcome and never complaining or blaming others. She was also extremely friendly toward her opponents. All of these qualities eventually benefited JoAnne. When she became famous, keeping her success in perspective was easy.

The Road to Excellence

When JoAnne went off to college at Arizona State University on full scholarship, she naturally chose to earn her bachelor's degree in physical education. While a student at Arizona State, she enjoyed her first substantial win, the national collegiate title. Then, in 1956, she reached the finals of the U.S. Women's Amateur, but she lost. She won the U.S. Girls' Junior Championship title instead. The following year, she won the U.S. Women's Amateur, becoming the second youngest at the time to do so. She went on to win the event a total of five times. Fans began calling her "The Great Gundy."

JoAnne enjoyed a brilliant twelve-year amateur career before turning professional. She played in the Curtis Cup from 1958 to 1964. She also won nearly every other important amateur championship at least once, including the Western Amateur, the Intercollegiate, the Pacific Northwest, the Eastern, and the Trans-Mississippi.

Basically a left-hander, JoAnne played right-handed golf. She was equally good at match and stroke play, and she became known as one of the longest hitters of all time among women golfers.

In 1963, JoAnne married Donald Carner, who became her best friend

Major Championship Victories

1956	U.S. Junior Girls
1957, 1960, 1962, 1966, 1968	U.S. Women's Amateur
1971, 1976	U.S. Women's Open
1975, 1978	Du Maurier Classic

Other Notable Victories

1958, 1960, 1962, 1964	Curtis Cup Team
1958-59	Pacific Northwest
1959	Western Amateur
1960	Intercollegiate
1961	Trans-Mississippi
1968	Eastern
1969	Burdine's Invitational
1970	Wendell West Open
1971, 1974	Bluegrass Invitational
1974	Desert Inn Classic
1974, 1976	Hoosier Classic
1975	All-American Classic
1977-78	Borden Classic
1980-81	Lady Keystone Open
1982	Henderon Classic
	McDonald's LPGA Kids' Classic
	Rail Charity Golf Classic
1982-83	Chevrolet World Championship of Women's Golf
1982, 1985	Elizabeth Arden Classic

and strongest critic. Don bought a golf course in Seekonk, Massachusetts, and the couple ran it together. JoAnne managed the snack bar and won tournaments during her vacations. For years, JoAnne had preferred to compete in amateur tournaments while beating the professionals in selected professional competitions. Don believed she ought to turn professional to prove herself as the best at the game. After she suffered a brain hemorrhage in late 1969, JoAnne became bored with amateur golf, so the couple hired a manager to run their golf course and headed off in their trailer, joining the professional circuit.

The Emerging Champion

Few women players have ever compiled the kind of amateur record that JoAnne Carner brought to the professionals. In her first professional seasons, however, her playing was not quite the same. She did not play as seriously as before, and somehow,

she lost her swing. Her career suffered. Although she was named rookie of the year in 1970, her winnings still did not cover her expenses. In 1970, she won only one tournament; in 1971, only two. Meanwhile, JoAnne worked hard to improve her swing. Sam Snead, her mentor and friend, counseled her on her swing technique. When she recovered her swing, it was stylistically similar to a man's. When she hit the ball, the ground shook. From then on, the Great Gundy became known as "Big Mamma." Her other nicknames included "Miss Slugs" and "Hot Pepper."

From that time on, JoAnne excelled. She finished in the top six for money winners eight times. She won the U.S. Women's Open twice, in 1971 and 1976, to become the only woman to have claimed victory in all three United States Golf Association (USGA) events: the junior, amateur, and open. In 1982, she was the LPGA player of the year for the third time and won the Vare Trophy as well. The following year, she won the World Championship of Women's Golf. In 1985, she won the Safeco Classic.

JoAnne once played Arnold Palmer in an exhibition game. After the two players teed off, Palmer walked up to the farthest ball, assuming it was his. Big Mamma had outdriven him by 20 yards. Along with Mickey Wright, JoAnne is believed to be the only woman who has ever been able to hit long irons as well as the best men golfers.

Eventually, JoAnne ranked among the LPGA's all-time money winners, earning more than $2 million. With her forty-three LPGA wins, she was inducted into the LPGA Hall of Fame in 1982 and into the World Golf Hall of Fame three years later.

Continuing the Story

As a player, Carner was consistent and durable. Possibly, her remarkable record derived from her stable home life. An extremely devoted wife, she was also the family breadwinner and a career woman. However, her marriage endured the kind of challenges that damaged marriages of other golfers on tour. JoAnne had no children or pets. Don accompanied her everywhere; the two of them were never apart more than ten days total in their marriage. Of all her nicknames, she preferred when Don affectionately called her "Curly."

JoAnne and Don liked to fish whenever they were not on the fairways. They had a mobile home hideaway in the Smoky Mountains of Tennessee, perched above the white waters of the Tellico River. They often spent Saturday nights around a bonfire at a fishing camp listening to bluegrass music. Don died in 2000; he and JoAnne had been happily married for thirty-six years. JoAnne moved to Palm Beach, Florida, where she snorkeled and fished from her 42-foot Hatteras boat.

In 1981, the USGA honored JoAnne with the Bob Jones Award for distinguished sportsmanship. Known for her unfailing sense of humor, JoAnne responded that she thought players had to be dead to win the award. In 1994, JoAnne captained the U.S. team to victory in the Solheim Cup. In 1999, she became the oldest player to make the cut at an LPGA major event, the Du Maurier Classic. She was named one of the LPGA's top fifty players in 2000. In 2001, the Palm Beach National Golf and Country Club announced the opening of the JoAnne Carner Golf Academy for Ladies. JoAnne became known as one of the top golf instructors for women. Even in her sixties, she continued to compete and even excel in women's competitive golf. JoAnne became the oldest player to make a cut on the LPGA Tour, the 2004 Chik-Fil-A Charity championship. In 2004, she made ten starts on the LPGA Tour.

Summary

One of the longest hitters of all time, JoAnne Carner became a leading money winner on the LPGA Tour. She showed tremendous longevity in her sport and exhibited professionalism at every stage of her career. Golf legend Nancy Lopez acknowledged JoAnne as a pioneer in women's golf. In addition to becoming one of golf's all-time greats, JoAnne was known for her exemplary sportsmanship, for which she received the Bob Jones Award.

Nan White, updated by Howard Bromberg

Additional Sources

"Carner Feels Her Age." *Golf Digest* 53, no. 48 (2000).

Golf Magazine's Encyclopedia of Golf: The Complete Reference. New York: HarperCollins, 1993.

Smith, Lissa, ed. *Nike Is a Goddess: The History of Women in Sports.* New York: Grove Atlantic, 2001.

"Three Eras, Aces." *Golf Digest* 51, no. 12 (2000).

Yocum, Guy. *My Shot: The Very Best Interviews from "Golf Digest" Magazine.* New York: Stewart, Tabori & Chang, 2007.

Records and Milestones

First woman to have won the USGA Girls' Junior, U.S. Women's Amateur, and U.S. Women's Open titles

In 1981, became the second player to cross the $1 million mark in career earnings

In 1986, became the second player in LPGA history to cross the $2 million mark

In 2004, at sixty-four years of age, became the oldest person to make the cut in an LPGA tournament

Honors and Awards

1970	LPGA Rookie of the Year
	Gatorade Rookie of the Year
	Golf Digest Rookie of the Year
1974	*Golf Digest* Most Improved Golfer
	Golf Digest Mickey Wright Award for Tournament Victories
1974, 1981-82	LPGA Player of the Year
	Rolex Player of the Year
1974, 1981-83	GWAA Player of the Year
1974-75, 1981-83	LPGA Vare Trophy
1976	Seagram's Seven Crowns of Sports Award
1981	Bob Jones Award
1982	Inducted into LPGA Hall of Fame
1985	Inducted into World Golf Hall of Fame
1987	Inducted into Sudafed International Women's Sports Hall of Fame
1988	Honored among *Golf Magazine*'s 100 Heroes of Golf
2000	Honored as one of LPGA's top fifty players

Billy Casper

Born: June 24, 1931
      San Diego, California
Also known as: William Earl Casper, Jr. (full
    name); Buffalo Bill

Early Life

William Earl Casper, Jr., was born June 24, 1931, in San Diego, California. His father, an amateur golfer, introduced him to golf when he was five. Billy showed a marked interest in golf from an early age and frequently practiced at a small course on his grandfather's ranch in New Mexico.

As Billy matured, his concentration on golf increased. During his high school years, he was captain of the golf team, and he earned money by working as a caddy at the San Diego Golf Club. He won a golf scholarship to attend the University of Notre Dame but left school after one year because of the severity of Indiana's weather. Rather than continue his college career elsewhere, he enlisted in the Navy. His naval service proved a help to his aspirations to a career as a professional golfer. He managed golf courses, taught the game, and gave exhibitions, mostly around his native San Diego. He was fortunate that his period of military service, which ended in 1955, occurred during a period in which the United States was not involved in combat.

The Road to Excellence

In essence, golf consists of two separate games: the play from tee to green and putting on the green. Most professionals are relatively equal in the first of these. Some golfers do indeed stand out even here: Jack Nicklaus drove with such power and accuracy that his second shot usually consisted of a short iron to the green. For the most part, however, players are bunched together before they reach the green.

Putting is all together another story. A par score of 72 strokes is based on 36 putts. A golfer who can score a significant number of one-putt greens can easily break par. Winners of golf tournaments frequently are on especially successful putting streaks.

Billy's putting distinguished him from his contemporaries. Since his early youth on his grandfather's ranch, he had practiced putting incessantly. He much preferred it to drills in other types of shots, which he found to be both boring and hard work. His putting skill paid handsome dividends, and he became recognized as the best putter in golf.

Billy's technique proved especially effective on long putts. He had a low, fast stroke reminiscent of the style of Bobby Locke, a South African golfer of the 1940's and 1950's. Billy's deadly accuracy on long putts enabled him to achieve immediate success on the professional tour.

Billy Casper playing a shot in 1966. (Popperfoto/Getty Images)

Major Championship Victories

1959, 1966	U.S. Open
1970	The Masters
1983	U.S. Senior Open

Other Notable Victories

1957	Phoenix Open
1958, 1963	Bing Crosby National Pro-Am
1961, 1963, 1965, 1967, 1969, 1971, 1973, 1975	Ryder Cup Team
1962, 1964	Doral Open
1962, 1968	Greensboro Open
1964, 1968	Colonial National
1965-66, 1969, 1973	Western Open
1965, 1969	Bob Hope Classic
1967	Canadian Open
1968	Greater Hartford Open
1968, 1970	Los Angeles Open
1970	IVB-Philadelphia
1971	Kaiser International
1973	Sammy Davis, Jr.-Greater Hartford Open
1974	Lancome Trophy
1979	Ryder Cup captain
1982	Merrill Lynch/Golf Digest Commemorative Pro-Am/Senior Tour
1984	Senior PGA Tour Roundup
1987	Del E. Webb Arizona Classic/Senior Tour
	Greater Grand Rapids Open/Senior Tour
1988	Mazda Senior Tournament Players Championship
	Vantage at the Dominion/Senior Tour
1989	Transamerica Senior Golf Championship

The Emerging Champion

Billy turned professional in 1955, soon after his discharge from the Navy. To raise expenses, he arranged with a consortium of businesspeople for a loan of one thousand dollars a month. In return, he promised the group 30 percent of his winnings as well as repayment of the loan. Their investment proved a sound one; within a few years, Billy had become one of the tour's leading money winners.

Billy's march to success culminated in his 1959 victory in the U.S. Open, the premier American tournament. Over the difficult New York course of Winged Foot, he needed only 114 putts for four rounds, an average of fewer than 30 per round.

Billy's initial success did not last long. He confronted several major problems. Although he was a genuine phenomenon in putting, other phases of his game were not as well developed. His fellow professionals frequently criticized him for his neglect of the tee-to-green part of golf. Not even Billy's near-miraculous putting compensated for deficiencies elsewhere in his game.

These deficiencies were difficult to remedy because Billy intensely disliked practice. Very unusual for a champion athlete, he was not a keen admirer of his own sport. To him, golf to him was a way of earning his living, not a vocation to be pursued with enthusiasm. He also suffered from an explosive temper and frequent attacks of nerves. As if this were not enough, Billy's weight sharply increased during his first few years on the tour. By 1964, he was more than 50 pounds overweight. He developed a number of allergies and became listless. Not surprisingly, from 1960 to 1963, he failed to play up to the level that had led to his U.S. Open triumph.

Continuing the Story

Billy showed that he had true championship quality by his manner of dealing with his problems. On the advice of a doctor, he embarked on a rigorous weight-reduction program, and he soon managed to shed his excess pounds. His new diet featured unusual foods such as buffalo and elk meat, a change that gained him much attention in the press and gave rise to his nickname "Buffalo Bill."

Although Billy disliked practice, he realized its necessity and succeeded in improving his tee-to-green shotmaking. To his great delight, his skill in putting did not desert him during his period of illness and lethargy. When his acknowledged supremacy in the area was combined with his new-found physical fitness and an overall improved game, the result was readily predictable.

Billy again became one of golf's leading players. In 1966, he won the U.S. Open a second time, defeating Arnold Palmer by four strokes in a playoff. For a number of years, he was at or near the top in money won and was a frequent tournament winner.

In 1981, Billy joined the PGA Senior Tour and won the U.S. Senior Open two years later. He won his ninth Senior Tour victory in 1989 at the Transamerica Senior Golf Championship. Billy played in only three official events on the Senior Tour in 1999 and 2000 but made frequent appearances in Legends of Golf tournaments. At the conclusion of his playing career, he focused his attention on designing golf courses.

Records and Milestones

Second player to reach $1 million in official tour earnings (1970)
PGA Tour's money leader (1966, 1968)
Won fifty-one events between 1956 and 1975, and was the money leader twice

Honors and Awards

1960, 1963, 1965-66, 1968	PGA Vardon Trophy
1966, 1968, 1970	*Golf Digest* Byron Nelson Award for Tournament Victories
1966, 1970	PGA Player of the Year
1968, 1970	GWAA Player of the Year
1971	GWAA Charlie Bartlett Award
1978	Inducted into World Golf Hall of Fame
1982	Inducted into PGA Hall of Fame

Summary

Like most golf champions, Billy Casper learned the game at an early age. Unlike most other outstanding players, his skill lay in one area—putting. He quickly became recognized as one of the greatest putters in the game, and his skill was sufficient to gain him two victories in the U.S. Open. After confronting serious health problems, he improved the remainder of his game and became one of the major golfers of the 1960's.

Bill Delaney

Additional Sources

Casper, Byron. *Billy Casper's Golf Tips*. Edinburgh: Pastime Publications, 2002.

_____. *Golf Shotmaking with Billy Casper*. Garden City, N.Y.: Doubleday, 1966.

_____. *The Good Sense of Golf*. Englewood Cliffs, N.J.: Prentice-Hall, 1980.

Davis, Seth. "Catching Up with . . ." *Sports Illustrated* 86, no. 25 (June 23, 1997): 8-10.

Golf Magazine's Encyclopedia of Golf: The Complete Reference. New York: HarperCollins, 1993.

Hack, Damon. "Decades After Casper's Victory, a Winning Strategy Endures." *The New York Times*, June 12, 2006, p. 2.

Hall, Martin. "How to Tame a Duck Hook." *Golf Magazine* 48, no. 3 (March, 2006): 74.

Yocum, Guy. *My Shot: The Very Best Interviews from "Golf Digest" Magazine*. New York: Stewart, Tabori & Chang, 2007.

Fred Couples

Born: October 3, 1959
     Seattle, Washington
Also known as: Frederick Stephen Couples (full name)

Early Life

Frederick Stephen Couples was born in Seattle, Washington, on October 3, 1959. He was an enthusiastic soccer and baseball player as a youth. During Fred's teens, Jefferson Park, a municipal golf course about two blocks from his home, became the center of his interest in golf.

As his golf skills developed, Fred enjoyed the fun and challenge of playing in competitive golf games with older boys and men. When he and his friend Jay Turner got jobs at the Jefferson Park driving range, Fred was allowed to hit golf balls for free. He loved to blast them as far as he could.

After completing St. George grade school, he attended O'Dea Catholic High School for Boys, a small school that was run by the Irish Christian Brothers. The school's golf coaches took the team to courses in the Seattle area and occasionally took members across the Puget Sound to play. Fred enjoyed these trips to new courses and became a skilled player.

The Road to Excellence

At the age of eighteen, Fred won the Washington State Open Golf Tournament as an amateur. He chose to attend the University of Houston and made the golf team as a freshman. He improved each year, and his college roommate Jim Nantz, who later became a network television sports announcer, predicted that some day Fred would win The Masters. Fred laughed and told Jim that he played golf solely for enjoyment. As he played against the best college players, however, and saw professionals play in Texas, he began to believe that he could compete at the professional level.

Fred met Deborah Morgan, his future wife, while they were students at Houston. During the summer of 1980, before his senior year, Fred went to California to visit her. While there, he inquired about playing in the Queen Mary Open Tournament in Long Beach. He was told that all the amateur openings were filled but that he could play as a professional. A friend paid his entry fee. Fred tied for sixth place. He repaid the loan, and his professional career had begun.

After finishing in fifty-third place on the Professional Golfers' Association (PGA) Tour list of money winners in both 1981 and 1982, Fred won his first PGA tournament, the Kemper Open, in 1983. The following year, he won the prestigious Tournament Players Championship and gained recognition as a bright young prospect. His smooth

Fred Couples watching his shot at a 2008 tournament. (Leslie Billman/Landov)

swing, powered by strong calf and thigh muscles, generated drives that made him one of the longest hitters on the tour.

Although he did not win again until the Byron Nelson Golf Classic in 1987, by the end of that year, he had earned more than a million dollars since joining the tour in 1981. He finished nineteenth in earnings in 1987, joining the elite players on the tour.

In 1989, Fred was chosen as a member of the U.S. Ryder Cup team. The Ryder Cup competition matches two teams of top-ranking professionals, one from the United States and one from Europe. Fred lost all of his matches. The European team retained the Ryder Cup, as the U.S. team was only able to tie in total match points. Fred was disappointed that he was not able to help the U.S. effort, but his fellow professionals Tom Watson and Raymond Floyd encouraged him to use the experience as motivation to become a tougher competitor. With golf instructors Paul Marchand and Dick Harmon, Fred worked earnestly on his swing and on his mental approach to the game.

The Emerging Champion

Fred realized that he needed to develop a reliable putting stroke, one on which he could depend under pressure. His improved putting helped him to

---

Major Championship Victories

1992	The Masters

Other Notable Victories

1983	Kemper Open
1984	Tournament Players Championship
1987	Byron Nelson Golf Classic
1990, 1992	Nissan Los Angeles Open
1991	B.C. Open
	Federal Express St. Jude Classic
1991, 1995	Johnnie Walker World Championship
1992	Nestlé Invitational
1992-95	World Cup Team
1993	Honda Classic
1994	World Cup Championship (Individual)
	Buick Open
1995	Dubai Desert Classic
1996	Tournament Players Championship
1998	Bob Hope Chrysler Classic
2003	Shell Houston Open
2007	Inducted into National Italian-American Sports Hall of Fame
2009	Presidents Cup team captain

---

build confidence in his game. That confidence led to one tournament victory in 1990 and three wins in 1991. Even more satisfying was his performance in the 1991 Ryder Cup matches. He won three matches and contributed to the close victory of the U.S. team. His consistent play on the PGA Tour also won him the Vardon Trophy for the lowest scoring average per round on the tour.

In 1992, Fred continued his strong play, winning the Nissan Los Angeles Open and the Nestlé Invitational in Orlando, Florida. In April, he achieved the goal that his friend Jim Nantz had predicted by winning The Masters at the Augusta National course in Georgia. During 1992, Fred's three-year cumulative record earned him the top position in the Sony World Rankings of players. He was also recognized as player of the year on the PGA Tour and again won the Vardon Trophy.

Continuing the Story

In 1992, in the midst of his rise to golf prominence, Fred and his wife, Deborah, separated after a marriage of eleven years. Fred's career could have taken a downturn, but with the support of his father, Tom, his mother, Violet, his sister Cindy, and loyal friends on the tour, Fred rededicated himself to making golf his life and his source of enjoyment. During 1993, he won the Honda Classic tournament and again represented the United States as a member of the Ryder Cup team.

Fred played on five Ryder Cup teams, won the World Cup Championship as an individual in 1994, and became the first player to win two Tournament Players Championships. He also recorded back-to-back victories on the PGA European tour in 1995, the first American to do so since Charles Coody in 1973.

Fred continued to play well in the new millennium. In nineteen events he entered in 2000, Fred had five top-ten finishes and eleven top-twenty-five finishes, and he earned nearly $1 million for the season. In 2003, Fred won the Shell Houston Open, his first PGA tournament victory in five years, and in 2005, he tied for third place at the British Open, equaling his highest finish in the tournament.

Summary

Fred Couples's skill, backed by the confidence that his talent, experience, and determination gave him, enabled him to compete successfully with the best players in his profession. His honesty, down-to-earth attitude, and desire to enjoy a simple, private lifestyle reflected his basic values.

Ray Sobczak

Honors and Awards

1989, 1991, 1993, 1995, 1997	Ryder Cup Team
1991-92	PGA Tour Player of the Year
	Vardon Trophy for lowest scoring average on tour
1992	PGA of America Player of the Year
1994, 1996, 1998, 2005	Member, U.S. Presidents Cup Team

Additional Sources

Bissell, Kathlene. *Fred Couples: Golf's Reluctant Superstar.* Lincolnwood, Ill.: Contemporary Books, 2000.

Couples, Fred, Guy Yocum, and Stephen Szurlej. "Fred Couples' Guide to Life." *Golf Digest* 51, no. 11 (2000).

Feinstein, John. "Semi-Retired." *Golf Magazine* 42, no. 9 (2000).

Marchand, Paul. "Boom-Boom's Basics." *Golf Magazine* 45, no. 11 (November, 2003): 79-80.

_____. "Fred Couples: Cool Customer." *Golf Magazine* 46, no. 8 (August, 2004): 50-53.

Ben Crenshaw

Born: January 11, 1952
   Austin, Texas
Also known as: Ben Daniel Crenshaw (full name)

Early Life

Ben Daniel Crenshaw was born January 11, 1952, in Austin, Texas, the third of three children. The Crenshaw family was well-off. Ben's father, Charles Edward Crenshaw IV, was an attorney prominent in local politics. Ben's mother, Pearl Johnson Crenshaw, was an elementary schoolteacher. Ben's father, an ardent amateur golfer, often took his youngest son with him when he played, and Ben, carefully following his father's instructions, quickly picked up the rudiments of the game. Ben had al-

ready started playing golf in elementary school, and by fourth grade, he had won his first tournament.

The Road to Excellence

Ben demonstrated from an early age that he had inborn talent for golf. He shot a 74, a score many golfers never reach in their lives, when he was ten years old. While he was still in his mid-teens, he won a number of local titles, including the state junior championship in 1967 and 1968, as well as three consecutive Austin city championships. He also captured his first national title in 1968, the Jaycees junior championship.

Ben had an outstanding teacher, Harvey Penick, the head professional at the Austin Country Club and one of the leading golf teachers in the United States. Penick emphasized improving the swing the golfer had already developed. When coaching Ben, he basically left things alone, providing useful tips and diagnosing the source of any problems.

Ben was lucky to have topflight competition and instruction so early in his life, but to take advantage of these opportunities, more than luck was needed. Fortunately for him, he had the necessary dedication for hours of daily practice. Ben participated in a number of other sports at Austin High School: He was on the track-and-field, basketball, football, and baseball teams. However, golf was always his first priority. He played one or two rounds every day for ten months a year.

By Ben's senior year in high school, his golfing talent began to attract wide public notice. In his first U.S. Open, he finished thirty-second, tied for top amateur. During the year, he won eighteen of nineteen tournaments he entered. After high school graduation, he enrolled at the University of Texas on a golf scholarship. In his freshman year, he won several championships, placed fifth at the U.S. Amateur Championship, and tied for twenty-seventh at the U.S. Open—accomplishments that earned him all-American honors.

Ben Crenshaw, who captained the U.S. Ryder Cup team in 1999. (Ralph W. Miller Golf Library)

Major Championship Victories

1984, 1995   The Masters

Other Notable Victories

1971-73	NCAA Championship
1972, 1988	World Cup Team
1973	San Antonio-Texas Open
	World Open
	Western Amateur
1976	Bing Crosby National Pro-Am
	Irish Open
1977	Colonial National
1979	Phoenix Open
1980	Texas State Open
1981, 1983, 1987, 1999	Ryder Cup Team
1983	Byron Nelson Classic
1986	Buick Open
1988	Doral Ryder Open
1990	Southwestern Bell Colonial
1992	Central Western Open
1993	Nestlé Invitational
1994	Freeport McMoran Classic
1995	PGA Grand Slam of Golf

In 1972, Ben took ten more championship titles and was selected for the U.S. World Amateur Cup team. The following year, he won ten championships in the course of clinching his third National Collegiate Athletic Association (NCAA) title. Torn between finishing his studies or joining the lucrative professional tour, Ben opted for the latter course.

The Emerging Champion

After turning professional in 1973, Ben immediately surpassed expectations. He won his first tournament, the San Antonio-Texas Open, and three weeks later, he won the prestigious World Open in North Carolina. In a mere six weeks, he pocketed more than $75,000 in prize money—a huge sum at that time. His fellow professionals hailed Ben as the next Arnold Palmer or Jack Nicklaus.

However, Ben's promising start soon encountered obstacles. A major blow was the sudden death of his mother, which shocked him and sent him into a tailspin for a time. Over the following few years on the tour, he went into a slump. His record was not bad, but he had not yet succeeded in becoming one of the game's superstars.

Ben's reaction to his problems showed he had an essential quality of a true champion. He did not give up; instead, he resolved to correct defects that

held him back. To do so, he sought instruction from Bob Toski, a former winner of the U.S. Open. By making a few changes in Ben's swing, Toski helped him to regain an outstanding rhythm. Toski also gave him valuable pointers on the mental side of golf. Ben was willing to pay the price of success, and his persistence paid off. By 1976, he was again viewed as an emerging superstar. In that year, he won three tournaments and finished second in The Masters.

Continuing the Story

From 1976 to 1982, Ben established a solid if not spectacular reputation as one of the tour's leading players. He won a number of tournaments, including the 1977 Colonial National Invitational, and consistently finished high on the annual money-winners list. However, the highest mark of success eluded him: He failed to win a major championship. Golfers' records of success in these events determine their positions among the legends of the game.

After 1982, the situation worsened for Ben. He went into another period of decline, and his career seemed over. He was again determined to overcome his problems. This time, he returned to his original instructor, Penick. Ben's comeback left no doubt about his status as one of golf's great players. In 1983, he finished second in The Masters, and in 1984, he won the tournament, defeating his archrival from high school, Tom Kite. At last, he had succeeded in winning a major.

After his triumph at The Masters, Ben's career continued in a pattern of slumps and comebacks.

Milestones

Placed third in the U.S. Open (1975)
Placed second in the Masters (1976, 1983)
Placed second in the British Open (1978-79)
Placed second in the PGA Championship (1979)

Honors and Awards

1974	*Golf Digest* Rookie of the Year
1976	*Golf Digest* Byron Nelson Award for Tournament Victories
	Golf Digest Most Improved Golfer
1989	GWAA Richardson award
	PGA Ed Dudley Award
1991	Bob Jones Award
2002	Inducted into World Golf Hall of Fame
2006	Kappa Alpha Order Sportsman of the Year

Part of the trouble was personal: In 1984, he divorced his wife. In 1985, he remarried. In 1986, he entered into partnership with Bill Coore, establishing Coore and Crenshaw, a golf-course design firm.

Throughout the 1980's, in spite of temporary difficulties, Ben continued to be recognized as an outstanding golfer. In 1989, he led The Masters after three rounds but was overtaken by Nick Faldo in the last round. In 1991, he received the Bob Jones Award for his distinguished sportsmanship. Between 1992 and 1995, he had one victory each year. In 1995, in one of his most memorable performances, Ben won his second Masters Championship a week after serving as pallbearer for longtime friend and teacher Penick.

After undergoing foot surgery in 1997 and disappointing performances in 1998 and 1999, Ben was named team captain for the 1999 Ryder Cup team. Ben played in eleven PGA tournaments in 2000, but he made the cut in only the GTE Byron Nelson Classic. In 2002, he was inducted into the World Golf Hall of Fame. In 2006, he was named Kappa Alpha Order sportsman of the year. After more than three decades on the professional tour, nineteen PGA victories, and more than $7 million in prize money, sweet-swinging Ben remained one of the most popular players on the professional circuit.

Summary

Few golfers have demonstrated their talent as early as Ben Crenshaw did. He did not rely solely on his inborn gifts but practiced incessantly. He announced his arrival as a professional in dramatic fashion, winning several tournaments in his first year. Although slumps impeded his career, his persistence secured him a place among the outstanding golfers of the 1970's and 1980's, and his leadership during the 1999 Ryder Cup Championship provided one of the most exciting tournaments in the history of the event.

Bill Delaney, updated by Jack Ewing

Additional Sources

Apfelbaum, Jim, ed. *The Gigantic Book of Golf Quotations.* New York: Skyhorse, 2007.

Crenshaw, Ben, with Melanie Hauser. *A Feel for the Game: A Master's Memoir.* New York: Broadway Books, 2002.

Curtis, Walter J., Sr. *History's Master Golfers.* Indianapolis: Curtis, 2003.

Ouimet, Francis. *A Game of Golf.* Boston: Northeastern University Press, 2004.

Puett, Barbara, and Jim Apfelbaum. *Golf Etiquette.* Rev. ed. New York: St. Martin's Press, 2003.

Strange, Curtis. "Twenty Questions with Crenshaw." *Golf Magazine* 41 (October, 1999): 120-124.

John Daly

Born: April 28, 1966
　　　Carmichael, California
Also known as: John Patrick Daly (full name);
　　Long John; the Lion

Early Life

John Patrick Daly was born in Carmichael, California, on April 28, 1966. His passion for golf began at the age of four when his father Jim, an engineer, gave him two cut-off golf clubs. This seemingly insignificant event began one of the most memorable careers in professional golf.

Because of his father's job, John, along with his family, was often required to move. Shortly after his family settled in Dardanelle, Arkansas, John began playing golf. The game provided a perfect outlet for him because, as a child, he had few friends. Golf

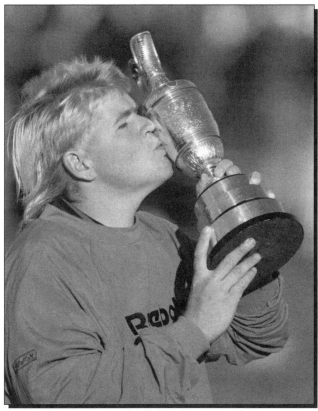

John Daly after winning the British Open at St. Andrews, Scotland, in 1995. (AP/Wide World Photos)

allowed John to play alone or with a group, whether they were his own age or adults.

The Road to Excellence

In his early teens, John studied the golf swing of Jack Nicklaus. While John's swing resembled his idol's, his backswing was longer. John had the ability to move the club further behind his head, allowing him to drive more force into the ball. This unique motion produced long drives and iron shots that floated high through the air.

Because of his swing, John regularly hit the ball further than most men. Despite using a set of basic clubs and balls, which he fished out of nearby ponds, he became consistent in his play. John practiced diligently, and at the age of twelve, he won the men's championship at the Lake of the Woods Country Club in Fredericksburg, Virginia. John's win caused members of the club to forbid teens from ever again entering the tournament.

In high school, John demonstrated remarkable athletic ability. He played baseball and lettered in football and golf at Helias High School in Jefferson City, Missouri. In golf, he was a Missouri state champion and won the Missouri Amateur Championship in 1983. In 1984, his parents moved to New Hampshire; John settled in Arkansas with his older brother Jamie. He won the 1984 Arkansas Amateur Championship and repeated as the winner of the Missouri Amateur Championship.

Success brought challenges to John. Once a good student, his grades began to drop because of his new fondness for alcohol and partying. However, his golf game did not suffer, and he was offered a golf scholarship to the University of Arkansas. John played three years at Arkansas before quitting after his junior year in 1987. He won the Missouri Open and decided to turn professional.

The Emerging Champion

In 1990, after a failed marriage and time spent playing in South Africa, John returned to the

PGA Tour Victories

1991	PGA Championship
1992	Broome County Open
1994	BellSouth Classic
1995	British Open
2004	Buick Invitational

United States. He won the Utah Classic, finishing the year in ninth place on the Ben Hogan Tour. In 1991, he played on the PGA Tour, but he was largely inconsistent. In August, John qualified as the final alternate in the last major tournament of the year: the PGA Championship at Crooked Stick Golf Club in Carmel, Indiana.

John was the improbable winner of the 1991 PGA Championship. His propensity for hitting long drives, often more than three hundred yards, coupled with his ability to hit short irons and wedges onto the green, allowed him to post low scores all four days of the tournament. With his unorthodox swing and enormous drives off the tee, John quickly became a crowd favorite, earning him the nickname of "Long John." Partly because of his underdog win, John was voted PGA rookie of the year, was given endorsements, and gained fame. However, in the years that followed, John became involved in several alcohol-related incidents, which caused the PGA Tour to suspend him twice.

Continuing the Story

In the first half of 1995, John exhibited the erratic behavior that had characterized him to that point. However, in July, when he arrived in St. Andrews, Scotland, for the British Open Championship he was clean, sober, and without expectations. The high winds and balmy weather that normally accompanied the tournament were nonexistent, giving him an advantage. John turned in another outstanding performance, hitting long drives on nearly every tee. He defeated Costantino Rocca in a playoff to win the tournament. The victory was John's second major championship before his thirtieth birthday, placing him in a class with legends

such as Jack Nicklaus, Tom Watson, and Johnny Miller.

In the 1990's, John's turbulent personal life overshadowed his golfing. His drinking habit resurfaced; he accrued gambling debts and suffered through a second divorce. John had several stints in rehabilitation centers to deal with his health and emotional problems. His golf game was erratic. In March, 1998, he had two consecutive fourth-place ties, in the Nissan Open and Honda Classic. The next week, he scored an 18 on a hole at the Bay Hill Invitational. In 2000, his worst year on the PGA tour, he failed to qualify for the final weekend in ten of twelve events.

In 2001, John won the BMW Championship on the European Tour and held a spot in the top fifty world rankings at the end of the year. He was in contention to win tournaments again. In 2004, he won the Buick Invitational, outlasting Chris Perry and Luke Donald in a playoff. The cheers he received from the crowd reinforced his status as a fan favorite.

Summary

John Daly has revolutionized the use of the long drive in modern professional golf and helped to popularize the sport worldwide. He is an athlete with impressive talent who attacks golf and life with equal passion. Despite his past off-course issues, he continued to be a major contender in the golf world.

Brian Culp

Additional Sources

Daly, John, and Glen Waggoner. *My Life in and out of the Rough: The Truth Behind All That Bull**** You Think You Know About Me.* New York: Harper-Collins, 2006.

Mahoney, Paul. "John Daly for President! The Superstar with the Common Touch Is Still the People's Champion." *Golf World,* May, 2004.

Newsham, Gavin. *John Daly: Letting the Big Dog Eat.* London: Virgin Books, 2003.

Wartman, William. *John Daly: Wild Thing.* New York: HarperPaperbacks, 1996.

Jimmy Demaret

Born: May 24, 1910
Houston, Texas
Died: December 28, 1983
Houston, Texas
Also known as: James Newton Demaret (full name)

Early Life

James Newton Demaret was born May 24, 1910, in Houston, Texas. He was one of nine children. Unlike many golfers who learn the game from their fathers, Jimmy was not in a position to take up hobbies. Early in life, he was faced with the need to earn enough money on which to live.

Occasionally people who rise to success from a difficult background are hard-driving and ruthless. Having known poverty, they will allow nothing to place them at risk of a return to that state. Jimmy had an entirely different attitude. He was a happy-go-lucky, friendly person who enjoyed parties and continually engaged in banter.

The Road to Excellence

Jimmy became interested in golf as a means of earning money, not as an activity valued for its own sake. Money was available through local tournaments and through gambling in rounds with wealthy amateurs. The game was not Jimmy's main source of funds, however: He worked as a night-club singer with a band.

The Texas courses had low, rolling areas near the green that demanded a delicate touch. Like his friend Jack Burke, Jimmy developed into an excellent wedge player. Because of the flat surfaces of the courses, a putter would often be used in shots to approach the green—the so-called "Texas wedge." Jimmy added this technique to his repertoire, further enhancing his skill in the short game. He was also superb with long irons.

Jimmy's ability and technique enabled him early to dominate Texas professional golf. He won a number of local tournaments, including the Texas Professional Golfers' Association (PGA) Championship five times in succession. In 1938, he decided to turn full-time professional. He won the im-

portant Los Angeles Open in his first full year on the circuit, 1939.

The Emerging Champion

As Jimmy rose to national prominence in the late 1930's, golf fans encountered a player the likes of whom they had never before seen. He specialized in colorful clothes—bright orange or blue trousers were favorites. To Jimmy, a golf cap was no mere ar-

Jimmy Demaret putting in preparation for The Masters in 1957. (Augusta National/Getty Images)

ticle of convenience but an opportunity to display a riot of colors. Conservative golfers, who might otherwise have protested, only shook their heads. By his constant good-natured conversation on the course, he charmed both galleries and his fellow professionals. Throughout his career, Jimmy was among the best-liked players in the game.

Jimmy demonstrated that he was much more than a comedian on the course. He soon proved to be one of the best golfers in the country. In 1940, he won The Masters, establishing a tournament record in the process. In the final 18 holes of the tournament, he scored an incredibly low 60. The Masters was the most important of the seven tournaments—six of them in row—he won in 1940.

Jimmy's ability reached its peak just before the United States entered World War II, and Jimmy served in the Navy during the years—the early 1940's—in which he would have had the best chance of dominating the game. As always, however, he was not discouraged. He emerged from military service with both his personality and his golf game intact.

Jimmy immediately resumed his rank among the leaders. He won The Masters again in 1947, and in 1948, he finished second in the U.S. Open. He became the first three-time winner of The Masters in 1950. He won the tournament with a strong closing round of 69. In 1947, he was the leading money winner. His purses totaled $27,936, a very high amount for golfers in the 1940's.

In spite of his success, two weaknesses plagued Jimmy's game. He devoted little time to practice, and he preferred late-night parties and dancing, no doubt reflecting his earlier career as an enter-

---

Major Championship Victories

1940, 1947, 1950	The Masters

Other Notable Victories

1934	San Francisco Match Play Championship
1934-38	Texas PGA Championship
1939	Los Angeles Open
1941	Argentine Open
1947, 1949, 1951	Ryder Cup Team
1949-50	Phoenix Open
1952	Bing Crosby National Pro-Am

---

tainer. Sam Snead once suggested that Jimmy's lack of practice made him play far below his potential.

Continuing the Story

Jimmy lacked the driving intensity characteristic of most champions: As long as he did well and enjoyed himself, he was content. His lack of aggressiveness made him especially vulnerable in match play. He was uninterested in struggling against an opponent face-to-face, and players more intent on victory could usually beat him. Once, after losing a match to Ben Hogan in the PGA Championship, he joked that the turning point of the match was Hogan's appearance on the course. Nevertheless, his ability enabled him to reach the semifinals of the PGA Championship four times.

A further obstacle confronted Jimmy. He had the misfortune to play golf at the same time as three of the foremost players of all time: Snead, Byron Nelson, and Hogan. Owing to the unusually difficult competition, Jimmy was unable to win a major title besides The Masters. An illustration of the forces with which he had to contend is the outcome of the 1948 U.S. Open. Jimmy broke the previous course record for the U.S. Open by three strokes, but Hogan broke it by five. Jimmy's best finish in the U.S. Open was his second place in the 1948 tournament; he finished fourth or better three times. Altogether, he won some forty tournaments in his career.

Jimmy did not resent having to play second fiddle to other golfers. He became Hogan's closest friend in golf and won six tournaments playing with Hogan as his partner. These events, called "four-balls," were matches in which the low scorer wins the hole for the two-person team. The two

---

Records and Milestones

Credited with forty-four tournament wins, not all of which are recognized by the U.S. PGA

In 1950, became the first golfer to collect three Masters titles

Came close to winning the U.S. Open several times: sixth (1946), second (1948), fourth (1953), third (1957)

Reached the PGA Championship semifinals four times

Honors and Awards

1947	PGA Vardon Trophy
1960	Inducted into PGA Hall of Fame
1983	Inducted into World Golf Hall of Fame

players were utterly opposed in temperament: Hogan was grim and taciturn and had a desire to win stronger than any other player of his time. Nevertheless, the two were fast friends.

After Jimmy's tournament days were over, he developed the Champions Golf Club with his lifelong friend Burke. Jimmy suffered a fatal heart attack in Houston, Texas, on December 28, 1983.

Summary

Jimmy Demaret honed his exceptional short-game play on the Texas semiprofessional circuit. He attracted national attention by his colorful dress and pleasant personality, but these should not hide the fact that he was one of the best golfers of the 1940's. Ben Hogan and others eclipsed him, but he did not mind. Had he required consolation, he could have looked to his three wins in The Masters.

Bill Delaney

Additional Sources

Companiotte, John, and Ben Crenshaw. *Jimmy Demaret: The Swing's the Thing*. Ann Arbor, Mich.: Clock Tower Press, 2004.

Golf Magazine's Encyclopedia of Golf: The Complete Reference. New York: HarperCollins, 1993.

Purkey, Mike. "Jimmy Demaret." *Golf Magazine* 35, no. 11 (November, 1993): 104-105.

Roberto De Vicenzo

Born: April 14, 1923
     Buenos Aires, Argentina
Also known as: Roberto Ricardo De Vicenzo (full
     name); El Maestro; the Master

Early Life
Roberto Ricardo De Vicenzo was born in 1923, in
Buenos Aires, Argentina. Growing up poor, he
made money as a caddy, meanwhile learning the
rules of golf and developing his physical and mental skills. He turned professional in 1938 and won
the Argentine Open and the Argentine Professional Golfers' Association Championship in 1944.
Further victories in those tournaments followed
during the 1940's, as did a victory in the Chilean
Open.

The Road to Excellence
In 1948, Roberto began establishing his reputation
beyond South America by finishing in a four-way tie
for third place at the British Open. In 1949, he
placed third, and in the following year, he placed
second. During the 1953 British Open, Ben Hogan
and Roberto were tied for first place at 214 after
three rounds. On the last round, however, Hogan
shot a 68, a course record, and Roberto, with a 73,
slipped into a sixth-place finish. In the 1956 British
Open, Roberto again played well, except for a 79 in
the third round, which caused him to finish third
instead of first.

Meanwhile, he won other tournaments during
the 1950's, including the Palm Beach Round
Robin and, with Henry Ransom, the Inverness Invitational Four-Ball. In 1957, Roberto also won the
Colonial National Invitational and the All-American Open. In addition to those victories, in 1953,
he and Antonio Cerdá won the Canada Cup for Argentina. Roberto also won open championships in
France, the Netherlands, Belgium, Mexico, and
Panama.

The Emerging Champion
Despite those wins and others, Roberto entered his
mid-forties without having won a major, one of the
world's four most important golf tournaments: the
British Open, The Masters, the U.S. Open, and the
PGA Championship. He continued to play well at
the British Open, finishing in the top four in 1960,
1964, and 1965. Then, in 1967, he played in his eleventh British Open, at Hoylake, England. At the end
of the second round, the defending champion,
Jack Nicklaus, led with a total of 140, one stroke
ahead of Roberto. In the third round, Roberto shot
an excellent 67 to pull three strokes ahead of
Nicklaus, who shot a 71. In the last round, Nicklaus
scored a 69, but Roberto, with a 70, held on to win
the tournament by two strokes. At the age of forty-
four years and ninety-two days, he became the oldest golfer to win the British Open since 1867.

The victory at Hoylake would have become the
best-known event in Roberto's career had it not
been for what happened the next year at Augusta,
Georgia, during The Masters. The fourth round
came on April 14, 1968—Roberto's forty-fifth
birthday. As play began that Sunday, Gary Player
held the lead at 210. Bob Goalby was tied with four
other competitors for second place at 211. Roberto
and Lee Trevino were tied at 212. For seventeen
holes, Roberto played brilliantly, finishing the first
nine holes with a 31 and shooting birdies on the
twelfth, thirteenth, and fifteenth holes. As the
spectators watching in person and on television
saw, Roberto also birdied the seventeenth hole,
with a score of 3. Despite a bogey on the eighteenth
hole, his apparent score for the last round was a su-

International Victories

1944-45, 1947-49, 1951, 1960, 1964-66, 1969, 1971-72, 1974, 1977, 1985	Argentine PGA Championship
1944, 1949, 1951-52, 1958, 1965, 1967, 1970	Argentine Open
1946, 1961	Chilean Open
1950	Dutch Open
	Belgian Open
1950, 1960, 1964	French Open
1951, 1953, 1955	Mexican Open
1952-53, 1971, 1973-74	Panama Open
1953, 1962	Canada Cup
1961	Colombian Open
1964	German Open
1966	Spanish Open
1972-73	Venezuelan Open

---

perb 65. He and Goalby tied for the lead and would compete in a playoff the next day to determine the championship.

After a delay, however, the announcement came that Goalby had won with a total score of 277, and that Roberto's score for the fourth round had to be counted as 66, making his tournament total 278. Roberto's playing partner and scorekeeper, Tommy Aaron, had recorded Roberto's score for the seventeenth hole as a 4 instead of a 3, and Roberto had signed and submitted the inaccurate scorecard. According to a rule of golf, if Roberto had submitted a scorecard with an incorrectly low score, he would have been disqualified. In this case, however, the rule said that the incorrectly high score had to stand. Some golfers would have thrown a public fit at what had happened, blaming everyone but themselves, but Roberto quickly acknowledged the mistake as his own. Already popular because of his affability, he quickly became one of the most admired professional golfers, and in 1970, the United States Golf Association presented him the Bob Jones Award to recognize his sportsmanship.

Continuing the Story

Despite disappointment at the 1968 Masters, Roberto did not retreat. On May 5, he won the Houston Champions International. The following year, he again won the Argentine PGA Championship; in 1970, he won both the Argentine Open and the individual title in the World Cup (the successor to the Canada Cup). During the 1970's, other victories in Latin American tournaments followed, including four in the Argentine PGA Championship.

In 1985, at the age of sixty-two, Roberto won the Argentine PGA Championship for the sixteenth time.

During the years he was playing in Latin America against golfers at the peaks of their careers, he also played in seniors' tournaments in the United States. In 1974, Roberto won the PGA Senior Championship; in 1979, he teamed with Julius Boros to win the Liberty Mutual Legends of Golf; and in 1980, he won the first U.S. Senior Open. Among his other victories as a senior golfer was one as late as 1991, with Charlie Sifford, in the legendary division of the Liberty Mutual Legends of Golf.

Summary

Roberto De Vicenzo entered the World Golf Hall of Fame in 1989 but did not officially retire from competition until 2006, when he was in his eighties. He won national titles in more than one dozen countries and a total of at least 230 tournaments throughout a career that seemed to defy age. A hero in Argentina, he was for decades the best South American golfer. For well-informed golfers and golf fans around the world, he was a model of perseverance and sportsmanship.

Victor Lindsey

Additional Sources

Barrett, Ted. *The Complete Encyclopedia of Golf.* Chicago: Triumph Books, 2005.

Palmer, Arnold. *Playing by the Rules: All the Rules of the Game, Complete with Memorable Rulings from Golf's Rich History.* New York: Pocket Books, 2002.

Sampson, Curt. *The Lost Masters: Grace and Disgrace in '68.* New York: Atria Books, 2005.

Ernie Els

Born: October 17, 1969
     Johannesburg, South Africa
Also known as: Theodore Ernest Els (full name);
   the Big Easy

Early Life

Ernie Els was born Theodore Ernest Els in Johannesburg, South Africa, and grew up in Kempton Park. His parents had two other children, Dirk and Carina. Ernie attended Delville Primary School and Jan De Klerk High School. His parents, Cornelius "Neels" and Hester Els, encouraged their children to participate in a variety of sports. At the age of four, Ernie started joining his father and brother on the golf course and began to caddy for them shortly thereafter. Ernie's first golf club was Kempton Park Golf Club. Early on, Ernie was active in tennis, rugby, cricket, and golf. A natural athlete, Ernie excelled in most sports and even won the tennis Eastern Transvaal Junior Championship at the age of thirteen. By the age of fourteen, he had decided to make golf his main focus. Gaining dominance did not take long: He won the 1984 Junior World Golf Championships in San Diego, California, beating future golf star Phil Mickelson in the age 13-14 category.

The Road to Excellence

After winning the Junior World Golf Championships, Ernie enjoyed success on the amateur circuit. His other notable amateur wins included the 1986 South African Boys Golf Championship, the 1986 South African Amateur Golf Championship, and the 1989 South African Stroke Play Championship. Ernie turned professional in 1989. For a couple of years, he played well but did not win any big tournaments. In 1990, he began working with well-known swing coach David Leadbetter. In 1991, Ernie had a professional win on the Southern Africa Tour (now Sunshine Tour); two years later, he won the Dunlop Phoenix Tournament in Japan. In 1994, golf fans took notice, as Ernie won his first major championship at the U.S. Open, defeating Colin Montgomerie and Loren Roberts in sudden death.

The Emerging Champion

Following his U.S. Open win, Ernie began to establish himself as an international player. He obtained the fitting nickname "the Big Easy" because of his physical size—6 feet 3 inches—his graceful swing, and his easygoing manner on the golf course. Unlike many golfers in the PGA, Ernie enjoyed playing tournaments not spon-

Ernie Els teeing off at the 2008 Singapore Open. (Vivek Prakash/ Reuters/Landov)

sored by the organization. He continued to win tournaments, too, including the Dubai Desert Classic on the European Tour, the World Match Play Championship twice, the Byron Nelson Classic, and the South African Open. In 1996, Ernie beat Vijay Singh to secure his third consecutive World Match Play Championship win, a feat unmatched by any other golfer.

Ernie established his position in golf history when he won his second major at the 1997 U.S. Open. Throughout the next few years, he added several other big victories to his list, including the Buick Invitational and the Johnnie Walker Classic. Following these wins, Ernie finished second in three majors—the British Open, The Masters, and the U.S. Open. In 2000, the European Tour honored Ernie with a lifetime membership because of his successful career. However, both 2000 and 2001 were disappointing years for Ernie because he could not produce a significant triumph.

Following those two lean years, Ernie made a

stellar comeback in 2002, with a big win over Tiger Woods in the Genuity Championship and his triumph in the British Open. The success in the British Open came after a tight four-man playoff during a period of time when Ernie had been criticized for lack of mental stamina. Also in 2002, Ernie won his fourth World Match Play Championship.

The next couple of years, Ernie built upon the successes of 2002. He earned his first European Tour Order of Merit and won two more World Match Play Championships in 2003 and 2004. He finished in the top twenty in all four majors of 2003. In 2004, he had sixteen finishes in the top ten and earned another European Tour Order of Merit.

Continuing the Story

In the latter half of the 2000's, Ernie became a member of golf's unofficial "Big Five," which included top money earners Tiger Woods, Vijay Singh, Retief Goosen, and Phil Mickelson. Ernie held his own among the top five despite a knee injury in 2005.

In 2007, Ernie announced that he had a three-year plan to finally beat Tiger Woods, a task that had been important to the South African golfer since he finished second to Woods more times than any other golfer. In the same year, Ernie's earned a record seventh World Match Play Championship.

In 2008, Ernie continued to be competitive, winning the Honda Classic in March. He also contributed articles to *Golf Digest* and tweaked his own game as his career matured. In April of 2008, he announced a change in swing coaches, from the legendary David Leadbetter to Butch Harmon. Furthermore, in 2008, Ernie began

Notable Victories

1991	Amatola Sun Classic
1992	South African Masters; Swazi Sun Classic; Goodyear Classic
1992, 1995, 1999	South African PGA Championship
1992, 1996, 1998	South African Open
1992, 2001	Tournament Players Championship
1993	Dunlop Phoenix Tournament
1994	Johnnie Walker World Championship; Sarazen World Open
1994-96, 2002-03, 2007	World Matchplay Championship
1994, 2002, 2005	Dubai Desert Classic
1994, 1997	U.S. Open
1995	Byron Nelson Classic; Bells Cup
1996	Johnnie Walker Super Tour Event
1996-97	Buick Classic
1997	PGA Grand Slam of Golf; World Cup of Golf
1997, 2003	Johnnie Walker Classic
1998	Bay Hill Invitational
1999	Nissan Open
1999-2000, 2002	Nedbank Golf Challenge
2000	Loch Lomond tournament; The International
2002	Genuity Championship; The British Open
2002-04	Heineken Classic
2003	Mercedes Championship
2003-04	Sony Open in Hawaii
2004	Scottish Open; Omega European Masters
2005	BMW Asian Open
	Qatar Masters
2006	Dunhill Championship
2007	South African Airways Open
2008	Honda Classic

his public support of autism research because his son was diagnosed with the disorder.

Summary

Beginning in the 1990's, Ernie Els became one of golf's toughest competitors. He possessed a positive public image as a calm, easy-going golfer with great finesse. Ernie's three major victories and record seven World Match Play Championships became his career highlights. He made societal contributions through his charitable organization, the Fancourt Foundation, which benefits underprivileged South African children. He also designed golf courses and started a well-respected wine-making company.

Valerie Brown

Additional Sources

Els, Ernie. *How to Build a Classic Golf Swing.* New York: HarperCollins, 1999.

Els, Ernie, and David Herman. *Ernie Els' Guide to Golf Fitness: Take Strokes off Your Game and Add Yards to Your Drive.* New York: Three Rivers Press, 2000.

Shipnuck, Alan. "Shot to the Top." *Sports Illustrated,* June 30, 1997.

Nick Faldo

Born: July 18, 1957
      Welwyn Garden City, Hertfordshire,
      England
Also known as: Nicholas Alexander Faldo (full
    name); Nasty Nick

Early Life

Nicholas Alexander Faldo was born July 18, 1957, in Welwyn Garden City, Hertfordshire, England. His parents, Joyce and George Faldo, tried to instill in their only child the ambition to be the best at what he did. While instruction in dancing, speaking, music, and modeling did not hold Nick's attention, individual sports such as swimming and cy-

Nick Faldo at the 1988 Masters. (Augusta National/ Getty Images)

cling did. In 1971, Nick was inspired while viewing the telecast of The Masters from the United States. After watching Jack Nicklaus play on the fairways and greens of the Augusta National course, Nick told his mother that he wanted to try golf.

The Road to Excellence

Within a year, Nick was playing to a seven handicap at the Welwyn Garden City golf club. Ian Connelly, the club professional, saw early signs of Nick's determination to master the game. One afternoon, Connelly taught Nick a drill for maintaining an easy tempo in his swing. That evening, as the teacher was leaving the parking lot, Nick called to him to show him how well he had learned the drill. Nick's determination and willingness to practice long hours showed remarkable results. Within four years of taking up golf, Nick became the dominant amateur player in Great Britain. At eighteen, he became the youngest player to win the English Amateur Championship.

Nick enrolled at the University of Houston in the United States with the intention of improving his play, but he found that golf coach Dave Williams's system did not mesh well with his own practice methods. He left Houston after one semester and joined the professional European golf tour at the age of nineteen.

The Emerging Champion

Nick's first full year as a professional was successful. He finished eighth on the Order of Merit, the system used to rank European golfers. In 1977, in his first Ryder Cup team competition against the United States, the twenty-year-old Nick won all three of his matches, including a victory over Tom Watson, one of the world's best players. Nick's overall performance in 1977 earned him recognition as rookie of the year on the European Tour. In 1978, Nick's success continued when he won the European Professional Golfers' Association (PGA) championship.

By 1983, Nick had emerged as the leading player in Europe; that year, he won five tournaments on the European Tour, ranked first on the Order of

Major Championship Victories

1987, 1990, 1992	British Open
1989-90, 1996	The Masters

Other Notable Victories

1977	Skol Lager
1978	Colgate PGA Championship
1980-81	Sun Alliance PGA Championship
1983	Paco Rabanne French Open
	Ebel Swiss Open-European Masters
1984	Heritage Classic
1987	Peugeot Spanish Open
1988	Volvo Masters
1988-89	Peugeot French Open
1989	Dunhill British Masters
	Suntory World Match Play Championship
1990, 1993	Johnnie Walker Asian Classic
1991-93	Carrolls Irish Open
1992	GA European Open
	Scandinavian Masters
	Toyota World Match Play Championship
1994	Alfred Dunhill Open
1995	Doral-Ryder Open
1997	Nissan Open
1998	World Cup of Golf (Team)
2006	The Royal Trophy, European Team

Merit, and became the first player on the tour to exceed £100,000 in earnings. Following this success, Nick began to look for further ways to improve his golf swing with the help of teaching professional David Leadbetter. Nick's height—6 feet 3 inches—and long legs—35-inch inseam—posed problems of balance in his full swing. By widening his stance to the approximate width of his shoulders, adjusting the flex in his knees to get an athletic posture rather than a stooped one, and setting his club angle early in the swing, Nick was able to improve his leg action and get a flatter swing. The new approach resulted in lower ball flight, a definite asset in windy conditions.

During the transition period in which Nick rebuilt his swing through countless hours of practice, his tournament results suffered. He was willing to endure the slump, however, in order to develop techniques necessary to win major championships.

Continuing the Story

In 1987, Nick's determination and persistence gained him recognition as a world-class player.

At the Spanish Open in Madrid, Nick scored his first victory in three years, then won the British Open at Muirfield. Setting his goals on major world championships, he won the French Open and the Volvo Masters in 1988. A loss to Curtis Strange in the 1988 U.S. Open only increased Nick's desire. In 1989, he won The Masters in the United States and then defended his title in 1990, by defeating Raymond Floyd in a playoff. He followed his Masters triumph by winning the 1990 British Open at the famous Old Course at St. Andrews, Scotland, giving Nick two major championships in one year. In 1992, he added a third British Open title to his record by winning at Muirfield again.

In 1989, Nick was voted the British Broadcast Corporation sports personality of the year in England, and in 1990, U.S. PGA player of the year. The 1993 Sony World Rankings showed Nick as the world's top professional golfer based on his three-year cumulative record, which included nine championships all over the globe. His wife, Gill, and three children provided the stability that enabled him to keep his life in perspective. However, Nick's marriage ended in 1995; he remarried in 2001.

In 1991, Nick set up a golf course design business, followed by a number of other ventures, including a coaching school and pro shops. This did not hinder his competitive golfing through the 1990's. He won major tournaments in every year between 1993 and 1998, including a dramatic third victory in The Masters in 1996. Down by 6 strokes to Australian Greg Norman, Nick shot a final round of 67 and won by 5 strokes.

In the Ryder Cup, Nick's performances over the twenty-year period from 1977 to 1997 were equally impressive. His career points were the most by any Ryder Cup player, as was the number of times he was selected. One of Nick's most crucial victories was against Curtis Strange in the penultimate

Honors and Awards

1977-97	Ryder Cup team
1987	Member of the Order of the British Empire
1989-90, 1992	European Golfer of the Year
1990	PGA Player of the Year
1997	Inducted into World Golf Hall of Fame
1998	Awarded Most Excellent Order of the British Empire (MBE)

match in the 1995 Cup. Nick was chosen to be the nonplaying captain for the Europeans for the 2008 Ryder Cup.

After 1998, Nick's participation in major championships declined, but he still placed in the top ten in championships held in 1999, 2000, 2002, and 2003. He became active in sports broadcasting, first for ABC and then for CBS.

Summary

Nick Faldo's willingness to refine and improve his playing techniques and his concentration made him a serious contender in every tournament in which he played. His ambition was matched by his success. Off the professional circuits, Nick contributed to golf through coaching schemes. In 1996, he started the Faldo Series of championships to assist young players in Europe. In 1997, he also set up the Faldo Golf Institute. He was awarded the Member of the British Empire (MBE) for his services to golf.

Ray Sobczak, updated by David Barratt

Additional Sources

Barratt, David. "Nick Faldo." *Golf Magazine* 40, no. 7 (1998).

Concannon, Dale. *Nick Faldo Driven: The Definitive Biography.* London: Virgin Books, 2001.

Faldo, Nick. *Faldo: In Search of Perfection.* London: Weidenfeld and Nicolson, 1994.

_____. *Life Swings: The Autobiography.* London: Headline Books, 2004.

Faldo, Nick, and Vivian Saunders. *Golf: The Winning Formula.* New York: Lyons & Burford, 1989.

Johnny Farrell

Born: April 1, 1901
    White Plains, New York
Died: June 14, 1988
    Boynton Beach, Florida
Also known as: Johnny Joseph Farrell (full name)

Early Life
Johnny Joseph Farrell was born in White Plains, New York, on April 1, 1901. He acquired an interest in golf as a teenager when he saw the first tournament ever run by the Professional Golfers' Association (PGA), held at the Siwanoy Country Club in New York. Johnny found tournament play exciting and immediately decided to become a professional golfer. He embarked devotedly on a training program that enabled him to master all aspects of golf. He secured a job as a caddy at the Westchester Golf Club and acquired a thorough knowledge of this and other New York courses. By the time he was twenty years old, Johnny was ready to commit to playing professionally.

The Road to Excellence
Johnny quickly demonstrated that he was capable of competing with the best professionals. In the 1922 U.S. Open, he finished eleventh, a good showing for a newcomer. In that tournament, he encountered a situation that plagued him throughout his golf career. Although an outstanding player, he was often upstaged by even better golfers. In the 1922 Open, his playing partner was another newcomer, Gene Sarazen, who astonished the golf world by winning the tournament. Sarazen, one of the greatest golfers of all time, was, however, not the most formidable obstacle standing in Johnny's way.

During the 1920's, golf was dominated by Bobby Jones. Although a number of other great golfers, such as Sarazen, Walter Hagen, and Tommy Armour, achieved enviable records during this decade, Jones was far and away the best. A lifelong amateur, he was ineligible to play in professional ranks. That was fortunate for the professionals, because Jones finished at or near the top of nearly every major tournament he entered. Most likely, Johnny Farrell would have achieved more had he not been faced with Jones during much of his career.

Johnny Farrell, who won the 1928 U.S. Open. (Ralph W. Miller Golf Library)

Johnny's golf game had both strengths and weaknesses. Although not an exceptionally long hitter from the tee, he was an excellent wood player. Even more important was his putting. In a par round of 72 shots, 36 strokes, or 2 per green, are allowed for putts. A golfer who excels at this "game within the game" is in a good position to better par, and the winner of a tournament often turns out to be a golfer on a streak of excellent putting. Few golfers of the 1920's, perhaps only Jones and Hagen, could match Johnny in this vital area. Against these many strengths stood an important weakness. Johnny was highly temperamental; frequently, he failed to perform well under pressure. Although his swing was easy and effortless, he required a great deal of time before each shot to calm himself. As a result, he was one of golf's slowest players.

The Emerging Champion

In spite of his problematic temperament, Johnny's skill and determination enabled him to acquit himself creditably on the course. In 1927, he won six tournaments in succession. In the 1927 PGA Championship, he seemed well on the way to victory. At that time, the PGA was a match play event, and Johnny's opponent in the final was the great Hagen. Except for his comparable putting excellence, Hagen's game was opposite to Johnny's. Hagen's swing was choppy, while Johnny's was smooth and elegant. Hagen was a master of psychological tactics and the best match player in golf. He almost always played at his best under pressure. At the end of the morning, Johnny was up by four strokes, normally a commanding lead. The players then broke for lunch; when play resumed, Hagen pulled out all the stops. The cunning tactician proved too much for the perpetually nervous Johnny, and Hagen, overcoming Johnny's lead, took the title.

Johnny refused to be discouraged by losing a major championship that was within his grasp. In the 1928 U.S. Open, he tied for first. After the first three rounds, Jones held his usual secure lock on the lead. Jones proceeded to suffer a rare slump and finished with a poor 77. Johnny had an excellent last round and managed to tie Jones. The winner of the tournament was decided by a 36-hole playoff. Johnny had the task of defeating the greatest golfer of the era in one-on-one play. Johnny demonstrated his niche among golf's outstanding players, turning in an excellent first round of 70, while Jones continued on his slump. Jones's poor play ended as suddenly as it had begun, and in the final 18 holes, he was clearly back in form. Johnny saw his first-round lead nearly erased. This time, Johnny overcame his unsteady nerves. He birdied the seventeenth hole and repeated the feat on the eighteenth, sinking a 7-foot putt. That enabled him to win the U.S. Open by one stroke. After Johnny's formidable achievement, many predicted that he would become Jones's successor as the game's premier player.

Continuing the Story

Although Johnny retained his smooth swing to the end of his career, his nervousness and poor health prevented him from reaching supremacy. He never again won a major title after his 1928 victory in the U.S. Open. He did, however, remain one of the top players on the circuit for many years. He finished in the top five in the U.S. Open on three occasions aside from his 1928 victory. He was once runner-up in the British Open, and he scored a number of high finishes in the PGA Championship, in which he played every year from 1922 to 1937. Johnny's smooth swing stood him in good stead, enabling him to play outstanding golf many more years than most of his contemporaries. During his years on the tour, the dapper Irishman was acclaimed golf's best-dressed player. He died on June 14, 1988, in Boynton Beach, Florida.

Summary

Johnny Farrell was entranced by golf as a youngster. He intended to become a professional golfer after he viewed his first tournament and joined the tour while barely out of his teens. He won recognition almost at once. He was an excellent putter and wood player, and his smooth swing attracted widespread admiration. He defeated the greatest golfer of the 1920's, Bobby Jones, to win the 1928 U.S. Open. He had a number of other successes, but poor nerves and intense competition kept him from additional major titles.

Bill Delaney

Additional Sources

Golf Magazine's Encyclopedia of Golf: The Complete Reference. New York: HarperCollins, 1993.

Rapoport, Ron. *The Immortal Bobby: Bobby Jones and the Golden Age of Golf.* Hoboken, N.J.: John Wiley & Sons, 2005.

Ray Floyd

Born: September 4, 1942
    Fort Bragg, North Carolina
Also known as: Raymond Loren Floyd (full
    name); Raymond Floyd

Early Life
Raymond Loren Floyd, the son of a U.S. Army officer, was born September 4, 1942, in Fort Bragg, North Carolina. From an early age, Ray displayed talent in athletics. Golf was not his first love; like many American boys, he dreamed of becoming a professional baseball player. Unlike most, he had the physical attributes to do it. He was exceptionally strong, fast, and agile.

Ray seemed well on his way to achieving his goal. However, he had played golf throughout his teenage years. He enjoyed the game and played exceptionally well. Eventually, golf supplanted baseball as Ray's sport of choice. In 1960, Ray won the National Jaycees Tournament. This proved that he had the ability to excel at golf; how far he could go in baseball was still unknown. He had the physical stature for baseball success, standing 6 feet tall and weighing 185 pounds, but he did not know if he had the ability to star in a sport in which nearly every player had exceptional physical talent. In golf, his prospects seemed better, and he joined the professional tour in 1963.

The Road to Excellence
In the 1960's, physical ability became more important in golf than in earlier eras. In the 1920's and 1930's, golfers played with wood-shafted clubs. Finesse and mastery of a variety of shots were more

integral than power. One of the greatest golfers of that era, Gene Sarazen, was 5 feet 6 inches tall. Another, Tommy Armour, had suffered lung damage from his subjection to a gas attack during World War I. The longest driver of the 1930's, Jimmy Thompson, was a minor golf figure.

After 1960, the situation changed. Golfers played with steel- and fiberglass-shafted clubs, far more powerful than the wooden predecessors. Most golf courses had better-conditioned fairways and less-threatening rough. Because landing in the rough was no longer the disaster it once was, golfers could swing with more abandon. The new style, into which Ray's game fitted perfectly, was best exemplified by Jack Nicklaus. He was able to drive the ball so far that, even on long par 4 and par 5 holes, he would need only a short second shot to reach the green. Ray, if not quite Nicklaus's equal in driving, nearly matched him in strength and exceeded him in body conditioning. Ray's power enabled him to play to perfection the new style that Nicklaus had pioneered.

The Emerging Champion
Because of his powerful swing, Ray seemed destined for immediate stardom. In 1964, he finished with an excellent score in the U.S. Open, winning favorable attention from many golf experts. He was overshadowed in that event by his playing partner, Ken Venturi, who won the tournament. The previous year, Ray had gained attention when he won the St. Petersburg Open. At the time, he was the second-youngest golfer to win a professional event in the history of American golf.

It seemed Ray lacked only the experience to be considered among golf's leaders. In 1969, Ray triumphed in the Professional Golfers' Association (PGA) Championship, one of golf's major events. Rather than mark the onset of his reign among the elect, the victory inaugurated a decline. Ray had to face two obstacles. Physical ability is sufficient for success, but constant practice is also necessary. In his first years on the tour, Ray proved unwilling to devote the time and effort needed to perfect his game. He spurned long hours at the practice tee,

---

Records and Milestones

Has won seventeen regular PGA Tour events

Honors and Awards

1963	*Golf Digest* Rookie of the Year
1983	PGA Vardon Trophy
1989	Ryder Cup team captain
	Inducted into World Golf Hall of Fame

instead devoting his time to parties and high living. The other obstacle cannot be blamed on Ray. During the 1960's, golf was dominated by Jack Nicklaus and Tom Watson. Nicklaus, considered by some to be the greatest golfer of all time, finished at or near the top of nearly every major tournament he entered. In the 1970's, Watson challenged Nicklaus for golf supremacy, engaging the "Golden Bear" in several classic duels for major titles. With these two in control, little room existed for others in the golf majors. Ray might have had a better record in the 1960's and 1970's if his path had not crossed Nicklaus's.

Continuing the Story

Because of Ray's reputation as a partygoer, many experts viewed him as a player unable to fulfill his early promise. He was seen as a good journeyman golfer who had won a major event, the PGA, by playing above his normal game. During the 1970's, he showed that he had a characteristic akin to most champion athletes: the ability to learn from mistakes. He embarked on the grueling hours of practice he had hitherto spurned. His decision to abandon his previous style of life was aided by the beginning of a strong and stable marriage. He began to excel in accuracy as well as in distance.

Even during his years of decline, Ray had almost always ranked among the leading money winners. After his calculated course of improvement, there was no room for doubt about Ray's standing. He won the 1976 Masters, and in 1982, he won the PGA tournament for the second time. His foremost achievement came in 1986, when he won the most important tournament in American golf, the U.S. Open. In winning this event, he demonstrated another quality of a true champion: the ability to play well under pressure. He won the event through an excellent final round, surpassing a number of players closely bunched together at the start of the final day of play.

Major Championship Victories

1969, 1982	PGA Championship
1976	The Masters
1986	U.S. Open

Other Notable Victories

1963	St. Petersburg Open
1969	American Golf Classic
1969, 1975, 1977, 1981, 1983, 1985, 1991	Ryder Cup team
1975	Kemper Open
1976	World Open
1977	Byron Nelson Classic
1978	Brazilian Open
1979	Greensboro Open
1980-81	Doral Eastern Open
1981	Canada PGA
	Manufacturers Hanover-Westchester Classic
	Tournament Players Championship
1982	Danny Thomas-Memphis Classic
	Memorial Tournament
1985	Houston Open

Senior Tour Victories

1992	GTE North Classic
	Ralphs Senior Classic
	Senior Tour Championship
1993	Gulf Stream Aerospace Invitational
	Northville Long Island Classic
1994	*Golf Magazine* Senior Tour Championship
	The Tradition
	Las Vegas Senior Classic
	Cadillac NFL Golf Classic
1995	PGA Seniors Championship
	Burnet Senior Classic
	Emerald Coast Classic
1996, 2000	Ford Senior Players Championship
2006	Wendy's Champions Skins Game

During the course of his years on the tour, Ray has been among the game's top total-money winners, winning more than $3 million in purses and triumphing in Europe as well as in the United States. He needed only a victory in the British Open to give him wins in all of golf's four major events, an achievement only a handful of great golfers accomplished.

In 1992, with victories in the Doral-Ryder Open and the Senior Tour Championship, Ray made history as the first PGA professional to win tournaments in both PGA and PGA Senior events in the same year. Ray won important tournaments every year until 1997, the first year since he joined the Senior Tour that he did not have a first-place finish. By 1998, he had passed the $11 million mark in career earnings. Appearing in only nineteen tournaments in 1999, Ray still managed to rank among the top thirty-one money earners. He finished the year with two second-place finishes and was the only senior player to make the cut at The Masters. In 2000, he won his second Ford Senior Players Championship and had nine top-twenty-five finishes, including six in the top ten. He continued to play well on the Senior Tour and, in 2006, won the Wendy's Champions Skins Game.

Summary

Ray Floyd's interest in golf as a teenager was surpassed by his enthusiasm for baseball. He almost embarked on a professional baseball career but was dissuaded at the last minute by his golfing prowess in college. His career as a professional golfer began well, but he soon slumped because of his aversion to practice. After overcoming this problem, Ray became one of the best golfers of the 1980's and one of the most successful senior players on the tour throughout the 1990's and 2000's.

Bill Delaney

Additional Sources

Barratt, David. "Nine Men Out." *Golf Magazine* 37, no. 6 (1995).

Floyd, Ray, and Larry Dennis. *From Sixty Yards In: How to Master Golf's Short Game.* New York: HarperPerennial, 1992.

Floyd, Ray, and Jaime Diaz. *The Elements of Scoring: A Master's Guide to the Art of Scoring Your Best When You're Not Playing Your Best.* New York: Fireside, 2000.

Golf Magazine's Encyclopedia of Golf: The Complete Reference. New York: HarperCollins, 1993.

Jim Furyk

Born: May 12, 1970
West Chester, Pennsylvania
Also known as: James Michael Furyk (full name)

Early Life

James Michael Furyk was born in West Chester, Pennsylvania. He was an active teen and participated in basketball and golf at Manheim High School. His basketball career may have taken precedence over his golf success if he had not earned a state championship in golf before graduation. His father, a golf professional at Uniontown Country Club in Pennsylvania, taught Jim to have patience and control in his golf game. Jim accepted a scholarship to play at the University of Arizona following his high school career.

The Road to Excellence

Because of Jim's 6-foot 2-inch frame, many in the golf world assumed Jim had power off the tee comparable to greats such as Tiger Woods and Phil Mickelson. However, at the beginning of Jim's col-

lege career, many in the golf community questioned his unorthodox stance and unusual swing. Prior to college, Jim had been coached only by his father. When approached to change his swing in college, and again later in life, Jim stuck to his beliefs, refusing to change his swing. Although his college career was a success by most standards, he first earned fame when he turned professional in 1992.

The Emerging Champion

In 1993, Jim earned his first win as a member of the Nationwide Tour, at the Nike Golf Mississippi Gulf Coast Classic. Following a successful Nationwide stint, Jim earned his playing card and moved onto the PGA Tour to face the best players in the game. Between 1994 and 1997, Jim won two tournaments. His first, the Las Vegas Invitational, came in 1995, and he ended that season as the thirty-third ranked golfer on tour. Following the 1995 campaign, Jim won the 1996 Hawaiian Open, beating Brad Faxon in a pressure-filled playoff round. Although Jim failed to win any notable tournaments in 1997, he finished fourth on the money list in the final PGA rankings. His most noteworthy victory came on June 15, 2003, when he became the U.S. Open champion, beating Stephen Leaney by three strokes. Jim did not garner the fame of Woods, Mickelson, Arnold Palmer, or other greats of the game, but his consistent play kept him in the top twenty of the earnings list beginning in 1997, with the exception of an injury-plagued 2004 campaign. Jim underwent wrist surgery in 2004 but returned the following season. Following the disappointing 2004 campaign, Jim won the Western Open in 2005, beating Tiger Woods by two strokes; won two events in 2006; and a earned repeat victory at the Canadian Open in 2007.

Jim Furyk teeing off at the thirteenth hole of the 2005 U.S. Open. (Andy Lyons/Getty Images)

Continuing the Story

Jim came up short of winning a major event in 2008; his best finish was a fifth-place tie in the U.S. Open. Despite his lack of multiple major-tournament victories, Jim became recognized for his swing and his friendly, yet competitive demeanor on the golf course. In forty-eight starts in the U.S. Open, Masters, British Open, and PGA Championship, Jim has earned one victory. Despite this, Jim managed to find golf success in other avenues of the game. He was a member of the 1997, 1999, 2002, 2004, 2006, and 2008 Ryder Cup teams; thanks to Jim's excellent play, the U.S. team won the event in 1999 and 2008. In addition, Jim was a member of the 1998, 2000, 2003, 2005, and 2007 Presidents Cup teams, earning victories in four of those years. Jim did all of this with a driving distance off the tee of nearly 9 yards less than the PGA competitive field average. However, his driving accuracy, greens-in-regulation percentage, and putts-per-round average are considerably better than those of his fellow competitors. The patience and concentration he learned at a young age carried over to his PGA career and aided in his success.

Summary

One of Jim's most noteworthy years on tour was 2006; he won the Vardon Trophy, which is awarded

Honors, Awards, Milestones

1997, 1999, 2002, 2004, 2006, 2008	U.S. Ryder Cup team
1998, 2000, 2003, 2005, 2007	Presidents Cup
2006	Vardon Trophy

annually by the PGA to the tour's leader in scoring average. Jim posted his career-best two victories in 2006 and finished the year earning more than $7 million on tour. His wife, Tabitha, and two children, Caleigh and Tanner, are his first priority. In 2008, preparing for the Ryder Cup at Valhalla golf course in Louisville, Kentucky, Jim excused himself from team preparations to be with his ailing wife, who was experiencing back pain. He returned to Valhalla days later to help lead the U.S. team to its first Ryder Cup Championship in nearly a decade. After a career-threatening injury in 2004, he battled back. He never changed his unorthodox swing and always found time to play both on the PGA and in events representing his country. He provided motivation to youth to battle through injury and obstacles and helped his communities in Pennsylvania and Ponte Vedra Beach, Florida, through multiple tournament and charity appearances.

Keith J. Bell

PGA Tour Victories

1995, 1998-99	Las Vegas Invitational
1996	Hawaiian Open
2000	Doral-Ryder Open
2001	Mercedes Championships
2002	Memorial Tournament
2003	U.S. Open
	Buick Open
2005	Western Open
2006	Wachovia Championship
2006-07	Canadian Open
2008	PGA Grand Slam of Golf

Additional Sources

Hopkins, John, Dave Anderson, and Martin Davis. *The Ryder Cup: Golf's Greatest Event: A Complete History.* Greenwich, Conn.: American Golfer, 2008.

Jacobsen, Peter, and Jack Sheehan. *Embedded Balls: Adventures on and off the Tour with Golf's Premier Storyteller.* New York: Putnam Adult, 2005.

Silver, Michael. "Father Knows Best: Jim Furyk Won the U.S. Open Using a Loopy Swing He Grooved Under the Tutelage of His Dad." *Sports Illustrated* 98, no. 25 (June 23, 2003): 34.

Retief Goosen

Born: February 3, 1969
      Pietersburg (now Polokwane), South
      Africa
Also known as: The Iceman; the Goose

Early Life

Retief Goosen was born on February 3, 1969, in Pietersburg (now Polokwane), South Africa. Retief's father, Theo Goosen, introduced him to golf at an early age. His father preached discipline and hard work on and off the golf course and never made things easy on his son. From an early age, Retief was a bit different. At the age of fifteen, he was struck by lightning while golfing with a childhood friend. His clothes and shoes disintegrated, and his watchband melted to his wrist. Several weeks after suffering a near-death experience, Retief was ready to get back on the course and resume his amateur career. He had no memory of the horrific event, but his father took his survival as a sign of good things to come.

The Road to Excellence

In 1990, soon after winning the South African Amateur Championship, Retief joined the professional tour. He won his first professional tournament at the Iscor Newcastle Classic in 1991. In 1992, he claimed another big professional victory, winning the European Qualifying School. His success continued in Europe, with victories virtually every year between 1991 and 2000. However, one thing continued to elude Retief. Whether right or wrong, golfers are measured by their success on the American tour, and Retief had yet to have any success in the U.S.-based tournaments. He set his sights on the U.S. Open, and his status soon changed.

The Emerging Champion

In 2001, Retief had his great breakthrough on American soil. Playing at a challenging Southern Hills Country Club, he appeared ready to win the U.S. Open. However, the final round proved difficult. Retief's putter failed him on the back nine. He had a three putt and missed a twelve-footer on the final hole, costing him the victory. Instead, he fell into an 18-hole playoff round with Mark Brooks, the 1996 PGA Championship winner. On Monday, Retief's putter did not fail him. He breezed to a 2-stroke victory in the playoff round and was crowned U.S. Open champion.

With his victory in a major tournament, Retief joined an elite group. However, as his nickname "The Iceman" implies, the pressure and expectations did not phase him. He finished the 2001 season with two additional wins and eleven top-ten finishes. He was at the top of the European Tour Order of Merit and was considered among Europe's top golfers, and his world ranking rocketed to number eleven.

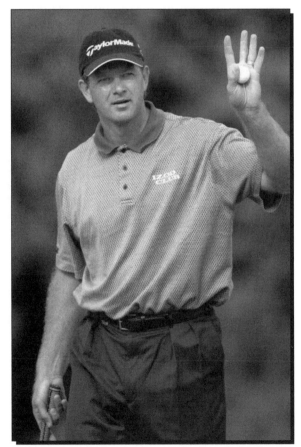

Retief Goosen acknowledges the gallery in 2002. (AP/ Wide World Photos)

PGA Tour and European Tour Victories

1996	Northumberland Challenge
1997, 1999	French Open
2000, 2003	Trophée Lancôme
2001	Scottish Open
	Madrid Open
2001, 2004	U.S. Open
2002	Johnnie Walker Classic
	BellSouth Classic
2003	Chrysler Championship
2004	European Open
	Tour Championship
2005	German Masters
	South African Airways Open
	International
2007	Qatar Masters

Retief's success continued. He won a tournament on the PGA European Tour every year between 1995 and 2005 and on the American tour every year between 2001 and 2005. In 2004, at Shinnecock Hills Country Club in New York, Retief won his second U.S. Open. His second major win rang in what became known as "The Big Five Era." The phrase referred to a period of time when men's professional golf was dominated by Tiger Woods, Vijay Singh, Ernie Els, Phil Mickelson, and Retief. The five golfers moved up and down the top five rankings, thoroughly dominating the game.

In 2006, Retief reached a career-high ranking, but by the end of that year, he began slumping. In 2007, he won the Qatar Masters, but his ranking dropped to number twenty-six in the world by season's end. He was forced to withdraw from the 2008 Qatar Masters because of complications related to laser eye surgery. He came back soon thereafter and returned to form by mid-2008.

Continuing the Story

As of 2008, Retief had won nine events on the Sunshine Tour in South Africa, fourteen events on the PGA European Tour, and six events on the PGA Tour. He won two U.S. Open Championships and finished in the top three at The Masters four times. While he had a brief slump in late 2006 and 2007, he played well in 2008 and won the Iskandar Johor Open in the Asian Tour. With his steady game and calm demeanor, Retief hoped to claim many more victories on both the European and the American tours.

Summary

Retief Goosen was one of four golfers who stood up to challenge the dominance of Tiger Woods at the beginning of the twenty-first century. He won two major tournaments and twice finished second at The Masters. In 2001, he was the PGA European Tour golfer of the year.

Theodore Shields

Additional Sources

Kalb, Elliott. *Who's Better, Who's Best in Golf? Mr. Stats Sets the Record Straight on the Top Fifty Golfers of All Time.* New York: McGraw-Hill, 2006.

Lewis, Chris. *The Scorecard Always Lies: A Year Behind the Scenes on the PGA Tour.* New York: Free Press, 2007.

Shipnuck, Alan. "Back from the Dead." *Sports Illustrated* 94, no. 26 (June 25, 2001): 56.

Walter Hagen

Born: December 21, 1892
    Rochester, New York
Died: October 5, 1969
    Traverse City, Michigan
Also known as: Walter Charles Hagen (full name); the Haig

Early Life

Walter Charles Hagen was born on December 21, 1892, in Rochester, New York. He was the second of five children of blacksmith William Hagen and his wife Louise (Balko) Hagen. As a boy, Walter was interested in baseball as well as golf. Because his fa-

Walter Hagen, who won eleven major championships. (Courtesy of Amateur Athletic Foundation of Los Angeles)

ther worked in East Rochester auto body shops for only eighteen dollars a week, Walter worked as a caddy at the age of nine. He earned ten cents a round with an occasional five-cent tip.

A natural athlete, Walter spent most of his time after school at the Rochester Country Club, frequenting the pro shop. His eagerness so impressed the club's golf pro that he made Walter his assistant. Walter mainly fixed golf clubs, but he also taught himself aspects of the game, such as how to grip the clubs for different shots. At the age of twelve, Walter decided that the country club was giving him all the education he needed, so he quit school to spend more time there. To supplement his income, he also worked part-time as a taxidermist, a garage mechanic, and a piano finisher.

The Road to Excellence

In 1913, Walter succeeded his boss, Andy Christie, as club professional. By then, he had learned much about the game from expert club professionals such as Christie and Al Ricketts. He later attributed his sportsmanship to these men. From them he learned not only golf but also the qualities and proper mannerisms and speech of a gentleman. In 1912, Walter entered his first tournament, the Canadian Open. He felt embarrassed to have to ask permission of his country club board of directors for the time off to play. It proved worthwhile, even though he only came in eleventh.

Walter was shorter than 6 feet, but somehow he always looked taller because he walked around a golf course as if he owned it. His confidence seemed unshakable and came from an oversized personality, which eventually gave rise to great achievements. Walter was considered an attractive player to watch—never monotonous, always exciting. He soon developed exceptional skills at putting and at making shots with irons, with few to equal him. He played his best golf on or near the green. Walter was a master at recovering from nearly impossible situations. He often found himself playing out of bunkers, so he became one of the most talented golfers ever at using a nine-iron to extract his ball from bunkers.

All aspects of Walter's life were exciting. He reveled in his image as a bad boy. Sometimes he had his caddy roll up his tuxedo into a ball, so that when he wore it on the course that morning, he would appear to have arrived from an all-night party. Other times he played in his dancing pumps. Later on, though, he no longer needed to fake his carousing, as he did it in style and in earnest.

The Emerging Champion

In 1914, a wealthy Rochester man sponsored Walter's entry into the U.S. Open tournament. The night before the tournament, Walter dined on bad lobster and was so ill he thought of dropping out of the game. He felt obligated to his sponsor, however, and played nevertheless. Even though he felt miserable, he managed to score a 68—one of the lowest scores in the history of the Open at the time—and won. Walter was a champion at last, at the age of twenty-one. In 1919, he won the U.S. Open again. Walter turned himself into one of the greatest shot makers in the history of golf. He won the British Open four times, in 1922, 1924, 1928, and 1929. Match play was his strongest suit. When the Professional Golfers' Association's (PGA's) tournaments were match tournaments, he won the PGA Championship five times—four of these wins in succession. Walter never won a U.S. or British Open in which his arch-competitor Bobby Jones played. This irritated Walter; however, only three

---

Honors, Awards, and Milestones

1921	U.S. Open runner-up
1923	PGA Championship runner-up
1926	British Open third-place finisher
1940	Inducted into PGA Hall of Fame
1962	GWAA Richardson Award
1974	Inducted into World Golf Hall of Fame

golfers have ever won more major titles: Jones, Jack Nicklaus, and Tiger Woods.

Continuing the Story

Not only Walter's talent for golf made him a success but also his attitude toward the game. Whereas other players would throw clubs and get angry when they made poor shots, Walter was not perturbed. He said he always expected to hit about seven bad shots in any round, so he was not bothered by them or by bad luck when it occurred.

Walter's flamboyant nature, combined with his love of living in style, served his sport well. Golf had long needed a high-profile player to boost its image—Walter was that man. He became a popular hero whom the common man could appreciate. He broke tradition in every way, and broke par as well. He revolutionized golf—then a sport for aristocrats only—not only with his showmanship and flashy clothes but also with his outrageous, nonchalant behavior. People related to him, and golf finally came into its own as a national spectator sport.

As a result, Walter has been called the father of professional golf. Before he came along, professionals were discriminated against by the members of their country clubs. Clubhouses were sanctuaries for members, and professionals were never allowed to set foot in them. Professionals were more like servants who instructed the rich about how to play. Walter changed that. With his wisecracks and antics, his Rolls Royce and color-coordinated golf outfits, he lived in the highest style and soon charmed the English upper class. The Prince of Wales invited him to lunch at the Royal St. George's clubhouse and indignantly insisted that the club's class-conscious steward serve him. Clubhouse doors opened to professionals in England and abroad. Walter had triumphed over snobbery for the benefit of all professionals to come after him.

Major Championship Victories

1914, 1919	U.S. Open
1921, 1924-27	PGA Championship
1922, 1924, 1928-29	British Open

Other Notable Victories

1916, 1921, 1926-27, 1932	Western Open
1918, 1923-24	North and South Open
1920	French Open
1923, 1929	Texas Open
1926	Eastern Open
1927, 1929, 1931, 1933, 1935, 1937	Ryder Cup Team playing captain
1931	Canadian Open

Walter was never beneath cashing in on his fame by endorsing clubs and golf equipment. When he retired, the Wilson Sporting Goods Company named a division after him and hired him to run it. Finally, when poor health caused Walter to quit playing golf entirely, he took up hunting and fishing and became an avid baseball fan. In 1956, his autobiography, *The Walter Hagen Story*, was published. He died of cancer on October 5, 1969, in Traverse City, Michigan.

Summary

Walter Hagen, one of golf's best players ever, appeared in more than twenty-five hundred exhibitions, from his first victory at the U.S. Open in 1914 until his retirement in 1929. He made a name for himself internationally by winning the British Open four times. He also played on the first six Ryder Cup teams and claimed five PGA titles, five Western Opens, and one Canadian Open. Walter is credited with popularizing golf through his showmanship.

Nan White

Additional Sources

Barkow, Al. *Best of Golf: Best Golfers, Courses, Moments, and More.* Lincolnwood, Ill.: Publications International, 2002.

Clavin, Thomas. *Sir Walter: The Flamboyant Life of Walter Hagen.* London: Aurum, 2006.

_____. *Sir Walter: Walter Hagen and the Invention of Professional Golf.* New York: Simon & Schuster, 2005.

Holanda, Raymond. *The Golfer of the Decade on the PGA Tour: From Walter Hagen in the 1920's to Tiger Woods in the 2000's.* New York: iUniverse, 2007.

Lowe, Stephen R. *Sir Walter and Mr. Jones: Walter Hagen, Bobby Jones, and the Rise of American Golf.* Ann Arbor, Mich.: Ann Arbor Media Group, 2004.

Pádraig Harrington

Born: August 31, 1971
Ballyroan, Dublin, Ireland

Early Life
Pádraig Harrington came from a sporting family: His father, Paddy, played Gaelic football for Cork. He attended Coláiste Éanna, the local high school, the same school Paul McGinley, another Ryder Cup player attended. Peter Lawrie, another Irish international, was also born at Ballyroan. The local area of Rathfarnham has many golf clubs, one of which, Stackstown, is where Pádraig learned golf. While playing golf as an amateur, he gained a degree in accounting. He and his wife Caroline, whom he married in 1997, had two children through 2008.

The Road to Excellence
Pádraig's first golfing successes were as an amateur. His earliest win was in 1991, when he won the Sherry Cup, followed by his 1994 win at the West of Ireland Amateur. In 1995, he won both the Irish Amateur Open and Irish Amateur Closed Championships, prompting him to turn professional. As an amateur he had also played three times in the Walker Cup for Great Britain and Ireland against the United States and was on the winning team in 1995.

Pádraig had some immediate successes as a professional and was chosen to represent Ireland in team events, including the Alfred Dunhill Cup, where he played every year from 1996 to 2000, and the World Cup, which he and McGinley won for Ireland in 1997, beating Scotland in the final. He also helped the Irish team to victory in the Seve Trophy event in 2002, 2003, and 2005. As an individual, his first success was in 1996, when he won the Peugeot Spanish Open on the European Tour. He was consistent on that tour for the next few years, without managing to win again. A fifth-place finish at the British Open in 1997 was his best major result during the time period.

The Emerging Champion
Major international recognition for Pádraig first came with his selection for the European Ryder Cup team in 1999. His team lost narrowly, but Pádraig broke even, 1-1-1, beating Mark O'Meara. He represented Europe in all the following Ryder Cups; his best result was in 2004, when he won 4 out of 5 matches. This was followed by a disastrous per-

Pádraig Harrington working his way out of a bunker. (Vivek Prakash/Reuters/Landov)

Notable Victories

Year	Tournament
1996	Peugeot Spanish Open
1998, 2004-05, 2007	Irish PGA Championship
2001	Volvo Masters
2002	BMW Asian Open
2002, 2006	Dunhill Links Championship
2003	Omega Hong Kong Open
2004	German Masters
2005	Honda Classic
	Barclays Classic
2007	Irish Open
2007-08	British Open
2008	PGA Championship

formance in 2006. He could manage only one draw in five games, even though his team won easily.

Beginning in 2000, he won regularly on the European Tour, though his attempts to enter the U.S. circuit were not quite so successful. His first victory in the United States was in a non-PGA tournament, the 2002 Target World Challenge. After slightly better seasons in the United States, he finally gained membership to the PGA Tour in 2005. He won his first major U.S. tournament in that year, the Honda Classic, beating Vijay Singh and Joe Ogilvie in a sudden-death playoff. He followed that with a dramatic, final-hole win in the Barclays Classic, beating Jim Furyk. His easy manners and calm demeanor won him popularity in the United States. His best major tournament results in the United States were fifth-place finishes at The Masters, in 2002 and 2008, and the U.S. Open, in 2000 and 2006.

On the European Tour, Pádraig had managed a fifth-place finish in the British Open of 1997 and 2002. In the latter year, he won his biggest prize money up to that time, approximately $250,000. Increasingly, he was making an impression in the Order of Merit, the European Tour's money list. Between 1996 and 2005, he finished in the top ten seven times. In 2005, he was fifth with winnings of approximately $17 million. However, the next year, Pádraig topped the list, beating Paul Casey on the last hole of the last tournament of the year.

Continuing the Story

In 2007, Pádraig earned his first victory in a major tournament. In the British Open, played at Carnoustie in Scotland, Pádraig

and Sergio Garcia had both scored 277, 7 strokes below par; both players missed winning chances on the last few holes. In the four-hole playoff, Pádraig gained a 1-stroke lead on the first hole and managed to maintain it. He had the satisfaction of beating Tiger Woods by 5 shots. Pádraig became the first Irishman since Fred Daly in 1947 to win the British Open. In the same year, Pádraig also won the Irish Open, again after a playoff, this time with Bradley Dredge, the Welsh champion.

Success at the British Open shifted Pádraig from a major European player to a recognized international star. Based on that success, he wrote his first book, the proceeds of which were directed to a charity he founded, the Pádraig Harrington Charitable Foundation. In 2008, Pádraig injured his wrist before the start of the British Open. However, he elected to defend his title. Recovering from a 2-stroke deficit on the final day of the tournament, Pádraig repeated as champion, besting Ian Coulter by 4 strokes. Later in the year, he added another major to his win total by capturing the PGA Championship.

Summary

Pádraig Harrington was the leader of the Irish renaissance of golfing that included players such as Paul McGinley, Peter Lawrie, Darren Clarke, Graeme McDowell, and Damsen McGrane. He helped build the prestige of the European circuit while continuing to be a popular member of the U.S. PGA Tour. He was seen as an excellent ambassador for European golf.

David Barratt

Additional Sources

Harrington, Pádraig. *Pádraig Harrington's Journey to the Open.* London: Bantam Press, 2007.

Reid, Philip. *The Jug: How Pádraig Harrington Won the 2007 British Open.* Dunshaughlin, County Meath, Ireland: Maverick House, 2007.

Honors and Awards

Year	Honor
1996-2000	Alfred Dunhill Cup team
1999, 2002, 2004, 2006, 2008	Ryder Cup team
2002-03, 2005	Seve Trophy tournament winner
2002, 2007	Radio Telefís Éireann Sports Person of the Year
2006	PGA European Tour Order of Merit
2008	PGA Tour Player of the Year

Hisako Higuchi

Born: October 13, 1945
       Kawagoe City, Saitama Prefecture, Japan
Also known as: Chako Higuchi

Early Life
Hisako "Chako" Higuchi was born in Kawagoe City, Saitama, Japan, on October 13, 1945. She was the youngest of six children. From early on and throughout her career, she was known as Chako, a common nickname for Japanese women named Hisako. At Nikaido High School in Tokyo, Chako was a track-and-field champion. In 1963, when one of her sisters became a locker-room attendant at a Tokyo golf course, Chako had her first chance to play golf. She became the caddy to one of Japan's most famous golfers at the time, professional-turned-teacher Torakichi Nakamura.

The Road to Excellence
Nakamura liked what he saw in Chako. He trained her diligently, building up her strength through daily running practice and developing her skills by making her drive approximately one thousand golf balls a day. On November 1, 1967, a few days after her twenty-second birthday, Chako turned professional.

Nakamura founded the Japan Ladies Professional Golf Association (JLPGA) and became its first chair in 1967. Chako was the league's first star player. In 1968, Chako won the first JLPGA Championship. She repeated this feat for an amazing seven consecutive years, until 1974. Also in 1968, Chako won the second major annual tournament, Japan's Women's Open Golf Championship (known as the Tokyo Broadcasting System Women's Open from 1968 to 1970). She compiled four consecutive wins in this tournament. On November 3, 1974, at twenty-nine years old, Chako won the third most important JLPGA tournament, the Ladies Professional Golf Association Japan Classic (renamed the Mizuno Classic in 1999) at Horyu Country Club, with a score of 218, four below par.

From 1968 to 1976, Chako was Japan's top-earning women's golf professional. Her financial compensation reflected the increase of money in-

Honors and Awards

Year	Award
1977	First Japanese woman to win LPGA Championship
1996	Became president of JLPGA
2003	Inducted into World Golf Hall of Fame
2008	Inducted into International Women's Sports Hall of Fame
	Ogino Ginko Merit Award

volved in Japan's professional women's golf. In 1968, Chako was the top earner, with 350,000 yen (under $1,000 at the time); by 1975, her earnings had risen to 8,428,233 yen (about $28,000 at the time).

The Emerging Champion
Reigning supreme at home, Chako began to play in foreign tournaments. She joined the international LPGA Tour in 1969, competing in the United States and Europe. In 1974, when the Wills Australian Ladies Open was launched at the Victoria Golf Club, Chako was its first winner, with a score of 219 over three rounds. With her win, Chako became a serious international contender in women's golf. In 1975, Chako married the golf professional Isai Matsui; however, she kept her professional name.

Chako's second big international triumph occurred on August 7, 1976, in Sunningdale, England. There, she won the Colgate European Open. In the four rounds, Chako scored a total of 284 on 72 holes, 6 strokes ahead of her two tied rivals. With this athletic feat, Chako made sports headlines around the world, and *The New York Times* published an action photograph of her.

Chako became undisputed champion on June 12, 1977, when she won the LPGA Championship at North Myrtle Beach, South Carolina. Chako, at 5 feet 6 inches and 124 pounds, used her trademark unorthodox technique: She rocked back and forth on her backswing and downswing, even losing sight of her ball at the apex of her backswing. On June 10, in the first round of the tournament, she came in second with a score of 71, one below par. Her score of 67 put her in the lead on the second round that day. The next day Chako was in a three-way tie with Judy Rankin and Pat Bradley; each player had 210 strokes. In the fourth and final round on June 12, Chako shot five birdies, two bogeys, and eleven pars for a total of 279. This earned Chako the championship; she bested her competitors, who were tied at 282, by 3 strokes. Back home in Tokyo, Chako was celebrated with a ticker-tape parade. She was the first Asian woman to win a major LPGA tournament.

Notable Victories

1968-71, 1974, 1976-77, 1980	Japan Women's Open Golf Championship
1968-74, 1976-77	JLPGA Championship
1970-73	JGP Ladies Open
1971-73, 1975-77, 1980	Tokai Classic
1972	JPGA Asahi Kokusai Tournament
1972-74	Mizuno Golf Tournament
1973	Matsushima Ladies Open
1973-74	World Ladies Golf Tournament
1974	Wills-Qantas Australian Women's Open
	Chikuma Kogen Ladies Open
	Tokyo Charity Classic
	Sunster Ladies Match
	LPGA Japan Golf Classic
1976	Sanpo Champions
	Miyagi TV Cup Ladies Open Golf Tournament
	European Open
1977	LPGA Championship
1978	Junon Ladies Open
1978-79	Shinkoh Classic LPGA Tournament
1978-79, 1983	Japan LPGA East vs. West
1979	Fuji Heigen Ladies Open
	Hokuriku Queens Golf Cup
	Toyotomi Ladies
1980	KBS Kyoto Ladies Golf Tournament
1981	Okinawa Makiminato Auto Ladies Tournament
	Tokushima Tsukinomiya Ladies Open Golf Tournament
	Pioneer Cup
1982	Hokuriku Queens Golf Cup
1982, 1984	Kumamoto Chuou Ladies Cup Golf Tournament
1983-84	Kibun Ladies Classic
1984	Paris Ladies Classic
	Ladies Open Golf Tournament
1985	Chukyo TV-Bridgestone Ladies Open
1986	Fujitsu Ladies
	Tsumura-Itsuki Classic
1987	Yamaha Cup Ladies Open
1990	Kohsaido Asahi Golf Cup

Continuing the Story

At home, Chako won the JLPGA Championship in 1976 and 1977, for a record nine titles. She also won the Japan's Women's Open Golf Championship in 1974, 1976, 1977, and 1980, for a total of eight victories. In 1978 and 1979, she was Japan's top women's golf money earner, with 18,399,345 yen (about $80,000 at the time). Her LPGA championship in 1977 earned her $22,500.

Chako's fellow women competitors deeply appreciated her professional ethics and her warm personality. Rankin admired Chako's superb tempo and great balance, and Carol Mann called her a fierce competitor, great athlete, and delightful companion off the course. Chako continued to do well in Japan and abroad throughout the 1980's. In 1987, at the age of forty-one, she took twenty months leave from golf when her daughter was born.

In 1994, Chako became chairwoman of the JLPGA, a position she still held in 2008. When she ceased formal competition in 1996, she had won sixty-nine times on the JLPGA Tour and become a superstar athlete in Japan. Chako remained actively involved in Japanese golf. In her honor, the JLPGA installed the Hisako Higuchi Kibun Classic tournament. With golfer Isao Aoki, Chako designed a golf course in Ibaraki Prefecture. Chako was inducted into the World Golf Hall of Fame in St. Augustine, Florida, on October 20, 2003. In the 2000's, she continued to play in the newly constituted Legends Tour of women ex-professionals.

On December 28, 2006, as chairwoman of the JLPGA, Chako had to ban Ai Takimaki from professional golf for ten years for cheating. When Chako's teacher Nakamura died on February 11, 2008, Chako held a joint memorial service for him given by the JLPGA and the Japan Professional Golfers' Association.

Summary

Hisako "Chako" Higuchi was Japan's first woman golfer of international fame. Her amazing series of successes in Japan and her victories in major tournaments on four continents made her a beloved sports star in Japan and in the golf community. Her success inspired other Japanese women golfers of subsequent generations, including fellow World Golf Hall of Fame athlete Ayako Okamoto and the rising champions of the 2000's, Ai Miyazato and Sakura Yokomine. Her personal integrity helped to heal golf's reputation after the Takimaki scandal.

R. C. Lutz

Additional Sources

"Chako Higuchi Captures LPGA Title by Three Shots." *The New York Times,* June 13, 1977.

"Mrs. Higuchi Wins by Six Shots at 284." *The New York Times*, August 8, 1976.

Ohno, Akira, et al. "Golf and Other Professional Sports." In *Sports in Japan.* Tokyo: Foreign Press Center, 2002.

Sirak, Ron. "The Price Is Right: Price, Diegel, and Higuchi Make Golf Hall of Fame." *Golf World* 56, no. 40 (May 9, 2003): 8.

Ben Hogan

Born: August 13, 1912
   Stephenville, Texas
Died: July 25, 1997
   Fort Worth, Texas
Also known as: William Benjamin Hogan (full
   name)

Early Life

William Benjamin Hogan was born on August 13, 1912, in Stephenville, Texas, the son of a blacksmith who died when Ben was nine years old. When Ben was twelve, his mother moved the family to Fort Worth, Texas, and Ben got a job as a caddy at Glen Garden Country Club for sixty-five cents a round, more money than he could make selling newspapers at the Union Station. For Ben, good things always came the slow and hard way. The unspoken rule among the caddies at Glen Garden was that a new boy had to fight with his fists for his right to work there. Ben passed that test. He was a natural left-hander, but when he decided to learn golf himself, the only secondhand clubs available were right-handed.

The Road to Excellence

It came as a considerable surprise to everyone at Glen Garden when, at fifteen, Ben somehow managed to tie for first with Byron Nelson in the annual Christmas Day caddy tournament. At nineteen, Ben turned professional, and the next winter he set out for Los Angeles and the professional tour with less than a hundred dollars in his pocket, counting on winning enough prize money to keep afloat. He lasted a month. The following winter, 1933, he took another shot at the circuit, lasting a little longer before he had to return home again. The next four years he remained in Fort Worth. He supported himself with odd jobs, while working daily on his game, refusing to alter his intention to make golf his career. Ben was dedicated. He wanted to be the best golfer ever. Ben's swing was not naturally flawless—he practiced for hours to perfect it.

In 1937, he rejoined the circuit as an improved golfer.

The Emerging Champion

In 1942, Ben entered the Army Air Corps, serving for three years. When he returned to civilian life and competitive golf in 1945, he quickly reaffirmed his position. By 1948, Ben had won much money, but only one major title had come his way. In May of that year, he captured the Professional Golfers' Association (PGA) Championship, but the long week of matches wore him out. The slight, 137-pounder was no longer young. A dozen years had passed since he had qualified to play in his first U.S. Open. The 1948 championship was played at

Ben Hogan, who won nine major championships. (Courtesy of Amateur Athletic Foundation of Los Angeles)

Major Championship Victories

1946, 1948	PGA Championship
1948, 1950-51, 1953	U.S. Open
1951, 1953	The Masters
1953	British Open

Other Notable Victories

1940	Greensboro Open
1940, 1942	North and South Open
1942, 1947-48	Los Angeles Open
1946	Texas Open
1946-47	Phoenix Open
1946-47, 1952-53, 1959	Colonial National
1946, 1948	Western Open
1948	Bing Crosby Pro-Amateur
1949	Bing Crosby Invitational
1951	World Championship

the Riviera Country Club in Los Angeles, a 7,020-yard course perfect for Ben's long shots and uncanny accuracy. Ben's total of 276 was 5 strokes better than Ralph Guldahl's eleven-year-old scoring record for the Open.

On the morning of February 2, 1949, Ben and his wife, Valerie, were driving their Cadillac across western Texas. Ben had started the new winter tour by winning two of the first four events. Now the Hogans were heading home to Fort Worth for a few weeks of rest. On the highway near the crossroad town of Van Horn, a Greyhound bus roared out of the morning haze and smashed head-on into the Hogans' car. In the crash, Ben suffered grave injury: a double fracture of the pelvis, a fractured collarbone, a broken left ankle, and a broken right rib. He was hospitalized in El Paso. A month after the crash, his already-serious condition took a turn for the worse. Phlebitis was causing blood clots in his legs. To halt the phlebitis, doctors performed a two-hour abdominal operation and tied off the principal veins in Ben's legs. The operation saved his life, but there was no chance of Ben defending his U.S. Open Championship.

Continuing the Story

By 1950, miraculously, Ben had returned. During the sixteen months since his accident, Ben had successfully completed a tedious and often painful convalescence. By June, Ben had won one tournament. The pain in Ben's legs still showed in his walk, and in the late rounds of a tournament, his game obviously suffered from his exhaustion. Ben won his second U.S. Open, and the following year, in 1951, he won his first Masters and another U.S. Open.

From time to time after Ben's recuperation, there were indications of a "new Ben," a more mellow player. When there was no golf to play, his manner was more outgoing than it had been formerly, and his conversation revealed a new warmth and depth. The exploits of Ben Hogan were viewed from two perspectives by the American public. Some saw him as a scientist-golfer working miracles of precision; others saw him as the hero of a heart-warming human-interest comeback story. The interest in Ben had a great deal to do with the boom that golf enjoyed in the United States in the mid-twentieth century.

In the 1950's, Ben found more ways to connect with America's enthusiasm for golf. In 1953, he founded the Ben Hogan Company, a manufacturer of golfing equipment, and in 1957 he coauthored the classic *Ben Hogan's Five Lessons: The Modern Fundamentals of Golf*. In 1971, he retired from professional golf with an impressive sixty-three tournament victories, including nine majors. He died on July 25, 1997, at the age of eighty-four.

Summary

Ben Hogan set a high standard for his golf game. His ability to overcome a life-threatening injury

Honors, Awards, and Milestones

1940-41, 1948	PGA Vardon Trophy
1940-42	PGA Tour money leader
1948, 1950-51, 1953	PGA Player of the Year
1952	Placed third in the U.S. Open
1953	Associated Press Male Athlete of the Year
	Hickok Belt
	Inducted into PGA Hall of Fame
	Professional Male Athlete of the Year
1954-55	Placed second in the Masters
1955	Placed second in the U.S. Open
1973	GWAA Richardson Award
1974	Inducted into World Golf Hall of Fame
1976	Bob Jones Award

and his superior skill on the golf course made him one of the most admired golfers in U.S. history.

Brooke K. Zibel

Additional Sources

Bertrand, Tom, and Printer Bowler. *The Secret of Hogan's Swing.* Hoboken, N.J.: J. Wiley & Sons, 2006.

Coyne, John. *The Caddie Who Knew Ben Hogan.* Irvine, Calif.: Griffin, 2007.

Davis, Martin. *Ben Hogan: The Man Behind the Mystique.* Greenwich, Conn.: American Golfer, 2002.

Dodson, James. *Ben Hogan: An American Life.* New York: Broadway Books, 2005.

Frost, Mark. *The Match: The Day the Game of Golf Changed Forever.* New York: Hyperion, 2007.

Hogan, Ben, and Herbert Warren Wind. *Ben Hogan's Five Lessons: The Modern Fundamentals of Golf.* New York: Simon & Schuster, 2006.

Leadbetter, David. *The Fundamentals of Hogan.* Chelsea, Mich.: Sleeping Bear Press, 2000.

Towle, Mike. *I Remember Ben Hogan: Personal Recollections and Revelations of Golf's Most Famous Legend from the People Who Knew Him Best.* Nashville, Tenn.: Cumberland House, 2000.

Vasquez, Jody. *Afternoons with Mr. Hogan: A Boy, a Golf Legend, and the Lessons of a Lifetime.* New York: Gotham Books, 2004.

Juli Inkster

Born: June 24, 1960
Santa Cruz, California
Also known as: Juli Simpson (birth name)

Early Life

Juli Simpson Inkster was born in Santa Cruz, California, on June 24, 1960. As the youngest and only female in a family of three children, Juli competed with her older brothers in all sports. Her parents moved to a home located next to the fairway of Pasatiempo Golf Club. Juli's tomboy nature kept her active in track, swimming, softball, basketball, and tennis, despite her employment at the Pasatiempo Golf Club clubhouse restaurant. As a teenager, she became interested in playing golf and practiced relentlessly, hitting balls at the driving range before and after school. Eventually, Juli had low enough scores to play competitively and made

Juli Inkster taking a chip shot in 2002. (AP/Wide World Photos)

the Harbor High School boys' golf team. The hobby soon became her first love: She competed hard and won numerous awards. Her golf game was good enough to garner attention from and a scholarship to San Jose State University.

The Road to Excellence

Juli was the star of San Jose State's golf team and earned all-American status for three years, 1979, 1981, and 1982. She set the women's record for most collegiate victories, winning seventeen tournaments during her four years at San Jose State. She was named the San Jose State athlete of the year in 1981 and later was elected to the San Jose State University Sports Hall of Fame. Juli worked tirelessly on her game because she believed that she could successfully compete with anyone in golf. She was named California's amateur golfer of the year in 1981; all-Nor-Cal in 1979, 1980, and 1981; and the Bay Area athlete of the year in 1982.

Juli's hard work and intelligent practice techniques won her national prominence, enabling her to compete in United States Golf Association (USGA) events and win the U.S. Women's Amateur title three years in a row. Juli was only the fifth woman in history to accomplish the latter feat. In 1982, Juli won the prestigious Broderick Award. This prize honors the most outstanding National Collegiate Athletic Association women athletes.

Juli's numerous championships earned her the right to play for the U.S. national team. In 1982, Juli was invited to join the U.S. Curtis Cup and World Cup teams while still in college; she represented the United States with great success. The U.S. Curtis Cup is a competition among the United States, England, and Ireland. The Women's World Cup is a challenge between players in the Ladies Professional Golf Association (LPGA) and the Ladies European Tour. She continued to win amateur competitions and soon realized that she had the ability to be a successful professional golfer.

The Emerging Champion

In 1983, Juli joined the LPGA Tour with momentum and confidence. She played in eight tournaments, and after only her fifth start, she won first place. In 1984, her official rookie season, she won two major championships—Nabisco Dinah Shore and the Du Maurier Classic. Juli captured the rookie of year award and was the tour's brightest young star.

Juli became known for her consistency as a golfer. Many of her greatest wins came against the best competitors in major events. She compiled thirty-one career LPGA and six non-LPGA victories. Juli was competitive in each decade in which she played; she won twelve times in the 1980's, nine in the 1990's, and nine more through 2008. Her competitive fire was well known. In 1992, she lost two emotional matches in playoffs: the Nabisco Dinah Shore and the coveted U.S. Open.

Continuing the Story

Despite her fast start, Juli had trouble balancing her home life and golf career from 1993 to 1997. Her children became her priority, and she had less time to devote to practice and competition. Although she wanted to put more effort into golf, Juli averaged only two wins a year until 1999, when she had five. Her victories, which included the LPGA Championship, completed a career Grand Slam, whereby a golfer wins all the major events. By doing so, she qualified for the World Golf Hall of Fame, to which she was elected in 2000. Juli was only the fourth woman to win a career Grand Slam. Her consistency and commitment helped her come from behind to beat Annika Sorenstam at the 2002 U.S. Open.

Juli became one of the all-time LPGA career-earnings leaders, with more than $11 million, and was part of seven Solheim Cup teams, an invitational match-play event between the United States and Europe. She remained allegiant to her first golf club, becoming Pasatiempo's touring professional. She maintained close contact with the staff and players at the club and resided in nearby Los Altos.

Summary

Juli Inkster followed her athletic dreams, becoming a golf champion. Her strong desire to excel provided her with a successful career in a sport which requires high technical skill and mental toughness. Crediting

her husband, Brian, for his superb coaching, Juli became a role model and leader for players on and off the course. She competed in charity golf tournaments, including a 2007 event to help raise money for the Alzheimer's Association. Her humility inspired many athletes to be the best.

Deborah Stroman

Additional Sources

"Juli Inkster." *Current Biography Yearbook*, 63, 2002.
McCord, Robert. *The Golf Book of Days: Fascinating Facts and Stories for Every Day of the Year.* Citadel Press, 2002.

LPGA Victories

Year	Event
1983	Safeco Classic
1984	Kraft Nabisco Championship
	Du Maurier Classic
1985-86	Lady Keystone Open
1986	Kemper Open
1986, 1988	Atlantic City LPGA Classic
1986, 1999-2000	McDonald's Championship
	Safeco Classic
1988-89	Crestar Classic
1989	Kraft Nabisco Championship
1991	Bay State Classic
1992	JAL Big Apple Classic
1997-98, 2000	Samsung World Championship of Women's Golf
1999	Welch's/Circle K Championship
	Safeway LPGA Golf Championship
1999-2000	Longs Drugs Challenge
1999, 2002	U.S. Open
2001	Electrolux USA Championship
2002	Chick-fil-A Charity Championship
2003	LPGA Corning Classic
	Evian Masters
2006	Safeway International

Honors and Awards

Year	Award
1982	Broderick Award
	Curtis Cup
1983	LPGA rookie of the year
1992, 1998, 2000, 2002-03, 2005, 2007	Solheim Cup
1999	Golf Writers Association of America female player of the year
2000	Inducted into World Golf Hall of Fame
2004	William and Mousie Powell Award

Hale Irwin

Born: June 3, 1945
    Joplin, Missouri
Also known as: Hale S. Irwin (full name)

Early Life

Hale S. Irwin was born on June 3, 1945, in Joplin, Missouri. Most outstanding athletes develop an interest in their sport at an early age, and Hale was no exception. Unlike most, he did not confine himself to a single sport. He excelled in basketball and football as well as in golf. By the time he attended Boulder High School—his family had moved to Colorado—he was on the school team in all of these sports.

After Hale graduated from high school, he enrolled in the University of Colorado. He managed to limit himself to two sports, golf and football. He came under the influence of the football coach, Eddie Crowder, who inspired him to pursue a professional career. In Crowder's opinion, Hale was the best athlete in the history of the state.

The Road to Excellence

Hale's background illustrates a change that has marked professional golf since the 1960's. During the 1920's and 1930's, golfers were not generally regarded as athletes, and it was possible for someone with a poor physique to play outstanding golf. The rotund Walter Hagen dominated professional golf in the 1920's. Paul Runyan, barely 5 feet tall, defeated the great Sam Snead for the Professional Golfers' Association (PGA) Championship in 1937. Ben Hogan won the U.S. Open in 1950, even though his recovery from a near-fatal automobile crash was far from complete. What counted for golf success was knowledge of course conditions and the ability to play a wide variety of shots. These skills required long years of experience to obtain; only rarely would a newcomer relying purely on his natural talent become a consistent winner.

Since the 1960's, conditions have changed. As the prizes and lucrative endorsement contracts have increased, golf has attracted players qualified for demanding physical sports. Hale, who might have become a professional football player, was at the forefront of this trend. Hale had great natural ability and an obsessive desire to be the best. His success was because of his determination. He practiced constantly. Often, he proceeded to the golf tee after a grueling session of football practice, re-

Hale Irwin, who won three U.S. Opens and two Masters. (Ralph W. Miller Golf Library)

Major Championship Victories

1974, 1979, 1990 U.S. Open

Other Notable Victories

1967	NCAA Championship
1971, 1973	Heritage Classic
1974-75	World Picadilly Match Play
1974, 1979	World Cup team
1975	Western Open
1975, 1977	Atlanta Classic
1975, 1977, 1979, 1981, 1991	Ryder Cup team
1976	Florida Citrus Open
	Glen Campbell Los Angeles Open
1977	San Antonio-Texas Open
1978	Australian PGA
1979	South African PGA
1981	Buick Open
	Hawaiian Open
1982	Brazilian Open
1983, 1985	Memorial Tournament
1984	Bing Crosby Pro-Am
1987	Fila Classic
1990	Buick Classic
1994	MCI Heritage Golf Classic

maining there until he had hit hundreds of balls. Given his physical talent and will to win, an outstanding career seemed assured.

The Emerging Champion

Although Hale was regarded as an outstanding professional prospect, he did not at once rise to supremacy. Two obstacles confronted him. The first of these was a flaw in his otherwise superb physical condition. The 6-foot-tall, 170-pound young athlete exercised constantly to maintain his fitness, but exercise could not change the fact that he had blurred vision. Since he was a boy, Hale had worn glasses when playing golf. Poor vision is an especially severe handicap on the green, because accurate putting demands attention to the contours of the grass. Hale could likewise do little about the other obstacle. During the 1960's, golf was dominated by Jack Nicklaus, one of the greatest golfers of all time. Other outstanding golfers, most notably Tom Watson, stood waiting in the wings. Even an athlete of Hale's ability required years of preparation before he could play on even terms with the likes of Nicklaus and Watson.

Hale resolved to confront these difficulties with constant practice. From his college years, his game has been characterized by extraordinary precision. He was not golf's longest driver or most accurate putter, but his ground swing always gave him a straight trajectory. Because of his consistency, Hale was able to place his shots where he had the best chance to reach the green, rather than having to scramble to extricate himself from trouble. His careful shot-making and ability to avoid poor shots was reminiscent of Ben Hogan, the greatest golfer of the 1950's.

Continuing the Story

Although Hale at first stood outside the elite circle of winners, headed by Jack Nicklaus, his persistence eventually paid off. He won the U.S. Open in 1974 and 1979. He remained a consistent winner

Senior Tour Victories

1995	Vantage Championship
1995, 1998-99	Ameritech Senior Open
1996	American Express Invitational
1996-97	PGA Seniors Championship
	LG Championship
	Vantage Championship
1997-98	Bank Boston Classic
	Las Vegas Senior Classic
1997, 1999	Burnet Classic
	Boone Valley Classic
1997, 2007	MasterCard Championship
1998, 2000	U.S. Senior Open
1998, 2002	Toshiba Senior Classic
	PGA Seniors Championship
	Energizer Senior Tour Championship
1999	Ford Senior Players Championship
1999-2000	Nationwide Championship
2000	BellSouth Senior Classic
	EMC Kaanapali Classic
2001	Siebel Classic
	Bruno's Memorial Classic
2001-03, 2005	Turtle Bay Championship
2002	ACE Group Classic
	3M Championship
2003	Kinko's Classic of Austin
2004	Liberty Mutual Legends of Golf
2005	PGA Seniors Championship
	Outback Steakhouse Pro-Am
	Wal-Mart First Tee Open at Pebble Beach
	SAS Championship

Honors, Awards, and Records

1975-78	Covered eighty-six tournaments without missing the thirty-six-hole cut—longest streak in PGA Tour history
1990	Oldest player ever to win the U.S. Open (age 45)
1992	Inducted into World Golf Hall of Fame
1996-98	Byron Nelson Award
1997-98	Senior Tour Player of the Year
2000	All-time leader in combined PGA and Senior PGA career earnings with over $20 million
2002	Inducted into University of Colorado Athletic Hall of Fame
2006	Inducted into Colorado State High School Athletic Hall of Fame

throughout the 1970's and 1980's. His steadiness accounted for his success in the Open and for his longevity as a topflight player.

Unlike Arnold Palmer, whose come-from-behind charges in the early 1960's delighted golf fans, Hale tended to win a tournament by assuming an early lead and retaining it for the duration. Difficult courses became his strength because his accuracy ensured that he would not have massive failures. Although his athletic ability and precise play made him a match for any of his contemporaries, he was not able to dominate the game in the style of Nicklaus. Other outstanding players—Seve Ballesteros, Ray Floyd, Greg Norman—had comparable abilities and skills. The parity of golf in the 1980's ensured that few golfers were able to win more than a handful of tournaments each year. Golf in the 1970's and 1980's was marked by stiffer competition than ever before. Even so, Hale remained among golf's best players. In 1992, he was inducted into the PGA World Golf Hall of Fame.

When Hale joined the Senior Tour in 1995, he had tremendous success, winning the Senior PGA Tour rookie of the year award. In 1999, he became the first player on the circuit to win five major tournaments three years in a row. He was the top Senior Tour player in 1997 and 1998, grossing more than $2 million in each of those years. In 1999, Hale had one of the most amazing years in Senior Tour history. From May to August, he won all five tournaments in which he played, with a scoring average of 68.51. He remained at the top of his game through 2000, winning four major tournaments and earning more than $2 million for the fourth straight year. In 2004, he won the PGA Senior Championship.

Summary
Through 2008, Hale Irwin won eighty-seven PGA and PGA Senior Tour events and appeared five times on the U.S. Ryder Cup team. He reached the $1 million mark in Senior Tour earnings faster than any other player in history and is the all-time money leader on the combined PGA and PGA Senior Tours, with more than $20 million in career earnings. After joining the Senior Tour, he was one of the most consistent players in the history of the tour.

Bill Delaney

Additional Sources
Fasciana, Guy S., Hale Irwin, and Terry Dill. *Golf's Mental Magic: Four Strategies for Mental Toughness.* Greenville, S.C.: Health and Performance Associates, 2000.

Irwin, Hale. *Hale Irwin's Smart Golf: Wisdom and Strategies from the "Thinking Man's Golfer."* New York: Quill, 2001.

"Pure Beauties." *Golf Magazine* 48, no. 6 (June, 2006): 125-131.

Sampson, Curt. "Hale Storms." *Golf Magazine* 46, no. 6 (June, 2004): 205-208.

Tony Jacklin

Born: July 7, 1944
Scunthorpe, North Lincolnshire, England

Early Life

Tony Jacklin was born into a poor family in Scunthorpe, North Lincolnshire, England, a mill and mining town. He was introduced to golf when he caddied for his father; he was hooked immediately by the game. He began to devote all his spare time to developing his game at the nearby golf course. He was largely self-taught. As a boy, he caddied for Bobby Locke when he visited the club. He also saw the British Ryder Cup team win at nearby Lindrick.

Tony managed to gain a handicap card and began playing in schoolboy and club tournaments, winning the Lincolnshire junior tournament at the age of thirteen. At fourteen, he left school, and by fifteen, he was good enough to play for the county. The next year, he won the Lincolnshire county championship. At seventeen years old, he became an assistant at the Potters Bar club outside London. Although he hated the conditions of the club, Tony was able to play in the various assistants national tournaments, which he began winning, culminating with the 1965 Gor-Ray tournament. Earlier, in 1963, he had been voted Sir Henry Cotton rookie of the year.

The Road to Excellence

Tony resigned from his job, and over the following few years, some of the club members financed him. His first British Open was in 1963 at Lytham St. Anne's golf club. He finished a creditable thirtieth place, winning £56 ($120 at that time). He decided to join the South Africa tour during the winter, winning only a minimal amount of money in the first season but considerably more the next.

In the summer of 1965, he met his first wife, Vivien, in Northern Ireland. They were married in the winter. It was a happy marriage; Vivien toured with Tony and later brought the couple's three children on tour. Tony improved rapidly, placing fifth in the British PGA Order of Merit in 1966. His first important international tournament was the Canada Cup. Soon, he was playing with the big international names, such as Jack Nicklaus and Arnold Palmer. He felt he had arrived: His confidence grew, his passion for the game was high, and his ambition was immense. He was the most promising young British player on the scene. This was confirmed when he received an invitation to the 1967 Masters at Augusta, Georgia, where he finished sixteenth.

In 1967, the British Open was held at the Hoylake golf club. Tony placed fifth in the event. Then, he returned to play in the United States, under the management of Mark McCormack and his company, International Management Group. Later in his career, Tony felt his contract with McCormack had been exploitative, especially when he was held back in Europe to launch the European PGA Tour. He would have preferred to stay in the United States. Tony's long and successful involvement with the Ryder Cup began that year in Houston, Texas. In his final match, he broke the course record of 64 with a hole in one.

The Emerging Champion

In 1968, Tony was transformed by playing in the United States. His became more professional and competitive. He returned to England for the British Open, again held at Lytham St. Anne's, and had rounds of 68, 70, and 70 for the first three days. On the fourth day, he played exceptionally and won the championship by two strokes. He was the first British golfer to win the British Open in eighteen years and was awarded the Order of the British Empire for his achievement.

PGA Tour and PGA Senior Tour Victories

1968	Jacksonville Open Invitational
1969	British Open
1970	U.S. Open
1972	Greater Jacksonville Open
1994	First of America Classic
1995	Franklin Quest Championship

European Tour Victories

1972	Viyella PGA Championship
1973	Italian Open
	Dunlop Masters
1974	Scandinavian Enterprise Open
1976	Kerrygold International Classic
1979	Braun German Open
1981	Billy Butlin Jersey Open
1982	Sun Alliance PGA Championship

At the 1969 Ryder Cup, the U.S. and European teams played equally well. In the final singles match, Tony played Nicklaus. At the last hole, Nicklaus conceded a 2-foot putt to Tony, thus tying the game and the tournament. Tony never forgot that gesture, and years later, Nicklaus and Jack opened a golfing complex in Florida called The Concession.

Equally satisfying for Tony was his victory at the 1970 U.S. Open, which was played in extremely difficult conditions. He became the first British player to win the U.S. Open since 1920. Over the next few major tournaments, Tony maintained a high standard of performance, though he never won another major golf tournament. In 1971, he came close to repeating as U.S. Open champion but lost at the seventeenth hole of the final round to Lee Trevino. Subsequently, he suffered from anxiety while putting, which led to a loss of confidence over the next few years. There were no sports psychologists then, and little assistance seemed available. Although he helped build the European PGA Tour and played in further Ryder Cups, his career stalled. At thirty-eight years old he decided to quit competitive golf.

Continuing the Story

Tony's experienced negatives and positives during the 1980's. He captained four highly successful Ryder Cup teams, which had expanded from a British to a European team. In 1985, for the first time in twenty-eight years, the British/European team beat the U.S. team; the team won the next two Ryder Cups as well. However, in 1988, Tony's wife died.

Furthermore, Tony experienced financial trouble because of bad investments.

Later, he met Astrid Waagen, and a second happy marriage ensued. The couple moved to the United States, where Tony played on the PGA Senior Tour for two years, finally settling in Bradenton, Florida. Business ventures picked up, and he was inducted into the World Golf Hall of Fame in 2002.

Summary

Tony Jacklin was the first of a new generation of European players who could compete with and defeat the American players in the United States. He brought a new degree of professionalism to the Ryder Cup, helping to make the event a popular and significant showcase. He also helped lay the foundation for a successful European PGA Tour. He set an example for younger European golfers, such as Seve Ballesteros, Jose-Maria Olazabal, Nick Faldo, and Bernhard Langer, each of whom dominated the world stage.

David Barratt

Additional Sources

Barratt, Michael, and Tony Jacklin. *Golf with Tony Jacklin: Step by Step, a Great Professional Shows an Enthusiastic Amateur How to Play Every Stroke of the Game.* London: A. Baker, 1970.

Jacklin, Tony, Peter Dobereiner, and Chris Perfect. *Jacklin's Golf Secrets.* London: Hutchinson, 1983.

Jacklin, Tony, with Curtis Gillespie. *My Autobiography.* London: Simon and Schuster, 2006.

Kahn, Liz. *Tony Jacklin: The Price of Success.* London: Hamlyn, 1979.

Trevillion, Paul. *Tony Jacklin at Play.* London: A. Baker, 1970.

Honors and Awards

1963	Sir Henry Cotton rookie of the year
1967, 1969, 1971, 1973, 1975, 1977, 1979	Ryder Cup
1970	Order of the British Empire
1983, 1985, 1987, 1989	Ryder Cup captain
1990	Commander of the British Empire
2002	Inducted into World Golf Hall of Fame

Bobby Jones

Born: March 17, 1902
    Atlanta, Georgia
Died: December 18, 1971
    Atlanta, Georgia
Also known as: Robert Tyre Jones, Jr. (full name)

Early Life

Robert Tyre Jones, Jr., was born in Atlanta, Georgia, on St. Patrick's Day, March 17, 1902. His father, Robert P. Jones, an attorney, was an accomplished amateur baseball player, and his mother, Clara, was a fine amateur golfer.

Bobby Jones, who competed as an amateur. (Courtesy of Amateur Athletic Foundation of Los Angeles)

Bobby not only grew up in an athletic family, but he also lived near a golf course, Atlanta's East Lake Golf Course. As a very young child, he spent much time watching the club professional, Steward Marden, teach his pupils. At the age of five, Bobby began to play golf—only nineteen years after golf had been introduced in the United States. He improved quickly as a golfer, imitating the swing of Marden, and soon entered amateur competition.

The Road to Excellence

At the age of thirteen, Bobby began to win many major amateur tournaments. In 1915, he defeated the top amateurs of the South in the prestigious Roebuck Invitational Tournament. The next year, at the age of fourteen, he qualified for the U.S. Amateur Championship at the Merion Cricket Club in Philadelphia, Pennsylvania, leading the field after the first qualifying round with a score of 74. He defeated Eben Byers, a former amateur champion, but was defeated by Bob Gardner in the third round.

Bobby's exceptional performance at such a young age brought him recognition as a child prodigy of golf. Bobby had difficulty with his temper, however. He was known as a perfectionist, and he often lost his temper on the golf course, throwing his clubs. From 1916 through 1922 Bobby had a difficult time—he competed in eleven national and international events but failed to win a tournament.

In 1923, at twenty-one years of age, Bobby entered the U.S. Open at Inwood Country Club on Long Island, New York. Here, he won his first major victory by defeating Bobby Cruikshank in a playoff.

Bobby continued to play as an amateur, but he pursued other interests in addition to golf. He married Mary Malone on June 17, 1924, and had three children: Clara, Robert Tyre III, and Mary Ellen. He was an outstanding student and earned a bachelor's degree in mechanical engineering from Georgia Technological Institute. He later earned another undergraduate degree in literature from Harvard and then studied law at Emory University in Atlanta. After completion of his studies, he passed the federal and state law examinations in 1928.

The Emerging Champion

As Bobby matured, he learned to control his temper in order to master golf. With his victory in the 1923 U.S. Open, he began a seven-year dominance of golf that culminated in the first Grand Slam, victories in the four major tournaments. In 1926, he became the first amateur in twenty-nine years to win the British Open. His splendid record during this period included five U.S. Amateur titles, four U.S. Open titles, three British Open titles, and one British Amateur title.

Throughout this period, Bobby continued to compete as an amateur against professional players in all open tournaments—those in which both professional and amateur players compete. His victories are even more impressive considering that he competed in a small number of events each year. At the age of twenty-eight, he retired from both national and international competition after eight years of participation.

Continuing the Story

After his Grand Slam in 1930, Bobby retired from competition and accepted a contract to make films on golf. He also joined his father in a land invest-

---

Major Championship Victories

1923, 1926, 1929-30	U.S. Open
1924-25, 1927-28, 1930	U.S. Amateur
1926-27, 1930	British Open
1930	British Amateur

Other Notable Victories

1917, 1920, 1922	Southern Amateur Championship

---

ment and development business and began to devote his energies to his law practice in Atlanta.

Bobby had severe back problems and played little golf in the 1930's. He continued to make contributions to golf, however. In 1930, he discovered a beautiful 365-acre plot of land near Augusta, Georgia, and began to plan a site for a golf course. He joined with Alister Mackenzie to design the world-famous Augusta National Golf Course and, with the assistance of Clifford Roberts, established The Masters, which is one of the major tournaments in golf today.

Bobby later served as a lieutenant colonel in World War II, and after the war he became an active member of the Republican Party. He later worked as a fund-raiser for Dwight D. Eisenhower's presidential campaign. In 1948, at the age of forty-six, he contracted syringomyelia, a crippling spinal cord condition, which caused his 1971 death at the age of sixty-nine.

Records and Milestones

In 1930, became the only golfer ever to win a recognized Grand Slam (four major championships in a single season)

Said to have holed a putt in excess of one hundred feet on the fifth green in the first round of the 1927 British Open

Never turned professional

Received the Freedom of the City Award

Honors and Awards

1926	World Trophy
1930	James E. Sullivan Award
1940	Inducted into PGA Hall of Fame
1958	GWAA Richardson Award
1974	Inducted into World Golf Hall of Fame

Summary

Bobby Jones is considered one of the greatest sports champions of the 1920's, a period that is considered the golden age of sport in the United States. In the 1920's, great sporting champions such as Jack Dempsey, Gertrude Ederle, and Babe Ruth achieved tremendous feats in their respective sports. Bobby's Grand Slam is considered by many to be the greatest achievement in the decade.

Bobby received wide recognition for his exceptional playing record. He was inducted into the World Golf and PGA halls of fame. He received the Freedom of the City Award at St. Andrews, Scotland, to become, with Benjamin Franklin, one of only two Americans to receive the award. Many people, however, consider his sportsmanship to be his greatest contribution to golf. His spirit of competition and code of conduct established a standard for other players. The course at Augusta and the annual Masters Tournament attest to his contribution to golf.

Susan J. Bandy

Additional Sources

Frost, Mark. *The Grand Slam.* London: Time Warner, 2005.

Keeler, O. B. *The Bobby Jones Story: The Authorized Biography.* Chicago: Triumph Books, 2003.

Lewis, Catherine M. *Bobby Jones and the Quest for the Grand Slam.* Chicago: Triumph Books, 2007.

_____. *Considerable Passions: Golf, the Masters, and the Legacy of Bobby Jones.* Chicago: Triumph Books, 2000.

Matthew, Sidney. *Bobby Jones Golf Tips: Secrets of the Master.* Secaucus, N.J.: Citadel Press, 2004.

Price, Charles. *A Golf Story: Bobby Jones, Augusta National, and the Masters Tournament.* Chicago: Triumph Books, 2007.

Rapoport, Ron. *The Immortal Bobby: Bobby Jones and the Golden Age of Golf.* Hoboken, N.J.: J. Wiley & Sons, 2005.

Betsy King

Born: August 13, 1955
       Reading, Pennsylvania

Early Life

Betsy King was born in Reading, Pennsylvania, on August 13, 1955, to Dr. and Helen Szymkowicz King. Sports came naturally to Betsy because both her parents were talented athletes. Her mother, a 1940 graduate of the University of Rhode Island, was elected to the university's athletics hall of fame as the best all-around athlete in her senior class. Betsy's father received a football scholarship to attend Dickinson College in Carlisle, Pennsylvania, although he later chose to pursue medicine.

Both parents had an influence on Betsy, which accounted for her fierce sense of competitiveness.

Betsy King. (Courtesy of LPGA)

When Betsy was little, she was the kind of child who ran around the yard so fast that her parents could not catch her. She grew up preferring to play with her brother rather than with dolls.

Because Betsy was nearsighted, she began wearing thick glasses when she was in the second grade, replacing them with contact lenses when she was sixteen. As a child, she was always a little shy and withdrawn, which fame as a golfer was destined to change.

The Road to Excellence

When Betsy first began playing golf seriously, she put her talent for self-control to work by setting a routine of playing five or six days each week. In addition, Betsy worked out regularly because she found that exercise and lifting weights strengthened her golf.

While attending Furman University, Betsy played with the Paladins, leading her team to the National Collegiate Athletic Association championship in 1976. That year, she was also the lowest scoring amateur at the U.S. Open.

Then, in 1977, she went on the professional tour. By the second year on the tour, she realized she was limited by her swing. She showed flashes of talent, such as when she finished second at the 1978 Borden Classic and the 1979 Wheeling Classic. However, in her first four years as a professional, she averaged 74.26 strokes per round. At that rate, she could barely make a living on the tour.

By 1980, Betsy knew she had to do something to change the situation. She met Chicago teaching professional Ed Oldfield, whom some called the swing architect. Oldfield was known for rebuilding the games of other top amateurs. Betsy met Ed during an embarrassing moment, when she was hitting shots so low to the ground that people joked and called them "worm-burners."

Oldfield analyzed Betsy's problems and found about twenty things wrong with her swing. Her chipping and putting strokes needed improvement, and Oldfield set about changing them. That winter, Betsy spent the off-season near Oldfield in Phoe-

Major Championship Victories

1986, 2000	LPGA Corning Classic
1987, 1990, 1997	Nabisco Dinah Shore
1989-90	U.S. Women's Open
1992	Mazda LPGA Championship

Other Notable Victories

1984, 1988-89	Women's Kemper Open
1985	Ladies' British Open
1985-86, 1988	Rail Charity Classic
1990	JAL Big Apple Classic
	Itoman World Match Play Championship
1992	Mazda Japan Classic
1995, 2001	ShopRite LPGA Classic
2000	Cup o' Noodles Hawaiian Ladies Open

nix, Arizona. Oldfield made drastic changes in Betsy's swing, breaking it down into bits and warning her it would get worse before it got better. Betsy practiced her swing mechanics, and her scoring average improved steadily, year by year.

The Emerging Champion

Finally, in 1984, Betsy was good enough to win her first Ladies Professional Golf Association (LPGA) tournament. That same year, she won another two tournaments, earning her first player of the year award as well as the money title. Her lessons with Oldfield were paying off at last.

In 1987, she won her first major tournament, the Nabisco Dinah Shore. In the following years, she compiled numerous wins, player of the year awards, and the LPGA Vare Trophy. Betsy had at last become the country's top woman golfer and perhaps the finest in the world.

Betsy continued to work out regularly in addition to playing golf, allowing her to put more power behind the ball. She also attributed her success not to positive thinking, as so many other professionals did, but simply to the mechanics of her swing.

In 1989, Betsy had another banner year with six major victories, including the U.S. Women's Open, for a total income of $654,132 in prize money. She had come a long way from the years when professional golf barely paid her bills.

Continuing the Story

Betsy considered 1980 to be the turning point in her life. Not only did she begin working with Oldfield that year, but she also became an ardent Christian. Her new philosophy had a beneficial effect on both her thinking and her playing.

After 1980, Betsy became the Fellowship of Christian Athletes' most vocal and successful member, donating 10 percent of her sizable income to the organization. Every summer, she did volunteer work for Habitat for Humanity, a Christian organization that builds houses for the needy. She and several members of the organization spent a week helping carpenters in the Tennessee mountains build houses. Despite sparse accommodations, unappetizing food, and grueling work, Betsy

Records and Milestones

Set season record earnings of $654,132 in 1989

First player in LPGA history to surpass the $5 million mark in career earnings

From 1984 to 1989, won twenty tournament titles, which gave her the distinction of being the most winning professional golfer during that period

First player in LPGA history to record four rounds in the 60's in a major championship (1992 Mazda LPGA)

Honors and Awards

1977	Furman University Athlete of the Year, Woman Scholar Athlete of the Year
1984	*Golf Digest* Most Improved Golfer
1984, 1989, 1993	LPGA Player of the Year
	Rolex Player of the Year
1985	South Carolina's Professional Athlete of the Year
1987	*Golf Magazine* and *Golf Illustrated* Player of the Year
	Samaritan Trophy
1987, 1993	LPGA Vare Trophy
1989	Founder's Cup
	Golf Digest-LPGA Founder's Cup Award
	Golf Digest Mickey Wright Award
	Golf World Player of the Year
	GWAA Female Player of the Year
1990-95	U.S. Solheim Cup Team
1995	Inducted into LPGA Hall of Fame
2001	Honorary doctorate degree from Albright College (Pa.)
	Indiana Sports Corporation's Pathfinder Award
	NCAA Silver Anniversary Award
2005	Thomas P. Infusino Award

always enjoyed the week enough to return annually.

Betsy was often unfairly portrayed in the media as an "ice queen" because of her undramatic and stoic personality. However, in golf, the ability to keep one's emotions under control is an enviable one and central to success on the fairways.

In 1992, Betsy continued to excel. She became the first LPGA player to record four sub-60 rounds in major tournament play with scores of 66-68-67-66 at the Mazda LPGA Championship, which she won. In 1995, she won her thirtieth major tournament at the ShopRite LPGA Classic, becoming the first player in LPGA history to cross the $5 million mark in earnings. She was inducted into the LPGA Hall of Fame. Betsy won the Nabisco Dinah Shore Tournament in 1997, her thirty-first tournament victory. After a winless streak of more than two years, she won her next tournament in 2000 at the Cup o' Noodles Hawaiian Classic and finished 2001 as a three-time winner of the ShopRite LPGA Classic.

As Betsy's playing career wound down, she sought another outlet in which to channel her energies. Betsy became committed to addressing poverty in Africa following a 2006 visit to Rwanda. Upon returning to her home in Scottsdale, Arizona, she began enlisting the support of fellow LPGA members to join her. Emerging from those conversations and as a tribute to her effectiveness in rallying support, Golf Fore Africa became a reality. This was a charitable effort of the LPGA designed to assist children orphaned by AIDS and families in need of medical attention. Betsy returned to Africa in 2007, accompanied by five LPGA members and the editor of *Golf World*. This resulted in widespread exposure through the golf community about the extent of the health crisis affecting Africa and helped raise money for health services and the construction of a medical clinic in Rwanda.

Summary

After seven years on the LPGA Tour without a single win, Betsy King made some radical changes in her swing and in her thinking. She went on to become one of the best women golfers in the world, with thirty-four career victories, three LPGA player of the year awards, and two Vare trophies. She captained the U.S. Solheim Cup team to victory in 2007, only the second win for the Americans on European soil and a fitting tribute to her six appearances in that event. After her playing days ended, Betsy channeled her competitive energies into Golf Fore Africa, a charitable arm of the LPGA seeking to enhance the lives of children in Africa who have been orphaned by the AIDS crisis.

Nan White, updated by P. Graham Hatcher

Additional Sources

Allis, Peter. *The Who's Who of Golf.* Englewood Cliffs, N.J.: Prentice-Hall, 1983.

DeMeglio, Steve. "Focus on Africa, Not Golf, for LPGA Veteran King." *USA Today,* June 6, 2008.

Golf Magazine's Encyclopedia of Golf: The Complete Reference. New York: HarperCollins, 1993.

McGovern, Mike. "A New World of Worries." *Golf World* 50, no. 17 (1996).

Murray, Jeff. "A Collapse in Corning." *Golf World* 53, no. 44 (2000).

Russel, Geoff. "Heading to Shore." *Golf World* 50, no. 34 (1997).

Tom Kite

Born: December 9, 1949
　　McKinney, Texas
Also known as: Thomas Oliver Kite, Jr. (full name)

Early Life

Thomas Oliver Kite, Jr., was born on December 9, 1949, in McKinney, Texas, a small town north of Dallas. Tom showed an interest in playing golf from the time he could walk. His father, a good golfer, encouraged Tom by providing him with a cut-down, wooden-shafted club.

When Tom was thirteen, he moved with his family to Austin, Texas. There his precocious golfing interests were developed by a professional golfer and teacher, Harvey Penick. Also, competition with another fine young Austin, Texas, golfer, Ben Crenshaw, helped to sharpen Tom's game.

The Road to Excellence

By the time Tom was in high school, he knew he wanted to be a professional golfer. At the same time, he was realistic about difficulties, such as his small physical stature at 5 feet 8 inches and 150 pounds, with which he had to contend to achieve his goal. Therefore, he learned to perfect his game with hard work, constant practice, and determination. This approach brought him success at both amateur and professional levels of competition.

As a student at McCallum High School in Austin, Tom was the Division AAAA state champion in 1967 and 1968. Between 1969 and 1972, he played on the golf team at the University of Texas at Austin under Coach George Hannon. Tom and his teammate Crenshaw led the Texas Longhorns to the National Collegiate Athletic Association (NCAA) championships in 1971 and 1972. A three-time all-American, Tom was individual cochampion with Crenshaw in the 1972 NCAA tournament.

Tom was successful in the major golf tournaments in which he played as an amateur. He was runner-up amateur at The Masters in Augusta, Georgia, in 1971 and 1972, and at the U.S. Open at Pebble Beach, California, in 1972. In 1970, Tom was second in the U.S. amateur tournament and a member of the U.S. World Cup team—made up of the four best amateurs in the nation—that competed in Madrid, Spain. In 1971, Tom was a member of the U.S. Walker Cup team at St. Andrews, Scotland.

The Emerging Champion

In 1972, Tom turned professional after completing his last year of eligibility for collegiate golf. As he began the demanding schedule of the professional tour, he realized that his swing needed adjustment. Tom enlisted the help of instructor Bob Toski, who taught him the correct mechanics of the swing. Although this step did not produce immediate tournament wins, it provided a crucial foundation for Tom's long-term achievements.

Tom Kite celebrating after sinking a putt in a 2004 tournament. (AP/Wide World Photos)

During the 1970's, consistency became the hallmark of Tom's professional career. He won only two tournaments—the Bicentennial Golf Classic in 1976 and the British Columbia Open in 1978—but he regularly appeared as a top finisher on the leader boards. He was named *Golf Digest*'s rookie of the year in 1973, and, from 1974 to 1990, he was among the top thirty in tournament earnings and often in the top ten.

Another dimension of Tom's game was sportsmanship. In 1979, he was given the Bob Jones Award by the United States Golf Association for distinguished sportsmanship in golf. Although this award arose from one incident at a tournament in 1978, when Tom gave himself a penalty stroke that cost him the championship, it was indicative generally of Tom's fair-minded attitude, making him one of the best-liked and most respected golfers on the tour.

Continuing the Story

During the 1980's, the solid foundation of Tom's golf game brought even greater success on the tour. Through long hours of practice, he developed a well-rounded game and the mental concentration necessary for consistent results. His philosophy of the game was basic and direct: "Excellence means lots of work." He also added that golf was not a natural sport. Therefore, the swing and strokes required constant attention to their execution. His goal was for a long-range career spanning several decades.

The statistics of Tom's game during the 1980's demonstrated how well he had done. In 1981 and 1989, he was the leading money winner on the tour, winning the Professional Golfers' Association (PGA) Arnold Palmer Award in 1981. In 1989, he won the PGA player of the year award. In 1981 and 1982, he won the Vardon Trophy for the best scoring average per round. He played on numerous national teams, including appearances in the Ryder Cup and World Cup.

Tom won a tournament in every year from 1981 through 1987. His best year in tournament wins was 1989, when he won the Nestlé Invitational at Bay Hill in Orlando, Florida; the Nabisco Championships at Hilton Head, South Carolina; and the Tournament Players Championship at Sawgrass in Ponte Vedra, Florida. The victory at the Players Championship was particularly significant because

Notable Victories

1971	Walker Cup team
1972	NCAA Championship
1976	IVB-Bicentennial Golf Classic
1978	British Columbia Open
1979, 1981, 1983, 1985, 1987, 1989	Ryder Cup team
1980	European Open
1983	Bing Crosby National Pro-Am
1984	Doral-Eastern Open
1984-85	World Cup team
1986	Western Open
1987	Kemper Open
1989	Nabisco Championships
	Nestlé Invitational
	Tournament Players Championship
1990	Federal Express St. Jude Classic
1991	Infiniti Tournament of Champions
1992	BellSouth Classic
	U.S. Open
1993	Bob Hope Chrysler Classic
	Nissan Los Angeles Open
1996	Oki Pro-Am (Spain)
2008	Boeing Classic

Senior Tour Victories

2000	Countrywide Tradition
	SBC Senior Open
2001	Gold Rush Classic
2002	MasterCard Championship
	SBC Senior Classic
	Napa Valley Championship
2004	3M Championship
2006	AT&T Classic
	Boeing Greater Seattle Classic

it attracts a prestigious field and was considered the "fifth major" among tournaments on the PGA tour.

One of the highlights of Tom's career came in 1992, when he won the U.S. Open, defeating Jeff Sluman with a final round score of 72 amid difficult weather conditions. Tom also finished second behind Tiger Woods in the 1997 Masters Championship. In the same year, he captained the U.S. Ryder Cup team to a narrow defeat, losing by only one point.

In 1998, Tom underwent eye surgery and struggled with his game, recording no victories and only four top twenty-five finishes in 1998 and 1999. In 1999, he joined the PGA Senior Tour and won two Senior Tour events in 2000, the Countrywide Tradition and the SBC Senior Open. Out of twenty events entered, Tom finished in the top twenty-five in eighteen of them. After struggling during the late 1990's, he improved his play dramatically.

Records and Milestones

Only player to win a tournament in every year from 1981 to 1987

Won the greatest number of official U.S. PGA prizes through 1989 ($5,600,691)

Honors and Awards

1971	Walker Cup team
1973	*Golf Digest* Rookie of the Year
1979	Bob Jones Award
1979, 1981, 1983, 1985, 1987, 1989, 1991, 1993, 1997	Ryder Cup team (captain in 1997)
1981	Arnold Palmer Award
	Golf Digest Most Improved Golfer Award
	GWAA Player of the Year
1981-82	PGA Vardon Trophy
1989	PGA Player of the Year
1989-90, 1992, 1994	Dunhill Cup team
2004	Inducted into World Golf Hall of Fame

Besides playing professional golf, family life was important to Tom. In 1975, he married Christy Brandt, who was also a good golfer. Tom had three children: a daughter, Stephanie Lee, born in 1981, and twin sons, David Thomas and Paul Christopher, born in 1984. Tom arranged his schedule so that he could spend as much time as possible in family activities such as coaching his sons' soccer team, working around his home in the yard, or at his hobby of golf-club repair.

Tom supported University of Texas athletic programs, taking a particular interest in both the men's and women's golf teams. He was active in efforts to raise funds for a women's golf scholarship in honor of his teacher Penick. He also enjoyed watching the Longhorn basketball teams.

Tom joined the Champions Tour, the circuit reserved for players who are at least fifty years of age, and won nine tournaments. In 2001, he won the Gold Rush Classic in California. In 2002, he was victorious three times and took home trophies from the SBC, the MasterCard Championship, and the Napa Valley Championship. In 2004, he won the 3M tournament in Minnesota. After a year drought, he won the Boeing Classic and the AT&T Classic. He went winless in 2007, but he finished second three times and seventh in season earnings.

Off the tour, Tom was an active ambassador who spent time emphasizing respect for the traditions and etiquette of golf, and was a role model for courtesy and sportsmanship. He worked to publicize the ideas of his longtime mentor Penick, who showed that golf transcends the realm of athletic competition to teach valuable, everyday lessons. Tom also contributed regularly to books dealing with swing mechanics, and he collaborated in several instructional videos.

Tom began designing golf courses in 1992, starting with one in his hometown of Austin. His most publicized project was Liberty National Golf Club in northern New Jersey, a course with the skyline of Lower Manhattan as its backdrop. Thanks to the Champions Tour and course-design projects, Tom continued the solid, consistent golf career he began in the 1970's.

Summary

Tom Kite was described as a thinking person's golfer. Through constant practice, mental tenacity, and sportsmanship, he set a standard of consistent excellence in golf. His high level of performance throughout his career ranks him as one of the outstanding players in the history of this sport.

Karen Gould, updated by Michael Polley

Additional Sources

Callahan, Tom. *The Bases Were Loaded (and So Was I): Up Close and Personal with the Greatest Names in Sports.* New York: Three Rivers Press, 2005.

Carrick, Michael, and Steve Duno. *Caddie Sense: Revelations of a PGA Tour Caddie on Playing the Game of Golf.* New York: St. Martin's Press, 2000.

Kite, Tom. *Fairway to Heaven: My Lessons from Harvey Penick on Golf and Life.* New York: William Morrow, 1997.

_____. Foreword to *Golf Etiquette.* New York: St. Martin's Press, 2003.

Toski, Bob, and Lorin Anderson. "Tom Kite." *Golf Magazine* 42, no. 9 (2000).

Bernhard Langer

Born: August 27, 1957
Anhausen, West Germany (now Germany)

Early Life

Bernhard Langer was born on August 27, 1957, in the small Bavarian town of Anhausen in West Germany (now in Germany). Bernhard's father was a Czechoslovak who had jumped a Soviet prisoner-of-war train to settle in Bavaria, where he worked as a house builder.

Bernhard started his golf career working as a caddy at the Augsburg Club. At the young age of nine, he walked five miles each day to work.

The Road to Excellence

Bernhard worked hard at the Augsburg Club, and he learned much as a caddy. In 1972, at the age of fifteen, he became an apprentice, training to play professional golf. Within seven years from the time he became a golf apprentice, Bernhard won his first professional golf tournament, the Cacharel under-twenty-five championship, by a margin of 17 strokes. In 1980, he became the first German to win a major tournament on the PGA European Tour when he won the Dunlop Masters.

Early in his career, Bernhard was handicapped by putting problems. On occasion, he actually hit the ball twice on a single stroke; sometimes he knocked a short putt erratically several feet past the hole. When asked about his inconsistent putting stroke, Bernhard described the feeling as one of intense pressure in the hands; at other times, he explained that he felt as if some other being had taken him over. Other golfers, including such greats as Sam Snead and Ben Hogan, have had similar putting problems. Typically, such golfers play confidently on long putts but are troubled by a jerking motion on short putts. Many golf experts attribute this to the fact that nerves take charge of the body's movement at such moments. Although he played well as a young professional, he continued to struggle with his putting. His troubles were especially evident at the Hennessy Matches in 1976, when he missed many of his shortest putts.

The Emerging Champion

Ironically, when Bernhard won his first major tournament, he did so with his putting. He beat Brian Barnes by 5 strokes and Nick Faldo by 8. He had rounds of 70, 65, 67, and 68—with 29, 25, 26, and 30 putts in each round, respectively. The total of 110 putts in a single tournament was thought to be a European Tour record.

As Bernhard gained more experience, his nerves settled. At the Hennessey Cup tournament in September, 1980, he tried using a different putter, one that had been designed for women. Bernhard liked the feel of the smaller club; he had the grip thickened, and with his new putter, he soon began to feel more confident in his putting.

After winning the Dunlop Masters, Bernhard finished third in the Lancôme tournament in France. Within two months, he had won more than $60,000 and established himself as one of the bright young stars of the European Tour. After the end of the European season in 1980, he won the Colombian Open and finished second in World Cup competition.

In 1981, Bernhard was even better. He finished in the top ten in

Honors and Awards

1976, 1978, 1980, 1982	Hennessy Cognac Cup
1976-80, 1991-93	World Cup Team
1981, 1984	European Order of Merit
1981-97, 2002, 2004	Ryder Cup Team
1985	Lancôme Trophy
1985-86	Nissan Cup team captain
1985-87, 1989	Four Tours World Championship team captain
1987	Kirin Cup team captain
1992, 1994, 2000	Alfred Dunhill
1994-96, 2006	World Cup
2000	Seve Trophy winner
2001	Inducted into World Golf Hall of Fame
2001-02	UBS Cup
2006	Honorary Officer of Most Excellent Order of the British Empire

fourteen of the seventeen tournaments he entered, six times as runner-up and twice as the winner. After placing second in the British Open at Sandwich, Bernhard won the German Open, leading throughout the tournament and becoming the first German to win his country's open. At the Benson & Hedges International Open that year, Bernhard caught the attention of worldwide television audiences when he climbed into the branches of a tree in which his ball had lodged and chipped onto the green. Tom Weiskopf prevailed, beating Bernhard by one stroke, but Bernhard then went on to win the Bob Hope British Classic. That year, Bernhard gained the first of many selections for the Ryder Cup European team.

Bernhard's putting problems returned in 1982, but they were not as severe as they had been in his early career. By 1982, Bernhard had earned respect as a golfer of world status and had amassed a growing army of fans in Germany. In 1982, he again won the German Open, beating Bill Longmuir at the first sudden-death hole. In 1985, he won his first major U.S. championship and first Grand Slam tournament by capturing first place in The Masters. He shot a closing round of 68, while Curtis Strange blew a 4-stroke lead on the final nine.

Continuing the Story

Despite his ongoing putting woes and his experiments to solve them, Bernhard continued to win tournaments. In 1993, he again won The Masters, finishing 4 strokes ahead of Chip Beck. With the victory, Bernhard joined Spain's Seve Ballesteros and England's Nick Faldo as the only non-U.S. golfers to become two-time Masters champions. Bernhard's winning total of 277 was one of the best scores in the sixty-year history of the prestigious tournament.

In the Ryder Cup, he made ten appearances, playing forty-two matches, winning half of them. One of the Cup's most dramatic games ever was Bernhard's last-game singles with Hale Irwin in 1991, which went to the last putt on the last green. However, he was unable to win the Cup.

In 1996, with the adoption of an unusual putter with a long broom-like handle, he improved his putting as well as his overall play. In 2000, Bernhard won the Murphy's Irish Open and finished in

Major Championship Victories	
1985, 1993	The Masters

Other Notable Victories	
1980	Colombian Open
	Dunlop Masters
1981	British Classic
1981-82, 1985-86, 1993	German Open
1983	Glasgow Classic
	Italian Open
	St. Mellion Tournament Players Championship
1984	French Open
1984, 1987	Irish Open
1984, 1989	Spanish Open
1984, 1992	Dutch Open
1985	Australian Masters
	European Open
	Sea Pines Heritage Classic
	Sun City Challenge
1987	Belgian Classic
	English PGA Championship
1990	German Masters
	Madrid Open
1993	Volvo PGA Championship
	Sea Pine Heritage Classic
1994	Murphy's Irish Open
1994, 2002	Volvo Masters
1995	Volvo PGA Championship
	Deutsche Bank Open TPC of Europe
	Smurfit European Open
1997	Conte of Florence Italian Open
	Benson and Hedges International Open
	Chemapol Trophy Czech Open
	Linde German Masters
2001	TNT Open
	Linde German Masters

a tie for eleventh place in the British Open. He finished in the top ten in four events in Europe.

In 2004, Bernhard's phenomenal success in the Ryder Cup was acknowledged by his appointment as European captain. He became the first German to gain this honor. On American soil, Europe trounced the United States by 18.5 points to 9.5 points. His captainship was praised for its modesty, wise partnering, and the insight he gave to players.

As Bernhard entered his fifties, he became more involved in the Senior Tour but continued his interest in The Masters. In 2008, he won the Casa Serena Open on the European Senior Tour. Throughout his career, he was one of the most consistent players in golf, remaining among the top thirty in the Order of Merit for many years. By 2008, he had recorded forty victories on the European Tour, three on the PGA Tour, three in the Champions Tour, and twenty-seven other tournament wins, for a total of 73 victories.

Summary

Bernhard Langer's perseverance and love of golf brought him a long way from his days as a young caddy. He overcame his early putting problems to become one of the world's most consistent and successful professional golfers. He helped put Germany on the map in golfing terms and did a great deal to encourage the sport in that country, helping found the Mercedes-Benz tournament there. He was a devout Catholic, a modest and wise man, and an excellent role model. In 1984, he married his wife Vikki, an American, and settled in Boca Raton, Florida. The couple had four children. In 2005, Bernhard played with his son Stefan in the MBNA Father/Son Championships and won. Stefan occasionally caddied for him.

Carol Blassingame, updated by David Barratt

Additional Sources

Langer, Bernhard. *My Autobiography*. London: Hodder & Stoughton, 2003.

_____. *While the Iron Is Hot*. London: Hutchinson, 1988.

Langer, Bernhard, and Vivien Saunders. *Langer on Putting*. London: Stanley Paul, 1987.

Richardson, Gordon. "Weekend at Bernie's." *Golf World* 51, no. 8 (1997).

Lawson Little

Born: June 23, 1910
    Newport, Rhode Island
Died: February 1, 1968
    Monterey, California
Also known as: William Lawson Little, Jr. (full name); Cannonball Little

Early Life

William Lawson Little, Jr., was the son of Colonel William Lawson Little of the United States Army Medical Corps and his wife. Lawson, Jr., was born at Fort Adams, the U.S. Army base at Newport, Rhode Island, on June 23, 1910. Because of his father's career, the family moved a great deal. Lawson spent his boyhood and adolescent years at a number of U.S. Army posts, including several in China. All of these bases had golf courses, and golf became Lawson's favorite form of recreation.

In the early part of the twentieth century, U.S. Army bases in countries such as China were rather small, and people from all Western nationalities tended to form friendships across national lines. Therefore, Lawson formed many golfing friendships with people from England and Europe.

The Road to Excellence

Lawson was short, but he developed powerful arms and shoulders through weightlifting and gymnastics exercises such as the parallel bars and the rings. Lawson's squat, muscular build allowed him to drive the ball unusually long distances on his tee shots. These drives were so fast and so strong that, early in his career, Lawson was nicknamed "Cannonball" Little.

Furthermore, Lawson had fine control over his muscles, and, once his ball was on the green, the "Cannonball" became a delicate and precise putter. Early in his career, Lawson also learned he could intimidate some of his opponents by adopting a fierce facial expression during the course of the game.

The Emerging Champion

In 1934, Lawson became a top international golfer. In that year he became the U.S. Amateur champion by defeating David Goldman, won the British Amateur Championship by defeating James Wallace, and was named a member of America's Walker Cup team—quite a year for a young man just out of college.

The next year, 1935, Lawson again won the amateur titles on both sides of the At-

Lawson Little. (Courtesy of Amateur Athletic Foundation of Los Angeles)

lantic. This alone ensured his place in golfing history; he was the first player to win both the U.S. and British titles in two consecutive years. In recognition of this accomplishment, the Amateur Athletic Union (AAU) named Lawson the 1935 winner of the James E. Sullivan Memorial Award, the highest honor for an amateur athlete.

Continuing the Story

In 1936, Lawson became a professional golfer and began playing in tournaments with cash prizes. He immediately made his mark on the professional golf world by winning the Canadian Open, setting a new record for the course on which it was played.

Each year Lawson traveled all over the United States, Canada, and England winning major tournaments. In 1939, World War II broke out in Europe, and Lawson had to restrict his play to North America. Even then his career bloomed. In 1940, eleven hundred people played in the qualifying rounds for the U.S. Open Tournament at Olympia Fields Country Club of Chicago. The lowest score on 36 holes was 134, shot by Lawson. In the tournament, Lawson tied Gene Sarazen, 287 strokes each, but Lawson won the tie-breaking round 70 strokes to 73.

Because of shortages of gasoline for travel and to emphasize the seriousness of the war, fewer golf

---

Honors and Awards

1934	World Trophy
	Hall of the Athlete Foundation Athlete of the Year
1935	James E. Sullivan Award
1961	Inducted into PGA Hall of Fame
1980	Inducted into World Golf Hall of Fame

---

tournaments were held after the United States entered World War II at the end of 1941. However, in 1942 and 1944, Lawson was ranked second only to the legendary golfer Ben Hogan. When the war was over, Lawson returned to international golfing and did well in the British Open in 1946 and 1947. In 1948, Lawson won his last major tournament, the St. Petersburg Open held at the Lakewood Country Club in St. Petersburg, Florida.

In 1951 and 1952, the Professional Golfers' Association (PGA) honored Lawson by naming him cochairperson in charge of organizing national tournaments. In 1961, Lawson was inducted into the PGA Hall of Fame at Pinehurst, North Carolina. He died in 1968.

Summary

Although physically strong, Lawson Little felt that much of his success was the result of his mental ability. Before teeing off, he always thought out his play and made allowances for unexpected circumstances.

Michael R. Bradley

Major Championship Victories

1934-35	U.S. Amateur
	British Amateur
1940	U.S. Open

Other Notable Victories

1934	Walker Cup Team
1936	Canadian Open
1940	Los Angeles Open
1941	Texas Open
1948	St. Petersburg Open

Additional Sources

Golf Magazine's Encyclopedia of Golf: The Complete Reference. New York: HarperCollins, 1993.

Kalb, Elliott. *Who's Better, Who's Best in Golf? Mr. Stats Sets the Record Straight on the Top Fifty Golfers of All Time.* New York: McGraw-Hill, 2006.

Strege, John. *When War Played Through: Golf During World War II.* New York: Gotham Books, 2005.

Nancy Lopez

Born: January 6, 1957
      Torrance, California
Also known as: Nancy Lopez-Knight (full name);
    Nancy Lopez-Melton

Early Life

Nancy Lopez was born January 6, 1957, in Torrance, California. She grew up in the southern New Mexico city of Roswell. This region of the country, with its abundance of sunshine and mild winters, provides a great environment for year-round outdoor sports activities. As a child, Nancy's small build led to her involvement in gymnastics and swimming. Her father, Domingo, was an avid golfer and took Nancy and her older sister Delma to the golf course with him almost every day. Nancy showed an immediate interest in golf, and her father gave her some clubs when she was only eight years old. She began hitting golf balls daily at the range and, by the time she was nine, she entered her first pee-wee tournament in Alamogordo, New Mexico, and won.

The Road to Excellence

By the time Nancy was a freshman in high school, she had distinguished herself as a junior golfer and had generated some controversy as well at Goddard High School. She was good enough to play on the boys' golf team, but girls were not permitted to play on boys' teams and there was no girls' team at the high school. Nancy's situation drew national attention, and within a year, girls were allowed to play on boys' teams in noncontact sports, such as golf, tennis, and track. Nancy not only made the team but also was its best golfer and led the team to two state championships. She was a pioneer in the rights of women to participate in school athletics. Because of Nancy's great ability, teachers and coaches realized that girls should have the same opportunities to participate in sports as boys.

In high school, Nancy dreamed of going to Arizona State University and playing on the Sun Devils' golf team. When it came time to pick a college, however, Nancy found that Arizona State did not have full scholarships for women's golf. Dale McNamara, the golf coach at Tulsa University in Oklahoma, had been reading about Nancy in golfing magazines for several years. She persuaded the Tulsa athletic department to provide a full scholarship for Nancy to play for the Golden Hurricanes.

Nancy Lopez teeing off in 1978. (AP/Wide World Photos)

The Emerging Champion

Nancy was an immediate sensation in college golf. The Tulsa women's team entered nine tournaments during the 1975-1976 season and won six of them. Nancy was the individual winner in six of the tournaments and led the team to a second-place national finish. She won the national championship as an individual, was second once in her two years of college golf, and was all-American both years.

In 1977, with her father's blessing and guidance, Nancy joined the Ladies Professional Golf Association (LPGA) as a touring professional and began a career as perhaps the greatest woman golfer ever. Nancy's first year on the professional tour was one of the most remarkable years for any athlete in any sport. As a rookie, at the age of twenty-one, she won nine tournaments, including five in a row. She set new records for the amount of prize money won in one year and had the lowest scoring average. She was unanimously named rookie of the year and player of the year, a first in professional golf. Her second year on the tour was just as successful. Nancy won eight tournaments and was named player of the year again. In that two-year period, Nancy elevated her status from golf superstar to sports legend. She single-handedly brought women's golf to a new level, making it popular as a spectator sport, and became a celebrity in the process.

Continuing the Story

To be a superstar at the age of twenty-one can burden one with huge responsibilities, and Nancy found that some of the other golfers on tour resented her great talent and success on the course and her popularity with the media. In addition, playing in a tournament every week and traveling all the time was not as glamorous as Nancy thought it would be. She met sportscaster Tim Melton in Cincinnati, and they were married in 1979. Nancy soon found that life as a sports superstar presented special problems in a relationship, and the marriage did not survive.

Although Nancy continued to win golf tournaments and became a spokesperson for women's golf, she still sought an identity away from the sport and the satisfaction and security of a family. In 1982, Nancy married Ray Knight,

who was a professional baseball star. Nancy needed the support of someone who understood the pressures of professional athletics.

Over the next four years, Nancy took time out from golf to have two daughters, Ashley Marie and Erinn. She and Knight managed to blend busy, glamorous sports careers with the happiness of a quiet home life. Nancy resumed her winning on the LPGA Tour and was inducted into the LPGA Hall of Fame in 1987.

In 1991, Nancy took time off to have her third child, another daughter, but still managed to play in eleven tournaments, with a win at the Sara Lee Classic. The following year, she recorded consecutive playoff victories in the Rail Charity Golf Classic and the PING-Cellular One LPGA Golf Championship. In 1993, she collected her forty-seventh career victory in a sudden-death playoff with Deb Richard in the Youngstown-Warren LPGA Classic.

After two years without a tour victory Nancy won the Chick-fil-A Charity Championship in 1997, bringing her total LPGA tournament victories to forty-eight. She also finished second in the U.S. Women's Open Championship, an event that she never won.

Nancy competed in few tournaments in 1999 and 2000 because of knee and gall-bladder surger-

---

Major Championship Victories

1978, 1985, 1989	LPGA Championship
1981	Colgate Dinah Shore

Other Notable Victories

1978-79	Colgate European Open
1979	Lady Keystone Open
1980	Women's Kemper Open
1980, 1992	Rail Charity Classic
1982-83	J & B Scotch Pro-Am
1983	Elizabeth Arden Classic
1984	Chevrolet World Championship of Women's Golf
1989	Atlantic City Classic
	Nippon Travel-MBS Classic
1990	MBS LPGA Classic
1991	Sara Lee Classic
1992	PING-Cellular One LPGA Golf Championship
1993	Youngstown-Warren LPGA Classic
1997	Chick-Fil-A Charity Championship

Records

Became the fastest LPGA player ever to reach the $200,000 and $400,000 marks in a single season

Became the second player in 1988 (Amy Alcott was the first) to cross the $2 million mark in career earnings

Holds the record for consecutive LPGA victories (5) (record shared with Annika Sorenstam)

Honors and Awards

1976	Tulsa University Female Athlete of the Year
1977	*Golf Digest* Rookie of the Year
1978	*Golf Digest* Most Improved Golfer
	LPGA Rookie of the Year
	Gatorade Rookie of the Year
1978, 1985, 1988	*Golf Digest* Mickey Wright Award for Tournament Victories
1978-79	GWAA Player of the Year
	Seagram's Seven Crowns of Sports Award
1978-79, 1985	LPGA Vare Trophy
1978-79, 1985, 1988	LPGA Player of the Year
	Rolex Player of the Year
1978-87	*Golf Magazine* Golfer of the Decade
1987	William and Mousie Powell Award
	Inducted into LPGA Hall of Fame
1989	Inducted into PGA Hall of Fame
1998	Bob Jones Award
2001	Inducted into Georgia Sports Hall of Fame
2005	Captain of Solheim Cup team
2007	ASAP Sports/Jim Murray Award

ies. During the LPGA's fiftieth anniversary celebration, she was named one of the LPGA's top fifty players. In 2002, she competed in only fourteen tournaments as part of her "Nancy Lopez Farewell Tour"; in the second round of the Jamie Farr Krogel Classic, she recorded her third hole in one. Two years later she was appointed captain of the 2005 U.S. Solheim Cup team, which regained the cup from the European team. In 2007, she was named captain of the 2009 PING U.S. Junior Solheim team and competed in some LPGA events, though without much success. When she retired from full-time participation in the LPGA, she had won forty-eight titles and was in sixth place on the all-time money list with more than $1 million.

Summary

Nancy Lopez was arguably the best woman golfer ever and was responsible for making the LPGA a success on television and on tour throughout the United States. Her dazzling smile and warm personality, combined with her tremendous athletic talent, made her one of the most popular women athletes of all time and an effective role model for millions of young people.

Henry A. Eisenhart, updated by Thomas L. Erskine

Additional Sources

Douglas, Delia D., and Katherine M. Jamieson. "A Farewell to Remember: Interrogating the Nancy Lopez Farewell Tour." *Sociology of Sport Journal* 23, no. 2 (2006): 117.

Hudson, David L. *Women in Golf: The Players, the History, and the Future of the Sport.* Westport, Conn.: Praeger, 2007.

Lopez, Nancy. *The Complete Golfer.* New York: Galahad Books, 2000.

O'Neil, Dana Pennett, and Pat Williams. *How to Be Like Women Athletes of Influence: Thirty-one Women at the Top of Their Game and How You Can Get There Too.* Deerfield Beach, Fla.: Health Communications, 2007.

Orr, Frank, and George Tracz. *The Dominators: The Remarkable Athletes Who Changed Their Sport Forever.* Toronto: Warwick, 2004.

Davis Love III

Born: April 13, 1964
  Charlotte, North Carolina
Also known as: Davis Milton Love III (full name)

Early Life

Davis Milton Love III was an active boy who played many sports with his brother Mark. His father, Davis Milton Love II, an accomplished professional golfer and head golf professional at the Atlanta country club, first introduced Davis to the game. Despite his golf pedigree, Davis still managed to take interest in other games and activities. He had a natural talent for golf but chose to spend most of his time playing ice hockey and exploring the outdoors. He skipped golf practice to hunt and fish with family friends. Eventually, golf became his passion and focus. With the encouragement and tutelage of his father, Davis competed and won golf events for Holy Innocents Episcopal High School. Inspired by the golf professionals he met at the country club and with his father while he played on the Professional Golfers' Association (PGA) Tour, Davis set his goal to compete at the top level. He earned a golf scholarship to the University of North Carolina at Chapel Hill (UNC).

The Road to Excellence

In only his first year as a Tar Heel at UNC, Davis was an all-American and Atlantic Coast Conference award winner. He repeated as all-American the next two years and won eight college golf tournaments, including the prestigious North and South Men's Amateur Golf Championship. Realizing his dream was at hand, Davis decided to turn professional after finishing his junior year of school. He played for the United States in the 1985 Walker Cup.

Davis's father died in an airplane crash and did not witness his son's first PGA championship, the 1987 MCI Heritage Golf Classic on Hilton Head Island in South Carolina. Davis's victory was surprising and was aided by the fact that the previous leader had struck his ball out-of-bounds. Although he did not win again that year, Davis gained invaluable experience: learning the process of competing, playing with the world's best golfers, and perfecting his game.

The Emerging Champion

Davis was always a strong competitor, but he played twelve years on the PGA Tour before winning a major championship. During the 1997 PGA Championship, Davis played nearly perfect golf and beat the runner-up by 5 strokes. He also won the prestigious Players Championship in 1992 and 2003. He earned more than $35 million dollars, making him one of the top career money leaders on the PGA Tour.

Davis broke many records and was recognized as one of the most efficient American golfers. He possessed the unique ability to excel with the long and

Davis Love III in 2002. (Mike Nelson/AFP/Getty Images)

short games of golf. He came close to beating the record for distance off of the tee. At the 2004 Mercedes Championship, Davis set his own personal record of 476 yards.

Davis compiled nineteen victories on the PGA Tour, including such notable events as the Dunhill Cup, World Cup of Golf, Ryder Cup, and Presidents Cup. Although he started a family and pursued other sports interests, Davis remained a contender in most golf tournaments. In 2001, he was inducted into the Georgia Golf Hall of Fame. In the official World Golf Rankings, Davis held a top-ten listing for more than 450 weeks; his highest career placement was third, reflecting his brilliance on the course. He became one of the PGA Tour's most popular players. Partly because of his friendship with another Tour player, David Duval, Davis started snowboarding. He enjoyed the daring challenge so much that he built a home in Sun Valley, Idaho, where he visited as much as possible to participate in extreme sports such as heli-boarding.

Continuing the Story

Davis may be best known for his team play. He was an instrumental part on numerous American golf teams that have competed against international teams. He became a cheerleader for his teammates and an accomplished winner. He partnered with Fred Couples to win four international competitions.

Greatly influenced by his father, Davis is a family man and enjoys spending time with his wife, Robin, and their two children, Alexia and Davis IV. Residing in St. Simons Island, Georgia, Davis participated in his children's activities and community

Honors and Awards	
1993, 1995, 1997, 1999, 2002, 2004	Ryder Cup Team
1997	Inducted into University of North Carolina Order of Merit
1998	Honorary chairman for PGA of America's National Golf Day
2001	Inducted into Georgia Golf Hall of Fame

projects. In 1994, his love of golf expanded to business development, as he and his brother founded Love Golf Design, a golf course architecture company. The firm designs courses throughout the southeastern United States. One of the company's signature courses is The Preserve, which is located near Davis's college hometown of Chapel Hill. The Preserve was designated as an Audubon International Certified Sanctuary Golf Course, reflecting Davis's love of the outdoors and the company's commitment to environmental issues.

Summary

In 1997, Davis Love III published the book *Every Shot I Take* to honor the influence his father had on his life. Davis learned to be a caring man on and off the golf course. His wife gave him a one-of-a-kind custom-made motorcycle, which he used to travel and participate in charitable events across the country. In July, 2005, Davis decided to help his friend, motorsport star, and fellow North Carolinian, Kyle Petty, riding his motorcycle 3,750 miles with more than two hundred friends, family, and supporters for the Chick-fil-A Kyle Petty Charity Ride Across America. This charitable effort demonstrated how Davis combines his athleticism, love of children, and thrill-seeking nature to help others.

Deborah Stroman

Additional Sources

Harmon, Claude. *The Four Cornerstones of Winning Golf: Butch Harmon Shares the Secrets He's Taught to Greg Norman, Davis Love III, and Tiger Woods.* New York: Fireside, 1998.

Love, Davis. *Every Shot I Take: Lessons Learned About Golf, Life, and a Father's Love.* New York: Simon & Schuster, 1997.

_____. "One, but Not Done." *Sports Illustrated* 104, no. 24 (June 13, 2006).

PGA Tour Victories	
1987, 1991-92, 1998, 2003	MCI Heritage Golf Classic
1990, 2003	The International
1992, 2003	Tournament Players Championship
	KMart Greater Greensboro Open
1993	Infiniti Tournament of Champions
	Las Vegas Invitational
1995	Freeport-McMoRan Classic
1996	Buick Invitational
1997	PGA Championship
	Buick Challenge
2001, 2003	AT&T Pebble Beach National Pro-Am
2006	Chrysler Classic of Greensboro

Lloyd Mangrum

Born: August 1, 1914
    Trenton, Texas
Died: November 17, 1973
    Apple Valley, California
Also known as: Lloyd Eugene Mangrum (full
  name)

Early Life

Lloyd Eugene Mangrum was born on August 1, 1914, in Trenton, Texas. The youngest of three

Lloyd Mangrum. (Courtesy of Amateur Athletic Foundation of Los Angeles)

brothers, he grew up on a dirt farm just outside the city. His older brother, Ray, eventually became a golf professional and won several Professional Golfers' Association (PGA) events, until a leg ailment forced him to quit. The Mangrum family was poor. Lloyd did not grow up with many toys; he mostly played outdoors on the family farm. When he was older, his impoverished father decided things might get better if the family moved to Dallas. There Lloyd dropped out of school before he was legally old enough to do so. The young boy began playing golf, not only for fun but also for money.

The Road to Excellence

At the age of fifteen, Lloyd turned professional. Playing golf earned him enough money to live on. The next year, at the age of sixteen, he paid his own way to Los Angeles, where he played against amateurs for five and ten dollars. A child of the Depression, Lloyd had to play golf to win money because it was the only way he could afford to play the game, and he did so at a time when golf was still considered a game primarily for the upper class.

Lloyd was an ornery, tough player—a maverick at the game. He had to be, because the men he played against were a rough bunch. One of his opponents, it turned out, was wanted for bank robberies. Another stuffed Lloyd's partner into a locker after losing to him. Once Lloyd gambled with a professional who lost by three putts. The man was so angry that he took his putter into the creek and jammed it knee-deep into the mud.

Because of the world in which he lived, Lloyd grew up fast. At the age of nineteen, he married Eleta, the operator of a beauty salon, who was eleven years older than Lloyd. She had three children, the eldest child only eight years younger than her new stepfather. Lloyd

Major Championship Victories

1946   U.S. Open

Other Notable Victories

Year	Event
1947, 1949, 1951, 1953	Ryder Cup team
1948	Greater Greensboro Open
1948, 1953	Bing Crosby National Pro-Am
1949, 1951, 1953, 1956	Los Angeles Open
1950	Eastern Open
1952-53	Phoenix Open
1952, 1954	Western Open
1953	Ryder Cup team captain

addressed Eleta as "Mother" and let her handle the handsome income his golf playing soon began to generate. In spite of the age difference, Lloyd and Eleta's marriage was successful.

The Emerging Champion

In order to secure backing for some of his tournaments, Lloyd went to his brother Ray, who was then a successful golfer himself. Ray is said to have pulled out a wad of bills and peeled off two one-dollar bills, telling his younger brother to get a job because he was not good enough at golf. However, by 1943, Lloyd had become a successful golfer. That year, he won four PGA events, the first four out of a total of thirty-six that he would win over the course of his lifetime.

Lloyd was drafted and served in the armed forces as an infantry sergeant on the front lines. Later, he was a member of a reconnaissance team that headed the 90th Division of General George S. Patton's Third Army on D day at Omaha Beach. After the ensuing battles, Lloyd was one of only two surviving members of his original platoon. For this and his multiple injuries, he was awarded two Purple Hearts.

After the war, Lloyd, the hero, returned to golf on the PGA Tour. It took him a while to get back into the game and to win enough to make a living. In 1946, he won the U.S. Open, and, by 1951, he led all the professionals, winning four tournaments for a grand total of $26,088. He was then able to buy his own airplane.

Although his career was interrupted by

World War II, Lloyd still made it to the top. In addition to winning many PGA events, he won the Vardon Trophy twice. He won the Los Angeles Open four times and was on four Ryder Cup teams, serving as captain once.

Continuing the Story

Golf professionals and teachers were amazed by Lloyd's success. To them, his game was nothing exceptional. Many of them could outdrive him and hit straighter. Somehow, the game just came naturally to him.

However it may have happened, Lloyd's putts, chips, pitches, and bunker shots were nearly matchless, and he was considered one of the least nervous of putters in golf history. In fact, he was known for his calmness on the fairways. A thin, leathery-looking fellow, he always managed to appear constantly bored, as if there were nothing better for him to do. He would even putt with a cigarette hanging out of his mouth.

Violence was a part of Lloyd's life, on and off the fairways. During one tournament, he received a telephone call threatening his life if he won the game. He refused to withdraw and went on to win, surrounded by uniformed police.

Eventually, by 1953, Lloyd became only an occasional winner. In 1949, his first book was published, *Golf, A New Approach.* In this book, Lloyd revealed that he deliberately tried to copy the short game of Johnny Revolta, the swing of Sam Snead, and the putting style of Horton Smith. On November 17, 1973, at fifty-nine years of age, Lloyd died at home in Apple Valley, California, of his twelfth heart attack. He was survived by his wife, Eleta, his son, Robert, and his two daughters, Reina and Shirley. Lloyd is a member of both the California Golf Hall of Fame and the PGA Hall of Fame.

Milestones

The Masters runner-up (1940)
Among the top ten money leaders between 1946 and 1954
Won four times in 1949; four times in 1950; five times in 1951; five times in 1952
Won a career total of thirty-four PGA tournaments

Honors and Awards

1951, 1953   PGA Vardon Trophy
1964   Inducted into PGA Hall of Fame

Summary

Lloyd Mangrum's golf successes were remarkable for a man whose career was interrupted by the war and by injuries sustained in battle. In addition to winning thirty-six PGA events, Lloyd won the 1946 U.S. Open, won the Vardon Trophy twice, and played on four Ryder Cup teams.

Nan White

Additional Sources

Barrett, Ted. *The Complete Encyclopedia of Golf.* Chicago: Triumph Books, 2005.

Kalb, Elliott. *Who's Better, Who's Best in Golf? Mr. Stats Sets the Record Straight on the Top Fifty Golfers of All Time.* New York: McGraw-Hill, 2006.

Mangrum, Lloyd. *Golf: A New Approach.* London: N. Kaye, 1949.

_____. *How to Play Better Golf.* Greenwich, Conn.: Fawcett, 1954.

Peper, George, and Mary Tiegreen. *The Secret of Golf: A Century of Groundbreaking, Innovative, and Occasionally Outlandish Ways to Master the World's Most Vexing Game.* New York: Workman, 2005.

Phil Mickelson

Born: June 16, 1970
San Diego, California
Also known as: Philip Alfred Mickelson (full name); Lefty

Early Life

Philip Alfred Mickelson seemed destined to play golf: He was born into a family with an enthusiasm for sports, and his birth announcement depicted a baby in diapers with a golf bag slung over his shoulder. Phil's father, Phil, Sr., was an accomplished amateur golfer, and his mother, Mary, won a number of gold medals as a member of the U.S. Senior Olympics basketball team. At the age of three months, Phil received his first golf club; by eighteen months, he was swinging it in the backyard. Although Phil was a natural right-hander in everything except golf, he developed his signature left-handed swing by facing and mimicking his father. As a youngster, Phil honed his golf game in his family's large suburban backyard that his father transformed into a training ground equipped with a regulation putting green and sand trap. At three years old, Phil played his first complete round of golf, and he earned his first trophy at the age of four when he won a local putting contest. By

the age of five, he was competing in local tournaments and had announced to his family that he wanted to be a golfer when he grew up. At seven years old, Phil scored his first birdie and played a below-par round at his local course. In 1980, when he was only ten years old, he beat his father for the first time.

The Road to Excellence

In 1981, Phil began playing on the San Diego junior golf circuit and soon emerged as one of the most gifted young golfers in Southern California. At the age of fourteen, he began working with Coach Dean Reinmuth, a partnership that lasted into Phil's professional career. By high school, Phil had quit playing other sports and focused solely on golf. Attending the prestigious University of San Diego High School, Phil had a stellar junior golf career. He won sixteen junior events in the San Diego area, captured twelve American Junior Golf Association (AJGA) tournaments, and earned three Rolex national player of the year awards (1986-1988).

Phil's success in the AJGA earned him a golf scholarship at Arizona State University. Coached by Steve Loy, Phil dominated the collegiate ranks as a Sun Devil. He won sixteen collegiate tournaments; won National Collegiate Athletic Association individual championships in 1989, 1990, and 1992; and was a first-team all-American all four years. While still a collegiate player, he captured the 1990 U.S. Amateur Championship, and as an amateur in 1991, he won the Northern Telecom Open, a PGA tournament.

The Emerging Champion

In 1992, Phil turned professional after graduating with a psychology degree from Arizona State University. Teamed with caddy Jim "Bones" Mackay, Phil strug-

Phil Mickelson at the 2008 Scottish Open. (Andrew Yates/AFP/Getty Images)

PGA Tour Victories

1991	Northern Telecom Open
1993	The International
1993, 2000-01	Buick Invitational
1994, 1998	Mercedes Championships
1995	Northern Telecom Open
1996	Nortel Open
	Phoenix Open
	Byron Nelson Golf Classic
	World Series of Golf
1997	Bay Hill Invitational
	Sprint International
1998, 2005, 2007	Pebble Beach National Pro-Am
2000	The Tour Championship
2000, 2005-06	BellSouth Classic
2000, 2008	Colonial
2001, 2002	Greater Hartford Open
2002, 2004	Bob Hope Classic
2004, 2006	The Masters
2005	FBR Open
	PGA Championship
2007	Tournament Players Championship
	Deutsche Bank Championship
2008	Northern Trust Open

Continuing the Story

Despite Phil's success on the tour, he had struggled in the major tournaments. While he was called "Lefty" as a term of endearment by the media, he also began to be known as the "best golfer to have never won a major." He had come close to victory several times. Between 1994 and 2003, he posted eight second- or third-place finishes in major tournaments. Finally, in 2004, he drained a 20-foot birdie on the eighteenth hole in the final round of The Masters to defeat Ernie Els for his first win in a major. He followed the 2004 Masters victory with a 2005 win at the PGA Championship and another win at The Masters in 2006. He nearly captured a fourth major at the 2006 U.S. Open, but a final-hole collapse cost him the tournament. He represented the United States in numerous international competitions. As an amateur, he twice played in the Walker Cup; as a professional, he played on seven Ryder Cup teams and seven Presidents Cups. In 2008, with Tiger Woods injured, Phil helped recapture the Ryder Cup for the United States.

Beyond golf, Phil became an accomplished pilot and writer. He flew himself to golf tournaments, and after winning the 2004 Masters, he coauthored, with Donald T. Phillips, *One Magical Sunday (But Winning Isn't Everything)*, a combination autobiography and account of his experience in winning the 2004 Masters. He and his wife, Amy, had three children: Amanda, Sophia, and Evan. Phil's older sister, Tina, was a PGA professional, and his younger brother, Tim, coached the golf team at the University of San Diego.

gled through his first year on the tour, missing the cut in nine out of seventeen tournaments. In 1993, however, he proved that his stellar junior career was not a fluke when he won two PGA events. His first professional victory, the Buick Invitational at Torrey Pines in San Diego, was held at the course on which he had played so many times as a junior golfer.

Phil became one of the most accomplished players on the PGA Tour. Beginning in 1996, he was ranked no lower than fifteenth in the World Golf Rankings, and he finished in second three times, behind Tiger Woods. Known for his aggressive and daring short game, especially his famous "Phil Flop" shot, Phil won at least one tournament each year between 1993 and 1998, including four wins in the 1996 campaign. After going winless in 1999, he bounced back with four wins in 2000. Other than a second winless season in 2003, he won at least two tournaments each year through 2008.

Summary

In 2008, Phil Mickelson's thirty-four PGA wins ranked him second among golfers active during his

Honors, Awards, and Milestones

1989, 1991	U.S. Walker Cup team
1990-92	NCAA individual champion
	Haskins Awards
1994, 1996, 1998, 2000, 2003, 2005, 2007	U.S. Presidents Cup team
1995, 1997, 1999, 2002, 2004, 2006, 2008	U.S. Ryder Cup team
1996	Byron Nelson Award
2004	ESPY Award: best championship performance
	ESPY Award: best male golfer

era. He ranked thirteenth on the all-time list. As the most accomplished left-handed golfer in history, Phil hoped to add to his string of PGA wins and continued to represent the United States in international competition.

Mark R. Ellis

Additional Sources

Hartman, Robert. *Leonard, Duval, Woods, and Mickelson: Masters of the Millennium—The Next Generation of the PGA Tour.* Champaign, Ill.: Sports, 1999.

Magee, David. *Endurance: Winning Life's Majors the Phil Mickelson Way.* Hoboken, N.J.: John Wiley & Sons, 2005.

Mickelson, Phil, with Donald T. Phillps. *One Magical Sunday (But Winning Isn't Everything).* New York: Warner Books, 2005.

Shipnuck, Alan. "Lefty Gets It Right: Phil Mickelson Is Striking the Ball Better than Ever, as Evidenced by His Players Win." *Sports Illustrated* 106, no. 21 (2007): 48.

_____. "Master Craftsman: The Way Phil Mickelson Won His Second Masters, His Best May Be Yet to Come." *Sports Illustrated* 104, no. 16 (2006): 34.

Byron Nelson

Born: February 4, 1912
    Near Waxahachie, Texas
Died: September 26, 2006
    Roanoke, Texas
Also known as: John Byron Nelson, Jr. (full
    name); Lord Byron

Early Life

John Byron Nelson, Jr., the top golfer of the late
1930's and 1940's, was born on February 4, 1912,
near Waxahachie, Texas, to John Byron and Madge
Marie Nelson. Byron's father was a grain merchant
in Fort Worth, Texas. The family lived in a
home near the Glen Garden Club of Fort
Worth, so when Byron was in his early teens,
he began caddying after school at the club's
golf course. Soon after, he learned the game,
and from then on, he practiced whenever
possible. When he was fourteen years old,
he and his friend, Ben Hogan, tied for the
caddy championship. Two years later, Byron
went on to win his first event, the Glen Garden Club's junior title.

At sixteen, Byron left the Fort Worth public schools to work as a file clerk for a bank-
ers' magazine and for the Fort Worth and
Denver Railroad. In his free time, he always
headed for the fairways.

The Road to Excellence

Byron's first important success as a golfer
came in 1930, at the age of eighteen. He captured the Southwest amateur crown, a triumph that hinted at what lay ahead for the
young Texas golfer.

Two years later, in 1932, Byron turned
professional. His early efforts at tournament
golf were not successful. Because of the Depression, in his first year, he won only $12.50.
He did, however, tie for third in the Texarkana Open. For five rather lean years, Byron
persisted. In 1933, as the professional at
the Texarkana Country Club, he earned a
monthly salary of $60. He married Louise
Shofner in June of the following year. To
supplement his small income, he also taught golf at
the Ridgewood, New Jersey, and Reading, Pennsylvania, country clubs. By the 1935 season, his income had jumped to $2,708, as he managed to win
the New Jersey Open. That win enabled him to continue to play golf for a living.

While teaching golf, Byron also worked on a
problem he had with his own swing. He discovered
that his swing had a troublesome hook and figured
out how to cure it. As a result, his performance improved, and he became a strong contender in tournament play from then on.

*Byron Nelson, who received a posthumous Congressional Gold
Medal in 2006.* (Courtesy of Amateur Athletic Foundation of Los
Angeles)

The Emerging Champion

Finally, in 1937, the years of perseverance paid off. Byron won his first major tournament, The Masters, where he exhibited exceptional putting skills, sinking a thirty-footer on the tenth hole. At last, his career was launched.

Only two years later, in 1939, Byron experienced his peak season. He won not only the U.S. Open but also the Western Open and the North and South Open. That same year, he earned the Vardon Trophy, for having the lowest scoring average, and came in second in the Professional Golfers' Association (PGA) Championship.

Tournament golf in the United States was suspended because of World War II, by which time Byron held an exceptional record of wins and had established himself as a top-ranking American golfer. Byron's war-year wins on the fairways often have been downplayed because so many excellent contenders were off fighting instead of teeing off. However, Byron, who was exempt from military service because of a blood-clotting condition, had proved himself as a consistent winner long before Pearl Harbor.

Byron spent the war years playing in golf exhibitions for the Red Cross or the United Service Organizations (USO). In 1944, he won seven of twenty-two events, compiled a scoring average of 69.67, and earned a record $37,900 in war bonds. The Associated Press (AP) voted him male athlete of the year. Over a period of eighteen months beginning

Major Championship Victories

1937, 1942	The Masters
1939	U.S. Open
1940, 1945	PGA Championship

Other Notable Victories

1937, 1939, 1947	Ryder Cup Team
1939	North and South Open
	Phoenix Open
	Western Open
1940	Texas Open
1941-42, 1944-45	All-American Open
1941, 1945	Greensboro Open
1945	Canadian Open
1945-46	Los Angeles Open
1948	Texas PGA Championship
1951	Bing Crosby Invitational
1955	French Open
1965	Ryder Cup nonplaying captain

the following year, he achieved his most memorable accomplishment. He won eighteen of thirty-five tournaments, eleven of them in a row. No golfer will probably ever match this record; since Byron, only Tiger Woods has won more than five consecutive tournaments (7). In 1945, Byron was an obvious choice for AP male athlete of the year.

Continuing the Story

After winning every title he could in the United States, Byron began to have severe problems with his back. Crawling out of bed each morning was agony. He would arrive at tournaments leaning on his wife, and later he began skipping some of them entirely. He was tired of having to shake hands and attend lunches and of attracting too much attention. He began to think more and more about ranching.

In 1946, exhausted after fourteen years of constant effort, Byron retired, a few weeks after his caddy accidentally kicked his ball and cost him the U.S. Open. For all his victories, he was not able to save anything from his professional career. He found more profitable work as a rancher-businessman, managing his eight-hundred-acre Hereford ranch near Roanoke, Texas. He became a golfing commentator on ABC television and was con-

Records and Milestones

Won a record eighteen tournaments (including one unofficial) in a single season, including a record eleven consecutive victories (Mar. 8, 1945, through Aug. 4, 1945)

Runner-up in the 1946 U.S. Open, the 1941 and 1947 Masters, and the 1939, 1941, and 1944 PGA Championships

Honors and Awards

1939	PGA Vardon Trophy
1944-45	Associated Press Male Athlete of the Year
1953	Inducted into PGA Hall of Fame
1968	Byron Nelson Golf Classic is first golf tournament named in honor of a player
1974	Inducted into World Golf Hall of Fame
	GWAA Richardson Award
	Bob Jones Award
1997	PGA Tour Lifetime Achievement Award
2006	Congressional Medal of Honor (posthumous)

sidered one of the best coaches in the United States.

Byron was one of the most influential figures in the evolution of the golf swing. He had a way of drawing back his club in a "one-piece" movement, with no single part of his body dominating the move. His swing included a full shoulder turn but a restricted hip turn, and an extra-straight left arm to keep the club face square and hit the ball with extra leg drive. His club then pulled into the ball on the downswing, rather than pushed into it. This kind of swing increased the chances of consistent hitting.

Summary

Byron Nelson's strength was his consistent, powerful playing ability, which often caused him to be described as a mechanical golfer. Although his career was brief, he won forty-nine PGA tournaments and every other golf title and award there was to win in the United States. He constantly set records. His 1945 consecutive-victory record may never be broken. In 2006, he was awarded the Congressional Gold Medal posthumously.

Nan White

Additional Sources

Companiotte, John. *Byron Nelson: The Most Remarkable Year in the History of Golf.* Chicago: Triumph Books, 2006.

Davis, Martin. *Byron Nelson: The Little Black Book—The Personal Diary of Golf Legend Byron Nelson: 1935-1947.* Arlington, Tex.: Summit, 1995.

_____. *Byron Nelson: The Story of Golf's Finest Gentleman and the Greatest Winning Streak in History.* New York: Broadway Books, 1997.

Nelson, Byron. *How I Played the Game.* Rev. ed. Lanham, Md.: Taylor, 2006.

Nelson, Byron, and Jon Bradley. *Quotable Byron: Words of Wisdom, Faith, and Success by and About Byron Nelson, Golf's Great Ambassador.* Nashville, Tenn.: TowleHouse, 2002.

Larry Nelson

Born: September 10, 1947
    Fort Payne, Alabama
Also known as: Larry Gene Nelson (full name)

Early Life

Larry Gene Nelson was born September 10, 1947, in Fort Payne, Alabama. Unlike many professional golfers who took up golf at an early age, Larry never gave much thought to golf as a youngster. Growing up in Acworth, Georgia, Larry concentrated on baseball and basketball. A good athlete, he played as both pitcher and shortstop for a championship team in the Georgia Colt League and lettered in both sports in high school. After graduating high school, Larry was enrolled at Southern Polytechnic State University. He had recently married when he was drafted to serve in the United States Army during the Vietnam War. While serving in Southeast Asia, Larry's interest in golf began to develop. At this time, he realized he could make a decent living playing golf and decided to give the game a try upon his return home.

Following his discharge from the Army, Larry worked as an illustrator for aerospace manufacturer Lockheed and enrolled at Kennesaw Junior College in Georgia. As a full-time student working seven days a week, he did not have much time for golf. That changed in 1969, when his course work was almost completed. With more free time, he frequented a local driving range. Soon Larry was working in pro Bert Seagrave's shop at the Pine Tree Club in Kennesaw. Golf was becoming more than a hobby; Larry was a natural at the sport.

The Road to Excellence

Larry learned to play golf by reading *The Modern Fundamentals of Golf* by Ben Hogan and by taking advice from Seagrave. He was a good study. His first time playing he scored below a 100, and he broke 70 within nine months. Now employed as the assistant to Seagrave at the Pine Tree Club, he was beginning to have confidence in the likelihood of becoming a club pro himself.

However, Larry was turned down when he applied for a position as a club pro. Friends, both un- derstanding of Larry's disappointment and confident in his playing ability, encouraged and financed a move to Florida so he could better develop his game in the hope of playing professionally. After arriving in Florida, he began participating in mini-tours. Then, in 1973, he completed the Professional Golfers' Association (PGA) Tour qualifying school and made the 1974 PGA Tour at the age of twenty-seven.

The Emerging Champion

Larry's start on the PGA Tour was not spectacular. He did not qualify in ten of eleven events and then failed to make the cut when he did qualify. He was, however, able to keep his tour card for the next season by finishing eighth at Jacksonville, winning $3,500.

In 1979, after several years of competing, Larry finally won on the tour, at both the Jackie Gleason-

---

PGA Tour Victories

1979	Jackie Gleason-Inverrary Classic
	Western Open
1980	Atlanta Classic
1981	Greater Greensboro Open
1981, 1987	PGA Championship
1983	U.S. Open
1984, 1987	Walt Disney World Golf Classic
1988	Georgia-Pacific Atlanta Golf Classic

Champions Tour Victories

1998	American Express Invitational
	Pittsburgh Senior Classic
1998, 2000	Boone Valley Classic
1999	GTE Classic
	Bruno's Memorial Classic
2000	Las Vegas Senior Classic
	Foremost Insurance Championship
	Bank One Senior Championship
	Vantage Championship
2000-01	FleetBoston Classic
2001	MasterCard Championship
	Royal Caribbean Classic
	Farmers Charity Classic
	SBC Championship
2003	Constellation Energy Classic
2004	FedEx Kinko's Classic
	Administaff Small Business Classic

Inverrary Classic and the Western Open. He finished the year second on the money list to Tom Watson. Also in 1979, Larry played for the U.S. Ryder Cup team for the first of three times. As a member of the team, he was the only golfer to win five matches in a single Ryder Cup tournament. Playing with partner Lanny Wadkins, he won four team matches and also won his singles match against Seve Ballesteros. These five victories started an unbeaten streak of nine that tied Larry with American Gardener Dickinson.

Continuing the Story

In 1980 and 1988, Larry won the Atlanta Classic on his home course, the Atlanta Country Club in Marietta, Georgia. His participation in the Atlanta Classic helped to elevate the status of the tournament to a major tour stop.

In 1997, Larry joined the PGA Senior Tour (renamed the Champions Tour in 2003) and won nineteen times. In the 2000 season, he was named senior player of the year, winning six events and $2.7 million, the second highest season total ever on the Champions Tour.

As a member of the Champions Tour, Larry participated in events with each of his two sons, Drew and Josh, both aspiring golfers. Larry joined Raymond Floyd as the only fathers to win the Father/Son Challenge with two different sons by winning the 2004 Office Depot Father/Son Challenge with son Drew and the 2007 Del Webb Father/Son Challenge with Josh.

Summary

In his career, Larry won three major tournaments, each during the 1980's: the U.S. Open in 1983 and the PGA Championship in 1981 and 1987. Only Jack Nicklaus, Seve Ballesteros, and Tom Watson won three or more majors during the 1980's. Larry was a three-time member of the U.S. Ryder Cup team—in 1979, 1981, and 1987—and he actively designed golf courses. He was elected and served twice as the player director of the PGA tournament policy board. Larry was elected to the Georgia Golf Hall of Fame in 1990 and inducted into World Golf Hall of Fame in 2006.

Michael D. Cummings, Jr.

Additional Sources

Feherty, D. *David Feherty's Totally Subjective History of the Ryder Cup.* New York: Rugged Land, 2004.

Golf Magazine's Encyclopedia of Golf: The Complete Reference. 2d ed. New York: HarperCollins, 1993.

Jarmin, C. M. *The Ryder Cup: The Definitive History of Playing Golf for Pride and Country.* Chicago: Contemporary Books, 1999.

Jack Nicklaus

Born: January 21, 1940
　　　Columbus, Ohio
Also known as: Jack William Nicklaus (full
　　name); the Golden Bear

Early Life

Jack William Nicklaus was born January 21, 1940, in Columbus, Ohio. He was the first of two children born to Louis Charles and Nellie Helen (Schoener) Nicklaus. His father was the owner of a chain of drug stores, a successful pharmacist in Columbus, and a former president of the Ohio Pharmacy Board. A personal friend of the legendary Ohio State University football coach Woody Hayes, Charlie Nicklaus had high hopes that Jack would one day play for the Buckeyes.

Jack attended Upper Arlington, Ohio, public schools and Ohio State University, which granted him an honorary doctorate later in his life. Jack was an all-around athlete, participating in a variety of sports. He played golf, baseball, football, and basketball in high school, although golf became his primary activity.

Jack was introduced to golf at the age of ten by his father, who was playing golf on the order of a physician to aid in the strengthening of a leg which had suffered injury. Jack's first nine holes resulted in a score of 51, and a golfing legend had begun.

The Road to Excellence

As a junior member of the Scioto Country Club in Columbus, Jack enrolled in a golf class taught by the club professional, Jack Grout. Grout encouraged young golfers to hit the ball as far as they could and to worry about control later. Under the guidance of Grout, who knew Jack was a talented young golfer, Jack became the best junior golfer in Ohio during the 1950's.

At the age of thirteen, Jack shot a round of 69 on the 7,095-yard course at Scioto. As a thirteen-year-old, Jack won the Ohio state junior championship for players aged thirteen to fifteen. He also won the Columbus junior match-play championship and competed into the fourth round of the United States Golf Association (USGA) juniors tournament.

During his four years at Upper Arlington High School in Columbus, Jack built an impressive list of accomplishments. At the age of fourteen, he was the Scioto junior club champion, the Columbus junior match-play champion, Columbus junior stroke-play champion, and a medalist in his tri-state high school championship.

The following year, Jack qualified for

Jack Nicklaus, who compiled the most PGA victories ever. (Courtesy of Amateur Athletic Foundation of Los Angeles)

the United States Amateur Championship for the first time and again won the Columbus junior match-play and stroke-play championships, along with the Columbus District Amateur Championship. Jack qualified for the U.S. Open for the first time in 1957, although he missed the cut by 10 shots after the first two rounds.

Jack's father initiated and supported Jack's involvement in the game during these early years. His father's values, strong character, and perspective were noted as significant to Jack's successes in life on and off the golf course.

The Emerging Champion

Jack chose to attend Ohio State University, although he received many scholarship offers from other schools. As a college student, he won the United States Amateur Championship twice, in 1959 and 1961, and was the runner-up to Arnold Palmer by 2 strokes in the 1960 U.S. Open in Denver, Colorado. This budding rivalry was captured on film and presented in a HBO documentary titled *Back Nine at Cherry Hills* (2008).

Leading an active college life and playing many sports while still a full-time student tended to keep Jack's school efforts at a minimum. Jack stated that not completing his undergraduate degree remained a source of regret.

Following his 1961 United States Amateur Championship win, Jack seriously considered turning professional. He was spending much of his time working on his golf game, and he was also working to support his new bride, Barbara, and his first of five children. Although Jack's father had hoped that Jack could remain an amateur golfer as the great Bobby Jones was able to do, Jack announced that he was turning professional on November 8, 1961.

What happened next was simply history in the making. Although he did not take the professional golf world by storm, Jack had a successful first year on the tour. In his first seventeen tournaments, he

Major Championship Victories

1959, 1961	U.S. Amateur
1962, 1967, 1972, 1980	U.S. Open
1963, 1965-66, 1972, 1975, 1986	The Masters
1963, 1971, 1973, 1975, 1980	PGA Championship
1966, 1970, 1978	British Open
1991, 1993	U.S. Senior Open

Other Notable Victories

1959, 1961	Walker Cup Team
1961	NCAA Championship
1963-64, 1966, 1971, 1973	World Cup Team member
1963-64, 1971, 1973, 1977	Tournament of Champions
1964	Phoenix Open
1964, 1968, 1971, 1975-76, 1978	Australian Open
1965	Memphis Open
1967, 1972	Westchester Classic
1967, 1972-73	Bing Crosby National
1967-68	Western Open
1968	American Golf Classic
1969	Andy Williams-San Diego Open
1969, 1971, 1973, 1975, 1977, 1981	Ryder Cup Team
1970-71	Byron Nelson Classic
1972, 1975	Doral-Eastern Open
1974, 1976, 1978	Tournament Players Championship
1975	Heritage Classic
1977-78	Jackie Gleason-Inverrary Classic
1982	Colonial National
1983, 1987	Ryder Cup Team captain
1990	Mazda Senior Tournament Players Championship
1990, 1995-96	Tradition at Desert Mountain, senior
1991	PGA Seniors Championship

had eight top-ten finishes and finished either first or second five times.

Jack's next tournament was one of the four major tournaments on the PGA tour—the U.S. Open. Jack defeated Palmer in a playoff to win the first of his record eighteen major titles on the PGA Tour.

In all, in 1962, his first year as a professional, Jack played in twenty-six U.S. events. Along with his win at the U.S. Open, he won the Seattle Open, Portland Open, and the World Series of Golf. Understandably, Jack was then chosen as the rookie of the year.

Continuing the Story

Through the 1990 season, Jack's first year of eligibility on the Senior or Champions Tour, Jack had won more than ninety tournaments worldwide. He

Records and Milestones

Co-holder (with Arnold Palmer) of the PGA Tour record for most consecutive years with a victory (seventeen), winning at least once every year from 1962 to 1978

First to reach $2 million, in 1973; $3 million, in 1977; $4 million, in 1983; and $5 million, in 1988; in PGA Tour career earnings

One of two golfers (Tiger Woods) to win all **four** major titles twice, while setting a record with eighteen major PGA tournament victories

Accumulated a total of seventy-three PGA tour victories and a total of nineteen international titles

Oldest winner of the Masters, in 1986, at forty-six years of age

Leading money winner of the PGA Tour (1964-65, 1967, 1971-73, 1975-76)

Honors and Awards

1962	PGA Rookie of the Year
	Golf Digest Rookie of the Year
1964-65, 1967, 1972-73, 1975	*Golf Digest* Byron Nelson Award for Tournament Victories
1967, 1972-73, 1975-76	PGA Player of the Year
1972, 1975-76	GWAA Player of the Year
1974	Inducted into World Golf Hall of Fame
1975	Bob Jones Award
1975-77	Seagram's Seven Crowns of Sports Award
1978	*Sports Illustrated* Sportsman of the Year
	GWAA Richardson Award
1980	Named Athlete of the Decade (1970's)
	Comeback of the Year Award
1982	Card Walker Award for outstanding contributions to junior golf
	Herb Graffis Award
1988	Named Golfer of the Century
1993	*Golf World*'s Golf Course Architect of the Year
1995	Inducted into Canadian Golf Hall of Fame
2000	PGA of America's Distinguished Service Award
	Memorial Tournament Honoree: Captains Club
	Payne Stewart Award
2001	ESPY: Lifetime Achievement Award
2003	Muhammad Ali Sports Legend Award
2005	Presidential Medal of Freedom

was second on the all-time tournament winners list, with seventy-three PGA Tour victories. Along with this, Jack was in second or tied for second fifty-six times and placed third or tied for third thirty-five times. He had the lowest career scoring average— approximately 70.5—and led the PGA Tour in career earnings for a number of years.

Besides his major championships, Jack finished second nineteen times, which set a record. On the PGA Senior Tour in 1990, Jack won two of his four tournament entries. From 1969 to 1987, he was a member of the U.S. Ryder Cup teams that competed against golfers from Europe; he served as a nonplaying captain of the team twice.

Jack won both the PGA Senior Championship and the U.S. Senior Open in 1991, and he won a second U.S. Senior Open in 1993. Following consecutive victories at the Tradition in 1995 and 1996, he had no tournament wins in 1997. An injured hip in 1998 hampered his play; nonetheless, he finished sixth at The Masters. He ended a remarkable streak of 154 consecutive appearances in major PGA tournaments when he decided not to compete in the PGA Championship in 1998.

Jack continued to play tournaments in 1999 and 2000, though he appeared in fewer events. His best finish was a tie for ninth at the 2000 Tradition. Jack increasingly turned his attention to golf-course design through his company, Golden Bear International. *Golf World* named him the golf-course architect of the year in 1993.

Summary

The Jack Nicklaus story was made more compelling by the fact that he was a devoted family man. As the father of five children, he was consistently an active parent. He was known for an ability to balance his golf career, family involvement, and business interests. His illustrious career ended in 2006, the year after he received the Presidential Medal of Freedom. Even with Tiger Woods as his heir apparent, Jack remained the greatest golfer ever to play the game. His records and list of achievements on and off the golf course left his legacy intact in the twenty-first century.

Hal J. Walker, updated by Kevin Eyster

Additional Sources

Andrisani, John. *The Nicklaus Way: An Analysis of the Unique Techniques and Strategies of Golf's Leading*

Major Championship Winner. New York: Harper-Collins, 2003.

Nicklaus, Jack, with Ken Bowden. *Jack Nicklaus: My Story*. New York: Simon & Schuster, 1997.

_____. *My Most Memorable Shots in the Majors*. Trumbull, Conn.: Golf Digest/Tennis, 1988.

Nicklaus, Jack, with David Shedloski. *Jack Nicklaus: Memories and Mementos from Golf's Golden Bear*. New York: Stewart, Tabori, and Chang, 2007.

O'Connor, Ian. *Arnie and Jack: Palmer, Nicklaus, and Golf's Greatest Rivalry*. New York: Houghton Mifflin, 2008.

Sampson, Curt. *The Eternal Summer: Palmer, Nicklaus, and Hogan in 1960, Golf's Golden Year*. New York: Villard, 2000.

Shaw, Mark. *Nicklaus*. Dallas, Tex.: Taylor, 1997.

Wukovits, John F. *Jack Nicklaus*. Philadelphia: Chelsea House, 1998.

Greg Norman

Born: February 10, 1955
 Mount Isa, Queensland, Australia
Also known as: Gregory John Norman (full name); the Shark

Early Life

Gregory John Norman was born on February 10, 1955, in Mount Isa, a small mining town in Queensland, Australia. His father was a mining engineer, but his sporting ancestry stemmed from his mother, who was an excellent amateur golfer. In spite of his family connection with golf, Greg did not take to the sport as a boy. In this, he differed from the typical outstanding athlete, who tends to realize an affinity for a sport from an early age.

Greg was not an athletic child by nature. In an effort to remedy his scrawny condition, he participated in a number of sports. He became an excellent rugby player and further developed his body by using a weight-training program. Interestingly, Greg switched from rough sports to what is considered a country-club sport.

Greg first realized his potential as a golfer during his teen years. After caddying for his mother, he decided to try the game. To his surprise, he discovered that he could drive the ball enormously far. At this point in his life, the ability to hit the ball a huge distance was more important to Greg than accurate play.

The Road to Excellence

Greg was fortunate to be mentored by Charlie Earp, the lead professional at the Queensland Club in Brisbane. Earp followed a course diametrically opposed to tradition. Most professionals would have discouraged Greg from his stress on power and worked at developing an accurate, grooved swing instead.

Earp encouraged Greg to continue to hit the ball as hard as he could. Greg often drove over 330 yards, an astonishingly long distance. Earp did not give up on developing greater accuracy for Greg. Rather, he recognized accuracy came with experience. Exactly as he and his coach expected, Greg developed into a very straight shooter. He did this by slightly shortening the distance of his average drive in order to maintain greater control. His drives averaged 280 yards, a distance that was still better than almost all other golfers.

Earp provided Greg with the opportunity to develop another key attribute of a golf champion: the psychology of a winner. He employed Greg as his assistant on a small salary. In order to increase his earnings, Greg frequently played in matches with members of the club. Because of golf's handicap system, in which the weaker player has a certain number of strokes automatically deducted from his score, the outcomes of the matches were not foregone conclusions. In order to win these matches—and he could not afford to lose—Greg had to shoot well under pressure. This early experience sharpened his concentration tremendously.

The Emerging Champion

Given Greg's natural talent and the skills he picked up from Earp, Greg quickly developed into an outstanding golfer. He became a scratch player—a

Australian Greg Norman. (Courtesy of PGA of America)

Major Championship Victories

1986, 1993   British Open

Other Notable Victories

1980	French Open
1980, 1983, 1986	Suntory World Match Play
1980, 1987, 1995-96	Australian Open
1981-82	Dunlop Masters
1984	Canadian Open
1984, 1986	Kemper Open
1988	MCI Heritage Classic
1990, 1993, 1996	Doral-Ryder Open
1990, 1995	Memorial Tournament
1992	Canadian Open
1994	Tournament Players Championship
1995	Canon Greater Hartford Open
1995, 1997	NEC World Series of Golf
1997	Fedex St. Jude Classic

golfer without a handicap—while still a teenager. In 1976, he turned professional and immediately made his presence known on the Australian tour.

To become an outstanding local player was one thing; to gain worldwide recognition was a much more demanding assignment. Greg's game had both strengths and weaknesses. One-half of the strokes of a par-72 round are allotted to putting, and in order to win a tournament, a golfer must usually shoot well below 36 putts per round. Greg was an indifferent putter, and, although at times he could putt well, this area of the sport was not his strength. His comparative lack of excellence in putting meant that, when matched with a golfer such as his hero, Jack Nicklaus, he was at a severe disadvantage. Nicklaus could equal Greg in power but was also one of the game's best putters. On the positive side, Greg's enormous power could not be overlooked. Although his aggressive style sometimes got him into trouble, he was arguably the longest accurate hitter of any golfer of the 1970's and 1980's.

Continuing the Story

Greg's rise to the top was fast and furious. After establishing a winning record in Europe and Asia, he came to the United States in 1981. He attracted attention quickly with a high finish in The Masters, one of golf's ma-

jor tournaments. In the next few years, Greg won six tournaments in the United States.

Perhaps more significantly, Greg's record in the rest of the world was unsurpassed. Throughout most of the early 1980's, Greg was at or near the top in monetary earnings and was usually among the leaders in year-round stroke average. He was also a perennial tournament winner.

Only one obstacle prevented Greg from unconditional recognition as a superstar. He needed to win one of golf's "majors"—the four most important tournaments for professional golfers. In 1986, Greg met the challenge when he easily won the British Open. He finished high in several of the other majors, and he frequently performed so well that he aroused talk of a Grand Slam—a victory in all of the majors in one year, a feat no professional golfer had ever attained.

After his 1986 win, Greg did not win another major tournament until 1993, when he recorded his second win at the British Open. Critics pointed to Greg's overly aggressive game and contended that

Records and Milestones

Winner of eighty-seven tournaments around the world

PGA Tour leading money winner (1986, 1990)

British Open, runner-up (1989)

Masters, runner-up (1986, 1987, 1996)

Won twenty-nine tournaments around the world (primarily Australia and Europe) before joining the American Tour full-time in 1984

First player on the PGA Tour to surpass $12 million in career earnings (1999)

U.S. Open, runner-up (1984, 1995)

Honors and Awards

1985-90, 1992, 1994-96	Dunhill Cup Team
1986, 1990	Arnold Palmer Award
1988	Metropolitan Golf Writers Association Mary Bea Porter Award
1989-90, 1994	PGA Vardon Trophy
1988, 1990, 1993-95	Byron Nelson Award
1986	BBC Sports Personality of the Year: Overseas Personality Award
1994-2000	Presidents Cup Team
1995	PGA Tour Player of the Year
2001	Inducted into World Golf Hall of Fame
2008	Golf Course Superintendents Association of America's Old Tom Morris Award

he often "choked" when faced with a close struggle to win. Like a true champion though, Greg invariably met his near-misses with his customary good nature. He refused to alter his daring style of play—Greg lost in a playoff at all four majors. However, in the early 1990's, Greg spent 331 weeks as the number-one player in the world.

In 1998, after several seasons of playing with shoulder pain, Greg decided to undergo surgery to remove bone spurs that caused tendinitis in his rotator cuff. Following his recovery from surgery, he won the Greg Norman Holden International in Australia. In 1999, despite a reduced schedule following his surgery, he became the first player on the Professional Golfers' Association Tour to surpass $12 million in career earnings. He also finished third at The Masters.

In 2000, Greg underwent surgery again, this time on his right hip. Greg was an Olympic torchbearer for the 2000 Olympic Summer Games in Sydney, Australia. The National Childhood Cancer Foundation (NCCF) honored him and his then-wife, Laura, with the Hands of Hope award for their help in raising $10 million for NCCF.

Amid criticism concerning his ability to play under pressure, Greg proved to be a dedicated professional. His eagle on the thirteenth hole of the 1999 Masters demonstrated the effectiveness of his aggressive play, and despite many disappointing finishes in 2000, he still finished eighty-fourth on the official money list with over $500,000 in earnings. In 2001, Greg was inducted into the World Golf Hall of Fame.

Greg also became a successful entrepreneur. At one point, his net worth was believed to be close to $500 million. His company, Great White Shark Enterprises, had a number of branches, including an apparel company, a production company, and a merchandising division. His company also developed resorts, with his signature golf courses.

Through his resort enterprise, Greg met Chris Evert, the former tennis champion, who became his fiancée. He had contracted her to build tennis academies at his resorts and the two quickly became more closely acquainted. The story made headlines in numerous sources, and in December 2007, the two announced that they had become engaged. On June 28, 2008, they wed in the Bahamas.

Summary

Like many other famous golfers, Greg Norman developed his interest and skill in golf through his early experience as a caddy. His outstanding advantage was in his powerful drives. Greg was fortunate to meet a teacher who had the patience to develop his accuracy without inhibiting his power. Although reputed to have a tendency to "choke" under intense pressure, Greg became one of the world's leading golfers during the 1970's and 1980's. His likable personality made him a favorite with fans.

Bill Delaney, updated by P. Huston Ladner

Additional Sources

Allis, Peter. *The Who's Who of Golf.* Englewood Cliffs, N.J.: Prentice-Hall, 1983.

Moriarty, Jim. "Norman Meets the Future of Aussie Golf." *Golf World* 61, no. 25 (February 15, 2008): 46.

Murphy, Austin. "A Taste for Profit." *Sports Illustrated* 105, no. 1 (July 3, 2006): 90-93.

Norman, Greg, and Don Lawrence. *Greg Norman, My Story.* London: Harrap, 1983.

St. John, Lauren. *Greg Norman: The Biography.* Sydney: Bantam, 1998.

Vigeland, Carl A. *Stalking the Shark: Pressure and Passion on the Pro Golf Tour.* New York: W. W. Norton, 1996.

Lorena Ochoa

Born: November 15, 1981
Guadalajara, Mexico

Early Life

Lorena Ochoa grew up in a five-bedroom house next door to the Guadalajara Country Club. Her father, Javier, was a real-estate developer, and her mother, Marcela, was an abstract artist. Lorena took up golf at the age of five, and for several years, she was the only female to play at the country club. Her mentor, Rafael Alarcón, played professionally in the 1980's and 1990's. As a child, Lorena sat and watched him practice. When Lorena was nine, Alarcón began to teach her the game. The third of four children and the oldest daughter, Lorena decided, at the age of twelve, to be the best player in the world. She won her first state event in golf at the age of six and her first national event at the age of seven. She won five consecutive Junior World Golf Championships. In 2000, she enrolled at the University of Arizona on a golf scholarship. She won National Collegiate Athletic Association (NCAA) player of the year awards in both 2001 and 2002, finishing as the runner-up both years for the NCAA national championship. She was named Pac-10 Conference freshman of the year in 2001 and first-team all-Pac-10 Conference in 2001 and 2002. In her sophomore year, Lorena had eight tournament wins in the ten events she entered. She set an NCAA record with seven victories in her first seven events. In 2001, Mexican president Vincente Fox presented Mexico's highest sports award to Lorena. She was the youngest athlete and the first golfer to ever receive the award.

The Road to Excellence

Lorena left the University of Arizona after her sophomore year to join the professional golf circuit. In the 2002 Futures Tour, she proved she was ready for the ranks of professional women's golf, winning three of ten events. In her rookie season on the LPGA Tour, Lorena had eight top-ten finishes and was named rookie of the year. In 2004, she won her first professional event, the Franklin American Mortgage Championship, becoming the first Mexican born player to win on the LPGA Tour. In 2006, her first round score of 62 in the Kraft Nabisco Championship tied a record for the lowest score ever by a golfer, of either sex, in a major tournament. In April, 2007, Lorena overtook Annika Sorenstam to become the number-one ranked female player in the world. The same year, she also became the first woman to earn more than $4 million in a single season. Despite Lorena's overwhelming early success, she had yet to win a major tournament. She had come close on a couple of occasions. Inevitably, golf pundits began to say that she could not win a major. However, Lorena may have been waiting for the right time and place. In August, 2007, she won the first professional women's golf tournament ever held at St. Andrew's in Scotland: the Women's British Open. Lorena had the distinction of winning her first major at the first women's professional tournament ever held at the world's most revered golf course.

Lorena Ochoa watching her shot at the 2008 Samsung World Championships. (John Green/CSM/Landov)

The Emerging Champion

Lorena reached $12 million in career earnings faster than any player in LPGA history. In 2008, she had already earned enough

LPGA Tour Victories

2004	Franklin American Mortgage Championship
	Wachovia Classic
2005-06	Wegmans LPGA
2006	LPGA Takefuji Classic
	Wendy's Championship for Children
	The Mitchell Company Tournament of Champions
2006-07	Samsung World Championship of Golf
2006-08	Sybase Classic
2006, 2008	Corona Championship
2007	Women's British Open
	Canadian Open
	Safeway Classic
	ADT Championship
2007-08	Safeway International
2008	HSBC Women's Champions
	Kraft Nabisco Championship
	Ginn Open
	LPGA Classic

points to be elected to the LPGA Hall of Fame. She had to wait until 2012 to be enshrined in the hall because she had not played the minimum ten years required to be inducted. In the middle of her success, Lorena awarded hundreds of scholarships to children between the ages of six and fifteen to attend La Barranca, a school in Guadalajara which Lorena supported. She was named to *Time* magazine's list of the world's one hundred most influential people.

At 5 feet 6 inches and 130 pounds, Lorena was surprisingly strong, averaging 271 yards for her driving distance. To stay in shape, Lorena ran six times each week, from 35 to 70 minutes, training with her brother and sister. In 2007, she had eight LPGA victories, and she finished as runner-up in five other tournaments. That same year, she won the Rolex player of the year award and was named by *Sports Illustrated* as the woman athlete of the year.

Continuing the Story

At many courses where Lorena played, the grounds and their surroundings were maintained by Spanish-speaking workers. Lorena, without seeking publicity, often made her way to the sheds and garages where these workers were headquartered, away from the course's public places. She took the time to thank these workers and to express her appreciation for all they do to make each tournament possible. Lorena made certain that these workers felt a

sense of pride in their work and understood their importance. Even in a country like Mexico, where golf is a minor sport, Lorena became one of the most popular figures in the nation.

Working with Alarcón, her coach, and Dave Brooker, her caddy, Lorena became the dominant player in her sport. Physically fit and confident, she made a game that can be extrememly difficult seem practically effortless. In April, 2008, at the Ginn Open in Reunion, Florida, Lorena won her fourth consecutive tournament. She followed this victory with her third consecutive Sybase Classic win in Clifton, New Jersey.

Summary

Lorena Ochoa, Mexico's greatest golfer of all time and one of its greatest sports heroes, became a phenomenon in the world of golf. The Lorena Ochoa Foundation, founded in 2004, was created with an emphasis on health and education issues for Mexican children. Lorena hoped to play a few more years and then retire to perhaps marry, raise a family, continue to work for her charities, and simplify her life.

Randy L. Abbott

Additional Sources

Anderson, Kelli. "Long Time Coming." *Sports Illustrated* 107, no. 6 (August 13, 2007): G6-G8.

Garrity, John. "Marching On." *Sports Illustrated* 108, no. 14A (April 8, 2008): 16-18.

Shipnuck, Alan. "Simply the Best." *Sports Illustrated* 108, no. 23 (June 9, 2008): 66-72.

Honors and Awards

1999	Mexico's sportswoman of the century
2001	Mexico National Sports Award
2002	Futures Tour rookie of the year
	Futures Tour player of the year
2003	LPGA rookie of the year
2006	Mexico athlete of the year
2006-07	Mexico national sports award
	Associated Press female athlete of the year
	LPGA player of the year
	LPGA Vare Trophy
	Golf Writers Association of America female player of the year
2007	Women's Sports Foundation sportswoman of the year
	Glamour magazine woman of the year
	EFE sportswoman of the year
	Heather Farr Player Award
2008	ESPY Award: best international athlete
	Time magazine one hundred most influential people in the world

Ayako Okamoto

Born: April 2, 1951
Akitsu (now Higashihiroshima),
Hiroshima Prefecture, Japan

Early Life

The daughter of an orange farmer, Ayako Okamoto was born in Akitsu (now Higashihiroshima), Hiroshima Prefecture, Japan, on April 2, 1951. As a young woman, Ayako worked for the Daiwabo textile company and played for company's softball team, becoming the star pitcher and helping her team win the Japanese national championship when she was twenty years old. While in Hawaii for a softball tournament, she noticed a golf course below her hotel window. She and her teammates decided to try the sport. Back in Japan, Ayako began learning and playing golf at a facility next door to her work. She played right-handed, although she had been a left-handed softball pitcher. At first, her parents did not want her playing golf. However, Ayako and her parents made an agreement that, if she did not become successful in golf by the time she was twenty-five, she would return home and do whatever they wished her to do.

The Road to Excellence

Ayako never had to fulfill her pledge to come home. By the time she was twenty-five years old, she had won her first tournament: the 1975 Mizunono corporation tournament. She was an all-star player the next year, won four tournaments in 1977, and won the KTV Ladies Classic in 1978. In 1979, at twenty-eight years old, she won the Japan Ladies Professional Golf Association (JLPGA) Championship. She had a three-round score of 17 under par, giving her a place in *The Guinness Book of Records*. By the time Ayako was thirty, she had become a superstar in Japan. She had won eight Japanese tournaments and topped the JLPGA money list.

Ayako was blessed with a natural swing and keen hand-eye coordination. She fulfilled the Japanese people's hope for a real golf hero. Ayako hosted a weekly television show, *Super Golf*, which was the highest-rated golf show in the country. Although she continued to enjoy impressive victories, includ-

ing the JLPGA Championship in 1982 and 1990, she decided to widen the scope of her career. She qualified for the American LPGA Tour on her first attempt. Between 1982 and 1992, Ayako had seventeen wins, the first of which was the 1982 Arizona Copper Classic.

The Emerging Champion

Having attained international status, Ayako consistently won on the LPGA Tour and in various tournaments in Japan. Although she did not win a major in the United States, she had three wins in 1984: the J&B Scotch Pro-Am, the Mayflower Classic, and the Hitachi Ladies British Open. The following year, she recorded her third career hole in one at the McDonald's Championship. Her two wins in

Ayako Okamoto in 1984. (Getty Images)

1986 were the Elizabeth Arden Classic and the Cellular One-Ping Golf Championship. In 1987, she was particularly successful. She won four tournaments, including the Kyocera Inamori Golf Classic, the Chrysler-Plymouth Classic, the Nestlé World Championship, and the Lady Keystone Open, which made her the LPGA Tour's fifteenth millionaire. She made the fourth hole in one of her LPGA career at the McDonald's Championship, and she became the first international player to be awarded the Rolex player of the year award.

In 1988, Ayako won the Orient Leasing Hawaiian Ladies Open, the Greater Washington Open, and the San Diego Inamori Golf Classic, at which she posted a career-low score of 63. She was the LPGA Corning Classic winner in 1989; the Sara Lee Classic winner in 1990, at which time she became the eighth LPGA Tour player to exceed $2 million in career winnings; and the McDonald's Championship winner in 1992, marking her seventeenth career title.

Continuing the Story

By 1993, the frequent travel to and from Japan, the constant attention of the Japan press, and a series of injuries had taken their toll. Ayako left the LPGA Tour in the United States to continue playing on the JLPGA Tour and in other events. In 1993, she won the Japan Women's Open and the Itoen Ladies tournament. The next year, she was victorious in the Tohato Ladies event and the Itoki Classic. In 1995, she participated in five competitions and finished in a tie for twenty-first at the U.S. Women's Open. She added the 1996 Fujjoi Sankei Ladies tournament, the 1997 Japan Women's Open, and the 1999 Katokichi Queens tournament to her list of victories.

In 2000, Ayako was recognized during the LPGA's fiftieth anniversary as one of its top fifty players and teachers. On September 14, 2004, the ministry of foreign affairs of Japan held an awards ceremony for the foreign minister's certificate of

LPGA Tour Victories

Year	Victory
1982	Arizona Copper Classic
1983	Rochester International
1984	J&B Scotch Pro-Am
	Mayflower Classic
	Hitachi Ladies British Open
1986	Elizabeth Arden Classic
	Cellular One-Ping Golf Championship
1987	Kyocera Inamori Golf Classic
	Chrysler-Plymouth Classic
	Lady Keystone Open
	Nestlé World Championship
1988	Orient Leasing Hawaiian Ladies Open
	San Diego Inamori Golf Classic
	Greater Washington Open
1989	LPGA Corning Classic
1990	Sara Lee Classic
1992	McDonald's Championship

commendation. To commemorate the 150th anniversary of the Japan-U.S. exchange, the ministry conferred commendations on three recipients, including Ayako, for contributions to Japan-U.S. relations. Less than a year later, on June 22, 2005, Ayako was elected to the World Golf Hall of Fame at a ceremony in Cherry Hills Village, Colorado. Subsequently, on November 14, in St. Augustine, Florida, she attended the induction ceremony. This honor made Ayako the third Japanese golfer to be inducted into the hall of fame. In addition to her seventeen LPGA wins in the United States, she scored forty-four victories in Japan and one in Europe.

Summary

Ayako Okamoto became a hero to the Japanese people early in her career. She did not play the game just for her own satisfaction; rather, she felt the responsibility to set a precedent for future generations of women golfers in Japan. She is counted among the top five women's golfers in the world.

Victoria Price

Honors and Awards

Year	Award
1987	LPGA player of the year
	LPGA money leader
	Japanese Prime Minister's Award
2005	Inducted into World Golf Hall of Fame

Additional Sources

"Ayako Okamoto Wins Hitachi British Women's Open Golf Tournament." *The New York Times*, October 7, 1984.

Nickerson, Elinor. *Golf: A Women's History.* Jefferson, N.C.: McFarland, 1987.

"Okamoto Wins by Shot." *The New York Times*, February 3, 1986.

Francis D. Ouimet

Born: May 8, 1893
    Brookline, Massachusetts
Died: September 2, 1967
    Newton, Massachusetts
Also known as: Francis Desales Ouimet (full
  name)

Early Life

Francis Desales Ouimet was born on May 8, 1893, in Brookline, Massachusetts. His future fame was built upon events that occurred during his early youth. Just about the time he was starting grade school, his family moved to a house in a thinly populated area of Brookline, across the street from the local country club. Francis's father, a working man, had no interest in golf. Were it not for the close proximity of the golf course, his children probably would have followed some other sport.

The Road to Excellence

Francis's first encounter with golf came as he walked the course with his brother Walter, looking for lost balls. Golf clubs were not so easily found. Only after Walter Ouimet became a caddy did the family get a golf club from one of the country club members who hired Walter. When his brother was working the course, young Francis would practice with their golf club. Across the street from the club, Francis was able to view the players who participated in the tournaments. He studied their move-

Francis D. Ouimet. (Ralph W. Miller Golf Library)

ments and was able to copy their swings. With practice, he found that he could hit a ball as straight and as true as some of the older players.

After learning that a local sporting equipment company would trade a good golf club for thirty-six golf balls, Francis and Walter used part of their large collection of found balls to trade for a couple of clubs. Shortly thereafter, the boys decided to use some of the land behind their house as a three-hole golf course. While primitive, and in no way comparable to the country club, the boys had a place to practice their shots and their putting. The greens were made of very short grass, and they used a tomato can sunk into the ground for the hole.

At the age of eleven, Francis followed his brother's footsteps and became a caddy at the club. He was able to get close-up views of his heroes, who were the elite of the game for that period of time. A member for whom he caddied gave Francis four additional clubs, and suddenly there was no stopping Francis. He usually practiced in the morning until the groundskeeper would hasten him off so that members could play.

The Emerging Champion

In 1910, at the age of seventeen, with money borrowed from his mother, Francis joined the Woodland Golf Club as a junior-member and attempted to qualify for the U.S. Amateur Championships. That year and for the next two, he failed in his quest to qualify by the same 1-stroke margin. In 1913, he finally made the grade. That year, the tournament was played in Brookline at the golf course across from where Francis grew up and lived. At this tournament, he made his mark not only in Massachusetts but also throughout the golfing world.

In addition to his natural ability and the long hours he spent practicing, Francis had one other great attribute: He had the ability to use his head. Even in defeat, he was able to learn some lesson and make sure that the errors he committed were not repeated in the future. He never tried to be like the other golfers but rather played the game as his abilities would allow. He had confidence in himself and knew his own limitations.

Major Championship Victories

1913 U.S. Open
1914, 1931 U.S. Amateur

Other Notable Victories

1914 French Amateur
1922-24, 1926, 1928, 1930, 1932, 1934 Walker Cup team
1936, 1938, 1947, 1949 Walker Cup nonplaying captain

Golf had been introduced to the United States at the beginning of the twentieth century, and it took about a dozen years for the game to gain some popularity. After the 1914 U.S. Amateur Championships, the game's popularity soared. Most of the credit belongs to Francis, who, against tall odds, beat two of the greatest golfers of that time, Britons Harry Vardon and Ted Ray.

No one had given young Francis any chance in this tournament. The critics seemed to be right when, with four holes left in the final round, Francis needed to play superb golf merely to tie Vardon and Ray. Playing the final four holes in one under par, Francis tied the other golfers and forced an eighteen-hole playoff the next day. The press and all the so-called experts discussed which of the two Englishmen would succeed the following day. They assumed that the pressure would get to the young American and that he would not be a factor. Showing great poise and determination, Francis proved them all wrong as he won the 1914 championships and started a new era in American golf.

Continuing the Story

Controversy entered the career of Francis when, in 1916, he was disbarred from the game by the United States Golf Association (USGA), the governing body of the sport. The USGA claimed that, by owning and operating a golf supply store, Francis was forfeiting his status as an amateur. For several years, Francis played only in tournaments sanctioned by a rival group, the Western Golfing Association (WGA). Only after World War I was his amateur status reinstated, and he was again allowed to play in the major tournaments. He won many important titles in his career, including the French Amateur and, for a second time, the U.S. Amateur, seventeen years after his initial victory, when most thought he was past his prime.

Francis was closely associated with the Walker Cup for many years and was captain of that team numerous times. His distinguished association with the game did not end when his playing career slowed. He was an active member of the USGA and was a leader in golf administration and legislation in the United States. In 1951, in recognition of his contributions to the sport and his close ties to Britain, he was elected captain of the Royal and Ancient Golf Club of St. Andrews, thus becoming the first non-Briton to hold that position. Francis died in 1967.

Summary

Francis D. Ouimet's golf game was always credited for its great consistency rather than the tremendous brilliance he had shown in his initial victory. His ability to play well under pressure made him a hero in the sport at a time when golf was just emerging. His passion for the game helped make golf a national sport for all to enjoy, not only a few. He was a true founder of the game in the United States.

Carmi Brandis

Additional Sources

Frost, Mark. *The Greatest Game Ever Played: Harry Vardon, Francis Ouimet, and the Birth of Modern Golf.* New York: Hyperion, 2002.

Herzog, Brad. *The Sports One Hundred: The One Hundred Most Important People in American Sports History.* New York: Macmillan, 1995.

Ouimet, Francis, Ben Crenshaw, and Dick Johnson. *A Game of Golf.* Reprint. Boston: Northeastern University Press, 2004.

Wade, Don. *Talking on Tour: The Best Anecdotes from Golf's Master Storyteller.* Lincolnwood, Ill.: McGraw-Hill/Contemporary, 2003.

Honors, Awards, and Milestones

Year	
1914	World Trophy
1923	British Amateur semifinalist
1940	Inducted into PGA Hall of Fame
1951	Elected captain of the Royal and Ancient Golf Club of St. Andrews—the first non-Briton to receive the honor
1956	Bob Jones Award
1957	GWAA Richardson Award
1974	Inducted into World Golf Hall of Fame

Se Ri Pak

Born: September 28, 1977
   Taejon, South Korea

Early Life

Se Ri Pak was born on September 28, 1977, in Taejon, South Korea. Her father, Joon Chul Pak, taught her to play golf when she was fourteen years old. While a student in high school, Se Ri excelled in track and played golf. As an amateur golfer, she won thirty tournaments.

The Road to Excellence

In 1996, Se Ri turned professional. As a member of the Korean Ladies Professional Golf Association, Se Ri played in fourteen events, winning six and placing in seven. She finished third in the Samsung World Championship of Women's Golf. In 1997, she moved to Orlando, Florida, and in 1998, she tried out for the Ladies Professional Golf Association (LPGA) tour. She won a position on the tour on her first try. In the same year that she qualified for the tour, she was awarded the Korean Order of Merit, the highest award that a Korean athlete can receive.

The Emerging Champion

In 1998, in her rookie year on the LPGA, Se Ri was a sensation. She participated in twenty-seven tournaments and finished second on the money list, earning $872,170. In May, she won the McDonald's LPGA Championship, becoming the youngest player ever to win that contest. In July, Se Ri was the youngest player to win the U.S. Women's Open (U.S. Open). She beat Jenny Chuasiriporn with a birdie on the second extra hole after both had shot 73 in regular play. Se Ri became only the third golfer in LPGA history to win both the LPGA Championship and the U.S. Open in the same year.

After victory at the U.S. Open, Se Ri received a congratulatory telegram from Korean president Kim Dae Jung, in which he hailed Se Ri as "the hope" of the Korean nation. Throughout her career, Se Ri experienced adulation from the Korean media and public but also felt pressured by Korea's expectations for her. She was flattered by Kim's telegram but also felt an increased amount of stress.

In addition to winning the LPGA Championship and the U.S. Open in 1998, Se Ri won the Jamie Farr Kroger Classic and the Giant Eagle LPGA Classic. At the former competition, she finished 10 under par and set the record for the lowest score ever in an LPGA contest; this record was broken later in the season. She was named the 1998 LPGA rookie of the year.

Continuing the Story

Se Ri had a spectacular rookie year but confronted many personal and business problems. Her father, who had taught her to play and who had managed

Se Ri Pak watching her tee shot at the Lexus Cup in 2008.
(Vivek Prakash/Reuters/Landov)

her career, often shared his eccentricities with the media, claiming he had been a Korean gangster. Se Ri had grown increasingly weary of his control of her life and management of her career and money. Eventually, she pulled away from him and insisted he give up his control.

In addition, Se Ri's relationships with both the Korean media and Samsung, her corporate sponsor, were tense. She often expressed confusion about the persona that Samsung wished her to display, and she had difficulty living up to the image that the Korean media presented of her. The Korean public wanted Se Ri to shine for Korea rather than leave her alone to play for her own glory.

Se Ri's personal and business problems may have affected her performance during the 1999 and 2000 tours. In 1999, she was unable to defend either her LPGA Championship or her U.S. Open title. She did not exhibit the spectacular play that she had shown in 1998. However, she did finish third on the LPGA money list in 1999. That year, she finished in the top ten in ten of the twenty-seven tournaments in which she participated.

In 2000, Se Ri was again third in LPGA money rankings, earning $550,000. At the end of that year her career earnings of $1,829,096 placed her fourth all-time. However, she won no tournaments in 2000. Her best showing that year was at the Jamie Farr Classic, in which she finished third and won $67,933. However, she won this tournament in 2001, 2003, and 2007.

In 2000, Se Ri dropped Butch Harmon as her coach. Her only criticism of Harmon was that he was too busy with Tiger Woods, his other famous student. Her new swing coach, Tom Creavy, remained her trainer through 2008.

From 2001 to 2003, Se Ri compiled a series of stunning victories. In 2001, she won the Women's British Open and placed second in the U.S. Open. Her biggest win in 2002 was the LPGA Championship. In 2003, she placed second in the Women's British Open. During this period she earned nearly $2 million annually, tripling her 2000 earnings. In 2003, she won the coveted Vare Trophy for a scoring average of 70.03. In 2004, winning the Michelob Ultra Open earned her sufficient points for the LPGA World Golf Hall of Fame, but she had to wait for her induction until fulfilling the ten-year LPGA membership requirement.

In 2005, Se Ri experienced physical and per-

Championships, Honors, and Awards

Year	Award
1998	LPGA Championship
	U.S. Women's Open
	Korean Order of Merit
	Rolex Rookie of the Year
	Giant Eagle LPGA Classic
1998-99, 2001, 2003, 2007	Jamie Farr Kroger Classic
2001	Women's British Open
2002	LPGA Championship
2003	Vare Trophy
2006	LPGA Championship
	LPGA Heather Farr Award
2007	Inducted into World Golf Hall of Fame

sonal crises. In addition to injuries to her left middle finger, neck, shoulder, and lower back, she suffered an emotional burnout. However, in 2006, Se Ri made another comeback. She won the LPGA Championship and received the LPGA Heather Farr Award. Her annual earnings were $884,961 after winning $62,628 the previous year. On November 12, 2007, Se Ri was inducted by Nancy Lopez into the LPGA World Golf Hall of Fame as the youngest living member and first Korean.

In April, 2008, Se Ri played strongly but tied for tenth place in her first major, the Kraft Nabisco Championship. She failed to make the cut at both the U.S. Women's Open and the Women's British Open. However, her luck changed at the CN Canadian Women's Open. On August 16, in the third round of the tournament, on the fifth hole, she scored her first hole-in-one at an LPGA tournament. She used a six-iron to ace the ball from 178 yards. On August 17, her second place finish elevated Se Ri's career earnings to $10,119,909. After eleven years as a professional, Se Ri became the fifth woman golf professional to earn more than $10 million in prize money.

Summary

Many consider the 5-foot 6-inch Se Ri Pak to be one of the most talented women ever to play golf. However, some believed that political and business pressures and personal problems affected her ability to concentrate and play well in 2000. Her stunning three-year run from 2001 to 2003 proved critics wrong. She emerged as the leader of a burgeoning flock of South Korean woman golfers. Her resiliency and maturity helped her overcome an inconsistent 2005 season, and her 2007 induction into the World Golf Hall of Fame cemented her reputation as a world-class player and role model.

Annita Marie Ward, updated by R. C. Lutz

Additional Sources

Bae, Jay-song. "Pak Se Ri: Ambition, Her Lifelong Companion." *Koreana* 18, no. 3 (Fall, 2004): 40-43.

Bamberger, Michael. "Yes Se Ri." *Sports Illustrated* 89 (August 3, 1998): 52-55.

Brubach, Holly. "The Woman Can Swing." *The New York Times Magazine*, October 18, 1998, p. 82.

Meyers, Kate. "A Hard-Won Peace." *Sports Illustrated Women* 4, no. 3 (May/June, 2002): 100-103.

"Pak Has Shown the Way for an Entire Nation; the Youngest Ever to be Inducted into the LPGA Hall of Fame." *Los Angeles Times*, November 11, 2007, p. D5.

Stewart, Mark. *Se Ri Pak: The Drive to Win*. Brookfield, Conn.: Millbrook Press, 2000.

Arnold Palmer

Born: September 10, 1929
  Youngstown, Pennsylvania
Also known as: Arnold Daniel Palmer (full name)

Early Life

Arnold Daniel Palmer was born in Youngstown, Pennsylvania, on September 10, 1929, and grew up in Latrobe, a small industrial community near Pittsburgh. Arnold's father worked at the Latrobe Country Club, eventually becoming the club's golf professional. Arnold's mother was also an avid golfer, so, not surprisingly, Arnold took to golf early.

Arnold Palmer, who was arguably the most popular and successful golfer in history. (Ralph W. Miller Golf Library)

Arnold received his first golf club when he was three years old. By the time he was nine, he shot a nine-hole round of 45—a better score than most who play golf for a hobby ever achieve. Arnold's father encouraged his son's interest in the game. In addition to instructing him in swing fundamentals, he impressed upon him the need to control his temper.

During high school, golf became Arnold's main interest, and he won several amateur tournaments. While playing in a junior tournament in Los Angeles, he struck up a friendship with Bud Worshan, the brother of Lew Worshan, a leading professional and winner of the U.S. Open. Bud encouraged Arnold to apply for a golf scholarship at Wake Forest University in North Carolina. Arnold followed his friend's advice, and his college years gave him the opportunity for further training and competition. After graduation, Arnold intended to remain an amateur. He obtained a business position that enabled him to play golf nearly every afternoon. But the attractions of a full-time career in golf proved too strong for him to overcome, and in 1954, he turned professional.

The Road to Excellence

Arnold's golf game differed greatly from the traditional style. Although Arnold had received professional instruction since his earliest youth, his swing violated many of golf's fundamentals. He lunged at the ball and finished his swing with an awkward follow-through. Because of his strength, he generated massive power. If, however, his swing was slightly off, he was liable to hit a very poor shot.

Some golfers thought the faults in his swing would prevent him from reaching the top level. Among his detractors was Gene Sarazen, a great golfer of the 1920's and 1930's, who predicted that Arnold's professional career would be a short one.

Arnold's initial lack of major success did not cause him to alter his ambition to become a great professional golfer. He faced an additional problem in this quest, a difficulty that was also his greatest strength as a player: He placed extremely high demands on his swing.

Arnold always took risks, aiming for the long drive instead of playing safe, even on very difficult holes. If in trouble, he tended to elect a risky shot to the green rather than the easy return to the fairway. Similarly, his putts were aimed directly at the hole; "lagging up" to the pin was not for him. If his first putt missed, Arnold was apt to find himself several feet behind the hole. Fortunately for him, he was one of the best long putters in the game.

The Emerging Champion

Arnold's odd swing and daring strategy gained him a wide following. The dominant golfer of the early 1950's was Ben Hogan. An icy perfectionist, Hogan aimed his shots precisely and knew the fundamentals of the swing better than anyone else. Although Hogan was widely respected, his taciturn demeanor did not encourage familiarity. Arnold, by contrast, was outgoing and friendly, and his lack of a perfect swing helped amateurs identify with him.

Arnold quickly attracted enormous galleries whenever he played. His fans acquired the nickname "Arnie's Army," and Arnold continued to draw a wide audience throughout his career. A dashing style and personable manner were not sufficient to account for his popularity. Arnold was, in fact, one of the greatest golfers of his time.

Arnold's first major victory came in 1958, at The Masters. He won the tournament by a single shot, defeating the previous year's champion, Doug Ford. Arnold's 1960 victory in the same tournament was even more memorable. One of the striking features of his game was his ability to come from behind when seemingly out of contention. His charges in a tournament's final round were one of the attractions to which his "army" looked forward. In 1960, he sank two long putts on the seventeenth and eighteenth holes, enough to give him the decision over the third-round leader, Ken Venturi.

Arnold had his best year as a player in 1960. Besides winning The Masters, he won the U.S. Open.

Major Championship Victories

1954	U.S. Amateur
1958, 1960, 1962, 1964	The Masters
1960	U.S. Open
1961-62	British Open
1980, 1984	Senior PGA Championship
1981	U.S. Senior Open

Other Notable Victories

1955	Canadian Open
1956	Eastern Open
1958	St. Petersburg Open
1960-62	Texas Open
1960, 1962, 1968, 1971, 1973	Bob Hope Desert Classic
1960, 1962-67	World Cup Team
1960, 1963	Pensacola (Monsanto) Open
1961-63	Phoenix Open
1961, 1963	Western Open
1961, 1963, 1965, 1967, 1971, 1973	Ryder Cup Team
1962	Colonial National
1962, 1965-66	Tournament of Champions
1962, 1967	American Golf Classic
1963, 1966-67	Los Angeles Open
1968	Kemper Open
1969	Heritage Classic
1971	Florida Citrus Invitational
	Westchester Classic
1975	Ryder Cup Team nonplaying captain
1984-85	Senior Tournament Players Championship
1996	Captain of Presidents Cup Team

Although at one point he was seven shots behind the leader, his final round was spectacular and gained him a two-stroke victory.

Continuing the Story

Arnold's style and success won a larger public for golf than the sport had ever known. His duels during the early 1960's with other notable golfers made golf a major television attraction. Among the foremost of his rivals was Billy Casper, whose controlled shot-making recalled Hogan. Arnold and Casper had their most remarkable duel in the 1966 U.S. Open. In the final round, Arnold had a seven-stroke lead with nine holes to play. This time Arnold's risk-taking style did not pay off. Several poor shots erased his lead, and Casper defeated Arnold the following day in a playoff.

In spite of his loss to Casper, Arnold remained the dominant golfer of the early 1960's, winning two British Opens and a fourth Masters. By the middle 1960's, however, Arnold was eclipsed by Jack Nicklaus, regarded as one of the foremost golfers of all time.

Arnold continued to win tournaments until 1973, but his ungainly swing proved increasingly unequal to the demands his risky style placed on it. His touch on long putts also lessened after the mid-1960's. He ceased to be a major force on the tour after this time, but his fans retained their devotion to him.

In 1994, Arnold made his final appearance at the U.S. Open after forty years of competing in the tournament. In 1996, he captained the U.S. team to victory in the Presidents Cup. Diagnosed with prostate cancer, Arnold underwent surgery in 1997 and radiation treatment in 1998. Following his treatment, he spearheaded the Senior Tour for the Cure program to raise awareness about prostate cancer.

Arnold's recovery from cancer and the death of his wife Winnie limited his appearances in Senior Tour events in 1999 to ten, his lowest total since 1983. In 2000, he reached a new milestone, playing in his one-thousandth tour event. He would later appear in his fiftieth Masters Tournament, the highest total in the history of the tournament. Apart from his remarkable success as a player, Arnold became a highly accomplished businessman, course designer, and aviator. His personal life continued to develop as well, and on January 26, 2005, Arnold married Kathleen Gawthrop in a private ceremony on the island of Oahu.

Less known than his commercial enterprises was his role in golf history, both in the United States and internationally. As a recognized participant in and witness to many notable events, he was frequently asked to write introductions for or contribute chapters to books on topics ranging from the major golf courses of China and the basics of the sport to biographies of famous golfers and histories of the sport in the United States.

Summary

Arnold Palmer's enthusiasm for golf and desire to excel compensated well for the defects in his swing.

Honors and Awards

1957, 1960-63	*Golf Digest* Byron Nelson Award for Tournament Victories
1960	Hickok Belt
	Sports Illustrated Sportsman of the Year
1960, 1962	PGA Player of the Year
1961-62, 1964, 1967	PGA Vardon Trophy
1969	GWAA Richardson Award
1970	Associated Press Athlete of the Decade (1960-69)
1972	Bob Jones Award
1974	Inducted into World Golf Hall of Fame
1976	GWAA Charlie Bartlett Award
1978	Herb Graffis Award
1980	Inducted into PGA Golf Professional Hall of Fame
	Arnold Palmer Award begun for PGA Tour's leading money winner
1983	Old Tom Morris Award
1996	Golfer of the Century
1998	PGA Tour Lifetime Achievement Award
2004	Presidential Medal of Freedom

He learned golf almost as soon as he could walk, and the game came naturally to him. As a result, he trusted his swing fully and played in a risky, aggressive style. His daring shots won him a wide audience and helped to establish golf as a major spectator sport. He was the foremost golfer of the period from 1958 to 1965 and remained one of the most popular and accessible sports figures in history.

Bill Delaney, updated by Robert B. Ridinger

Additional Sources

Hauser, Thomas. *Arnold Palmer: A Personal Journey.* San Francisco: Collins, 1994.

McCormack, Mark H. *Arnold Palmer: The Man and the Legend.* London: Cassell, 1967.

Palmer, Arnold. *Arnold Palmer: Memories, Stories, and Memorabilia from a Life on and off the Course.* New York: Stewart, Tabori & Chang, 2004.

_____. *Playing by the Rules: All the Rules of the Game, Complete with Memorable Rulings from Golf's Rich History.* 2d ed. New York: Atria Books, 2004.

Palmer, Arnold, and James Dodson. *A Golfer's Life.* New York: Ballantine Books, 2000.

Sampson, Curt. *The Eternal Summer: Palmer, Nicklaus, and Hogan in 1960, Golf's Golden Year.* New York: Villard, 2000.

Sounes, Howard. *The Wicked Game: Arnold Palmer, Jack Nicklaus, Tiger Woods, and the Story of Modern Golf.* New York: William Morrow, 2004.

Grace Park

Born: March 6, 1979
   Seoul, South Korea
Also known as: Park Ji-eun (birth name); Birdie
   Queen; Flat Screen; Major Queen; Sleeper

Early Life
Grace Park, who was born Park Ji-eun in Seoul, South Korea, moved with her family to Hawaii when she was twelve years old. Eventually, the family moved to and settled in Phoenix, Arizona. Grace grew up in a family of avid golfers and played her first 18 holes of golf at the age of nine. She won her first tournament at eleven. She enjoyed living in Hawaii, where she had an aunt, but without any relatives or friends she had trouble fitting into the Caucasian world of Phoenix. In addition, she struggled to learn English. However, this difficult situa-

Grace Park at the 1999 U.S. Women's Open. (Luke Frazza/AFP/Getty Images)

tion helped her focus on golf. She credited her father in particular for inspiring her and telling her that in order to succeed she needed to sacrifice. When Grace was still in high school and only seventeen years old, she was asked to compete against famous golfer Laura Davies in a long-drive competition. Although Grace did not win, she had impressive results.

The Road to Excellence
In 1994, Grace was named the Rolex junior player of the year, an award she received again in 1996. Also in 1996, she received the Dial Award as top female high school scholar-athlete in the United States. The same year, she received the Rolex Eleanor Dudley college player of the year award. Before Grace became a professional golfer in 1999, she had been an impressive amateur golfer for years and won most of the major amateur championships in 1998, including the U.S. Women's Amateur Championship. In 1999, she tied for eighth as an amateur at the U.S. Women's Open.

The Emerging Champion
Grace became highly regarded for her long drives, fierce sense of competition, and her vivacious beauty. She attended Arizona State University on a full scholarship, but she graduated from Ewha Woman's University in Seoul in 2003. In 1998, while a freshman at Arizona State, she was named player of the year and an all-American. Furthermore, she swept all the major amateur competitions, including the U.S. Women's Amateur Championship, becoming the first player to do so since 1938. In 2003, in addition to the one win, she also had five second-place finishes, four third-place finishes, and nineteen top-ten finishes, before losing to Annika Sorenstam in a playoff at the LPGA Championship.

Continuing the Story
As a professional golfer, Grace decided to play on the Futures Tour in 1999. She was immediately successful and won five of the next ten tournaments that she entered. She finished as the top money-

Futures Tour Victories

1999	Betty Puskar Golf Classic
	YWCA Briarwood Open
	SmartSpikes Classic
	Carolina National Classic
	Greater Lima Open

LPGA Tour Victories

2000	Kathy Ireland Greens.com Classic
2001	Office Depot Championship
2002	World Ladies Match Play Championship
2003	Michelob Light Open at Kingsmill
2004	Kraft Nabisco Championship
	CJ Nine Bridges Classic

Summary

Golf had an upsurge in popularity in Asia in the latter part of the 1990's. Korean women, in particular, became successful golfers. Grace Park said that Korean culture places great value on dedication and discipline, and she credited her parents with helping her achieve her goals. She loved the pressure of the professional sporting life and the competition, which is what drove her to practice and work hard. "Hurricane Grace," as her friends called her, overcame many obstacles, including coming to a new country and learning a different language. From a young age, she dedicated herself to golf and became an inspiration to young athletes everywhere.

M. Casey Diana

winner. That year, she was named both rookie of the year and player of the year. However, shortly after Grace turned professional, speculation emerged that she had reached the peak of her golfing career. Grace attributed her decline to the fact that she simply missed college and wanted to live a more normal life. However, she soon came to realize that a top woman golfer was all she really wanted to be. She also came to realize that winning at golf involved a high degree of mental preparation.

After refocusing on the sport, Grace headed straight toward stardom. In 2002, a new coach and trainer helped her refocus, and she became successful on the LPGA Tour. At this time, she also became a popular fashion icon. Grace's first major match was the 2004 Kraft Nabisco Championship, which she won. She went on to win at least one LPGA tournament each season from 2000 to 2004. In 2004, she earned the prestigious Vare Trophy for her low scoring average.

However, after 2005, Grace's progress as a professional golfer came to a sudden stop. She suffered first from a back injury and then from a neck injury that prevented her from practicing. Consequently, in 2005, she managed to have only four top-ten finishes, and in 2006, she did not play for three months and did not rank in the top ten.

Additional Sources

Buren, Jodi, and Donna A. Lopiano. *Superwomen: One Hundred Women, One Hundred Sports.* New York: Bulfinch Press, 2004.

O'Neil, Dana Pennett, and Pat Williams. *How to Be Like Women Athletes of Influence: Thirty-one Women at the Top of Their Game and How You Can Get There Too.* Deerfield Beach, Fla.: Health Communications, 2007.

O'Reilly, Jean. *Women and Sports in the United States: A Documentary Reader.* Boston: Northeastern, 2007.

Sanson, Nanette. *Champions of Women's Golf: Celebrating Fifty Years of the LPGA.* Naples, Fla.: Quailmark Books, 2000.

Woolum, Janet. *Outstanding Women Athletes: Who They Are and How They Influenced Sports in America.* Phoenix, Ariz.: Oryx Press, 1998.

Honors and Awards

1996	Dial Award
1998	*Golfweek* College Player of the Year
	Eleanor Dudley College Player of the Year
1999	LPGA Rookie of the Year
	LPGA Player of the Year
2004	Vare Trophy

Willie Park, Sr.

Born: June 30, 1834
    Wallyford, near Musselburgh, Scotland
Died: July 25, 1903
    Edinburgh, Scotland

Early Life

Willie Park, Sr., was born on June 30, 1834, in Wallyford, a Scottish village near Musselburgh and Edinburgh. His birthplace is on the side of the Firth of Forth opposite that of St. Andrews, the legendary home of golf. It was a fitting place for Willie to grow up, as he was to become the first winner of golf's first major tournament, the Open Championship, which later became known as the British Open outside Great Britain.

Willie was the brother of Mungo Park (evidently named after the Scottish explorer of Africa), another noted golfer and Open champion, and the father of Willie Park, Jr. (1864-1925), who won the Open Championship twice. Willie's son also became the first professional player to write a monograph on the game of golf and become a noted golf-course architect. Another brother, David, also became a respected golfer.

The Road to Excellence

The game of golf originated in Scotland and was played at Musselburgh at least as early as the year 1672. According to legend, Mary, Queen of Scots played there more than a century earlier. In the early twenty-first century, the Musselburgh golf course was still used and ranked as the world's oldest course still in use.

Musselburgh was also home to two families who played significant roles in the early development of modern golf. One of these families was the Parks. The son of a farm laborer, Willie began his golfing career as a caddy during an era in which golfers used hickory-shaft golf clubs to hit featherie balls, which were made of goose feathers bound tightly in leather. In those days, some of the best golfers were caddies. By the time he competed for the first Open Championship in 1860, he was able to use the recently invented gutta percha balls.

The Emerging Champion

The first Open Championship took place at the Prestwick course in South Ayrshire. Only eight players—all either professional golfers or caddies—participated. The tournament committee was concerned that the professional players might not compete in the proper spirit of the game, so gentlemen markers were appointed to ensure that the rules of the game were strictly followed. The competition consisted of three rounds of twelve holes each, all to be completed in a single day. Although the event took place in mid-October, when days were noticeably shortening, the entire field completed all 36 holes before darkness fell.

Willie won the tournament with an aggregate score of 174, beating his major challenger, "Old" Tom Morris, who represented Prestwick, by 2 strokes and Andrew Strath, a St. Andrews player, by 6. The other competitors were Robert Andrew of Perth, William Steel of Bruntsfield, Charles Hunter of Prestwick St. Nicholas, and George D. Brown of Blackheath.

Continuing the Story

After the inaugural Open Championship, Willie went on to win the tournament three more times, in 1863, 1866, and 1875. He was also the runner-up four times. He achieved all his other Open victories at Prestwick. His brother Mungo won the Open in 1874 and his son Willie, Jr., won it in 1887 and 1889.

Over a period of twenty years, Willie posed a standing challenge, which he first posted in the pages of *Bell's Life* magazine, that he would take on any golfer in the world for a prize of one hundred pounds—a substantial sum during the late nineteenth century. According to an unsubstantiated report, Willie occasionally played challenge matches using only one hand and standing on only one leg while taking his strokes.

Willie's most frequent and fiercest opponent was Tom Morris, Sr. (1821-1908), who was known as "Old Tom Morris" to differentiate him from his son, Tom Morris, Jr., another noted golfer. Like Willie, both Old Tom and his son won the Open Championship four times each. On the whole,

Milestones

1860	Won the first British Open
1863, 1866, 1875	Won the British Open
2005	Inducted into World Golf Hall of Fame

Willie and Morris shared golfing honors fairly evenly over the years and enjoyed a mutually respectful relationship. However, a serious controversy arose between them on one occasion. During a match played at Musselburgh, an official stopped play because of the unruly behavior of Willie's staunch fans. When Morris refused to finish the contest, Willie completed the closing holes on his own and claimed the prize.

In 1870, Willie established his own club and ball-making company, which he based in nearby North Berwick. That time period was the start of an era that saw a rapid growth in the export of Scottish-made golf equipment throughout the world. Willie's business expanded quickly to include facilities in Musselburgh and Edinburgh. Willie also took up golf-course design and the reconstruction of existing courses. He provided advice on green-keeping and supplied golf clubs and balls of the finest quality. Willie designed several golf courses but never achieved the reputation in this field that his son later enjoyed. Willie, Jr.'s masterpiece is the Sunningdale Old Course, which opened in 1901 near the famous Ascot Racecourse in Berkshire, England.

Summary

When Willie Park, Sr., died in 1903, he was rightly regarded as one of the greatest golfers of the nineteenth century. Both a powerful striker of the ball and a noted putter, he deserves his place alongside the other great Scottish pioneers of modern golf. In 2005, he was inducted into the veteran's category of the World Golf Hall of Fame in St. Augustine, Florida. A suite in the conference wing of the Old Course Hotel in St. Andrews bears his name.

Alan Bairner

Additional Sources

Baddiel, Sarah. *Golf: The Golden Years—A Pictorial Anthology.* London: Studio Editions, 1989.

Campbell, Malcolm, and Glyn Satterley. *The Scottish Golf Book.* Edinburgh, Scotland: Lomond Books, 2001.

Elliott, Alan, and John Allan May. *Golf Monthly Illustrated History of Golf.* London: Hamlyn, 1990.

Ironside, Robert, and Harry Douglas. *A History of the Royal Musselburgh Golf Club 1774-1999.* Musselburgh, East Lothian, Scotland: Royal Musselburgh Golf Club, 1999.

Park, Willie, Jr. *The Art of Putting.* 1920. Reprint. Edinburgh: Luath Press, 2007.

Henry Picard

Born: November 28, 1906
    Plymouth, Massachusetts
Died: April 30, 1997
    Charleston, South Carolina
Also known as: Henry Gilford Picard (full name);
    the Hershey Hurricane; Pick

Early Life

Henry Gilford Picard was born on November 28, 1906, in Plymouth, Massachusetts. A good student through grade school and high school, he intended to study accounting in college. However, his plans changed when, as a teenager, he began caddying and serving as a steward at the Plymouth Country Club. While working, he learned the finer points of golf. Donald Binton, Henry's boss and the head professional at the country club, asked the youngster if he would like to accompany him and work at the Charleston Country Club in South Carolina over the winter. Henry asked his father what he thought of the idea; the elder Picard considered the opportunity to be a wonderful learning experience. Thus, Henry headed south with Binton.

The Road to Excellence

By 1925, nineteen-year-old Henry had become a professional at the Charleston Country Club. That same year, he won his first professional tournament, the Carolinas Open, and repeated as champion of the event the following year. He dreamed of touring as a professional.

By 1931, Henry had become the head professional at Charleston. However, he was told that because of the Depression, the club could no longer afford his salary. Many businesses in the area had gone bankrupt, and membership had decreased. For Henry, the news was ill-timed: His wife Annie "Sunny" Addison was expecting the first of the couple's four children, the couple's bank had failed, and they had no money on hand.

Luckily, Henry's pleasant, modest disposition had earned him many friends in the community, and they helped to ensure that the young golfer would not only survive but also achieve his goal of becoming a touring professional. Whenever he played a par round of golf, his friends in the community paid him $5. He earned an additional $5 for each stroke under par. Henry realized that if he did not perform well, his family would starve. Therefore, he quickly learned to golf under pressure. In 1932, he earned his first PGA Tour victory, a three-way first-place tie with Al Watrous and Al Houghton at the Mid-South Open.

The Emerging Champion

Henry remained the professional at Charleston through 1934. In the meantime, he repeated as Carolinas Open champion in 1932 and 1933. In 1934, the year he moved to Pennsylvania to become head pro at the Hershey Country Club, he captured his second PGA Tour event, the North and South Open.

Selected for the 1935 U.S. Ryder Cup team to compete in match play against European professional golfers, Henry felt the need to improve his game. Therefore, one month before the tournament, he began taking lessons from Alex Morrison, a leading golf instructor. Henry hit hundreds of golf balls while practicing a foot roll that added distance and accuracy to his drives.

PGA Tour and Other Victories

1925-26, 1932-33, 1937	Carolinas Open
1932	Mid-South Open
1934, 1936	North and South Open
1935	Agua Caliente Open
	Atlanta Open
1935-37	Miami International Four-Ball
	Tournament of the Gardens Open
1935, 1939	Metropolitan Open
	Inverness Invitational Four-Ball
1936-37	Hershey Open
1937	St. Augustine Pro-Amateur
	Argentine Open
1938	Pasadena Open
	The Masters
1939	Thomasville Open
	Scranton Open
	PGA Championship
1939, 1941	New Orleans Open
1941	Harlingen Open-Texas
1945	Miami Open

The results of all Henry's practice became apparent immediately. In 1935, Henry won championships at five professional events: the Agua Caliente Open, the Tournament of the Gardens Open, the Atlanta Open, the Metropolitan Open, and the Inverness Invitational Four-Ball. This season was the first of a five-year run in which he scored at least two victories each year. A thumb injury suffered during his victory at the 1938 Pasadena Open forced him to change from an overlapping to an interlocking grip. However, the change in technique made no difference: Henry's winning streak culminated in the most victories in 1939, when he was the PGA's leading money-winner. Along the way, he triumphed in several major events: the 1937 Argentine Open, the 1938 Masters, and the 1939 PGA Championship, in which he won by 1 stroke in an exciting playoff against reigning champion Byron Nelson.

Continuing the Story

Henry continued to compete in PGA events on the circuit, but his career as a leading competitor was ending as younger golfers rose through the ranks. Henry had two victories in 1941 and won his final event, the Miami Open, in 1945. Though he participated in the U.S. Open until 1959 and The Masters until 1969, he never again finished higher than sixth place before retiring from the PGA Tour in 1973.

Known for his generosity, Henry, through his gentle suggestions, exerted a profound influence on other golfers who later became famous. He persuaded Sam Snead to turn professional. He also helped correct Ben Hogan's hook and showed him how to hit with more power. Hogan later dedicated a golfing instruction book, *Power Golf*, to Henry. Furthermore, in 1941, when Henry left the Hershey Country Club to become head professional at Twin Hills Golf and Country Club in Oklahoma City, Oklahoma, he recommended Hogan as his replacement.

Honors and Awards

1935, 1937	U.S. Ryder Cup Team
2006	Inducted into World Golf Hall of Fame

In his later years, Henry served as golf professional at the Country Club of Harrisburg, Pennsylvania, Canterbury Golf Club in Cleveland, Ohio, and Seminole Golf Club in Palm Beach, Florida, before returning to the Charleston Country Club. There, in the early 1970's, he helped instruct Beth Daniel, who later became a member of the Ladies Professional Golf Association (LPGA) Hall of Fame. Even after his retirement, Henry kept playing well into his eighties. He died April 30, 1997, at the age of ninety. Henry, a member of the PGA Golf Professional Hall of Fame, was inducted posthumously into the World Golf Hall of Fame in 2006.

Summary

A leading golfer on the PGA Tour from the mid-1930's until the early 1940's, Henry Picard won a total of twenty-seven PGA Tour events and two major championships: the 1938 Masters and the 1939 PGA Championship. A member of U.S. Ryder Cup-winning teams in 1935 and 1937, he was also instrumental in helping to improve the play of other golfers, including Sam Snead, Ben Hogan, and Beth Daniel.

Jack Ewing

Additional Sources

Bowden, Ken. *Teeing Off: Players, Techniques, Characters, and Reflections from a Lifetime Inside the Game.* Chicago: Triumph Books, 2008.

Frost, Mark. *The Match: The Day the Game of Golf Changed Forever.* New York: Hyperion Books, 2007.

Lawrenson, Derek. *The Complete Encyclopedia of Golf.* London: Carlton, 2002.

Gary Player

Born: November 1, 1935
     Johannesburg, South Africa
Also known as: Gary Jim Player (full name);
    Black Knight; Mr. Fitness

Early Life

Gary Jim Player, the youngest of three children, was born in Johannesburg, South Africa, on November 1, 1935. Gary's father, Harry, worked as a foreman in a gold mine. The family was not poor, but they were not rich either. When Gary was eight years old, his mother died of cancer. As the youngest child, Gary was the most affected by his mother's death. He was able to deal with his loss, however, thus beginning a lifelong struggle to win despite the challenge or the challenger.

The Road to Excellence

One factor in Gary's determination to succeed was his smaller size in comparison to the rest of his family. His older brother Ian never let Gary use his size as an excuse for failure. Determined to be better than bigger athletes, Gary participated in every sport available. He was voted the best all-around athlete at his school.

Because his father was an excellent golfer, Gary began to follow him onto the course. Although Gary was untrained, his potential was obvious and he soon began to receive lessons. Once he began taking lessons, Gary also began to date his teacher's daughter. Obviously, playing golf was an attractive proposition for the young South African.

Almost immediately, Gary began to compete in amateur tournaments. He was not very successful at first, but he soon decided to become a professional golfer. He practiced constantly and followed a carefully designed plan of exercise and diet to make up for his size and strength.

Gary's victory in a professional tournament at the age of nineteen persuaded his father to borrow money so his son could compete in his first tournament outside South Africa. Gary won the tournament and used his winnings to go to Great Britain.

Gary did not win any tournaments that year, but he did win enough prize money to meet his expenses. His time spent in Britain helped him to decide that playing golf would be his life's work.

Gary Player, who along with Arnold Palmer and Jack Nicklaus, was part of the "big three" in golf during the 1960's. (Ralph W. Miller Golf Library)

The Emerging Champion

Few people thought Gary would succeed as a professional golfer. He was too short and he was from South Africa, which was a difficult challenge because many fans were not happy with the way the South African government treated the majority of its population. Segregation of the races, called apartheid, became increasingly unpopular, and Gary was sometimes the subject of physical and verbal abuse.

Although Gary was not successful at first on either the British or American tour, he continued to improve his game. In 1959, he became the youngest player to win the British Open since 1868. He then made a determined effort to succeed on the American tour. In 1961, he won The Masters. He was also the leading money-winner on the tour.

Gary followed his victory in The Masters by winning the Professional Golfers' Association (PGA)

Championship in 1962. He was only one tournament away from winning the four major tournaments of the Grand Slam of golf—the British Open, U.S. Open, the PGA Championship, and The Masters. In 1965, he won the U.S. Open.

Continuing the Story

Gary, along with Arnold Palmer and Jack Nicklaus, was part of the "Big Three" of international golf during the 1960's. Unlike Palmer and Nicklaus, however, Gary did not restrict himself to American and British tournaments. Though he won more tournaments off the American tour than on it, Gary consistently placed in the top five when he did play on the American tour. He did not win every tournament, but he definitely made money.

In 1972, Gary won the PGA Championship for the second time. Then, a serious operation made it impossible for him to play for more than a year. In 1974, Gary bounced back from his illness with victories in the British Open and The Masters.

In 1985, Gary joined the PGA Senior Tour, a series of tournaments for players near retirement. He succeeded in popularizing the tournaments on the new tour. When he was joined by Palmer and Nicklaus, the prizes offered on the tour became big.

Gary was always a subject of controversy. He upset many people with questions and requests for advice. One British professional told him he should learn the game before entering tournaments. Gary was not discouraged, however. At the end of each tournament, he would play a special round to correct his mistakes. He was among the first to insist that golf required athletic training.

Gary became a successful golfer, but it was not easy. He spent time on airplanes flying to tournaments around the world while other golfers practiced. Still, his career achievements are impressive. Gary won nine major tournament titles and 163 tournaments around the world. He was the first player from outside the United States to top the money list for the American tour.

The list of Gary's achievements in golf

Major Championship Victories

1959, 1968, 1974	British Open
1961, 1974, 1978	The Masters
1962, 1972	PGA Championship
1965	U.S. Open
1986, 1988, 1990	Senior PGA Championship
1987-88	U.S. Senior Open

Other Notable Victories

1956, 1960, 1965-69, 1972	South African Open
1958, 1962-63, 1965, 1969-70	Australian Open
1960, 1967, 1971-74	Dunlop Masters
1964	Pensacola (Monsanto) Open
1965-66, 1971, 1973	Picadilly Match Play
1965, 1977	World Cup Team
1969, 1978	Tournament of Champions
1970	Greater Greensboro Open
1972, 1974	Brazilian Open
1974	Danny Thomas-Memphis Open
	Memphis Classic
1978	Houston Open
1987	Mazda Senior Tournament Players Championship
	Paine Webber World Seniors Invitational
1988	Southwestern Bell Classic, senior tour
1988-89	GTE North Classic, senior tour
1989	RJR Championship, senior tour
1991	Royal Caribbean Classic
1993, 1995	Bank One Classic
1998	Northville Long Island Classic

is considerable. His nine major PGA golf titles tie him with Ben Hogan for fourth all-time, and he finished in the top ten in thirty-seven major tournaments. Gary also recorded victories in twenty-seven consecutive years, a record that bests the second-place player by ten years. However, Gary is more than a man who won golf tournaments and titles. He also helped young golfers on the tour. In 1965, he donated the money from the U.S. Open to the American junior golf program and to cancer research.

Outside of playing golf, Gary has been involved in golf-course design and real estate. He has been widely recognized for his contributions to golf. He was chosen as the South Africa athlete of the twentieth century and received the Payne Stewart Award in 2006. In 2007, he made his fiftieth appearance at The Masters.

Summary

By conventional standards, Gary Player should not have been able to succeed as a golfer. Nevertheless, in terms of both longevity and success, he became one of the greatest golfers ever; he ranks with Ben Hogan, Arnold Palmer, Jack Nicklaus, Bobby Jones, and Tiger Woods. He is an inspiration to those who are told they cannot succeed because they are not like everyone else.

J. K. Sweeney

Additional Sources

Beaumont, Forrest. *In the Presence of Gary Player: A Perspective on the Life and Philosophy of One of the World's Greatest Golfers.* Hatfield, South Africa: Umdaus Press, 2004.

Player, Gary. *Fit for Golf.* New York: Simon & Schuster, 1995.

_____. *The Golfer's Guide to the Meaning of Life.* Emmaus, Pa.: Rodale, 2002.

Player, Gary, and Floyd Thatcher. *Gary Player, World Golfer.* London: Pelham, 1975.

Player, Gary, and Mike Wade. *Bunker Player.* New York: Broadway Books, 1996.

Player, Gary, Chris Whales, and Duncan Cruickshank. *The Complete Golfer's Handbook.* Guilford, Conn.: Lyons Press, 2000.

_____. *Gary Player's Top Golf Courses of the World.* London: New Holland, 2007.

Records and Milestones

Won more than 160 events worldwide

Became the first foreigner to win the Masters and the PGA Championship and the first foreigner since Ted Ray (in 1920) to win the U.S. Open

One of only five men to win the modern Grand Slam (the others being Gene Sarazen, Ben Hogan, Jack Nicklaus, and Tiger Woods)

Winner of South African Open thirteen times since 1956

Leading money winner on the PGA Tour (1961)

Only player in the twentieth century to win the British Open in three different decades

Best year on Regular Tour was 1978 with earnings of $177,336

Oldest player ever to make the cut in the British Open (age fifty-nine in 1995)

Oldest player ever to make the cut in The Masters (age sixty-two in 1998)

Honors and Awards

1961	*Golf Digest* Most Improved Golfer
1967	Bob Jones Award
1973	GWAA Charlie Bartlett Award
1974	Inducted into World Golf Hall of Fame
1975	GWAA Richardson Award
1990, 2000	South African Sportsman of the Century
1995	Awarded the Order of Ikhamanga (in gold)
2003	Laureus Lifetime Achievement Award
2006	Payne Stewart Award
2007	Inducted into African American Sports Hall of Fame

Sandra Post

Born: June 4, 1948
       Oakville, Ontario, Canada

Early Life

Sandra Post was born on June 4, 1948, in the affluent community of Oakville, Ontario, Canada, a suburb of Toronto. The area was conducive to farming the land and yachting on Lake Ontario. A Canadian who wishes to enjoy the pleasures of golf must endure long winter months of cold weather or move south. The Post family took an annual vacation to sunny Florida. Sandra's father, Cliff, played golf for its challenge and social value. He introduced his daughter to the game when she was only five years old. The young girl followed her dad around the golf course, striking the ball a short distance with a short club. Those joyous days of warm weather and frolic set the stage for the development of a golf champion.

The Road to Excellence

Tutored by her father, Sandra learned the fundamentals of a golf swing. Her progress led to precision shots struck with an aggressive style of play. Soon, competitions became a proving ground to test her development.

As a teenager, Sandra won the Ontario Junior Championship and the National Junior Championship of Canada for three straight years. The triple winner took her consistently aggressive style south to the United States, where she won the South Atlantic Title. In 1968, convinced that her golfing skills had reached a level comparable with that of the best women players in North America, Sandra turned professional.

Confident of her ability, Sandra approached the U.S. tour without hesitation. She felt that, to earn a living, she would have to know when to be aggressive and attack a golf course and when to be patient when the risk of hitting a difficult shot would be taking too great a chance.

The nineteen-year-old Sandra tested her plan at the Ladies' Professional Golf Associa-

tion (LPGA) Championship. A major tournament, the LPGA Championship is ranked along with the U.S. Open as one of the most prestigious titles. The 1968 LPGA Championship was played at the Pleasant Valley Country Club in Sutton, Massachusetts. On a demanding golf course and in an important tournament, Sandra displayed remarkable poise for one so young. With so much pressure, she was not expected to perform well enough to tie for the lead at the conclusion of regulation play, but there she was, in an eighteen-hole playoff with the formidable Kathy Whitworth. Sandra managed her emo-

Sandra Post, who was the best Canadian golfer in the 1970's. (Ralph W. Miller Golf Library)

Major Championship Victories

| 1968 | LPGA Championship |
| 1978-79 | Colgate Dinah Shore |

Other Notable Victories

1978	Lady Stroh's Open
1979	ERA Real Estate Classic
	Lady Michelob
1980	West Virginia Classic
1981	McDonald's Kids Classic

Time healed the back condition, and Sandra approached the 1973 competitive campaign excited but cautious. She played a tempered game to test her back muscles. Although she did not achieve a tournament victory, she did finish well enough to rank twenty-third on the money-winners list. By the conclusion of the 1974 season, she had improved to fifteenth on the list. She continued to be a member of the top fifteen money winners over the next seven years.

Continuing the Story

Sandra earned a reputation for striking accurate irons and having the ability to play position golf on tight courses. On the par 3 eighth hole at the 1973 Colgate Dinah Shore, she hit an iron shot that struck the green 10 feet below the flagstick. The ball took a bounce, one hop, and rolled into the cup. The hole in one was worth a new car and five thousand dollars.

In 1978, Sandra scored a rare double, in both victories and shot performance. Playing a par 5 hole in two strokes is statistically more difficult than making a hole in one. Sandra holed a number 3 wood shot from more than 200 yards to score a memorable double eagle. That same year, the Colgate Dinah Shore became her second tournament victory. Once again, she was extended beyond regulation play and responded with a victory over

tions well enough to win the playoff by seven strokes. A major championship in her first year as a professional golfer brought Sandra earnings plus rookie of the year honors.

The Emerging Champion

Sandra's first major victory was a springboard to the Ladies' World Series of Golf. The tournament was only in its fourth year and had sponsor problems that ultimately caused its discontinuation. However, the World Series was the most financially rewarding tournament on the LPGA Tour. Participants included the top two players on the money-winning list, Mickey Wright and Sandra Haynie; the defending champion, Kathy Whitworth; the Canadian Open Champion, Carol Mann; the U.S. Open Champion, Susie Berning; and Sandra, as the LPGA Champion.

Only the best players on the women's tour could play for the $10,000 first prize, and Sandra was part of this elite group. She felt that luck had played a major part in her playoff win at the LPGA. However, when she took an early lead in the 36-hole World Series, skill was a prominent factor. A bogey late in the first round placed Sandra four shots off the lead. Whitworth's two scores of 69 subdued the field and won the tournament, but Sandra had proven to be capable of playing with the best golfers on tour.

Placing thirteenth on the 1968 money-winning list excited Sandra. The future looked bright until back problems struck her down. Lower back and hip-muscle spasms are common symptoms associated with the golf swing. Sandra's aggressive approach and limber swing had contributed to her injury. Her competitive level suffered for three long years.

Milestones

Won both the Ontario and Canadian Junior Championships three times each as an amateur

Member of LPGA Board of Directors

Honors and Awards

1968	Gatorade Rookie of the Year
	Golf Digest Rookie of the Year
	LPGA Rookie of the Year
1979	Canada's Female Athlete of the Year
	Lou Marsh Trophy as Canada's Outstanding Athlete of the Year
1988	Elected to the Canadian Sports Hall of Fame
	Elected to the Royal Canadian Golf Association Hall of Fame
1999-2000	Captain of the Canadian team in the inaugural Nation's Cup between Canada and the United States
2003	Member of the Order of Canada

Penny Pulz of Australia on the second extra hole. Another victory at the Lady Stroh's Open moved Sandra into seventh place on the money-winners list. It had been her best year to date, and 1979 would be even better.

A second victory at the Colgate Dinah Shore made Sandra the first champion to defend her title in that tournament. Two more victories and a total of twelve top-ten finishes moved her into second place on the money-winners list. Ordinarily, her performance for the season would have placed her on top of the golfing world, but there was another newcomer, Nancy Lopez, who had taken the top spot.

Her performance in 1979 brought Sandra recognition as Canada's female athlete of the year and the outstanding athlete of the year. She retired from the competitive circuit following the 1983 season and made her home in Boynton Beach, Florida. Teaching golf, writing a column for the Canadian golf magazine *Score*, and travel filled her busy schedule. In 1999, Sandra captained the Ca-

nadian team in the inaugural Nation's Cup between Canada and the United States. She was selected as captain again the following year. In 2003, she became a member of the Order of Canada.

Summary

Sandra Post attacked a golf course and made her aggressive approach pay off handsomely. She finished in the top twenty-five money-winners on tour for nine straight years and was the best Canadian golfer during the 1970-1979 decade.

Thomas S. Cross

Additional Sources

Allis, Peter. *The Who's Who of Golf.* Englewood Cliffs, N.J.: Prentice-Hall, 1983.

Golf Magazine's Encyclopedia of Golf: The Complete Reference. New York: HarperCollins, 1993.

Post, Sandra, and Loral Dean. *Sandra Post and Me: A Veteran Pro Takes a New Golfer from First Swing to Tournament.* Toronto: McClelland & Stewart, 1998.

Nick Price

Born: January 28, 1957
     Durban, South Africa
Also known as: Nicholas Raymond Leige Price
    (full name)

Early Life

Nicholas Raymond Leige (Nick) Price was born in South Africa of British parentage on January 28, 1957. The youngest of three boys, Nick moved with his family to racially tense Rhodesia (now Zimbabwe) when he was still young. His father was a proud man of high principles who influenced his son greatly. However, he died of lung cancer when Nick was just ten years old.

Living in a mild climate, Nick played many sports, but golf became his true passion. At the age of eight, he was hitting plastic balls into tomato cans buried in his neighbors' gardens. In one day, he and his friends played as many as 144 "holes" in their "garden" tournaments. He was naturally left-handed, but his brother, Tim, persuaded him to start playing right-handed so they would not have to share the same clubs. Even after changing his swing, Nick soon developed into an excellent ama-

teur player. By the age of seventeen, his reputation earned him an invitation to the Junior World Golf Championships in San Diego, California. Nick won the event, convincing him that he could become a professional golfer.

The Road to Excellence

Before Nick could pursue his dream of golfing full time, he had to complete a two-year stint of military service in the Rhodesian air force. The country, at that time, was in the midst of a bloody civil war. Many of Nick's companions were killed or injured, and he was fired upon several times. The experience gave him a lifelong appreciation that there were many more important things than golf.

With his service completed, Nick was free to turn professional, which he did in 1977. His first professional tournament was the South African PGA in October of that year. He finished seventeenth, earning prize money equal to two months' salary for him in the air force. A year later, he joined the European PGA Tour. In 1979, Nick notched his first championship, winning the 1979 Asseng Invitational in South Africa. He won at least one tournament in Europe or Africa in each of the next three years.

Nick's playing remained too erratic, however, to win on the American PGA Tour. He was capable of going on a brilliant run of four birdies only to follow that with four consecutive bogeys. Nick turned to David Leadbetter to help him polish his game. Using a more economical motion in his swing, Nick began to develop greater consistency, but he lost yardage off the tee. In 1982, the hard work paid off at the British Open at Royal Troon. There, Nick was poised to win his first major championship as he held a 3-stroke lead with six holes to play. However, inexperience got the better of him, and he finished the last four holes 3 over par, ultimately losing by 1 stroke to Tom Watson. The defeat was a crushing one, but it heralded Nick's arrival as a major player.

The Emerging Champion

Not long after, Nick won his first PGA event, the 1983 World Series of Golf. However, several years

---

Major Championships

1992	PGA Championship
1994	British Open
	PGA Championship

PGA Tour Victories

1983	World Series of Golf
1991	Byron Nelson Classic
	Canadian Open
1992	Texas Open
1993	Players Championship
	Greater Hartford Open
	Western Open
	St. Jude Classic
1994	Honda Classic
	The Colonial
	Western Open
	Canadian Open
1997	MCI Classic
1998	St. Jude Classic
2002	The Colonial

passed before his next PGA victory. At the 1988 British Open at Royal Lytham and St. Annes, Nick again found himself with a lead going into the last round. This time he scored well. However, the great Spanish champion Seve Ballesteros played one of the best rounds of his life and snatched away the tournament. Nick was devastated by the loss but knew he was ready for a breakthrough.

At 6 feet tall and 190 pounds, Nick had the build of an athlete. Though all parts of his game were solid, his incredible accuracy off the tee set him apart from other golfers. With great strength and speed, he could consistently drive the ball with machine-like precision. Not only was his play recognized but also his kindness and easygoing attitude. He earned the reputation of one of the nicest guys in professional golf.

After a couple of disappointing years, Nick began winning often. After a drought of eight years, he won two PGA Tour events in 1991, the Byron Nelson Classic and the Canadian Open. Then, starting in August of 1992, Nick went on an incredible run. It started with a 3-stroke victory in the PGA Championship played at Bellerive in St. Louis, Missouri. At last, Nick had brought home a major championship trophy.

Nick continued his excellent form when he won the Players Championship by 5 strokes in the spring of 1993. Later that summer, he notched three consecutive PGA Tour victories and ended up leading the money list with more than $1.4 million in winnings. By year's end, Nick was the number-one ranked player on the PGA circuit.

Continuing the Story

In 1994, Nick had one of the best years of his career as well as one of the best in PGA history. After the near-misses of 1982 and 1988, Nick was ready to win the elusive British Open. This time he was the one who came from behind: He was down 3 strokes to Jesper Parnevik with only six holes to play. He birdied the sixteenth hole; then, on the seventeenth, he sank a 50-foot putt for an eagle. He closed out the match with a par to beat Parnevik by 1 stroke.

A month later, at the PGA Championship at Southern Hills, Nick won more easily, cruising to a 6-stroke victory over Corey Pavin. The victory rep-

Honors and Awards	
1982-83	Sunshine Tour Order of Merit
1993-94	PGA Tour Player of the Year
1993, 1997	PGA Vardon Trophy
1994, 1996, 1998, 2000, 2003	International Team for the President's Cup
1997	Byron Nelson Award
2002	ASAP Sports/Jim Murray Award
2003	Inducted into World Golf Hall of Fame
2005	Bob Jones Award

resented his second PGA Championship and third major championship in three years. Adding to these triumphs, Nick won four other PGA events in 1994, including his second Canadian Open. Between 1992 and 1994, he won sixteen of the fifty-four tournaments in which he played worldwide. He was named to the international team for the Presidents Cup, the first of three such appearances in the 1990's. At the age of thirty-seven, Nick was the best player in the world. He won the 1994 PGA Tour player of the year award, topped the PGA Tour money list in 1993 and 1994, and was ranked number one for forty-three weeks.

In the following years, Nick experienced a series of setbacks. A recurring sinus problem hampered him for several years, and the death of his long-time caddy, Squeeky Medlen, in 1997, affected him deeply. With the support of his wife, Sue, and children, Gregory, Robyn, and Kimberly, Nick regained some of the form he had shown in 1994. He won the 1997 MCI Classic and the 1998 St. Jude Classic as well as racking up several top-ten finishes. After 1999, he had six top-ten finishes in the four major tournaments.

In his book *The Swing* (1997) he outlined his ideas on the two-plane swing that made him more accurate off the tee and improved his iron play. Twice the winner of the Vardon Trophy, given to the player with the lowest scoring average, he was on the international squad in the Presidents Cup competition five times. His behavior off the greens also has been recognized: In 2002, he was the first recipient of the ASAP Sports/Jim Murray Award for professional players working with the media; in 2005, he won the Bob Jones Award for sportsmanship in golf.

In addition to playing golf, Nick kept busy by designing golf courses, one of which was in Mareazul,

Mexico, and creating a line of high-end golf apparel through his Nick Price Design.

Summary

By winning four PGA tournaments and two major championships in 1994, Nick Price put together one of the best years any professional golfer had ever had. Along with Tiger Woods, Nick shared the record of fifteen PGA victories as the most by any player in the 1990's. He became the world's number-one player but always carried himself with humility and grace. As such, he was one of the best-liked men on the PGA Tour and a favorite with fans around the world.

John Slocum, updated by Thomas L. Erskine

Additional Sources

Bamberger, Michael. *The Green Road Home: A Caddie's Journal of Life on the Pro Golf Tour.* New York: Thunder's Mouth Press, 2006.

Blauvelt, Harry. "Price Chances to Win Major Are Dwindling." *USA Today,* July 22, 2002, p. 12c.

Dobereiner, Peter. "Ranking Price's 1994 Season in History." *Golf Digest* 46, no. 1 (January, 1995): 28.

Huggan, John. "No More Mr. Nice Guy." *Golf Digest* 46, no. 6 (June, 1995): 196.

Price, Nick, and Lorne Rubenstein. *The Swing: Mastering the Principles of the Game.* New York: Knopf, 1997.

Richardson, Gordon. "Long Time Coming." *Golf World* 50, no. 28 (February 21, 1997): 35.

Judy Rankin

Born: February 18, 1945
   St. Louis, Missouri
Also known as: Judith Torluemke (birth name)

Early Life

Judy Rankin was born Judith Torluemke on February 18, 1945, in St. Louis, Missouri. Until Judy came along, St. Louis had been known primarily for professional baseball teams. As the city would learn, a golf prodigy was developing in the community. The only child in a close-knit family, Judy was dependent on her father. Her mother died from a brain tumor, and the family income was barely enough to cover daily expenses. Mr. Torluemke sacrificed much time and what money he had to develop his daughter's golf talent.

With his support and tutelage, Judy began playing golf at the age of six. Judy and her father spent hours on the practice range, where he taught her the fundamentals of the golf swing. Her enthusiasm for the game grew to the point where she could strike nine hundred practice shots per session without tiring. With competent instruction and so much practice, Judy became good in a short time.

The Road to Excellence

A hole-in-one contest sponsored by the city newspaper drew Judy to her first golf competition. Just under four feet in height and weighing 42 pounds, she used a driver on the 102-yard hole, while most of her opponents hit short irons. She won the women's division with the shot closest to the pin. Afterward, she told newspaper reporters that her dad had confidently told her that she could win and she believed everything he said.

The unorthodox grip Mr. Torluemke taught his daughter was the reason for the distance Judy was able to hit a golf ball. Her right hand was turned so that the palm was facing straight up. The common method was to have the right palm facing the target. Setting the right hand as Judy did should have created a boomerang of a hook. However, her left wrist and hand were strong enough to resist rolling over at impact. The outcome was a well-controlled hook with much distance.

Judy won the National Pee Wee Championship for ten- to twelve-year-olds when she was eight. At the ages of nine and ten years old, she won the same tournament. At that point she weighed 60 pounds and could drive a golf ball 170 yards and score consistently in the 80's.

Sponsors for the Pee Wee Championship established a thirteen- to fifteen-year-old playing category. Judy won the new category as an eleven-year-old. Three years later, she be-

Judy Rankin. (Ralph W. Miller Golf Library)

Major Championship Victories

1976   Colgate Dinah Shore
1977   du Maurier Classic

Other Notable Victories

1970   Lincoln-Mercury Open
1973   American Defender
         Lady Carling Open
1976   Babe Zaharias Invitational
         Borden Classic
         Burdine's Invitational
1978-79 WIU Classic

came the youngest and lightest golfer to win the Missouri State Women's Amateur Championship. That same year, 1959, the petite girl with the strong golf game entered the U.S. Women's Open. Not quite 5 feet tall and weighing 80 pounds, the small golfer gave the tournament registration clerk the impression that she wanted to enter her mother in the tournament.

The Emerging Champion

Having the determination to achieve a goal is a fundamental trait of the successful athlete. Following her third Pee Wee victory, Judy stated that she would enjoy becoming a great golfing champion. That was her humble way of forecasting the goal she was determined to achieve.

The site for the 1961 U.S. Women's Open was the difficult Baltusrol Country Club in Springfield, New Jersey. Judy's home course, the Triple "A" Golf Club, was an unsuitable course to use as a practice ground. The holes were easy, lacking distance, rough, or water hazards. Undaunted, Judy took full advantage of the Triple "A" practice facilities, and that summer, her performance at the Open indicated the determination of a potential champion. During the second round of play, she took a triple bogey six on the par-3 fourth hole. Angry at herself but determined, she birdied the next hole. Three additional birdies sandwiched around a double bogey and five bogeys gave her a final score of 78. Among eighty-three participants, her score was one of only eighteen to break 80 strokes for the day. The little sixteen-year-old had finished the most important tournament of her young career in a respectable twenty-fifth place.

After becoming the Missouri amateur cham-

pion for a second time, Judy turned professional. In 1962, she joined the Ladies' Professional Golf Association (LPGA) tour. Although she did not win a tournament for six years, she placed forty-first on the money-winners list for that first season.

Those early years on the tour were filled with emotion. Judy struggled with playing golf for a living. She underestimated her potential and lost substantial leads in the last few holes of a tournament. Reflecting back on those early years, she acknowledged the mistake of spending more time on deciding what to wear for the day than how to play the game. Emotional maturity in the following years, combined with her golfing talent, placed Judy in the top nine money-winners in every year from 1970 to 1977.

Continuing the Story

The professional golf tour had always been lucrative. In 1976, it reached its zenith. That year, Judy became the first woman to win more than $100,000 in a season. With six victories to her credit, she was named Rolex player of the year. Established in

Records and Milestones

Became the first professional woman golfer to win more than $100,000 in one year (1976)

Accumulated twenty-six victories between 1968 and 1979

Won seven tournaments in 1976 and set a new single-season record earnings total of $150,734

Following season won five more tournaments and earned $122,890

At least one win each season from 1970 to 1979

Honors and Awards

1973, 1976-77   LPGA Vare Trophy
1976-77   GWAA Player of the Year
            LPGA Player of the Year
            Rolex Player of the Year
1977   Seagram's Seven Crowns of Sports Award
1987   Inducted into Texas Golf Hall of Fame
1993   Inducted into All-American Collegiate Golf Hall of Fame
1996, 1998   Captain of U.S. Solheim Cup Team
2000   Inducted into LPGA Tour Hall of Fame, "veteran" category
            Inducted into World Golf Hall of Fame
2002   Bob Jones Award

1966, the award is given to the most consistent player on tour, based on points awarded for finishing in the top five players of each official tournament. Judy received the Vare Trophy, named in honor of Glenna Collett Vare, for the low scoring average, 72.25 strokes per round, she had maintained throughout the year.

Judy was pleased to be at the top of her profession, but she was determined to play even better. The year 1977 became her career season. Averaging 72.16 strokes per round earned her the Vare Trophy and player of the year honors for the second year in a row. Beside winning five tournaments and leading the money-winning list once again, she completed an 18-hole round at the Bent Tree Classic in Florida by scoring nine birdies. Only a few golfers, male or female, have ever accomplished the level of play required to perform so well.

Back problems limited Judy's play after the success of 1977. She retired from active competition following the 1983 season. Not a person to be slowed by injury, she replaced the golf club with a microphone and became one of a very few female television golf commentators. Also a devoted wife and mother, Judy always was determined to do her best.

Judy was selected as captain of the 1996 and 1998 U.S. Solheim Cup teams, leading them to victory in both years. In 2000, the LPGA voted the twenty-six-time tour champion into the LPGA Tour Hall of Fame under the "veteran" category, which was established in 1999. That same year, she was also inducted into the World Golf Hall of Fame. In 2002, she received the Bob Jones Award. Judy became a respected ABC Sports golf analyst for men's and women's golf tournaments.

Summary

For most athletes, obtaining championship status requires good coaching, many hours of practice, and the determination to succeed. Judy Rankin's father helped instill these attributes in his daughter. His training taught Judy how to win golf tournaments at an early age. She became a fierce competitor who knew her capabilities and had the confidence to persevere. Golf's "Shirley Temple" to the Pee Wee set, Judy was a champion golfer in the 1970's and a respected teacher and analyst thereafter.

Thomas S. Cross

Additional Sources

Clay, Jonathan, and Tom Smith. *My Best Day in Golf: Celebrity Stories of the Game They Love.* Kansas City, Mo.: Andrews McMeel, 2003.

Rankin, Judy, and Michael Aronstein. *A Natural Way to Golf Power.* New York: Harper & Row, 1976.

Rankin, Judy, and Peter McCleery. *A Woman's Guide to Better Golf.* Chicago: Contemporary Books, 1995.

Sherman, Adam. *Golf's Book of Firsts.* North Dighton, Mass.: JG Press, 2004.

Sirak, Ron, and Tim Rosaforte. "Highest Rankin." *Golf World* 53, no. 41 (2000).

Verdi, Bob. "Judy Rankin." *Golf Digest* 49, no. 9 (1998).

Gene Sarazen

Born: February 27, 1902
    Harrison, New York
Died: May 13, 1999
    Naples, Florida
Also known as: Eugenio Saraceni (birth name)

Early Life

Gene Sarazen was born Eugenio Saraceni on February 27, 1902, in Harrison, New York. His father had been forced by financial need to abandon his studies in Rome for the priesthood. He immigrated to the United States and worked as a carpenter. He always regretted his failure to pursue his scholarly career and was a bitter and unhappy man.

As a result, Gene and his father had a poor relationship. Gene worked as a caddy at local golf clubs but did not take up the game seriously until the conflict with his father worsened. This further break took place after the entry of the United States into World War I in 1917. Gene's father secured a job for Gene at a local shipyard after urging him to quit school. In part because of the hard labor required, Gene developed pneumonia. After his recovery, he abandoned his job and decided to become a professional golfer, much to his father's displeasure.

The Road to Excellence

Gene Sarazen—a name which he adopted after turning professional—had a number of qualities that marked him for greatness. He was aggressive and cocky with a fierce will to win. He was capable of spectacular shot-making under pressure.

Gene's golf matched his temperament. He punched his shots so that they had a low trajectory, enabling him to ignore unfavorable wind conditions. Although only 5 feet 6 inches tall, he was immensely strong, and his fast hand action enabled him to generate highly powerful shots. His best clubs were the fairway woods, in the use of which he became one of the two or three best of all time. Putting was not his strength, but Gene's method of dealing with this weakness was characteristic. He spent hours practicing this aspect of his game until it became a real weapon in his arsenal.

The Emerging Champion

In 1922, Gene emerged as a major presence in golf. He won the U.S. Open, held at the difficult Skokie course near Chicago. How he won the tournament exemplifies his personality. He made a study of

Gene Sarazen, who was the first to accomplish golf's Grand Slam.
(Courtesy of Amateur Athletic Foundation of Los Angeles)

Major Championship Victories

1922, 1932	U.S. Open
1922-23, 1933	PGA Championship
1932	British Open
1935	The Masters
1954, 1958	Senior PGA Championship

Other Notable Victories

1925	Metropolitan Open
1927-28, 1939	Metropolitan PGA Championship
1927, 1929, 1931, 1933, 1935, 1937	Ryder Cup Team
1930	Western Open
1934	Hawaiian Open
1936	Australian Open
1954	International Seniors

Continuing the Story

Gene's way of coping with his slump showed his immense dedication. In spite of his success—his slump was by most golfers' standards a period of great success—he decided to revamp his game completely. He had come to adopt an outside-in trajectory on his swing that, he believed, was responsible for inadequate control of the club. He thought that an inside-out swing was more suited to his game and embarked on the endless hours of practice required to alter his swing.

Gene also endeavored to improve his play in sand bunkers. To this end, he invented a new golf club, the sand wedge, which proved much more efficient than the earlier niblick and soon became a standard item.

In the 1932 British Open, Gene again had Daniels as his caddy. This time he followed his adviser's suggestions and triumphed in the tournament. He also won the U.S. Open that year, doing so by one of his come-from-behind charges.

Gene's most famous victory took place in the 1935 Masters. As the tournament neared its end, Gene needed to birdie three of the last four holes in order to secure a tie with Craig Wood, who had already finished his round. On the fifteenth hole, Gene used his skill with fairway woods to full effect. He sank his second stroke, a 250-yard shot to green, giving him a double-eagle 2 on the par-5 hole. This was sufficient to give him his tie with Wood, whom he bested in the playoff.

An unusual feature of Gene's game was his longevity as a topflight golfer. In 1940, he tied for the

the course in the week preceding the event and memorized the contours of the greens. As a result, he was among the tournament's leaders after three rounds, a position he had never before attained in the U.S. Open.

The young player, undaunted by the U.S. Open's prestige, proceeded to play the last round in aggressive fashion; he finished with a 69, a good enough score to win the tournament outright. He avoided a playoff by a daring approach to the last green.

In the same year, Gene won the Professional Golfers' Association (PGA) Championship. At that time, the PGA Championship was a match play event, in which golfers faced each other head-to-head. Walter Hagen was generally regarded as the greatest of all match players. Gene was immune to the pressure and dispatched Hagen, a feat he repeated in an arranged match for the "World's Golf Championship."

In 1923, Gene's game slumped, and he finished poorly in the U.S. Open. He revived by the time of the PGA Championship and again defeated Hagen in the final. Gene appeared set for a long reign at golf's pinnacle, but the remainder of the 1920's proved a disappointment. He did not win any other major titles in that decade. In part, the reason for his fall was precisely the source of his strength. His aggressive game sometimes got out of control. In the 1928 British Open, he missed a chance to win by ignoring the advice of his experienced caddy Skip Daniels. He attempted a risky shot that failed, and his seven on the hole cost him the tournament.

Records and Milestones

First player to win all four major (Grand Slam) golf tournaments
Placed second in the British Open (1928), third (1931, 1933)
Placed second in the U.S. Open (1934, 1940), third (1926)

Honors and Awards

1932	Associated Press Male Athlete of the Year
1940	Inducted into PGA Golf Professional Hall of Fame
1965	GWAA Richardson Award
1974	Inducted into World Golf Hall of Fame
1984	Charlie Bartlett Award
1988	Old Tom Morris Award

U.S. Open with Lawson Little. Although he lost the playoff, his achievement was remarkable. He was thirty-eight years old at the time, in golf a quite advanced age.

Perhaps even more amazing was his performance in the 1958 British Open. He finished only 10 strokes behind the winner. He ended in a tie for sixteenth place with Bobby Locke, the previous year's victor. Gene also became the first player older than sixty to make the cut at The Masters.

Summary

Gene Sarazen became one of the greatest golfers of the 1920's and 1930's by a combination of aggressive temperament and physical ability. His strength and speed enabled him to risk shots that other golfers dared not attempt. He played best when under pressure, and his dashing style gained him wide publicity as well as seven major championships.

Bill Delaney

Additional Sources

Barkow, Al. *Best of Golf: Best Golfers, Courses, Moments and More.* Lincolnwood, Ill.: Publications International, 2002.

Barkow, Al, Gene Sarazen, and Mary Ann Sarazen. *Gene Sarazen and Shell's Wonderful World of Golf.* Ann Arbor, Mich.: Clock Tower Press, 2003.

Olman, John M. *The Squire: The Legendary Golfing Life of Gene Sarazen.* Cincinnati: Author, 1987.

Sarazen, Gene. *Gene Sarazen's Common Sense Golf Tips.* Chicago: Reilly & Lee, 1924.

Sarazen, Gene, and Peggy Kirk Bell. *Golf Magazine's Winning Pointers from the Pros.* New York: Harper & Row, 1965.

Sarazen, Gene, and Roger P. Ganem. *Better Golf After Fifty.* New York: Harper & Row, 1967.

Sarazen, Gene, and Herbert W. Wind. *Thirty Years of Championship Golf: The Life and Times of Gene Sarazen.* New York: Prentice-Hall, 1950. Reprint. London: A & C Black, 1990.

Patty Sheehan

Born: October 27, 1956
Middlebury, Vermont

Early Life

Patty Sheehan was born October 27, 1956, in Middlebury, Vermont, to Bobo Sheehan, a college sports coach, and Leslie Sheehan, a nurse. When Patty was ten years old, the Sheehan family moved from Vermont to Nevada.

At one year of age, Patty started skiing. By age four, she was ski racing and also playing golf. Patty learned to feel comfortable on skis by walking around with shortened skis on her feet. Her parents were avid skiers and often skied with Patty standing between their legs. Patty's parents provided great support for her athletic efforts. Her father taught her the value of top-level performance by telling her to do her best in whatever she did.

As a child, Patty admired skiers such as Nancy Green, a Canadian who won the World Cup in 1968. She also admired some of the college athletes on her father's ski team. By age thirteen, Patty was a nationally ranked junior skier. Soon, however, her desire to excel in skiing diminished. At the same time, her interest in golf began to resurface.

The Road to Excellence

After moving from Vermont to Nevada, the Sheehan family lived on a golf course, providing Patty with many chances to practice and play. By the age of fifteen, Patty began to compete in golf tournaments.

As a young woman, Patty was winner of the Nevada State Amateur Championship from 1975 through 1978, and she won the California Amateur Championship in 1978 and 1979. Patty reached the pinnacle of her amateur career when she claimed the 1980 AIAW National Championship while attending San Jose State University. Patty was also a member of the U.S. Curtis Cup team in 1980, winning all four of her matches.

The Emerging Champion

After completing her college years at San Jose State, Patty joined the Ladies Professional Golf Association (LPGA) tour in 1980. Her talents were almost immediately evident. She captured the attention of golf fans by winning the LPGA rookie of the year award. In the following year, her second on tour, she achieved her first tour victory in the Mazda Japan Classic.

By 1983, other LPGA golfers were made even more aware that they had a serious contender at any tournament in which Patty Sheehan played.

Patty Sheehan celebrating a victory in 1996. (Otto Greule, Jr./ Getty Images)

She captured four tournaments that year, including her first major title, the LPGA Championship. In addition, she collected $255,185 and won the Rolex player of the year award. Patty's momentum continued into 1984, when she won four more tournaments, including another LPGA Championship, and was awarded the Vare Trophy for the low-scoring average of the year at 71.40.

In 1986 and 1987, the tournament wins continued; moreover, Patty received recognition as an outstanding person away from the golf course. In 1986, she was selected as the Samaritan Award winner. In 1987, she was among eight athletes selected by *Sports Illustrated* for the "sportsman" of the year award, an honor given to athletes who practice the ideal of sportsmanship away from the playing arena. Patty was also recognized for her work with troubled teenagers in Santa Cruz County.

Continuing the Story

The year 1989 provided the greatest challenge of Patty's career, as she experienced two devastating setbacks within ten months. In October, the San Francisco earthquake severely damaged her house, leaving her temporarily homeless. In July, she blew an 11-stroke lead during the final round of the U.S. Women's Open. Reflecting on the year, Patty said, "I had to overcome a lot of psychological hurdles—bad memories and bad thoughts."

Patty rebounded from the obstacles of 1989 the next year by becoming the second woman to cross the $700,000 earnings mark in a season, collecting $732,618. That same year, she posted a career best scoring average of 70.62 and won five titles. She was

Major Championship Victories

1983-84, 1993	LPGA Championship
1992, 1994	U.S. Women's Open
1996	Nabisco Dinah Shore Championship

Other Notable Victories

1980	AIAW National Championship
1981, 1988	Mazda Japan Classic
1982	Orlando Lady Classic
1982-83	Inamori Classic
1982, 1990	Safeco Classic
1983	Corning Classic
1983-84	Henredon Classic
1984	Elizabeth Arden Classic
	McDonald's Kids Classic
1985	J&B Scotch Pro-Am
1985-86, 1988	Sarasota Classic
1986	Konica San Jose Classic
	Kyocera Inamori Classic
1989-90, 1992	Rochester International
1990	Jamaica Classic
	McDonald's Championship
	Ping-Cellular One Golf Championship
1991	Orix Hawaiian Ladies Open
1992	Jamie Farr Toledo Classic
1993	Standard Register Ping
1995	Rochester International

also a member of the victorious inaugural U.S. Solheim Cup team.

The 1991 season had its ups and downs for Patty. The ups included career-win number twenty-six and a total of twelve top-ten finishes. The downs came in the second half of the season, when Patty suffered from tendinitis in her left index finger. Despite the physical pain, Patty recorded her second hole in one at the Women's Kemper Open and crossed the $3 million mark in career earnings.

Three wins in 1992 brought Patty within one victory of qualifying for membership in the LPGA Hall of Fame. In her U.S. Women's Open victory, she showed nerves of steel and great determination. She birdied the final two holes of regulation to force an eighteen-hole playoff against Juli Inkster, which Patty won.

As the 1993 season began, many wondered when the knicker-clad, energy-packed Patty Sheehan would break through the door for victory number thirty, the number of LPGA wins required for hall-of-fame

Honors and Awards

1980	Curtis Cup Team
	LPGA Rookie of the Year
1983	LPGA Player of the Year
1984	Vare Trophy
1986	Samaritan Award
1987	*Sports Illustrated* Co-Sportsman of the Year
1990	Inducted into Collegiate Hall of Fame
1990, 1992, 1994, 1996, 2002-03	U.S. Solheim Cup Team
1993	Inducted into LPGA Hall of Fame
1994	Flo Hyman Award
	LPGA's Top 50 Players
2002	Patty Berg Award
2002-03	Captain of U.S. Solheim Cup Team

admission. Patty was consumed with thoughts about the hall of fame. She later recalled, "I thought about it every day, but not in a negative way. I knew it was attainable. I just had to stay out of the way and let it happen." Following her own advice, she produced an impressive five-stroke victory in the Standard Register Ping tournament.

Patty kept thinking about the importance of the thirtieth victory, even though she tried to block those thoughts from her mind. However, the pressure also helped; Patty acknowledged that she had an enhanced "focus" during the final stretch toward the hall of fame. She attributed the increased concentration to the heightened level of competition on the LPGA Tour. That level of competition brought out her best play, as she finished the final hole by making her fifth birdie of the round and shooting a tournament-record 17 under par. Later that season, she became the thirteenth woman inducted into the LPGA Hall of Fame. In 1994, she captured her second U.S. Women's Open title.

In 1996, Patty won her sixth major tournament at the Nabisco Dinah Shore Championship, bringing her career win total to thirty-five. She contin-

ued to play in tournaments in the following years, posting several top-ten finishes in 1998 and 1999. In 2000, Patty became interested in course design and did some consulting work for a new course in Angels Camp, California. She continued to appear in LPGA tournaments, firing a season-low 67 in the first round of the Firstar LPGA Classic. In 2002 and 2003, she captained the U.S. team at the Solheim Cup.

Summary

Patty Sheehan's talent and determination brought her to the pinnacle of success in her field. Even after she attained LPGA Hall of Fame status, she remained a top competitor, as she continued to follow her father's advice to do her best in everything.

Judy C. Peel

Additional Sources

McCord, Robert. *The Golf Book of Days: Fascinating Facts and Stories for Every Day of the Year.* Secaucus, N.J.: Citadel Press, 2002.

Sheehan, Patty, and Betty Hicks. *Patty Sheehan on Golf.* Dallas, Tex.: Taylor, 1996.

Charlie Sifford

Born: June 2, 1922
      Charlotte, North Carolina
Also known as: Charles Luther Sifford

Early Life

Charles Luther (Charlie) Sifford was born on June 2, 1922, in Charlotte, North Carolina, the third of six children. His father, Rosco, worked as a laborer in the local fertilizer plant, and his mother Eliza, was a homemaker. Charlie knew he wanted to golf at an early age. The type of work his father did, carting around heavy loads of manure at the factory, did not appeal to Charlie. Little did he know that his love of golf would greatly impact the history of professional sports.

Charlie began his career in golf at the age of ten at the Carolina Country Club, an all-white club near his house. By the time Charlie was thirteen, he was the best caddy at the club, He did so well that he earned almost as much money as his father. Eventually, his interest in the game led him to play more. Using clubs that the members of the country club loaned to him, Charlie, self-taught, could hit far and straight and produce low scores.

In his teens, Charlie, as an African American, began to experience the type of racial discrimination prevalent during the time period. Even though he was well respected and popular, club members complained that Charlie and the other African American caddies should not be allowed to play on the course. One day, his supervisor told him that certain individuals threatened to physically assault him and the African American caddies if they continued to play. After a confrontation with a white shop owner who had verbally mistreated him, Charlie, and a friend, decided to move north.

The Road to Excellence

Charlie arrived in Philadelphia in 1940. He lived with his uncle and worked as a shipping clerk. He soon began golfing at Cobbs Creek, the local public course. As he discovered, Cobbs Creek was a golf course open to everyone, complete with a pro shop and a clubhouse. The course was also the unofficial home turf to the best black golfers in the city. Since black golfers were shut out of whites-only tournaments and clubs, at Cobbs Creek, black golfers could meet and conduct tournaments of their own. Charlie's golf game improved significantly in the presence of skilled players.

After serving as a member of the 24th Infantry in the Army in Okinawa, Japan, during World War II, Charlie returned to the United States and traveled as a professional. He became the private golf professional for the big-band leader, Billy Eckstine. Later, he joined the United Golf Association (UGA), since he could not compete on the PGA Tour because of racial discrimination. The UGA provided a mini-tour for black players; the most

Charlie Sifford. (Augusta National/Getty Images)

important tournament was the National Negro Open. In 1952, Charlie won the first of six National Negro Opens.

The Emerging Champion

Discouraged by the PGA rules that excluded people of color, Charlie challenged the "Caucasian clause" in place in professional golf. Charlie was often compared to Jackie Robinson, who was the first African American to integrate Major League Baseball. However, Charlie's situation was unique. Baseball was a team sport; Charlie was left to fight his battles alone.

Despite his success, life on the road was not easy. At the Phoenix Open in 1952, Charlie and his playing foursome, which included boxer Joe Louis, found the first hole on the course vandalized. He constantly received death threats, was taunted, and was refused access to the facilities of his competitors. However, Charlie was undaunted. In 1957, he won the Long Beach Open; in 1960, he won the UGA National Negro Open again. In the same year, Charlie finally earned his playing card, becoming the first African American to be granted this status.

Continuing the Story

Even after his best years in golf, Charlie won on the PGA Tour. In 1967, he won at the Greater Hartford Open at the age of forty-five. During this tournament he defeated great players such as Arnold

Milestone

First African American to be inducted into the World Golf Hall of Fame (2004)

Palmer, Lee Trevino, Gary Player, Tom Weiskopf, and Raymond Floyd. Two years later, in 1969, Charlie won the Los Angeles Open in a playoff against Harold Henning. Established as a player, he finally began garnering the respect he deserved. In 1975, he won the PGA Senior Tour Championship; later, he became an original member of the Senior PGA Tour. In 2004, Charlie was elected to the World Golf Hall of Fame. Such an accomplishment was fitting for a man who fought impossible obstacles and broke through racial barriers to do what he loved.

Charlie, with his trademark cigar sticking from the side of his mouth, won more than $340,000 on tour, a substantial sum in those days. Charlie was widely acknowledged as the Jackie Robinson of golf. His story is one of dedication, patience, and perseverance.

Summary

Charlie Sifford was one of the first African Americans to play on the PGA Tour and the first to win a tour event. He played in a challenging time in U.S. history and became a symbol of determination and courage. Charlie's achievements were many and benefited African Americans, golf, and the United States.

Brian Culp

Notable Victories

Year	Event
1952-56, 1960	United Golf Association National Negro Open
1956	Rhode Island Open
1957	Long Beach Open
1960	Almaden Open
1963	Puerto Rico Open
1967	Greater Hartford Open Invitational
1969	Los Angeles Open
1971	Sea Pines
1975	Senior PGA Championship
1980	Suntree Classic

Additional Sources

Lacy, Tim. "It's About Time." *Afro-American Red Star* 113, no. 16 (December, 2004).

Rasbury, Marc. "Dr. Charles Sifford Came Before Tiger." *New York Beacon* 14, no. 26 (July, 2007).

Sifford, Charles, and Jim Gullo. *Just Let Me Play: The Story of Charlie Sifford, the First Black PGA Golfer.* Latham, N.Y.: British American, 1992.

Vijay Singh

Born: February 22, 1963
Lautoka, Fiji
Also known as: The Big Fijian

Early Life
Vijay Singh was born in Lautoka, Fiji, on February 22, 1963. He came from modest beginnings. In fact, as a child, Vijay practiced golfing with coconuts because his family could not afford to buy golf balls. Vijay's father, Mohan, was an airline technician. However, he also taught golf. Mohan helped Vijah to mimic the swing of Tom Weiskopf, a golfer

Vijay Singh waits for play at the Mercedes-Benz Championship tournament in Maui, 2009. (Stan Badz/US PGA Tour/Getty Images)

on the PGA Tour who had won the British Open. Weiskopf's swing was the model through which Vijay constructed his own swing. As a boy, Vijay also pursued the other popular sports of his region, such as snooker, cricket, soccer, and rugby. However, golf was the activity at which he most excelled.

The Road to Excellence
In 1982, Vijay joined the Asian Tour. However, he did not win his first tournament until the 1984 Malaysian Open. Four years passed before Vijay won another tournament. Unfortunately for Vijay, his career ran into trouble. Vijay allegedly doctored his scorecard in order to make the cut of an event. He was suspended from the Asian Tour and publicly embarrassed. He then took a job at a Malaysian golf club, saved money, and continued to practice and gain experience. Once he had saved enough money, he began entering tournaments again. In 1988, Vijay won his second event, the Nigerian Open. Also in 1988, he entered the European Tour Qualify School and joined the European Tour. In 1989, he won four tournaments on the European Tour. He played on the tour for five years and won thirteen times. However, more than a decade passed before Vijay had his breakthrough in the world of golf.

The Emerging Champion
In 1993, Vijay brought his game to the American shore, joining the PGA Tour. He won the Buick Invitational and was named PGA rookie of the year. He was competitive but did not win often over the following five years. His first major victory came at the 1998 PGA Championship. Then, in 2000, he won The Masters. In 2001, he began to gain a reputation as the hardest working man on the PGA Tour. He played every week, and he usually played well. While he did not win any tournaments in the 2001 season, he had fourteen top-ten finishes, which landed him at number four on the money list for the year. In 2002, he won twice, at the Shell Houston Open and at the Tour Championship. Those victories were the beginning of an amazing few years for Vijay.

PGA Tour Victories

1993, 1995, 2006	Buick/Barclays Classic
1995, 2003	Phoenix Open
1997	Memorial Tournament
1997, 2004-05	Buick Open
1998	The International
1998, 2004	PGA Championship
1999	Honda Classic
2000	The Masters
2002	The Tour Championship
2002, 2004-05	Shell Houston Open
2003	Byron Nelson Championship
	John Deere Classic
	FUNAI Classic at the Walt Disney World Resort
2004	Pebble Beach National Pro-Am
	HP Classic of New Orleans
	Bell Canadian Open
	84 Lumber Classic
	Chrysler Championship
2004, 2008	Deutsche Bank Championship
2005	Sony Open in Hawaii
	Wachovia Championship
2007	Mercedes Championship
	Arnold Palmer Invitational
2008	WGC-Bridgestone Invitational

In 2003, Vijay had his most successful year. He won four tournaments and had an amazing eighteen top-ten finishes. For the first time in his career, he was the number-one player on the PGA money list, with the second highest total in PGA history. His ability to win tournaments and to be competitive in the ones he did not win, propelled him into rarified air.

If the golf world was impressed with Vijay's gritty performance in 2003, it had to be amazed by his excellence in 2004. That year, Vijay won an astounding nine tournaments and had eighteen top-ten finishes. He was number one on the money list again, earning a record $10,905,166. He had twelve consecutive top-ten finishes, which was the most by any golfer since 1975. He ended the year winning his second major tournament, the PGA Championship. Most significant, he took control of the number-one ranking from Tiger Woods. In twenty-two hard fought years, Vijay had gone from an unknown rookie on the Asian Tour to the number-one golfer in the world.

Continuing the Story

During the 2005 season, Vijay and Woods traded the number-one ranking back and forth; Woods ended on top. However, Vijay had made his mark. In April of 2005, he was elected into the World Golf Hall of Fame. His induction made him the youngest living member of the hall. With eighteen wins, Vijay had more than any other man in PGA history after turning forty.

In 2008, Vijay was ranked number three in the world, behind Woods and Phil Mickelson. He figured to remain a force in the world of golf for years to come. With his persistence and constant training he was certain to make another run at the number-one ranking.

Summary

Vijay Singh influenced the golf world immensely. With hard work and dedication, he was able to accomplish his goals. Though he was disgraced and suspended from the Asian Tour as a young golfer, he was later the number-one ranked golfer on the PGA Tour. He was, perhaps, the most consistent golfer of his generation.

Theodore Shields

Additional Sources

Mizell, Hubert. "Experience a Good Teacher." *St. Petersburg Times*, April 10, 2000.

Rees, Peter. "Golf's Humble Fijian: Vijay's Rise to Number One." *Pacific Magazine* (November 1, 2004).

Spander, Art. "Singh Hits Top Note but Stays Man of Mystery." *The Daily Telegraph*, December 31, 2004.

Honors and Awards

1993	PGA Rookie of the Year
2003-04	PGA Tour leading money winner
2004	Byron Nelson Award
	PGA Tour Player of the Year
	PGA Vardon Trophy
	Twelve consecutive top-ten finishes, the most by any golfer since 1975
2005	Inducted into World Golf Hall of Fame
	Became youngest living member of the World Golf Hall of Fame
2008	Most PGA Tour wins after forty years old (eighteen)

Marilynn Smith

Born: April 13, 1929
    Topeka, Kansas
Also known as: Miss Personality

Early Life
Marilynn Smith was born in Topeka, Kansas, in 1929. She loved playing sandlot baseball with her friends, but in doing so, she picked up some bad habits, including a colorful vocabulary of words unacceptable in polite society. One day, when she came home from a disappointing baseball game, she spewed out a string of invectives that shocked her mother, who told her husband about it that evening.

Marilynn's father suggested that Marilynn, then twelve, take up golf, which he considered a more genteel sport than baseball. Although Marilynn initially considered golf a noncompetitive sport, once she began to play at the Wichita Country Club, of which her father was a member, she was disabused of that notion. She showed a natural aptitude for golf and was encouraged by her parents to continue her participation.

The Road to Excellence
In 1946, Marilynn's amateur career received a considerable boost when, at seventeen, she earned her first of three victories in the Kansas Women's Amateur competition. In 1949, while still an undergraduate at the University of Kansas, she won the National Collegiate Athletic Association Championship, which completed her amateur career. She finished her college education in 1951, majoring in physical education and journalism. As a professional golfer, she won twenty-one Ladies Professional Golf Association (LPGA) Tour titles, including championships in 1963 and 1964.

Women's golf had been organized by the Women's Professional Golf Association (WPGA), but by 1949, that organization was declining. The threatened collapse of the WPGA motivated a group of female golfers, persuaded that they could succeed as professionals, to find an alternative: They founded the LPGA at the Women's U.S. Open in Wichita, Kansas, in 1950.

Assuming a leadership role in the founding of the LPGA, Marilynn displayed tact and diplomacy, which won her the moniker of "Miss Personality." Her colleagues shared a genuine respect and fondness for her. They appreciated her willingness to work hard behind the scenes, avoiding the spotlight herself, in order to establish the most successful women's sports association in existence. Marilynn served as the LPGA's secretary in 1957 and as its president from 1958 to 1960.

The Emerging Champion
In 1954, Marilynn won her first tournament in Indiana's Fort Wayne Open. In 1963, after serving as secretary and president of the LPGA, she was named the most improved player in women's golf. In 1971, playing in the Lady Carling Open, she became the first player in the history of the LPGA to score a double-eagle, 3 strokes under par.

In 1961, Marilynn won more than $10,000 for the first time; the following year, her winnings were up to $12,075. In 1964, she earned $21,691, a phenomenal amount at that time in women's golf.

Marilynn's winnings stayed in five figures every year between 1961 and 1973, but dropped to hundreds rather than thousands of dollars by 1978.

LPGA Tour Victories

Year	Tournament
1954	Fort Wayne Open
1955	Heart of America Open
	Mile High Open
1958	Jacksonville Open
1959	Memphis Open
1962	Sunshine Open
	Waterloo Open
1963	Eugene Ladies Open
	Cavern City Open
1963-64	Titleholders Championship
1963, 1965	Peach Blossom Open
1964	Albuquerque Pro-Am
1966	St. Petersburg Women's Open
	Louise Suggs Delray Beach Invitational
1967	St. Petersburg Orange Classic
	Babe Zaharias Open
1968	O'Sullivan Open
1970	Women's Golf Charities Open
1972	Pabst Ladies Classic

Despite this decline in earnings, Marilynn earned respectable amounts of money for more than a decade. Her dedication to the game was complete and genuine, so her satisfaction came from advancing the cause of women's professional golf.

Even as her competitive golfing career reached its end, Marilynn experienced a number of triumphs. In 1979, she received the first Patty Berg Award for her overall service to professional women's golf. In 1981, during the Kemper Women's Open, she scored the fifth hole in one in her LPGA career. In 1983, she was the recipient of the *Golf Digest* LPGA Founders Cup for her overall charitable service.

In 1987, Marilynn was recognized by the Vincent Lombardi Tournament of Champions for her leadership role in sports and her general charitable efforts. During the 1990's, she was an active participant in the Sprint Titleholders Senior Challenge, an unofficial event for seniors.

Continuing to teach golf and actively involved in managing the Marilynn Smith Golf Classic, in 2000, Marilynn was one of six inaugural inductees into the LPGA Teaching and Club Professionals Hall of Fame. On October 30, 2006, Marilynn received what was probably her greatest honor: induction into the World Golf Hall of Fame, in recognition of her lifetime achievement in the sport.

Continuing the Story

Marilynn remained active as she entered her eightieth year. In 2007, she and fellow LPGA founder Louise Suggs raised the U.S. flag at the opening of the Solheim Cup in Sweden. She was named one of the LPGA's top fifty players during the organization's fiftieth anniversary commemoration in 2000. Also, she established the Marilynn Smith Scholarship for the benefit of young women with the potential to be golf champions, and she oversaw the administration of this scholarship.

Marilynn was active during the 1950's in promoting the LPGA by participating in radio and

Honors and Awards

1950	Cofounder of the LPGA
1958-60	LPGA president
1963	LPGA most improved player
1979	Patty Berg Award
1983	*Golf Digest* LPGA Founders Cup
1987	Vincent Lombardi Tournament of Champions Award
1991	Inducted into Kansas Golf Hall of Fame
1994	Inducted into Texas Golf Hall of Fame
1999	Inducted into Kansas University Sports Hall of Fame
2000	Inducted into Kansas Sports Hall of Fame
	Inducted into LPGA Teaching and Club Professionals Hall of Fame
	LPGA Fiftieth Anniversary Fifty Greatest Players
2005	Inducted into Wichita Sports Hall of Fame
	Inducted into Wichita East High School Sports Hall of Fame
2006	Inducted into World Golf Hall of Fame
	Pinnacle Award

television shows and remained an active participant in various talk shows in the twenty-first century for the same purpose. She was extremely interested in politics in the United States, particularly as it pertained to women and gender equality.

Summary

The greatest significance that can be drawn from Marilynn Smith's life is that people can be as productive working behind the scenes as they can by assuming center stage. Ever self-effacing, Marilynn was sincerely devoted to advancing her sport and to creating a place for women among golf professionals. She succeeded admirably through her intelligence and her true dedication to golf.

R. Baird Shuman

Additional Sources

Crosset, Todd. *Outsiders in the Clubhouse: The World of Women's Golf.* Albany: State University of New York Press, 1995.

Ireland, Mary Lloyd, and Aurelia Nattiv, eds. *The Female Athlete.* Philadelphia: W. B. Saunders, 2002.

Norwood, Joe, Marilynn Smith, and Stanley Blicker. *Joe Norwood's Golf-o-Metrics.* 2d ed. Las Vegas, Nev.: Norwood, 1992.

Sam Snead

Born: May 27, 1912
    Ashwood, Virginia
Died: May 23, 2002
    Hot Springs, Virginia
Also known as: Samuel Jackson Snead (full
    name); Slammin' Sam

Early Life
Samuel Jackson Snead was born on May 27, 1912, in Ashwood, Virginia. With his four older brothers and one sister, Sam grew up on a farm. Although the family was not destitute, there was little money for travel or for leisure activities. Sam enjoyed hunting and fishing, activities he continued long after leaving home. He credited squirrel hunting with developing his accurate eye, which proved to be of great value on the golf course.

Sam's oldest brother, Harold, was Sam's mentor. They made golf clubs out of tree branches, and under Harold's tutelage, Sam showed great aptitude for the game. By age twelve, he was caddying on the nearby Homestead Hotel golf course, earning some much desired pocket money. Surprisingly, he did not excel in the game while in high school.

The Road to Excellence
At Valley High School in nearby Hot Springs, Sam was an all-around athlete. He participated successfully in track, boxing, football, baseball, and basketball. His high school coach convinced Sam to avoid liquor and tobacco, and he abstained from both throughout his career.

In 1935, Sam became an assistant golf professional at White Sulphur Springs, West Virginia, earning $25 a week, and in 1936, he was promoted to teaching professional at Cascades Inn in Hot Springs. He turned professional in 1937, placing seventh at the Los Angeles Open and first in the Oakland Open, where he became an overnight sensation. That same year, he won the Bing Crosby Invitational, the Miami Open, and the St. Paul and Nassau Opens. He was runner-up in the U.S. Open, phenomenal for a relative newcomer to professional golf.

Sam ended 1937 as the third-highest golfer in money won, with $10,243. In 1938, he was the number-one money winner, with $19,334, and the most popular golfer on the circuit, drawing big crowds wherever he played. Fred

Sam Snead. (Ralph W. Miller Golf Library)

Corcoran, the Professional Golfers' Association (PGA) tournament manager, recruited Sam for the professional tour, recognizing his skills.

The Emerging Champion

Sam had a good year in 1938. He won the Canadian Open and came in second in the U.S. Open and the PGA tournament. He won the Vardon Memorial Trophy for the lowest strokes-per-round average in PGA-sponsored competition that year, the first of four such awards.

Sportswriters noted Sam's golf skills, citing his

"swing of beauty" as both functional and artistic. Sam also had a grass-roots appeal, his folksy manner endearing him to spectators. He was a colorful player, always friendly and a pleasure to watch. At first, the press referred to him as "the hillbilly from the backwoods of Virginia," but soon he was affectionately nicknamed "Slammin' Sam" by both press and fans.

Sam served in the Navy from 1942 to 1944 and was unable to play professionally; however, overall, the 1940's were a successful decade for him. He won the Canadian Open in 1940 and 1941, the PGA Championship in 1942, and the Portland and Richmond Opens in 1944. A high point was his victory in the British Open in 1946, the first time the title returned to the United States since 1933.

In spite of Sam's many tournament wins, he sometimes lost "sure" matches because of erratic putting, often losing by two, three, or four strokes. In 1949, a fine record subdued the talk that he choked in "clutch" situations, as he won both the PGA Championship and The Masters and began a fantastic run of wins.

Major Championship Victories

1942, 1949, 1951	PGA Championship
1946	British Open
1949, 1952, 1954	The Masters
1964-65, 1967, 1970, 1972-73	Senior PGA Championship

Other Notable Victories

1937	Oakland Open
1937-38, 1941, 1950	Bing Crosby Pro-Am
1937, 1939, 1941, 1947, 1949, 1951, 1953, 1955	Ryder Cup Team
1938	Westchester 108 Hole Open
1938, 1940-41	Canadian Open
1938, 1946, 1949-50, 1955-56, 1960, 1965	Greater Greensboro Open
1939, 1941-42	St. Petersburg Open
1941, 1950	North and South Open
1944	Portland Open
	Richmond Open
1945	Pensacola Open
1945, 1950	Los Angeles Open
1946	World Championship of Golf
1948, 1950	Texas Open
1949-50	Western Open
1950	Colonial National Invitation
1952	All-American Open
	Eastern Open
1956, 1960-61	World Cup Team
1961	Tournament of Champions
1964-65, 1970, 1972-73	World Seniors Championship
1969	Ryder Cup nonplaying captain
1980	*Golf Digest* Commemorative, senior tour
1982	Legends of Golf, senior tour (with Don January)

Continuing the Story

In the 1950's, Sam's chief rival was another golfing great, Ben Hogan. The two monopolized The Masters: Sam won in 1949, 1952, and 1954, and Ben won in 1951 and 1953. Clearly, Sam was at his peak, but he never won the big one: The U.S. Open. In spite of his more than one hundred tournament victories, Sam was badgered repeatedly for his failure to win the U.S. Open, although he was runner-up four times. He did not, however, let this failure deter him from enjoying golf and continuing to play in the manner that brought him much fame and money. He played to the best of his ability and continued his winning ways well into his sixties.

Until Arnold Palmer began dominating golf in the 1960's, Sam remained the leading money-winner and the most popular figure on the professional tour. He also took great pride in the fact that he helped bring prestigious foreign titles to the United States. In 1946, he won the British Open and, between 1937 and 1955, he was a Ryder Cup team member eight times, playing singles and in foursomes. His record was impressive: five wins and one loss in singles play and five wins and one loss in the foursomes.

Age did not slow Sam much. He had a good year in 1955, winning four open tournaments. In 1956, he won the Greensboro Open. In 1965, at the age of fifty-two, he won the Greensboro Open again and, at the age of sixty-two, tied for third in the 1974 National PGA. The "swing of beauty" had not deserted him.

Records and Milestones

PGA Tour money leader (1938, 1949-50, 1955)

Credited with at least 135 wins worldwide, including a record 84 on the PGA tour

Became oldest champion at an official PGA Tour event, winning the 1965 Greater Greensboro Open at age fifty-two years and ten months

One of the founders of the Senior Tour

Honors and Awards

1938, 1949-50, 1955	PGA Vardon Trophy
1949	PGA Player of the Year
1953	Inducted into PGA Golf Professional Hall of Fame
1974	Inducted into World Golf Hall of Fame
1984	GWAA Richardson Award
1998	Received PGA Tour Lifetime Achievement Award

Summary

In 1953, with Ben Hogan and Byron Nelson, Sam Snead was elected to the PGA Golf Professional Hall of Fame. He continued playing tournaments well into the 1970's, earning respectable scores and much adulation from fans. Fittingly, Sam won the first Legends of Golf tournament held in Austin, Texas, in 1978. The Golfers' Creed views the game as "a contest, calling for courage, skill, strategy, and self-control"—all of which Sam had in abundance.

S. Carol Berg

Additional Sources

Barkow, Al. *Sam: The One and Only Sam Snead.* Ann Arbor, Mich.: Sports Media Group, 2005.

"Sam Snead on How to Shake the Shanks." *Golf Magazine* 49, no. 4 (April, 2007): 63.

Snead, Sam, and George Mendoza. *Slammin' Sam.* New York: Donald I. Fine, 1986.

Snead, Sam, and Francis J. Pirozzolo. *The Game I Love: Wisdom, Insight, and Instruction from Golf's Greatest Player.* New York: Ballantine Books, 1997.

Snead, Sam, and Al Stump. *The Education of a Golfer.* New York: Simon & Schuster, 1962.

Towle, Mike. *I Remember Sam Snead: Memories and Anecdotes of Golf's Slammin' Sammy.* Nashville, Tenn.: Cumberland House, 2003.

Yocum, Guy. *My Shot: The Very Best Interviews from Golf Digest Magazine.* New York: Stewart, Tabori & Chang, 2007.

Annika Sorenstam

Born: October 9, 1970
Bro, near Stockholm, Sweden

Early Life

Annika Sorenstam was born in Bro, near Stockholm, Sweden, on October 9, 1970, to Tom and Gunilla Sorenstam. Annika's younger sister, Charlotta, also grew up to be a professional golfer. Instead of ice skating, skiing, or tobogganing, Annika preferred golf, a sport usually associated with warmer climates than that of Sweden. Annika began to play when she was twelve years old.

Before Annika began playing golf, she participated in tennis, a sport that could be played indoors as well as outdoors. While she was considered a good athlete, she never reached a top-ten ranking as a junior tennis player in the city of Stockholm. So she turned to golf, a game she could practice on her own. In later life, she developed a reputation as something of a loner, and in this, golf suited her well.

The Road to Excellence

Annika was a member of the Swedish national golf team, with which she came under the tutelage of head coach Pia Nilsson. Annika's training came primarily from the Swedish Golf Federation. The guidance of Nilsson, emotional support from her parents, and her own abilities and belief in her skills paved the way to greater opportunities. The training Annika received from the Swedish Golf Federation resulted in a scholarship to the University of Arizona at Tucson.

At the university she was a two-time all-American golfer and world amateur champion in 1992. She won seven collegiate honors, including the National Collegiate Athletic Association championship and the college player of the year award. After an excellent amateur career she turned professional in 1993.

The Emerging Champion

Annika's two years of competitive collegiate experience helped to hone her skills, and when she quit the University of Arizona in 1992, her future looked bright. In 1993, she established herself as rookie of the year on the Women Professional Golfers' European Tour. That same year she joined the Ladies Professional Golf Association (LPGA), competed in three events, and earned nearly $50,000.

In 1994, Annika was named Rolex rookie of the year on the basis of three top-ten finishes. She earned numerous victories and awards that year. She competed in nineteen events, with three victories, and earned $366,533, making her the season's leading money winner. She won the Samsung World Championship with a 45-foot chip shot in a sudden-death playoff. In 1995, Annika rose above the competition, winning the Heartland Classic by 10 strokes. She earned nearly $700,000 and recognition as the season's top money-winner. Sweden honored her as its athlete of the year.

In 1996, she won her second world championship and the Core States Betsy King Classic, finishing all four rounds in the 60's. She successfully

Annika Sorenstam in 2006. (Scott Halleran/Getty Images)

LPGA Victories

1995	U.S. Women's Open	2001 (cont.)	BMO Canadian Women's Open
	GHP Heartland Classic		Cisco World Match Play Championship
	Samsung World Championship		Mizuno Classic
1996	U.S. Women's Open	2002	LPGA Takefuji Classic
	Core States Betsy King Classic		Kraft Nabisco Championship
	Samsung World Championship		Electrolux Championship
1997	Chrysler-Plymouth Tournament of Champions		Kellogg Classic
	Hawaiian Ladies Open		Evian Masters
	Longs Drugs Challenge		ShopRite Classic
	J.C. Penney-LPGA Skins Game		Williams Championship
	Michelob Light Classic		Safeway Classic
	Betsy King LPGA Classic		Samsung World Championship
	ITT Tour Championship		Mizuno Classic
2000	Welch's/Circle K Championship		ADT Championship
	Standard Register Ping	2003	The Office Depot
	Nabisco Championship		Kellogg Classic
	The Office Depot		LPGA Championship
2001	Welch's/Circle K Championship		Women's British Open
	Standard Register PING		Safeway Classic
	Kraft Nabisco Championship		Mizuno Classic
	The Office Depot	2004	Safeway International
	Chick-fil-A Championship		The Office Depot

2004 (cont.)	LPGA Corning Classic
	LPGA Championship
	John Q. Hammons Hotel Classic
	Samsung World Championship
	Mizuno Classic
	ADT Championship
2005	MasterCard Classic
	Safeway International
	Kraft Nabisco Championship
	Chick-fil-A Championship
	ShopRite Classic
	LPGA Championship
	John Q. Hammons Hotel Classic
	Samsung World Championship
	Mizuno Classic
	ADT Championship
2006	MasterCard Classic
	U.S. Women's Open
	State Farm Classic
2008	SBS Open at Turtle Bay
	Stanford International Pro-Am
	Michelob ULTRA Open at Kingsmill

defended her title at the U.S. Women's Open, and her career earnings topped the $1 million mark. She also earned a second Vare Trophy for achieving the season's lowest scoring average. Her career earnings passed $2 million after she won the Longs Drugs Challenge and the J. C. Penney-LPGA Skins Game in 1997. That same year she also was victorious in the Chrysler-Plymouth Tournament of Champions, the Michelob Light Classic, and the Hawaiian Ladies Open.

In 1998, Annika continued winning and finished the season as the first golfer in LPGA history to have a scoring average below 70. By 1999, her career wins totaled eighteen. She played twenty-one tour events and earned $837,314. In 2000, she played in twenty LPGA Tour events, and she finished first in five of them. For the year, she earned more than $1 million.

In 2001, Annika began the season in spectacular fashion by winning four consecutive LPGA tournaments. In the Standard Register Ping, in Phoenix,

Arizona, she became the first LPGA player in history to score under 60 in an 18-hole round by shooting a 59, 13-under par, in the second round. She also tied the LPGA record of 28 for nine holes. Annika won the Kraft Nabisco for the first time in 2001. She won this major championship again in 2002 and 2005.

International Victories

1994	Australian Ladies Open
	LPGA Rookie of the Year
1995	Australian Ladies Masters
	Sweden's Athlete of the Year
1997	Hisako Higuchi Kibun Classic
1998, 2002	Compaq Open
2002, 2004	ANZ Ladies Masters
2003	Nichirei Cup
2004	HP Open
2005-06	Scandinavian TPC
2006	Women's World Cup of Golf
2006-07	Dubai Ladies Masters
2008	Suzhou Taihu Ladies Open

Continuing the Story

In 2003, Annika made history by competing on the men's tour at the Bank of America Colonial golf tournament. She became the first woman to participate in a PGA event since Babe Zaharias in 1945. While there was some controversy surrounding this event, Annika was cheered by the fans on the course. Beginning in 2003, she captured the LPGA Championship three years in a row. In 2003, she also won the Women's British Open for the first time. She won her tenth major championship in 2006 with her victory at the U.S. Women's Open. In 2007, a neck injury forced Annika to take time off from golf. During the year, she did not win any LPGA tournaments. In May of 2008, she announced her retirement from professional golf effective at the end of the 2008 season. During her remarkable career, Annika won ninety tournaments around the world, including seventy-two LPGA events.

Summary

Early in life, Annika Sorenstam demonstrated skills in golf, a sport not usually associated with the snow and cold of Scandinavia. When she had gone as far as she could in her native country, she continued to hone her skills at the University of Arizona. After two years at the university, she left campus life and turned professional. In the LPGA, she established

Honors and Awards	
1987-92	Swedish National Team
1993	WPGET Rookie of the Year
1994	LPGA Rookie of the Year
1994, 1996	U.S. Solheim Cup Team
1995-96, 1998, 2001, 2005	Vare Trophy
1995, 1998, 2001-05	Rolex Player of the Year
1997	LPGA Player of the Year
2003	Inducted into World Golf Hall of Fame
	Patty Berg Award
2003-05	Associated Press Female Athlete of the Year
2003, 2005	European Player of the Year

herself as one of the great woman golfers of all time. Over the length of her career, Annika was named player of the year a record ten times and earned more than $22 million on the LPGA tour.

Albert C. Jensen, updated by Jeffry Jensen

Additional Sources

Babineau, Jeff. "Annika Sorenstam." *Golf Magazine* 40, no. 7 (July, 1998): 136-137.

Burnett, Jim. *Tee Times: On the Road with the Ladies Professional Golf Tour.* New York: Scribner, 1997.

Riner, Dax. *Annika Sorenstam.* Minneapolis: Twenty-first Century Books, 2007.

Sorenstam, Annika. *Golf Annika's Way.* New York: Gotham Books, 2004.

Woods, Bob. *Annika Sorenstam.* Chanhassen, Minn.: Child's World, 2007.

Payne Stewart

Born: January 30, 1957
    Springfield, Missouri
Died: October 25, 1999
    Mina, South Dakota
Also known as: William Payne Stewart (full name)

Early Life
William Payne Stewart was born on January 30, 1957, to William Louis Stewart and Bee Payne Stewart in Springfield, Missouri. The youngest of three children, Payne showed more interest than his sisters in following his father's footsteps on the golf course. He received his first set of golf clubs, when he was four, from his father, who was an accomplished amateur golfer.

The Road to Excellence
Payne was an all-around athlete while growing up. He played Little League baseball, basketball, and football. His main interest, however, remained golf. By junior high he had won several local tournaments.

In his freshman year of high school, Payne joined the golf team. Early evidence indicated that golf was Payne's best sport. He had a natural, fluid motion in his swing. By the end of his freshman year, Payne and his father had established a plan. He was going to play golf professionally.

During breaks from school, Payne and his father often played at Hickory Hills Country Club. They also matched Payne's extraordinary golfing ability against other players. At this time, Payne honed his competitive edge. He learned that if you play well, you get paid. If you do not, you go home with nothing.

Payne was offered a golf scholarship to Southern Methodist University (SMU) in Texas. At SMU, he majored in business. During his senior year, Payne won three tournaments. After graduation, he won the Missouri state amateur title.

The Emerging Champion
After graduating from SMU in 1979, Payne played in the PGA Tour Qualifying School, attempting to earn his PGA Tour card, which would allow him to compete with professionals. However, Payne did not make the cut. Realizing that he had to do something to earn money while he waited for his next chance at the school, Payne got a job at a local department store. This type of work was not for him, so Payne took the advice of a friend and joined the eleven-event Asian Golf Tour, playing throughout Southeast Asia, Indonesia, and India. His father and five other men formed a partnership to sponsor Payne on the tour.

Payne Stewart hugging his trophy after winning the 1999 U.S. Open. (AP/Wide World Photos)

161

PGA Tour Victories

1982	Quad Cities Open
1983	Walt Disney World Classic
1987	Hertz Bay Hill Classic
1989	MCI Classic
	PGA Championship
1990	MCI Classic
	Byron Nelson Classic
1991, 1999	U.S. Open
1995	Houston Open
1999	Pebble Beach Pro-Am

International Victories

1981	Indian Open (Asia)
	Indonesian Open (Asia)
1982	Coolangatta-Tweed Head Classic (Australia)
1990	World Cup (Individual)
1991	Heineken Dutch Open (Europe)
1993	Hassan II Trophy (Morocco)

During the tour, Payne sharpened his skills, made lasting friendships, and developed a reputation as a prankster. He also learned that the game was not about perfection, it was about getting the job done.

In 1980, Payne tried for the PGA Tour card a second time but again missed the cut. Undaunted, he continued playing abroad. Finally, in 1981, Payne earned his tour card. Having won the Indian Open and the Indonesian Open, Payne was invited to play in the British Open that same year. He finished last.

Continuing the Story

During the 1980's, the PGA Tour had a qualifying system in which members had to qualify on Monday in order to play each week. Payne did not pass a Monday qualifier until March of 1982. In April of 1982, he won his first PGA tournament at the Magnolia Classic in Mississippi. However, since the match was played at the same time as The Masters in Georgia, this did not count as a win for Payne.

About this time, Payne developed his unique style of dress on the links. He often wore knickers, knee socks, and a tam-o'-shanter while playing. He received a lot of ribbing from his fellow golfers, but positive response from the fans and media. Even his game benefited. "When I put my work

clothes on," he once said, "I get all fired up." It may have been a coincidence, but that year Payne won his first official PGA tournament, at the Quad Cities Open in Illinois, wearing his trademark outfit.

Payne played well over the next several years, finishing second in six PGA tournament events in 1984. In 1986, he earned sixteen top-ten finishes, a PGA Tour record at the time. Although Payne was playing well, he was not winning. In 1984 and 1986, he set records for the most money ever won without winning a tournament. He came back in 1987, winning the Hertz Bay Hill Classic in Orlando, his hometown.

In 1988, Payne continued to play well but still was not winning. On the advice of a good friend, he visited a sports psychologist. The doctor noticed that Payne was having difficulty focusing on anything for too long. Payne was diagnosed with attention deficit disorder. He tried taking prescription drugs, but they did not work for him. Instead, he and his coaches developed a routine to help him focus on the easier, mundane shots.

By 1989, Payne was affectionately known as "the best player never to have won a major." Determined to shake this unofficial title, Payne won the PGA Championship that year—his first major. He then went on to win the U.S. Open at Hazeltine in 1991.

The highlight of Payne's career came in 1999, when he once again won the U.S. Open. Also important to Payne were his five chances to play in the Ryder's Cup, the biannual tournament pitting the best golfers in the United States against those from Europe.

At the request of a longtime friend, Payne became involved in planning golf courses. During a trip to Dallas to visit a new course, the plane Payne was on crashed in Mina, South Dakota, on October 25, 1999.

Honors and Awards

1979	All-American
	Missouri Amateur Champion
1987, 1989, 1991, 1993, 1999	Ryder Cup Team
1988	All-Around category winner Nabisco Statistics
1989	Nabisco Statistics scoring leader
1991-93	Skins Game winner
2001	Inducted into World Golf Hall of Fame

Summary

Payne Stewart was spontaneous, outspoken, charitable, and extremely confident, and he always wore his emotions on his sleeve. He was never afraid to shed a tear of joy, or sadness, in front of others. He was also a devoted son, husband, and father. Payne always considered his ability to play golf a God-given talent and was not ashamed to proclaim his faith in public. His strong family life, along with his faith in God, were what kept him going through the ups and downs of life as a professional golfer.

Maryanne Barsotti

Additional Sources

Arkush, Michael. *I Remember Payne Stewart.* Nashville, Tenn.: Cumberland House, 2000.

Chastain, Bill. *Payne at Pinehurst: The Greatest U.S. Open Ever.* New York: Griffin, 2005.

Guest, Larry. *The Payne Stewart Story.* Kansas, Mo.: Andrews McMeel, 2002.

McNew, Monte. *Golf in the Ozarks.* Charleston, S.C.: Arcadia, 2006.

Stewart, Tracey. *Payne Stewart: The Authorized Biography.* Nashville, Tenn.: Broadman and Holman, 2000.

Curtis Strange

Born: January 30, 1955
    Norfolk, Virginia
Also known as: Curtis Northrup Strange (full
    name); Brutus

Early Life
Curtis Northrup Strange was born on January 30, 1955, in Norfolk, Virginia. His father was a golf professional. Curtis spent part of his boyhood doing chores around the professional shop for his dad. When he was seven, he began to play golf. By eight years of age, he was playing at the White Sands Country Club in Virginia Beach every day. At the age of fourteen, Curtis lost his thirty-nine-year-old father to cancer. This tragedy left him determined to succeed at golf.

Curtis Strange, who, in 1989, became the first golfer in almost forty years to win consecutive U.S. Opens. (Ralph W. Miller Golf Library)

The Road to Excellence
In college at Wake Forest University in Winston-Salem, North Carolina, Curtis was nicknamed "Brutus" by his fraternity brothers. His golf game was formidable. He won the 1973 Southeastern Amateur tournament at the age of eighteen. He was National Collegiate Athletic Association (NCAA) champion and Western Amateur champion in 1974. In the NCAA Championship, at the last hole, he needed to make an eagle 3 on a water-guarded par 5 to win the individual title and carry his team to victory. Curtis used a 1-iron to bring the ball to within 10 feet of the hole and sank the putt. He won the Eastern Amateur in 1975, which his father had won in 1957. Also in 1975, he was North and South Amateur champion. That same year, he was on the Walker Cup team, taking 3½ points of a possible 4. In addition, he was 1974 college player of the year and 1975 and 1976 the Virginia amateur champion. In 1976, he again won the North and South Amateur Championship and decided to turn professional after a short but brilliant amateur career.

During this period of time, he met his wife, Sarah. They were married and later had two sons, Thomas Wright III and David Clark.

The Emerging Champion
In the spring of 1977, Curtis attended golf qualifying school and turned professional. Curtis's first two years as a professional resulted in his lowest rankings and money winnings as a professional golfer. He ranked eighty-seventh and eighty-ninth in 1977 and 1978, respectively. He won useful, although not large, sums of money before breaking into the top sixty. In his third year as a professional, Curtis jumped to twenty-first in the rankings, and in his fourth year, he was up to number three. After that, he became a big money winner and a highly consistent player. He won his first tournament in 1979, the Pensacola Open, with a 62 in the third round. He won the Houston Open and the Westchester Classic the following year when, with $271,888, he was third in winnings and third in stroke average. At the age of twenty-

seven, in 1983, he was destined to become a major-championship winner and a frequent tournament winner.

Curtis did not win a tournament in 1981 or 1982, but topped $200,000 in winnings both years. He lost in a playoff for the 1981 Tournament Players Championship. In 1982, he set a new income high for a nonwinner, with winnings of $263,378, and was third in stroke average. In 1983, Curtis won the Sammy Davis, Jr. Greater Hartford Open. In 1984, he won the LaJet Classic. Curtis had another big year in 1985, winning the Honda Classic, Panasonic-Las Vegas Invitational, and Canadian Open. That year at The Masters, everything was going right. He said, "I had blinders on and I was making a lot of birdies starting Friday morning and continuing on until the very end Sunday." He did not finish with a win, one of the rare occasions on which Curtis did not come through in the "clutch."

Continuing the Story

In 1986, Curtis won the Houston Open, and in 1987, he won the Canadian Open, the Federal Express-St. Jude Classic, and the NEC World Series of Golf. Curtis's strength was his control. He did not make long drives, although he could on occasion, but he could drive straight, especially under pressure.

Major Championship Victories

1988-89	U.S. Open

Other Notable Victories

1974	NCAA Championship
	World Amateur Cup
1975-76	North and South Amateur
1979	Pensacola Open
1980	Manufacturers Hanover Westchester Classic
	Michelob-Houston Open
1983	Sammy Davis, Jr. Greater Hartford Open
1983, 1985, 1987, 1989	Ryder Cup Team
1985	Panasonic-Las Vegas Invitational
1985, 1987	Canadian Open
1986	Houston Open
1988	Memorial Tournament
	Nabisco Championship
	Independent Insurance Agent Open
1993	Greg Norman's Holden Classic

Records and Milestones

PGA Tour leading money-winner (1985, 1987-88)

Set a record on the PGA Tour in 1987, winning $925,941

First player in Tour history to exceed $1 million in official earnings in a single season (1989). He won four times that year and collected $1,147,644

Honors and Awards

1974	College Player of the Year
1980	*Golf Digest* most improved player
1985, 1987	*Golf* magazine Player of the Year
1985, 1987-88	Arnold Palmer Award
	Golf Writers Player of the Year
	Golf Digest Byron Nelson Award
1988	PGA Player of the Year
2000, 2002	U.S. Ryder Cup Team Captain
2007	Inducted into World Golf Hall of Fame

Curtis was ranked fifth, third, and eleventh in driving accuracy on the tour during 1988, 1989, and 1990. He was a good iron player, making many holes from the fairway. He ranked as high as twelfth in greens hit in regulation in 1987. He proved to be a deadly putter. He was among the top twenty in the tour's putting statistics in 1989.

In 1988, Curtis won the Independent Insurance Agent Open, the Memorial Tournament, and the Nabisco Championship at Pebble Beach, his biggest money day. There he birdied the second extra hole to defeat Tom Kite. The victory was worth $360,000 plus the season-long bonus money of $175,000. His most important victory of the year was the U.S. Open. In 1988, he was the obvious choice for player of the year. His victory at the Country Club in Brookline, Massachusetts, was in a playoff over Nick Faldo, 71 to 75. In 1989, he played brilliantly through the final holes at Oak Hill in Rochester, New York, to win again. He became the first since Ben Hogan, in 1950-1951, to win the title in back-to-back years.

In 1990, when Curtis teed off at Medinah, he was attempting something few golfers have had an opportunity to accomplish: winning three consecutive U.S. Open titles. The last man to make the attempt was Ben Hogan in 1952. Curtis's bid for a third consecutive U.S. Open title was not successful, as he shot an opening 73 followed by a second round of 70.

In 1994, he came close again to winning the U.S. Open when he missed the playoff by one stroke.

In 1999, Curtis was selected to captain the 2000 U.S. Ryder Cup team—he was the cocaptain of the team two years later. That year he also had three top twenty-five finishes. In 2000, his best finish was a tie for fifteenth at the MCI Classic. In 2005, he started playing on the Champions Tour. He was inducted into the World Golf Hall of Fame in 2007.

Summary

Curtis Strange won seventeen tournaments on the PGA Tour. He can be counted as one of the all-time greats in golf. He won twelve times on the PGA Tour in six years. He was a three-time winner of the Arnold Palmer Award as leading money winner. In 1989, he became the first player in tour history to exceed the $1 million mark in official earnings in a single season. He won four times that year and collected $1,147,644. From childhood to adulthood, Curtis worked on mastering the skills of the sport, competing and sharing his knowledge with others. His outstanding professional career was highlighted with back-to-back U.S. Open wins.

Judy C. Peel

Additional Sources

Strange, Curtis, and Kenneth Van Kampen. *Win and Win Again: Techniques for Playing Consistently Great Golf.* Chicago: Contemporary Books, 1990.

Wade, Don. *Talking on Tour: The Best Anecdotes from Golf's Master Storyteller.* Lincolnwood, Ill.: McGraw-Hill/Contemporary, 2003.

Yocum, Guy. *My Shot: The Very Best Interviews from Golf Digest Magazine.* New York: Stewart, Tabori & Chang, 2007.

Marlene Streit

Born: March 9, 1934
      Cereal, Alberta, Canada
Also known as: Marlene Stewart Streit (full name)

Early Life

Marlene Stewart Streit was born in Cereal, a small village in central Alberta, Canada. She began to work as a caddy, carrying golf clubs for other golfers, when she was only thirteen years old and became a golfer herself at the early age of fifteen. Her golf instructor was well-known golf professional Gordon McInnis, Sr., and he taught her to play at the Lookout Country Club golf course in Fonthill, Ontario, Canada. Marlene learned quickly; from the beginning, she had the makings of a champion golfer. However, her success came earlier than anyone expected. In 1956, Marlene graduated from Rollins College, a liberal arts school located in Winter Park, a suburb of Orlando, Florida.

The Road to Excellence

Marlene played junior golf in Fonthill before winning her first Canadian Ladies Amateur Golf Championship at the young age of seventeen. She won the Canadian Ladies Amateur Golf Championship eleven times between 1951 and 1973. To everyone's amazement, she broke into the international amateur circuit as a teenager and won the British Ladies Amateur Golf Championship in 1953. The same year she graduated from college, the physically diminutive Marlene won the National Collegiate Athletic Association (NCAA) Women's Championship. She rose to the top of her sport early and remained there.

The Emerging Champion

Although the temptation arose to turn professional, Marlene chose to remain an amateur throughout her entire career. She never became a professional golfer because she grew up at a time when becoming a profes-

sional player was not a common occurrence for female players. Marlene was a member of the Canadian team at the World Amateur Golf Team Championships in 1966, 1970, 1972, and 1984.

Marlene was the first golfer to win the Australian, British, Canadian, and U.S. Women's Amateur Golf Championships. Between 1951 and 2003, she won every significant amateur title available. A remarkable champion, her victories included at least one major national or international title every ten years. She added twenty amateur and four senior Canadian women's titles to her list of winnings. In all, Marlene accumulated twenty-four national titles. Only two other golfers, Mabel Thomson and Ada Mackenzie, who each attained

Marlene Streit chipping from the rough at a 1967 tournament. (AP/Wide World Photos)

five titles, even came close to Marlene's total of career victories.

In 2004, the Golf Association of Ontario honored Marlene for her induction into the World Golf Hall of Fame. Present for the announcement were hall-of-fame members Ben Crenshaw, Hale Irwin, Tony Jacklin, Carol Mann, Lee Trevino, and hall-of-fame global ambassador Gary Player. Marlene was the first Canadian player inducted into the World Golf Hall of Fame.

Amateur Victories

1951-57, 1963, 1968	Canadian Ladies Golf Association Close
1951, 1954-56, 1958-59, 1963, 1968-69, 1972-73	Canadian Ladies Golf Association Open
1953	British Ladies Golf Championship
1956	NCAA Women's Championship
	U.S. Women's Championship
1956, 1974	North and South Women's Championship
1963	Australian Women's Golf Championship
1985, 1987-88, 1993	Canadian Ladies Golf Association Senior Women's
1985, 1994, 2003	U.S. Senior Women's Golf Championship

Continuing the Story

In September of 2003, Marlene shocked the golf world by claiming her third U.S. Senior Women's Amateur Golf Championship, becoming the oldest competitor to win the competition. For more than half a century, she was Canada's best female amateur golfer.

Marlene settled in Unionville, Ontario, just north of Toronto, and played golf at York Downs. Marlene said her success stemmed from simply remaining calm. She was rarely intimidated when outside her native Canada and played well against such American champions as Babe Didrikson Zaharias. She once claimed that she was successful primarily because she simply did not like to lose. In addition, Marlene credited her successful career in golf to the fact that she never attempted to change her swing.

Summary

Marlene Streit won all of the world's most prestigious amateur golfing titles and positioned herself as a true legend in the history of women's golf. She won the Canadian, U.S., British, and Australian amateur championships. In addition, she captured eleven Canadian Ladies Open Championships during her career. A powerful competitor, Marlene was noted for her fierce pride and her will to win. She is perhaps the greatest golfer Canada has ever produced.

M. Casey Diana

Additional Sources

Barclay, James A. *Golf in Canada: A History.* Toronto: McClelland & Stewart, 1992.

Buren, Jodi, and Donna A. Lopiano. *Superwomen: One Hundred Women, One Hundred Sports.* New York: Bulfinch Press, 2004.

O'Neil, Dana Pennett, and Pat Williams. *How to Be Like Women Athletes of Influence: Thirty-one Women at the Top of Their Game and How You Can Get There Too.* Deerfield Beach, Fla.: Health Communications, 2007.

O'Reilly, Jean. *Women and Sports in the United States: A Documentary Reader.* Boston: Northeastern, 2007.

Sanson, Nanette. *Champions of Women's Golf: Celebrating Fifty Years of the LPGA.* Naples, Fla.: Quailmark Books, 2000.

Honors, Awards, and Milestones

1951, 1956	Lou Marsh Trophy
1962	Inducted into Canada's Sports Hall of Fame
1963	First golfer to win Australian, British, Canadian, and U.S. Women's Amateur Golf Championships
1967	Officer of the Order of Canada
1971	Inducted into Canadian Golf Hall of Fame
	Inducted into Royal Canadian Golfing Association Hall of Fame
2000	Inducted into the Ontario Golf Hall of Fame
	Canadian Ladies Golf Association female amateur golfer of the century
2004	Inducted into World Golf Hall of Fame
2006	Member of the Order of Ontario

Louise Suggs

Born: September 7, 1923
     Atlanta, Georgia
Also known as: Mae Louise Suggs (full name);
   Miss Sluggs

Early Life

The daughter of a baseball player and golf course manager, Mae Louise Suggs was born in Atlanta, Georgia, on September 7, 1923, to Johnny and Marguerite Suggs. By the age of ten, Louise was playing golf with her father in Lithia Springs, an Atlanta suburb. They played when the course was closed to the public. During the early 1940's, a

professional career in golf was not an option for women. Furthermore, Louise's parents would not have allowed their unmarried daughter to travel alone to play golf. Thus, Louise worked as a file clerk for Gulf Oil Corporation; the job did not last, however, as her employers agreed that she was probably better at golf than at filing.

The Road to Excellence

When Louise was thirteen, Martha Daniels, hailed as the best woman golfer in Georgia at the time, observed that she was hitting balls with ideal form. Daniels was so impressed with Louise's skill that she took her to the Georgia state women's tournament. Louise won the Georgia State Amateur Championship held in Columbus, Georgia, in 1940, when she was seventeen—about the time that she graduated as high school valedictorian. In 1942, she won this championship again. Thus, at nineteen, she was already the dominant woman golfer in the southern United States.

Louise continued to establish her career and won the Southern Amateur Championship in 1941 and 1947. Three times she won the North and South Women's Amateur Golf Championship: in 1942, 1946, and 1948. In 1946 and 1947, she won both the Western Amateur Championship and the Western Open, a major championship. In 1946, Louise also won the Titleholders Championship, later designated a women's major championship. The next year, she won the United States Women's Amateur Golf Championship. During her final year as an amateur, Louise won the British Ladies Amateur Golf Championship and represented the United States on the 1948 Curtis Cup team, her final win as an amateur.

The Emerging Champion

On July 8, 1948, Louise turned professional and won the Belleair Open competition. In 1949, she added four wins: the

Louise Suggs cleaning her shoes after completing a round at the 1947 Women's Western Amateur golf tournament. (AP/Wide World Photos)

LPGA Tour Victories

1941, 1947	Southern Amateur Championship
1942, 1946, 1948	North and South Women's Amateur Championship
1946, 1954, 1956, 1959	Titleholders Championship
1946-47, 1949, 1953	Women's Western Open
1948	Belleair Open
1949, 1952	U.S. Women's Open
	All-American Open
	Muskegon Invitational
1950	Chicago Weathervane
	New York Weathervane
1951, 1954	Carrollton Georgia Open
1952	Jacksonville Open
	Stockton Open
	All-American Women's Open
	Betty Jameson Open
1952-53	Tampa Open
1953	Phoenix Weathervane
	San Diego Open
	Bakersfield Open
	San Francisco Weathervane
	Philadelphia Weathervane
	144-Hole Weathervane
1953-54	Betsy Rawls Open
1954	Sea Island Open
1954, 1958	Babe Zaharias Open
1955	Los Angeles Open
	Oklahoma City Open
	Eastern Open
	St. Louis Open
1955, 1958, 1960	Triangle Round Robin
1956	Havana Open
	All-American Open
1957	LPGA Championship
	Heart of America Invitational
1958	Gatlinburg Open
	French Lick Open
1959-61	Dallas Civitan Open
1959, 1962	St. Petersburg Open
1960	Youngstown Kitchens Trumball Open
1960-61	San Antonio Civitan
1961	Royal Poinciana Invitational
	Golden Circle of Golf Festival
	Kansas City Open

Jacksonville Open, the Tampa Open, the Stockton Open, the All-American Women's Open, the Betty Jameson Open, and the U.S. Women's Open, a major championship.

In 1953, Louise compiled nine victories, including the Women's Western Open, a major championship. She broke her own LPGA scoring record to win the Tampa Open and won additional tournaments, including the Betsy Rawls Open; the Phoenix Weathervane, in a tie with Patty Berg; the San Diego Open; the Bakersfield Open; the San Francisco Weathervane; the Philadelphia Weathervane; and the 144-Hole Weathervane. She was also the leading money-winner in 1953. Other accomplishments that year included the publication of a book, *Par Golf for Women,* and an award by the LPGA, the Vare Trophy, given for excellence in scoring.

Continuing the Story

In 1954, about halfway through her professional career, she continued to excel. She claimed the Titleholders Championship, a major win, in addition to winning the Sea Island Open, the Betsy Rawls Open, the Carrollton Georgia Open, and the Babe Zaharias Open. In 1955, Louise won the Los Angeles Open, the Oklahoma City Open, the Eastern Open, the St. Louis Open, and the Triangle Round Robin. The next year she was the winner at the Havana Open, the All-American Open, and the major Titleholders Championship.

In 1957, Louise added the prestigious LPGA Championship and the Heart of America Invitational to her list of victories. She served as LPGA president from 1955 to 1957. She compiled four LPGA wins in 1958: the Babe Zaharias Open, the Gatlinburg Open, the Triangle Round Robin, and the French Lick Open. In 1959, she was victorious at the St. Petersburg Open, the Dallas Civitan Open, and, for the fourth time, the Titleholders Championship. In 1960, Louise won four more competitions. In 1961, she became the first woman to defeat male pros when she shot 1 stroke better than Dub Pagan and 2 strokes better than Sam Snead at the Royal Poinciana Invitational. She also won competitions in the Golden Circle of Golf Festival, the Dallas Civitan Open, the

All-American Open; the Muskegon Invitational; and two major championships, the U.S. Women's Open, by a record 14 strokes, and the Western Open. In 1950, Louise, along with twelve other female golfers, helped establish the Ladies Professional Golf Association (LPGA). She also won the Chicago Weathervane and the New York Weathervane Championships. By this time, Louise had proven herself throughout the golf community. Following a win in the Carrollton Georgia Open that year, she won six championships in 1952: the

Kansas City Open, and the San Antonio Civitan that year.

Louise's professional career ended in 1962. She won the St. Petersburg Open and was scheduled to play later in Milwaukee, Wisconsin. When she became ill and was unable to attend the event, she was fined $25 for failing to appear. She felt that this was unfair and, as a matter of principle, retired to Delray Beach, Florida, and Sea Island, Georgia, where she taught golf, conducted clinics, and played in exhibitions.

Louise was bestowed with many honors. In 1966, she was inducted into the Georgia Sports Hall of Fame and was an inaugural inductee into the LPGA Tour Hall of Fame in 1967. In 1979, she became the first female to be inducted into the World Golf Hall of Fame. In 2000, the Louise Suggs Rolex rookie of the year award, given to the best first-year player on the LPGA Tour, was named in her honor. She was also the 2007 recipient of the Bob Jones Award, given by the United States Golf Association to recognize distinguished sportsmanship in golf.

Summary

Not only was Louise Suggs a key figure in the creation and success of the LPGA Tour, but she also

Honors and Awards

1948	Curtis Cup Team
1953	LPGA Tour Vare Trophy
1953, 1960	LPGA Tour money leader
1966	Inducted into Georgia Sports Hall of Fame
1967	Inducted into LPGA Tour Hall of Fame
1979	Inducted into World Golf Hall of Fame
2000	Louise Suggs Rolex Rookie of the Year Award created
2007	Bob Jones Award

was one of its most successful participants. Such feats as winning an LPGA Tour event three consecutive years, all four majors in existence during her career, and the 1949 U.S. Women's Open by 14 strokes—a record not broken until Tiger Woods's 15-stroke win in 2000—helped to assure visibility and respect for women's golf.

Victoria Price

Additional Sources

Nickerson, Elinor. *Golf: A Women's History.* Jefferson, N.C.: McFarland, 1987.

Stevens, Peter F. "Lady Killer." *Golf* 44, no. 11 (November, 2002).

Suggs, Louise. *Par Golf for Women.* New York: Prentice-Hall, 1953.

Lee Trevino

Born: December 1, 1939
      Dallas, Texas
Also known as: Lee Buck Trevino (full name);
      the Merry Mex; Super Mex

Early Life
Lee Buck Trevino was born on December 1, 1939, into a fatherless home on the outskirts of Dallas, Texas. Lee and his two sisters were raised by his mother Juanita and their maternal grandfather Joe Trevino, who worked as a gravedigger. The family lived in a four-room shack, without electricity or plumbing, which was located next to the Glen Lakes Country Club.

When Lee was six years old, he began to look through the fence separating his frame house from the country club to watch the men playing golf. He found an old golf club, cut it down to his size, and played a two-hole course he designed in his front yard.

After completing the seventh grade, Lee quit school and worked as a caddy at Glen Lakes Country Club. At the end of each day, Lee played a few holes. At the age of fifteen, Lee played his first complete 18 holes of golf and shot a 77.

The Road to Excellence
Lee was only seventeen when he lied about his age to join the United States Marine Corps. He served four years with the Marines. While playing on the Third Marine Division golf team, Lee began taking golf seriously.

After Lee was discharged from the Marines in 1961, he worked at Hardy's Driving Ranch and Pitch 'n' Putt course, operated by Hardy Greenwood. Lee needed additional income to survive, so he hustled golfers by offering to play them by using a Dr. Pepper bottle as a club. He wrapped tape around the neck of the Dr. Pepper bottle so it did not slip. Lee hit the golf ball with a baseball swing and putted croquet style. In three years, Lee claimed, he never lost a bet playing golf with a Dr. Pepper bottle.

Martin Lettunick, a millionaire, heard about Lee and convinced him to move to El Paso. Lee arrived at El Paso with fifty dollars in his pocket. Lettunick helped him get a job as assistant professional at Horizon Hills Country Club. Lee's salary was thirty dollars a week. During Lee's off hours at Horizon Hills, he practiced continuously. Most days, he hit a minimum of five hundred balls.

The Emerging Champion
In 1966, Lee earned his Class A card, which enabled him to play in professional golf tournaments. Lee's

Lee Trevino, who rose from humble beginnings to become one of the most celebrated golfers in history. (Ralph W. Miller Golf Library)

172

Major Championship Victories

1968, 1971	U.S. Open
1971-72	British Open
1974, 1984	PGA Championship
1990	U.S. Senior Open

Other Notable Victories

1967	Metropolitan Golf Writers Association Rookie of the Year
1968	Hawaiian Open
1968-71, 1974	World Cup Team
1969, 1971, 1973, 1975, 1979, 1981	Ryder Cup Team
1971-72, 1980	Danny Thomas-Memphis Classic
1971, 1977, 1979	Canadian Open
1972	Greater Hartford Open
1973	Doral-Eastern Open
	Jackie Gleason-Inverarry Classic
1975	Florida Citrus Open
1976, 1978	Colonial National Invitation
1978	Lancome Trophy
1980	Tournament Players Championship
	San Antonio, Texas, Open
1981	MONY Tournament of Champions
1985	Ryder Cup team captain
1990, 1995	Transamerica Senior Golf Championship
1991	Aetna Challenge
1991-93	Vantage of the Dominion
1992	The Tradition
	Las Vegas Senior Classic
1992, 1994	Senior PGA Championship
1993	Nationwide Championship
1993, 2000	Cadillac NFL Golf Classic
1994	Royal Caribbean Classic
	Paine Webber Invitational
	Bell Atlantic Classic
	Bell Southern Senior Classic
1994-95	Northville Long Island Classic
1996	Emerald Coast Classic
	Australian PGA Seniors Championship
1998	Southwestern Bell Dominion
2000	Cadillac NFL Golf Classic

first professional tournament was the 1966 U.S. Open at the Olympic Country Club in San Francisco. He tied for fifty-fourth place and won $600. Lee's wife sent in the registration fee for the 1967 U.S. Open. Golfers must qualify for this tournament by playing 2 rounds of golf. Lee qualified with the lowest score in the United States by shooting a 69 and a 67 for a total of 136. He finished in fifth place in the 1967 U.S. Open, played at Baltusrol Country Club, and won $6,000. Lee won a total of $28,000 that year and was named rookie of the year by the Metropolitan Golf Writers Association.

In 1968, Lee had his first great year on the Professional Golfers' Association (PGA) tour. By U.S. Open time in June, he had pocketed $54,000. Lee won the U.S. Open, played at Oak Hill Country Club in Rochester, New York, and was the first person to shoot all 4 rounds in the 60's. He also tied Jack Nicklaus's U.S. Open record of 5 under par 275. Lee was only the third person to make the U.S. Open his first major tournament win. The win in the 1968 U.S. Open pushed him into golf stardom.

Lee won the 1968 Hawaiian Open, which was worth $25,000 in prize money. In 1968, Lee won a total of $132,127, which placed him sixth on the money list. Several people thought Lee was merely lucky, but he proved them wrong by demonstrating his ability as one of the greatest golfers in history. In 1970, Lee won more prize money than any other professional golfer, with $157,037. That was the only year he led the PGA in money won. He finished second on the money list three times.

Lee was known as "the Merry Mex" or "Super Mex" for his ability to talk and joke on the golf course. Lee relieved stress by telling a joke or making light of a golf shot.

In 1975, Lee was struck by lightning while playing at the Western Open near Chicago. The lightning struck a nearby lake, traveling through the ground to where Lee was leaning on his golf club. Lee almost died from the electrical shock. The shock also caused a problem in Lee's back. In 1976, he had an operation to correct a herniated disk in his back. Lee's back became a constant problem after that time.

Continuing the Story

In 1980, at the age of forty and in spite of his back problem, Lee had a great year. He won three tournaments and $385,814. For the fifth time, he won the Vardon Trophy, the award given for the lowest stroke average per round; his stroke average of 69.73 was the best on the PGA circuit in thirty years. Lee did not miss a cut in twenty-one tournaments and finished in the top five eleven times.

By 1984, Lee had gone three and one-half years without a tour victory. In one of the outstanding sports stories of the year, Lee turned this situation around by winning his second PGA Championship. At the age of forty-four, Lee defeated Gary Player and Lanny Wadkins at Shoal Creek by shooting all 4 rounds in the 60's.

Lee joined the Senior Tour in 1989, and in 1990, he earned both the tour's rookie of the year and player of the year awards. In his first year as a senior, he won the U.S. Senior Open and the Transamerica Senior Golf Championship. By 2007, Lee had accumulated twenty-nine Senior Tour victories, including two victories at the Senior PGA Championship in 1992 and 1994.

Summary

Lee Trevino's humble beginnings had a lasting effect on his entire life. He never forgot that he was a fatherless Mexican American with a seventh-grade education who was raised with too little food and even less money. Lee believed in working hard. Lee has a true love of golf. He is perhaps one of the few senior tour players who would play for the love of the game even if no prize money were available.

Peter W. Shoun

Additional Sources

Kramer, Jon. *Lee Trevino.* Austin, Tex.: Raintree Steck-Vaughn, 1996.

Trevino, Lee, and Sam Blair. *The Snake in the Sandtrap (and Other Misadventures on the Golf Course).* New York: Holt, Rinehart, and Winston, 1985.

_____. *They Call Me Super Mex.* New York: Random House, 1982.

Wade, Don. *Talking on Tour: The Best Anecdotes from Golf's Master Storyteller.* Lincolnwood, Ill.: McGraw-Hill/Contemporary, 2003.

Yocum, Guy. *My Shot: The Very Best Interviews from Golf Digest Magazine.* New York: Stewart, Tabori & Chang, 2007.

Records and Milestones

Twenty-nine wins on the PGA tour

First golfer to win at least $1 million on the Senior Tour

PGA Tour leading money-winner (1970)

Finished second on the earnings list three times

Honors and Awards

Year	Award
1967	*Golf Digest* Rookie of the Year
1970-72, 1974, 1980	PGA Vardon Trophy
1971	Hickok Belt
	Sporting News Man of the Year
	Golf Digest Byron Nelson Award for Tournament Victories
	PGA Player of the Year
	Associated Press Male Athlete of the Year
	Sports Illustrated Sportsman of the Year
	GWAA Player of the Year
1972	GWAA Charlie Bartlett Award
1980	GWAA Ben Hogan Award
1981	Inducted into World Golf Hall of Fame
1985	GWAA Richardson Award
	Ryder Cup captain
1990	Senior PGA Tour Player of the Year
	Senior PGA Tour Rookie of the Year
1990-92	Byron Nelson Award
1990, 1992	Arnold Palmer Award
1990, 1992, 1994	Jack Nicklaus Trophy

Harry Vardon

Born: May 9, 1870
       Grouville, Jersey, Channel Islands
Died: March 20, 1937
       Totteridge, Herefordshire, England

Early Life

Harry Vardon was born May 9, 1870, in Grouville, Jersey, one of the Channel Islands in the English Channel. He was one of seven sons born to a professional gardener. He attended the village school along with his brothers. The Royal Jersey Golf Club lay over the Grouville Common area, and at the age of seven Harry had his introduction to golf as a caddy.

Childhood in the Channel Islands gave Harry limited opportunities to play golf. His brother Tom was influential in continuing Harry's involvement with the game. They made their own clubs from materials that were readily available; blackthorn was popular for the shafts and bent oak roots served as the club heads. The two materials were crudely united with nails and string. Later on, the brothers acquired real heads from broken clubs and attached them to the blackthorn shafts. The grip was smaller than what was common for the times. The grip had no felt or leather, so the boys modified the traditional ten-finger grip by wrapping their thumbs the top of the shaft. Thus, they established a new technique to avoid getting sore hands.

The Road to Excellence

By age twenty, Harry had played only two or three dozen times, usually on public holidays. Following the lead of his brother, who was making money at golf, Harry was appointed professional and greenskeeper at a new course named the Studby Royal Club at Ripon, Yorkshire.

Harry moved to Bury Club, Lancashire, where he played the first professional match of his life against Sandy Herd, who was then at Herdersfield Club. Herd won easily. From Bury Club, Harry became the professional at Ganton. In 1893 at Prestwich, he played his first British Open Championship to no great effect. J. H. Taylor made his first appearance that year and won the next two Opens in 1894 and 1895. Harry finished fifth in his second year at the British Open. In 1895, he led after the first round but finished ninth.

The Emerging Champion

Taylor was the biggest name in golf at the time. In 1896, about a month before the British Open, the Ganton members raised the money for a challenge

Harry Vardon, who was one of the early champions in golf and helped popularize the sport outside of Scotland. (Courtesy of PGA of America)

match between Harry and Taylor. Harry won by 8 and 6 strokes. The two next went to play the British Open. Harry began with an 83 to trail Taylor by 6 strokes. Harry was still behind by 3 with a round to go. The final day, Harry and Taylor finished in a tie. After a thirty-six-hole playoff, Harry had won his first British Open by a 4-stroke margin.

Harry was one of the game's greatest innovators in terms of technique. The grip he used, with forefinger and little finger interlocking and thumbs on top of the shaft, was called the "Vardon Grip" at the time and later the "interlocking grip." Although the grip probably originated with a gifted amateur player named Johnny Laidlay, and was used by Taylor, it was Harry who was imitated.

When Harry came to prominence, the ideal swing was long with a tendency toward flatness. The idea was to hit the ball low. Harry showed that an upright swing with a high-ball trajectory worked well. As his reputation grew, other players began to copy his style. Many commented that he had the most graceful and easy swing that golf had yet seen. On the "take away," he had a full shoulder and hip turn around a straightened right leg, which ended with his back turned toward the hole.

Harry's play was most noted for accuracy. Some said he could not play the same golf course twice because his ball would land in his own divots. This statement was incorrect, however, because Harry seldom took divots, preferring to shave the top of the turf.

By the end of the century, Harry was considered the greatest of the "Great Triumvirate," which also included Taylor and James Braid. He was playing at the peak of his game.

From his first British Open win in 1896, Harry went on to win a record six British Open Championships, in 1896, 1898, 1899, 1903, 1911, and 1914.

Major Championship Victories

1896, 1898-99, 1903, 1911, 1914	British Open
1900	U.S. Open

Other Notable Victories

1911	German Open
1912	British Professional Match Play

He was runner-up in 1900, 1902, and 1912. During a nearly year-long tour of the United States in 1900, he won the U.S. Open as well. Astonishingly, he lost only one exhibition game during the time that he was touring the United States. Challenge and exhibition matches were played by golf professionals of the day, rather than the tournament format that became prevalent in the 1900's.

Continuing the Story

Harry placed second to Herd in the British Open of 1901. Herd used a wound rubber ball for the first time while Harry used the gutta-percha ball, said to be the only one available at the time. During the 1903 British Open win, Harry felt so ill he believed he would not be able to finish. Shortly after the event, he entered a sanatorium, suffering from tuberculosis. Thereafter, he suffered from the disease, and some have traced his decline in putting to that cause. Harry's putting became so poor as a result of his affliction that it was difficult for people to believe that he had been a major golfer. In the 1920's, Gene Sarazen thought Harry was the worst putter he had ever seen. He remarked that Harry did not three putt, he four putt.

Harry may have been as good a putter as anyone, but, because of illness and age, he began to have more and more difficulty with short putts. Even during his early playing days, however, it was noted that putting had seemed to be his weakness. Harry died on March 20, 1937, in Totteridge, Herefordshire, England.

Summary

At the peak of his career from 1896 to 1914, Harry Vardon was one of the dominant players in golf. He was considered the best of the "Great Triumvirate" play-

---

Records and Milestones

Won a record six victories in the British Open

British Open runner-up (1900, 1902, 1912), third (1906, 1913), second (1920)

French Open runner-up (1912, 1914), third (1909-10)

Trophies for low-scoring average on the PGA and European tours were named in his memory

Honors and Awards

1974   Inducted into World Golf Hall of Fame

---

ers. He was also a catalyst for change not only in style and technique but also in popularizing golf. A game that had begun as a strictly Scottish pursuit had gained worldwide popularity, much of which can be attributed to Harry's admirable style and travel throughout the United States.

Judy C. Peel

Additional Sources

Frost, Mark. *The Greatest Game Ever Played: Harry Vardon, Francis Ouimet, and the Birth of Modern Golf.* New York: Hyperion, 2002.

Howell, Audrey. *Harry Vardon: The Revealing Story of a Champion Golfer.* 2d ed. Stroud, Gloucestershire, England: Tempus, 2001.

Vardon, Harry. *Birdies Eternal: A Treasury of Timeless Tales and Tips from Harry Vardon, Golf's Great Champion for the Ages.* Nashville, Tenn.: Towle-House, 2001.

———. *The Complete Golfer.* Rev. ed. Trumbull, Conn.: Golf Digest/Tennis, 1986.

———. *The Gist of Golf.* New York: Doran, 1922.

———. *How to Play Golf.* Philadelphia: G. W. Jacobs, 1916.

Glenna Collett Vare

Born: June 20, 1903
New Haven, Connecticut
Died: February 3, 1989
Gulf Stream, Florida
Also known as: Glenna Collett (birth name)

Early Life

Glenna Collett was born on June 20, 1903, in New Haven, Connecticut. Growing up in the neighboring state of Rhode Island, she spent her earliest years enjoying the competitiveness of all athletics. Although she excelled at swimming and diving, her favorite sport was baseball. In fact, she played baseball so well that she became an important member of her brother's team.

The social attitudes of pre-World War I New England did not include athletics as a recommended endeavor for the daughters of wealthy parents.

Glenna Collett Vare. (Ralph W. Miller Golf Library)

Glenna's natural athletic ability and desire to participate in sports caused her parents to worry about their "tomboy" daughter, so her mother took Glenna to the tennis courts, a socially acceptable game for women at the time. Glenna learned to play tennis well, but when her father took her to the golf course, she was captivated by the game and its challenge. Early success at hitting a golf ball inspired Glenna to study and practice the game at every opportunity.

The Road to Excellence

Glenna played her first round of golf at the age of fourteen. It took several years of play and practice before she would became a competitive force. Even when her skill level had reached its peak, she had to overcome the mental difficulties of performing in pressure situations.

During the 1921 Berthellyn Cup competition in Philadelphia, Glenna was matched against the English golfing star Cecil Leitch. Major golf tournaments during that era used the common match-play scoring system. A match pits one player against another over a scheduled number of holes, usually eighteen. Holes are won by the player scoring fewer strokes than the opponent. In her role of underdog, Glenna decided to match her opponent stroke for stroke rather than attempt more difficult shots to win outright. To her credit, the new strategy carried the match to the final hole, where she sank a 10-foot putt for a one-hole victory.

Glenna had known the competitive pressure of golf but had never been able to handle it until her victory in the Berthellyn Cup. Learning how to win the difficult matches was the last piece of the puzzle. Armed with mental confidence and physical skill, she was poised to challenge the best golfers in the world.

The Emerging Champion

In her nineteenth year, Glenna won the North and South and the Eastern Amateur Championships. Her performance caught the pub-

Major Championship Victories

1922, 1925, 1928-30, 1935   U.S. Women's Amateur Championship

Other Notable Victories

1921	Berthellyn Cup
1922-24, 1927, 1929-30	North and South Amateur Championship
1922-24, 1927, 1932, 1935	Eastern Amateur Championship
1923-24	Canadian Amateur Championship
1925-27	French Amateur Championship
1932, 1934, 1936, 1938, 1948	Curtis Cup Team
1950	Curtis Cup nonplaying captain

lic's attention. An excellent golf swing, combined with the good looks of the all-American girl, made Glenna popular with the sporting world. Her manner and etiquette on or off the golf course were pleasant, gracious, and all business. She enjoyed playing competitive golf and doing it well. Reports state that she once drove the golf ball a distance of 307 yards, proof that she had a sweet golf swing as well as a winning way.

Glenna won fifty-nine out of sixty matches in 1924. The one defeat was administered by Mary Kimball Browne on the nineteenth hole of the semifinals at the Women's National Golf Championship. So many victories by one person should be hailed as a brilliant athletic achievement, and rightly so, but Glenna's single defeat should be noted for the reason that Browne was better known for her tennis play. Browne ranks as the only person in history to reach the final round of competition in both the National Tennis and Golf Championships in the same year.

Glenna devastated the best women golfers in the United States, winning the National Women's Amateur Championship six times and finishing as runner-up on three separate occasions during the period from 1922 to 1935. This accomplishment has no equal in amateur golf. However, even her eloquent swing and admirable distance were not enough to conquer the world of golf.

Glenna's nemesis proved to be the celebrated English golfer Joyce Wethered, later to become the Lady Heathcoat-Armory. In the summer of 1925, she and Glenna matched scores for the first time at the British Women's

Championship. Although Glenna played well enough to beat most opponents, Wethered played fifteen of the holes in an average of 4 shots, a rare standard for the time. A second match four years later at St. Andrews, Scotland, has been reported by witnesses to be the best women's match ever played. Glenna played the first nine holes of the morning round in 34 shots, magnificent for the time. She seemed to be an easy winner after moving to a lead of five holes, but Wethered answered with a blistering 73 strokes over the next eighteen holes. By the time the players reached the seventeenth hole of the afternoon round, Wethered was ready to close out Glenna. Gracious in defeat, Glenna acknowledged the other's brilliant play. These worthy opponents met once more in the first Curtis Cup Match of 1932. Again, the English golfer prevailed in repelling the American's challenge.

Continuing the Story

Considered the greatest American woman golfer of the 1920's and 1930's, Glenna is given credit for changing country club tradition. She proved women capable of playing a quality game of golf when she became the first to break 80 strokes, with a score of 79 shots, in qualifying for the 1924 U.S. Women's Amateur Championship.

In 1931, Glenna became the wife of Edwin H. Vare, Jr., of Philadelphia. By 1935, Glenna, the mother of two children, was back on the competitive circuit. That year at Interlachen Country Club in Minnesota, Glenna won her sixth U.S. Women's Amateur Championship. Her opponent and runner-up was the young, but soon to be famous, Patty Berg.

Curtis Cup competition did not become a presti-

Milestones

LPGA prize for low-scoring average named after her (Vare Trophy)

British Open Amateur Championship runner-up (1929-30)

Honors and Awards

1965	Bob Jones Award
1975	Inducted into World Golf Hall of Fame
1981	Inducted into Sudafed International Women's Sports Hall of Fame

gious event until 1932. The biannual tournament, between the best amateurs of the United Kingdom and the United States, consists of single matches and foursomes played over a two-day period. Glenna had the honor of playing or serving as team captain on six separate occasions. While Glenna was a participant in the tournament, the American team won all but the 1936 competition, which finished in a tie.

As the years passed, there were fewer competitive days but more work days. Glenna did not play as much, but she showed her giving personality by working to develop the game. As a member of the United States Golf Association (USGA), she served on various committees for fifty years, all for the purpose of advancing the quality of women's golf. To crown her achievements and sportsmanship in the game, the USGA presented Glenna with the Bob Jones Award in 1965.

The Vare Trophy, named in her honor, is awarded once a year to the woman professional golfer averaging the lowest strokes-per-round figure. Because Glenna is credited with opening golf to women, recognition by the professional tour was most appropriate. She died in Gulf Stream, Florida, on February 3, 1989.

Summary

Glenna Collett Vare always remained close to her roots. She kept her membership current at the Point Judith Country Club in Narragansett, Rhode Island, throughout her playing career. The club championship was a scheduled event on her calendar for sixty-two consecutive years.

Golf became a universal sport for women when Glenna first strolled down the fairway. Her quality play and etiquette forced skeptical male players to accept women as capable golfers. An amateur who earned international admiration, Glenna had many golf authorities labeling her as the "female Bobby Jones" of golf.

Thomas S. Cross

Additional Sources

Layden, Joseph. *Women in Sports: The Complete Book on the World's Greatest Female Athletes.* Los Angeles: General, 1997.

McCord, Robert. *The Golf Book of Days: Fascinating Facts and Stories for Every Day of the Year.* New York: Citadel Press, 2002.

Woolum, Janet. *Outstanding Women Athletes: Who They Are and How They Influenced Sports in America.* Phoenix, Ariz.: Oryx Press, 1998.

Tom Watson

Born: September 4, 1949
    Kansas City, Missouri
Also known as: Thomas Sturges Watson (full name)

Early Life

Thomas Sturges Watson was born on September 4, 1949, in Kansas City, Missouri. His father, an insurance executive, was an avid amateur golfer, and Tom became a caddy for his father at the Kansas City Country Club at the age of six.

Tom displayed both talent and enthusiasm for golf, and by his teen years had won several amateur tournaments. He came under the influence of Stan Thirsk, the professional at the Kansas City club, who taught him the basic swing Tom used throughout his career.

Tom Watson, who was the PGA player of the year six times. (Ralph W. Miller Golf Library)

The pattern of early interest and talent is standard among topflight golfers, but in one aspect Tom's development was unusual. He attended Stanford University and graduated with a degree in psychology in 1971. His university career was not a sideline to his pursuit of athletic excellence; quite the contrary, Tom manifested high intelligence as well as physical skill. In golf, he became known as a thinking person's player.

The Road to Excellence

Because of his talent, intelligence, and keen desire to win, Tom soon attracted attention after he turned professional in 1972. He put in countless hours of practice and became known for his extraordinary seriousness about his game.

In 1973, he seemed destined for early triumph. Playing in the U.S. Open at Winged Foot, in Mamaroneck, New York, Tom led the tournament for three rounds. He collapsed in the final round with a disastrous 79 and won no tournaments during the entire year.

At this point, Tom came into contact with Byron Nelson, an outstanding player of the 1930's and 1940's, who is regarded as one of the foremost golfers of all time. Nelson advised Tom about technical faults in his swing. Principally, Tom was failing to shift his weight properly from right-to-left during the downswing. His quick swing tempted him to avoid the necessary weight shift.

Nelson also gave Tom advice about the psychological side of golf. He urged him not to despair over his collapse during the 1973 U.S. Open. Such things happen to nearly every golfer, but the true test of a champion is how he or she copes with them.

The Emerging Champion

Tom showed he had taken Nelson's lessons to heart. He made the necessary changes in his swing and established him-

Major Championship Victories

1975, 1977, 1980, 1982-83	British Open
1977, 1981	The Masters
1982	U.S. Open

Other Notable Victories

1974, 1977, 1984	Western Open
1975, 1978-80	Byron Nelson Golf Classic
1977	Wickes-Andy Williams San Diego Open
1977-78	Bing Crosby National Pro-Am
1977, 1981, 1983, 1989	Ryder Cup Team
1979, 1982	Sea Pines Heritage Classic
1979, 1996	Memorial Tournament
	Tournament of Champions
1980	Andy Williams-San Diego Open
1980, 1982	Glen Campbell-Los Angeles Open
1980, 1984	MONY Tournament of Champions
1981	Atlanta Classic
1987	Nabisco Championship of Golf
1992	Hong Kong Open
1997	Dunlop Phoenix (Japan)
1998	MasterCard Colonial
1999	Bank One Championship
2000	IR Senior Tour Championship
2001	Senior PGA Championship
2002	Senior Tour Championship at Gaillardia
2003	JELD-WEN Tradition
2003, 2005, 2007	Senior British Open
2005	Charles Schwab Cup Championship
2007	Outback Steakhouse Pro-Am

Tom could not equal Nicklaus's last 2 rounds. He scored a 70 and 67, however, and thus lost only one stroke of his lead, even after Nicklaus's surge. Tom had conclusively shown that he could withstand pressure.

Tom repeated his triumph over Nicklaus at the 1977 British Open. The two were paired for the last 2 rounds. Nicklaus shot a 65, only to be matched by Watson. Not to be outdone, Nicklaus returned the next day to shoot a 66. Watson responded with a 65, winning the tournament by a stroke. During the 1970's and early 1980's, Tom became the tour's leading money-winner, supplanting Nicklaus, and won two Masters and five British Opens.

Continuing the Story

One essential for a great golfer had eluded Tom: victory in the U.S. Open, the most important American tournament. Every great American player except Sam Snead had won this event. Tom's turn came in 1982. In that year, the U.S. Open was played at the difficult Pebble Beach course in California, a site Tom knew well. At the end of 3 rounds, Tom seemed in a good position to win the event. Once more, the great Nicklaus proved to be the ma-

self as one of the outstanding golfers of the 1970's. In 1977, he won both the British Open and The Masters, two of the four tournaments that constitute golf's major championships.

Even more significant than Tom's victories were the circumstances under which he achieved them. In both events, he was locked in rivalry with Jack Nicklaus, generally considered one of the top two or three golfers of all time. In the 1977 Masters, Tom held a 3-stroke lead over Nicklaus after the first thirty-six holes of play. Nicklaus proceeded to shoot the next 2 rounds in 70 and 66. The latter score was astonishingly low, because in major championships, the courses are exceptionally difficult and subpar scores are rare.

Records and Milestones

Won thirty-four times on the PGA Tour

PGA Tour money leader five times (1977-80, 1984)

Biggest year was 1980, when he won six times on the tour in addition to winning the British Open, and won a record $530,808 First player to break the $500,000 mark in earnings

Honors and Awards

1974	*Golf Digest* most improved player
1977-79	PGA Vardon Trophy
1977-80	GWAA Player of the Year
1977-80, 1982, 1984	PGA Player of the Year
1977-81, 1984	*Golf Digest* Byron Nelson Award for tournament victories
1978-79	Seagram's Seven Crowns of Sports Award
1987	Bob Jones Award
1988	Inducted into World Golf Hall of Fame
1991	GWAA Richardson Award
1992	Old Tom Morris Award
1993	Ryder Cup captain
2001	Inducted into Bay Area Sports Hall of Fame

jor obstacle. Nicklaus had a characteristically excellent final round. Finishing before Tom, Nicklaus watched from the clubhouse to see whether Tom could hold on to his lead. Once more, Tom proved equal to the pressure. At the seventeenth hole, he sank a long second shot to give him a birdie. This shot proved enough, and he won the U.S. Open by two strokes.

During the early 1980's, Tom seemed established as the foremost golfer in the world. Not only had he won a number of major titles, he had also bested Nicklaus in several head-to-head confrontations. Although he by no means always defeated Nicklaus, he seemed to hold the edge in their rivalry.

However, Tom's play during the late 1980's did not equal the supreme achievements of his struggles with Nicklaus. Although Tom continued to do well throughout the 1980's, he was not able to establish a long-standing dominance over the game in the style of Nicklaus. Nevertheless, he remained a threat in any tournament he entered.

Tom had limited success on the PGA Tour during the early 1990's. He won the Memorial Tournament in 1996 and the MasterCard Colonial in 1998. In 1999, Tom joined the Senior Tour. Playing in only two official events in his first year, he won one and finished in the top twenty-five in the second. Tom also played in thirteen PGA tournaments.

In 2000, Tom had greater success in both PGA and PGA Senior Tour tournaments. He shot a final round 66 to win the IR Senior Tour Championship. He had two second-place finishes and lost two play-offs for second place. On the PGA Tour, Tom's best finish was a tie for ninth at the PGA Championship. In 2001, Tom finished in a tie for eighth place at the MasterCard Championship.

In 2002, Tom won the PGA Senior Championship. He was victorious in both the 2003 and 2005 Senior British Open. In 2007, Tom won the Outback Pro-Am, the Senior British Open, and the Legends of Golf, and finished in the top ten in eight other tournaments. The following year, he defended his Outback Pro-Am title, finishing nine strokes under par.

In early 2003, Bruce Edwards, Tom's long-time caddy, announced that he had been diagnosed with Lou Gehrig's disease. That year, Edwards continued to caddy for Tom, and both men devoted a great deal of time to fundraisers to help find a cure to the debilitating and fatal disorder. Tom received a special exemption to the U.S. Open that year, and his outstanding play in the early rounds, assisted by an ailing Edwards, was a thrilling and emotional event. The disease prevented Edwards from traveling to Britain, where Tom won the first of his three Senior British Opens. At the end of the season, Watson announced that he was donating his million dollar season bonus to medical research. In April, 2004, Edwards became the only caddy to win the prestigious Ben Hogan Award, but he was too ill to attend the ceremony, and died the next day.

Tom designed six golf courses, including one in Ireland and one in Japan. Although the days when he battled weekly with Nicklaus for the title of top player were long gone, he remained one of the most popular players in golf as the twenty-first century unfolded.

Summary

Tom Watson showed unusual talent and enthusiasm for golf from his early youth. His ability was combined with high intelligence and the determination to devote unlimited time toward perfecting his game. In his early years as a professional, he became a protégé of Byron Nelson, who advised him on his swing. Tom became the golfer of the 1970's, doing so in dramatic fashion. He defeated Jack Nicklaus by close scores in several major championships.

Bill Delaney, updated by Michael Polley

Additional Sources

Corcoran, Mike. *Duel in the Sun: Tom Watson and Jack Nicklaus in the Battle of Turnberry.* Lincoln: University of Nebraska Press, 2005.

Feinstein, John. *Caddy for Life: The Bruce Edwards Story.* Boston: Little, Brown, 2004.

Golf Magazine's Encyclopedia of Golf: The Complete Reference. New York: HarperCollins, 1993.

"Not So Elementary, Watson." *Golf Magazine* 49, no. 3 (March, 2007): 131.

Spearman, Mitchell. "Big Play." *Sports Illustrated* 107, no. 5 (August 6, 2007): G14.

Watson, Tom, and Nick Seitz. *Tom Watson's Getting Back to Basics.* New York: Pocket Books, 1992.

_____. *Tom Watson's Strategic Golf.* Turnbull, Conn.: Golf Digest, 1993.

Karrie Webb

Born: December 21, 1974
Ayr, Queensland, Australia
Also known as: Karrie Anne Webb (full name)

Early Life

Karrie Anne Webb was born on December 21, 1974, in Ayr, Queensland, Australia, to Robert and Evelyn Webb, and was the oldest of three children. Karrie's parents and maternal grandparents were golfers, and at the age of four, Karrie was on the course playing with them. On her eighth birthday, Karrie received her first pair of real golf clubs and started taking lessons with her neighbor Kelvin Haller soon thereafter. Even before reaching adolescence, Karrie had decided that she wanted to become a professional golfer. She worked on her swing, played in amateur golf tournaments, and soon became one of the best golfers in her area.

The Road to Excellence

Karrie fell in love with golf at a young age. Haller, who taught himself how to play the game and worked at the local golf course, started giving Karrie casual lessons of golf. Soon, golf became a serious activity for Karrie. By the age of twelve, she knew she wanted to be a professional golfer, and by her teens, she was competing in amateur tournaments. She quickly became one of the best golfers in her area; from 1992 to 1994, Karrie represented Australia in amateur international competitions. In her last year as an amateur, Karrie won the Australian Strokeplay Championship, one of the most prestigious amateur events on the international circuit. In October of 1994, two months before her twentieth birthday, Karrie turned professional and was on her way to becoming one of the greatest women's golfers ever to play the game. She spent a year playing golf in Europe and on the Future's Tour in the United States, where she gained valuable experience. This journey helped her progress to the highest level of professional women's golf.

The Emerging Champion

Despite her age, Karrie started her professional career strongly. In 1995, only a couple months after turning professional, Karrie became the youngest winner of the Weetabix Women's British Open. That same year, she qualified for the Ladies Professional Golf Association (LPGA) Tour on her first attempt, despite having a broken bone in her wrist.

The next year, despite some personal problems, Karrie surprised the golf world yet again. She won the Health South Inaugural, which was only her second tournament with the LPGA, and went on to win three more titles that year. Karrie's success was growing quickly. Not only had she become the first female player ever to win more than $1 million in a season, but also she was the first rookie, male or female, to win that amount of money. Karrie had

Karrie Webb teeing off at the 2000 U.S. Women's Open. (Tannen Maury/AFP/Getty Images)

Major Championships

1999	Du Maurier Classic
2000-01	U.S. Women's Open
2000, 2006	Kraft Nabisco
2001	LPGA Championship
2002	Women's British Open

Other LPGA Victories

1995, 1997	Weetabix British Open Championship (not major at the time)
1996	HealthSouth Classic
	Sprint Championship
	ITT LPGA Tour Championship
1996-97	Safeco Classic
1997-98	MBNA America Classic
1998-2000	Australian Masters
1999	Standard Register Ping
	Mercury Championship
1999-2000	Office Depot Invitational
1999, 2002	Wegmans LPGA
2000	LPGA Takefuji Classic
	Nabisco Championship
	Oldsmobile Classic
	AFLAC Tournament of Champions
2001	ADT Championship
2003	John Q. Hammons Hotel Classic
2004	Kellog-Keebler Classic
2006	Kraft Nabisco Championship
	Michelob Ultra Open at Kingsmill
	Evian Masters
	Longs Drugs Challenge
	Mizuno Classic

placed herself among the top golfers in the world, and she had only been competing at that level for one year. A rivalry between Karrie and Annika Sorenstam, often referred to as the best women's golf player in the history of the game, had developed; this rivalry established Karrie as one of the best in the sport.

Continuing the Story

Karrie was playing better than ever. In 1996, along with her major achievements on the course, Karrie received the ESPY award for female golfer of the year. The success did not stop there, and in 1999, Karrie won her first major championship at the Du Maurier Classic. She was also awarded her first LPGA Tour player of the year award. In the following years, Karrie continued to win major championships, including the U.S. Women's Open, two years in a row, and consecutive Vare Trophies and player of the year titles. In 2000, Karrie had already

earned enough points to qualify for the LPGA Tour Hall of Fame. However, she could not be inducted because she did not meet the ten-year membership requirement.

In 2001, Karrie reached a milestone in her career. She won the LPGA Championship to become the youngest winner of the LPGA career Grand Slam. Furthermore, Karrie was victorious at the 2002 Women's British Open, which meant that she had completed a super career Grand Slam. She won every available major championship in women's golf. In 2005, Karrie finally become a member of the World Golf Hall of Fame. At the age of thirty, she was the youngest golfer to be inducted at the time. Her talent, strong work ethic, and her childhood aspirations enabled her to reach her amazing heights of achievement at such a young age.

Summary

From her introduction to golf to her induction into the LPGA Tour Hall of Fame, Karrie Webb kept her love for the game and her desire to be the best. The basis for Karrie's success was her close relationship with her coach and family and her motivation to continually improve. She is considered one of the best golfers in the history of the game, comparable to Annika Sorenstam and Tiger Woods, and debatably one of the greatest female athletes in the world.

Deborah Stroman

Additional Sources

Happell, Charles. *Karrie Webb*. Melbourne: Legend Books, 2002.

Stringham, Joan, and Mary Keller. *Famous Female Sports Stars*. Scottsdale, Ariz.: Remedia, 2001.

Tresidder, Phil. *Karrie Webb: The Making of Golf's Tigress*. Sydney: Pan Macmillan Australia, 2000.

Honors and Awards

1995	Ladies European Tour Rookie of the Year
1996	LPGA Rookie of the Year
	ESPY Female Golfer of the Year
1997, 1999-2000	Vare Trophy
1999-2000	LPGA Tour Player of the Year
2000	Golf Writers Association of America Female Player of the Year
2005	Inducted into World Golf Hall of Fame

Kathy Whitworth

Born: September 27, 1939
      Monahans, Texas
Also known as: Kathrynne Ann Whitworth

Early Life

Kathrynne Ann Whitworth was born on September 27, 1939, in Monahans, Texas. Her family did not stay long in Texas, but moved to Jal, New Mexico, where her father became the proprietor of a hardware store. Kathy was an overweight teenager. Nevertheless, sports came naturally to her. When she was fifteen, her tennis partners introduced her to golf. Golf proved to be the one sport that helped her to lose weight.

Kathy Whitworth. (Ralph W. Miller Golf Library)

The Road to Excellence

At the Jal Country Club, Kathy studied with golf teacher Harry Loudermilk until he taught her all he knew. When Kathy was ready for more advanced teaching, Loudermilk sent her to Harvey Penick in Austin, Texas. Kathy's supportive mother drove Kathy faithfully the four hundred miles to Austin at regular intervals until Kathy graduated from high school.

By the time Kathy enrolled in a junior college in Odessa, Texas, she had lost 50 pounds. She was still sensitive about her weight, costing her the self-confidence necessary to win at golf. Consequently, when she withdrew from college to turn professional, she failed miserably. She then took a year off from professional competition to lose weight and practice her game.

Back on the tour in 1959, Kathy kept losing during her first three months. Again she thought about quitting. However, her family supported her. They encouraged her, gave moral support, and arranged for financial backing because she was not yet earning any winnings. Kathy continued on the tour, in spite of a discouraging start. It proved to be a good thing that she did.

The Emerging Champion

By the end of Kathy's first season on tour, she had recorded a scoring average of 80.30 strokes per round, and she had earned some winnings, although only $1,217. It took another two years before she was good enough to pay her own bills, and a total of four years on tour before she made a name for herself.

In 1962, Kathy at last won her first two events and came in second in eight others; for this she was named most improved professional of the year. In 1963, Kathy won eight tournaments and netted $27,000 dollars in winnings. She was thrilled.

The next year, she won $40,000. By 1965 and 1966, she ranked number one among women golf professionals in terms of highest cash winnings and lowest scoring average. She averaged 72.61 and 72.81 strokes per round in the Ladies Professional Golf Association (LPGA). As a result, during both years, the Associated Press voted her female athlete of the year.

Kathy Whitworth had made it, but she had a remaining goal: to win the U.S. Women's Open, the one championship title she coveted. Many experts said that Kathy was the best under pressure of anyone who ever played on the tour. Whenever she had the chance to play for the U.S. Open title, however, she became tense and made too many mistakes.

When she lost the Open in 1972, she decided to change her swing to a more traditional motion. This cost her. Then she called on her old golf teacher Harvey Penick, whose instruction pulled her out of her slump. That season, Kathy played superb golf and won $85,000. She continued winning for a career total of more than eighty-eight tournaments.

Continuing the Story

Kathy was always fascinated by golf because she felt it impossible to master. She certainly mastered many of its shots, however. Although she was primarily recognized as a long-ball hitter, her strength was the putt. She never seemed to make mistakes on the green or to have to three-putt. She sank her ball every time. On the fairways, she was so focused

Major Championship Victories

1965-66	Titleholders Championship
1967	Western Open
	Colgate Dinah Shore
1967, 1971, 1975	LPGA Championship

Other Notable Victories

1963	Carvel Open
1965	Lady Carling Midwest Open
1966	Sutton Lady Carling
1966, 1968	Baltimore Lady Carling
1967	Columbus Lady Carling
	Los Angeles Open
1968-70, 1974	Orange Blossom Classic
1969	Atlanta Lady Carling
	Wendell West Open
1971	Lady Carling
1976	Bent Tree Classic
1977	American Defender Classic
1981	Kemper Open

on scoring that she never cared about style, or relating to onlookers. She no longer worried about her appearance, and she turned out to be a trim, 5-foot 9-inch golfer, weighing 145 pounds.

Kathy served as president of the LPGA for many years. She worked to persuade major companies to sponsor the organization's tournaments and to enhance its prizes. Later, as a role model for younger golfers, she became a golf teacher, living in Richardson, Texas.

After 1985, Kathy was no longer able to finish in the top ten. Much of her $1.7 million in winnings was lost when she became the victim of an investment scam. She still had her wealth of knowledge, however, and students who idolized her for her concentration, consistency, and coolness under pressure.

Kathy continued to appear in selected tournaments throughout the 1990's and early 2000's. She competed in the Sprint Senior Challenge from 1991 to 1995 and again in 1997. In each event, she finished in the top five, including two second-place finishes. She was also selected as the team captain in the inaugural Solheim Cup Tournament in 1990 and in 1992. She retired in 2005.

Records and Milestones

Leading money-winner eight times (1965-68, 1970-73)
Recorded lowest scoring average seven times (1965-67, 1969-72)
First player to cross the $1 million barrier in career earnings (1981)
Most career tournament victories among all golfers, men and women, 88 (2001)

Honors and Awards

1960, 1962	*Golf Digest* Most Improved Player
1965-66	Associated Press Female Athlete of the Year
1965-67, 1969-72	Vare Trophy
1965-68, 1971-73	*Golf Digest* Mickey Wright Award for Tournament Victories
1966-69, 1971-73	LPGA Player of the Year
	Rolex Player of the Year
1968-77	*Golf* magazine Golfer of the Decade
1972-73	GWAA Player of the Year
1975	Inducted into LPGA Tour Hall of Fame
1982	Inducted into World Golf Hall of Fame
1984	Metropolitan Golfwriters and Golfcasters Golf Tee Award
	Inducted into Sudafed International Women's Sports Hall of Fame
1986	GWAA Richardson Award
	William and Mousie Powell Award
1992	Solheim Cup team captain

Summary

Kathy Whitworth overcame her weight problem to become the leading money-winner of the women's professional golf tour, winning nearly every major LPGA title. She was chosen as the Associated Press female athlete of the year twice and the LPGA's player of the year seven times. For her lowest scoring average, she earned the Vare Trophy seven times. Her eighty-eight tournament titles are more than any other golfer, male or female, in history.

Nan White

Additional Sources

Golf Magazine's Encyclopedia of Golf: The Complete Reference. New York: HarperCollins, 1993.

Hudson, David L. *Women in Golf: The Players, the History, and the Future of the Sport.* Westport, Conn.: Praeger Publishers, 2007.

Whitworth, Kathy. *Kathy Whitworth's Little Book of Golf Wisdom: A Lifetime of Lessons from Golf's Winningest Pro.* New York: Skyhorse, 2007.

Whitworth, Kathy, and Rhonda Glenn. *Golf for Women.* New York: St. Martin's Press, 1992.

Michelle Wie

Born: October 11, 1989
     Honolulu, Hawaii
Also known as: Michelle Sung Wie (full name);
   Wie Seong-mi (Korean name)

Early Life
Michelle Sung Wie was born on October 11, 1989, in Honolulu, Hawaii. Her father, Byung-Wook "B. J.," and her mother, Hyun-Kyong "Bo" Wie, were first-generation South Korean immigrants to the United States. When Michelle was only four years old, her parents introduced her to golf; she immediately took to the game. Her father became her first coach and caddy.

In 2000, at the age of ten, Michelle first gained attention as an athlete when she became the youngest golfer to qualify for the United States Golf Association (USGA) Women's Amateur Public Links Championship. Winning the 2000 Honolulu Mayor's Cup highlighted Michelle's sudden appearance as a preteen golf star.

The Road to Excellence
In 2001, at eleven years old, Michelle confirmed her emerging reputation as a golf prodigy. After winning the Hawaii State Junior Golf Association's Tournament of Champions, she became the youngest player to win the Jenny K. Wilson Invitational, Hawaii's most prestigious women's amateur tournament. She also was the youngest ever to win the Hawaii State Women's Stroke Play Championship.

A year later, in 2002, Michelle defended her Junior Golf Association title and achieved a stunning 13-stroke victory in the Hawaii State Open Women's Division. She became the youngest player to participate in an LPGA tournament, the Takefuji Classics, but missed the cut by 3 strokes.

At thirteen, Michelle experienced an exceptionally successful year that brought her U.S. media attention. At that time, she became the youngest player to enter an LPGA major tournament, the Kraft Nabisco Championship. She tied for ninth place with a par score of 288 and a superb third round of 6-below par. Next, Michelle scored her biggest triumph as an amateur, winning the USGA

Women's Amateur Public Links Championship on June 22, 2003. At the U.S. Women's Open, she tied for thirty-ninth place.

The Emerging Champion
By 2004, Michelle was widely known beyond her native Hawaii. At fourteen, she attracted fellow young teens to the game of golf, which, in turn, gained a new audience. That year, Michelle was the youngest player to participate in the Curtis Cup. Her 2-2 record helped the U.S. team to achieve victory.

Michelle also dared to compete against adult male golfers. She became the first woman to qualify for a PGA tournament, the Sony Open in Hawaii. She missed the cut by just 1 stroke and caused a me-

Michelle Wie at the 2006 Evian Masters. (Dean Mouhtaropoulos/Getty Images)

Milestones

Year	Age	Achievement
2000	10	Youngest golfer to qualify for USGA championship
2001	11	Youngest golfer to win Jenny K. Wilson Invitational
		Youngest golfer to win Hawaii State Women's Stroke Play Championship
2002	12	Youngest golfer to participate in a major LPGA tournament
2003	13	Won USGA Women's Amateur Public Links Championship
2004	14	Youngest female player in a PGA Tour event
		Laureus Newcomer of the Year Award
2005	15	Turned professional
		Signs multimillion-dollar sponsorship deals
2006	16	Made cut in four LPGA tournaments
		First female medalist in local qualifier for Men's U.S. Open

dia stir. Her fourth place at the Kraft Nabisco Championship and her tie for eleventh at the U.S. Women's Open put her among the top twenty in two LPGA majors.

In 2005, at the Sony Open, Michelle played against men again. As Michelle grew to 6 feet 1 inch, her swing gave her drives sufficient power. However, she missed the cut by 7 strokes. Michelle competed in all four LPGA majors and made the cut in each. She missed winning the McDonald's LPGA Championship by only 3 strokes, placing second.

Michelle turned professional on October 5, 2005, six days before her sixteenth birthday. She received sponsorships with Nike and Sony that were reportedly worth an annual amount of $10 million. However, that October, her first tournament as a professional ended on a sour note when she was disqualified from the Samsung World Championship. Allowed to move the ball from an unplayable position against a penalty, Michelle's new placement was a few inches closer to the hole than the old lie, violating golf's Rule 20-7. In her second professional tournament, she missed the cut by 1 stroke.

Continuing the Story

In 2006, Michelle had a stellar year. She played and made the cut in all four LPGA major tournaments. She tied for third place at the Kraft Nabisco, tied for fifth at the LPGA Championship, tied for third at the U.S. Women's Open, and tied for twenty-sixth at the Women's British Open. Against men,

Michelle did not play well. Her best result was a tie for thirty-fifth place at the SK Telecom Open in South Korea.

In 2007, Michelle had her worst season to date. In January, she missed the cut at the men's Sony Open in Hawaii. Then, while running, she fell and hurt her right wrist. A month later, she fractured her left wrist. After too brief a recuperation, Michelle competed in May in the Ginn Tribute Hosted by Annika. Trailing badly, Michelle hurt her wrist again at the sixteenth hole and withdrew from the tournament. While her playing partner Janice Moodie confirmed Michelle's injury, some alleged Michelle's withdrawal was a strategic move to avoid the Rule of 88. If a player scores as high as 88 in a round, she is banned from all of that year's LPGA tournaments.

Next, Michelle finished a disappointing eighty-fourth at the LPGA Championship. Then, for the first time, she missed the cut at an LPGA major, the Women's British Open. While earning $19 million in sponsorships, Michelle won only $23,024 in prize money in 2007.

In 2008, Michelle launched her comeback. A Stanford freshman, she played again, but was humbled by her bad experience. In May, she placed sixth at the Ladies German Open. Michelle qualified for the U.S. Women's Open with a second-place showing at Rockville, Maryland, on June 9. At the U.S. Women's Open, she shot 5 over par at the ninth hole in the first round. With a score of 156 after the second round, Michelle was 10 over par and had 6 strokes too many to make the cut. However, her resilience and unvanquished optimism were promising signs for the future.

In August, 2008, Michelle finished tied for twelfth place at the CN Canadian Women's Open, which was not enough to qualify her for the 2009 LPGA Tour on exemptions. She took the long-delayed step to earn a starting position the regular way: competing in the LPGA qualifying tournaments nicknamed "Q-School." In September, 2008, at the LPGA Sectional Qualifying Tournament in California, on the same Mission Hills golf course where Michelle's bright career was launched at the age of thirteen, she tied for fourth place among 164 contenders. This success enabled her to compete in the LPGA Final Qualifying Tournament held at Daytona Beach, Florida, in December, 2008. Her tie for seventh place in that tournament qualified her to play as a full member of the 2009 LPGA Tour.

Summary

Michelle Wie's stellar athletic start fascinated a whole generation of young teens. Her early victories against older players and successful matches with male players turned her into golf's teen heroine. Michelle showed character when she recovered from her injury-plagued year of 2007. She matured as a person and athlete. Her remaining challenge was to make a mark as an adult athlete and prove wrong those who begrudged her for having earned more than $30 million in sponsorship money before turning twenty-one years old.

R. C. Lutz

Additional Sources

Bamberger, Michael. "The Lost Year of Michelle Wie." *Sports Illustrated* 107, no. 26 (December 31, 2007): 69.

Chu, Jeff. "Ten Questions for Michelle Wie." *Time* 167, no. 14 (April 3, 2006): 8.

Dorman, Larry. "Recovery Shot for Wie." *The New York Times,* June 29, 2008, p. 7L.

Mario, Jennifer. *Michelle Wie: The Making of a Champion.* New York: St. Martin's Griffin, 2006.

Tiger Woods

Born: December 30, 1975
      Cypress, California
Also known as: Eldrick Tont Woods (full name)

Early Life

Eldrick Tont "Tiger" Woods was born to Earl Woods, a retired African American lieutenant colonel in the Army, and his wife, Kultida Punsawad, a native Thai and a secretary for the army. Tiger's parents met when Earl served in Thailand during the Vietnam War. Their only child was named Eldrick but soon was called Tiger, a nickname Earl had bestowed upon Colonel Nguyen Phong in recognition of Phong's bravery.

Earl became an enthusiastic golfer months before his retirement from the Army and soon transferred this enthusiasm to Tiger, who often sat in a high chair in the garage while Earl practiced his swing. Before Tiger was two years old, Earl had modified a golf club to the boy's height. Tiger showed prodigious skill in using this improvised club. By the time he was two, Tiger appeared with Bob Hope on *The Mike Douglas Show,* where he showed his prowess in putting and won over the audience with his natural charm. When Tiger was five, a story about him and his remarkable ability appeared in *Golf Digest.* He also appeared on the television show *That's Incredible.* Earl devoted himself fully to grooming Tiger to be a world-class golfer.

The Road to Excellence

Tiger's career began remarkably early. By age two, he could hit a golf ball a considerable distance. By three, he mastered difficult shots that included chipping golf balls out of sand traps. At the age of four, he scored a forty-eight on the back nine holes at the Navy Golf Course, a respectable score for adult golfers.

Earl had three children from an earlier marriage, but Tiger was Earl and Kultida's only child. Earl lavished single-minded attention on his son, recognizing that the child was a prodigy, a virtual Mozart of golf. Nevertheless, Earl did not pressure his son to excel in the game. Tiger grew up in a warm and supportive atmosphere.

Attending high school in Cypress, California, a city in which the Woodses were the first nonwhite residents, Tiger played baseball, basketball, and football. By the time Tiger entered high school, Cypress had become a racially mixed community. Al-

Tiger Woods at the 2008 U.S. Open. (Louis Lopez/CSM/Landov)

PGA Tour Victories

1996	Las Vegas Invitational	2000 (cont.)	PGA Championship	2005 (cont.)	British Open Championship
	Walt Disney World/Oldsmobile Classic		WGC NEC Invitational		NEC Invitational
1997	Mercedes Championship		Bell Canadian Open		American Express Championship
	The Masters	2001	The Masters	2006	Buick Invitational
	GTE Byron Nelson Golf Classic		Bay Hill Invitational		Ford Championship at Doral
	Motorola Western Open		The Players Championship		British Open Championship
1998	BellSouth Classic		Memorial Tournament		Buick Open
1999	Buick Invitational		NEC Invitational		PGA Championship
	Memorial Tournament	2002	Bay Hill Invitational		Bridgestone Invitational
	Motorola Western Open		The Masters		Deutsche Bank Championship
	PGA Championship		U.S. Open Championship		American Express Championship
	WGC NEC Invitational		Buick Open	2007	Buick Invitational
	National Car Rental Golf Classic/ Disney		American Express Championship		WGC-CA Championship
	The Tour Championship		Buick Invitational		Wachovia Championship
	WGC American Express Championship	2003	Accenture Match Play Championship		Bridgestone Invitational
2000	Mercedes Championship		Bay Hill Invitational		PGA Championship
	AT&T Pebble Beach National Pro-Am		Western Open		BMW Championship
	Bay Hill Invitational Memorial Tournament		American Express Championship		The Tour Championship
	U.S. Open Championship	2004	Accenture Match Play Championship	2008	Buick Invitational
	British Open Championship	2005	Buick Invitational		Accenture Match Play Championship
			Ford Championship at Doral		Arnold Palmer Invitational
			The Masters		U.S. Open Championship

though Tiger demonstrated a considerable talent in a variety of sports, his single-minded passion was for golf. Endless practicing became the happiest part of his day.

The Emerging Champion

Tiger was popular in school, was a solid student, and was a valued athlete. While still in high school, he accumulated numerous trophies. He set many records, including winning three consecutive United States Junior Amateur Championship victories and becoming the youngest golfer to win a championship at the age of fifteen. In 1994, he became the youngest player to win a United States Amateur Golf Championship.

Upon completing high school, Tiger won a golf scholarship to Stanford University, enrolling in the fall of 1994 as an economics major. During his freshman year, he defended his amateur title and also played in The Masters tournament, the only junior contender to make the cut. During his sopho-more year, he continued to maintain a B average while winning tournaments throughout the United States. Although he was successful as both a student and an athlete, Tiger decided to leave Stanford to pursue golf exclusively. He experienced considerable anguish deciding whether to continue at Stanford or turn professional. However, he was undoubtedly swayed by two major endorsements that came to him, one from Titleist, worth $20 million, and one from Nike, worth $40 million.

Continuing the Story

Earl had conditioned Tiger to concentrate fully on his game. He frequently did things to distract his son as he played, such as coughing, jingling coins in his pocket, and doing other things that might rattle a typical golfer. Tiger learned to ignore such distractions, a skill that gave him an edge over his competitors. In 1997, he demonstrated his prowess by becoming the youngest person to win The Masters, achieving the lowest score in the tournament's history at 12 strokes below par. He was the first person of color to win The Masters.

Following this victory, Tiger played on the American teams for the Ryder Cup and the Presidents Cup. In 1999, he won the PGA Championship. His winnings continued into the 2000 and 2001 seasons, during which he won an incredible number of tournaments. His father, whose health was failing, did his best to attend each tournament in which Tiger participated. He continued to do so until 2006, when he died, leaving Tiger devastated.

Honors and Awards

1992	*Golf Digest, Golfweek,* and *Golf World* Top Amateur Player
1993	*Golf World* Top Amateur Player
1994	*Golf World* Man of the Year
	U.S. World Amateur Team
1995	Walker Cup Team
1996	Collegiate Player of the Year
	PGA Rookie of the Year
	Sports Illustrated Sportsman of the Year
1997, 1999-2003, 2005-2006	PGA Player of the Year
1997, 1999, 2002, 2004, 2006	Ryder Cup Team
1997, 2001, 2003, 2005-07	PGA of America and Golf Writers Association of America Player of the Year
	First golfer selected Associated Press Male Athlete of the Year in 26 years
	Sports Star of the Year Award, given to athletes who combine excellence in their sport with significant charitable endeavors
1998	Dunhill Cup Team
1998-2007	Mark H. McCormack Award
1998, 2000, 2003, 2005, 2007	The Presidents Cup Team
	PGA Grand Slam of Golf winner
1999	World Cup Team
1999-2003, 2005-07	Byron Nelson Award
1999-2003, 2005, 2007	PGA Vardon Trophy
	AP Athlete of the Year
2000	CNN-*Sports Illustrated* Sportsman of the Year
2001-02, 2005-07	PGA Tour Money Leader
2006	Associated Press Male Athlete of the Year

Records and Milestones

1993	First golfer to have won three U.S. Junior Amateur Championships
1994	Became youngest winner of U.S. Amateur
1996	Became first player to win three consecutive U.S. Amateur titles (1994, 1995, 1996)
	Joined Jack Nicklaus and Phil Mickelson as the only players to win NCAA and U.S. Amateur in same year
	Set U.S. Amateur records for consecutive match-play victories (18) and winning percentage (.909)
1997	Associated Press named Tiger's Masters win the top sports story of 1997
	Masters Tournament rounds of 70-66-65-69-270 set 72-hole record
	Masters Tournament 12-stroke margin of victory set a Masters record
1998	Eighth athlete to be named a permanent Wheaties representative, after Bob Richards (1958), Bruce Jenner (1977), Mary Lou Retton (1984), Pete Rose (1985), Walter Payton (1986), Chris Evert (1987), and Michael Jordan (1988)
2000	Became the first player at the U.S. Open to finish 72 holes at double digits, under par
2001	The first golfer to be the defending champion of all four major tournaments (The Masters, the British Open, the U.S. Open, and the PGA Championship) at the same time
2002	Youngest golfer to win seven PGA major-tournament championships
2004	The first golfer to accumulate more than $40 million in career
2005	The third player (after Jack Nicklaus and Arnold Palmer) to win at least four Masters Tournaments
	Second golfer to win all four major tournaments multiple times
	Most PGA Tour victories before the age of thirty, 34
2006	The youngest golfer to reach 50 PGA tournament wins
2008	The first player to have multiple streaks of five straight PGA Tour victories

Tiger became the youngest golfer to complete a career Grand Slam—victories at the British Open, The Masters, the PGA Championship, and the U.S. Open—and as of 2008, ranked second behind Jack Nicklaus for wins in major tournaments.

As Tiger continued to compile victories, at the urging of South Africa's president Nelson Mandela, he used his celebrity to better the lives of others. Tiger founded the Tiger Woods Foundation, overseen initially by his father. The aim of this organization is to help young people by providing for their educations.

Summary

Tiger Woods's greatest social contribution was his excellence as a golfer, which opened the sport to people of various ethnicities. Despite the social implications of his achievements, Woods declined to be politically involved in matters of race and gender, both salient issues in the world of golfing as blacks and women sought admission to segregated country clubs.

R. Baird Shuman

Additional Sources

Bradley, Michael. *Tiger Woods*. New York: Marshall Cavendish, 2004.

Gates, Henry Louis, and Evelyn Brooks Higginbotham, eds. *African American Lives*. New York: Oxford University Press, 2004.

Glaser, Jason. *Tiger Woods*. New York: PowerKids Press, 2008.

Goodman, Michael E. *Tiger Woods*. Mankato, Minn.: Creative Education, 2004.

Kearns, Brad. *How Tiger Does It: Put the Success Formula of a Champion into Everything You Do*. New York: McGraw-Hill, 2008.

Rosaforte, Tim. *Raising the Bar: The Championship Years of Tiger Woods*. New York: St. Martin's Press, 2000.

Whitaker, Matthew C. *African American Icons of Sport: Triumph, Courage, and Excellence*. Westport, Conn.: Greenwood Press, 2008.

Mickey Wright

Born: February 14, 1935
         San Diego, California
Also known as: Mary Kathryn Wright (full name)

Early Life

Mary Kathryn Wright was born in San Diego, California, to attorney Arthur Wright and Mary Kathryn Wright on February 14, 1935. With the same legal name as her mother, she soon became known as "Mickey." She grew into an adolescent with a larger-than-ordinary body. Her friends at school sometimes teased her, calling her "Moose." This teasing gave her an inferiority complex and motivated her to outshine everyone at some skill in order to feel good about herself.

Golf proved to be Mickey's niche. Luckily for her, she was already good at it. Her father was an amateur golfer, and he had encouraged her to practice on a driving range since she was nine years old. By the age of eleven, Mickey played her first round and scored 145. At twelve, she broke 100; at thirteen, she was already down to 80 strokes per round. For years, she had been reading everything she could about golf and keeping scrapbooks of the famous golfers she idolized.

The Road to Excellence

Mickey played in her first tournament in San Diego when she was fifteen. She shot a 70. By the next year, she was beating the male professionals at her local course. At one point, her elbow kept flying out too much on the backswing. Professional Paul Runyan showed her how to weaken her grip to fix that. Mickey's mother made her an elastic band that let her arms swing freely but would not allow her elbows to separate. Mickey practiced by the hour, wearing the contraption. By 1952, she had progressed so well and quickly that she was able to claim victory at the United States Golf Association's Junior Girls' Championship.

Mickey enrolled at Stanford University. When summer came, she was back on the links, proving herself as the best-scoring amateur in the U.S. Open, as well as the St. Petersburg Open and the Tam O'Shanter tournaments. She was also the runner-up in the U.S. Amateur. After only one year in college, she convinced her father to let her take a leave of absence from school in order to play as an amateur on the professional tour that coming winter. Mickey did so well on the tour that, when she calculated what she would have earned had she played as a professional instead of as

Mickey Wright. (Ralph W. Miller Golf Library)

Major Championship Victories

1958-59, 1961, 1964	U.S. Women's Open
1958, 1960-61, 1963	LPGA Championship
1961-62	Titleholders Championship
1962-63, 1966	Western Open
1973	Colgate Dinah Shore

Other Notable Victories

1960	Eastern Open
	Memphis Open
1961, 1963	St. Petersburg Open
1961, 1963, 1966	Mickey Wright Invitational
1963	Babe Zaharias Open
1966-67, 1969	Bluegrass Invitational
1967	Baltimore Lady Carling
	Pensacola Invitational

an amateur, she saw that it made sense for her to immediately switch to professional status.

The Emerging Champion

As a professional, Mickey earned an excellent income right from the start. When she was twenty years old, she earned $7,000, and then in the next two years, $8,500 and $12,000, respectively. By 1958, she was winning major tournaments like the Ladies Professional Golf Association (LPGA) Championship and the U.S. Open.

Later in that year, though, she went into a slump during the St. Petersburg Open. Her roommate Betsy Rawls recognized Mickey's self-pity for what it was and snapped her out of it. Rawls made Mickey see that she could blame her performance on no one but herself.

In 1960, Mickey began to work with her new golf teacher Earl Stewart, the professional at the Oak Cliff Country Club in Dallas, Texas. Mickey moved to Dallas to be near him. As a first and essential lesson, Stewart taught Mickey how to relax her perfectionist attitude toward work. He wanted her to play one shot at a time without getting emotionally involved in the shots to come or those behind her. Stewart's primary assistance was psychological, but he also worked on Mickey's swing.

As a result of Stewart's tutelage, Mickey won the Vare Trophy for lowest average strokes per round in 1960. For the next three years, no one surpassed her average. The following year, she achieved a re-

markable feat: She was the winner of the U.S. Women's Open, the LPGA Championship, and the Titleholders Championship.

The year 1963 proved to be Mickey's greatest year ever and represented one of the greatest years ever achieved by a woman golfer. Mickey won thirteen major tournaments, for a lifetime total of fifty-three tournament victories, including her fourth LPGA title. In addition, her average score was 72.81, the lowest among all her competitors, for the fourth time. The Associated Press polled sports editors nationwide for their annual selection of female athlete of the year. Mickey was the easy choice.

Continuing the Story

Between 1961 and 1964, Mickey's income rose from $18,000 to $31,269, surpassing that of all other women golfers. In addition to her place at the top of LPGA money-winners, Mickey was also the best long-ball hitter. She surprised many male professionals, who never thought they would see a woman hit the ball 300 yards. Mickey consistently

Records and Milestones

Eighty-two career victories

Won a record thirteen victories in 1963

Tour's leading money-winner four times (1961-64)

Had at least one tournament victory a year (1956-70)

Only woman golfer to win the U.S. Women's Open and the LPGA Championship in the same year twice (1958, 1961)

Her collection of four U.S. Women's Open titles is a record shared with Betsy Rawls

Honors and Awards

1957	*Golf Digest* Most Improved Golfer
1958, 1960-64	*Golf Digest* Award for Tournament Victories
1958-67	*Golf* magazine Golfer of the Decade
1960-64	Vare Trophy
1963-64	Associated Press Female Athlete of the Year
1964	Inducted into LPGA Tour Hall of Fame
1976	Inducted into World Golf Hall of Fame
1981	Inducted into Sudafed International Women's Sports Hall of Fame
1999	Associated Press Female Golfer of the Century
2000	*Golf Digest* greatest woman golfer of all time and ninth-greatest golfer of all time

hit drives averaging 225 to 270 yards. Once, aided by a strong wind, she overshot the green of a 385-yard hole. Mickey was a strong, 5-foot 9-inch golfer; she was no longer self-conscious about her size, a trim figure at 150 pounds.

Mickey's swing was considered the best of all time. Golfers everywhere marveled at her grace and balance and at how well her swing was synchronized. She never appeared to be swinging hard, yet she could hit as far as the men professionals. She was the Jack Nicklaus of women's driving.

Later, Mickey went into the brokerage business, while living in Port St. Lucie, Florida. When she injured her back, she stopped playing golf regularly. Though she made her last official LPGA Tournament appearance in 1980, Mickey competed in the Senior Sprint Challenge from 1993 to 1995. She finished in the top five each year, including a second-place finish in 1994. Her paycheck from that event was $30,000, the largest of her career.

Summary

Mickey Wright was the greatest long-ball hitter in the history of women's golf. She is often considered the finest woman golfer ever. She won both the LPGA title and the U.S. Women's Open four times and the Vare Trophy five years in a row. For two years in succession, she was named female athlete of the year by the Associated Press. She was the first woman ever to win as many as thirteen major tournaments in a single year. Mickey has the second-highest number of tournament titles, 82, behind Kathy Whitworth, and in 1999, the Associated Press named her golfer of the century. For all of her achievements in golf, she was inducted into the LPGA Tour Hall of Fame.

Nan White

Additional Sources

Cherney, Ron, and Michael Arkush. *My Greatest Shot: The Top Players Share Their Defining Golf Moments.* New York: HarperResource, 2004.

Glenn, Rhonda. *The Illustrated History of Women's Golf.* Dallas, Tex.: Taylor, 1991.

Golf Magazine's Encyclopedia of Golf: The Complete Reference. New York: HarperCollins, 1993.

Hudson, David L. *Women in Golf: The Players, the History, and the Future of the Sport.* Westport, Conn.: Praeger, 2007.

Sommers, Robert. "Mickey Wright: Open Greatness." *Golf Magazine* 37, no. 12 (December, 1995): 84-85.

Wright, Mickey. *Play Golf the Wright Way.* Dallas, Tex.: Taylor, 1990.

Babe Didrikson Zaharias

Born: June 26, 1911
Port Arthur, Texas
Died: September 27, 1956
Galveston, Texas
Also known as: Mildred Ella Didriksen (birth name); Babe Didriksen; Mildred Ella Zaharias
Other major sports: Track and field, basketball, and softball

Early Life

Mildred Ella "Babe" Didriksen was born on June 26, 1911, in Port Arthur, Texas. She was the sixth of seven children born to Ole and Hannah Did-

riksen—Mildred changed the "e" in her parents' Norwegian name to an "o" later in her life. Mildred's parents were poor but strict. Her father had worked as a cabinetmaker on ships at sea while in Norway but later made a meager wage as a furniture refinisher. Her mother was a housekeeper and took in washing and ironing from neighbors to help the family survive. The family moved to Beaumont, Texas, when Mildred was three years old.

Mildred's father was a fitness fanatic. He required each of his seven children to exercise and to play sports. Her mother had been an excellent skater and skier in Norway. Mildred's father built playing fields and exercise equipment of all kinds for his children. With four brothers and two sisters plus many neighbor boys and girls in the yard at all times, Mildred competed in numerous sports.

Some reports claim Mildred was called Babe because she was the baby of the family. Others say it was because she hit a baseball like Babe Ruth.

The Road to Excellence

Through her years at Magnolia Grade School, Babe competed on even terms with the boys. She also played the harmonica for three years on a weekly radio show and was an excellent student. She won first prize at the Texas State Fair for a dress she made.

While at South Junior High School, Babe decided she wanted to become the greatest athlete who ever lived, and while playing basketball for Beaumont Senior High School, she made all-city and all-state. Colonel Melvin J. McCombs, the coach of one of the best women's amateur basketball teams in the nation, convinced Babe to play for his team, the Golden Cyclone Athletic Club, which was sponsored by the Employers Casualty Company of Dallas. The Employers Casualty Company hired Babe as a typist and a player on its basketball, track, and other sports teams.

Babe Didrikson Zaharias, who was a multisport athlete but earned her greatest fame as a golfer. (AP/Wide World Photos)

Major Championship Victories (Golf)

Year	Competition
1940, 1944-45, 1950	Western Open
1946	U.S. Women's Amateur
1947	British Open Amateur Championship
1947, 1950, 1952	Titleholders Championship
1948, 1950, 1954	U.S. Women's Open

Other Notable Victories

Year	Competition
1940, 1944, 1951-52	Texas Open
1948, 1950-51, 1954	All-American Open
1948, 1951	World Championship
1949	Eastern Open
1953	Babe Zaharias Open

Babe became an all-American in basketball while leading the team to the national championship. She also won medals in ice skating and swimming.

The Emerging Champion

In the spring of 1929, Babe talked McCombs into starting an Employers Casualty Company track team because she wanted to try track. She practiced in the afternoon and again at night. She wanted to try every event. In 1929, track competitors were allowed to enter as many events as they desired. By this time, Babe had grown into a 5-foot 4-inch, 105-pound, muscular athlete.

Babe won eight of the ten events she entered in the Texas State Track and Field Championships. In 1929, she broke the world javelin record with a throw of 133 feet 3¼ inches. In 1930, her baseball throw of 296 feet set a women's record. In 1932, Babe became the best female track and field athlete in the United States and then in the world. The National Championships and the 1932 Olympic trials were combined into one meet held at Northwestern University.

Babe entered the meet as a one-woman team representing the Employers Casualty Company. She entered eight of the ten events, winning five and placing in two others. She set world records in the hurdles, with a time of 12.1 seconds, and the javelin, with a toss of 139 feet 3 inches, and tied Jean Shiley with a world-record high jump of 5 feet 3¾ inches. Babe scored 30 points and won the meet by herself, beating the second-place team—twenty-two women representing the Illinois Athletic Club—by 8 points.

Continuing the Story

A few weeks later, Babe was off to Los Angeles for the 1932 Olympics. In 1932, women's Olympic track and field consisted of only five individual events. Each person was allowed to enter no more than three of the events. Babe chose the javelin, the hurdles, and the high jump.

Babe's first throw in the javelin was a world record of 143 feet 4 inches. In the 80-meter hurdles, she broke a second world record with a time of 11.7 seconds. In the high jump, she tied for first place at a world-record height of 5 feet 5 inches. A judge disqualified her from first place, contending that her head passed over the bar before the rest of her body, which was not allowed in those days. She settled for the silver medal.

Babe's great dedication to practice, determination to succeed, and athletic ability resulted in her first of six Associated Press female athlete of the year awards. She had become a star.

At first, Babe tried many different activities, attempting to capitalize on her Olympic fame. She is often considered to be the greatest woman athlete of all time. She toured the country with Babe Didrikson's All-Americans, a basketball team. She was the only woman on the team. She traveled with the bearded House of David baseball team. She was a pitcher and the only woman on the team. She

Major Championships (Track and Field)

Year	Competition	Event	Place	Time/Distance/Height
1930	National AAU Outdoor Championships	Javelin throw	1st	133' 3"
1931	National AAU Outdoor Championships	80-meter hurdles	1st	12.1
		Long jump	1st	17' 11½"
1932	Olympic Games	80-meter hurdles	Gold	11.7 OR
		High jump	Silver	5' 5"
		Javelin throw	Gold	143'4" WR, OR
	National AAU Outdoor Championships	80-meter hurdles	1st	12.1
		High jump	1st	5' 3¾" WR
		Shot put	1st	39' 6¼"
		Javelin throw	1st	139' 3" WR

Notes: OR = Olympic Record; WR = World Record

pitched in a Major League Baseball exhibition game during spring training.

After the Olympics, Babe became a golfer. She practiced unceasingly, sometimes for as many as ten hours a day. Often her hands bled, and she bandaged them and kept practicing. She was a long hitter from the beginning, often out-driving men players. Her short game needed a great amount of practice, and she was determined to become a good player around the greens and to control her tee shots.

In 1934, Babe entered her first golf tournament, shooting a 77 to win first place. During the next twenty years, Babe won fifty-three major golf tournaments all over the world. Between 1946 and 1947, she won seventeen straight titles, a record no one else has matched.

In 1938, Babe met and married wrestler George Zaharias. He gave up his career to help Babe continue her golf career.

Babe was voted the outstanding female athlete of the first half of the twentieth century. In 1953, she learned that she had cancer. Through several cancer operations, she fought the disease valiantly. She won the U.S. Women's Open and four other golf tournaments in 1954. After a courageous fight, Babe Didrikson Zaharias died of cancer on September 27, 1956.

Milestones

LPGA leading money-winner four consecutive years (1948-51)

First American golfer to capture the British Open Amateur Championship since it began in 1893

Garnered thirty-one victories out of one hundred twenty-eight LPGA events during her eight-year career

Founder and Charter Member of the LPGA

Named "Golfer of the Decade" (1948-57) by *Golf* magazine

Honors, Awards, and Records

Year	
1929	Set world record in the javelin throw (133′ 3¼″)
1932, 1945-47, 1950, 1954	Associated Press Female Athlete of the Year
1950	Associated Press Outstanding Female Athlete of the Half-Century
1951	Inducted into LPGA Hall of Fame
1954	GWAA Ben Hogan Award
	GWAA Richardson Award
	Vare Trophy
1957	Bob Jones Award
1974	Inducted into National Track and Field Hall of Fame
	Inducted into World Golf Hall of Fame
1977	Inducted into PGA Golf Professional Hall of Fame
1980	Inducted into Sudafed International Women's Sports Hall of Fame Pioneer
1983	Inducted into U.S. Olympic Hall of Fame

Summary

Babe Didrikson Zaharias became an outstanding athlete because of her intense desire to be the best woman athlete in the world. Her parents gave her a good foundation and, using her great competitive desire, she achieved her goal.

Walter R. Schneider

Additional Sources

Cayleff, Susan E. *Babe: The Life and Legend of Babe Didrikson Zaharias*. Rev. ed. Urbana: University of Illinois Press, 1996.

Dure, Jane. "Female Athlete of the Century." *Texas Monthly* 27, no. 12 (December, 1999): 152-153.

Hutchison, Kay Bailey. *American Heroines: The Spirited Women Who Shaped Our Country*. New York: William Morrow, 2004.

Johnson, William O., and Nancy P. Williamson. *Whatta-Gal! The Babe Didrikson Story*. Boston: Little, Brown, 1977.

Tricard, Louise M. *American Women's Track and Field: A History, 1895 Through 1980*. Jefferson, N.C.: McFarland, 1996.

Zaharias, Babe Didrikson, and Harry T. Paxton. *This Life I've Led: My Autobiography*. Reprint. New York: Dell, 1975.

Tennis

Andre Agassi

Born: April 29, 1970
     Las Vegas, Nevada
Also known as: Andre Kirk Agassi (full name)

Early Life

Andre Kirk Agassi was born on April 29, 1970, in Las Vegas, Nevada, to Emmanuel "Mike" Agassi, a showroom captain at a casino, and Elizabeth "Betty" Dudley Agassi, who worked for the state of Nevada. Andre was the youngest of four children: He had a brother, Philip, and two sisters, Rita and Tamee. Andre's dad had been born in Iran and had boxed for his native country in the 1948 and 1952 Summer Olympics. Of Armenian descent, he had immigrated to the United States during the mid-1950's.

Andre's father had been fascinated with the game of tennis since he was a child and hoped that one of his children would one day be a tennis champion. After Mike and Betty married, they settled in Las Vegas because the climate allowed for tennis to be played year-round; all of the Agassi children were taught to play. From the time Andre was a baby, he was groomed to be a tennis champion. By age two, he was able to serve the ball on a tennis court.

The Road to Excellence

Andre's father was confident that hard work and training would make Andre into a tennis star. At the age of four, Andre got the chance to practice with tennis great Jimmy Connors during a Las Vegas hotel exhibition. He practiced relentlessly on the family's backyard court. At the age of seven, he entered his first tennis tournament, a ten-and-under event. Andre won this tournament and the next eight tournaments that he entered.

When Andre was thirteen, his parents decided that he should attend the fa-

mous Nick Bollettieri Tennis Academy in Bradenton, Florida. However, Andre had a hard time adjusting to life away from home, and he became moody and difficult to coach. Eventually, he overcame his frustrations, and he grew not only as a tennis player but also as an individual. While he was at the Bollettieri Academy, he continued his academic studies with the help of private tutors. On the tennis court, he was not winning consistently, but Bollettieri believed in Andre's potential. The

Andre Agassi serving to John McEnroe at the 1992 Wimbledon semifinal match. (AP/Wide World Photos)

coach persuaded the Nike shoe company to offer Andre an endorsement contract, and, in 1986, Andre turned professional. With the $25,000 endorsement fee from Nike, he was able to play in all the major tennis tournaments.

The Emerging Champion

At 5 feet 11 inches and 150 pounds, Andre needed to become stronger if he wanted to compete successfully against seasoned professionals. He was noted for his aggressive play, but his results on the court tended to be erratic. Having been taught at an early age to hit the ball as hard as he could, Andre needed to learn to control his blistering ground strokes. When he was focused, his ground strokes, especially his return of serve, could defeat even the most seasoned veteran.

In Andre's first two professional tournaments, he won more than $11,000. He had the skill and a flair for the game that made stardom a real possibility, but he needed to learn patience. He was still a teenager, and the pressure of professional tennis was making life difficult for him. Andre struggled through much of the first half of 1987, and he contemplated giving up the game. Through the efforts of the professional tennis tour's traveling minister,

---

Major Championship Victories and Finals

1990-91	French Open finalist
1990, 1995	U.S. Open finalist
1992	Wimbledon
1994, 1999	U.S. Open
1995, 2000-01	Australian Open
1999	French Open
	Wimbledon finalist
2002, 2005	U.S. Open finalist
2003	Australian Open

Other Notable Victories

1987	Sul American Open
1988	U.S. Indoor Championship
1990	ATP Tour World Championship
1990, 1992	On victorious U.S. Davis Cup Team
1990, 1994	Canadian Open
1990, 1995-96	Lipton International Players' Championship
1996	Gold medal, Olympic men's tennis singles
2002	Rome Open
	Madrid Open
2003	Miami Open
2004	Cincinnati Open

Fritz Glauss, Andre renewed his Christian faith. With a newfound ability to put tennis in perspective, he became more relaxed when he competed. In November, 1987, he won his first professional title, beating Luiz Mattar in the finals of the Sul American Open in Itaparica, Brazil.

By the end of 1987, Andre's ranking had risen to twenty-fifth in the world. He was finally on the verge of becoming one of the top players on the Association of Tennis Professionals (ATP) tour. In addition to his aggressive tennis game, Andre developed a flashy court presence that excited fans. He wore brightly colored clothes that irritated the more conservative elements in the game, but his showmanship caught on with the crowds. Andre was becoming famous for more than his ability to play tennis. In 1988, he captured six titles and reached the semifinals of both the U.S. Open and the French Open. The ATP and *Tennis* magazine both named Andre the most improved player of the year for 1988, and his ranking soared all the way to third in the world.

Continuing the Story

Andre always seemed to be in the spotlight. Major companies paid him millions of dollars to use and endorse their products. However, Andre wanted more than to be a celebrity; he wanted to be considered a great tennis player. To earn such recognition, he had to win one of tennis's four Grand Slam tournaments. In 1990 and 1991, he reached the finals of the French Open but lost on both occasions. In 1990, he also reached the finals of the U.S. Open, where he played another American, Pete Sampras. Andre was no match for Sampras and his blistering serves, however, and he lost in straight sets. Tennis critics were beginning to wonder if Andre could win a major tournament.

Because Andre's tennis strength was his ground stroke, experts believed that he had his best chance of winning a Grand Slam title on the clay courts of the French Open. Andre, however, surprised everyone at the 1992 Wimbledon Championships by winning his first Grand Slam title on the grass courts of the All England Lawn Tennis and Croquet Club. Grass courts normally favor players who have a big serve, but Andre's return of serve was up to the challenge, and he defeated Goran Ivanišević in a dramatic five-set match.

Afterward, Andre struggled to equal the inten-

Honors, Awards, and Milestones

Youngest man to earn top-ten world ranking, at age seventeen
The only male tennis player to be ranked in the top ten in three different decades
In 2003, became the oldest number-one ranked male player ever

1988	ATP Most Improved Player
	Tennis magazine Most Improved Player
1995, 2001	ATP Arthur Ashe Humanitarian of the Year
1999	ITF World Champion
	ATP Player of the Year
2000	ESPY Award: Outstanding Men's Tennis Performer of the Year
2000, 2003	ESPY Award: Best Male Tennis Player

sity that won him Wimbledon in 1992. After severing his association with Bollettieri in the summer of 1993, he needed to replenish his strength before he could compete at top form. After having wrist surgery in December, 1993, he returned to the tour in early 1994. In September, he reaffirmed his place among the game's elite by downing Michael Stich for the U.S. Open title.

In 1995, Andre started the year by capturing a Grand Slam singles title at the Australian Open. He won seven titles and ended the year ranked number two in the world. He won a gold medal in singles at the 1996 Summer Olympics held in Atlanta, Georgia. A wrist injury sidelined him for most of 1997, and his ranking dropped to 141 in the world.

Andre showed amazing determination and fought hard to reclaim his position as one of the top players. In 1999, he won the French Open and the U.S. Open. He also reached the finals at Wimbledon. By winning the French Open, he became only the fifth man to win all four Grand Slam singles titles in his career. The other four were Don Budge, Fred Perry, Rod Laver, and Roy Emerson. Andre ended 1999 as the number-one ranked player in the world. In 2000, he won the Australian Open despite the fact that he had trouble focusing on tennis: Both his older sister and his mother were diagnosed with breast cancer. A car accident in which Andre hurt his back also hindered his play during the year, but he managed to defend his Australian Open title in 2001.

In 2001, Andre married tennis great Steffi Graf. They have two children. He won his last Grand Slam title in 2003 at the Australian Open. Because of various debilitating back problems, he retired from professional tennis in 2006. Over the length of his remarkable career, he won eight Grand Slam singles titles and more than $30 million in career earnings. In 1994, he founded the Andre Agassi Charitable Foundation, which raised millions of dollars to help at-risk children of Las Vegas.

Summary

Andre Agassi proved himself to be both a great competitor and a great showman. He changed the way many tennis fans viewed the game, making image part of the mix whenever he stepped onto a tennis court. He became only the fifth male tennis player to win a career Grand Slam.

Jeffry Jensen

Additional Sources

Bauman, Paul. *Agassi and Ecstasy: The Turbulent Life of Andre Agassi.* Chicago: Bonus Books, 1997.

Chambure, Alexandre de. *Andre Agassi: Through the Eyes of a Fan.* Los Angeles: ICCS, 2007.

Christopher, Matt. *On the Court with Andre Agassi.* Boston: Little, Brown, 1997.

Cobello, Dominic, with Mike Agassi. *The Agassi Story.* Toronto: ECW Press, 2008.

Collins, Bud. *Total Tennis: The Ultimate Tennis Encyclopedia.* Toronto: Sports Media, 2003.

Knapp, Ron. *Andre Agassi: Star Tennis Player.* Springfield, N.J.: Enslow, 1997.

Arthur Ashe

Born: July 10, 1943
     Richmond, Virginia
Died: February 6, 1993
     New York, New York
Also known as: Arthur Robert Ashe, Jr. (full name)

Early Life

Arthur Robert Ashe, Jr., was born in Richmond, Virginia, on July 10, 1943. When Arthur's father was appointed a public parks supervisor, the family moved to a modest home near Brookfield. This provided Arthur and his brother Johnny with access to a swimming pool, ball fields, and basketball and tennis courts. When he was six, Arthur's mother died. Arthur and his brother grew closer to their father, and the boys were expected to spend their time at home or at the park. Arthur had routine chores that taught him the meaning of hard work and discipline. As an African American, Arthur faced challenges in which this strong background helped him to succeed.

The Road to Excellence

While playing at the tennis courts, Arthur attracted the attention of Ronald Charity, who taught tennis for the city recreation department. Charity became Arthur's first tennis instructor and an early role model. Charity's interest in Arthur included encouragement and support, especially when Arthur faced the difficulties of limited opportunities to develop his potential. When not playing with Charity or his friends, Arthur watched the best tennis players at Richmond's Byrd Park. Arthur, however, was restricted from playing with whites in Richmond and other places.

Charity arranged for Arthur's participation in area tournaments sponsored by the American Tennis Association (ATA). Arthur worked hard to be a good tennis player; he even won a tournament three weeks after breaking his collar bone. By the age of ten, Arthur was the most promising young black tennis player in Richmond. Due to his success in these local tournaments, Charity introduced Arthur to Dr. Robert Johnson of Lynchburg, Virginia.

Johnson was recognized as one of the leading developers of black tennis talent in the country. One of his students was Althea Gibson. Arthur spent the next eight summers with Johnson and other young tennis players, practicing and playing tournaments throughout the nation. Arthur returned to Richmond, lived with his family, and attended school after these summers. He even played briefly on Walker High School's basketball and baseball teams. Tennis, however, was Arthur's main interest.

Arthur Ashe, who was a writer, activist, and champion tennis player. (AP/Wide World Photos)

Johnson developed Arthur's ground strokes and serve, which were the basis for Arthur's future successes. Arthur was known as much for his intelligence and composure on the court as for his aggressive style of play. Under Johnson's guidance, Arthur won his first ATA Championship in 1955.

In 1960, Arthur moved to St. Louis, Missouri, and improved his game, especially his volley, by playing year-round on the wooden court of the armory. Arthur won the U.S. Interscholastic Championship Boys' Singles in the summer of 1961, fulfilling a dream for himself and Johnson since African Americans were not even allowed to enter that tournament ten years earlier.

The Emerging Champion

Arthur's tennis career continued under the leadership of Coach J. D. Morgan of the University of California at Los Angeles (UCLA). Though pressures were often tough, Arthur received support from Coach Morgan and Pancho Gonzales, who recognized the obstacles Arthur had overcome and still faced. By the time he graduated, Arthur had won the National Collegiate Athletic Association (NCAA) Championship and risen to a number two national ranking.

Arthur remained an amateur even after his biggest win—the 1968 U.S. Open. This was the first year that amateur tennis players competed with professionals. Arthur's five-set victory over Tom Okker was a turning point for tennis. If tennis was going to be popular outside of country clubs, it needed a leader with whom people could identify and admire. Arthur's personable style, coupled with his emergence as one of the top players in the world, boosted the sport's popularity.

Though Arthur did not dominate tennis through-

Major Championship Victories and Finals

1966-67	Australian Championship finalist
1968	U.S. National Championship
	U.S. Open
	U.S. Open doubles finalist (with Andres Gimeno)
1970	Australian Open
	French Open doubles finalist (with Charlie Pasarell)
1971	Australian Open finalist
	French Open doubles (with Marty Riessen)
	Wimbledon doubles finalist (with Dennis Ralston)
1972	U.S. Open finalist
1975	Wimbledon
1977	Australian Open doubles (with Tony Roche)

Other Notable Victories

1955, 1960-62	ATA Championship
1961	U.S. Interscholastic Championship
1965	NCAA Championship
	NCAA Championship doubles (with Ian Crookenden)
1967, 1975	U.S. Clay Court Championship
1968-70	On winning U.S. Davis Cup team
1970	U.S. Clay Court Championship doubles (with Clark Graebner)
1970-71	U.S. Indoor Championship doubles (with Stan Smith)
1972	U.S. Pro Indoor doubles (with Bob Lutz)
1975	WCT Finals
	Pacific Southwest Open

---

out his playing career, he collected wins over the greatest names in the sport as he boomed serves from his "rug-beater" racket. Recognizing that professional tennis players needed coordinated leadership to help ensure their livelihood, Arthur contributed to the formation of the Association of Tennis Professionals (ATP) and served as its president in 1975.

Arthur played on ten Davis Cup teams from 1963 to 1978, compiling a then-record twenty-seven singles victories against only five losses. Arthur's most notable victory came against a powerful Jimmy Connors at the 1975 Wimbledon. Long known for a hard-hitting style of play, Arthur stunned everyone by winning with soft, low, and wide-reaching shots that frustrated his opponent. Arthur's four-set win was a testimony to his concentration, commitment, and adaptability, and it established him as the premier player in tennis.

Continuing the Story

As great as 1975 was for Arthur, within eighteen months he had career-threatening heel surgery and eye problems, which left him ranked 257th in the world. Ever the optimist and supported by many, including

---

Honors, Awards, and Milestones

1963-65	All-American
1963, 1965-70, 1975, 1977-78	Davis Cup team
1975	Ranked number one in the world
1979	ATP Comeback Player of the Year
1981-85	U.S. Davis Cup team captain
1985	Inducted into International Tennis Hall of Fame

his new wife, Jeanne Marie, whom he married on February 20, 1977, Arthur played his way back into the top ten rankings. This earned him comeback player of the year honors in 1979.

A heart attack at the age of thirty-six ended his competitive career. But Arthur soon redirected his energies into promoting tennis for inner-city youth and capably representing his sport and his country throughout the world. He served as a goodwill ambassador and human rights advocate on visits to Africa.

Arthur was a columnist for *The Washington Post*, a television commentator, a lecturer at Yale University, and the author of *A Hard Road to Glory* (1988), a black sports history work in three volumes. The same poise and dignity he brought to the sport was once again seen on the tennis court, as he was Davis Cup team captain from 1981 to 1985, winning two championships.

Summary

Arthur Ashe was a pioneer for his race and his sport during critical times of change in the United States. Arthur has been greatly admired by many for his accomplishments both on and off the court. As an athlete, he rose to the top of his sport and is remembered as much for how he won as what he won; as a person, he continued to help others find opportunities to experience their own successes.

P. Graham Hatcher

Additional Sources

Ashe, Arthur. *Days of Grace: A Memoir.* New York: Alfred A. Knopf, 1993.

_____. *A Hard Road to Glory: A History of the African American Athlete.* Rev. ed. New York: John Wiley & Sons, 2007.

Djata, Sundiata A. *Blacks at the Net: Black Achievement in the History of Tennis.* Syracuse, N.Y.: Syracuse University Press, 2006.

Harris, Cecil, and Larryette Kyle-DeBose. *Charging the Net: A History of Blacks in Tennis from Althea Gibson and Arthur Ashe to the Williams Sisters.* Chicago: Ivan R. Dee, 2007.

Steins, Richard. *Arthur Ashe: A Biography.* Westport, Conn.: Greenwood Press, 2005.

Towle, Mike. *I Remember Arthur Ashe: Memories of a True Tennis Pioneer and Champion of Social Causes by the People Who Knew Him.* Nashville, Tenn.: Cumberland House, 2001.

Wiggins, David Kenneth. *Out of the Shadows: A Biographical History of African American Athletes.* Fayetteville: University of Arkansas Press, 2006.

Juliette Atkinson

Born: April 15, 1873
    Rahway, New Jersey
Died: January 12, 1944
    Lawrenceville, Illinois
Also known as: Juliette Paxton Atkinson (full
    name); Mrs. Buxton (married name); Mrs.
    Hockery (married name)

Early Life
Juliette Paxton Atkinson was born in Rahway, New Jersey, a few years after the American Civil War. She was the first of two daughters born to Civil War veteran Jerome Gill Atkinson and his wife, Kate McDonald Atkinson. Juliette's sister, Kathleen Gill Atkinson, was born in 1875. Her father served as a battlefield surgeon in the war and later became a successful physician in private practice. Always diminutive—she grew to only five feet tall—Juliette nonetheless began participating in sports at an early age. Raised in an affluent environment, she learned to swim when only five years old. Later, she took up cycling, bowling, basketball, and golf. Most significantly, Juliette and her younger sister taught themselves how to play tennis.

The Road to Excellence
As a teen, Juliette joined the Kings County, New York, tennis club and began winning local tournaments. She picked up many prizes awarded at such contests: jeweled rings, gold hair combs, lamps, brooches, and trophy cups. During the early 1890's, she began to compete on a national level and soon excelled at the U.S. Open tournament (then known as the U.S. Women's National Singles Championship). The event, which was first staged in 1881, featured only men's singles matches until 1887, when women's singles were included. Women's doubles championships were added in 1889 and mixed doubles in 1892.

Juliette began her tennis career by playing women's doubles and then mixed doubles. In 1894, she teamed with women's singles champion Helen Hellwig to win the U.S. Open women's doubles championship. The victory was the first of five straight U.S. Open doubles titles for Juliette, out of a total of seven such championships she captured between 1894 and 1902. She played with five different partners over that time span. In 1897 and 1898, her partner in the national women's doubles championship was her younger sister, Kathleen.

Not content to dominate women's doubles, Juliette also competed in the U.S. Open mixed doubles. With partner Edwin P. Fisher, she swept to three straight titles from 1894 to 1896. After her successful debut, at the 1894 tournament, Juliette looked for new challenges. The following year, she won the U.S. Open women's singles title.

The Emerging Champion
At the 1895 U.S. Open tennis championships, Juliette and Kathleen were the first sisters to play against one another in the tournament. Juliette beat Kathleen in the semifinals in 1895 and 1897. In the finals, Juliette faced Helen Hellwig, a formidable foe, the 1894 singles champion, and Juliette's partner for the doubles titles in both 1894 and 1895. Juliette—one of the first women to charge the net and engage in prolonged, blistering volleys—swamped Hellwig in straight sets, 6-4, 6-2, and 6-1, to win her first individual U.S. Open title.

In the 1896 finals Juliette, who had sprained an ankle in a riding accident, lost to Elisabeth Moore in four sets. In 1897, she got her revenge, besting Moore in a tough, five-set match. In 1898, she won her third and final U.S. Open singles title in five grueling sets—6-3, 5-7, 6-4, 2-6, and 7-5—against Californian Marion Jones. With a total of fifty-one games, the match was the longest ever played in the

---

U.S. Championships Record (now U.S. Open)

1894-96	Mixed-doubles
1894-98, 1901-02	Doubles
1895, 1897-98	Singles
1896	Singles runner-up
1974	Inducted into International Tennis Hall of Fame

women's national singles tournament. Though the U.S. Open was her premier event, Juliette also participated in other tennis tournaments, including the Cincinnati Masters, the oldest tennis tournament in the United States to still be played in its original city. There, however, she did not fare as well. In the 1899 finals, she lost in four sets to Myrtle McAteer, who partnered with Juliette for the 1901 U.S. Open women's doubles victory. In 1901, she was defeated by Winona Closterman in three sets at the Cincinnati Masters.

Continuing the Story

By 1902, Juliette had collected thirteen U.S. Open titles—seven women's doubles, three mixed doubles, and three women's singles—and dozens of lesser awards. At thirty years of age, she retired from competition.

After leaving center court, Juliette fell into obscurity; little is known about her later years. Her mother died in 1901. Her father remarried to Julia A. Imlay and lived until 1930. Juliette married twice, first to George Buxton and later to Henry Hockery. Whether or not she had children is unknown. Juliette died January 12, 1944, at the age of seventy-one. Her sister Kathleen survived her and lived to the age of eighty-one, before dying in 1957. Juliette was posthumously elected to the International Tennis Hall of Fame in 1974.

Summary

A dynamic player in the early period of women's tennis, Juliette Atkinson proved that small stature was no hindrance to playing championship-caliber tennis. A national tennis champion in women's singles, women's doubles, and mixed doubles, she was one of the first female players to play stylistically like a man. Juliette, not content to stay at the baseline and trade lobs, was never afraid to rush the net, to volley, and to make winning smashes. Demonstrating superior athleticism during nearly a decade of competition at the U.S. Open, she pioneered a style that helped later women tennis players succeed at the sport.

Jack Ewing

Additional Sources

King, Billie Jean, and Cynthia Starr. *We Have Come a Long Way: The Story of Women's Tennis.* New York: McGraw-Hill, 1988.

Lumpkin, Angela. *Women's Tennis: A Historical Documentary of the Players and Their Game.* Albany, N.Y.: Whitston, 1981.

Mangan, J. A., and Roberta J. Park. *From Fair Sex to Feminism: Sport and the Socialization of Women in the Industrial and Post-Industrial Eras.* London: Frank Cass, 1987.

Porter, David L. *Biographical Dictionary of American Sports.* Westport, Conn.: Greenwood Press, 1992.

Bunny Austin

Born: August 26, 1906
      London, England
Died: August 26, 2000
      Coulsdon, Surrey, England
Also known as: Henry Wilfred Austin (full name)

Early Life
Henry Wilfred "Bunny" Austin was born in London, on August 26, 1906. His father Wilfred was a talented athlete in many sports and was Bunny's first coach. His older sister Joan won national championships in tennis and served as Bunny's mixed-doubles partner. He received the nickname "Bunny" from a cartoon rabbit in the paper named Wilfred. Bunny pursued a number of sports during his years

Bunny Austin playing at the All England Tennis Club, Wimbledon, in 1928. (AP/Wide World Photos)

at Repton School and achieved some eminent results as a cricketer. By the time he left for Pembroke College at the University of Cambridge, he had determined to make tennis his primary sport.

The Road to Excellence
Bunny won the British school boys' tennis championship in four different years, 1921 and 1923 to 1925. He captained the Cambridge varsity tennis team and won a couple of national tournaments in 1927. He even qualified for the English Davis Cup team in his first year at Cambridge, but he turned down the invitation on the advice of his father, who felt that Bunny's studies deserved attention. While Bunny was at Cambridge, he worked enough academically to receive a degree in history.

For much of his life, Bunny weighed the claims of tennis against those of his profession and other responsibilities. He met his wife Phyllis on an ocean cruise and became greatly involved with her role as an actress. She came from a Jewish family and appeared in early films directed by Alfred Hitchcock. The couple had two children and received plenty of attention in the social columns of newspapers at the time.

In 1929, Bunny met Fred Perry, the fellow British tennis player with whose career his own was to be linked. Perry had a more powerful game than Bunny and became the most successful English player of the twentieth century. Bunny continued to have mixed results over the next few years, with losses brought about by injury and a lack of stamina. He had beautiful strokes but never an overpowering game, resulting in many prolonged matches.

The Emerging Champion
Also in 1929, Bunny advanced to the semifinals of Wimbledon, the first of ten consecutive Wimbledon tournaments in which he advanced to the quarterfinals or beyond. In 1930, he was ranked ninth in the world, and two years later, he succeeded in reaching the finals at Wimbledon. That year, his competition was Ellsworth Vines, a power player from the United States; Bunny was over-

whelmingly defeated, winning only six games. He admitted that he could not keep up with Vines's power and was thinking of giving more serious attention to his career as a stockbroker.

The next year was perhaps the most successful in Bunny's tennis career. He did not get back to the finals at Wimbledon, but he and Perry teamed up to take the Davis Cup away from the French, who had held it for six years. The French team included many champions from the 1920's, but, even playing in Paris, it could not overcome the British team's youth. The British controlled the Davis Cup for four years, with Bunny and Perry managing to fend off challenges from the Americans. Bunny was distinctly more successful in Davis Cup events than he was in the major singles championships. His game was more suited to singles than to doubles, so even in the Davis Cup, the doubles responsibilities were left to others.

One of the turning-points in his career was also a fashion statement. Before Bunny's time, men's tennis players wore long trousers on the court. This was perceived as the attire of a gentleman in a traditional game. Bunny decided that the perspiration that the trousers retained in long matches contributed to his problems with stamina, and he started to play in shorts. While he had been concerned about the reaction from the traditionalists, no negative consequences materialized, and shorts have been the attire of choice ever since.

Continuing the Story

Bunny enjoyed the international travel and attention that came with his Davis Cup victories, but he recognized how much of that success was because of Perry, who won Wimbledon three years in a row. During that time, Bunny was unable to return to the finals. Then, when Perry turned professional after the 1936 season, even the Davis Cup triumphs came to an end. At that time only amateurs were allowed to play in the Davis Cup and the main international tournaments, so Perry was lost to the British team. Bunny continued to play in various events and returned to the Wimbledon finals in 1938. He lost, however, to the American Don Budge, even more decisively than against Vines six years before. The following year, he was eliminated in the third round. His career as an international tennis player was over.

Bunny, however, had been active in various

Milestones

British school boys' tennis champion (1921, 1923-25)

Beginning in 1929, advanced to ten consecutive Wimbledon quarterfinals

Two-time Wimbledon runner-up (1932, 1938)

Davis Cup champion (1933-36)

Inducted into International Tennis Hall of Fame (1997)

---

causes during his playing days, and those were enough to keep him busy. He and Perry had made a public protest over the German refusal to allow Jewish players on its Davis Cup team. He also became one of the spokesmen for the movement known as "Moral Re-Armament" that looked to a return to religion as an alternative to the increasing militarism of the 1930's. Bunny spent a fair amount of time working in London on theater designed to reinforce some of the claims that Moral Re-Armament was making.

In 1943, Bunny traveled to the United States on behalf of Moral Re-Armament and did not return to England until 1961. When he was drafted into the American military, the heart ailment he had since his Cambridge days kept him from active service. On returning home, he found that his move to the United States had affected his celebrity, but he lived long enough to regain popular affection. In 2000, despite residing in a nursing home, he took part in a parade of former champions at Wimbledon in a wheelchair. He died shortly thereafter.

Summary

During his entire career, Bunny Austin was an outstanding example of a gentleman tennis player. He was able to play at the top of his game in certain settings and that enabled him, even after his tennis career was over, to retain the public eye for other causes.

Thomas Drucker

Additional Sources

Austin, Henry Wilfred, and Phyllis Konstam. *A Mixed Double*. London: Chatto & Windus, 1969.

Mason, Tony. "Henry Wilfred Austin." In *Oxford Dictionary of National Biography*, edited by H. C. G. Matthew and Brian Harrison. 2d ed. Oxford: Oxford University Press, 2004.

Potter, E. C., Jr. *Kings of the Court*. New Brunswick, N.J.: A. S. Barnes, 1963.

Tracy Austin

Born: December 12, 1962
      Palos Verdes, California
Also known as: Tracy Ann Austin Holt (full
    name); Tracy Ann Austin (birth name)

Early Life
Tracy Ann Austin was born on December 12, 1962, the youngest of George and Jeanne Austin's five children. Tracy's father, a nuclear physicist, and her mother, who worked at the pro shop of a local tennis club, played tennis for recreation. Her older sister, Pam, and two of her brothers, Jeff and John, played professional tennis. Tracy started playing with a cut-down racket when she was two years old. By age five, she could rally with adult players.

The Road to Excellence
Tracy continued her precocious development as a tennis player. She was coached by Vic Braden and, from around 1970, by Robert Lansdorp, a Dutch tennis professional. She entered her first tennis tournament at the age of seven, and, although she lost to older and stronger players, she was soon winning junior titles. Between 1974 and 1977, when she was eleven to fourteen years old, she won ten national junior titles in various age group divisions. She also played in exhibition matches. In one of these matches, the thirteen-year-old Tracy defeated Bobby Riggs, a former U.S. Open champion and the loser in the famous 1973 "Battle of the Sexes" match with Billie Jean King.

In January, 1977, at the age of fourteen, Tracy entered the qualifying rounds for a women's professional tournament, the Avon Futures, in Portland, Oregon, and won. She maintained her amateur status while playing in professional tournaments, including Wimbledon, where she lost in the second round to Chris Evert, the defending champion.

Tracy Austin backhands the ball to Martina Navratilova at the 1979 U.S. Open. (AP/Wide World Photos)

Major Championships

1978-79	Federation Cup
1978-79, 1981	Wightman Cup
	Italian Open, singles
1979	U.S. Open, singles
1980	Wimbledon, mixed doubles
	Federation Cup
1981	U.S. Open, singles
	Canadian Open

She also reached the quarterfinals of the U.S. Open in 1977. In 1978, she balanced her athletic life—playing professional tournaments, and competing in junior tournaments—with her academic life—attending school at Rolling Hills High School, where she maintained an "A" average. She reached the fourth round at Wimbledon, ultimately losing to Martina Navratilova, and the quarterfinals at the U.S. Open, losing to Evert. However, she won the junior singles titles at both Wimbledon and the U.S. Open.

The Emerging Champion

After competing successfully in professional tournaments as an amateur for two years, Tracy decided to turn professional in October, 1978. He decision was validated by her numerous victories in 1979. In March of 1979, she reached the finals of the Avon Championship in New York, where she lost to Navratilova. In May, she won the Italian Open, her first major international victory, by defeating Evert and ending Evert's 125-match winning streak on clay courts. Although Tracy had been troubled by a leg injury, she reached the semifinals at Wimbledon, eventually falling to Navratilova.

In 1979, Tracy's most important win was the U.S. Open, where she defeated Navratilova in the semifinals and Evert in the finals. At sixteen years, nine months old, she was the youngest player to win the U.S. Open. The Associated Press named her female athlete of the year.

In 1980, although Tracy continued to win a number of tournaments, she began to be bothered by back injuries and sciatic nerve pain. She reached the semifinals of both Wimbledon and the U.S. Open, and she and her brother John won the mixed doubles title at Wimbledon, the first brother-sister pair to win this title. In 1980, she also became the number-

one ranked player, the youngest woman to reach the top at that time.

Much of the first half of 1981 was spent trying to heal her injuries. With the help of a new coach, Marty Riesen, she was able to regain her form by later in the summer. She won the Canadian Open and then defeated Navratilova in a close three-set match to win her second U.S. Open championship.

Continuing the Story

By age eighteen, Tracy had reached a peak in her sport, and she seemed to have a great future in professional tennis ahead of her. However, her injuries persisted. She played off and on through the early 1980's, but she was never able to recover consistently enough to challenge successfully in the major Grand Slam tournaments. Tracy never officially retired, always hoping, and on occasion trying, to return to professional tennis. In 1989, she played World Team Tennis with the New Jersey Stars. However, serious hopes for a comeback vanished when she was severely injured in an automobile accident that required surgery on her right knee and almost a year of intensive therapy. Recognition of her achievements in tennis came in 1992, when she became the youngest person to be inducted into the International Tennis Hall of Fame in Newport, Rhode Island.

Tracy remained involved with tennis. She sponsored a charity tournament in Southern California and participated in other charity tennis events. During the 1980's, she began working in tennis broadcasting, doing tennis features for ABC-TV, and she was a commentator and tennis analyst for NBC, USA, and other television networks. She has participated in the senior women's professional tour. She and her husband Scott Holt had three sons.

Summary

Tracy Austin was the first teenage athlete to achieve success in women's professional tennis. Small and

Honors and Awards

1979	Youngest winner of the U.S. Open
1979, 1981	Associated Press Female Athlete of the Year
1980	Ranked U.S. and world number one
	Women's Sports Foundation Sportswoman of the Year
1992	Inducted into International Tennis Hall of Fame

slight, about 5 feet 4 inches tall, she gave a youthful appearance with her pigtails and eyelet tennis dresses. Although burnout was cited as a reason for her lack of longevity on the women's tennis circuit, the real problem was a succession of injuries that were difficult to overcome. In the few years in which she was able to play relatively injury-free, she competed at the highest level, winning many tournaments, consistently defeating other top tennis professionals such as Martina Navratilova and Chris Evert, and capturing two Grand Slam singles titles at the U.S. Open.

Karen Gould

Additional Sources

Austin, Tracy, and Christine Brennan. *Beyond Center Court: My Story.* New York: William Morrow, 1992.

Austin, Tracy, and Steve Eubanks. *I Know Absolutely Nothing About Tennis: A Tennis Player's Guide to the Sport's History, Equipment, Apparel, Etiquette, Rules, and Language.* Nashville, Tenn.: Rutledge Hill Press, 1997.

Dwyre, Bill. "Austin Remains Quite a Winner." *Los Angeles Times,* July 21, 2005, p. D4.

Wertheim, L. Jon. "Tracy Austin: Out of Pinafores." *Sports Illustrated* 105, no. 1 (July 3, 2006): 114.

Boris Becker

Born: November 22, 1967
      Leimen, Germany
Also known as: Boris Franz Becker (full name)

Early Life

Boris Franz Becker was born in Leimen, a short distance southwest of Heidelberg, West Germany (now Germany), on November 22, 1967. He was the son and only child of Karl-Heinz Becker and Elvira Becker. The father, an architect, designed the tennis center in his town. By the time Boris was three, the senior Becker was training him in tennis, for which Boris displayed a remarkable aptitude. At the age of nine, Boris was playing in national tournaments sponsored by the West German Tennis

Boris Becker playing Andre Agassi at a 1988 tournament. (Diane Johnson/WireImage/Getty Images)

Federation. Local trainers, who recognized the boy's unique ability, selected him for one-on-one training. Intensely competitive, Boris always played an aggressive game. During this early period, Boris was also an avid soccer player. By age twelve, however, his sole athletic interest was tennis. He worked daily with trainer Günther Bosch, mastering the fundamentals of the game and developing an impressive ability to serve and volley.

The Road to Excellence

Boris's devotion to tennis was intense. Early on, he was suspended from the West German Tennis Federation's youth program for a temper tantrum. This suspension apparently chastened the young player, because after that, he was generally polite and decorous on the courts. In 1982, Boris became Germany's junior tennis champion, retaining that status for the next two years. In 1983, he advanced as far as the runner-up spot in his first important international competition, the U.S. Junior Championship. The following April, Bosch brought his protégé to the attention of Ion Tiriac, the former Romanian Davis Cup player who had gained renown as the coach of such tennis stars as Guillermo Vilas, Björn Borg, and Ilie Nastase. Tiriac questioned whether Boris had the temperament to endure the trials and pressures of the professional tennis tour, but after conferring with the sixteen-year-old's parents, he became the youth's manager.

Once Boris graduated from the local *Realschule* in 1984, Tiriac set him on a grueling tournament schedule in order to see if Boris would break under the strain. During the next year, Boris's serve became the most intimidating aspect of his game; he was able to propel the ball across the net at 150 miles an hour. Boris quickly rose from 566th place in the Association of Tennis Professionals to 65th. Playing doubles with Wojteck Fibak, Boris scored a number of wins, although he had not yet won a singles title. He entered the Australian Open, but he was forced to withdraw from Wimble-

Major Championship Victories and Finals

1985-86, 1989	Wimbledon
1988, 1990-91	Wimbledon finalist
1989	U.S. Open
1991, 1996	Australian Open
1992	Gold medal, Olympic men's tennis doubles

Other Notable Victories

1986	Canadian Open
	Volvo International
1986, 1989, 1992	Paris Indoor
1988	WCT Finals
1988-89	German Davis Cup team
1988, 1990	U.S. Hardcourt Championship
1988, 1990-91, 1994	Stockholm Open
1988, 1992, 1995	The Masters/ATP Tour Championship
1989	Paris Open
	U.S. Pro Championship
1992	Mercedes Super 9

Honors, Awards, and Milestones

1985	Youngest winner of the Wimbledon singles title
	Rolex Rookie of the Year
	German Davis Cup team
2003	Inducted into International Tennis Hall of Fame

don because of a torn tendon in his left ankle that required surgery.

The Emerging Champion

When Boris returned to the tour, he attracted attention by defeating Stefan Edberg and winning the young master's crown in world competition. He continued on the Grand Prix circuit during the ensuing months, then, in June, 1985, he beat Johan Kriek, 6-2, 6-3, in the Stella Artois Grass Court Championships in England. However, people were not betting on Boris to win, or to come close to winning, the men's singles at Wimbledon.

Wimbledon was tailor-made for Boris, whose strength in serving and volleying was well suited to its grass courts. Boyish looking with freckles, a mop of reddish blond hair, and an infectious smile, Boris won over the spectators with his acrobatics, his risk-taking, and his obvious command of the game. He defeated five formidable opponents, despite having twisted his ankle in a set against Tim Mayotte that required him to adapt to playing with this painful impediment. Finally, beating Anders Jarryd, 3-6, 7-6, 6-3, 6-3, Boris was up against Kevin

Curren, who had defeated Jimmy Connors and John McEnroe. He wore Curren down, defeating him 6-3, 6-7, 7-6, 6-4, to become—at that time—the youngest single men's champion of the world at the age of seventeen. Despite his record-breaking victory, Boris had not yet played the four top-seeded players in the world: Ivan Lendl, Mats Wilander, McEnroe, and Connors. Skeptics predicted that he would get his comeuppance when he played against them.

Continuing the Story

Tennis gurus began to speculate not only on how Boris would fare against the top-seeded players but also on how he would hold up under the mental strain of competition. Some, observing his self-assurance, expected that, when faced with self-doubts, he would ultimately break emotionally. Although this did not happen, Boris's play after Wimbledon was inconsistent. He had some notable successes on clay, hard, and grass courts, but between August, 1985, and March, 1986, he did not win a single tournament title and was trounced by Joakim Nystrom, Lendl, and others.

Boris turned around, however, to defeat Lendl soundly in the Volvo-Chicago Tennis Tournament in March, 1986, having first beaten Connors in the semifinals. Nevertheless, Boris showed a disturbing tendency to lose in the early rounds of matches, then to recover. His own explanation of this phenomenon was that consistency comes with age. He also explained that some of his disappointing performances in his home country were the result of the high expectations of the German people. They did not leave him alone, making it difficult for him to concentrate.

In 1986, Boris again took the men's singles honors at Wimbledon, defeating Lendl, 6-4, 6-3, 7-5. Lendl, however, turned the tables by defeating Boris in the 1986 Volvo International competition. Boris was also defeated in the 1987 Australian Open. Shortly after this, Bosch resigned as Boris's coach, citing Boris's lackadaisical attitude. In 1991, Boris won the Australian Open and made it to the finals of Wimbledon in July, before suffering defeat to Michael Stich, a fellow German.

At the 1992 Summer Olympics in Barcelona, Spain, Boris won a men's doubles gold medal playing with Stich. He married Barbara Feltus in December, 1993. In 1996, he won his second Australian Open title by beating Michael Chang in four sets. In 1999, he lost to Patrick Rafter in the fourth round at Wimbledon. This was the last time the three-time Wimbledon champion played on the grass courts where he became a star tennis player. In 1999, Boris decided to retire from the tennis circuit and, in 2003, he was inducted into the International Tennis Hall of Fame. Boris wrote an autobiography called *The Player*, in which he discloses intimate details of his life in the spotlight.

Summary

Boris Becker, facing the problem of almost instant celebrity, spent considerable time adjusting to the demands of a tennis professional. Because he was a champion, he was frequently in the public eye.

However, the affable German with the rocket serve handled the distractions well enough to have earned a place among the best in professional tennis.

R. Baird Shuman

Additional Sources

Becker, Boris. *The Player.* London: Bantam, 2005.

Breskvar, Boris, with Ulrich Kaiser. *Boris Becker's Tennis: The Making of a Champion.* Champaign, Ill.: Leisure Press, 1987.

Collins, Bud. *Total Tennis: The Ultimate Tennis Encyclopedia.* Toronto: Sport Media, 2003.

Fein, Paul. *Tennis Confidential: Today's Greatest Players, Matches, and Controversies.* Washington, D.C.: Brassey's, 2002.

Phillips, Caryl. *The Right Set: A Tennis Anthology.* New York: Vintage Books, 1999.

James Blake

Born: December 28, 1979
      Yonkers, New York
Also known as: James Riley Blake (full name)

Early Life

James Riley Blake was born in Yonkers, New York, on December 28, 1979, but grew up in Fairfield, Connecticut. James has mixed racial heritage. His late father, Thomas, Sr., was African American, while his mother, Betty, was a Caucasian from England. At young ages, James and his older brother Thomas exhibited interest in tennis. Developing as an athlete was more physically challenging for James than for Thomas. James suffered from scoliosis, a curvature of the spine, and he had to wear a back brace several hours a day to help alleviate the condition. Despite his medical problem, he was determined to succeed on the tennis court. Both James and Thomas enrolled in the Harlem Junior Tennis Program in New York City. There, the boys received quality instruction that conformed to the Blake family's middle-class budget.

The Road to Excellence

When he completed high school, James followed his brother to Harvard University. Both brothers received tennis scholarships and each eventually earned all-American status. Thomas graduated in 1998 and began a career as a professional player. James, the more talented, if less physically imposing, of the two, decided to become a professional before receiving a degree. In his sophomore year, he became the number-one player in the National Collegiate Athletic Association rankings, prompting his decision to forego the remainder of college. He began competing in tournaments sponsored by the leading tour for male players, the Association of Tennis Professionals (ATP), as well as in minor-league tournaments conducted by other organizations.

Like other male players of African descent, James's success was often measured against that of Arthur Ashe—the greatest African American male tennis player in history. In his early career, James did not approach Ashe's venerated status. James's professional career got off to a slow start; the transition from college phenomenon to successful professional was neither quick nor easy.

The Emerging Champion

James often competed in minor-league tournaments, a typical experience for professional players at the beginning of their careers. The prize money offered in such events is not great, but the competition is of lesser quality than in larger tournaments. In this way, a new professional competitor is able to earn match victories for ranking points. After becoming more comfortable and successful competing at this level, a player can progress to other venues where the money, competition, and ranking points are all greater. The rise to the top of the rankings, consequently, is usually a slow and tedious process. This was the case with James. He won several of these minor-league contests but was

James Blake. (Ahmed Jadallah/Reuters/Landov)

ranked only 293 in the world at the end of 1999 and 212 the following year.

In August, 2002, in Washington, D.C., James finally won a singles title in an ATP event. However, he did not win another until 2005. Interestingly, he had more success in doubles play during the early years of his professional career, winning five tournaments between 2002 and 2004 with a variety of partners. Winning a doubles title is a significant achievement, but many players who aspire to win singles events play fewer doubles matches as their success in singles play increases. Early in their careers, these players often lose in the first and second rounds of tournaments and, thus, need the doubles experience to stay competitive and to win extra money. However, when players' successes in singles increases, they avoid playing doubles in order to rest for the extra singles matches they are playing. James followed this pattern to singles success. He rarely played doubles after 2004.

Continuing the Story

In May, 2004, James's career almost came to an end. While practicing for a tournament in Rome, Italy, he lunged for a ball and slammed into one of the metal posts that hold the net in place. The impact broke one of his vertebrae. Doctors were not sure if he would ever be able to perform as an athlete again. To recuperate, James had to exercise more and practice tennis less. His recovery was slow. However, when he returned to the ATP tour, he experienced more success in singles than he ever had before. In 2005, he won two singles championships and finished the year ranked number twenty-four in the world. The following year, he won five tournaments and soared to a ranking of number four.

Despite making millions of dollars and ranking near the top of the tennis ratings, as of 2008, James had failed to add a victory in a Grand Slam event— the Australian Open, the U.S. Open, the French

Association of Tennis Professionals Victories

Date	Tournament
2002	Cincinnati Masters, doubles (with Todd Martin)
	Legg Mason Tennis Classic
2003	Tennis Channel Open, doubles, (with Mark Merklein)
2004	SAP Open, doubles (with Mardy Fish)
	U.S. Men's Clay Court Championships, doubles (with Mardy Fish)
	BMW Open, doubles (with Mark Merklein)
2005-06	Stockholm Open
2005, 2007	Pilot Pen Tennis
2006	Tennis Channel Open
	Indianapolis Tennis Championships
	Thailand Open
2006-07	Medibank International

Open, and Wimbledon—to his resume. Winning a single's title at one of those tournaments is every tennis player's dream and secures his or her place in sports history. James not only has failed to win one of these coveted tournaments but also has not made the final round of any of them. Many tennis observers have predicted that he will win one or more of these events at some point in the future.

Summary

James Blake has been ranked highly, and he has won several tennis tournaments. He has established himself as the third best male tennis player of African descent, behind Arthur Ashe and Yannick Noah. As his career continues, each victory will add to his legacy. Whether he can match or surpass the achievements of Ashe and Noah, however, is undetermined.

Roger D. Hardaway

Additional Sources

Blake, James, with Andrew Friedman. *Breaking Back: How I Lost Everything and Won Back My Life.* New York: HarperCollins, 2007.

Bodo, Peter. "Stepping Up." *Tennis,* April, 2002.

Wertheim, L. Jon. "The Late Bloomer." *Sports Illustrated* 106, no. 2 (January 15, 2007).

Björn Borg

Born: June 6, 1956
  Södertalje, Sweden
Also known as: Björn Rune Borg (full name)

Early Life

Björn Rune Borg was born on June 6, 1956, in Södertalje, Sweden—a suburb of Stockholm. Björn was an only child whose first love was ice hockey. He was the starting center for Södertalje's junior ice hockey team by the time he was nine. One day, however, his father won a city championship in table tennis. The prize was a tennis racket, and Björn's father passed the racket on to his son. Björn soon discovered that he loved tennis more than ice hockey. For weeks he used the family garage door as a backstop. When Björn was eleven, Percy Rosburg, a nationally known tennis coach, came to Södertalje looking for players to try out for the Swedish national tennis team. Rosburg was impressed with Björn's ability and asked if he wanted to become his pupil. Björn was quick to accept the offer, even though it meant a ninety-minute train ride to get to Stockholm.

The Road to Excellence

Björn was an unorthodox player. He used a two-handed grip at all times and did this because his first racket was too heavy. As his strength developed, however, he was able to hit his forehand shots with one hand. Still, he continued to use two hands for his backhand, even though his coaches advised against the practice. Despite this flaw in his game, Björn began to win tournaments. When he was thirteen he was the national junior champion in the age thirteen and fourteen division. Björn was a success as a tennis player but not as a student. At the age of fifteen, he felt he had to make a choice between school and tennis.

Soon after leaving school in 1972, Björn competed in the Madrid Grand Prix. He won the junior title in Madrid. He also won the junior crowns at Berlin, Barcelona, Milan, Wimbledon, and Miami. He was, therefore, considered the junior world champion. Björn also participated in the international Davis Cup competition. He won both his singles matches against opponents from New Zealand and became a national hero. Lennart Bergelin, leader of the

Björn Borg sinking to his knees after winning his fifth consecutive Wimbledon title in 1980. (Rob Taggart/Hulton Archive/Getty Images)

Swedish Davis Cup team, soon became Björn's coach. Bergelin helped Björn to become a good tournament player. He insisted that players practice every day and believed that a tournament player must concentrate solely on tennis. Björn was willing to do this, and in 1972, at the age of sixteen, he became a professional tennis player.

The Emerging Champion
Once Björn decided to become a professional tennis player, however, he faced a tremendous problem. In order to compete, a player must have enough money to travel and pay other expenses. Björn's family was not wealthy, and he was not old enough to find a job. Fortunately for Björn, the Swedish Tennis Association was able to persuade Scandinavian Airlines to donate the money Björn needed to compete. Björn did not win many tournaments in his first year on the international tennis circuit. Still, he was able to refine his game and develop the self-confidence he needed to succeed. Although he was still very young, Björn was able to ignore distractions that upset other, older players.

Major Championship Victories and Finals

1974-75, 1978-81	French Open
1976-80	Wimbledon
1976, 1978, 1980-81	U.S. Open finalist
1981	Wimbledon finalist

Other Notable Victories

1974	U.S. Clay Court Championship
1974-76	U.S. Pro Championship
1974, 1978	Italian Open
1974, 1978-79	Swedish Open
1975	On winning Swedish Davis Cup team
1976	WCT Finals
1977	U.S. National Indoors
1977, 1979-80	WCT Monte Carlo
1978	WCT Tournament of Champions
1979	Canadian Open
1980-81	The Masters

Honors, Awards, and Milestones

1972-80	Swedish Davis Cup team
1979-80	Ranked number one by ATP
1981	Ranked number one by Sweden
1987	Inducted into International Tennis Hall of Fame

When he appeared in the 1973 Wimbledon tournament, he became famous. His youth and his behavior on the court caught the attention of the audience and reporters. He was surrounded by fans whenever he left his hotel. He became a tennis superstar. The next year, 1974, he won the Italian Open and became the youngest player to win a major international tournament. Two weeks later, he became the youngest player to win the French Open. His victories, however, exhausted him, and he was eliminated from the 1974 Wimbledon competition. However, he recovered to win the U.S. Pro Championship. In 1975, Björn won the French Open and the U.S. Pro Championship again. He failed, however, to advance to the final round at Wimbledon.

The next year, Björn opened the season with a victory in the World Championship of Tennis (WCT) but then lost the French Open. This defeat was, however, a blessing in disguise. Björn used the time to prepare a devastating first serve to use at Wimbledon. He became the youngest Wimbledon champion in forty-five years. He was also the first in twenty-three years to complete the tournament without losing a single set.

Continuing the Story
Björn's victory at Wimbledon was followed by yet another loss in the U.S. Open. Björn played at his peak in the U.S. Open, and the tiebreaker round with Jimmy Connors was a legendary match. Nevertheless, he was defeated and was to be defeated repeatedly in the U.S. Open. He won Wimbledon five times. He captured the French Open on six occasions—four of those in succession. However, he never won the U.S. Open, and despite his considerable acclaim as a tennis player, he did not win the Grand Slam of tennis.

Björn was not, by conventional standards, a great tennis player. He was, however, a superb athlete, and his concentration on the task at hand was absolute. Björn did not go on the attack, but waited calmly on the defensive and wore his opponents down. Such an approach, although successful and profitable, took its toll physically and emotionally. In 1983, at the age of twenty-seven and after fifteen years of competition, Björn retired. In 1991, he decided to live the comfortable life his hard work had earned for him and for his family. He made a brief return to the professional men's tour. In 1993, Björn began playing on the Worldwide Senior Tennis Circuit.

Summary

Björn Borg was the first legitimate international tennis superstar. He made recreational tennis into a multimillion-dollar industry. His example also led many young players to professional careers much earlier than was the case before he left the amateur ranks. Bjorn ranked among the best tennis players of his time and set the bar for the subsequent generation of players, such as Pete Sampras and Roger Federer.

J. K. Sweeney

Additional Sources

Borg, Björn, and Eugene L. Scott. *My Life and Game.* New York: Simon & Schuster, 1980.

Buckley, James, and David Fischer. *Greatest Sports Rivalries: Twenty-five of the Most Intense and Historic Battles Ever.* New York: Barnes & Noble, 2005.

Collins, Bud. *Total Tennis: The Ultimate Tennis Encyclopedia.* Toronto: Sport Media, 2003.

Folley, Malcolm. *Borg Versus McEnroe: The Greatest Rivalry, the Greatest Match.* London: Headline, 2006.

Orr, Frank, and George Tracz. *The Dominators: The Remarkable Athletes Who Changed Their Sport Forever.* Toronto: Warwick, 2004.

Robson, Douglas. "The Fall." *Tennis,* September, 2006, 83.

Jean Borotra

Born: August 13, 1898
    Domaine du Pouy, France
Died: July 17, 1994
    Arbonne, France
Also known as: Jean Robert Borotra (full name);
    the Bounding Basque

Early Life

Jean Robert Borotra was born on August 13, 1898, near the Spanish border in Domaine du Pouy, France. He was the son of Henri Borotra and Marguerite Revet. Jean was a country boy who was always active. He became internationally known as "the Bounding Basque," and that description fitted the style he had developed at a young age. Jean first learned tennis by playing with his brothers, Fred and Édouard. He began playing in obscure tournaments in the Basses-Pyrénées area, in the province of Pelote. Jean was an unorthodox player. Part of his training was traveling either on foot or by bicycle approximately seven miles to and from school. He seemed to have a never-ending supply of energy and enthusiasm for life and the sports he played.

The Road to Excellence

Jean developed a style of tennis that was uniquely his own. In the early tournaments in his native Basque region, his intensity and flair made him a crowd favorite. He seemed to be in constant motion. Jean always attacked, which was not the norm for tennis in his day. He even grunted when he served. Once he discovered how useful the volley could be, he became the first outstanding serve-and-volley proponent in the game. Jean attracted even broader attention when he played in a 1921 tournament in Paris. His aggressive playing style and his dramatic attire—he wore a blue beret—made him stand out.

In 1922, Jean was named to the French Davis Cup team. His reputation as an intense net player made him a feared competitor. Not until 1923 did the French Davis Cup team include all the members of what became known as the "Four Musketeers." The other Musketeers were Jacques Brug-

non, Henri Cochet, and René Lacoste. Brugnon was a doubles specialist, while the other two competed with Jean for the major singles titles throughout the rest of the 1920's and into the 1930's. There was a definite theatrical quality to Jean's game; the more a crowd cheered for him, the better his performance. He loved to dazzle an audience, and was capable of doing so.

The Emerging Champion

Jean won his first Grand Slam singles titles in 1924, when he captured both the French and Wimbledon Championships. He was more than a tennis player, though. At the age of twenty-two, Jean had first traveled to Paris to attend the famous engineering college École Polytechnique. He was a whirlwind both on and off the court. Always believing in the benefits of fitness, Jean went through a rigorous routine of physical exercises. He lived life with the same abandon with which he played tennis. Not only did he receive a degree in engineering, but he also earned a doctorate in law.

The Four Musketeers won their first Davis Cup in 1927, and they did not relinquish the Cup until the British defeated the quartet in 1933. Each year from 1924 until 1932, one of the Musketeers won the French singles title. In 1931, Jean won the French Championship. He was able to win Wimbledon again in 1926, and he won his only Australian Championship singles title in 1928. The only Grand Slam singles title that eluded him was the U.S. National Championship (now U.S. Open). Jean did have a good deal of success in the U.S. Indoor Championship, winning that title four times; he won every odd year from 1925 to 1931. In his career, Jean won many French and British indoor titles, and he is considered by many experts to be the best indoor tennis player of all time.

Continuing the Story

Jean seemed to have a flair for the dramatic and was not above distracting his opponent with some curious antics on the court. He attempted to be a crowd pleaser at all times. His most effective shot was the high backhand volley, and he was so proficient at this stroke that it became known as the "Borotra Prod." Jean's flair was evident off the court also; he was very witty and charming. Never one to slow down, Jean raced from a business meeting to a train station and off to a tennis match. He won his last Grand Slam title in 1933, by capturing the Wimbledon doubles with fellow Musketeer Brugnon.

In 1940, Jean became France's general commissioner for general education and sports. He served in that capacity until 1942, when he was captured by the German Gestapo and deported during World War II. For his military efforts, Jean was made a Commander of the British Empire and received the Croix de Guerre. He also received a medal for escaping from the Germans and a medal for resisting deportation.

After the war, Jean again played on the French Davis Cup team. In 1948, at the age of fifty, he and Marcel Bernard won the U.S. Indoor Championship doubles title; Jean's physical fitness regimen had kept him in fine shape. In 1976, Jean and the other Musketeers were inducted into the International Tennis Hall of Fame in Newport, Rhode Island. Jean was still able to compete in veteran tennis tournaments when he was in his seventies. He died in 1994.

Summary

Jean Borotra was a wonderful showman and a great athlete, and he gave the tennis world some of its most memorable displays of prowess. With Jean and the other Musketeers, France was a top tennis power during the late 1920's and early 1930's. Tennis fans around the world loved the country boy from the Basque region.

Jeffry Jensen

Additional Sources

Collins, Bud. *Total Tennis: The Ultimate Tennis Encyclopedia.* Toronto: Sport Media, 2003.

Faure, Jean-Michel. "National Identity and the Sporting Champion: Jean Borotra and French History." *The International Journal of the History of Sport* 13, no. 1 (1996): 86.

Parsons, John. *The Ultimate Encyclopedia of Tennis: The Definitive Illustrated Guide to World Tennis.* London: Carlton, 2006.

Major Championship Victories and Finals

Year	Event
1924-25, 1928-29, 1934, 1936	French Championship doubles (with René Lacoste, Jacques Brugnon, and Marcel Bernard)
1924, 1926	Wimbledon
1924, 1927, 1934	French Championship mixed doubles (with M. Bordes; with Colette Rosambert)
1924, 1931	French Championship
1925	Wimbledon mixed doubles (with Suzanne Lenglen)
1925, 1927, 1929	Wimbledon finalist
1925, 1929	French Championship finalist
1925, 1932-33	Wimbledon doubles (with Lacoste and Brugnon)
1926	French Championship mixed doubles finalist (with Mrs. Le Besnerais)
	U.S. National Championship finalist
	U.S. National Championship mixed doubles (with Elizabeth Ryan)
1927	French Championship doubles finalist (with Lacoste)
1928	Australian Championship
	Australian Championship doubles (with Brugnon)
1934	Wimbledon doubles finalist (with Brugnon)

Other Notable Victories

Year	Event
1925, 1927, 1929, 1931	U.S. Indoor Championship
1927-32	On winning French Davis Cup team
1935, 1938, 1948-49	British Covered Court Championship
1948	U.S. Indoor Championship doubles (with Marcel Bernard)
1956	U.S. Grass Court Championship-Men's 45 doubles (with Harry Hopman)

Honors, Awards, and Milestones

French Davis Cup team (1922-47)

Légion d'Honneur

Croix de Guerre

Commander of the British Empire

Inducted into International Tennis Hall of Fame (1976)

Don Budge

Born: June 13, 1915
        Oakland, California
Died: January 26, 2000
        Scranton, Pennsylvania
Also known as: John Donald Budge (full name)

Early Life

John Donald Budge was born on June 13, 1915, in Oakland, California. A shy redhead with freckles, Don grew up in a family of modest means, in which all members were athletically inclined. His father, John Budge, was a former world-class soccer player with the renowned Glasgow Rangers, before he emigrated from Scotland for health reasons. As a boy, Don had no interest in tennis. In fact, he scorned it. He was good at baseball, though, and was a tough left-handed hitter, a fact that later accounted for his remarkable backhand strokes in tennis. Whenever he started to play tennis, the tall, lanky boy soon got bored and headed out to the ballpark. Don's older brother, Lloyd, however, was an avid tennis player. One evening over dinner, when Don was fifteen years old, Lloyd chided him until Don impulsively agreed to enter the California state boys' championship that was to be held the following week.

The Road to Excellence

After only one week of practice, Don entered his first tennis tournament and won. He was exhilarated. Three years later he went on to win both the senior and junior California championships in one season. Even in those early days as an amateur, Don was an impressive player—steady yet explosive. He was tall and slender yet extremely strong. His strength in tennis was his sustained power. His backhand had a freedom of motion that was envied by every player who ever watched him. Originating from his baseball days, his mighty backhand stroke was guided by his left hand.

By the time he was nineteen, Don's game sufficiently impressed Walter Pate, the man in the best position to help Don's career. Pate thought Don was the player who could help bring the Davis Cup back to his team. When Pate was made team captain, he accepted on the condition that Don be part of the team, ahead of the older players. Don began working on his problems as a player. Pate felt his forehand needed work. Champion Fred Perry gave Don tips for his footwork. Fellow teammate Sidney Wood straightened out his forehand and encouraged him to choose one grip instead of experimenting with many.

The Emerging Champion

Don's tennis skills were still in the developmental stage in 1935, when Pate entered him in the Davis

Don Budge, who was the first tennis player to complete a Grand Slam. (Courtesy of Amateur Athletic Foundation of Los Angeles)

Major Championship Victories and Finals

1935	U.S. National Championship doubles finals (with Gene Mako)
1936	U.S. National Championship finalist
	Wimbledon doubles finalist (with Sarah Palfrey Fabyan)
1936, 1938	U.S. National Championship doubles (with Mako)
1937-38	U.S. National Championship
	U.S. National Championship mixed doubles (with Fabyan and Alice Marble)
	Wimbledon
	Wimbledon doubles (with Mako)
	Wimbledon mixed doubles (with Marble)
1938	French Championship
	Australian Championship

Other Notable Victories

1937-38	On winning U.S. Davis Cup team
1940, 1942	U.S. Pro Championship
1940-42, 1947, 1949	U.S. Pro Championship doubles (with Fred Perry, Bobby Riggs, and Frank Kovacs)
1947	World Professional Singles Tournament
1948-50, 1953	World Professional Doubles Tournament (with Perry, Pancho Gonzales, and Frank Sedgman)

Cup singles against Australia. Leg cramps nearly finished him in a draining four-hour match against Jack Crawford, but in a last-ditch effort, he won, and his team went on to play the British for the Cup. The team, however, lost. Soon there was no one around who could compete with Don, except Perry, who shortly turned pro. This left Don to lead the way to another Davis Cup. First, however, he had to beat the German Gottfried von Cramm, in a match considered by many as the most dramatic and finest Davis Cup encounter ever played.

During the match, von Cramm received a long-distance call from none other than Adolf Hitler, who wanted von Cramm to restore national honor and demonstrate his racial superiority. The call put undue pressure on the German player, known for his anti-Nazi sympathies. When, in the end, Don won the match, von Cramm embraced his opponent and declared the match the finest he had ever played, and within the year, von Cramm was interned in a Nazi prison. Don set records as the first player ever to win the French, British, Australian,

and American national championships in a single year. Thus, Don completed the first Grand Slam in tennis history.

Continuing the Story

Late in 1938, the year Don scored his unprecedented Grand Slam, American sportswriters voted him the country's top athlete, amateur or professional. In succeeding years, only Rod Laver matched his achievement by completing a Grand Slam in 1962 and 1969. Consequently, Don was more than ready to turn pro. For three glorious years he went on to dominate the pros just as he had the amateurs. He toured with Ellsworth Vines, then Perry, Bobby Riggs and Frank Kovacs, and finally Bill Tilden.

Soon after, Pearl Harbor cut short Don's professional career, when he joined the Air Force. Five years later, when he returned to the grass courts, his game was not the same. He was still young—only thirty-one—but no longer able to take on Riggs during their two-month tour. Don's brief tennis career had come to a close. Many believe Don was one of the best ever even though his achievement lasted only a few short years. In those years, Don's triumphs included the return of the Davis Cup to the United States in 1937, after a decade of losses to France and England; his Grand Slam a year later; and his invincibility at Wimbledon and Forest Hills, where he rarely ever lost even a set. Despite all this, Don claimed the greatest thrill of his life was meeting Pablo Casals, a cello virtuoso, who gave Don a private concert in return for the pleasure of watching him play tennis.

Records and Milestones

Turned professional in 1938
U.S. Davis Cup team (1935-38)
First to win the Grand Slam (1938)

Honors and Awards

1936-38	Ranked number one by the USTA
1937-38	Associated Press Male Athlete of the Year
1964	Inducted into National Lawn Tennis Hall of Fame

Summary

During his two all-conquering years, Don Budge was the world's top tennis amateur at Wimbledon and Forest Hills. He was the first player ever to win the French, British, Australian, and American national championships in a single year. His two-year reign at the top, in which he did not lose a single match that mattered, stands as one of the great all-time sports achievements.

Nan White

Additional Sources

Collins, Bud. *Total Tennis: The Ultimate Tennis Encyclopedia.* Toronto: Sport Media, 2003.

Deford, Frank, Mark Mravic, and Richard O'Brien. "What Might Have Been." *Sports Illustrated* 92, no. 5 (February 7, 2000): 32-33.

Finn, Robin. "Don Budge, First to Win Tennis's Grand Slam, Dies at Eighty-four." *The New York Times,* January 27, 2000, p. B7.

María Bueno

Born: October 11, 1939
    São Paulo, Brazil
Also known as: María Esther Audion Bueno (full name)

Early Life

María Esther Audion Bueno was born on October 11, 1939, in São Paulo, Brazil. María lived with her parents and her elder brother in an attractive downtown house that was opposite a large sports club. María's father, Pedro, played tennis as a hobby, and when María was six years old he presented her with a tennis racket. She loved the game immediately and spent every possible minute practicing at the sports club. She played against her father and her brother Pedrinho, who was also a tennis enthusiast. When María was twelve, she won a girls' tennis tournament in São Paulo, as well as a swimming competition.

The Road to Excellence

From an early age María was determined to be the best. She studied the techniques of the great tennis players and particularly admired Bill Tilden, a famous tennis star from the 1920's. María tried to copy his service style from pictures she saw in books. She also attended tennis tournaments in her hometown and quietly learned from close observation of leading players in action. She never took formal tennis lessons or had a personal coach. In 1954, when she was only fourteen years old, María became the women's tennis champion of Brazil. The following year she represented her country at the Pan-American Games in Mexico City, Mexico. She won international tournaments in Venezuela and Argentina, and in 1957, she traveled to the United States, where she won the Orange Bowl junior championship in Miami, Florida. In spite of these early tennis successes, María did not neglect her education. Her father wanted her to become a teacher, and she attended

college with that goal in mind. Having secured her teacher's certificate, she taught in elementary school, but tennis was still her first love.

The Emerging Champion

In 1958, María played in thirty-two tournaments, winning eighteen of them. Her victories included the Italian Championship in May, her first major title. With her partner, Althea Gibson, she also won the women's doubles title at Wimbledon, England. Sportswriters and fans across the world, excited by María's graceful and skillful game, began predicting that she would become the next great woman

María Bueno, who won five major championships in the 1960's.
(Courtesy of International Tennis Hall of Fame)

Major Championship Victories and Finals

1958, 1960, 1963, 1965-66	Wimbledon doubles (with Althea Gibson, Darlene Hard, Billie Jean Moffitt, and Nancy Richey)
1959-60, 1964	Wimbledon
1959-60, 1967	Wimbledon mixed doubles finalist (with Neale Fraser, Robert Howe, and Ken Flethcher)
1959, 1963-64, 1966	U.S. National Championship
1960	French Championship doubles (with Hard)
	French Championship mixed doubles (with Howe)
	Australian Championship doubles (with Christine Truman)
1960-62, 1967-68	U.S. National Championship doubles (with Hard, Richey, and Margaret Court)
1960, 1968	U.S. National Championship finalist
1964	French Championship finalist
1965	Australian Championship finalist
1965, 1967	Wimbledon finalist
1967	Wimbledon doubles finalist (with Richey)
1968	U.S. Open doubles (with Court)

Other Notable Victories

1958, 1961, 1965	Italian Championship
1962	Italian Championship doubles (with Hard)
1963	Pan-American Games gold medalist
1964-65	Irish Championship

tennis player. The experts were proved right the next year, when María's talents reached full bloom. In 1959, she won the two most coveted titles in the game. In July, she became the women's singles champion at Wimbledon, defeating American Darlene Hard by the score of 6-4, 6-3. In September, María won the U.S. National Championship by beating Christine Truman of Great Britain, 6-1, 6-4. She became a national heroine in Brazil; a postage stamp was issued with her picture on it, and a statue of María was erected in São Paulo.

At this time, María was playing consistently brilliant tennis. She had learned not to get upset when decisions went against her, and her all-around game had no weaknesses. She had a strong service, and her ground strokes were faultless. She was also a very exciting player to watch, in part because she brought a new daring to the women's game. At a time when women's matches tended to feature long rallies with each player remaining on or near the baseline, María was always ready to follow up her service by advancing toward the net. She then won points with devastating volleys sent out of the reach of her opponent. María was a great adventurer on the court and never put safety first. She went for spectacular shots that skimmed just above the tape and brought chalk up from the lines. The fans loved her. In 1960, María retained the women's singles title at Wimbledon, beating the South African player Sandra Reynolds, 8-6, 6-0. In a surprise result, though, María's old rival, Darlene Hard, defeated her in the final of the U.S. National Championship.

Continuing the Story

With the entire world of tennis at her feet, María was struck a devastating blow in May, 1961, when she contracted hepatitis, a serious liver disease. She did not compete in any tennis tournaments until April of the following year. When she played at Wimbledon in June, 1962, it was obvious that she had not fully recovered from her illness. The luster had gone from her game, and she was beaten in the semifinals by Věra Suková, of Czechoslovakia.

The following year, María was eliminated in the quarterfinals at Wimbledon by Billie Jean Moffitt (later King). María's admirers wondered whether she would ever win a major tournament again. She did not give up, however, and in September, 1963, she regained her form and swept to a 7-5, 6-4 victory over Australia's Margaret Smith (later Court) in the final of the U.S. Open. The brilliant María was back, and at Wimbledon the following year she recaptured the singles title with another victory

Honors, Awards, and Milestones

1959-60	Ranked number one in the world
1978	Inducted into International Tennis Hall of Fame
1993	Inducted into New York Museum and Sports Hall of Fame
2003	Given the Jean Borotra Sportsmanship Award
2006	Received Raccheta D'Oro Award

over Smith. The intense rivalry between María and Smith was one of the main features of women's tennis in the mid-1960's.

At the U.S. Open at Forest Hills, New York, in September, 1964, María underlined her return to form by trouncing Carol Caldwell Graebner 6-1, 6-0—the most one-sided women's final at Forest Hills for forty-eight years. In 1965, Smith won back the Wimbledon singles title, and María also lost her U.S. Open title to King. In 1966, however, María triumphed again, beating the American Nancy Richey to win her fourth U.S. singles title. After this success the ascendancy in women's tennis passed decisively to Court and King. In 1968, María's last major title came when she teamed with her former rival Court to win the U.S. women's doubles title for the fourth time. She retired from tennis in 1971. After retiring from competitive tennis, María became active with celebrity and charity tennis events.

Summary

María Bueno was one of the all-time great women tennis players. She had grace, flair, and imagination. There was an artistry about her game that made her a joy to watch. She was often compared with many great players from an earlier time, such as the French star Suzanne Lenglen and American Alice Marble.

Bryan Aubrey

Additional Sources

Collins, Bud. *Total Tennis: The Ultimate Tennis Encyclopedia.* Toronto: Sport Media, 2003.

Wancke, Henry. "María Bueno: Still a Champion." *Forty-fiver* (Autumn, 2006).

Jennifer Capriati

Born: March 29, 1976
New York, New York
Also known as: Jennifer Marie Capriati (full
name)

Early Life

Jennifer Marie Capriati was born on March 29,
1976, in New York, New York, to Stefano Capriati, a
professional tennis instructor and former motion-
picture stuntman, and Denise Capriati, an airline
flight attendant. The Capriatis were a true tennis
family; Denise was taking tennis lessons from
Stefano on the courts in New York only 17 hours before Jennifer was born.

Jennifer Capriati at the U.S. Open in 1999. (Carol
Newsom/AFP/Getty Images)

Jennifer picked up a tennis racket for the first
time when she was three years old. At four, she began hitting tennis balls on a regular basis. The family then moved to Lauderhill, Florida, to be in a
year-round tennis environment. Stefano asked
Jimmy Evert, the father of tennis star Chris Evert, to
begin coaching Jennifer. He agreed and coached
Jennifer for five years. Jennifer became friends
with Chris and practiced with her often. In 1987,
the tennis star gave her a bracelet inscribed, "Jennifer, Love, Chris"; Jennifer wore the bracelet during
all of her tennis matches.

Tennis, however, was only part of Jennifer's life.
She attended the Palmer Academy and consistently earned A's. She also attended the Saddle-
brook International Tennis Center in Wesley Chapel, Florida.

The Road to Excellence

At the age of twelve, Jennifer began winning many
amateur tournaments, and she often beat girls who
were much older than she was. In 1988, she won the
national eighteen-and-under clay-court and hardcourt championships as well as the junior championships at the French Open and the U.S. Open.
The International Tennis Federation ranked her
second among eighteen-and-under players.

Jennifer's obvious ability at so young an age excited tennis fans, who expected great things from
her as a professional. In 1990, the Women's International Tennis Federation ruled that the earliest a
young player could become a professional was in
the month the player turned fourteen. The rule
was made to protect players from injury at a young
age.

In preparation for Jennifer's professional career, her parents took her to a sports-medicine
clinic in Virginia to evaluate her physical development in order to prevent injuries. In November of 1989, she played an exhibition match against
twenty-five-year-old Laura Gildemeister, who
was ranked in the top twenty-five professionals.
Thirteen-year-old Jennifer won the match by the
score of 6-4, 6-1, confirming her professional-level
ability. Jennifer then got a chance to hit with the

legendary tennis player Martina Navratilova. Although they did not keep score, Jennifer experienced the power of Navratilova's ground strokes and serve.

The Emerging Champion

On March 6, 1990, in the month of her fourteenth birthday, Jennifer made her debut as a professional in the Virginia Slims Tournament in Boca Raton, Florida. She beat four seeded players before losing to Gabriela Sabatini in the finals. The media was calling her the "eighth-grade wonder" and the "next Chris Evert." She also played doubles in the same tournament with the great Billie Jean King, but they lost in the second round of the competition.

Like Evert, Jennifer developed a two-handed backhand and learned to rally endlessly from the baseline, but she hit her ground strokes with more power and came to the net more often than her idol did. Her serve was clocked at an average of 94 miles per hour, and she showed her cool nerves in pressure situations.

In 1990, Jennifer lost to Monica Seles in the finals of the French Open, becoming the youngest Grand Slam runner-up in history. She also lost to Navratilova in the Family Circle Cup finals that year. In October, she won her first professional tournament, the Puerto Rican Open, and was ranked eighth in the world. *Tennis* magazine named her the 1990 rookie of the year.

Milestones

At age fourteen became youngest Grand Slam semifinalist

Youngest competitor in Wightman Cup history

Honors and Awards

1989	*Tennis* magazine Junior Player of the Year
	U.S. Olympic Committee Tennis Athlete of the Year
	World Tennis Junior Player of the Year
1990	*Tennis* magazine/Rolex Watch Female Rookie of the Year
	WTA Most Impressive Newcomer
1996	WTA Comeback Player of the Year
2001	WTA Player of the Year
	ITF World Champion
	Associated Press Female Athlete of the Year

Notable Victories

1988	U.S. Clay Court 18s
	U.S. Hard Court 18s
1989	French Open Junior
	U.S. Open Junior
1990	Puerto Rican Open
1991	Players' Challenge
1991-92	Mazda Tennis Classic
1992	Gold Medal, Olympic women's tennis
1993	New South Wales Open
1999	Strausbourg
	Bell Challenge
2001	Australian Open
	French Open
2002	Australian Open

Continuing the Story

Before the 1991 season, Jennifer began to work with weights in order to develop a more powerful serve and quicker footwork. Tom Gullikson of the United States Tennis Association, a former professional player, became her coach. In the past, she had trouble beating the game's top players such as Sabatini and Seles. Before the 1991 season, however, she told reporters that she had changed by becoming meaner, saying, "I like fighting."

In the 1991 quarterfinals at Wimbledon, Jennifer beat Navratilova in two sets, 6-4, 7-5, to advance to the semifinals against Sabatini. Even though she lost, 6-4, 6-4, she became the youngest player ever to reach the Wimbledon semifinals. In August, she won the Mazda Classic, beating Seles in the finals. A week later, she won the Players' Challenge over Katrina Maleeva. In 1991, Jennifer was gaining confidence. She won more than $600,000 in prize money, and her ranking rose to sixth in the world.

Jennifer tried to live as normally as possible. She visited friends, went to the malls to shop, used her money in practical ways, and continued to make the honor roll at school. In fact, the older players on the tour helped her with her homework. She faxed her homework to school when she was on tour.

The highlight of Jennifer's young career came in 1992, when she won the gold medal in women's tennis at the Barcelona Olympics. She defeated

Steffi Graf in the final match, 3-6, 6-3, 6-4, by constantly pounding her ground strokes to Graf's backhand. Jennifer's proudest moment was to be able to represent the United States in the medal ceremony at the Olympics.

After losing in the first round of the U.S. Open in 1993, Jennifer stopped playing on the women's tour. She did not return to the tour until November, 1994. In May of that year, she had been arrested for possession of marijuana. Whether or not stardom had come to Jennifer too soon, she definitely was troubled and unable to compete at her best. In 1996, she returned to competitive tennis with more focus and inner resolve. Jennifer won her first singles titles since 1993 at Strasbourg, France, and Quebec City, Canada, in 1999. She won the SEAT Open in 2000.

Jennifer surprised everyone, including herself, by winning the 2001 Australian Open. After an inability to reach the semifinals in five appearances, she won her first grand slam title by beating Martina Hingis after defeating both Seles and Lindsay Davenport. She followed up her victory by winning the French Open, defeating Kim Clijsters in the final. After reaching the semifinals at Wimbledon and the U.S. Open, she became the number-one women's player in the world in late 2001. In 2001 and 2002, she was the number-one player at different times, sharing the honor with Hingis, Davenport, and Venus Williams. She was named the Associated Press's female athlete of the year in 2001.

In 2002, she repeated as the Australian Open champion, defeating Hingis again, despite having to fight off four match points. As a result of her suc-cess, she was named the ESPY player of the year. In 2003, she won fourteen professional titles, but did not fare well in the Grand Slam events, only reaching the semifinals at the U.S. Open. She was beset by shoulder problems in 2004, when she made the semifinals at the French Open and the U.S. Open and the quarterfinals at Wimbledon. She played her last match, in Philadelphia, late in the year. She had arthroscopic surgery in 2005 and a third shoulder surgery in 2007.

Summary

Even in a sport dominated by young players, Jennifer Capriati stood out. Her natural skills were augmented by ceaseless training and fierce determination to make her the youngest Olympic tennis champion and youngest professional ever. She demonstrated her courage and determination by making one of the best comebacks in women's tennis. Had she not suffered shoulder injuries, she might have continued to win titles.

Kathy Davis, updated by Thomas L. Erskine

Additional Sources

Green, Carl R., and Roxanne Ford. *Jennifer Capriati.* New York: Crestwood House, 1994.

Lakin, Pat. *Jennifer Capriati: Rising Star.* Vero Beach, Fla.: Rourke, 1993.

Phillips, Dennis J. *Women Tennis Stars: Biographies and Records of Champions, 1800s to Today.* Jefferson, N.C.: McFarland, 2008.

Scott, Glenn, and Matt Christopher. *On the Court with Jennifer Capriati.* Boston: Little, Brown, 2004.

Michael Chang

Born: February 22, 1972
 Hoboken, New Jersey
Also known as: Michael Te-Pei Chang (full
 name); Zhang Depei

Early Life

Michael Te-Pei Chang was born to Joe and Betty Chang in Hoboken, New Jersey, on February 22, 1972, the younger of two sons. His brother, Carl, was also a tennis player; Michael, however, rose to tennis prominence. His parents—both research chemists who met on a blind date in New York City in 1966—had a strong work ethic, which they instilled in both sons. Michael's father was a self-taught tennis player and introduced the boys to the game. In 1977, the Changs decided to relocate the family from New Jersey to St. Paul, Minnesota, where the brothers quickly began defeating the local competition in tennis matches. By the time the family moved to San Diego a few years later, Carl and Michael had developed reputations as great tennis competitors. Dubbed "The Chang Gang,"

Michael Chang at the 1990 French Open. (Focus on Sport/Getty Images)

the brothers beat most of their age-group competition near their home in Placentia, California.

The Road to Excellence

Michael's movement on the court and tireless work ethic allowed him to compensate for his diminutive size. By the time he was ten years old, he had grown to 5 feet 7 inches tall—he grew only 2 more inches by adulthood. Most of the world's greatest tennis players have been taller. By age fifteen, he had made a name for himself in the junior ranks by beating future American champions Pete Sampras and Jim Courier. In 1987, Michael became the youngest player in seventy years to win a main draw match at the U.S. Open—beating Paul McNamee in the first round—and the youngest to reach a tour semifinal.

The Emerging Champion

All eyes turned to Michael when he entered the 1989 French Open as an unknown seventeen-year-old and silenced the naysayers who believed his size hindered him from becoming a tennis champion. No American man had won the French Open since Tony Trabert in 1955, and Michael—ranked nineteenth in the world entering the tournament—was not the player most thought would end the losing streak.

With uncharacteristic grit and steely concentration, Michael bested his competition to set up a dramatic match against top-ranked Ivan Lendl in the Round of 16. In a marathon match that lasted more than three hours and had the crowd on its feet, Michael dove to the ground for balls, pumped his fists with each point won, and played through severe leg cramps in the fifth set to defeat Lendl 4-6, 4-6, 6-3, 6-3, 6-3. He went on to capture the French Open title, ending a thirty-four-year drought for the Americans in the tourna-

Major Championships

1988	San Francisco	1995	Hong Kong
1989	French Open		Tokyo Indoor
	London Indoor		Atlanta
1990	Toronto		Beijing
1991	Birmingham	1996	Indian Wells
1992	San Francisco		Washington
	Indian Wells		Los Angeles
	Key Biscayne	1997	Memphis
1993	Jakarta		Hong Kong
	Osaka		Indian Wells
	Cincinnati		Orlando
	Kuala Lumpur		Washington
	Beijing	1998	Boston
1994	Jakarta		Shanghai
	Philadelphia	2000	Los Angeles
	Hong Kong		
	Atlanta		
	Cincinnati		
	Beijing		

ment and catapulting Michael into the international spotlight. With his victory, Michael also became the first Asian American to win a Grand Slam tennis title. Over his career, Michael compiled a 662-312 record, but never duplicated the fantastic run he made in Paris.

Continuing the Story

During his career, Michael earned nearly $20 million in prize money and won thirty-four singles titles. Although the French Open was his greatest achievement, Michael remained competitive. In 1994, he reached the quarterfinals of Wimbledon and, in 1995, reached the quarterfinals of the U.S. Open. His best results outside of the French Open came in 1996, when he reached the finals of both the Australian Open and the U.S. Open. A year later, Michael reached the semifinals of the U.S. Open, only to lose in straight sets to eventual champion Patrick Rafter, a difficult loss since Michael was ranked a career-high number two in the world, and American rivals Sampras and Andre Agassi had already been knocked out of the tournament.

In 1998, Michael suffered injuries to his left knee and right wrist that knocked him further back from his usual competitive results on the tour. In 1999, he fell to number fifty in the rankings. He officially retired in 2003, but joined Jim Courier's senior tour in 2006. He remained busy with other endeavors as well: He wrote an autobiography and coached Chinese tennis player Peng Shuai.

Summary
Beginning in 1991, Michael Chang was coached by his brother. In fact, he traveled the tennis circuit with the same entourage that was with him his entire life. His parents were often seen in the players' box rooting him on. A devout Christian, Michael often credited his faith and love of his family with helping him to overcome the hardships he faced during his tennis career.

A. K. Ruffin

Additional Sources
Bunn, Debbie. "Serving His God." *Challenge Newsline* 39 (July, 2004): 8.

Chang, Michael, and Mike Yorkey. *Holding Serve: Persevering on and off the Court*. London: Hodder Christian, 2003.

Collins, Bud, and Zander Hollander, eds. *Bud Collins' Modern Encyclopedia of Tennis*. 2d ed. Detroit: Visible Ink Press, 1994.

Deitsch, Richard, Hank Hersch, and Mark Bechtel. "Q and A: Michael Chang." *Sports Illustrated* 98, no. 14 (April 7, 2003): 28.

Kim Clijsters

Born: June 8, 1983
  Bilzen, Belgium
Also known as: Kim Antonie Lode Clijsters (full name)

Early Life

On June 8, 1983, in Bilzen, Belgium, Kim Antonie Lode Clijsters was born into an athletic family: Her father was a renowned soccer player and her mother was a gymnast. Kim inherited an athletic build from her father and flexibility from her mother, helping her to become the number-one tennis player in the world on two separate occasions.

Kim's father was Lei Clijsters, one of the Belgium's best soccer players ever. Her mother was Els Vandecaetsbeek, an accomplished artistic gymnast. At the age of five, Kim was already on the tennis court developing her game. Kim's younger sister Elke also enjoyed tennis. The two sisters, both infused with an intense competitive streak, became each other's best practice partner.

The Road to Excellence

By age six, Kim began playing competitive tennis. With the help of her first coach, Bart Van Kerckhovan, she flourished and won the Belgian Junior National Championship at the age of eleven. Three years later, Kim joined the Flemish Tennis Federation, aiding her competitive career. There, she met Carl Maes, who became her coach and helped to usher her into the professional leagues.

In 1998, Kim began playing in the junior Grand Slam tournaments. She reached the finals at Wimbledon and won both the French and U.S. Opens as a doubles participant. In addition to her success abroad, at the age of fifteen, Kim became the youngest Belgian national tennis champion ever. The following year, she turned professional and began entering tournaments. Her results that first year were modest, but she had strong showings. She won her first career singles title in Luxembourg. Kim ended the year with a respectable ranking inside the top fifty, which garnered her recognition as the Women's Tennis Association's promising newcomer of the year.

The Emerging Champion

The following year, Kim backed up her status as a rising star. However, not until the 2001 season did Kim emerge as one of the best. At the French Open that year, Kim reached her first Grand Slam final. She lost, but she gained recognition as one of the more formidable opponents on the tour.

Over the next couple of years, Kim continued to rise in the rankings. The 2003 season was considered her best. During the year, she won nine singles

Kim Clijsters in 2007. (Paul Yeung/Reuters/Landov)

and seven doubles tournaments. She reached the finals of both the French and U.S. Opens. During that year, she attained the number-one world ranking. She was the first woman to be ranked number one without having won a Grand Slam title.

Though Kim lost the overall top ranking, she ended 2003 in second. In 2004, Kim looked strong at the Australian Open, reaching the finals. Following that tournament, her career changed. Not too long after the Australian Open, Kim was defending her title in Indian Wells, California, when she began having problems with her wrist. The injury eventually required surgery and kept her out of action for almost the entire year.

Continuing the Story

In 2005, Kim returned to the court and displayed the same abilities that she had previously. She again won at Indian Wells and, along the way, defeated five of the world's top six players. Her greatest triumph came at the U.S. Open that year, where she was finally able to win her first Grand Slam. She ended the year ranked second and was named the comeback player of the year for the 2005 season.

The following year, Kim completed her comeback by regaining the number-one ranking. In doing so, she became the first tennis player to rise from outside the top one hundred to number one in a year's time. For the remainder of the 2006 season, Kim played impressively; she continued to advance in tournaments. However, she did not complete the year because her wrist injury again became an issue, and she withdrew from the U.S. Open, unable to defend her title.

Though Kim attempted to come back from her injury, playing in tournaments at the end of the 2006 season and during the 2007 season, her results were not to her expectations. On May 6, 2007, Kim announced her retirement from professional tennis.

Summary

Kim Clijsters played with smooth ground strokes and a strong defensive style. She was able to use this type of game to reach the world number-one ranking twice—in 2003 and 2006. On the court, she was known for doing the splits in an effort to reach a bit farther. Kim was also a gracious competitor and frequently earned the WTA

Women's Tennis Association Victories

Year	Tournament
1999	Fortis Championships Luxembourg
2000	Tasmanian International
	Sparkassen Cup
2001	Bank of the West Classic
	Sparkassen Cup
	Fortis Championships Luxembourg
2002	Betty Barclay Cup
	Porsche Tennis Grand Prix
	Fortis Championships Luxembourg
	Home Depot Championships
2003	Adidas International
	Pacific Life Open
	Telecom Italia Masters
	Ordina Open
	Bank of the West Classic
	JPMorgan Chase Open
	Porsche Tennis Grand Prix
	Fortis Championships Luxembourg
	WTA Tour Championships
2004	Open Gaz de France
	Proximus Diamond Games
2005	Pacific Life Open
	NASDAQ-100 Open
	Hastings Direct International Championships
	Bank of the West Classic
	JPMorgan Chase Open
	Rogers Cup
	U.S. Open
	Fortis Championships Luxembourg
	Gaz de France Stars
2006	J&S Cup
	Bank of the West Classic
	Gaz de France Stars
2007	Medibank International

---

sportsmanship award. Unfortunately for the sport, Kim retired at a relatively young age.

P. Huston Ladner

Additional Sources

Deitsch, Richard. "Gracious Goodbye." *Sports Illustrated* 106, no. 20 (May 14, 2007).

Wertheim, L. Jon. "Comeback Kim." *Sports Illustrated* 102, no. 15 (April 11, 2005): 87.

Honors and Awards

Year	Award
2000	WTA Newcomer of the Year
2001-04, 2006-07	Karen Krantzcke Sportsmanship Award
2005	Belgian Sportswoman of the Year
	International Tennis Writers Association (ITWA) Player of the Year
	ITWA Ambassador for Tennis
2006	WTA Player of the Year
	WTA Comeback Player of the Year

Henri Cochet

Born: December 14, 1901
      Lyons, France
Died: April 1, 1987
      St. Germain-en-Laye, France
Also known as: Henri Jean Cochet (full name);
    Ball Boy of Lyon; le Magicien

Early Life

Henri Jean Cochet was born on December 14, 1901, in Lyons, France. He was introduced to tennis at the age of seven. His father was the manager of the Lyons Lawn Tennis Club, and Henri acted as ball boy, so that he could get a closer look at the tennis matches. After the matches were over, he picked up an old racket and practiced against the wall. Henri practiced against a wall for two years before he was allowed to play on the courts with school friends. He loved the game and made steady improvement until he was the best young player in Lyons. Henri was thirteen when World War I started and the club was used by army trucks as a garage. After the war, he went back to playing tennis with more enthusiasm than ever.

The Road to Excellence

Henri stood only 5 feet 6 inches tall, and he usually found himself playing opponents who were larger and stronger. This challenge was a good experience for him, since it toughened his game and his resolve. Henri was becoming adept at taking the ball early and rushing to the net. Touch and timing were his greatest assets. In 1920, he won the Lyons Championship for the first time. His game was ready for Paris and beyond.

In 1921, Henri went to Paris, and entered its covered court championship. He and another unknown at the time, Jean Borotra, met in the final, and Henri prevailed easily. Borotra, along with Jacques Brugnon and René Lacoste, joined with Henri to become known as the Four Musketeers. These four players helped France to dominate the tennis world during the late 1920's and the early part of the 1930's. In 1922, Henri and Borotra became members of the French Davis Cup team, and a year later, all the Four Musketeers competed for their country on the team.

Henri won his first of five French Championships in singles in 1922. Always a quiet man, who, at times, gave the impression of disinterest during a match, Henri surprised many an opponent with his capacity to turn the tide in his favor with his seemingly effortless strokes. He was not one for hard practice or for un-

Henri Cochet, who was one of the "Four Musketeers" of French tennis. (Courtesy of International Tennis Hall of Fame)

Major Championship Victories and Finals

1922, 1926, 1928, 1930, 1932	French Championship
1926, 1928	Wimbledon doubles (with Jacques Brugnon)
1927	U.S. National Championship mixed doubles (with Eileen Bennett)
1927, 1929	Wimbledon
1927, 1930, 1932	French Championship doubles (with Brugnon)
1927, 1931	Wimbledon doubles finalist (with Brugnon)
1928	Wimbledon finalist
	U.S. National Championship
1928-29	French Championship mixed doubles (with Bennett)
1932	U.S. National Championship finalist
1933	French Championship finalist

Other Notable Victories

1920-22	Lyons Championship
1927-32	On winning French Davis Cup team
1937	Professional World Doubles Tournament (with Bill Tilden)
1950	British Covered Court Championship doubles (with Jaroslav Drobny)

necessary movement during a match. Timing was the key to his game, and he was able to refine it to near perfection.

The Emerging Champion

In 1923, Henri played on the French Davis Cup team against Denmark, Ireland, and Switzerland, but he did not travel to the United States or to Wimbledon to compete for the championships there. Henri lost to Lacoste in the 1924 French Championships and to Vincent Richards in the finals of the Olympics. Most observers could see that Henri was not himself and that he was not in good health. For some months he suffered from influenza. As a natural player when his game was on, he was almost unbeatable; when his game was off, however, he became prey to many of lesser abilities. In 1925, Henri did not play any Davis Cup matches and entered a minimum number of tournaments. Journalists were even beginning to talk of him as nearing the end of his career.

Henri was not on his way out, but about to start

the greatest phase of his career. In 1926, he beat both Richards and Lacoste to capture the French Championship singles title. The most stunning match of the year was Henri's victory over Bill Tilden in the quarterfinals of the U.S. National Championship at Forest Hills, New York. Lacoste eventually won the title, but Henri had served notice that he was back and playing inspired tennis.

Henri had won the Wimbledon doubles title that year, but it was not until 1927 that he broke through to take the singles title. He won Wimbledon in a dramatic fashion by rallying back from having lost the first two sets of each of his last three matches. He played Frank Hunter, Tilden, and Borotra in a row and snatched victory out of the jaws of defeat in each match. With Henri and the other Musketeers on the French Davis Cup team, France won its first Davis Cup by defeating the United States. France did not surrender the Cup until 1933.

Continuing the Story

The Four Musketeers dominated tennis in 1928. Henri won both the French and U.S. singles titles, while Borotra won in Australia, and Lacoste beat Henri to win Wimbledon. The French ruled the tennis world, and Henri was the greatest of the French. Tilden stated that Henri was possibly the best ever to play the game. In 1929, Henri became even more indispensable to the Davis Cup team with the retirement of Lacoste. Henri also captured his second Wimbledon singles title that year. His amateur career lasted through 1932 after he had amassed two Wimbledon titles, five French Championship singles titles, and one U.S. National Championship. Henri turned professional after France lost to Great Britain in the Davis Cup competition in 1933.

Henri's professional career could not live up to the standards he had set during his amateur days. Henri got the chance to play Tilden again, since Tilden had already turned professional, but the natural gifts and inspiration that had taken him to the top of the amateur ranks were not there with the same intensity. His professional career was of little consequence, and after World War II, Henri was reinstated into the amateur ranks. The glory years were over, but he did manage to win a number of tournaments. He won his last title of significance in 1950, when he and Jaroslav Drobny captured the British Covered Court Championship doubles title.

Henri made the most of his time outside competitive tennis, never really giving up the hold that the game had on him, through activity in various tennis organizations. He ran a successful sporting goods business and also traveled as a French representative of the Ministry of National Education. After a long illness, Henri died on April 1, 1987, in St. Germain-en-Laye, France.

Summary

Most experts agree that Henri Cochet was a tennis genius. His strokes looked effortless and his timing was impeccable. No one else could hit low volleys or half-volleys with the precision that Henri did. Along with the other members of the Four Musketeers, Henri took French tennis to the pinnacle during the late 1920's and early 1930's. Neither France nor any other country has produced another all-court player who looked as naturally suited to the game as Henri.

Jeffry Jensen

Honors, Awards, and Milestones

French Davis Cup team (1922-33)
Turned professional in 1933
Légion d'Honneur
Served as president of the International Lawn Tennis Club of France
Inducted into International Tennis Hall of Fame (1976)

Additional Sources

Collins, Bud. *Total Tennis: The Ultimate Tennis Encyclopedia.* Toronto: Sport Media, 2003.

Fein, Paul. *Tennis Confidential: Today's Greatest Players, Matches, and Controversies.* Washington, D.C.: Brassey's, 2002.

Parsons, John. *The Ultimate Encyclopedia of Tennis: The Definitive Illustrated Guide to World Tennis.* London: Carlton, 2006.

Wilner, Barry, and Ken Rappoport. *Harvard Beats Yale 29-29, and Other Great Comebacks from the Annals of Sports.* Lanham, Md.: Taylor Trade, 2008.

Maureen Connolly

Born: September 17, 1934
    San Diego, California
Died: June 21, 1969
    Dallas, Texas
Also known as: Maureen Catherine Connolly
    (full name); Little Mo

Early Life

Maureen Catherine Connolly was born on September 17, 1934, in San Diego, California. Her parents were Martin J. Connolly and Jassamine Connolly. Horses were Maureen's chief childhood passion until, at ten years of age, her family moved to a house near some municipal tennis courts. The pro there, Wilbur Folsom, became so accustomed to seeing a small, curly-haired girl peeking through the fence watching people play that he invited her inside and hit some balls to her. Folsom was so impressed with Maureen's natural ability that he offered to give her lessons. He switched her from a left-handed to a right-handed player, and after several months of coaching, he entered her in a tournament where she reached the finals. Tennis became Maureen's main pursuit.

The Road to Excellence

The next year, the famous Eleanor Tennant became Maureen's teacher and coach. "Teach" Tennant had developed such champions as Helen Wills, Al-

ice Marble, and Pauline Betz. Tennant, well known not only for her coaching but also for her skills as an analyst and psychologist, brought Maureen along slowly and deliberately. Besides the tennis coaching, she gave Maureen exercises to strengthen her arm and wrist. These exercises are considered a routine aspect of a tennis workout today but were a novelty back in the 1940's. Tennant also had Maureen take dance lessons to improve her footwork.

Maureen practiced hard, usually three to four hours a day, until she had molded herself into a highly capable player. By the time Maureen was fifteen, she not only had won fifty titles but also had become the youngest girl up to that time to win the coveted National Junior Championships, for players eighteen years of age and under. She won that title again the next year, 1950, when she was sixteen; she also competed on the women's circuit. She did so well that she was tenth in the women's rankings of 1950.

Noticed by the press, she was dubbed "Little Mo" or "Mighty Little Mo," a playful contemporary comparison with the powerful battleship *Missouri*, or "Big Mo." Her nickname was attributed to the fact that even though she was only 5 feet 5 inches in height, similar to the guns of the *Missouri*, she shot down her opponents with her outstanding powerful forehand and backhand drives.

The Emerging Champion

In 1951, Maureen did not defend her National Junior title because the date of the championship conflicted with the U.S. National Championship at Forest Hills, New York. She won this tournament and at seventeen was the second youngest player at the time to win the title. That year, she was selected for the Wightman Cup team and was the youngest to make the team. Moreover, she repeated as a member of the team in 1952, 1953, and 1954, and in four years of Wightman Cup play, she never lost a match.

Many wondered what made this teenager so successful against more experienced players. Not only was Maureen skillful, but also her outstanding concentration, coupled with her tremendous drive to win, made her a great champion.

Major Championship Victories and Finals

1951-53	U.S. National Championship
1952-54	Wimbledon
1953	Australian Championship
	Australian Championship doubles (with Julia Sampson)
1953-54	French Championship
1954	French Championship doubles (with Nell Hall Hopman)
	French Championship mixed doubles (with Lew Hoad)

Other Notable Victories

1951-54	Member of winning U.S. Wightman Cup team
1953	Italian Championship doubles (with Sampson)
1953-54	U.S. Clay Court Championship
1954	Italian Championship
	U.S. Clay Court Championship doubles (with Doris Hart)

Records and Milestones

Nationally ranked number one (1951-53)
U.S. Wightman Cup team (1951-54)
Ranked number one in the world (1952-54)
First woman to win the Grand Slam (1953)

Honors and Awards

1952	Service Bowl Award
1952-54	Associated Press Female Athlete of the Year
1968	Inducted into National Lawn Tennis Hall of Fame

Continuing the Story

In 1952, Maureen retained her U.S. title and won Wimbledon also; the Associated Press (AP) named her female athlete of the year. In addition, she was presented the Service Bowl Award by the United States Lawn Tennis Association (USLTA), given to the person who makes the most noticeable contribution to the sportsmanship, fellowship, and service of tennis.

The next year, 1953, after winning the Australian Championship, Maureen won the French Championship, repeated as winner at Wimbledon, and was victorious again at the U.S. National Championship at Forest Hills. By winning these four major championships in one year, she won the Grand Slam of tennis and accomplished what only one other person, Don Budge, had ever done. Significantly, Maureen lost only one set in achieving this feat.

At the end of 1953, Maureen was selected again by the Associated Press as the female athlete of the year, was ranked number one by the USLTA, and was listed as number one in the world. At the age of twenty, in 1954, she won her second French Championship and her third consecutive Wimbledon and was predicted to repeat her victory at Forest Hills. However, as Maureen was riding her new horse before the tournament, a speeding truck frightened the animal and Maureen was thrown against the truck, broke her right leg, and severed all the muscles in her calf. Even though she could not compete in the remaining tennis tournaments that year, for the third straight year the Associated Press voted her female athlete of the year.

Maureen tried every form of rehabilitation, but it soon became obvious that her leg was severely damaged. In January, 1955, the sad announcement was made that she would never play competitive tennis again.

What Maureen would have achieved had she not been injured before she was twenty-one years of age is speculation. Amazingly, from September, 1951, when she won her first United States National Championship, to July, 1954, when she won her third Wimbledon title, she had lost only one match anywhere in the world, and that was in 1954, in California. Though her career was cut short, Maureen is regarded as one of the greatest women tennis players to have ever played the game.

Summary

In 1955, Maureen Connolly married Norman Brinker, a former member of the U.S. equestrian team, whom she had met several years before while she was out riding. They settled in Dallas, Texas, and had two daughters.

Maureen was elected to the National Lawn Tennis Hall of Fame in 1968, and in 1969, knowing she had terminal cancer, she created the Maureen Connolly Brinker Foundation to help promote promising junior players. Also in 1969, the USLTA established the Maureen Connolly Brinker Award to be presented each year at the Girls' Nationals to the player who exhibited exceptional ability, sportsmanship, and competitive spirit. Maureen hoped to present the first award to be given in August, but she died on June 21, 1969, at the age of thirty-four.

Perhaps the best tribute to her brief career is by Lance Tingay, the tennis authority of the *London Telegraph*: "Whenever a great player comes along, you have to ask: Could she have beaten Maureen? In every case the answer is, I think not."

Joanna Davenport

Additional Sources

Collins, Bud. *Total Tennis: The Ultimate Tennis Encyclopedia.* Toronto: Sport Media, 2003.

Conner, Floyd. *Tennis's Most Wanted: The Top Ten Book of Baseline Blunders, Clay Court Wonders, and Lucky Lobs.* Washington, D.C.: Brassey's, 2002.

Parsons, John. *The Ultimate Encyclopedia of Tennis: The Definitive Illustrated Guide to World Tennis.* London: Carlton, 2006.

Sherrow, Victoria, ed. *Encyclopedia of Women and Sports.* Santa Barbara, Calif.: ABC-Clio, 1996.

Woolum, Janet. *Outstanding Women Athletes: Who They Are and How They Influenced Sports in America.* Phoenix, Ariz.: Oryx Press, 1998.

Jimmy Connors

Born: September 2, 1952
     East St. Louis, Illinois
Also known as: James Scott Connors (full name);
   Brash Basher of Belleville; Jimbo

Early Life

James Scott Connors was born on September 2, 1952, in East St. Louis, Illinois. Jimmy was the second son of Gloria Connors, a tennis pro, and James Connors, Sr., a toll booth manager. Jimmy and his older brother John grew up in East St. Louis and Belleville, Illinois.

Jimmy was first encouraged to play tennis as a preschooler, when his small hand could barely grasp a sawed-off racket. His mother and grandmother, Bertha Thompson, a tournament player, were his major tennis supporters. Jimmy always had a passion for tennis and from the beginning he credited his love for the sport as his greatest motivation.

The Road to Excellence

Jimmy practiced constantly and played from morning until night if allowed. His dedication from the outset was tireless, and no obstacles could block his improvement. Split-second timing and a two-handed backhand became the left-handed Jimmy's trademarks, as taught by his mother. Jimmy learned to strike the tennis ball on the rise to keep his opponent from getting prepared. Jimmy was small for his age, and his success was largely dependent on speed, agility, and quickness.

At the age of eight, Jimmy entered major tournaments for boys. His first championship was in the ten-and-under category in the Southern Illinois tournament. During his sophomore year at Assumption High School in St. Louis, Jimmy chose to play amateur tennis on the junior United States Lawn Tennis Association (USLTA) circuit. He believed he would improve faster on this circuit than if he played for his high school team.

In 1968, Jimmy won the sixteen-and-under U.S. National title against a much more expe-

rienced opponent. Jimmy then moved up to the junior level a full year early, to continue to challenge himself against the toughest possible opponents. At this point, Jimmy decided he needed both a coach and the opportunity to play more.

Francisco "Pancho" Segura became Jimmy's coach. At seventeen years old, Jimmy moved with his mother to Los Angeles to be close to Segura. Jimmy attended Rexford High School in the mornings and played tennis in the afternoon.

In 1970, Jimmy had a great year. He won the Junior National Hardcourt Championship and the Junior National Clay Court Championship that year. He was also a member of the Junior Davis Cup

Jimmy Connors striking the ball at the 1976 Wimbledon tournament. (Hulton Archive/Getty Images)

team and went to the semifinals in the Junior Outdoor Nationals.

Attending the University of California at Los Angeles (UCLA) in 1970-1971, Jimmy won the National Collegiate Athletic Association (NCAA) Championship against Roscoe Tanner. Jimmy was the first freshman ever to win the NCAA title. At the time, he was ranked first nationally in junior tennis and fourteenth as an adult.

The Emerging Champion

After he won the NCAA Championship as a freshman, great things were expected of Jimmy. A slumping second year in college and his passion for greatness caused him to consider turning professional. Playing in a tournament in Maryland, Jimmy made it to the finals against Ilie Nastase. Jimmy lost, and had to turn down a large prize check to retain his amateur status. The experience helped convince him to turn professional. After discussing the move with his mother, Jimmy competed professionally the next week in Jacksonville, Florida.

Showing the mark of a future superstar, Jimmy won his first tournament as a professional and took home a check for three thousand dollars for four days' work. At the next tournament, in Virginia, Jimmy showcased his outstanding talent and won again. Jimmy quickly became the hottest player on the circuit, and his years of hard work and determination were paying off.

By March of 1972, Jimmy had made the Davis

Major Championship Victories and Finals

1973	Wimbledon doubles (with Ilie Nastase)
1974	Australian Open
1974, 1976, 1978, 1982-83	U.S. Open
1974, 1982	Wimbledon
1975	U.S. Open doubles (with Nastase)
1975, 1977	U.S. Open finalist
1975, 1977-78, 1984	Wimbledon finalist

Other Notable Victories

1971	NCAA Championship
1973	U.S. Pro Championship
1973-75, 1978-79, 1983-84	U.S. Indoor Championship
1974	U.S. Clay Court Championship doubles (with Nastase)
1974-75	U.S. Indoor Championship doubles (with Frew McMillan and Nastase)
1974, 1976, 1978-79	U.S. Clay Court Championship
1975	U.S. Indoor Championship doubles (with Nastase)
1976, 1978-80	U.S. Pro Indoor Championship
1977, 1980	WCT Finals
1978	The Masters
1978-79	U.S. National Indoor Championships
1979	WCT Tournament of Champions
1980	Seiko World Super Tennis Classic
1982	Pacific Southwest Open

Cup team, representing the United States. Jimmy played his first Wimbledon that same year, bowing out in the quarterfinals. In his first year as a professional, Jimmy had seventy-five victories, the highest total among all American male professionals. Jimmy also finished second on the money list with ninety thousand dollars in prize money that year.

Jimmy's quick start and enormous success his first year as a professional, 1973, provided increasing challenges. A roller-coaster year was highlighted by his victory in the U.S. Pro Championship. Jimmy was the youngest winner ever of this championship.

The year 1974, perhaps Jimmy's best, resulted in many important victories. Jimmy won 99 of 103 matches that year, including his first Wimbledon, U.S. Open, and Australian Open titles. The attributes that defined Connors's

Honors and Awards

1972	Rolex Rookie of the Year
1974	Player of the Year Award
1974-78	Ranked number one by the Association of Tennis Professionals
1982	International Tennis Federation Player of the Year
1991	Domino's Pizza Team Tennis Male Rookie of the Year
1998	Inducted into International Tennis Hall of Fame

Milestones

109 professional titles
10 Grand Slam titles
U.S. Davis Cup team (1972, 1976, 1981, 1984)

style—an offensive mind-set, intense concentration, crisp ground strokes, great return of service, and precision timing—were on display in 1974.

Between the years 1974 and 1978, Jimmy was known as the most consistent player in men's tennis. "Jimbo" won more than fifty tournaments. In 1984, he became the first player to win one hundred singles titles.

Continuing the Story

Although the emergence of tennis greats Björn Borg and John McEnroe in the late 1970's and early 1980's made Jimmy less dominant, he remained ranked in the top five in the world for many years. Jimmy had established himself as one of the greatest U.S. players ever.

One of Jimmy's trademarks, in conjunction with his aggressiveness and spirited play, was his "fiery" attitude on the tennis courts. Jimmy was perceived as a loner within the tennis world and cultivated a "bad boy" image. This eventually became his greatest strength; Jimbo always provided a gutsy performance. Jimmy's driving spirit kept him competitive throughout the 1980's, well past his physical prime. He extended his tennis involvement as a television commentator during the latter part of his competitive career.

In the tennis world, Jimmy will be remembered for his great service returns, tireless attack, spirited play, and tenacious attitude every time he stepped on the court. His competitive instinct was again demonstrated in dramatic fashion at the 1991 U.S. Open. Through the first several rounds, thirty-nine-year-old Jimmy electrified the crowd and it appeared that he might actually go on to win his

sixth U.S. Open title. In the quarterfinals, however, Jimmy ran out of miracles, losing in three sets to American Jim Courier. Jimmy began playing on the Worldwide Senior Tennis Circuit in 1993. In 2006, Conners announced his new role as coach for Grand Slam tennis champion Andy Roddick.

Summary

Jimmy Connors remained competitive throughout the 1980's and into the 1990's. Even though his play was a few notches below that of the Jimbo of old, he remained an inspiration for younger players. Jimmy's style of play made him as successful as an entertainer as he once was as a competitor. Jimmy's personality and determination will live on in the tennis world. His long list of on-court accomplishments, coupled with his spirit and drive, will long be remembered. His style and aggressive approach will be undoubtedly emulated by future generations of tennis players.

Hal J. Walker

Additional Sources

Busch, Jim, and Diane Busch. *Jimmy Connors, a Biography: Eye of the Tiger.* Pittsburgh, Pa.: Dorrance, 1998.

Collins, Bud. *Total Tennis: The Ultimate Tennis Encyclopedia.* Toronto: Sport Media, 2003.

Drucker, Joel. *Jimmy Connors Saved My Life: A Personal Biography.* Toronto: Sportclassic Books, 2008.

"Great Shots." *Tennis* (January, 2006): 20.

Phillips, Caryl. *The Right Set: A Tennis Anthology.* New York: Vintage Books, 1999.

Wolff, Alexander. "Jimbo." *Sports Illustrated* 101, no. 8 (August 30, 2004): 82.

Jim Courier

Born: August 17, 1970
      Sanford, Florida
Also known as: James Spencer Courier, Jr. (full name)

Early Life

James Spencer Courier, Jr., was born on August 17, 1970, in Sanford, Florida, to James Spencer Courier, Sr., a marketing executive, and Linda Courier, an elementary-school media specialist. Jim was the second of three children in a family that included an older sister, Audra, and a younger brother, Kris. Growing up in Dade City, Florida, Jim got his competitive spirit from his father, who had been a baseball pitcher at Florida State University.

Baseball was Jim's first love. However, at the age of seven, his great-aunt, Emma Spencer, introduced Jim to tennis. His aunt, who had been a women's tennis coach, ran the Dreamworld Tennis Club out of her home in Sanford. In addition to the fundamentals of the game, she taught Jim how to behave on a tennis court. By the time Jim was eleven, he was ready for formal tennis training. He was sent to the legendary Australian tennis instructor Harry Hopman, who ran a tennis academy in Largo, Florida.

The Road to Excellence

Hopman was so impressed with how Jim hit the ball that he waived all fees and decided to instruct the boy for free. Jim remained under Hopman's tutelage for two years. The intense training paid off when Jim reached the finals of the fourteen-and-under division of the Orange Bowl Junior Championships, the pinnacle of junior tennis. Jim's game caught the attention of famous coach Nick Bollettieri, who offered Jim a full scholarship to his tennis academy in Bradenton, Florida. While attending the academy, Jim trained with another

future tennis great, Andre Agassi. Jim sometimes became frustrated at all the personal attention that Agassi got from Bollettieri, but he continued to work hard.

Power was the main component of Jim's tennis game when he was a teenager. He patterned his two-handed backhand stroke on a baseball swing. There was nothing subtle about his game. Jim hit the ball hard, and if that did not work, he hit the

Jim Courier celebrating his semifinal victory at the 1991 French Open. (Derrick Ceyrac/AFP/Getty Images)

Major Championship Victories and Finals

1991	U.S. Open finalist
1991-92	French Open
1992-93	Australian Open
1993	French Open finalist
	Wimbledon finalist

Other Notable Victories

1989	Swiss Indoors
1991	Lipton International
1991, 1993	*Newsweek* Champions Cup
1992	Japan Open
	Salem Open
1992-93	Italian Open
1992, 1995	Winning U.S. Davis Cup team member
1993	Kroger/St. Jude International
	RCA/U.S. Hardcourts

ball even harder. By winning in his age group at the 1986 and 1987 Orange Bowl Junior Championships, Jim became the first player since Björn Borg to win consecutive Orange Bowl titles. He was winning some matches on desire alone; he had not learned yet how to win by playing the intelligent shot instead of the power shot. In 1988, Jim decided to join the professional tour. Although he did not win any tournaments that year, he raised his Association of Tennis Professionals (ATP) ranking to forty-third in the world.

The Emerging Champion

In 1989, Jim finally won his first professional tournament, defeating Stefan Edberg in the finals of the Swiss Indoors in Basel, Switzerland. With the victory, Jim's world ranking rose to number twenty-four. Although Jim was steadily moving up in the rankings, his one-dimensional approach to the game prohibited him from rising much above twentieth in the world. Jim was a fierce competitor, but he got so tense on the court during a match that it became impossible for him to adjust his game to his opponent or to a particular situation in a match. Jim understood that a change was necessary, but he needed some expert guidance.

Although he was still taking instruction from Bollettieri, Jim knew that the association was not benefiting him. Early in 1990, he formally cut his ties with Bollettieri and looked to find a coach who could devote enough time to improve Jim's chances of cracking the top ten. In José Higueras, Jim found a coach who was up to the task. Under Higueras's guidance, Michael Chang had won the 1989 French Open. Jim began training with Higueras and college coach Brad Stine in 1990, and they set out to transform Jim's tennis strategy.

Jim had won or lost matches based on his powerful baseline game. Higueras and Stine wished to make Jim an all-court player. They wanted him to introduce variety into his game and to employ tactics to defeat an opponent. In 1991, Jim began to make successful use of what his new coaches had taught him. He won three tournaments that year, including the prestigious French Open, one of tennis's four Grand Slam tournaments. In the French Open final, Jim defeated Andre Agassi in a thrilling five-set match.

Continuing the Story

Because of his strong showing in 1991, Jim became the second-ranked player in the world. His willingness to work hard and never quit had pushed him to the top of the tennis game. In Jim, Higueras and Stine had found a student who was willing to learn, willing to put in long hours to get results. In January, 1992, Jim won the Australian Open, another Grand Slam event, by defeating the then-number-one player in the world, Stefan Edberg, in four sets.

With the help of this victory, Jim became the first American to be ranked number one since John McEnroe in 1985. Jim solidified his number-one ranking by winning a second French Open, and he capped off the year by helping the United States to defeat Switzerland in the Davis Cup.

Jim started 1993 by defending his Australian Open title. At the French Open, however, he was stunned by little-known Sergei Bruguera in a dramatic five-set final. In June, 1993, Jim reached his

Honors and Awards

1991	ATP Most Improved Tour Player
1992	ATP Tour Player of the Year
	Jim Thorpe Player of the Year
2005	Inducted into International Tennis Hall of Fame

first Wimbledon final, but he lost a tough four-set match to fellow American Pete Sampras. By the end of September, Jim had lost his number-one ranking to Sampras, who had also won the U.S. Open. Jim finished the year ranked third in the world behind Sampras and Germany's Michael Stich. Although he had lost his number-one ranking, he had established himself as a tough champion who remained an important force in professional tennis. In May, 2000, Jim decided to retire from competitive tennis.

Jim stayed busy after he retired. He remained involved in tennis as a television commentator, started an event promotion company called Inside-Out Sport and Entertainment, and founded the charitable organization Courier's Kids to promote youth tennis. In 2005, Jim became a member of the International Tennis Hall of Fame.

Summary

Jim Courier combined a wonderful work ethic with raw athletic talent to rise to the top of the tennis world. Always willing to give his best effort on the court, Jim was a gritty champion and one of the best tennis players of the 1990's.

Jeffry Jensen

Additional Sources

Applebaum, Michael. "Courier Seeks Success on Other Side of Sports." *Brandweek* 45, no. 32 (September 13, 2004): 16-18.

Bodo, Peter. "So Long, Sport." *Tennis* (October, 2000): 24.

Courier, Jim. "Special Tribute: Pete Sampras and Andre Agassi." *Tennis* (August, 2003): 50.

Evans, Richard. *The ATP Tour: Ten Years of Superstar Tennis.* New York: Universe, 1999.

Margaret Court

Born: July 16, 1942
     Albury, New South Wales, Australia
Also known as: Margaret Smith Court (full name); Margaret Smith (birth name)

Early Life

Margaret Smith was born in the small town of Albury, New South Wales, Australia, on July 16, 1942. Albury is located approximately two hundred miles north of the city of Melbourne, Australia. Margaret was the youngest of the four children of Lawrence and Maud Beaufort Smith. Her father worked as a foreman for a plant that produced dairy products. Margaret was good in a number of sports as a child.

The Smiths lived across the street from the Albury and Border Lawn Tennis Association tennis courts. Because Margaret and her friends were not allowed to play on the grass courts of the club, they had to sneak onto the courts. They attempted to play out of sight of the club professional Wal Rutter, who, if he caught them, would chase them off the premises. The friends whom Margaret played against were all boys. Margaret and her playmates could stay out of sight of Rutter if they played on a court that he could only partially view. Because Margaret was a girl, she was placed at the net on one side of the court while the boys blasted balls toward her from the other side. This early introduction to net play helped Margaret become confident in her volley.

The Road to Excellence

Margaret first played tennis left-handed, but her friends teased her so much that she was forced to learn how to play tennis with the racket in her right hand. At the age of ten, Margaret started attending a tennis clinic on Saturday mornings at the club across the street. She was so good that the instructors used her to show the other students how to hit the ball. Rutter organized competitions among the students, and Margaret was good enough to win her age division the next four years. She was starting to believe that tennis was going to play a large part in her future. As a teenager, Margaret won most of the senior division tennis championships in New South Wales and Victoria. Increasingly, her attention was focused on tennis instead of her schoolwork. Every chance she got, Margaret hit with Rutter or any other adult who took the time to play with her.

A major turning point in Margaret's

Margaret Court, who won the Australian Open eleven times. (Courtesy of International Tennis Hall of Fame)

development came when she was invited to be coached by one of Australia's great tennis players Frank Sedgman. Margaret had to move to the Melbourne area where her sister June lived. The move was a big one for Margaret because she was an extremely shy young woman. Margaret lived with her sister in the Melbourne suburb of Auburn and started an intensive training regime under the watchful eye of Sedgman. The program included lifting weights and sprinting.

By the time of the Australian Championships in 1960, Margaret had developed powerfully toned arms and legs. At the age of seventeen, she won her first Australian Championship by defeating the talented Brazilian María Bueno in a tough, three-set match. With the victory in hand, Margaret became the youngest player to win the tournament.

The Emerging Champion

Sedgman was somewhat surprised at what his pupil had accomplished. However, he knew that Margaret could conquer the wider tennis world through hard work and emotional maturity. Following his advice, she did not travel outside Australia for another year, at which time he felt she was finally ready to handle the pressure outside the isolated Australian environment. In 1961, Margaret made her first appearance at Wimbledon, where she reached the quarterfinals. She was not disappointed with the results, but she was determined to do better the next time. The experience of competing at Wimbledon was somewhat unsettling for someone still very shy and not used to the tournament's pageantry.

In 1962, after capturing her third Australian title and winning both the French and Italian championships, the twenty-year-old Margaret was ready to make a serious run for the Wimbledon crown. She lost to the young American, Billie Jean Moffitt (later Billie Jean

Major Championship Victories and Finals

1960-66	Australian Championship
1961-63, 1965	Australian Championship doubles (with Mary Carter Reitano, Robyn Ebbern, and Lesley Turner)
1961-65	U.S. National Championship mixed doubles (with Robert Mark, Fred Stolle, Ken Fletcher, and John Newcombe)
1962, 1964	French Championship
1962, 1965, 1968-69	U.S. National Championship
1963	U.S. National Championship finalist
1963-64	Australian Championship mixed doubles (with Fletcher)
	Australian Open mixed doubles (with Fletcher)
1963-65	French Championship mixed doubles (with Fletcher)
1963, 1965-66, 1968, 1975	Wimbledon mixed doubles (with Fletcher and Marty Riessen)
1963, 1965, 1970	Wimbledon
1963, 1968	U.S. National Championship doubles (with Ebbern and María Bueno)
1964-66	French Championship doubles (with Turner and Judy Tegart)
1964, 1969	Wimbledon doubles (with Turner and Tegart)
1964, 1971	Wimbledon finalist
1965	French Championship finalist
1966, 1971	Wimbledon doubles finalist (with Tegart and Evonne Goolagong)
1968-70, 1973	U.S. Open doubles (with Bueno, Virginia Wade, and Tegart-Dalton)
1969	French Open mixed doubles (with Riessen)
1969-71, 1973	Australian Open
	Australian Open doubles (with Tegart-Dalton, Goolagong, and Wade)
1969-70, 1972	U.S. Open mixed doubles (with Riessen)
1969-70, 1973	U.S. Open
	French Open
1971	Wimbledon mixed doubles finalist (with Riessen)
1973	French Open doubles (with Wade)

Other Notable Victories

1961, 1964	Italian Championship mixed doubles (with Roy Emerson and John Newcombe)
1962-64	Italian Championship
1963-64	Italian Championship doubles (with Ebbern and Turner)
1964-65, 1968, 1971	On winning Australian Federation Cup team
1968	Italian Open doubles (with Wade)
	Italian Open mixed doubles (with Riessen)
1970	Canadian Open
1970, 1972, 1975	Canadian Open doubles (with Rosie Casals, Goolagong, and Julie Anthony)

King), in the first round. The pressure of a number one seeding at Wimbledon had been too much for Margaret. However, she won her first United States National Championship in September of 1962. Because she had won three of the Grand Slam tournaments—the Australian, French, and U.S. championships—she was ranked first in the world at the end of the year. The only Grand Slam championship that had eluded her was Wimbledon. Margaret finally won her first Wimbledon singles title the next year by defeating Moffitt by the scores of 6-3, 6-4.

From 1960 to 1966, Margaret won seven consecutive Australian singles titles and four Australian doubles titles. She won Wimbledon again in 1965, which meant that during the early 1960's Margaret captured two French Championships, two U.S. National Championships, and two Wimbledon titles. By the end of 1966, Margaret had won everything for which a tennis player could hope. The years of playing had taken their toll, but it still came as a shock to the tennis world when Maragret announced her retirement from tennis.

Continuing the Story

After retiring, Margaret went back to Australia and, with Helen Plaisted, she opened a boutique by the name of "Peephole." The shop was located in the Western Australian city of Perth. Margaret met wool broker and yachtsman Barry Court, and they were married on October 28, 1967. Through the encouragement of her husband, she decided to return to active tennis competition in 1968. Traveling with her husband, Margaret was more relaxed, and playing tennis was not as all-consuming as it had been in the past. In 1969, she regained her top form, when she won all the Grand Slam singles titles except for Wimbledon. The next year, however, was her greatest. Margaret's newfound confidence helped her to become only the second woman in the history of tennis to win all the major championship singles titles in one calendar year. She played one of her greatest matches against Billie Jean King in the Wimbledon final. The match lasted almost three hours before Margaret prevailed by the score of 14-12, 11-9.

Milestones

Australian Federation Cup team (1962-65, 1968-69, 1971)

Grand Slam mixed doubles (1963, with Ken Fletcher)

Grand Slam (1970)

66 Grand Slam titles

Honors and Awards

1979   Inducted into International Tennis Hall of Fame

1986   Inducted into Sudafed International Women's Sports Hall of Fame

---

In 1972, Margaret gave birth to a son, Daniel, and resumed her tennis career as soon as she could later that year. The next year is remembered for her match with Bobby Riggs in what was billed as the "Battle of the Sexes." The aging tennis great and hustler got the better of Margaret and defeated her on May 13, 1973. Always a reserved individual, she felt ill at ease in such a circus-like event. In more familiar surroundings, she won her ninth Australian title, her fifth French title, and her fifth U.S. title. Margaret retired from tennis in 1977, with a total of sixty-six Grand Slam titles, including singles, doubles, and mixed doubles. After retiring, she served as a minister for a nondenominational Christian church in Australia.

Summary

Margaret Court was inducted into the International Tennis Hall of Fame in 1979. During her career, she was ranked number one in the world seven times. This quiet woman from Australia was one of the all-time greatest champions, and in some experts' minds, Margaret was the best woman player to ever walk onto a tennis court.

Jeffry Jensen

Additional Sources

Collins, Bud. *Total Tennis: The Ultimate Tennis Encyclopedia.* Toronto: Sport Media, 2003.

John, Emma. "Nice Guys Win, Too." *New Statesman* 136, no. 48 (June 25, 2007): 51-53.

Oldfield, Barbara. *A Winning Faith: The Margaret Court Story.* Tonbridge, England: Sovereign World, 1993.

Lindsay Davenport

Born: June 8, 1976
      Palos Verdes, California
Also known as: Lindsay Ann Davenport (full name); the Dav

Early Life

Lindsay Ann Davenport was born on June 8, 1976, the third child of Ann and Wink Davenport. Her parents were both volleyball players; her father had been a member of the U.S. volleyball team in the 1968 Olympics. Both of Lindsay's older sisters,

Lindsay Davenport earning another victory. (Roberto Schmidt/ AFP/Getty Images)

Shannon and Leiann, played volleyball in college. As a child, however, Lindsay was drawn to tennis. At the age of seven, she began playing on the hard courts of Southern California near her home. With her natural athletic ability, she developed the classic hard, flat ground strokes that became the foundation of her game.

The Road to Excellence

As Lindsay started competing in junior tennis matches, her abilities became recognized. In 1991, when she was fifteen, she was named female junior player of the year by *Tennis* magazine. In 1992, she fulfilled her promise in international junior competition, winning the U.S. Open junior singles and doubles titles as well as the Australian Open junior doubles. She was a finalist in junior singles at the Australian Open and in junior doubles at the French Open. Lindsay participated in the player development program sponsored by the United States Tennis Association.

By 1993, Lindsay had reached a level that made turning professional a logical step, which she took on February 22, 1993. Her first two seasons were learning experiences. She divided her time between tennis and school until she graduated from Murrieta Valley High School in 1994. At the same time, she was becoming accustomed to life on professional tennis tours. In 1993, she won her first professional tournament, the European Open, in Strasbourg, France, moving her ranking into the top thirty players. She was named 1993 rookie of the year by *Tennis* magazine. By 1994, she was ranked among the top-ten female professional tennis players.

The Emerging Champion

Although Lindsay was successful as a professional tennis player, she still had much unrealized potential. She was tall, almost 6 feet 3 inches. She had penetrating, hard ground strokes and a good net game. At the same time, she was not quick around the court, and her serve did not utilize the natural asset of her height.

In 1996, several things happened that helped Lindsay raise the level of her game to championship status. First, she started working with a new coach, Robert Van't Hof. He helped her improve her conditioning and strengthen her serve. Second, she won her first Grand Slam title, the French Open doubles, paired with Mary Joe Fernandez. Her confidence received a great boost when she participated in the 1996 Olympic Games in Atlanta, Georgia. The coach for the U.S. women's tennis team was the legendary tennis star Billie Jean King. She bolstered Lindsay's belief in her ability as a player. Lindsay won the gold medal in women's singles at the 1996 Olympics. En route to her victory, she defeated a number of highly ranked players, including Arantxa Sanchez-Vicario in the finals.

In 1997, she continued to play, winning several tournaments. At the U.S. Open she took the doubles title with Jana Novotná. In 1998, her game began to peak. She was a semifinalist at the Australian Open and the French Open and a quarterfinalist at Wimbledon, but she remained winless in Grand Slam events. Later in the summer she began playing the best tennis of her life, feeling like she was "in the zone." She won three hard-court tournaments in California and defeated Martina Hingis, the number-one ranked player. Her confidence was brimming as she came into the U.S. Open. At this Grand Slam tournament, she finally achieved her breakthrough by defeating Hingis in the finals. About six weeks later, in October, 1998, she became the top-ranked singles player in women's tennis.

Lindsay had hoped to carry her high level of play into the next season. She reached the final of the end-of-year Chase Championships but lost to Hingis. In January of 1999, she reached the semifinals at the Australian Open but lost in a tight three-set match. A wrist injury hampered her for several months, but she put in a good performance to reach the quarterfinals at the French Open.

Continuing the Story

At the 1999 Wimbledon tournament, Lindsay surprised everyone by capturing her second Grand Slam on grass, not her favorite surface. She won convincingly, not losing a set and defeating Novotná, the defending champion, in the quarterfinals, and Steffi Graf, a seven-time Wimbledon winner, in the final. She and her partner, Corina Morariu, also captured the doubles title.

Lindsay was not able to defend her 1998 U.S. Open victory, losing in a close match in the semifinals to the eventual champion, Serena Williams. She ended the year by winning the Chase Championships, dominating Hingis in three out of five sets. In addition, she began the 2000 season by winning her third Grand Slam event, the Australian Open. By late spring, she had regained the number-one ranking; went on to win tournaments in Indian Wells, California; Linz, Austria; and Philadelphia, Pennsylvania; and finished the year at number one. Popular with fans and players, she was reelected to the Women's Tennis Association (WTA) Players Council in 2002. The following year she married Jon Leach, an investment banker, former all-American tennis player, and brother of tennis professional Rick Leach.

Although Lindsay did not win any Grand Slam titles in 2004 and 2005, she did win thirteen titles during those two years, despite recurring back injuries. In 2005, *Tennis* magazine voted her twenty-ninth of the forty greatest tennis players. In late 2006, she took a break from tennis to have her first child, Jagger Jonathan. However, by the end of the year, she had returned to the courts and won tournaments in Bali, Indonesia, and Quebec City, Canada. In recognition of her accomplishment, the

Major Championships

1996	Olympics singles
	French Open doubles (with Mary Joe Fernandez)
1997	U.S. Open doubles (with Jana Novotná)
	Chase Championships doubles
1998	U.S. Open singles
	Chase Championships doubles
1999	Wimbledon singles
	Wimbledon doubles (with Corina Morariu)
	Chase Championships singles
2000	Australian Open singles
	Indian Wells singles
	Indian Wells doubles
	Federation Cup
2001	Tokyo (Pan Pacific) singles
	Zurich singles
	Zurich doubles
2003	Tokyo (Pan Pacific) singles
	Indian Wells doubles
2004	Tokyo (Pan Pacific) singles
	San Diego singles
2005	Zurich singles

Honors and Awards

1991	*Tennis* magazine Female Junior Player of the Year
1993	*Tennis* magazine Rookie of the Year
1993-2000	United States Federation Cup Team
1996	Gold medal, Olympic women's singles tennis
1998	WTA Tour Player of the Year
	Diamond Aces Award
	Tennis magazine Player of the Year
1999	Best Female Tennis Player ESPY Award
2000	Prix Orange Award Winner, French Open
2004	International Tennis Writers Association Women's Ambassador for Tennis Award, cowinner
2007	March of Dimes Sportswoman of the Year
	United States Tennis Association (USTA) President's Award
	WTA Comeback Player of the Year

WTA voted her the 2007 comeback player of the year.

In 2008, she won tournaments in Auckland, New Zealand, and Memphis, Tennessee. As of 2008, she had won fifty-five WTA singles titles, thirty-seven WTA doubles titles, three Grand Slam singles titles, and three Grand Slam doubles titles. She was the runner-up in four Grand Slam singles events and the runner-up in ten Grand Slam doubles events. She earned more than $22 million in WTA events, replacing tennis great Graf as the leading money winner in women's tennis. Unlike most other women tennis players, she was almost as successful in doubles as she was in singles.

Summary

Lindsay Davenport was a commanding presence in women's tennis during the 1990's and the early twenty-first century. She was not a teenage phenomenon; rather, her game matured at a steady pace. She did not seek attention and publicity, letting her athletic talent and achievement speak for her. Her results in 2000, particularly her third Grand Slam title, demonstrated that she had earned a place among the great players of women's tennis. Her achievements after 2000 solidified her status as one of the greatest women's tennis players in history.

Karen Gould, updated by Thomas L. Erskine

Additional Sources

Greer, Jim. "The Nice Girl Who Finished First." *Tennis*, September, 1999, 52-56.

McCann, John T. *Lindsay Davenport*. New York: Chelsea House, 2001.

Phillips, Dennis J. *Women Tennis Stars: Biographies and Records of Champions, 1800s to Today*. Jefferson: N.C.: McFarland and Company, 2008.

Price, S. L. "Standing Tall." *Sports Illustrated* 89, no. 12 (September 21, 1998): 60-63.

Sven Davidson

Born: July 13, 1928
    Borås, Sweden
Died: May 28, 2008
    Arcadia, California

Early Life

Sven Davidson was born in Borås, Sweden, on July 13, 1928. He was an avid tennis player as a youth. By the time he was in his late teens, he was one of the top tennis players in Sweden. In 1947, he was Sweden's junior champion. Because a professional tennis circuit did not exist in Sven's playing days in the same manner that it did later, he played out his career as an amateur. Events at that time did not provide monetary compensation to the victors; they were merely played for the love of the game and competition.

The Road to Excellence

Sven's tennis career lasted from 1948 until 1961, the most successful portion of which was between 1953 and 1958. During this time span, Sven was consistently ranked in the world's top ten. In 1957, he reached as high as number three. This same year, he won the French Open. He advanced to three consecutive French Open finals in his career. He was the first Swede to win the French Open, but he was not the last. Several decades later, Bjorn Borg won an unprecedented six French Open titles. However, Sven opened the door for Swedish players in major tennis tournaments.

Along with his prowess as a singles player, Sven was a prodigious doubles player. In 1958, he won the Wimbledon doubles championship with his partner Ulf Schmidt. Sven was also Sweden's greatest Davis Cup player. From 1950 to 1961, Sven had a combined record of 62-23 for Sweden's Davis Cup team; he was 39-14 in singles and 23-9 in doubles. He won a total of twenty-six Swedish Tennis Championships. He became Sweden's all-time Davis Cup doubles winner. His playing career essentially ended in 1961. Though he won just one major singles tournament and one major doubles tournament, in Sweden, Sven was the greatest player of his generation and became a revered citizen.

The Emerging Champion

While Sven had an extremely successful tennis career, his greatest accomplishments came after he stopped competing. Between 1960 and 1964, Sven covered tennis on Swedish television. However, what Sven was doing behind the scenes forever and monumentally changed the game of tennis. He, and numerous others, had been pushing for tennis to change from a strictly amateur sport to a professional one. There was professional tennis before and during Sven's days, but it was vastly different from what followed. Once players turned professional, they could no longer play in the major championship tournaments, which were reserved strictly for amateurs. Professional players toured in groups and were completely controlled by their managers. Sven felt that the major tennis events should feature all of the world's great tennis players and not just the amateurs. He also believed that such tournaments could generate enough income to provide ample prize money to free players from the control of managers. As history shows, Sven was correct. In effect, his goal was to turn the professional players into independent entities, open to play in any tournament in which they wished to play. Thus, the phrase "open era" of tennis came about.

Continuing the Story

Sven also played a critical role in the creation of the Stockholm Open tennis tournament. In 1969, the Stockholm Open became the first northern European tennis tournament with official prize money. Also around this time, Sven initiated the first general meeting of the International Tennis Federation (ITF). Along the line of Sven's ideas, the goal

Honors, Awards, and Milestones

1947	Swedish junior champion
1950-61	Member of Sweden's Davis Cup team
1955, 1956	French Championship (later French Open) finalist
1957	French Championship (later French Open) winner
1958	Wimbledon doubles championship (with Ulf Schmidt)
2007	Inducted into International Tennis Hall of Fame

of the federation was to create a cohesive set of rules and regulations to govern professional tennis around the globe. Those first general meetings of the ITF resulted in the modern form of tennis organization. In a sense, Sven, and the others in those first meetings, invented modern tennis. From the late 1960's to the early 1970's, tennis players went from either unpaid amateurs or tightly controlled professionals to free agents who could play where and when they desired. During the 1970's, the popularity of professional tennis exploded. All of the great players in the world were permitted to play in all of the major tournaments. The purses for the athletes increased dramatically. Tennis became a sport in which the athletes could make millions of dollars and become household names throughout the world. Modern players owed a great debt to the work of Sven and his efforts to implement an open form of competition.

Sven was inducted into the International Tennis Hall of Fame in 2007. He remained involved in international and Swedish tennis until his death in May of 2008. He died of pneumonia after he was di-agnosed with the early stages of Alzheimer's disease in 2007. He was married to his wife Mary for fifty-one years and left behind two daughters, one son, and two grandchildren.

Summary

Sven Davidson's significance was immense and of historical importance. Without his work and the work of others involved during the early days of the International Tennis Federation, open era tennis might never have happened. Though Sven won only two major tournaments as a player, his greatest impact was his willingness to initiate change in the structure of professional tennis.

Theodore Shields

Additional Sources

Collins, Bud, and Zander Hollander. *Bud Collins' Modern Encyclopedia of Tennis*. Detroit: Gale Research, 1994.

Goldstein, Richard. "Sven Davidson, Seventy-nine, Hall of Famer in Tennis, Dies." *The New York Times*, June 7, 2008.

Elena Dementieva

Born: October 15, 1981
    Moscow, Russia, Soviet Union (now in
    Russia)
Also known as: Elena Vyacheslavovna Dementieva
    (full name); Yelena Dementyeva

Early Life
Elena Vyacheslavovna Dementieva was born in Moscow, Soviet Union (now in Russia), on October 15, 1981, the younger of Viacheslav and Vera Dementieva's two children. Both parents were recreational tennis players, and they wanted their children to participate in the sport. When Elena was seven years old, her parents tried unsuccessfully to

enroll her in the Dynamo Club and the Red Army Club. The family was informed that Elena needed a year of development before she could be enrolled. Elena joined in the Spartak Club instead.

The Road to Excellence
Elena's first coach at the Spartak Club was Rauza Islanova, the mother and coach of Marat Safin and a particularly tough mentor. Training started early in the day and continued for many hours. After she lost a match, Elena was afraid to talk with her coach. Islanova instilled a sense of discipline and perseverance in Elena. After three years of training at the Spartak Club, Elena was admitted to the Red Army Club, where she trained under Sergei Pashkov.

By the time she was thirteen, Elena was among the top four under-14 female tennis players in Russia. Among her competitors were Anna Kournikova, Ekaterina Sysoeva, and Anastasia Myskina. At the age of thirteen, she won her first international tournament, Les Petit As, in France. She continued to improve her performance, working on her footwork and serves. In 1995, she began playing on the International Tennis Federation (ITF) tour. The next year, Elena won her first professional singles title on the ITF tour, in Jürmala, Latvia. She won another title in Istanbul, Turkey, in 1997. She also entered the top five hundred of the World Tennis Association (WTA) rankings that year. In 1998, Elena won another ITF singles title in Buchen, Germany. On August 25, 1998, Elena turned professional.

The Emerging Champion
Elena continued to improve her ranking in 1999, and by the end of the year, she was ranked sixty-second in the world. She represented Russia in the Federation Cup final against the United States. Elena upset Venus Williams in the final match to score Russia's only point. Also in 1999,

Elena Dementieva at the 2008 Beijing Olympic Games in Beijing, China. (Clive Brunskill/Getty Images)

she qualified for the Australian Open, the French Open, and Wimbledon. She received direct entry to the U.S. Open. Elena's rank rose as high as twelve during the 2000 season; she won more than forty singles matches and earned more than $600,000. Elena became the first Russian woman to reach the semifinals at the U.S. Open, eventually losing to Lindsay Davenport. She won a silver medal at the 2000 Olympics in Sydney, Australia, losing to Venus Williams in the gold-medal match. Her performance during the year earned her accolades as the WTA tour's most improved player.

In 2001, Elena became Russia's top-ranked tennis player, a position that had been held by Kournikova since 1997. She remained ranked among the top twenty players in the world through the year, peaking at number eight. However, she was slowed by a shoulder injury, which caused her to change her serve motion. She reached the finals in two WTA events, losing at the Mexican Open in Acapulco and at the Kremlin Cup in Moscow. Elena reached the third rounds of both the Australian Open and Wimbledon. She lost in the fourth round at the U.S. Open.

In 2002, Elena's ranking slipped because she only reached one final. She was more successful in doubles with her partner Janette Husarova. At the beginning of the year, Elena was ranked ninety-fourth, but by the end of the year, she reached sixth place. She won titles at Berlin, Germany; San Diego, California; Moscow; and at the WTA Tour Championships at the end of the season.

In 2003, Elena focused on her singles game, reaching number eight in the world rankings by September. She won three tournaments, earning almost $900,000 in prize money, and reached the doubles semifinals at Wimbledon with her partner Lina Krasnoroutskaya.

Continuing the Story

Elena had a successful year in 2005, becoming the sixth-ranked player in the world. She reached the finals in Miami, Florida, losing to Serena Williams. At the French Open, Elena reached her first Grand Slam final before losing to Anastasia Myskina. She lost in the first round at Wimbledon. At the U.S. Open, she reached the finals, losing to Svetlana Kuznetsova in straight sets.

In 2005, Elena also reached six semifinal rounds, including at the U.S. Open. Elena was involved in

some controversy at the U.S. Open when in the semifinals, Mary Pierce required twelve minutes of on-court medical treatment. Elena lost the momentum in the match waiting for play to resume. That same year, she reached the U.S. Open doubles final. Participating with the Russian team in the Federation Cup, she helped her team win the championship, beating France 3-2 in the final.

Elena finished 2006 with a top-ten ranking. She won singles titles at the Pan Pacific Open in Tokyo and in Los Angeles. In winning the Pan Pacific Open, she defeated Martina Hingis. Elena qualified for the year-ending WTA Tour Championships for the seventh straight year, becoming the only active player to do this.

In 2007, she finished out of the top ten for the first time in five years. Elena won two titles and reached the semifinals in three tournaments. Early in the season, she left the tour for nine weeks because of a rib fracture. After returning to the tour, she won the title at Istanbul. In the fall, she defeated Serena Williams for the Kremlin Cup title in Moscow. However, Elena failed to earn a spot at the end-of-year WTA Tour Championships.

Elena had a successful start to the 2008 season; she was ranked eleventh in the world. In March, 2008, she defeated Svetlana Kuznetsova to claim the title at the Dubai Tennis Championships. She lost in the quarterfinals of the French Open but rose to a number-five ranking one week later.

Women's Tennis Association Victories

Date	Location
2002	German Open, doubles (with Janette Husarova)
	Acura Classic, doubles (with Husarova)
	Kremlin Cup, doubles (with Husarova)
	WTA Tour Championships, doubles (with Husarova)
2003	Bausch & Lomb Championships, Amelia Island
	Ordina Open, doubles (with Lina Krasnoroutskaya)
	Wismilak International
	China Open
2004	Gaz de France Stars
2005	East West Bank Classic, doubles (with Flavia Pennetta)
2006	Pan Pacific Open
	JPMorgan Chase Open
2007	Istanbul Cup
	Kremlin Cup
2008	Barclay's Dubai Tennis Championships

Summary

When she turned professional, Elena Dementieva was often compared to her countrywoman Anna Kournikova because of her model-like good looks. Unlike Kournikova, she has been able to win consistently on the tennis circuit. Through early 2008, Elena had won nine singles titles and six doubles titles, earning more than $9 million. Her success was limited in part because of her serve, a feature of her game that she did not like to practice. She made up for this weakness with her aggressive baseline play and forehand returns. Along with her cohort of Russian beauties, such as Kournikova and Maria Sharapova, and female tennis players from other countries, Elena attracted a large number of new fans to women's tennis.

John David Rausch, Jr.

Additional Sources

Deitsch, Richard. "The Annadote." *Sports Illustrated* 93, no. 10 (September 11, 2000): 72.

Wood, Barry. "Dementieva: Will She Be Good for Kournikova?" *Tennis World*, November/December 2000, 6-9.

Margaret Osborne duPont

Born: March 4, 1918
    Joseph, Oregon
Also known as: Margaret Evelyn Osborne duPont
    (full name); Margaret Evelyn Osborne (birth
    name)

Early Life

Margaret Evelyn Osborne was born on March 4, 1918, in Joseph, Oregon, to Charles Marcus St. Lawrence Osborne, a farmer and garage manager, and Eva Jane Osborne. Margaret spent her early years on the family farm in Oregon. When she was nine, the family moved to Spokane, Washington, where Margaret saw tennis played for the first time. She became fascinated with the game, so her mother bought her a racket and encouraged her to play.

When Margaret was ten years old, the family moved to San Francisco. She played tennis on the public courts at Golden Gate Park. As Margaret's tennis began to improve, her mother suggested that they find a coach who could help to develop and refine her game. Margaret received her first formal tennis lessons when she was seventeen. Since the family had little money, Margaret helped to pay for the lessons by writing tennis articles for her coach.

The Road to Excellence

One day while Margaret was practicing, Hazel Wightman—a tennis champion, teacher, and founder of the Wightman Cup championship—saw her play. Hazel commented that Margaret was too nice and that she lacked the "killer instinct" to be a top competitor. Margaret was challenged rather than discouraged by Hazel's comments. She vowed to improve her game and enter a national competition. In 1936, at eighteen, she won the national girls' singles and doubles titles. By the time she was twenty, Margaret was ranked seventh among women players.

Even though Margaret had won national titles and received national ranking, she was always calm and steady when competing. These were the characteristics that later helped her to cope with the rigorous demands of top-level competition. Her game continued to improve, and she developed a reputation for playing her best tennis under pressure. Between 1940 and 1945, just as Margaret's game began to reach its peak, several important tennis competitions were suspended because of World War II. One competition that continued was the United States National Championship. During the war, many women tennis stars worked in factories and offices or served as volunteers. Margaret worked as a shipbuilding clerk eight hours a day, six days a week, practicing tennis after work. She joined another California tennis player, Louise Brough, entertaining soldiers with tennis exhibitions at more than fifty military bases.

The Emerging Champion

Margaret's play surprised competitors and tennis fans unfamiliar with California-style tennis. Unlike many women champions before her, she was a serve-and-volley player, rather than a baseline player. She developed a hard, fast serve, which she combined with well-placed net volleys that fea-

---

Major Championship Victories and Finals

1941	U.S. National Championship doubles (with Sarah Palfrey Cooke)
1942-50, 1955-57	U.S. National Championship doubles (with Louise Brough)
1943-46	U.S. National Championship mixed doubles (with William Talbert)
1944, 1947	U.S. National Championship finalist
1946-47, 1949	French Championship doubles (with Brough)
1946, 1948-50, 1954	Wimbledon doubles (with Brough)
1946, 1949	French Championship
1947	Wimbledon
1948-50	U.S. National Championship
1949-50	Wimbledon finalist
1950	U.S. National Championship mixed doubles (with Kenneth McGregor)
1956	U.S. National Championship mixed doubles (with Ken Rosewall)
1958-60	U.S. National Championship mixed doubles (with Neale Fraser)
1962	Wimbledon mixed doubles (with Fraser)

tured slices and topspins. She was known for tactical ability, and her skilled shot placement won many points.

During the 1940's and 1950's, Margaret ranked among the top players in the world. Her years of training, excellent all-around game, love of tennis, and calm disposition placed her in championship company. In 1941, teamed with Sarah Palfrey Cooke, Margaret won her first U.S. National Championship in doubles. From 1942 to 1950, she joined Louise Brough in winning the U.S. women's doubles title for an unprecedented nine consecutive years. During her career, Margaret was ranked in the world's top ten fourteen times. She was ranked number one in the United States from 1948 to 1950.

Margaret continued her winning ways in mixed doubles, playing with tennis champions William Talbert, Kenneth McGregor, Ken Rosewall, and Neale Fraser. Her championship play extended to Europe, where she won the French Open singles championship in 1946 and 1949, and the French doubles title, with Brough, in 1946, 1947, and 1949.

Margaret's success continued in England, where she won the Wimbledon doubles title in 1946, and the singles title in 1947. In 1949 and 1950, she lost the singles championships to her doubles partner, Brough. Their singles rivalry did not affect their play as a team, however. From 1946 to 1954, they won five Wimbledon doubles championships.

In 1947, Margaret married William duPont, Jr., a wealthy businessman, avid horseman, and tennis enthusiast. Marriage provided Margaret with additional personal and financial support to sustain a successful career in competitive tennis. In 1946, she was selected for the Wightman Cup team, captained by the same Wightman who had previously questioned Margaret's championship ability. During the 1940's and 1950's, the Wightman Cup players were known for their powerful serves and "killer" overhead shots. A writer for *The Times* of London commented that perhaps no other woman's serve had ever traveled as fast as Margaret's. From 1946 to 1962, she achieved one of the finest Wightman Cup records, remaining unbeaten in ten singles and eight doubles competitions. During this time, she was captain for the U.S. Wightman Cup team nine times.

Margaret's style of play helped to launch a new era in women's tennis. Her strong forehand, powerful serve, precise volleys, and attacking style of net play became the standard for women's competition.

Continuing the Story

Margaret dominated U.S. women's singles from 1948 to 1950; her doubles and mixed doubles titles success extended from 1941 to 1962. Her record in the U.S. championships may never be surpassed. In all, she won twenty-five U.S. titles—three in singles, thirteen in doubles, and nine in mixed doubles. Another of her records is the nineteen-year span between her first U.S. title, in 1941, and her last in 1960—when she was forty-two years old.

Although Margaret had humble beginnings playing on public courts and paying for her own lessons, she had the talent and temperament to make her a champion. Her mother, her husband, and Wightman greatly influenced Margaret in her rise to the top, a position she held for more than two decades.

Summary

Margaret Osborne duPont's strong serve and forehand, aggressive volley, and net play combined to make her successful. Her mastery of tennis basics, calm temperament under pressure, and exceptional skill made her a top individual competitor and a perfect doubles partner.

Barbara J. Kelly

Additional Sources

Collins, Bud. *Total Tennis: The Ultimate Tennis Encyclopedia.* Toronto: Sport Media, 2003.

Johnson, Anne Janette. *Great Women in Sports.* Detroit: Visible Ink Press, 1996.

Smith, Lissa, ed. *Nike Is a Goddess: The History of Women in Sports.* New York: Grove Atlantic, 2001.

Françoise Durr

Born: December 25, 1942
       Algiers, Algeria
Also known as: Frankie

Early Life

Françoise Durr was born on December 25, 1942, in Algiers, Algeria. Her father, George Durr, was an engineer and officer in the French air force, and her mother, Delphine Blanc, was a tennis champion. Soon after the Durrs married in 1936, they moved to Tours in the Loire Valley and then to Arcachon in the southwestern part of France. Stationed in Morocco when France fell to German invaders in 1940, Durr relocated his family to Algeria, where Françoise was born. Though Françoise's father survived the war, he was killed in an airplane accident when Françoise was four years old. Her mother chose to remain in Algeria to be near her family. However, during the late 1950's, she was finally forced to return to France by the increasingly violent Algerian independence movement.

Françoise began her tennis career at the Lawn Tennis Club of Oran, where her mother had started as well, and was coached by her mother's first teacher, Joseph de Stopla. Though tennis was a family obligation, Françoise quickly showed the strength, extraordinary ability, and passion for the sport that her mother and Stopla could nurture and develop. While her brother and sister remained recreational players, Françoise was groomed for a career in the sport.

The Road to Excellence

While developing her tennis skills, Françoise did not neglect her academic training. She was a good student during her time at the Sainte Jeanne d'Arc Institute, a Catholic school in Oran. However, tennis quickly became the center of her life. Using an unusual grip that extended her thumb along the shaft of the racket and gave her added accuracy and strength, she won the French junior championships in 1959 and 1960 and the senior champi-

Françoise Durr at Wimbledon in 1972. (Frank Tewkesbury/Hulton Archive/Getty Images)

onships in 1962. By the end of 1962, she was ranked eighth in the world among women tennis players.

The Emerging Champion

Reserved, polite, and perhaps a little shy, Françoise acquired a reputation in French tennis as a consummately professional player. She earned selection to the French Federation Cup team from 1963 to 1967. In 1966, she won the Swiss international championships singles title, the Holland international championships singles and doubles titles, and the London Queen's Club tournament in singles. The following year, she won the Western Australia Championships in women's singles; the French Championship in singles and doubles; and the German international singles championships. Her impressive victory over Lesley Turner Bowrey in women's singles at the 1967 French Championship paved the way to her eight doubles titles at that tournament in following years and made her famous.

Continuing the Story

At the end of 1967, Françoise was ranked third in the world and had reached the peak of her amateur career after representing France in South America, the United States, South Africa, Japan, India, and Europe. In 1968, she turned professional and continued to perform impressively. From 1968 to 1971, she achieved victories in doubles and mixed doubles at the French international championships. In 1969, she also won the doubles titles at the Switzerland, South Africa, Belgium, Italy, and United States international championships. In 1970, she won the doubles in Monte Carlo, Monaco, and the opens of Toronto, Canada, and Christchurch, New Zealand. She continued to play competitively, winning the U.S. international championships in doubles in 1972 and the Paris, Stockholm, and London tournaments in 1975. Though she lost six times in the finals at Wimble-

Major Doubles Titles

1967, 1970-71	French Championships (with Gail Chanfreau)
1968-69	French Championships (with Ann Haydon-Jones)
1968, 1971, 1973	French Championships mixed (with Jean Claude Barclay)
1969, 1972	U.S. Open (with Darlene Hard and Betty Stöve)
1976	Wimbledon mixed (with Tony Roche)

don, her career was anything but a failure. In 1976, she finally achieved a Wimbledon victory in mixed doubles, playing with Tony Roche.

In an era of emotionally flamboyant tennis players, Françoise was famous for a single and endearing quirk: She entered the court with her dog, Topspin, who carried her racket and then waited patiently for her to finish the match. In 1975, she married Boyd Browning.

Summary

Françoise Durr's highest achievement was a world ranking of third in 1967. During her career, she won eleven Grand Slam doubles titles; five French Open doubles titles, with three different partners; and a total of twenty-six singles titles and forty-two doubles titles. She defeated some of the best women players of her time, including Billie Jean King, Evonne Goolagong, and Martina Navratilova. Françoise was captain of the French tennis team from 1980 until 1999 and the first technical director of women's tennis for the French Tennis Federation. She retired in 2002 but still played in the seniors tennis league, the championship of which she and her teammates won in 2002, 2003, and 2006. In 2003, she was inducted into the International Tennis Hall of Fame. Two years later, she was awarded the Federation Cup award of excellence from the International Tennis Hall of Fame and the International Tennis Federation.

Denyse Lemaire and David Kasserman

Additional Sources

Durr, Françoise. *Doubles Strategy: A Creative and Psychological Approach to Tennis.* New York: David McKay, 1978.

Schwabacher, Martin. *Superstars of Women's Tennis.* New York: Chelsea House, 1996.

Taggart, Lisa. *Women Who Win: Female Athletes on Being the Best.* Berkeley, Calif.: Seal Press, 2007.

Honor and Awards

1988	Women's Tennis Association Tour Honorary Membership Award
2003	Inducted into International Tennis Hall of Fame
2005	Fed Cup Award of Excellence

Stefan Edberg

Born: January 19, 1966
     Västervik, Sweden
Also known as: Stefan Bengt Edberg (full name)

Early Life
Stefan Bengt Edberg was born in Västervik, Sweden, on January 19, 1966. His father Bengt was a local policeman. Barbro Edberg, Stefan's mother, agreed with her husband that they should borrow money on their house to pay for their son's tennis lessons and to travel to international tournaments. In Sweden, the local tennis club charged about ten dollars a year for membership. It cost only fifty cents to play, but lessons became expensive as Stefan's skills advanced. Swedish children attended school until four every afternoon and participated in athletics outside school hours.

Stefan's taciturn temperament was a reflection of his parents'. He was given neither to significant emotional swings nor to displays of temper on the courts. He was taught to control his emotions. Only once, when he was fourteen, did Stefan yield to them: Disappointed by his play, he tried to break his aluminum racket by throwing it against a wall.

The Road to Excellence
In 1983, Stefan, quickly advancing beyond local play, became the first player ever to win a junior grand slam. He beat Boris Becker in the Wimbledon Junior Men's Singles. His early conviction to show few emotions on the court carried over into his professional career, which began in 1984, although sometimes his demeanor seemed to belie his frustration or discouragement when his game was going poorly.

Blond, boyish in appearance, and known for his droll humor, Stefan projected an innocence and casualness in public. Stefan knew he was a good tennis player, but he remained modest. In the back of Stefan's mind lurked the specters of countrymen Björn Borg, who had won the Italian Open, and Mats Wilander, who had won the French. Therefore, the Milan Open in 1984, was important to Stefan. He defeated Wilander, a native of Smoland, the same small district in which Stefan's hometown lay. When Stefan played in the U.S. Open later in the year, however, John McEnroe defeated him soundly.

The Emerging Champion
After the U.S. Open, Stefan teamed with Anders Jarryd and beat McEnroe and Peter Fleming in the

Stefan Edberg wins at Wimbledon in 1988 after defeating Boris Becker. (AP/Wide World Photos)

267

Major Championship Victories and Finals

1985, 1987	Australian Open
1987	U.S. Open doubles (with Anders Jarryd)
1987, 1996	Australian Open doubles (with Jarryd and Petr Korda)
1988, 1990	Wimbledon
1989	Wimbledon finalist
	French Open finalist
1990, 1992-93	Australian Open finalist
1991-92	U.S. Open

Other Notable Victories

1984	Gold medal, Olympic men's tennis singles (demonstration sport)
	Milan Open
1984-85	On winning Swedish Davis Cup team
1985, 1987	U.S. Indoor Championship
1988	Swiss Indoor Championship
	Bronze medal, Olympic men's tennis singles
1989	The Masters
1990	ATP Championship

Continuing the Story

In 1989, problems developed in Stefan's personal life, and it was not an easy year for him. He lost two Grand Slam finals and failed to prevail in five other major contests, presumably because his personal problems affected his play. The situation came to a head when Stefan lost to Jimmy Connors in straight sets at the U.S. Open. Pickard knew Stefan needed to get back in stride, and Stefan, with his typical dedication and stoicism, devoted himself to intensive practice. Stefan began to emerge from his slump by defeating Ivan Lendl and Boris Becker in the Masters Tournament. In 1990, he played in the Australian Open, but illness caused him to lose to Lendl by default. In the French Open some weeks later, both Stefan and Becker were poised to rob Lendl of his number-one spot in world tennis. Both lost in the first round, however, and Pickard told his protégé in strident tones what was wrong with his game.

Stefan left France immediately for England to prepare for Wimbledon, determined to hone his game to the kind of perfection required to win. He defeated Becker in five sets, to become number one in world tennis. The Wimbledon contest was called for rain with Stefan in the lead. The twenty-four hour delay on Sunday apparently worked to Stefan's advantage; he remained calm and controlled and came back on Monday in full command of his game. His serves were impeccable, his volleys impressive. Even his forehand rose to new heights. In the semifinals of the 1991 Wimbledon, Stefan lost to the unlikely eventual champion Michael Stich of Germany. A few months later, however, Stefan was back in top form during the U.S. Open, with a dazzling three-set triumph over

1984 men's doubles of the Davis Cup final between the United States and Sweden. At about this time, Tony Pickard became Stefan's coach, which marked a turning point in Stefan's professional career. Pickard, a sales representative for products that Stefan endorsed, helped Stefan advance to the next level of professional excellence.

Realizing that, despite his obvious talent, Stefan had never really been pushed, Pickard, a close and dependable friend of the young player, put him under incredible pressure and taught him effective techniques with which to handle that pressure. Pickard helped Stefan capitalize on his strengths: a strong serve-and-volley game and his one-handed backhand. Pickard also helped Stefan with his forehand shots, not among his notable assets.

In 1985, the year after he turned professional, Stefan, largely through Pickard's effective training program, won the Australian Open and helped Sweden's Davis Cup team prevail over West Germany. He also won the all-German Championship over Becker in 1988. From 1985 to 1990, Stefan was consistently among the world's top five players, creeping up to second in 1987. Ivan Lendl was first.

Honors, Awards, and Milestones

1984-96	Swedish Davis Cup team
1988-90	Adidas Sportsman of the Year
1990	Player of the Year
1990-91	Ranked number one by ATP
1996	ATP begins awarding Stefan Edberg Sportsmanship Award
2004	Inducted into International Tennis Hall of Fame

American Jim Courier. Stefan had won his fifth Grand Slam singles title and his seventh Grand Slam title overall. Afterward, he called the match the best one he had ever played.

Summary

As the foremost tennis player in the world in 1990, Stefan Edberg won impressive cash prizes, making him one of the tennis world's highest earners. He was also well rewarded for his endorsements. Despite the fame and wealth, Stefan valued the relative anonymity of his quiet lifestyle. He retired in 1996, with an impressive career singles record of 806-270. His gracious demeanor and court etiquette as a player were formally recognized when the Association of Tennis Professionals renamed its prize for sportsmanship the "Stefan Edberg Sportsmanship Award." In 2004, Edberg was inducted into the International Tennis Hall of Fame.

R. Baird Shuman

Additional Sources

Collins, Bud. *Total Tennis: The Ultimate Tennis Encyclopedia.* Toronto: Sport Media, 2003.

Evans, Richard. *The ATP Tour: Ten Years of Superstar Tennis.* New York: Universe, 1999.

Fein, Paul. "Stefan Edberg: The Gentleman Champion." *Scandinavian Review* 92, no. 2 (Autumn, 2004): 52-60.

Parsons, John. *The Ultimate Encyclopedia of Tennis: The Definitive Illustrated Guide to World Tennis.* London: Carlton, 2006.

Roy Emerson

Born: November 3, 1936
      Blackbutt, Queensland, Australia
Also known as: Roy Stanley Emerson (full name);
  Emo

Early Life

Roy Stanley Emerson was born on November 3, 1936, in Blackbutt, in the outback of Queensland, Australia. As a young boy, his duty was to milk the cows every morning. The family dairy farm was about eight hundred acres in size. Roy learned early to be responsible and to work hard. The family farm had a tennis court, and Roy began to play on it at the age of eight. The court was popular with all members of the Emerson family, including Roy's sister Daphne, who became an excellent player in her own right. By the age of eleven, Roy had already started winning tennis trophies. He impressed his father so much that the family moved to Brisbane so that Roy could take advantage of the opportunities offered by a larger city.

The Road to Excellence

Before moving his family to Brisbane, Roy's father consulted Norman Brimson, who, as Roy's coach in Blackbutt, saw great potential in the young player. Because the Emersons were financially well off, Roy was able to attend private schools, where he developed solid academic skills while continuing to improve his athletic ability. Roy was a talented athlete in many sports. He ran the 100-yard dash in 10.6 seconds when he was fourteen. The family ethic that Roy had learned on the outback farm served him well as he moved up in the Australian tennis ranks. He was selected for the Queensland senior team at the relatively young age of fifteen. Roy trained and practiced religiously. On the tennis court, no one was in better shape than Roy.

Roy was exposed to the international world of tennis at the age of seventeen under the legendary Australian tennis coach and Davis Cup captain Harry Hopman. For a boy from the outback of Australia, it was definitely a learning experience. His eyes were opened to the world around him, but he never lost sight of his tennis game and the sacrifice necessary to reach the top of his chosen sport. Roy had to rely on superior fitness to wear down his opponents. His quickness and agility were used to defeat adversaries who possessed greater technical skills. The culmination of all his efforts was in 1961, when he won his first Australian Championship at the age of twenty-four.

The Emerging Champion

Even though Roy did not win his first major singles title until 1961, he had already proven to be a solid doubles player. In 1959, Roy and Neale Fraser

Roy Emerson at the U.S. Championships in 1962. (Courtesy of Amateur Athletic Foundation of Los Angeles)

had teamed to win doubles titles at Wimbledon, the U.S. National Championship, and the Italian Championship. In 1960, they won the French Championship and the U.S. National Championship. Roy was not only developing as a champion player, but he was also becoming recognized as a marvelous sportsman. His behavior was always impeccable, and he received a number of awards for his good sportsmanship.

Under the management of Hopman, the Australian tennis world was blossoming. A talented group of players was rising to the top ranks and included some of the greats of the game. In the 1950's, Ken Rosewall and Lew Hoad were the big names of Australian tennis. In the 1960's, Roy joined a group of prominent, up-and-coming Australian tennis players that included Rod Laver, Mal Anderson—who was to marry Roy's sister Daphne—Fred Stolle, Tony Roche, and John Newcombe.

Like his contemporaries, Roy left his mark on the game. Besides winning the Australian singles title in 1961, Roy also won the U.S. National Championship singles title. In 1962, Roy was runner-up to Laver in the Australian, French, and U.S. singles finals. Laver also won the Wimbledon title that year and, therefore, won the tennis Grand Slam. Laver was only the second man in the history of tennis to win all four Grand Slam singles titles in the same year. Many believed that Roy had a good chance of duplicating Laver's feat. With Laver joining the professional circuit in 1963—and therefore becoming ineligible to compete for the major titles—Roy had his best chance to win the Grand Slam. However, the closest Roy came to winning all four Grand Slam titles in one year was in 1964. The only title that escaped him that year was the French Championship.

Continuing the Story

Roy may have never held all four Grand Slam titles in the same year, but he is one of only five tennis players to win all four titles in a career. The other four are Fred Perry, Don Budge, Laver, and Andre Agassi. In 1967, Roy won his last major singles titles. In that year, he won the Australian, French, and

Major Championship Victories and Finals

1959-60, 1965-66	U.S. National Championship doubles (with Neale Fraser and Fred Stolle)
1959, 1961, 1971	Wimbledon doubles (with Fraser and Rod Laver)
1960-65	French Championship doubles (with Fraser, Laver, Manual Santana, Ken Fletcher, and Stolle)
1960-61, 1964-65	Australian Championship doubles finalist (with Fraser, Marty Mulligan, Fletcher, and Stolle)
1961, 1963-67	Australian Championship
1961, 1964	U.S. National Championship
1962	U.S. National Championship finalist
	Australian Championship finalist
	French Championship finalist
1962, 1966	Australian Championship doubles (with Fraser and Stolle)
1963, 1967	French Championship
1964-65	Wimbledon
1967	French Championship doubles finalist (with Fletcher)
1968-69	French Open doubles finalist (with Laver)
1969	Australian Open doubles (with Laver)
1970	U.S. Open doubles finalist (with Laver)

Other Notable Victories

1959-62, 1964-67	On winning Australian Davis Cup team
1959, 1961, 1966	Italian Championship doubles (with Fraser)
1964	Canadian Championship
1967	German Championship
1971	U.S. Pro Championship doubles (with Laver)
1986	Grand Masters Championship doubles (with Stolle)

German singles titles. In his career, he won all the Grand Slam singles titles at least twice, for a total of twelve. Roy also totaled sixteen doubles titles in the four major tournaments. In 1968, he joined the professional ranks, and after professionals were finally allowed to compete for the major titles, he and Laver teamed to win the 1969 Australian Open doubles title and the 1971 Wimbledon doubles title. Always loyal to Australia, Roy competed on its Davis Cup team from 1957 to 1967. A devoted family man, Roy and his wife, Joy, and their children settled in Brisbane in the early 1960's, near his parents. Roy worked in public relations and competed in the Legends Tour. By the 1980's, Roy lived in Newport Beach, California.

271

Summary

Roy Emerson established himself as one of the greats of tennis. Between 1961 and 1967, he was never ranked lower than number four in the world and he was ranked number one twice. Never a boastful person, Roy was somewhat of an unknown champion. However, he stood in elite company as one of only five men to win all four Grand Slam singles titles. He was an example of what hard work and determination can do for a tennis player who may not be the most naturally talented athlete. His position in tennis is secure and his versatility as a player almost unequaled.

Jeffry Jensen

Additional Sources

Collins, Bud. *Total Tennis: The Ultimate Tennis Encyclopedia.* Toronto: Sport Media, 2003.

LeCompte, Tom. "Legend for Hire." *Tennis* 36 (July, 2000): 20.

Parsons, John. *The Ultimate Encyclopedia of Tennis: The Definitive Illustrated Guide to World Tennis.* London: Carlton, 2006.

Chris Evert

Born: December 21, 1954
    Fort Lauderdale, Florida
Also known as: Christine Marie Evert (birth name); Chris Evert Lloyd; Chrissie; Ice Maiden; Ice Princess

Early Life

Christine Marie Evert was born on December 21, 1954, in Fort Lauderdale, Florida. She was the daughter of tennis teaching professional Jimmy Evert and his wife, Colette. The second child in a family of five children and the oldest daughter, Chris was brought up in a strict, lower-middle-class Catholic family. She attended St. Thomas Aquinas High School in Fort Lauderdale. Chris's father gave Chris her first tennis lessons in the summer before her sixth birthday. When she first started practicing, she was unable to return enough balls to hit with other children. Chris sacrificed many hours of summer fun to practice tennis. When school started, she practiced after school and on weekends. Her father sacrificed also by working overtime at the courts to pay for the cost of his children's tennis training.

The Road to Excellence

Chris learned to play on clay courts. This surface was perfect for her style because she was not aggressive or powerful. She was, however, accurate and hit the ball hard and with pace. She played with a two-handed backhand because she was small and lacked the strength to hold her racket in one hand. Chris's father taught her that the player with the fewest errors is usually the winner and that a player should remain emotionally stable on the court. Her style of play, which was based on this philosophy, enabled her to make few errors and to defeat many opponents.

In 1962, during the week of her eighth birthday, Chris competed in her first tournament, the Orange Bowl Junior Tourna-

ment in Miami, Florida. She and her partner won the doubles championship. Chris won her first singles tournament at the age of ten. Her excellent baseline game was a result of many hours of practice, which helped her to perfect her strokes and to develop the mental toughness she needed to win matches. Because she was so controlled on the court, Chris was dubbed the "Ice Maiden." Chris continued to compete in junior tournaments in Florida throughout the 1960's. In 1968, she won the fourteen-and-under national singles tournament. In 1970, at the age of fifteen, Chris won her first major tournament. She defeated Margaret Court, who was ranked number one in the world, at a clay court tournament in North Carolina.

Chris Evert during the semifinal round of Wimbledon in 1976. She defeated Evonne Goolagong in the final round to win her second of three Wimbledon titles. (Courtesy of Amateur Athletic Foundation of Los Angeles)

The Emerging Champion

After defeating Court, Chris competed on the U.S. team that won the 1971 Wightman Cup. She also competed in her first U.S. Open at Forest Hills, New York, where she established herself as a player who would help change women's tennis forever. In 1972, on her eighteenth birthday, Chris turned professional. She was ranked third in the world and reached the semifinals of her first Wimbledon and U.S. Open. In 1973, she reached the first two of her thirty-four Grand Slam finals. In 1974, at nineteen years of age, she won her first Wimbledon. Chris was ranked number one in the world in 1975, 1976, 1977, 1978, 1980, and 1981. From 1974 to 1981, Chris won twelve of her eighteen Grand Slam singles titles, including Wimbledon three times, and the U.S. Open five times.

In the spring of 1980, she won the French and Italian Opens, reached the finals of Wimbledon, won her fifth U.S. Open championship, and won a Grand Slam title. In 1981, Chris won her third Wimbledon crown. This was the seventh and last year she was ranked number one in the world. From 1982 to 1986, Chris was number two in the world, behind Martina Navratilova, and increased her Grand Slam titles to thirteen in thirteen years. Chris shared four Grand Slam titles with Navratilova in 1982, but defeated her to claim the 1982 Australian Open title. Chris defeated Navratilova in the French Open in 1985 and 1986, and in the 1985 Virginia Slims of Florida tournament. Chris lost to Navratilova at Wimbledon in 1978, 1982, 1985, and 1988. The intense rivalry between the two kept Chris competing in the 1980's when she might have quit professional tennis.

In 1987, Chris lost in the quarterfinals of the U.S. Open for the first time in seventeen U.S. Opens. She also lost in the first round of the Virginia Slims Championships. She reached her last Grand Slam final at the 1988 Australian Open. She also made it to the semifinals of Wimbledon and the U.S. Open in 1988. In the spring of 1989, Chris got to three finals in a row. She also made it to the semifinals of the 1989 Wimbledon championships and the quarterfinals of the U.S. Open. It ap-

peared that 1989 would be the first year in her professional career that she did not win a tennis tournament. In October, however, she won five straight Federation Cup matches and helped the U.S. team win the competition in Tokyo.

Continuing the Story

After Chris Evert officially retired from professional tennis in October, 1989, she was remembered for her many accomplishments and contributions. Chris missed tennis as well. Tennis helped her to excel and gain the confidence she needed to overcome her shyness. Chris's first marriage was to tennis player John Lloyd. After competing as Chris Evert-Lloyd for several years, she was divorced from Lloyd in 1987. The following year she married former Olympic skier Andy Mill and later had three sons. Although retired, she remained a touring professional for the Polo Club in Boca Raton, Florida. In 2006, her second marriage ended; soon

Major Championship Victories and Finals

1973	French Open finalist
1973, 1978-80, 1982, 1984-85	Wimbledon finalist
1974-75	French Open doubles (with Olga Morozova and Martina Navratilova)
1974-75, 1979-80, 1983, 1985-86	French Open
1974, 1976, 1981	Wimbledon
1974, 1988	Australian Open finalist
1975-78, 1980, 1982	U.S. Open
1976	Wimbledon doubles (with Navratilova)
1979, 1983-84	U.S. Open finalist
1982, 1984	Australian Open

Other Notable Victories

1971-73, 1976-77, 1979-85	On winning U.S. Wightman Cup team
1972-73, 1975, 1977	Virginia Slims Championship
1972-75, 1979-80	U.S. Clay Court Championship
1974-75	Italian Open doubles (with Morozova and Navratilova)
1974-75, 1980-82	Italian Open
1974, 1980, 1984-85	Canadian Open
1977-82, 1986	On winning U.S. Federation Cup team
1978	U.S. Indoor Championship
1980	Player's International
1983, 1985	German Open

after, she announced her engagement to golf legend Greg Norman, whom she married in June, 2008. Chris has also stayed active in tennis through her charity work and as a tennis commentator for network television. Chris was a unanimous selection to the International Tennis Hall of Fame in 1995.

Summary

Chris Evert became a world-class athlete because she was motivated, controlled, and had excellent concentration and consistent strokes. Few players in the history of tennis played as skillfully and successfully for so many continuous years as Chris did. She won with humility and lost with dignity.

Jane Kirkpatrick

Additional Sources

Buren, Jodi, and Donna A. Lopiano. *Superwomen: One Hundred Women, One Hundred Sports.* New York: Bulfinch Press, 2004.

Collins, Bud. *Total Tennis: The Ultimate Tennis Encyclopedia.* Toronto: Sport Media, 2003.

Howard, Johnette. *The Rivals: Chris Evert Versus Martina Navratilova—Their Epic Duels and Extraordinary Friendship.* New York: Broadway Books, 2005.

Segura, Melissa. "Chris Evert, Tennis Champion." *Sports Illustrated* 101, no. 12 (September 27, 2004): 24-26.

Milestones

U.S. Wightman Cup team (1971-73, 1975-85)

56-match win streak in 1974

Ranked number one by WTA (1975-78, 1980-82)

U.S. Federation Cup team (1977-82, 1986-87)

157 professional singles titles

21 Grand Slam titles

125-match win streak on clay from 1973 to 1979

Honors and Awards

1971	Lebair Sportsmanship Trophy
	Maureen Connolly Brinker Award
1974-75, 1977, 1980	Associated Press Female Athlete of the Year
1976	*Sports Illustrated* Sportswoman of the Year
1979	Karen Krantzcke Sportsmanship Award
1981	WTA Player of the Year
	Women's Sports Foundation Professional Athlete of the Year
	Inducted into Sudafed International Women's Sports Hall of Fame
1982	Service Bowl Award
1985	Women's Sports Foundation Greatest Woman Athlete of the Last 25 Years
1990	Flo Hyman Award
1995	Inducted into International Tennis Hall of Fame

Roger Federer

Born: August 8, 1981
    Basel, Switzerland
Also known as: Magician of Precision; Rogi;
    Federer Express; Basel Dazzle; Swiss Who
    Can't Miss; Lord of the Swings

Early Life
Roger Federer was born on August 8, 1981, in Basel, Switzerland, to Robert Federer and Lynette Durand Federer. His parents worked for Ciba-Geigy, a pharmaceutical company. They met in South Africa while Robert Federer was there on a business trip. Roger has an older sister, Diana, who

Roger Federer, who won five consecutive Wimbledon Championships. (Steve Crisp/Reuters/Landov)

was born in 1979. He and Diana spent their childhood years in Münchenstein, a suburban community near Basel. The family enjoyed playing tennis whenever possible. While Roger also enjoyed playing soccer, he showed a definite aptitude for tennis. When he had reached eight years old, he was good enough to join Basel's junior tennis program. The young Roger admired the German tennis star Boris Becker. As a child, Roger had difficulty controlling his emotions. He became upset if his hero Boris did not win, and he lost his temper if he himself hit a bad shot. Roger's parents became concerned with their son's inappropriate behavior. To help solve this problem, Roger was introduced to a coach who changed his whole approach to tennis.

The Road to Excellence
At the age of ten, Roger came under the tutelage of Peter Carter, a former tennis player from Australia. For the next few years, Roger spent more time with his new coach than he did with his own family. In addition to focusing on improving Roger's ground strokes and serve, Carter introduced him to a more positive mental approach to the game. Roger was taught the importance of controlling his temper and of not wasting so much emotional energy during matches. By the time he was a teenager, he had matured dramatically and seemed prepared for new challenges.

In 1994, Roger accepted an invitation to train at the Swiss National Tennis Center located in Ecublens, Switzerland. While he returned home on weekends, during the week, Roger was at the center. Since Roger spoke German, and French was spoken at the center, he felt out of place. After three years at Ecublens, he was ready to leave and find a new facility more suited to his needs. He chose a training center in Biel, Switzerland, where he could once again work with

Grand Slam Results

1998	Wimbledon junior
2003-07	Wimbledon
2004-08	U.S. Open
2004, 2006-07	Australian Open
2008	Wimbledon finalist
2009	French Open

Carter. By 1998, Roger had established himself as one of the top junior players in the world. During the year, he won the junior Wimbledon titles in both singles and doubles and the coveted Orange Bowl. For his accomplishments on the junior circuit, he was named the International Tennis Federation (ITF) world junior tennis champion of 1998.

The Emerging Champion

Before the end of 1998, Roger played in some Association of Tennis Professionals (ATP) tour events. He was a quality player but needed to play many more ATP matches before he could become a true champion. In 1999 and 2000, he continued to move up in the rankings even though he had yet to win an ATP title. At the end of 2000, he was ranked twenty-ninth in the world. In early 2001, he finally broke through by capturing the title in Milan. He also competed on the Swiss Davis Cup team against the United States in February of 2001. Roger was instrumental in Switzerland's 3-2 Davis Cup victory over the United States. By the end of 2001, he was ranked number thirteen in the world.

Roger was poised to become a top-ten player. In 2002, he rose to number six by winning three titles. His brilliant shotmaking, his focus, and his total control of the moment, were all elements that helped him become number one in the world and to win several Grand Slam tournaments. In 2003, Roger broke through with his victory over Mark Philippoussis in the final at Wimbledon. In addition to his straight-set victory at Wimbledon, Roger won several other titles during 2003. In February, 2004, he became ranked number one in the world. He held onto this ranking until August 17, 2008. While he had established himself as a tough competitor, he proved just how spectacular a champion he could be with the remarkable year he had in 2004.

In 2004, Roger won three Grand Slam titles. He defeated Marat Safin to capture the Australian Open, beat Andy Roddick to capture his second Wimbledon, and defeated Lleyton Hewitt to capture the U.S. Open. The only Grand Slam title to elude him was the French Open. With these victories, Roger was beginning to flirt with tennis history. Even with all his success, he still worked hard to become a more complete player. Critics and fans alike spoke of Roger as an artist, not merely as a champion tennis player.

Continuing the Story

In 2005, Roger won his third Wimbledon title and his second U.S. Open. However, he still could not find success on the red clay of Roland Garros. At the French Open, he did not even make it to the finals. A young Spaniard by the name of Rafael Nadal had burst onto the tennis scene. Nadal won the 2005 French Open in dramatic fashion and looked to be the player who could compete against Roger for supremacy on the court. Roger was the all-court specialist, while Nadal was the clay-court specialist. In 2006, Roger once again won three Grand Slam titles. He also made the finals of the French Open, only to lose to Nadal in four sets.

Honors, Awards, and Milestones

2003-04	Association of Tennis Professionals European Player of the Year
2003-04, 2006-07	Switzerland Athlete of the Year
2004	*Sports Illustrated* Tennis Player of the Year
2004-06	International Tennis Writers Association Player of the Year
2004-08	Most U.S. Open titles in a row
2005	Named Ambassador of United Nations for physical education
2005-06	U.S. Sports Academy Most Outstanding Athlete
2005-08	Association of Tennis Professionals Player of the Year
	Stefan Edberg Sportsmanship Award
2006-07	First man to advance to final match of all Grand Slam singles tournaments in consecutive seasons
2006-08	Laureus World Sportsman of the Year
2007	Arthur Ashe Humanitarian of the Year award
	Tennis Player of the Year
2008	Gold medal, Olympic doubles (with Stanislas Wawrinka)

Roger returned the favor by beating Nadal in the finals at Wimbledon. A rivalry was building.

In 2007, Roger had another extraordinary year. He won three more Grand Slam titles and again made the finals of the French Open only to lose to Nadal. In a dramatic finals at Wimbledon, Roger beat Rafael in five hard-fought sets. By the end of 2007, Roger had twelve Grand Slam singles titles. This left him only two behind Pete Sampras, who finished his illustrious career as the all-time leader with fourteen. Many believed that within a short period of time Roger would break Sampras's record and become the holder of the most Grand Slam singles titles for a man. However, in 2008, not everything went as planned. Roger only advanced to the semifinals at the Australian Open. With this loss, his string of ten consecutive Grand Slam finals was broken. By March, Roger revealed that he was suffering from mononucleosis. Whether a loss of energy was hindering his play or not, Roger was not winning with the same frequency as he had in the past. At the 2008 French Open, he was badly beaten by Nadal in the finals.

With only two Grand Slams tournaments left in 2008, Roger hoped to reclaim his competitive edge at Wimbledon. He also hoped to capture his sixth consecutive Wimbledon title. In what has been called one of the greatest tennis matches in modern tennis history, Nadal defeated Roger in five sets. For the tennis world, the event was an extraordinary advertisement for all that was good about the sport. Many hoped that both of these fierce competitors would duel once again in the finals of the U.S. Open. However, Nadal was beaten in his quarterfinal match. Roger prevailed, though, by defeating Novak Djokovic in the finals. While 2008 did not turn out exactly as he had hoped, Roger was pleased to win his fifth U.S. Open in a row. Furthermore, he and his partner, Stanislas Wawrinka, won the gold medal in men's doubles at the 2008 Summer Olympics.

During the following year, 2009, Roger made another impressive run in the Grand Slam events. After losing to Nadal in five hard-fought sets in the finals of the Australian Open, he finally captured his first French Open title by defeating Robin Söderling in straight sets. This victory tied him with Pete Sampras for the most Grand Slam singles titles (fourteen) for a man. In July, he set a new record for men by reaching his twentieth Grand Slam final at Wimbledon. In a match even more dramatic than his 2008 loss to Nadal, Roger beat Andy Roddick in five grueling sets that lasted well over four hours. The record-breaking fifth set alone stretched to thirty games and lasted ninety-five minutes, with Roger finally prevailing by a score of 16-14. The win gave him his fifteenth Grand Slam singles title and sole possession of the all-time men's record.

Summary

In relatively few years, Roger Federer has established himself as one of the all-time great tennis players. His style of play is pure artistry. His ground strokes, both forehand and backhand, are so precise that opponents are often forced into defensive positions. Blessed with a excellent serve and fine touch at the net, Roger has proved himself a dangerous adversary on all court surfaces. More importantly, however, he has become a true tennis great because of his keen mental acumen on the court. In addition to his unparalleled achievements on the tennis court, Roger has also involved himself with charities, including the Roger Federer Foundation that he founded in 2003. In 2006, he became a UNICEF Goodwill Ambassador.

Jeffry Jensen

Additional Sources

Bowers, Chris. *Fantastic Federer.* London: John Blake, 2006.

Labrecque, Ellen. *Roger Federer.* Mankato, Minn.: Child's World, 2008.

Savage, Jeff. *Roger Federer.* Minneapolis: Lerner, 2009.

Stauffer, René. *The Roger Federer Story: Quest for Perfection.* Washington, D.C.: New Chapter Press, 2007.

Althea Gibson

Born: August 25, 1927
　　　Silver, South Carolina
Died: September 28, 2003
　　　East Orange, New Jersey
Other major sport: Golf

Early Life

Althea Gibson was born on August 25, 1927, in Silver, South Carolina. Althea's parents lived in a small cabin and worked as sharecroppers on a five-acre farm, but after three years of bad weather ruined their crops and broke them financially, the Gibsons and three-year-old Althea moved to New York City. When Althea's father found work in a garage, the Gibsons moved to an apartment in the poor, predominantly black Harlem area of New York. Life was better for the Gibsons in Harlem than it had been in South Carolina, but it was far from good. Althea grew up playing in the poverty-stricken streets, and she skipped school on a regular basis.

The Road to Excellence

When Althea was about nine, the police blockaded the street in front of her home and designated the area a Police Athletic League "play street." Althea learned to play basketball, stickball, and paddle tennis in the street. She played all sports well, but soon became the neighborhood champion in paddle tennis. Althea won her first athletic medals representing her neighborhood in competition with other Harlem play streets.

The community recreation director, Buddy Walker, was so impressed with Althea's success in paddle tennis that he lent her a regulation tennis racket and encouraged her to learn tennis. A schoolteacher saw her play and arranged for her to begin lessons with Fred Johnson, a professional instructor at a tennis club. Althea, tall and muscular, quickly learned to hit the tennis ball with power and accuracy. She also learned the footwork, strategy, and etiquette of tennis. In just one year, Althea won the girls' singles in the New York State Open Championship.

The members of the tennis club took up a collection and paid Althea's way to Pennsylvania to compete in the 1942 American Tennis Association's (ATA) national girls' championships. The ATA sponsored tennis competition for African Americans because segregation was still common in many aspects of American life. African American players were not permitted to play in competitions sponsored by the United States Lawn

Althea Gibson, who was the first African American woman to compete in professional tennis. (Courtesy of International Tennis Hall of Fame)

Major Championship Victories and Finals

1956	French Championship
	French Championship doubles (with Angela Buxton)
1956-58	Wimbledon doubles (with Buxton, Darlene Hard, and María Bueno)
1957	Australian Championship finalist
	U.S. National Championship mixed doubles (with Kurt Nielsen)
	Australian Championship doubles (with Shirley Fry)
1957-58	Wimbledon mixed doubles finalist (with Neale Fraser and Nielsen)
	Wimbledon
	U.S. National Championship

Other Notable Victories

1947-56	ATA Championship
1948-50, 1952-55	ATA Championship mixed doubles (with R. Walter Johnson)
1957	On winning U.S. Wightman Cup team

Tennis Association (USLTA). Althea came in second in the 1942 ATA girls' championship. The competition was cancelled the next year, after America's entry into World War II, but Althea won the ATA girls' championships in both 1944 and 1945.

The Emerging Champion

By the 1946 ATA tournament, Althea had turned eighteen and was eligible to compete in the women's singles. Although she lost in the finals, her play attracted the attention of two doctors, named Eaton and Johnson, who were tennis supporters. They saw her potential and offered her a scholarship to an African American college where she could compete in a challenging intercollegiate tennis program.

The offer was altered when the doctors learned that Althea had never finished high school. Althea moved to Wilmington, North Carolina, and lived with Dr. Eaton's family. There she finished high school and practiced tennis on the Eaton's backyard tennis court. In the summers, she moved to the Lynchburg, Virginia, home of Dr. Johnson and traveled with him to summer tournaments. The doctors paid all of Althea's expenses. The plan sounded great, but Althea was uneasy about the prospect of living in small Southern towns. The person who convinced her to accept the doctors' generous offer was the famous boxer Sugar Ray Robinson. "You'll never amount to anything just banging around from one job to an-

other like you been doing," he said. "No matter what you want to do, you'll be better at it if you get some education."

For the next four years, Althea worked hard on both her tennis and schoolwork. She returned to the ATA championships each of the next ten years, and won the women's singles championships every time. She also began college at Florida A & M University. Althea was undeniably the best African American woman tennis player in the country.

In 1950, Alice Marble, a famous and respected American tennis player, wrote an editorial for the *American Lawn Tennis* magazine. She challenged USLTA officials to allow Althea Gibson to test her tennis ability against the best white players in the United States National Championship at Forest Hills. That August, Althea Gibson received an invitation to Forest Hills. She played well, but only won one match at the tournament that year. Meanwhile, Althea continued to break racial barriers in tennis tournaments around the country. She graduated from college and took a job as a physical education instructor.

In 1955, Althea was invited to join a group of other young American tennis players on a goodwill tour of Southeast Asia sponsored by the U.S. State Department. She played well during the six-week tour, received praise for her aggressive serve-and-volley style of play, and learned a lot about other countries. In 1956, Althea traveled abroad again and won the French National Championship, her first major tennis title and the first win for an African American player in any of the major interna-

Honors, Awards, and Milestones

1957	Babe Didrikson Zaharias Trophy
1957-58	Associated Press Female Athlete of the Year
	U.S. Wightman Cup team
1971	Inducted into International Tennis Hall of Fame
1980	Inducted into International Women's Sports Hall of Fame
1991	Given NCAA Theodore Roosevelt Award (first female recipient)
1995	Inducted into Intercollegiate Tennis Association (ITA) Women's Hall of Fame
2002	Inducted into National Women's Hall of Fame
2007	Inducted into U.S. Open Court of Champions

tional singles tennis championships. Althea was on her way to true stardom.

In 1957 and again in 1958, Althea impressed the world with wins at both Forest Hills and Wimbledon, the site of the all-England tennis championships. Althea received personal congratulations from the queen of England and the president of the United States. She rode in parades and starred in newsreels and television, and received the Babe Didrikson Zaharias Trophy as the 1957 woman athlete of the year.

Continuing the Story

Althea was extremely proud of her successes as an athlete, but she yearned to do other things also. In particular, Althea dreamed of becoming a famous singer. She recorded an album of popular ballads and even sang on national television on *The Ed Sullivan Show.*

In 1958, Althea surprised the world by announcing her retirement from amateur tennis. She then sang in nightclubs, wrote two autobiographical books, and acted in a movie. Althea did not, however, achieve any lasting success in any of these endeavors. By 1961, deeply in debt, Althea accepted a position in the business world as a community relations representative. In that job, she excelled as a public speaker. She was also appointed to advise the New York State Recreation Council in their development of public recreation programs for children.

Althea was always an athlete at heart, though, and in the 1960's she returned to competition in a new sport. Again she broke racial barriers. She was the first African American to qualify for the Ladies Professional Golf Association (LPGA) circuit. Her golf successes never matched her tennis successes,

and eventually she dropped out of professional golf competition. In 2007, four years after her death, Althea was inducted into the U.S. Open Court of Champions.

Summary

Althea Gibson will always be regarded as one of the most outstanding American tennis players, and she will always be respected for her personal courage and initiative. Althea broke racial barriers in both tennis and professional women's golf. She also displayed courage and initiative; she always tried new things, such as singing, writing, acting, and working in the business world. Althea never backed down from a challenge.

Kathleen Tritschler

Additional Sources
Barber, Terry. *Althea Gibson.* Edmonton: Grass Roots Press, 2007.

Gray, Frances Clayton, and Yanick Rice Lamb. *Born to Win: The Authorized Biography of Althea Gibson.* Hoboken, N.J.: John Wiley & Sons, 2004.

Harris, Cecil, and Larryette Kyle-DeBose. *Charging the Net: A History of Blacks in Tennis from Althea Gibson and Arthur Ashe to the Williams Sisters.* Chicago: Ivan R. Dee, 2007.

O'Neil, Dana Pennett, and Pat Williams. *How to Be Like Women Athletes of Influence: Thirty-one Women at the Top of Their Game and How You Can Get There Too.* Deerfield Beach, Fla.: Health Communications, 2007.

Schoenfeld, Bruce. *The Match: Althea Gibson and a Portrait of a Friendship.* New York: Amistad, 2005.

Wiggins, David Kenneth. *Out of the Shadows: A Biographical History of African American Athletes.* Fayetteville: University of Arkansas Press, 2006.

Pancho Gonzales

Born: May 9, 1928
     Los Angeles, California
Died: July 3, 1995
     Las Vegas, Nevada
Also known as: Richard Alonzo Gonzales (full
    name); Richard Alonzo González; Pancho
    Gonzalez

Early Life

Richard Alonzo "Pancho" Gonzales was born on
May 9, 1928, in Los Angeles, California. He was one
of seven children, and although he grew up during
the Great Depression, he never really knew poverty. His family always had plenty of food and clothing available but indulged in few luxuries. Tennis
lessons with a top teaching professional were out
of the question. Therefore, Pancho played and
learned tennis in the public parks of Los Angeles.

Pancho is one of the most talented players who ever lived, and
although he never had a formal
tennis lesson, his style was classic. Pancho, a Mexican American, went on to become one of
the best amateur and the best
professional tennis player in the
world.

The Road to Excellence

Pancho had practically no tournament competition when he
was growing up, but he was a
great player. At the age of nineteen, he played his first major
tournament. He defeated Herb
Flam, the National Junior Champion, in the final of the Southern California Championships.
This was the first in a long series
of championship wins that established Pancho as a world-class
player. After that victory, he decided to compete on grass and
clay courts on the major Eastern
circuit. Up to that point, he had
only played on hardcourts, but he earned the ranking of seventeen nationally. In 1948, he again played
the Eastern circuit. By this time he was unbeatable.

Pancho, a controversial personality, accomplished a great deal for tennis. He was admired by
every top player and had no critics. He stands alone
as a stylist, an unrelenting competitor, and a winner. He was always disciplined, dedicated, and determined, which accounts for his success on the
court. Pancho had the temperament of a lion and
took advantage of opponents' weaknesses. He appeared to have a sixth sense that gave him the advantage over all other players.

The Emerging Champion

In 1948 and 1949, Pancho won the U.S. National
Championship in singles at the Westside Tennis
Club in Forest Hills, New York. He also won the

Pancho Gonzales. (Courtesy of Amateur Athletic Foundation of Los Angeles)

U.S. Indoor Championship for 1949 and the U.S. Clay Court Championship for both 1948 and 1949. Pancho was equally proficient at doubles: In 1949, he won the Wimbledon doubles title with Frank Parker. He won the Professional World Doubles Tournament with Don Budge in 1950 and with Pancho Segura in 1951 and 1952. He and Jack Kramer together laid the foundation for modern professional tennis. They traveled around the world with the pro tour throughout the 1950's and into the 1960's. As a result of their efforts, open tennis finally became lucrative, and in 1968, the first U.S. Open was held at Forest Hills. Pancho's magnetism and dynamic personality had provided the two items that tennis had needed for years, spectators and money. Stadiums, arenas, and parks throughout the country finally attracted vast audiences. As a result, more people participated, donated funds for youth development, and, in general, worked to promote the sport.

Major Championship Victories and Finals

1948-49	U.S. National Championship
1949	Wimbledon doubles (with Frank Parker)
	French Championship doubles (with Parker)

Other Notable Victories

1948-49	U.S. Clay Court Championship
1949	On winning U.S. Davis Cup team
	U.S. Indoor Championship
	U.S. Indoor Championship mixed doubles (with Gussie Moran)
1950-52	Professional World Doubles Tournament (with Don Budge and Pancho Segura [twice])
1950-52, 1956	London Pro Championship
1953-59, 1961	U.S. Pro Championship
1964	U.S. Pro Indoor Championship
1967	New York Professional Championship
1968	Birmingham Professional Classic
1969-70	Howard Hughes Invitational
1969, 1971	Pacific Southwest Open
1969, 1972	Pacific Southwest Open doubles (with Ron Holmberg and Jimmy Connors)
1970	Paris Open Indoor doubles (with Ken Rosewall)

Honors, Awards, and Milestones

1949	U.S. Davis Cup team
1968	Inducted into International Tennis Hall of Fame

For more than twenty years, Pancho was a champion in the truest sense of the word and his initiative, motivation, or drive never diminished. In 1971, at forty-three years of age, he pushed himself harder than he had ever done before, as was evidenced by his Davis Cup play that year. Pancho's dedication to tennis was not completely selfish. He conducted clinics, talked to American youngsters, and spent time at his tennis ranch for children in California. Pancho realized that the future of tennis lay in the hands of its young people. Many of the attributes that made Pancho a champion were the same needed to be a good citizen and student. His love of fair play, drive to excel, power of endurance, and excitement for life were just a few of his remarkable characteristics. After winning his first two amateur titles, Pancho turned pro and ruled professional tennis for the next ten years. Many experts believe that if open tennis had come in the early 1950's, Pancho would have been ranked as the world's greatest player. One of Pancho's greatest attributes was his resilience.

Continuing the Story

In 1960, Pancho began his semiretirement, which meant that he came out of retirement at almost yearly intervals. In 1961, he came out of retirement to beat Frank Sedgman 6-3, 7-5, and win the U.S. Pro Championship for the eighth time. In May, 1964, having played only one tournament in the previous three years, he won the U.S. Pro Indoor Championship by defeating Rod Laver, Lou Hoad, and Ken Rosewall in successive days. In 1967, at thirty-nine years of age, a graying and gaunt Pancho beat Rod Laver in the final of the New York Professional Championship.

In 1968, at the age of forty, Pancho won the Birmingham Pro Classic by beating Roy Emerson in straight sets. In 1969, he took the Howard Hughes Invitational in Las Vegas by beating a young Arthur Ashe 6-0, 6-3, 6-4, and defeated Cliff Richey in the Pacific Southwest Open. In 1970, he won the Howard Hughes Invitational again, defeating Rod Laver 6-1, 7-5, 5-7, 6-3; in 1971, the "Old Lion," at the age of forty-three, kept a young Jimmy Connors at bay to win the Pacific Southwest Open again. In 1972, at forty-four years of age, he was still the ninth ranked professional in America. After 1970, Pancho served as tennis director at Caesars Palace in Las Vegas, Nevada.

Summary

Pancho Gonzales was a legend who won tournaments over top-notch opponents. He was a man to be admired and appreciated because he made tennis more exciting and raised its cultural signifi-

cance. He was elected to the International Tennis Hall of Fame in 1968.

Joseph Beerman

Additional Sources

Collins, Bud. *Total Tennis: The Ultimate Tennis Encyclopedia.* Toronto: Sport Media, 2003.

Parsons, John. *The Ultimate Encyclopedia of Tennis: The Definitive Illustrated Guide to World Tennis.* London: Carlton, 2006.

Price, S. L. "The Lone Wolf." *Sports Illustrated* 96, no. 26 (June 24, 2002): 68-76.

Evonne Goolagong

Born: July 31, 1951
      Griffith, New South Wales, Australia
Also known as: Evonne Fay Goolagong Cawley
   (full name); Evonne Goolagong Cawley;
   Evonne Fay Goolagong (birth name)

Early Life

Evonne Fay Goolagong was born on July 31, 1951, in the small town of Griffith, in New South Wales, Australia. She was the third of eight children born to Kenneth and Linda Goolagong, both of aboriginal ancestry. Evonne spent most of her childhood in the small farming community of Barellan, where her father worked as a sheepshearer, farm laborer, and mechanic. The family was poor; they lived in a tumbledown wooden building and sometimes went without meals.

The Road to Excellence

Evonne became fascinated by tennis at an early age. Her favorite toy was an old tennis ball that she carried with her constantly. By the time she was five, she was earning money retrieving balls at the Barellan War Memorial Tennis Club. When she was six, she began devoting all her spare time to practicing on the dirt courts. Noticing her dedication and her natural ability, W. C. Kurtzman, president of the tennis club, began teaching Evonne the fine points of the game. At the age of nine, Evonne attracted the attention of Vic Edwards, Australia's foremost tennis coach. When Evonne was ten, Edwards took her and her parents to a tournament. Though Edwards had mistakenly entered Evonne in an adult competition, she won the women's singles title.

Edwards began seriously coaching Evonne when she was eleven, and the town of Barellan paid many of her expenses as she earned wider notice. In 1965, she won the under-fifteen championship of New South Wales and was compared to Margaret Court, an Australian Wimbledon champion. At fourteen, Evonne moved in permanently with the Edwards family and received more intense training. Evonne also received the same schooling as the Edwardses' daughters, including secretarial

training, just in case she could not make her living from tennis. By sixteen, Evonne had won all the Australian junior titles without losing a set and, between 1968 and 1970, won eighty-eight championships on the Australian circuit. In 1970, she toured Europe and won seven of the twenty-one tournaments she entered.

The Emerging Champion

The combination of natural talent and excellent coaching was readily apparent in Evonne, but many wondered if her good nature would be a drawback in competition. She seemed to lack the killer instinct, the ruthless determination to win, which characterized many champions. Evonne triumphed over Rosemary Casals at the British Open championship in April, 1970, only to lose at Wimbledon two months later. Then, on February 1, 1971, Evonne captured the first major victory of her career when she defeated Court at the Victo-

Evonne Goolagong. (Courtesy of International Tennis Hall of Fame)

rian Open Championship. Later that year, at Wimbledon, perhaps the most important tennis tournament in the world, Evonne was seeded third. She defeated second-seeded Billie Jean King, a former Wimbledon winner, in only fifty-six minutes. During this tournament, Evonne was focused; her mind seemed to be concentrated on her ability to win, and nothing distracted her from that goal. At the finals on July 2, 1971, Evonne defeated Court to become the Wimbledon Champion at the age of nineteen, three years ahead of her coach's expectations.

Continuing the Story

Evonne's career, however, was not marked only by victories. Soon after her Wimbledon win, she lost both the Irish Open in Dublin and the North of England championships, though she came back to win the Dutch Open in August, 1971. The death of her father, in October, 1974, disrupted her American tour. When Evonne married Roger Cawley, a British businessman, in 1975, many doubted that she would be able to continue her career. "She can either give herself to love or to tennis, but not both," Vic Edwards said. However, Evonne surprised many fans when, in 1976, she was not only runner-up at both Wimbledon and the U.S. Open but also won a second Wimbledon championship in 1980, after the birth of her daughter in 1977.

In 1980, she helped to design a new style of brassiere for women tennis players and for other active women. She also endorsed a book, *Australian Dreaming: Forty Thousand Years of Aboriginal History* (1979), by Jennifer Isaacs, the profits from which would be used to encourage Aborigines to develop their arts and better themselves economically. After retiring from competitive tennis in 1983, Evonne remained active with tennis through product endorsements, a few Virginia Slims Legends Tour events each year, and her work with the Federation Cup Foundation and the Indigenous Sports Program in Australia.

Summary

Evonne Goolagong was one of the first women athletes able to combine winning sports careers with marriage and motherhood. In addition to her two Wimbledon championships, she was a runner-up at Wimbledon three times and the U.S. Open four times. By proving that it could be done, she was an encour-

---

Major Championship Victories and Finals

1971	French Open
	Wimbledon doubles finalist (with Margaret Court)
1971, 1974-75, 1976	Australian Open doubles (with Court, Margaret Michel, and Helen Gourlay)
1971, 1980	Wimbledon
1972	French Open mixed doubles (with Kim Warwick)
	Wimbledon mixed doubles finalist (with Warwick)
	French Open finalist
1972, 1975-76	Wimbledon finalist
1973-76	U.S. Open finalist
1974	Wimbledon doubles (with Michel)
1974-77	Australian Open

Other Notable Victories

1971, 1973-74	On winning Australian Federation Cup team
1972-73	Canadian Open
	Canadian Open doubles (with Court and Michel)
1973	Italian Open
1973, 1979	U.S. Indoor Championship
1974, 1976	Virginia Slims Championship

---

agement and an inspiration to a new generation of women athletes.

Mary Johnson

Additional Sources

Collins, Bud. *Total Tennis: The Ultimate Tennis Encyclopedia.* Toronto: Sport Media, 2003.

Parsons, John. *The Ultimate Encyclopedia of Tennis: The Definitive Illustrated Guide to World Tennis.* London: Carlton, 2006.

Smith, Lissa, ed. *Nike Is a Goddess: The History of Women in Sports.* New York: Grove Atlantic, 2001.

Honors, Awards, and Milestones

1971	Associated Press Female Athlete of the Year
1971-76	Australian Federation Cup team
1980	Karen Krantzcke Sportsmanship Award
1988	Inducted into International Tennis Hall of Fame
1989	Inducted into Sudafed International Women's Sports Hall of Fame

Steffi Graf

Born: June 14, 1969
Mannheim, West Germany (now in
Germany)
Also known as: Stephanie Maria Graf (full
name); Fraulein Forehand

Early Life

Stephanie Maria Graf was born on June 14, 1969, in
Mannheim, a large industrial city in West Germany
(now in Germany). Her parents, Peter and Heidi
Graf, were semiprofessional tennis players. She has
a younger brother, Michael. From about the age of
three, Steffi showed an interest in playing tennis.
She began hitting balls against the living room wall
and across a makeshift "net" of string between two
chairs. As her exceptional ability in the sport became apparent, her father moved the family to
Brühl, a suburb of Mannheim, where he opened a
tennis club and school. Under her father's coaching, Steffi posted impressive wins in junior competition by the time she was twelve years old. Her most
notable successes were winning the Orange Bowl
twelve-year-olds tournament in 1981, the European fourteen-and-under tournament, and the European Circuit Masters in 1982.

Steffi Graf backhanding the ball in the semifinal match of the 1993 U.S. Open.
(Don Emmert/AFP/Getty Images)

The Road to Excellence

At the age of thirteen, Steffi became a professional
on the international women's tennis tour. While on
the tour, she studied with a tutor. Her off-court interests included reading novels and books on current
events, shopping, and popular music. In the early
years of her professional tennis career, Steffi's game
advanced consistently, and she climbed steadily up
the computer rankings. At the 1984 Olympic Games
in Los Angeles, she won the tennis competition,
which was then played as a demonstration sport.

In 1985, building on her Olympic triumph, she
did well in Grand Slam tournaments and reached
the semifinals of the U.S. Open. In 1986, although
she failed to win a Grand Slam tournament, she
won eight other tournaments, defeating several
top-ranked players. For these achievements, she
was ranked number three and was named West
German sportswoman of the year.

Steffi's steady rise was based on elements that
ensured her continued success as an athlete. First,
she was motivated by a sheer love of tennis. Second,
she benefited from strong family support. Third,
and most important, she devoted much time to
practice and training. As a result, she perfected
powerful strokes, especially her
forehand and serve. She brought
great concentration, discipline,
and determination to her game.
As Steffi said: "All I want[ed] to
do [was] play good tennis and
have fun. I want[ed] so much to
hit it hard—and have it go in."

The Emerging Champion

In 1987, Steffi's potential came
to fruition. During that spring,
she won several major tournaments, including the Lipton International Players Championship, the Italian Open, and the
Ladies German Championship.
Most important, she won her
first Grand Slam tournament,
the French Open, defeating the

Major Championship Victories and Finals

1986-87, 1989	French Open doubles finalist (with Gabriela Sabatini)
1987-88, 1993, 1995-96, 1999	French Open
1987, 1990, 1994	U.S. Open finalist
1987, 1999	Wimbledon finalist
1988	Wimbledon doubles (with Sabatini)
1988-89, 1991-93, 1995-96	Wimbledon
1988-89, 1993, 1995-96	U.S. Open
1988-90, 1994	Australian Open
1989-90, 1992	French Open finalist
1993	Australian Open finalist

Other Notable Victories

1986	U.S. Clay Court Championship
	U.S. Clay Court Championship doubles (with Sabatini)
1986-89	German Open
1987	Italian Open
1987-88	Lipton International Players Championship
1987, 1989, 1993, 1995-96	Virginia Slims Championship (later the Chase Championships)
1988	Lipton International Players Championship doubles (with Sabatini)
	U.S. Hardcourt Championship
	Gold medal, Olympic women's tennis singles
1990	Canadian Open

number-one player, Martina Navratilova, in a hard-fought three-set match. Although Steffi lost the Wimbledon and U.S. Open finals to Navratilova, her record for the year—including a win at the final tournament of the season, the Virginia Slims Championship—established her as the number-one ranked player in women's professional tennis for 1987.

In 1988, Steffi dominated women's tennis with an outstanding, record-breaking year. In addition to winning several other tournaments, Steffi earned a place in tennis history by winning the calendar Grand Slam: The Australian Open, the French Open, Wimbledon, and the U.S. Open. She was only the fifth tennis player, man or woman, to accomplish this impressive feat. Steffi made this accomplishment even more historic by winning the gold medal in women's

tennis at the 1988 Olympic Games in Seoul, South Korea. By winning the Olympic title in the first year that tennis was again a recognized event, Steffi became the only tennis player in history to win the "Golden Slam." After she won the U.S. Open, she told the press that it was a "relief" to win the Grand Slam. "Now, there's nothing else that people can tell me I have to do."

Continuing the Story

Through 1990, Steffi Graf maintained her position as the top-ranked women's tennis player. She had to face, however, significant challenges as she matured both personally and athletically. In tennis, younger players keep the competition strong. In 1989, Steffi won three Grand Slam tournaments and the Virginia Slims Championship, but she lost in the French Open final to the younger Spaniard, Arantxa Sanchez-Vicario. The following year, 1990, was difficult for Steffi. She dealt with a broken thumb on her racket hand, a serious sinus condition that required surgery, and a personal crisis within her family. Although she won many of the tournaments she entered, she lost three of the four Grand Slam tournaments.

Despite these setbacks, Steffi maintained the strong competitiveness and sportsmanship that characterized her playing. She also continued working on her game with her coaching practice partner, Pavel Slozil, to strengthen weaker areas of her game and to increase her versatility. She won her first Grand Slam title since the 1990 Australian Open by capturing the 1991 Wimbledon singles title.

Honors, Awards, and Milestones

1986	West German Sportswoman of the Year
1987-88	International Tennis Federation Player of the Year
1987-90, 1993-95	WTA Player of the Year
1987-91	Ranked number one in the world
1988	Grand Slam
1989	Sportswoman of the Year
	Associated Press Female Athlete of the Year
1994, 1996-97	ESPY Outstanding Women's Tennis Performer of the Year
1995-96	*Tennis* magazine Player of the Year
2004	Inducted into International Tennis Hall of Fame

During the 1990's, Steffi proved to be one of tennis's all-time great champions. From 1992 through 1999, she won thirteen Grand Slam singles titles, including four Wimbledon titles, four French Open titles, three U.S. Open titles, and one Australian Open title. Dramatically, she won her last Grand Slam singles title of her illustrious career at the 1999 French Open by beating Martina Hingis in three sets. Steffi decided to retire from the women's tour in 1999. In 2001, Steffi married fellow tennis superstar Andre Agassi. The couple had their first child the same year and their second child two years later. Steffi has been awarded numerous tennis-related honors, including induction into the International Tennis Hall of Fame in 2004.

Summary

Steffi Graf's accomplishment in winning the 1988 "Golden Slam" assured her place in tennis history. During her career, she won more than one hundred singles titles, including twenty-two Grand Slam singles titles. With these twenty-two Grand Slam titles, Steffi ranked second all-time behind Margaret Court, who had twenty-four. Steffi's style of tennis—a combination of hard, powerful strokes, exceptional foot speed, and great intensity—left a lasting mark on the sport.

Karen Gould

Additional Sources

Collins, Bud. *Total Tennis: The Ultimate Tennis Encyclopedia.* Toronto: Sport Media, 2003.

Heady, Sue. Steffi: *Public Power, Private Pain.* Rev. ed. London: Virgin, 1996.

O'Neil, Dana Pennett, and Pat Williams. *How to Be Like Women Athletes of Influence: Thirty-one Women at the Top of Their Game and How You Can Get There Too.* Deerfield Beach, Fla.: Health Communications, 2007.

Parsons, John. *The Ultimate Encyclopedia of Tennis: The Definitive Illustrated Guide to World Tennis.* London: Carlton, 2006.

Rutledge, Rachel. *The Best of the Best in Tennis.* Brookfield, Conn.: Millbrook Press, 1998.

Justine Henin

Born: June 1, 1982
    Liège, Belgium
Also known as: Justine Henin-Hardenne
    (married name used 2002-2007, now
    divorced); Juju

Early Life

Justine Henin was born on June 1, 1982, in Liège, Belgium. The daughter of José Henin and Françoise Rosière, she spent her childhood in Rochefort, a small town in the southern part of Belgium, where she was a gifted student and enjoyed soccer and tennis. However, she lived her childhood in

Justine Henin hoisting her 2007 French Open trophy.
(Cynthia Lum/WireImage/Getty Images)

the shadow of an earlier tragedy, as did her sister Sarah and brothers David and Thomas. Nine years before Justine was born, her older sister Florence died in a hit-and-run automobile accident, prompting her parents to be understandably overprotective of their other children. In 1995, the family suffered another traumatic event: Justine's mother succumbed to intestinal cancer at the age of forty-eight. The loss contributed to the difficult relationship Justine had with her father and siblings in the following years.

The Road to Excellence

At the age of four, Justine began playing table tennis at home. Only a year later, she graduated to tennis, playing on a nearby court. Displaying a natural ability for the game, she soon became a member of the Rochefort tennis club, where she consistently outplayed her opponents. Her parents recognized her capability and enrolled her in formal training at Ciney, a town in the same region of Belgium. Instructed by increasingly more talented coaches, Justine began winning tournaments. Her mother was encouraged by Justine's success and prompted her to join the French Tennis Federation, where she trained with Jean-Pierre Collot, Luc Bodart, and Michel Mouillard for two years. In 1996, the Argentine Carlos Rodriguez became Justine's coach, developing her tennis style, her technique, and, in particular, her one-handed backhands and her forehand ground strokes.

In 1997, Justine won the junior girls' singles title at the French Open at Roland Garros. Following that victory, she entered international competitions and won five International Tennis Federation tournaments. Her potential as a world-class player had become apparent to all; she soon left school to devote herself to a career in professional tennis. Three years later, just before her seventeenth birthday, she won her debut Woman Tennis Association (WTA) event at the Belgian Open in Antwerp.

The Emerging Champion

In 1997, she met Pierre-Yves Hardenne, whom she married five years later in a lavish ceremony held at the castle of Lavaux-Sainte-Anne, not far from Rochefort. The upward trajectory of her life and career appeared unstoppable. The following year, in October, 2003, she became the number-one female tennis player in the world.

However, this first pinnacle of Justine's success was short-lived. In early 2004, she contracted a cytomegalovirus infection that required weeks of treatment before her immune system finally returned to normal. Fighting back from illness, in August, at the Summer Olympic Games in Athens, Greece, she won a gold medal, defeating Anastasia Myskina in the semifinal and Amelie Mauresmo in the final. At the start of 2005, Justine suffered another setback: a fractured kneecap and an injured hamstring, which required intensive physical therapy for rehabilitation. Moving to Monaco from Belgium to take advantage of a more advantageous tax structure, she and her husband became increasingly estranged. A separation early in 2007 led to divorce in April. The difficulties she faced in her relationships with her father, siblings, and husband, though serious, were no more able to derail her tennis career than the physical injuries and disease that she endured.

Continuing the Story

In 2007, Justine became one of the first women tennis players to win more than $5 million, and in 2008 was named player of the year by the WTA for the second time—the first was in 2004. Also in 2008, Justine began the year successfully. By April, she has won more than 83 percent of the 15 matches she played and was the leading player in the WTA with 6,105 points, ahead of her closest competitor,

---

Honors and Awards

2002-03, 2006-07	European Sports Press Union European Sportswoman of the Year
2003-04, 2006-07	Belgian Sportswoman of the Year
2003, 2006-07	International Tennis Federation World Champion
2004, 2008	Women's Tennis Association Player of the Year
	Gold medal, Olympic women's tennis singles
2006	UNESCO Champion for Sport
2007	Belgian Sports Personality of the Year
	United States Sports Academy Female Athlete of the Year
2008	Laureus World Sportswoman of the Year

Ana Ivanovic, by almost 1,900 points. Despite this success, in May, 2008, Justine announced her retirement from professional tennis.

From 1999 to 2006, Justine's percentage of victories increased from about 70 to 90. She won 41 singles titles in 132 tournaments, including seven Grand Slam victories. She was the winner of the French Open in 2003, 2005, 2006, and 2007; the German Open in 2002, 2003, and 2005; the Australian Open in 2004; and the U.S. Open in 2003 and 2007. In the 2007 U.S. Open, she defeated Serena and Venus Williams and Svetlana Kuznetsova.

Justine and her coach Carlos Rodriguez opened a tennis school in Limelette, Belgium, where they hoped to develop the next generation of tennis stars. Furthermore, in 2004, Justine established a foundation called Justine's Winners' Circle, her personal version of the Make-a-Wish foundation, which cares for children with severe illnesses.

Summary

Beset by personal tragedy, illness, injury, and familial discord, Justine Henin persevered in a technically demanding sport and rose to an elite level. At the same time, she managed to avoid the total self-absorption common in sports stars and worked to provide for others the benefits that her tennis career has garnered for her.

Denyse Lemaire and David Kasserman

Grand Slam Results

2001	Wimbledon (finalist)
2003, 2005-07	French Open
2003, 2007	U.S. Open
2004	Australian Open
2006	Australian Open (finalist)
	Wimbledon (finalist)
	U.S. Open (finalist)

Additional Sources

Antoun, Rob. *Women's Tennis Tactics.* Champaign, Ill.: Human Kinetics, 2007.

Ryan, Mark. *Tie-Break! Justine Henin-Hardenne, Tragedy, and Triumph.* London: Robson Books, 2004.

Wertheim, Jon. *Venus Envy: Power Games, Teenage Vixens, and Million-Dollar Egos on the Women's Tennis Tour.* New York: HarperCollins, 2002.

Martina Hingis

Born: September 30, 1980
Košice, Czechoslovakia (now in Slovakia)
Also known as: Swiss Miss

Early Life

Martina Hingis was groomed to be a tennis star from the moment she was born. Her mother, Melanie Molitor, was among Czechoslovakia's top twenty-five tennis stars, and her father, Karol, was a former amateur tennis player and tennis-club administrator. Her parents even named their daughter after tennis great Martina Navratilova.

As a young child, Martina spent four to five hours a day on the tennis courts where her mother taught. Her father adapted a tennis racket to fit Martina. She started playing on the courts when she was just three years old.

Coached by her mother, Martina made her first tournament appearance at the age of four and won her first competition after turning six. Her parents divorced when she was four, and at the age of seven, Martina moved with her mother to Trubbach, Switzerland. She did not speak German, used in the local area, but learned the language within just three months. She later learned English and some French.

The Road to Excellence

By the age of eight, Martina was winning against sixteen-year-olds; at the age of ten, she was capturing national and international tournament titles. In that same year, 1990, she beat her mother, who was once ranked tenth in Czechoslovakia, for the first time. In 1993, at the age of twelve, Martina became the youngest Grand Slam junior champion ever, winning the 1993 Junior French Open.

By the time she was fourteen, Martina had nearly run out of junior players good enough to challenge her. Therefore, only four days after her fourteenth birthday, she turned professional. This move ignited a debate about whether such a young player should shoulder so much responsibility or be permitted to play at the professional level. She left public school to attend a private school, a change that allowed her more time to compete in tennis. Unlike many successful young athletes driven to excel in a single sport, she remained well-rounded, participating in numerous outside activities, including skiing, ice skating, basketball, soccer, swimming, and horseback riding.

The Emerging Champion

In 1996, at the age of fifteen, the right-handed Martina captured the Wimbledon doubles crown with Helena Suková, beating Meredith McGrath and Larisa Neiland. That same year, Martina became the youngest tennis player of either sex to make more than $1 million in prize money. By age sixteen, Martina had become the youngest woman tennis player ever to be ranked number one in the

Martina Hingis at the 2007 China Open. (Xinhua/Landov)

world by the Women's Tennis Association (WTA). She also became the youngest player in more than one hundred years to earn a Grand Slam title when she won the 1997 Australian Open. In the tournament, she took every set and defeated the two top-ranked players, Steffi Graf and Monica Seles.

In 1997, Martina won the Wimbledon singles championship, despite playing on a grass court, which she disliked. She was also the 1997 U.S. Open singles champion and won the Australian Open doubles competition with Natasha Zvereva. She might have won the 1997 French Open as well, were it not for a fall from a horse prior to the tournament, which required Martina to undergo arthroscopic knee surgery. Although she defeated her onetime idol Monica Seles for the second time, she lost the 1997 French Open final to ninth-ranked Iva Majoli in a major upset.

At one point during the 1997 WTA tour, Martina won thirty-seven consecutive matches and became the first woman to win back-to-back-to-back tournaments played on three separate continents: the 1997 Australian Open (Australia), the Tokyo Pan-Pacific Open (Asia), and the Open Gaz de France (Europe).

Continuing the Story

The Associated Press named Martina its 1997 female athlete of the year; in January, 1998, *Tennis* magazine named her its 1997 player of the year. *Tennis* also named Martina's mother coach of the year. However, in late 1998, Martina lost her number-one ranking to Lindsay Davenport, causing some experts to claim Martina was not taking her practice routine seriously. While she won the 1998 Wimbledon doubles championship with Jana Novotná, the Australian Open singles championship, the Australian Open doubles competition with Mirjana Lučić, and the U.S. Open doubles competition with Novotná, she finished the year ranked second in the world. In 1999, she regained her number-one singles ranking, however, winning both Wimbledon and the Australian Open singles competitions and the Australian Open doubles competition with Anna Kournikova. Martina held that ranking again at the end of the 2000 season.

In 2001, though Martina began the year by reaching the Australian Open finals, the remainder of her year was a disappointment. In October, she underwent surgery on her right ankle and was

finished for the year. The ankle injury was a harbinger: Though she played part of the 2002 season, she had surgery on her left ankle and did not complete the year.

In 2003, at the age of twenty-two, after attempting to recuperate from her injuries, Martina announced her retirement. She had been ranked number one in the world for a total of 209 weeks. However, her desire to play tennis did not dissipate. After spending two years away from the intense competition of the professional level and rehabilitating physically, Martina began to play again. In

Major Championships

Year	Championship
1996	Wimbledon doubles (with Helena Suková)
1997	Australian Open
	Australian Open doubles (with Natasha Zvereva)
	Wimbledon
	U.S. Open
	Paris Indoors
	Paris Indoors doubles
	Hilton Head
	Hilton Head doubles
1998	Australian Open
	Australian Open doubles (with Mirjana Lučić)
	Wimbledon doubles (with Jana Novotná)
	U.S. Open doubles (with Novotná)
	French Open doubles
	Canadian Open doubles
	Chase Championships
	Indian Wells
1999	Australian Open
	Australian Open doubles (with Anna Kournikova)
	Wimbledon
	Chase Championships doubles
	Hilton Head
	Indian Wells doubles
	Italian Open doubles
	German Open
	Canadian Open
2000	French Open doubles
	Chase Championships
2001	Hopman Cup mixed doubles
2002	Australian Open doubles
	Tokyo (Pan Pacific), Japan
2006	Rome, Italy
	Australian Open mixed doubles
2007	Tokyo (Pan Pacific), Japan

Honors and Awards

1995	WTA Tour Most Impressive Newcomer
	Tennis magazine Female Rookie of the Year
1996	WTA Tour Most Improved Player
	Swiss Olympic Team
	Swiss Federation Cup Team
1997	WTA Tour Player of the Year
	International Tennis Federation Player of the Year
	Tennis magazine Player of the Year
	Associated Press Female Athlete of the Year
1998	WTA Tour Doubles Team of the Year (with Jana Novotná)
1999	WTA Tour Doubles Team of the Year (with Anna Kournikova)
2000	World Tennis Association (WTA) Tour Diamond ACES Award
2006	WTA Comeback of the Year
	Laureus World Comeback of the Year

2005, she played sparingly and with decent results; she announced that she would return for the 2006 season.

Throughout the 2006 and 2007 seasons, Martina showed flashes of her previous greatness. However, she was inconsistent, even though she was ranked as high as sixth. She was unable to compete with the stronger players that had emerged during her retirement.

Her final exit from professional tennis was a strange one: She left amid allegations of cocaine use, stemming from a drug test at Wimbledon. She vehemently refuted the results. Though the WTA banned her for two years, Martina announced her permanent retirement.

Summary

At 5 feet 6 inches, Martina Hingis was not exceptionally large or powerful by tennis standards. Tennis experts credit her intelligence on the court, excellent shot selection, and ability to anticipate her opponents' moves for making her such a tough competitor. Donna Doherty in *Tennis* magazine noted that she "reintroduced to women's tennis the game of angles and the art of thinking ahead like a chess player." Martina was known for her self-confident manner both on and off the court. She was credited with bringing new popularity to women's professional tennis during the late 1990's. At her peak, Martina was one of the most graceful players ever.

Cheryl Pawlowski, updated by P. Huston Ladner

Additional Sources

Clarey, Christopher. "Drug Test Hastens Retirement for Hingis." *The New York Times*, November 2, 2007.

Kimmelman, Michael. "Return, Hingis." *The New York Times*, August 20, 2006.

Leand, Andrea. "Second to None." *Tennis*, April, 1999, 34.

Starr, Mark. "Martina Redux." *Newsweek*, June 2, 1997.

Lew Hoad

Born: November 23, 1934
　　　Glebe, New South Wales, Australia
Died: July 3, 1994
　　　Fuengirola, Spain
Also known as: Lewis Alan Hoad

Early Life

Lewis Alan Hoad was born in Glebe, New South Wales, Australia, on November 23, 1934. He was born within three weeks of Ken Rosewall, another Australian tennis player, who was to be Lew's greatest rival during his amateur career. Lew's father, Alan Hoad, had been an athlete in his youth, but it was Bonnie Hoad, Lew's mother, who steered him toward tennis. She joined the local tennis club when Lew was nine, and he began to play immediately. He soon won a number of local titles, including several doubles championships partnered with Ken Rosewall. By the age of eighteen, he and Rosewall were already recognized as tennis's "Whiz Kids."

The Road to Excellence

The key to Lew's quick success was primarily his extraordinary strength. Although not exceptionally large—he was 5 feet 11 inches and usually played at a weight of about 170 pounds—he was, in the opinion of many experts, the strongest man ever to play the game. Lew's game, even as a young man, reflected his power. He had probably the hardest serve among his contemporaries. He disdained long rallies and slashed at the ball, hoping for an immediate winner. His was a dangerous style, but with Lew's power, it was often successful.

　　Lew confronted two obstacles on his road to the top, neither of which he was ever able to overcome completely. He was unable to concentrate totally on winning. Instead, he would often lose interest in matches, especially against inferior players. To combat these lapses, Lew trained with Harry Hopman, one of tennis's greatest teachers and the coach of the Austra-

lian national team. Hopman was renowned for the large number of Davis Cups won by his teams. He was a disciplinarian, however, and Lew did not like his rigid methods. The other obstacle Lew confronted was his frequent doubles partner, Ken Rosewall. In contrast to Lew's power game, Rosewall's game stressed speed, accuracy, and strategy. In their many meetings, Lew followed his usual tactics: He tried to blast the ball. Rosewall met Lew's charges with his customary accurate returns, and neither player was able to establish a convincing superiority.

The Emerging Champion

In spite of his problems, Lew's astonishing power propelled him into the game's top ranks. He estab-

Major Championship Victories and Finals

1953	French Championship doubles (with Ken Rosewall)
1953, 1956-57	Australian Championship doubles (with Rosewall and Neale Fraser)
1954	French Championship mixed doubles (with Maureen Connolly)
	U.S. National Championship doubles finalist (with Rosewall)
1955	Australian Championship finalist
1956	French Championship
	Australian Championship
	Wimbledon doubles (with Rosewall)
	U.S. National Championship finalist
	U.S. National Championship doubles (with Rosewall)
1956-57	Wimbledon

Other Notable Victories

1953, 1955-56	On winning Australian Davis Cup team
1956	Italian Championship
1957	Italian Championship doubles (with Fraser)
	London Pro Championship doubles (with Fraser)
1957, 1959, 1961-62, 1964, 1966	Professional World Doubles Tournament (with Rosewall and Tony Trabert)

lished himself in 1953, when he was only nineteen. In that year, Australia was down 2-0 to the United States in the Davis Cup. Lew faced Tony Trabert, the U.S. National champion and a much more experienced player. Lew electrified the partisan Melbourne crowd by defeating Trabert in five sets. Australia went on to win the Cup. The year 1954 was a relatively poor one for Lew, but in 1955 he again displayed his mastery in the Davis Cup. This time he defeated Trabert in straight sets, and Australia won the Davis Cup by a score of 5-0 over the United States.

In 1956, Lew had his greatest triumph as an amateur. He overcame his spotty concentration and won three of the four tournaments that make up tennis's Grand Slam. He won the Australian Open, the French Open, and Wimbledon. In the Wimbledon finals, he demolished his rival Rosewall in four sets. Although behind in the third set, Lew surged ahead winning five straight games in which his play was nearly flawless. However, Rosewall proved Lew's nemesis once more at the U.S. National Championship. His victory deprived Lew of the Grand Slam, tennis's greatest achievement.

Continuing the Story

In his last tournament as an amateur, Lew won the 1957 Wimbledon Championship, losing only one set in the entire tournament. Afterward, the opportunity to make money as a professional proved too great to resist, and Lew gave up his amateur standing. Lew signed with Jack Kramer, the leading promoter of professional tennis, who arranged for Lew to play a series of matches against Pancho Gonzales. The matches were the greatest challenge Lew faced as a player. Gonzales was for many years the best player in the game, and his serve matched Lew's in speed. Gonzales lacked Lew's powerful

Honors, Awards, and Milestones

1953-56	Australian Davis Cup team
1980	Inducted into International Tennis Hall of Fame

groundstroke, but he made up for it with his will to win.

At first, Lew met the challenge successfully. He led 18 to 9 in the series of matches with Gonzales and seemed well on the way to dethroning the professional champion. Unfortunately for Lew, his back became stiff, and his lead over Gonzales evaporated. His back problem never went away, and Lew always had to play second fiddle to Gonzales. His physical difficulties became so severe that he was forced to retire from tennis in the mid-1960's. At his best, Lew was unbeatable, a fact that even Gonzales acknowledged.

Summary

Lew Hoad rose to tennis stardom as a teenager, primarily because of his immense power. His fierce attacks made him a favorite with audiences, and he was among the best players of his era. His two greatest rivals, Ken Rosewall and Pancho Gonzales, prevented him from achieving uncontested supremacy. At the top of his game, however, Lew was able to defeat them, as well as anyone else who came his way.

Bill Delaney

Additional Sources

Drucker, Joel. "The Comet." *Tennis,* July, 2007, 56.

Hoad, Jenny, and Jack Pollard. *My Life with Lew.* London: HarperSports, 2002.

Phillips, Caryl. *The Right Set: A Tennis Anthology.* New York: Vintage Books, 1999.

Ana Ivanovic

Born: November 6, 1987
Belgrade, Yugoslavia (now in Serbia)

Early Life

Ana Ivanovic was born November 6, 1987, in Belgrade, Yugoslavia (now in Serbia). Her family consists of her mother Dragana, a lawyer, her father Miroslav, a businessman, and her younger brother Milos. As a child, Ana grew up in a country that was bombed regularly. However, she was able to distract herself by watching tennis on television. At the time, Monica Seles was Serbia's most famous tennis star. Ana's adoration of Seles led her to want to play tennis; she began playing before she was five. After seeing a commercial for a tennis school, she memorized the number and tried to persuade her parents to let her enroll. Her mother thought that dance school was a better choice, but Ana prevailed.

The Road to Excellence

Sports were not the most important issue in a country under strife. Ana initially learned the game of tennis in an empty swimming pool. Often that meant that chasing down a wide shot resulted in crashing into the wall. The dedication and the sacrifice eventually paid off.

Much like the circumstances in which Ana had to practice, getting to tennis matches was equally difficult. Because of the lack of flights out of Belgrade, Ana and her mother traveled to Budapest, a seven-hour bus ride, to go to tennis tournaments outside the country. At these tournaments, Ana displayed talent, but she was unspectacular overall.

The Emerging Champion

Ana's fortunes began to change when a Serbian tennis instructor introduced her to a potential benefactor in Dan Holzman, a Swiss businessman. Ana and her mother visited Holzman in Basel, Switzerland. He offered to pay for Ana's expenses if she repaid him later. This helped Ana get a coach and receive top-notch training. The total amount that Holzman spent was $500,000.

The training enhanced Ana's abilities. On August 17, 2003, she turned professional at the age of fifteen. In 2004, she reached the finals of the junior Wimbledon tournament. This result garnered her notice in the tennis world. However, the match that established her as a rising talent was the one in which she forced Venus Williams into two tie-breaks in Zurich, Switzerland.

In 2005, Ana continued to climb in the rankings, winning her first career singles title in Canberra, Australia. She improved throughout the year, advancing to the semifinals in a number of tournaments. The following year, Ana played well and advanced deeply in tournaments. In 2006, she won another singles title: the Canada Masters, in Montreal. She finished the year ranked number fourteen in the world. Also during 2006, she began signing endorsement deals. Her multimillion-dollar sponsorship with Adidas al-

Ana Ivanovic swinging away at the 2005 U.S. Open. (AP/Wide World Photos)

Notable Victories

2005	Canberra International
2006	Canada Masters
2007	German Open
	JPMorgan Chase Open
	Fortis Championships Luxembourg
2008	Pacific Life Open
	French Open
	Generali Ladies Linz

lowed her to pay back Holzman, who became her manager.

Continuing the Story

Ana had a difficult start in 2007. Her results in her first few tournaments were not great. At the end of the first major, the Australian Open, after losing in the third round, she announced that she had fired her coach. Her results after the coaching change were mixed. She played decently for the first few matches but showed improvement when the tour entered its clay-court season, winning her first tournament on that surface in Berlin.

In 2007, Ana continued her strong clay-court play and advanced to the French Open final, losing to Justine Henin. This result was her best in a major at that point. Though she sustained a knee injury in the summer of 2007, she returned to the tour after a brief hiatus and won the East West Bank Classic in Carson, California. She continued to play well throughout the rest of year, finishing with a career-high ranking of four, which raised expectations for 2008.

The year began well, as Ana reached the finals of the first major, the Australian Open, but she lost to Maria Sharapova. At the next major, the French Open, Ana finally fulfilled her promise. She earned her first major-tournament victory, defeating Dinara Safina. With the win, she also gained the number-one ranking in women's tennis.

Summary

Standing 6 feet 1 inch, and possessing a serve that often reached 130 miles per hour, Ana Ivanovic became a force on the women's tennis tour. While her stay at the number-one ranking was short-lived, she remained in contention to win any event she entered. At a young age, with an improving game, she was poised to challenge Maria Sharapova for the top spot among the her generation's tennis champions.

P. Huston Ladner

Additional Sources

Bodo, Peter. "When Ana Ivanovic Serves, You Better Duck." *The New York Times Magazine,* June, 2008.

Gregory, Sean. "Bombs Away." *Time,* 171, no. 26 (June 30, 2008): 48-49.

Honors and Awards

2005, 2007	Women's Tennis Association Most Improved Player
2007	Karen Krantczke Sportsmanship Award
	International Women of Courage Award, nominee
2008	International Sports Press Association (AIPS) Women's Tennis Player of the Year
	Michael Westphal Award

Billie Jean King

Born: November 22, 1943
      Long Beach, California
Also known as: Billie Jean Moffitt King (full
   name); Billie Jean Moffitt (birth name)

Early Life

Billie Jean Moffitt was born on November 22, 1943, in Long Beach, California. She is the first child of Willard J. Moffitt and his wife and has a younger brother, Randy. As a child, Billie Jean played softball, and at her father's fire department picnics, the men often asked her to play on their teams. She soon realized that there was no future for her in that sport, so her parents suggested she take up tennis. She was enrolled in the city's tennis program at the age of eleven, surprising her parents with her enthusiasm and her drive to excel.

The Road to Excellence

Billie Jean fell in love with tennis, using money earned at odd jobs to buy her racket, and spending hours hitting balls to improve her performance. She entered her first tournament at the age of eleven, defeating a University of Southern California (USC) junior, though she was so inexperienced she did not even realize that a match consisted of winning two sets. She continued to work on her own performance until a friend introduced her to tennis great Alice Marble, who agreed to coach Billie Jean for six months in 1958.

Billie Jean's skills improved remarkably under Marble's coaching, and she won her first title in 1958, winning the Southern California championship for girls fifteen and under. Her performance was still erratic, and though Billie Jean hated to lose, she knew that it was through losing that she would learn to win.

In 1960, Billie Jean's national ranking jumped from nineteenth to fourth, and she captured the attention of Frank Brennan, who then became her coach. In 1961, she and Karen Hantze Susman became the youngest team ever to win the women's doubles title at Wimbledon. The following year at Wimbledon she won a sensational singles victory over Margaret Smith (later Margaret Court), the top-seeded women's tennis player, though she did

Billie Jean King. (Volvo Women's Tennis Cup)

not win the title. She repeated her doubles victory, however, again with Hantze Susman.

When Billie Jean entered Los Angeles State College, she found she had little time to keep up with her tennis practice. Only after becoming engaged to Larry King did she decide to pursue her career in tennis and went to spend three months training with Mervyn Rose in Australia.

The Emerging Champion

Rose not only put Billie Jean on an exercise and drill program to regain the conditioning she had lost while in college, but he also shortened all of her strokes and concentrated on the weakest part of her game: the ground strokes. Though she lost the New South Wales championship to Margaret Smith, in December, 1964, the United States Lawn Tennis Association (USLTA) ranked Billie Jean second among American women.

In 1965, Billie Jean defeated every American rival she opposed, though she lost at Wimbledon to Maria Bueno, and she lost again to Margaret Smith. On September 17, 1965, Billie Jean and Larry King were married, and in December, she shared top ranking with Nancy Richey.

Billie Jean had a winning season in 1966; she attributed this to her determination to concentrate on her game. Her doubles success showed her keen tactical sense, and her improved concentration increased her ability to win singles matches. Though hampered by illness, she continued to develop her game, winning tournament after tournament. With Martina Navratilova, she shares the record of twenty Wimbledon titles (six singles, ten doubles, and four mixed doubles) and is ranked as one of the greatest women's tennis players of all time. She also became the first woman tennis player to earn more than $100,000 in a year.

Continuing the Story

Billie Jean considers her intensely competitive spirit one of her strongest characteristics. Although she continued to play competitively well into her late thirties and early forties, Billie Jean has done more than simply win tennis championships. Long bothered by the inequitable prize values between men's and women's tennis tournaments, she organized a boycott of women players against USLTA tournaments in 1972. She further drew attention to the deficit by staging a match against Wimbledon's 1939 men's champion Bobby Riggs and soundly defeating him. She promoted women in sports by hosting Col-

---

Major Championship Victories and Finals

1961-62, 1965, 1967-68, 1970-73, 1979	Wimbledon doubles (with Karen Hantze Susman, Maria Bueno, Rosie Casals, Betty Stove, and Martina Navratilova)
1963, 1969-70	Wimbledon finalist
1964, 1967	U.S. National Championship doubles (with Hantze Susman and Casals)
1964, 1976	Wimbledon doubles finalist (with Hantze Susman and Stove)
1965	U.S. National Championship finalist
1966-68, 1972-73, 1975	Wimbledon
1966, 1978	Wimbledon mixed doubles finalist (with Dennis Ralston and Ray Ruffels)
1967	U.S. National Championship
	U.S. National Championship mixed doubles (with Owen Davidson)
1967, 1970	French Championship mixed doubles (with Davidson and Bob Hewitt)
1967, 1971, 1973-74	Wimbledon mixed doubles (with Davidson)
1968	U.S. Open finalist
	Australian Open
1968, 1973, 1975, 1979	U.S. Open doubles finalist (with Casals and Navratilova)
1969	Australian Open finalist
	Australian Open doubles finalist (with Casals)
1970	French Open doubles finalist (with Casals)
1971-72, 1974	U.S. Open
1971, 1973, 1976	U.S. Open mixed doubles (with Davidson and Phil Dent)
1972	French Open
	French Open doubles (with Stove)
1974, 1978, 1980	U.S. Open doubles (with Casals and Navratilova)
1975, 1977-78	U.S. Open mixed doubles finalist (with Fred Stolle, Vitas Gerulaitis, and Ruffels)

gate's television special "The Lady Is a Champ," and was a sports commentator for ABC from 1975 to 1978.

Billie Jean also helped to launch a magazine called *Woman Sports* and established both the World Team Tennis League and the Women's Professional Softball League. In addition, she wrote a book about her own life, appropriately called *Billie Jean* (1982). She continued to work for women's equality in the world of sports, aligning herself with Navratilova and others who fought for personal freedom. During the 1990's, Billy Jean worked as a commentator for Home Box Office (HBO) and coached the American Federation Cup Women's Tennis Team. She also coached the American Olympic women's tennis team at the 1996 and 2000 Summer Olympics. She has won numerous awards for her contributions to tennis. In 2006, the USTA National Tennis Center—the home of the U.S. Open tennis tournament—was renamed the USTA Billie Jean King National Tennis Center.

Summary

Billie Jean King is one of the top-ranked female tennis players of all time. She holds a record twenty Wimbledon titles and has become a force both on and off the courts. She used her success on the court to highlight women's and human rights.

Mary Johnson

Additional Sources

Buren, Jodi, and Donna A. Lopiano. *Superwomen: One Hundred Women, One Hundred Sports.* New York: Bulfinch Press, 2004.

"Great Shots: The Forehand Volleys of Billie Jean King and Amelie Mauresmo." *Tennis*, July, 2006, 26.

King, Billie Jean, and Frank Deford. *Billie Jean.* New York: Viking Press, 1982.

Roberts, Selena. *A Necessary Spectacle: Billie Jean King, Bobby Riggs, and the Tennis Match That Leveled the Game.* New York: Crown Publishers, 2005.

Weinberg, Robert S., Billie Jean King. *Tennis: Winning the Mental Game.* Oxford, Ohio: Miami University, 2002.

Other Notable Victories

1961-67, 1970, 1977	On winning U.S. Wightman Cup team
1963, 1966-67, 1976-79	On winning U.S. Federation Cup team
1966	U.S. Hardcourt Championship doubles (with Rosie Casals)
1966-67	U.S. Indoor Championship mixed doubles (with Paul Sullivan)
1966-68, 1971, 1974	U.S. Indoor Championship
1966, 1968, 1971, 1975, 1979, 1983	U.S. Indoor Championship doubles (with Casals, Martina Navratilova, and Sharon Walsh)
1970	Italian Open
	Italian Open doubles (with Casals)
1970-71	British Covered Court Championship
1971	German Open
	German Open doubles (with Casals)
1974	Virginia Slims Championship doubles (with Casals)
1980	Avon Championship doubles (with Navratilova)
1982	U.S. Open Women's 35

Milestones

U.S. Wightman Cup team (1961-67, 1970, 1977-78)

U.S. Federation Cup team (1963-67, 1976-79)

39 Grand Slam titles

Honors and Awards

1967, 1973	Associated Press Female Athlete of the Year
1972	*Sports Illustrated* Sportswoman of the Year
1976	*Time* magazine Woman of the Year
1980	Inducted into Sudafed International Women's Sports Hall of Fame
1987	Inducted into International Tennis Hall of Fame

Jack Kramer

Born: August 1, 1921
      Las Vegas, Nevada
Also known as: John Albert Kramer (full name)

Early Life

The son of a Union Pacific railroad engineer, John Albert Kramer was born on August 1, 1921, in Las Vegas, Nevada. As a child, Jack actively played many sports—baseball, football, and basketball. He did not, however, play tennis. In fact, he thought he might make a career in Major League Baseball.

A football injury caused Jack to eventually take up tennis. One afternoon, Jack cracked his ribs and broke his nose in a scrimmage. Jack's parents were distressed and sought to persuade him to take up a safer sport. Although Jack was convinced that tennis was not a strong man's game, he eventually tried the sport when he was fourteen.

By then, his parents had moved to San Bernardino, California, so Jack joined the Southern California Tennis Association's junior development program. He trained under director Perry Jones, a man who was influential in the development of many tennis champions. Every day, Jack took a ninety-minute streetcar ride to Beverly Hills for a tennis lesson with Jones. There, he met an automotive engineer and tennis enthusiast named Clifton Roche, who also proved to be instrumental in the boy's career.

The Road to Excellence

For years, Roche had been devising a geometrical theory of tennis. From him, Jack learned a theory of angles that increased his chances of gaining and holding superior court position. This theory consisted of the mathematical soundness of hitting the ball at certain angles. As a result, placement soon won out over power in Jack's game. For example, by placing the ball into the far corner he could swing an opponent wide off the court, shortening the angle of return. Later known as "percentage tennis," this theory of play included the tactics of hitting every forehand approach shot down the line, serving at three-quarter speed to the backhand, and coasting on the opponent's delivery until the opportunity came for the break. Jack's use of angles made him nearly unbeatable.

Jack's tennis game made such swift progress during his early teenage years that by 1935, when he was fourteen, he won the national boys' singles title. He won the national interscholastic championship when he was seventeen. Later that same year, Jack tried for the U.S. National Championship men's title at Forest Hills, in Queens, New York. However, the night before he played, he ate some hot, spicy food that upset his stomach and interfered with the next day's performance. Nevertheless, he played well enough to be invited to try out for the 1939 U.S. Davis Cup team.

The Emerging Champion

By then, Jack was number fifteen in the national rankings. He had earned a reputation for playing a nerveless game of controlled aggression. His big

Jack Kramer dashing toward the net to return a ball. (Hy Peskin/Getty Images)

Major Championship Victories and Finals

1940-41, 1943, 1947	U.S. National Championship doubles (with Ted Schroeder and Frank Parker)
1941	U.S. National Championship mixed doubles (with Sarah Palfrey Cooke)
1946-47	U.S. National Championship
	Wimbledon doubles (with Tom Brown and Bob Falkenburg)
1947	Wimbledon

Other Notable Victories

1941	U.S. Clay Court Championship doubles (with Schroeder)
1946-47	On winning U.S. Davis Cup team
1947	U.S. Indoor Championship
	U.S. Indoor Championship doubles (with Falkenburg)
1948	U.S. Pro Championship
	U.S. Pro Championship doubles (with Pancho Segura)

serve, combined with his big volley, became known as the "big game." That year, he was chosen as a Davis Cup player against Australia. At seventeen years of age, he was then the youngest ever to play in the renowned event.

Jack played tennis for three more years before joining the Coast Guard in 1942. During that time, he won twelve doubles championships in fifteen tournaments, toured South America, and won the U.S. National Championship doubles at home. Before entering the service, the energetic young man won ten straight singles crowns and nearly became America's best tennis player. Just before the nationals, however, he succumbed to appendicitis and missed the chance to win.

World War II interrupted Jack's tennis career for two years. Then, barely out of uniform, Jack was so impatient to get back to the game that, at Wimbledon, he wrecked an uncalloused hand on new tennis rackets and lost his match. Characteristically, he turned such a defeat to an advantage, remarking later that whenever he was in a difficult situation, he simply recalled the pain and frustration he had felt at the time and recognized that things were not as bad as they had been at the Wimbledon defeat. After Wimbledon, however, Jack went on to win nearly everything: the U.S. National Championship singles at Forest Hills twice, the U.S. doubles four times, the Wimbledon doubles twice, and the Davis Cup.

Continuing the Story

With no serious challenges left to beat, Jack decided to turn professional. By then, he had achieved everything he could as an amateur. He was also tired of eking out a living relying on his job with a meat-packing company for a meager $60 a week. So Jack made the big switch to the pros, where he continued to dominate the tennis tournaments of his time—not just as the star attraction but in a new role as well: as promoter.

In this new guise, Jack found a unique way to hold the public's interest—by breaking up championship Davis Cup teams to form his own tour of handpicked opponents. He achieved this by simply offering the champions a guaranteed minimum and a percentage of total receipts—an offer no one could refuse. Eventually, he built up a team of superb young pros and began to tour with all of them in a kind of round-robin tournament. Thus, Jack originated a different type of professional tour.

Jack dabbled in other enterprises as well. He bought real estate, stocks, racehorses, and an oil well. His best-known ventures were his sporting goods and sportswear businesses. People from coast to coast wore sports shirts that carried his name and logo. Jack's income soared to more than $200,000 a year.

Eventually, Jack left the promotion tour to an association of the players, as he felt his presence might lessen the harmony between the pros and amateurs. He became a tennis commentator on the television networks. He then turned his attention to speaking out against the problems of amateur tennis and appealed for open tournaments. He helped broaden the professional base with these open tournaments. When open tennis was finally introduced in 1968, he had done more than anyone to popularize it.

Honors, Awards, and Milestones

1939, 1946-47	U.S. Davis Cup team
1946-47	Ranked number one in the world
1968	Inducted into National Lawn Tennis Hall of Fame

Summary

Jack Kramer's records include only two U.S. and one Wimbledon singles titles. Nevertheless, he ranks as one of tennis's all-time stars. As a player, Jack revolutionized tennis. He popularized the terms "big game," "attack," and "percentage tennis." His theory of modern tennis changed the face of the game forever. When he switched from player to promoter, he helped the game evolve to a whole new dimension.

Nan White

Additional Sources

Collins, Bud. *Total Tennis: The Ultimate Tennis Encyclopedia.* Toronto: Sport Media, 2003.

Kramer, Jack, and Frank Deford. *The Game: My Forty Years in Tennis.* London: Deutsch, 1981.

Parsons, John. *The Ultimate Encyclopedia of Tennis: The Definitive Illustrated Guide to World Tennis.* London: Carlton, 2006.

Phillips, Caryl. *The Right Set: A Tennis Anthology.* New York: Vintage Books, 1999.

René Lacoste

Born: July 2, 1904
     Paris, France
Died: October 12, 1996
     Paris, France
Also known as: Jean René Lacoste (full name);
   the Crocodile

Early Life

Jean René Lacoste was born on July 2, 1904, in Paris, France. It seemed unlikely that René, the son of a wealthy automobile manufacturer, would ever turn to athletic endeavors with any serious commitment. He did not receive any encouragement to participate in sports from his father, who wanted him to take over the family business when he was

René Lacoste, who won seven Grand Slams in the 1920's. (Courtesy of International Tennis Hall of Fame)

old enough. His father did not believe that his son should be distracted by frivolous activities.

René traveled with his father to London when he was fifteen and saw a tennis court for the first time. René was intrigued by what he saw and asked his father if he could buy a tennis racket so that he could learn the game. His father was against the idea. When his father finally gave in to his persistent son, he told René that if he wanted to play tennis, then he should strive to be the best. He gave his son five years to accomplish this task.

The Road to Excellence

René began taking lessons, and it became obvious that he was not naturally gifted. If he were to improve, it would be through hard work. René was a bright and ambitious young man. He began keeping a chart of the progress he was making and also started a notebook in which he wrote down the strengths and weaknesses of the opponents he played. He made slow but steady progress. Whenever he lost to someone he felt was of lesser ability, he would work even harder to improve his game. Because he had no family responsibilities, René was able to devote endless hours to practice. His hours spent on the court began to make up for what he lacked in natural talent. René was in the process of developing a strong baseline game in which strategy played a major role. He won because he could cover the court and because he always knew his opponent's game backward and forward.

Always serious and reserved, René treated tennis as if it were a science. He was a good observer, and he read everything he could about tennis. His health was never 100 percent perfect; one of the reasons he took up tennis was to make himself stronger. He finally had made enough progress at his game and was impressive enough to be named to the French Davis Cup team in 1923. The team consisted of the French players who would become known as the Four Musketeers. The other three members were Jacques Brugnon, Jean Borotra, and Henri Cochet. The Musketeers dominated the tennis world during the late 1920's and the early 1930's.

The Emerging Champion

Three of the Musketeers, including René, would win the majority of the Grand Slam singles titles over the next few years. Only Brugnon, who was a doubles specialist, did not vie for the major singles titles. René had won the French Indoor singles title by the time he was eighteen, having defeated another one of the Musketeers, Jean Borotra. In 1924, René lost in the finals at Wimbledon to Borotra. A competitive but friendly rivalry developed among the Musketeers. René had to work much harder than the other members of the group, for he was the least naturally gifted. He believed that cutting down on the number of errors one made during a match was far more crucial than trying to hit more winners. René became known as the "Crocodile" because he was as persistent as people thought a crocodile would be.

In 1925, René turned the tables on Borotra and won both the French and Wimbledon singles titles. He and Borotra also teamed to capture the Wimbledon doubles title. His patient and self-disciplined brand of tennis began to pay large dividends. In 1926, René finally made it to the top of the rankings. That year, René also won his first U.S. National Championship in singles and also beat

Bill Tilden in Davis Cup competition—the first time that Tilden had ever lost a Davis Cup match. René's tenacious baseline game was too much even for the legendary Tilden.

Continuing the Story

One of René's greatest victories over Tilden was in the 1927 U.S. National Championship. At thirty-four, the experienced Tilden attacked René as hard as he could but to no avail. René, at twenty-two, did not crack and played a nearly flawless match, winning in straight sets 11-9, 6-3, 11-9. He played error-free tennis and, therefore, was able to retain his U.S. title.

René's tennis career did not last much longer. He had also won the French Championship singles title in 1927; but the next year, the only major title he won was Wimbledon. Tilden beat René in a 1928 Davis Cup encounter, but the French captured a second Davis Cup in a row over the United States. This was the last time that René competed for France on the Davis Cup team. In 1929, after winning the French Championship title for the third time, he decided to bow out of competitive tennis.

In 1930, René started a career in the automotive and aerospace industry. He also married Simone Thion de la Chaume that year, and in the course of their marriage they had four children. Besides tennis, René is famous for designing the Lacoste crocodile shirts, which are sold all over the world. He also founded the La Chemise Lacoste Company and was the first person to invent a nonwood tennis racket, which was manufactured under license by Wilson Sporting Goods.

Major Championship Victories and Finals

1923	French Championship doubles finalist (with Henri Cochet)
1924	Wimbledon finalist
1924-25, 1929	French Championship doubles (with Jean Borotra)
1924, 1926, 1928	French Championship finalist
1925	Wimbledon doubles (with Borotra)
1925, 1927, 1929	French Championship
1925, 1928	Wimbledon
1926-27	U.S. National Championship
	U.S. National Championship mixed doubles finalist (with Hazel Wightman)

Other Notable Victories

1925, 1927, 1929	French International Championship
1926	U.S. Indoor Championship

Summary

René Lacoste's tennis career was short, but in that short period of time, he managed to rise to the top. As a member of the legendary Four Musketeers, he helped put the French at the top of the tennis world. Although not as naturally gifted as many of his contemporaries, René's determination and cool, steady style of play made him one of the most feared competitors of his day. He proved that a baseline player could beat a serve-and-volley player on any surface. If not for poor health, there is no telling how many more Grand Slam titles the Crocodile could have won.

Jeffry Jensen

Additional Sources

Collins, Bud. *Total Tennis: The Ultimate Tennis Encyclopedia.* Toronto: Sport Media, 2003.

Kapferer, Patricia, and Tristan Gaston-Breton. *Lacoste the Legend.* Paris: Cherche Midi, 2002.

Lacoste, Jean René. *How to Play Tennis.* London: E. J. Burrow, 1930.

_____. *Lacoste on Tennis.* New York: William Morrow, 1928.

Parsons, John. *The Ultimate Encyclopedia of Tennis: The Definitive Illustrated Guide to World Tennis.* London: Carlton, 2006.

Rod Laver

Born: August 9, 1938
      Rockhampton, Queensland, Australia
Also known as: Rodney George Laver (full
    name); the Rocket

Early Life
Rodney George Laver was born on August 9, 1938, in Rockhampton, in the cattle country of Queensland, Australia. He was the youngest of three boys born to Roy Laver, a cattle rancher with a passion for tennis.

Rod's eldest brother, Trevor, was six years older than Rod; the middle brother, Bob, was four years older. Their father considered the elder boys to be much better prospects at the sport than Rod, who was always small in size. Even as an adult, Rod stood only 5 feet 7½ inches and weighed just 145 pounds—very small for a tennis professional. The three brothers played tennis for hours on a clay court at home that their father had made by flattening out anthills and pounding the dirt to a smooth, hard finish. In later years, Rod remembered it as the best clay court on which he had played.

The Road to Excellence
Charlie Hollis, a local coach, did not agree with Roy Laver's assessment of the tennis ability of his three sons. By the time Rod was ten, Hollis thought he had the best potential of the three boys. Hollis was impressed by the calm temperament Rod had inherited from his mother. Both of Rod's brothers had quick tempers like their father, and Hollis considered a hot temper to be a liability in tennis.

Hollis coached Rod for four years. Even at this early age, Rod got out of bed at 5:00 A.M. to practice for two hours before school. When Rod reached fourteen, Hollis brought him to Harry Hopman, one of the greatest tennis coaches in the world. Hopman coached all the great Australian tennis stars of the 1950's and 1960's, and all of them were afraid of him. When he saw the scrawny, shy Laver for the first time, he nicknamed him "Rocket" as a joke, and the name stuck.

Hollis and Hopman shared coaching duties until Rod reached eighteen. That year he entered the French Championships and Wimbledon only to be beaten in the first round in both. In North America he was more successful, winning both the Canadian and American junior championships. Over the following three years his progress was sure and steady. He always worked hard at maintaining his fitness, and Hopman continued to drive him to his physical limits with punishing drills.

Rod Laver reaching to return the ball in the finals of Wimbledon in 1968.
(AFP/Getty Images)

The Emerging Champion

Rod's emergence as one of the top tennis players of all time was slow in coming. It took him three years to win his first major championship. Before 1962, he had reached seven major championship finals in all and won only two of them. Some people wondered if he had the nerve to be a true champion.

Though a great natural player, Rod had to work hard to climb to the top. In 1960, he won the Australian Championship by beating his fellow countryman Neale Fraser in five sets. Fraser, however, got his revenge by defeating Rod at Wimbledon and Forest Hills, site of the U.S. National Championship, in the same year.

In 1961, Rod lost in both the Australian and the U.S. finals to Roy Emerson, but he did win Wimbledon, beating Chuck McKinley in the final. He had finally arrived as a champion, though he was still only one among many.

To remedy this, Rod announced that he wanted to win the Grand Slam in 1962. The Grand Slam was made up of four major tournaments: The Australian and French Championships, Wimbledon, and the U.S. National Championship. Only one player, Don Budge, had ever won all four in the same year.

Rod met his great rival, Emerson, in three of the four finals and beat him in all of them. In the French, his greatest scare came in the semifinal against Neale Fraser, who led 5-4 in the fifth set. At Wimbledon, Rod beat Marty Mulligan in three sets, and at Forest Hills he beat Emerson in four. He had achieved a feat most great players of the past had failed to accomplish.

Continuing the Story

In 1963, Rod turned professional to join big names like Lew Hoad, Ken Rosewall, and Pancho Gonzales. At that time no professional tennis players were allowed to enter the major tournaments. However, the standard of professional play was considerably higher, and Rod suffered badly over the first three months. He averaged only one win every five matches. As usual, though, Rod responded to the challenge with dedication. He trained to reach top physical fitness and practiced relentlessly on his weak second serve and his volley. Rod's work paid off, and he became one of the top professionals along with Ken Rosewall.

Though Rod was small, one aspect of his physique stood out: his left arm, the arm with which he

Major Championship Victories and Finals

1959-60	Wimbledon finalist
	Wimbledon mixed doubles (with Darlene Hard)
1959-61	Australian Championship doubles (with Bob Mark)
1960	U.S. National Championship doubles finalist (with Mark)
1960-61	U.S. National Championship finalist
1960, 1962	Australian Championship
1961	French Championship doubles (with Roy Emerson)
	French Championship mixed doubles (with Hard)
1961-62, 1968-69	Wimbledon
1962	U.S. National Championship
	French Championship
1968	French Open finalist
1969	Australian Open
	Australian Open doubles (with Emerson)
	U.S. Open
	French Open
1970, 1973	U.S. Open doubles finalist (with Emerson)
1971	Wimbledon doubles (with Emerson)

Other Notable Victories

1959-62, 1973	On winning Australian Davis Cup team
1962	Italian Championship doubles (with John Fraser)
	Italian Championship
1964, 1966-69	U.S. Pro Championship
1964-67, 1970	Professional World Singles Tournament
1965, 1967	Professional World Doubles Tournament (with Earl Buchholz and Andres Gimeno)
1970	Canadian Open
	Pacific Southwest Open
1970-71	U.S. Pro Championship doubles (with Emerson)
1971	Italian Open
1972, 1974	U.S. Pro Indoor Championship
1973	Canadian Open doubles (with Ken Rosewall)
1973, 1976	U.S. Pro Indoor Championship doubles (with Emerson and Dennis Ralston)
1984	Grand Masters Championship

Records and Milestones

Only man to win two Grand Slams (1962, 1969)
Australian Davis Cup team (1959-62, 1973)

Honors and Awards

1961-62, 1968-69 Ranked number one in the world
1981 Inducted into International Tennis Hall of Fame

played. He developed it from an early age by constantly squeezing a tennis ball off court.

In 1968, professionals were finally invited to compete at Wimbledon. After five years away, Rod again had the chance to play in a big championship. He proved his worth by winning Wimbledon that year, beating another Aussie, Tony Roche, in the final. As in 1961, Rod publicly declared his intention to win the Grand Slam in 1969.

The 1969 Australian Championships final between Rod and Tony Roche took place in 105-degree heat over four hours. In the fifth set, the players were even until Roche got upset over a line call and lost the match. Rod, who never allowed bad line calls or adverse weather to upset him, then made good on his prediction, going on to win in France, Wimbledon, and Forest Hills to become the only player to win all four grand slam tournaments within a single calendar year twice.

Rod remained a top player for several years after his 1969 triumph, but he did not capture any more Grand Slam victories. In the late 1970's, he began a successful career on the Carte Blanche Tennis Legends circuit, competing in seniors events against

some of his old rivals. In 1981, Rod was inducted into the International Tennis Hall of Fame. In 1998, he suffered a moderate hemorrhagic stroke. He began an intensive therapy regimen in order to regain his speech and ability to walk. In 2000, Melbourne Park's court—the home of the Australian Open—was named Rod Laver Arena.

Summary

Though his achievements probably rank him above all players, Rod Laver was not a born champion. He developed his natural abilities through hard work and steely determination. A champion by his deeds, not his words, he always carried himself like a champion: He never showed tiredness or anger or lost his ability to focus on the game.

Philip Magnier

Additional Sources

Collins, Bud. *Total Tennis: The Ultimate Tennis Encyclopedia.* Toronto: Sport Media, 2003.

Crothers, Tim, and John Garrity. *Greatest Athletes of the Twentieth Century.* Des Moines, Iowa: Sports Illustrated Books, 1999.

Laver, Rodney George, and Bud Collins. *The Education of a Tennis Player.* New York: Simon & Schuster, 1973.

_____. *Rod Laver's Tennis Digest.* Chicago: Follett, 1975.

Parsons, John. *The Ultimate Encyclopedia of Tennis: The Definitive Illustrated Guide to World Tennis.* London: Carlton, 2006.

Phillips, Caryl. *The Right Set: A Tennis Anthology.* New York: Vintage Books, 1999.

Ivan Lendl

Born: March 7, 1960
Ostrava, Czechoslovakia (now in Czech Republic)

Early Life

Ivan Lendl, born in Ostrava, Czechoslovakia, on March 7, 1960, grew up in a structured environment both within his family and within an authoritarian nation. The only child of Jiri Lendl, a lawyer, and his wife, Olga, a secretary, Ivan was taken to tennis matches in his stroller. His father ranked fifteenth among Czechoslovakian men players, his mother second among women players. Tennis was in the family's blood.

Jiri used his keen mind to outwit opponents. Olga, however, was a dogged player, hounding her opponents to physical exhaustion. Ivan's game was more like his mother's than his father's. Lacking the notable endowments in tennis of such players as John McEnroe or Boris Becker, Ivan acknowledged early that only relentless training would transform him into the champion he wanted to be.

Before her child was six, Olga saw to it that he received that training. When he was eight, his coach was pairing him with older, stronger players. Ivan's worst punishment for misbehavior was to be kept away from the tennis courts.

The Road to Excellence

Olga Lendl was her son's most challenging early tennis opponent. When, at fourteen, he finally beat her for the first time, he burst with pride. The next year, he was excused from school to play tournaments in the United States. Always self-motivated, he studied on his own while he was on tour, returning to school to take examinations, on which he scored well. A strong student in mathematics, he was skeptical about the facts of history.

Traveling in the West, Ivan questioned the socialism that prevailed in Czechoslovakia. His sights were already on the West when he won the junior title at Wimbledon at eighteen years old. In 1978, Ivan returned to Czechoslovakia to begin a short-lived career as a university student, which he ended voluntarily when he began winning important matches. For his required military service, he was made an officer, playing tennis and representing his nation in the Davis Cup matches.

The Emerging Champion

In 1978, Ivan won the Italian, French, and Wimbledon junior singles; In 1980, he won the Spanish and Canadian open singles. By that time he was

Ivan Lendl playing in the French Open in 1994. (Clive Brunskill/ Getty Images)

ranked sixth in world tennis. The following year, the 6-foot 2-inch Ivan—intense and serious, seldom smiling in public—again won the Canadian and Spanish open singles, as well as the South American Open singles.

The budding champion continued to pile victory upon victory in succeeding years, claiming such prestigious wins as the French Open, the Monte Carlo Open, the Canadian Open, the Australian Open, the Stockholm Open, and various World Championship of Tennis singles tournaments, including The Masters singles.

Ivan spent considerable time in the United States on tour. He frequently visited Wojtek Fibak, his coach and business manager for five years, at his home in Greenwich, Connecticut. In 1981, Ivan bought a 16,000-square-foot Georgian mansion in Greenwich and took permanent residence status in 1987, sharing the house with Samantha Frankel, whom he married in 1989. Fibak's wife had introduced the shy, withdrawn Ivan to Samantha when she was a fourteen-year-old schoolgirl from St. Maarten attending the Spence School.

In order for Ivan to be qualified to represent the United States in Davis Cup matches and in the 1988 Olympic Games, a bill was put before Congress in the late spring of 1988 to grant Ivan full citizenship before he would normally have been eligible for it. The bill cited his continued residence in the United States and gave his income as more than $1,000,000 a year.

Continuing the Story

Ivan, always a loner, was already one of the world's best tennis players when the gregarious Fibak began coaching him around 1980. Fibak realized, however, that Ivan's only real asset was his formidable forehand. Ivan rushed the net whenever he had the opportunity, but his volley, serve, and backhand were shabby.

Major Championship Victories and Finals

1981, 1985	French Open finalist
1982-84, 1988-89	U.S. Open finalist
1984, 1986-87	French Open
1985-87	U.S. Open
1986-87	Wimbledon finalist
1989-90	Australian Open

Other Notable Victories

1980	On winning Czechoslovakian Davis Cup team
1980-81, 1983, 1989	Canadian Open
1982	WCT Finals
	ATP Championship
1982-83, 1986-87	The Masters
1982, 1990	WCT Tournament of Champions
1983	Italian Open
1985	U.S. Clay Court Championship
1986	U.S. Pro Indoor Championship

Fibak taught Ivan how to strengthen his game from the baseline and how to succeed by staying close in points until he could press through to a win. Fibak's chief aim was to toughen Ivan up mentally, to make his tennis more like his father's than his mother's. Fibak taught Ivan to be a more unemotional player and to increase his concentration, which made him a daunting opponent and resulted in his long string of significant victories.

In 1990, Ivan was still winning such tournaments as the Australian Open and the Stella Artois Grass Court Championships. He predicted he had four of five years of competitive playing left.

Although he won both the U.S. and French Opens three times and the Masters five times, and although he became one of the leading all-time prize-money winners in tennis, Ivan never won the Wimbledon men's singles. He played better on clay than on grass, a fact that he whimsically admitted in 1983, when he skipped Wimbledon, blaming an allergy to grass.

Ivan was consistently intense in his training routine. He monitored his diet closely, having his blood chemistry checked frequently to ensure that he was experiencing no nutritional deficiencies. The term "obsessive" was thus applied to Ivan.

Ivan had little patience with players who were not stalwart in their routines, dismissing all female players except Steffi Graf and Martina Navratilova because, in his eyes, they did not pay sufficient attention to keeping themselves fit. After retiring

---

Honors, Awards, and Milestones

1979	Rolex Rookie of the Year
1979-83	Czechoslovakian Davis Cup team
1985-87	International Tennis Federation Player of the Year
1985-87, 1989	Ranked number one by the ATP
2001	Inducted into International Tennis Hall of Fame

from competitive tennis in 1994, Ivan pursued golf with the same single-minded determination that pervaded his tennis game. He played on the Buy.Com Tour and hoped to earn the right to play on a professional golf tour. In April, 2000, Ivan won the Childrens' Medical Center Celebrity Classic in Richmond, Virginia. In 2004, he staged the "Ivan Lendl Celebrity Golf Tournament," a charity event.

Summary

Above all else, Ivan Lendl was a realist. Because he had an objective view of both his abilities and his limitations, he was able to hone his abilities and overcome the limitations he recognized in himself. Fibak tried to turn him into a machine, and Ivan accepted the necessity of the coaching method. From 1980 to 1993, he was the only tennis player to win at least one tournament in each year. Hard work made it possible for Ivan to rank as one of the top tennis players of all time, a fact that was recognized when he was inducted into the International Tennis Hall of Fame in 2001.

R. Baird Shuman

Additional Sources

Araton, Harvey. "Agassi's Run No Surprise to Lendl." *The New York Times*, September 2, 2005, pp. D1-D2.

Collins, Bud. *Total Tennis: The Ultimate Tennis Encyclopedia*. Toronto: Sport Media, 2003.

Lendl, Ivan, and George Mendoza. *Hitting Hot: Ivan Lendl's Fourteen Day Tennis Clinic*. New York: Random House, 1986.

Lendl, Ivan, and Eugene L. Scott. *Ivan Lendl's Power Tennis*. New York: Simon & Schuster, 1983.

Parsons, John. *The Ultimate Encyclopedia of Tennis: The Definitive Illustrated Guide to World Tennis*. London: Carlton, 2006.

Suzanne Lenglen

Born: May 24, 1899
        Compiègne, France
Died: July 4, 1938
        Paris, France
Also known as: Suzanne Rachel Flore Lenglen
    (full name); the Goddess of Tennis

Early Life

Suzanne Rachel Flore Lenglen was born in Compiègne, France, on May 24, 1899, to Charles and Anaïs Lenglen. Charles operated a prosperous business he inherited from his father. Soon after Suzanne was born, Charles sold the business, and the Lenglens moved to a villa in Maretz-sur-Matz, near Compiègne, where they spent the summer months. Their winter months were spent in Nice in the south of France.

Suzanne became a big, strong girl who had unusual athletic ability, exceeding boys her age in athletic pursuits. In Nice, she excelled in diabolo, a popular game among European children that involves a spinning top held on a string between two sticks. She studied dance in Nice as well.

The world's best tennis players often played in Nice in the winter, and Suzanne's father soon became interested in the game. In June of 1910, he presented Suzanne with her first tennis racket. Soon she became interested in the game and three months later entered her first tournament, winning four rounds to capture second place.

The Lenglens continued to return to Nice every fall and joined the prestigious Nice Tennis Club. Suzanne was coached by her father, who prescribed rigorous physical conditioning and conducted long practice sessions. In Nice, Suzanne played with some of the best male players on the French Riviera to perfect her game.

The Road to Excellence

In 1913, at the age of fourteen, Suzanne surprised everyone by winning the women's championship of the Nice Tennis Club;

she was later selected to represent the club in a contest against an Italian club, where she won one match after another. In 1914, she entered the Carlton Club tournament in Cannes, where she faced the world's top women players. Suzanne won the event, beating Mrs. R. J. Winch, an Englishwoman and former Wimbledon player, in three sets. With those victories, Suzanne became the most popular player in southern France.

As she celebrated her fifteenth birthday, Suzanne entered the World Hardcourt Championship at the Stade Français in Saint Cloud, a suburb of Paris. She continued to be victorious, winning the world titles in singles and doubles while placing second in mixed doubles.

Suzanne's father would not allow her to enter the tournament at Wimbledon in 1914. He wanted

Suzanne Lenglen, who was one of the first women's tennis players to gain international fame. (Courtesy of International Tennis Hall of Fame)

her to wait one more year before facing Dorothea Chambers, the winner of six Wimbledon singles titles. However, World War I brought about the suspension of the tournaments at Saint Cloud and Wimbledon, and Suzanne had to wait until 1919 to reenter international competition. Suzanne's reputation had already been established, however.

The end of World War I brought with it a sense of relief, a desire to forget and escape the memories of the war. Sports became widely popular, and the 1920's became known as the Golden Age of Sport, an era of unprecedented athletic achievements as well as glamorous and flamboyant heroes. Suzanne soon shared the spotlight with such notable champions as Gertrude Ederle, Bobby Jones, Jack Dempsey, and Babe Ruth.

The Emerging Champion

Suzanne received widespread recognition as France encouraged athletic competition for women after the war. In 1919, as a representative of France, Suzanne entered Wimbledon. Interest in seeing the young tennis prodigy brought many spectators to the All England Tennis Club, and gate receipts in-

Honors, Awards, and Milestones

| 1978 | Inducted into International Tennis Hall of Fame |
| 1984 | Inducted into Sudafed International Women's Sports Hall of Fame |

creased dramatically. Suzanne won easily in the first rounds, defeated Elizabeth Ryan in a difficult semifinal match, and, in the final, faced the defending champion Dorothea Chambers, a forty-year-old who had won seven singles titles. The match lasted three sets, requiring forty-four games—a record that stood until 1970—and Suzanne defeated the long-reigning champion.

With her first Wimbledon victory, Suzanne became a star. She dramatically changed tennis attire and play for women. At Wimbledon, she had not worn the customary corset. She later replaced the long pleated skirt with a short silk one and the hat with a colorful bandeau. Her new attire gave her the freedom that her leaping, whirling, and balletic style of play required.

The following year, Suzanne defeated Chambers 6-3, 6-0, and won the gold medal in singles and mixed doubles play in the Olympic Games. In 1921, she continued her reign as queen of tennis with victories at the Hardcourt Championships and at Wimbledon. However, later that year, she lost—by default because of illness—to Molla Mallory at Forest Hills. She regained her crown by defeating Mallory at Wimbledon the next year. In 1924, she defended her titles at the Hardcourt Championships but withdrew from Wimbledon, again because of illness; she returned to win both titles in 1925.

The next year brought the culminating victory of Suzanne's career. On February 16, 1926, she entered the long-awaited match with Helen Wills, the reigning American champion. In a hard-fought, controversial match, she defeated Wills in straight sets, retaining her title as world hard champion. Later that year, Suzanne returned to Wimbledon in pursuit of her seventh title. However, she had a dispute with the tournament organizers, kept the Queen of England waiting, and withdrew from the tournament.

Continuing the Story

In 1926, Suzanne signed a professional contract with C. C. Pyle to begin the Suzanne Lenglen North American Tour, the first professional tour in

Major Championship Victories and Finals

1919-23, 1925	Wimbledon
1919-23, 1925-26	Wimbledon doubles (with Elizabeth Ryan)
1920-23, 1925-26	French Championship
1920, 1922, 1925	Wimbledon mixed doubles (with Gerald Patterson, Pat O'Hara Wood, and Jean Borotra)
1925-26	French Championship doubles (with Didi Vlasto)
	French Championship mixed doubles (with Jacques Brugnon)

Other Notable Victories

1914, 1921-22	World Hardcourt Championship doubles (with Ryan and Germaine Golding)
1914, 1921-24	World Hardcourt Championship
1920	Gold medal, Olympic women's tennis singles
	Gold medal, Olympic mixed doubles (with Max Decugis)
1921, 1922-23	World Hardcourt Championship mixed doubles (with Decugis and Henri Cochet)

the United States. On October 6, 1926, she made her debut at Madison Square Garden, in New York, as the first professional tennis player. However, the tour was opposed by the United States Tennis Association, difficulties arose between Suzanne and Pyle, and the tour ended in February of 1927.

Suzanne returned to France, but the French Tennis Federation refused to rank her, declaring her ineligible for amateur competition. She continued to play professional tennis for a few months and then retired from competition. She wrote several books about tennis and a collection of short stories, *The Love Game* (1925). She later opened a tennis school in Paris. During the Wimbledon competition of 1938, Suzanne became extremely ill and died of pernicious anemia on July 4.

Summary

Suzanne Lenglen became a world champion in 1914, before her fifteenth birthday. She was the French singles, doubles, and mixed doubles champion in 1920-1923, 1925, and 1926. In 1920, she was Olympic singles and mixed doubles champion. She was Wimbledon champion six times, winning in 1919-1923 and in 1925. She was also the doubles champion in those years and mixed doubles champion in 1920, 1922, and 1925. For seven years she was nearly invincible. Suzanne single-handedly revolutionized women's tennis, altering the style of play and attire. She embodied the liberation of women and the brilliance and flamboyance of the Golden Age of Sport. For her many achievements and contributions, she was named to the International Tennis Hall of Fame in 1978 and to the International Women's Sports Hall of Fame in 1984.

Susan J. Bandy

Additional Sources

Engelmann, Larry. *The Goddess and the American Girl: The Story of Suzanne Lenglen and Helen Wills.* New York: Oxford University Press, 1988.

Phillips, Caryl. *The Right Set: A Tennis Anthology.* New York: Vintage Books, 1999.

Smith, Lissa, ed. *Nike Is a Goddess: The History of Women in Sports.* New York: Grove Atlantic, 2001.

Wallechinsky, David, and Jaime Loucky. *The Complete Book of the Olympics: 2008 Edition.* London: Aurum Press, 2008.

John McEnroe

Born: February 16, 1959
      Wiesbaden, West Germany (now in
      Germany)
Also known as: John Patrick McEnroe, Jr. (full
      name); Johnny Mac; Super Brat

Early Life

John Patrick McEnroe, Jr., was born on February 16, 1959, in Wiesbaden, West Germany (now in Germany), where his father served in the United States Air Force. He was the first of John Patrick and Kay McEnroe's three sons. John was nine

John McEnroe momentarily sits out while Ilie Nastase refuses to play at the 1979 U.S. Open. (AP/Wide World Photos)

months old when the family relocated to Flushing in Queens, New York. When John was four, the family moved to Douglastown, Queens, where John grew up.

John discovered tennis when he was eight. His family joined the Douglastown Club, which had five tennis courts. When John showed an interest in tennis, his father began to play with him and regularly defeated him.

John attended Buckley Country Day School near his home until he was thirteen. He was a model child who was chiefly concerned with doing well in school and sports. He attended Trinity School, the oldest continuously operated school in Manhattan, from which he graduated in 1977. He played tennis, football, and soccer at Trinity. Although he was already playing in significant tennis tournaments, John never missed school and never fell behind in his academic work.

After Trinity, John attended Stanford University, where he was on the tennis team. He won the National Collegiate Amateur Athletic (NCAA) Championship as a freshman. By 1978, however, tennis came to assume so important a role in John's life that he left Stanford to join the professionals.

The Road to Excellence

While he was still at Trinity School, John won several U.S. junior singles and doubles matches. By 1977, he had won the junior titles in the French Open mixed doubles and singles. The next year, having become a professional, he won the Italian Indoor Doubles Championship. He defeated Tim Gullikson in both the Stockholm Open and the Benson & Hedges Championships at Wembley in the same year. He also beat Dick Stockton in the TransAmerica Open. In 1979, he beat Vitas Gerulaitis in the U.S. Open and Arthur Ashe in the Masters.

John, shorter than most of his peers and pudgy in his early teens, had an intensity that became legendary among tennis fans. His furrowed brow bespoke a seriousness and competitiveness seldom seen even in championship tennis circles. His jutting lip and chin suggested unbending determination.

The Emerging Champion

Björn Borg was in many ways John's most formidable opponent. Therefore, beating him in the World Championship of Tennis finals of 1979 was particularly sweet. The victory marked an important prelude to other impressive victories that placed John first among American tennis players and eventually first among all tennis players.

John defeated Borg in five sets in the men's singles of the U.S. Open the following year and again in 1981. He also prevailed at the U.S. Open in 1984. In 1981, John claimed his most important victory over Borg at Wimbledon, where he and Peter Fleming had already taken the men's doubles titles in 1979 and 1981. He trounced Borg in the men's singles and won again in 1983 and 1984.

These victories over Borg were more important to John than his conquest of Jimmy Connors in the 1980 U.S. Indoor Championship men's singles in Memphis, Tennessee, or of Vitas Gerulaitis in the Custom Credit Australian Indoor Championship men's singles in Sydney, Australia, the same year, impressive as these victories were.

After winning the U.S. Pro Indoor Championship from 1982 to 1985 and the U.S. Indoor Championship in both 1980 and 1983, John slackened his pace during his courtship of actress Tatum O'Neal, which resulted in their marriage in 1986. The couple and their children settled in Malibu, California.

John prevailed, nevertheless, in the men's singles competitions of the AT&T Challenge of 1987, in the Japan Open the following year, and in the U.S. Hardcourt Championship of 1989. Fatherhood made John more attentive to his behavior on court. He began to create a more favorable image. Although his marriage ended in 1994, John said that rearing children helped him to become a more real person.

Continuing the Story

In 1988, when John played at Wimbledon after a two-year absence, he was in excellent form. He was, however, eliminated early in the competition and left England bemoaning the kind of tennis being played and muttering darkly about the future of the sport. The game of power and pace at which players like Boris Becker, Stefan Edberg, and Ivan Lendl excelled was a new brand of championship tennis that clearly delineated a new generation of tennis champions.

John may have mellowed through the years, but he did not lose his ar-

---

Major Championship Victories and Finals

1977	French Open mixed doubles (with Mary Carillo)
1978, 1982	Wimbledon doubles finalist (with Peter Fleming)
1979-81, 1984	U.S. Open
1979, 1981, 1983, 1989	U.S. Open doubles (with Fleming and Mark Woodforde)
1979, 1981, 1983-84, 1992	Wimbledon doubles (with Fleming and Michael Stich)
1980	U.S. Open doubles finalist (with Fleming)
1980, 1982	Wimbledon finalist
1981, 1983-84	Wimbledon
1984	French Open finalist
1985	U.S. Open finalist

Other Notable Victories

1978	NCAA Championship
1978-79	Italian Indoor Championship doubles (with Fleming)
1978-80	The Masters doubles (with Fleming)
1979	WCT World doubles (with Fleming)
1979, 1981-82	On winning U.S. Davis Cup team
1979, 1981, 1983-85	WCT Finals
1979, 1984	Canadian Open doubles (with Fleming)
1979, 1984-85	The Masters
1980	U.S. Indoor Championship doubles (with Brian Gottfried)
	U.S. Clay Court Championship doubles (with Gene Mayer)
1980-81	WCT Tournament of Champions doubles (with Fleming)
1980, 1982, 1984	U.S. Pro Indoor doubles (with Fleming)
1980, 1983	U.S. Indoor Championship
1981	ATP Championship
1981, 1982	ATP Championship doubles (with Ferdi Taygan and Fleming)
1982-85	U.S. Pro Indoor
1984-85	Canadian Open
1989	U.S. Hardcourt Championship

---

dor. In 1992, John teamed with German Michael Stich to win the doubles title at Wimbledon in dramatic fashion with a 19-17 fifth set. In 1993, he retired from the men's tour and became a tennis sportscaster for the USA Network. In 1994, he began playing on the Worldwide Senior Tennis Circuit. He was inducted into the International Tennis Hall of Fame in 1999. He was also named captain of the U.S. Davis Cup team in that same year, but he resigned from the position in 2000. A man of many interests, John also owned an art gallery in New York City and was involved with many charities through his own foundation.

In 1997, John married rock musician Patty Smyth. They have two daughters. In addition to his business endeavors and charity outlets, John established himself as a brilliant tennis analyst on both network and cable television. He also found the time to compete on the senior tennis circuit. In 2006, he returned to the ATP tour. John and Jonas Bjorkman played doubles together at the SAP Open in San Jose, California. In dramatic fashion, they won the tournament. Amazingly, this was the first title that John had won since 1992. With this victory, he had won doubles titles during the 1970's, the 1980's, the 1990's, and the 2000's. He also became the oldest player to win a prominent tournament in thirty years. His boundless curiosity and willingness to take on new challenges made him one of the most fascinating public figures in twentieth and twenty-first century American culture.

Summary

Recognized as an unusually complex individual, John McEnroe was a fierce competitor who expected perfection from himself on the court. Considered by many authorities to be one of the true geniuses of tennis, John left an indelible mark on the game that he loved. He will be remembered as one of the best doubles players to ever play the game. His impact on tennis goes beyond just the court. Always forthright and articulate, John injected fresh and sometimes controversial ideas into tennis. He was a unique kind of champion who asked for better from himself and from those who dared to stand in his way.

R. Baird Shuman, updated by Jeffry Jensen

Honors and Awards

1978	All-American
1978-84, 1987-91	Davis Cup team
1979-81, 1983-85	Ranked number one by the ATP
1981	Associated Press Male Athlete of the Year
1983-84	International Tennis Federation Player of the Year
1999	Inducted into International Tennis Hall of Fame
2001	Received RTS Television Sport Award: Best Sports Pundit
2003	Inducted into Laureus World Sports Academy
2006	Received Eugene L. Scott Award

Additional Sources

Adams, Tim. *On Being John McEnroe.* New York: Crown, 2003.

Drucker, Joel. "Mac the Nice." *Tennis* 35 (June, 1999).

Esterow, Milton. "John McEnroe: From Center Court to Soho." *ARTnews* 95 (April, 1996).

Evans, Richard. *McEnroe, Taming the Talent.* Lexington, Mass.: S. Greene, 1990.

Leand, Andrea. "Watch Your Back Mac." *Tennis* 36 (February, 2000).

Lidz, Franz. "An Invasion of Privacy." *Sports Illustrated* 85 (September 9, 1996).

McEnroe, John, with James Kaplan. *You Cannot Be Serious.* New York: G. P. Putnam's Sons, 2002.

Scanlon, Bill, Sonny Long, and Cathy Long. *Bad News for McEnroe: Blood, Sweat, and Backhands with John, Jimmy, Ilie, Ivan, Bjorn, and Vitas.* New York: St. Martin's Press, 2004.

Alice Marble

Born: September 28, 1913
    Beckwourth, California
Died: December 13, 1990
    Palm Springs, California

Early Life

Alice Marble was born on September 28, 1913, in Beckwourth, California, the fourth of five children. Life was hard in the early years; her father, a farmer, died when she was only six. By this time, the family had moved to San Francisco, and Alice's eldest brother, Dan, and her mother, Jessie, worked to support the family. Dan was seven years older than Alice and helped guide her toward a career in tennis. Alice spent her spare time playing baseball, which was her first love. At this time, however, it was unusual for girls to play baseball. Dan gave Alice her first tennis racket and paid for her to join a tennis club. By this time, Alice was sixteen years old.

The Road to Excellence

Alice began to practice regularly, curtailing the usual social engagements of a teenager in favor of the disciplined life of a serious athlete. She quickly became good enough to start playing junior tournaments, and she won the state junior tournament in 1931, at the age of seventeen. Next, Alice sought out Eleanor Tennant, the woman who was to be her coach. "Teach" Tennant was the leading coach of her day. She had several movie stars as her pupils, including Carole Lombard and Errol Flynn.

Tennant immediately recruited Alice as her pupil, and in return, Alice performed secretarial duties for her coach. The system paid dividends because a year later, Alice rose to number seven in the national rankings and won her first significant tournament—the state women's

Alice Marble. (Courtesy of Amateur Athletic Foundation of Los Angeles)

championship. Later in 1932, Alice took lessons from another coach, Harwood White, who helped her learn some new stroke techniques that greatly improved her game.

Alice continued to advance, and in 1933, she was chosen to play for the U.S. Wightman Cup team in the annual challenge match against Great Britain. She had risen to number three in the United States, behind the great contemporaries Helen Wills Moody and Helen Jacobs. In that year, Alice first contracted the illness that dogged her for most of the next two years. Playing in Easthampton, Long Island, Alice collapsed because of sunstroke after playing 108 games in 104 degrees Fahrenheit. Although she quickly recovered, more serious illness was around the corner.

The Emerging Champion

Following this incident, Alice became anemic, a condition resulting from a deficiency of iron in the body. Alice felt tired most of the time and was not able to play her best tennis.

In 1934, the Wightman Cup team made a trip to France. That was exceptional, since the team usually played only against Great Britain and had not traveled to the continent of Europe before. The six-day trip by ocean liner, the excitement of a new language, and the strange red clay court surface took their toll on Alice.

Alice was playing in the Stade Roland Garros in Paris when, once again, she collapsed on the court. Some thought she had tuberculosis, a lung disease that was often fatal in those days. A later diagnosis, however, revealed pleurisy, less dangerous but still a serious and painful illness. She was told by two doctors that she would never play tennis again. Alice was hospitalized, first in Paris and then in Los An-

Major Championship Victories and Finals

1936, 1938-40	U.S. National Championship
	U.S. National Championship mixed doubles (with Gene Mako, Donald Budge, Harry Hopman, and Bobby Riggs)
1937-38, 1939	Wimbledon mixed doubles (with Budge and Riggs)
1937-40	U.S. National Championship doubles (with Sarah Palfrey Fabyan)
1938-39	Wimbledon doubles (with Helen Jacobs)
1939	Wimbledon

Other Notable Victories

1933, 1937-39	On winning U.S. Wightman Cup team
1940	U.S. Clay Court Championship
	U.S. Clay Court Championship doubles (with Mary Arnold)

Honors, Awards, and Milestones

1933-34, 1937-39	U.S. Wightman Cup team
1936-40	Nationally ranked number one
1939-40	Associated Press Female Athlete of the Year
1964	Inducted into National Lawn Tennis Hall of Fame
1984	Service Bowl Award

geles, where she spent several months recovering in a sanatorium. As she convalesced, Alice started to do secretarial work for Tennant. She gradually got stronger and never let go of her dream to play tennis again. Almost a year later, Alice was back on court—as her coach's assistant—helping to give lessons to movie-star pupils such as Marlene Dietrich.

Continuing the Story

Despite the reservations of officials of the U.S. Lawn Tennis Association, Alice resumed her career in 1935. She and her coach Tennant were inseparable, and their hard work was rewarded when Alice won the California State Championships that year. This win was a turning point for Alice. Her repertoire of shots widened as she capitalized on the developments made with her other coach, Harwood White, three years earlier. Unlike other women players of her day, she possessed a hard American twist serve that she often followed with secure volleys. Her ground strokes were not always as powerful as those of her backcourt rivals, but her agility and determination in the attack made up for anything she lacked.

Few women had attempted to play this type of game before, and Alice seemed to draw inspiration from the male players of her day, such as Fred Perry and Don Budge, as she leapt for overheads and constantly hit the ball on the rise.

Alice's first taste of major success came in 1936, when she won the U.S. National Championship, beating Helen Jacobs in the final. Three more U.S. National Championship victories came in 1938, 1939, and 1940.

In 1939, Alice won not only the singles but also the doubles and the mixed doubles at Wimbledon, the British national championship. In 1939 and 1940, Alice Marble was totally dominant and received the Associated Press female athlete of the year award in both years.

In 1940, Alice turned professional and toured with Mary Hardwick, Donald Budge, and Bill Tilden. She also made her debut as a singer, performing at the Waldorf Astoria Hotel in New York City. She died on December 13, 1990, in Palm Springs, California.

Summary

Alice Marble's dominance was based on her strong serve and incisive volleys. Her style paved the way for postwar women champions such as Margaret Osborne and Louise Brough. If the war years had not intervened, it is certain that Alice would have won even more major titles. She overcame not only some illustrious rivals but also severe ill health. Alice was a pivotal figure in women's tennis in the twentieth century.

Elizabeth C. E. Morrish

Additional Sources

Davidson, Sue. *Changing the Game: The Stories of Tennis Champions Alice Marble and Althea Gibson.* Seattle, Wash.: Seal Press, 1997.

Fein, Paul. *Tennis Confidential: Today's Greatest Players, Matches, and Controversies.* Dulles, Va.: Potomac Books, 2008.

Gray, Frances Clayton, and Yanick Rice Lamb. *Born to Win: The Authorized Biography of Althea Gibson.* Hoboken, N.J.: John Wiley & Sons, 2004.

Helen Wills Moody

Born: October 6, 1905
 Centerville (now Fremont), California
Died: January 1, 1998
 Carmel, California
Also known as: Helen Newington Wills Moody
 Roark (full name); Helen Newington Wills
 (birth name); Little Miss Poker Face; Queen
 Helen

Early Life
Helen Newington Wills was born on October 6, 1905, in Centerville (now Fremont), California. Her parents were Dr. and Mrs. Clarence Wills. When she was very young, the family moved to Berkeley, California, where Helen was raised in a privileged social environment.

As a small child, Wills learned tennis from her father, and as a present for her fourteenth birthday, she was given a membership in the Berkeley Tennis Club. Soon she was playing every day, receiving help from William Fuller, the volunteer coach at the club who also arranged matches for her. Next, she started entering local tournaments and was soon winning them all.

The Road to Excellence
In 1921, when Helen was fifteen, she was sent east to play in the National Junior Tournament for girls 18 and under and to play on the women's circuit. She won the National Junior Championship and did extremely well in the other tournaments. Her career as an outstanding tennis player had begun.

The next year, 1922, Helen again won the National Junior Singles title and also won the National Junior Doubles with Helen Hooker. In the U.S. National Championship singles she reached the finals, where she was beaten by the defending champion, Molla B. Mallory. The defeat bothered Helen and motivated her to practice even harder when she returned to California. However, she did win the U.S. National Championship doubles title paired with Marion Z. Jessup. At the end of the year, when the United States Lawn Tennis Association (USLTA) released the rankings of the top ten women, seventeen-year-old Helen was rated third.

In 1923, Helen won the U.S. National Championship singles title, beating Mallory in the finals, and earned the number-one ranking. She was also selected as a member of the inaugural U.S. Wightman Cup team to play in an annual match between the top women players of the United States and England.

By this time, the press had given Helen the nickname "Little Miss Poker Face" for her incredible concentration on the court coupled with her expressionless behavior. They soon had to call her "Queen Helen," because for the next fifteen years she was the outstanding figure in women's tennis.

The Emerging Champion
In 1924, Helen traveled overseas and played at Wimbledon. She reached the finals, where she lost in three sets to the best British player, Kitty McCane, but she won the doubles title playing with

Helen Wills Moody in 1938. (AFP/Getty Images)

Hazel Wightman, donor of the Wightman Cup. Then she and Wightman went to Paris for the 1924 Olympic Games, where Helen won two gold medals, one in singles and one in doubles paired with Wightman.

Returning home to the United States, Helen accomplished a "hat trick" by winning all three titles at the U.S. National Championships: The singles, the doubles with Wightman, and the mixed doubles with Vincent Richards. When the rankings came out for 1924, Helen was number one again.

Continuing the Story

Helen won the U.S. National Championship singles five more times—in 1925, 1927, 1928, 1929, and 1931; she did not enter the 1926, 1930, and 1932 tournaments. In 1933, her last year in the U.S. Championship singles, she played in her most controversial match. Losing in the finals to her perennial rival, Helen Jacobs, she claimed she was ill and defaulted. Critics still wonder if she pretended to be sick to avoid outright defeat.

Helen won the U.S. National Championship doubles title two more times, once with Wightman and once with Mary K. Browne. In 1928, she won another mixed-doubles title, this time with John B. Hawkes. At Wimbledon, Helen Wills won the singles championship eight times. Her record of eight wins was not broken until 1990, when Martina Navratilova won her ninth Wimbledon singles title.

Major Championship Victories and Finals

1922, 1924, 1926, 1928	U.S. National Championship doubles (with Marion Zinderstein Jessup, Hazel Wightman, and Mary K. Browne)
1922, 1933	U.S. National Championship finalist
1923-25, 1927-29, 1931	U.S. National Championship
1924	Wimbledon finalist
1924, 1927, 1930	Wimbledon doubles (with Wightman and Elizabeth Ryan)
1924, 1928	U.S. National Championship mixed doubles (with Vincent Richards and John B. Hawkes)
1927-30, 1932-33, 1935, 1938	Wimbledon
1928-30, 1932	French Championship
1929	Wimbledon mixed doubles (with Francis T. Hunter)
1930, 1932	French Championship doubles (with Ryan)

Other Notable Victories

1923, 1927, 1929, 1931-32, 1938	On winning U.S. Wightman Cup team
1924	Gold medal, Olympic women's tennis singles
	Gold medal, Olympic doubles (with Wightman)

Milestones

U.S. Wightman Cup team (1923-25, 1927-32, 1938)
U.S. Wightman Cup team captain (1930, 1932)
30 Grand Slam titles

Honors and Awards

1923-31	Nationally ranked number one
1927-33, 1935, 1938	Ranked number one in the world
1935	Associated Press Female Athlete of the Year
1938	Comeback Player of the Year
1959	Inducted into National Lawn Tennis Hall of Fame
1981	Inducted into Bay Area [California] Sports Hall of Fame

After a two-year layoff between 1935 and 1937, Helen Wills competed at Wimbledon for the last time in 1938, and she defeated Jacobs in the final. Helen's victory after her long layoff earned her the comeback player of the year award.

In the French Championships, she won the singles three times and the doubles twice, both times with Elizabeth Ryan as a partner, and she played on the Wightman Cup teams ten times, serving as captain in 1930 and 1932.

Helen married Fred Moody, a California stockbroker, in 1929. In 1937, they divorced, and she married Aidan Roark, a writer and polo player. When she retired from tennis in 1938, Helen participated in few events connected with the game. She was an accomplished artist whose works were exhibited in galleries all over the world. She also wrote several books; the best known was her autobiography, *Fifteen-thirty: The Story of a Tennis Player* (1937). Later, she retired to live a quiet, private life in California.

Summary

Helen Wills Moody competed for eighteen years, and for most of those years she dominated women's tennis, winning thirty national and international championships. Between 1927 and 1933 she did not lose a set in singles; she won 180 matches in a row until the default to Helen Jacobs at the U.S. Championships. The USTA listed her in its top-ten rankings nine times, seven of those years at number one. In world rankings she was number one for nine years. Some tennis experts rate her as the most controlled champion the game has ever seen. In 1959, the National Lawn Tennis Hall of Fame inducted Helen, calling her "the greatest woman player in the annals of lawn tennis."

Joanna Davenport

Additional Sources

Engelmann, Larry. *The Goddess and the American Girl: The Story of Suzanne Lenglen and Helen Wills.* New York: Oxford University Press, 1988.

Orr, Frank, and George Tracz. *The Dominators: The Remarkable Athletes Who Changed Their Sport Forever.* Toronto: Warwick, 2004.

Wills, Helen. *Fifteen-thirty: The Story of a Tennis Player.* New York: Charles Scribner's Sons, 1937.

Wimmer, Dick, ed. *The Women's Game.* Short Hills, N.J.: Burford Books, 2000.

Carlos Moya

Born: August 27, 1976
Palma de Majorca, Spain
Also known as: Carlos Moya Llompart (full name); Charlie

Early Life

Carlos Moya Llompart was born on August 27, 1976. He was the third and youngest child of Andreu Moya and Pilar Llompart. His parents, who owned a hotel, often played tennis, and Carlos grew up with a racket in his hands. When Carlos was six years old, Jofre Porta began coaching him. Carlos also played soccer and basketball, which contributed to developing his athletic abilities and conditioning.

The Road to Excellence

As a boy, Carlos won a number of local and regional tournaments. By the time he was twelve, he began to show exceptional promise as a tennis player. When he was a teenager, he was coached by Alberto Tous, a former tennis professional from Majorca. Carlos won many junior tournaments in the Balearic Islands off the coast of Spain, where Majorca is located, and he also reached the semifinals of the Spanish junior tennis championships.

Carlos and his coach knew that to achieve major success as a tennis player, Carlos needed more intensive training and rigorous competition. At the age of seventeen, he moved to Barcelona to train at the Saint Cugat High Performance Center, where he began working with Juan Bautista Avendaño, as well as other coaches. He was also able to raise the level of his game through competition with highly ranked Spanish players who trained at the center in Barcelona.

In 1994, Carlos started to play professional tennis on the Association of Tennis Professionals (ATP) tour. He began by entering Challenger Series tournaments on the satellite circuit, primarily in Spain. Victories in several of these tournaments brought his ranking to number 346. He continued this path in 1995. By the end of that year, he had won his first regular ATP tournament in Buenos Aires, Argentina, and his ranking had climbed to 63.

In 1996, Carlos became a respected player on the ATP international circuit, maintaining his ranking in the top thirty. He entered the four Grand Slam tournaments for the first time, losing in the first round at the Australian Open and at Wimbledon and in the second round at the French Open and the U.S. Open. However, he reached the semifinals or finals of several other tournaments, and he won the Spanish Championships and the Croatia Open. In addition, he joined an elite group of Spanish players in Davis Cup competition. The experience that he gained, along with his hard work and talent, made him poised to become one of the best players on the men's professional tennis tour.

The Emerging Champion

All the potential and early success came together for Carlos in 1997, when he emerged as a top contender for major professional tennis championships. At the Australian Open, he was a surprising finalist. En route to the final, he defeated several top players, including Boris Becker of Germany and Michael Chang of the United States. Although Carlos lost in the final to number-one ranked Pete Sampras, his strong showing at this Grand Slam tournament demonstrated that he had become a major force in professional tennis. He did not do as well in the other Grand Slam events that year, but he won several professional tournaments and ended the year ranked seventh in the world.

Carlos's best Grand Slam season came in 1998 with his most important professional victory, at the French Open. The red-clay courts of the Roland Garros Tennis Center, where this Grand Slam tournament is played, are a favorite surface for Spanish

---

Major Championships

1998   French Open

Other Notable Victories

1998   Monte Carlo Masters
2002   Cincinnati Masters
2004   Rome Masters

players. Carlos had to defeat several highly ranked clay-court players, including Chilean Marcelo Ríos and his countrymen and friends Félix Mantilla in the semifinals and Alex Corretja in the finals. He won three other tournaments, reached the semifinal of the U.S. Open, and was a finalist at the ATP Tour World Championship in Hanover, Germany, where the tables were turned when he lost to Corretja. He ended the year ranked fifth in the world, and by the early part of 1999, his continuing high level of performance lifted him to the number-one ranking on the ATP tour.

Continuing the Story

Carlos's position as the number-one male professional tennis player was a short one, lasting only a few weeks, because he had no victories in several of the major tournaments in the spring of 1999. More important, he suffered a stress fracture of his vertebrae, which caused him to miss about eight months for recuperation through the later part of 1999 and into the 2000 season. Additional injuries to his toe and finger frustrated his efforts at a comeback.

During the early twenty-first century, Carlos worked hard to regain his competitive edge. He won one title in 2000 on clay courts at Estoril, Portugal, and one title in 2001, also on clay courts, at Umag, Croatia. By the end of 2001, Carlos had raised his ranking to number nineteen in the world. In 2002, he won four titles and proved to himself and to the tennis world that he had fought his way back. As further evidence of his comeback, he rose to a number-five ranking by the end of 2002. He remained ranked in the top ten into 2005. One of his proudest moments on the court took place in 2004, when he helped Spain to capture the Davis Cup by defeating the United States. His victories over Andy Roddick and Mardy Fish

were crucial in Spain's 3-2 victory. Although his ranking fell out of the top ten after 2005, Carlos continued to remain a fierce competitor and a dangerous opponent. After winning the title at Chennai, India, in 2005, he was generous enough to donate his prize money to the victims of the 2004 Indian Ocean earthquake and tsunami. In 2007, Carlos won his twentieth career singles title by beating Andrei Pavel in the finals of the Studena Croatia Open.

Summary

Spain has produced a number of excellent professional tennis players, but most of them have specialized in clay-court tennis, which emphasizes ground strokes, fitness, patience, and endurance. Carlos Moya had these characteristics as a tennis player, but he developed a more versatile, all-court game, and he was equally comfortable playing at the net. The flair of his game and his versatility made him more than just a clay-court player. His demonstrated ability to win on a variety of surfaces brought him a Grand Slam championship and, for a short period, the number-one ranking in men's professional tennis. He achieved a high level of performance in his sport, and he continued to work toward improving his record in tennis.

Karen Gould, updated by Jeffry Jensen

Additional Sources

Bodo, Peter. "Spanish Fly." *Tennis* 34, no. 7 (November, 1998).

Clarey, Christopher. "Fiesta at the French." *Tennis* 34, no. 4 (August, 1998).

_____. "Moya Wins, and Spain Takes Cup Once Again." *The New York Times*, December 6, 2004.

Malinowski, M. "The World According to Carlos Moya." *Tennis* 35, no. 8 (October, 1999).

Rafael Nadal

Born: June 3, 1986
      Manacor, Majorca, Spain
Also known as: Rafael Nadal Parera (full name);
    the Bull; Gladiator; the King of Clay; Rafa;
    Rafi; El Niño

Early Life

Rafael Nadal Parera was born on June 3, 1986, in Manacor, on the island of Majorca, in Spain, to Sebastián Nadal and Ana María Parera. Rafael has a younger sister, María Isabel. When Rafael was only three years old, he was introduced to tennis by his uncle, Toni Nadal, who was a professional tennis player himself. Toni remained Rafael's principal coach. Although Rafael was right-handed, Toni encouraged him to play tennis with his left hand. With a two-handed backhand, Toni believed that the shot would be strengthened by the power of Rafael's naturally strong right arm. As with most European players, Rafael grew up playing primarily on clay courts. He learned the importance of

Rafael Nadal concentrating on the ball during his semifinal match at the 2008 French Open. (Mike Hewitt/Getty Images)

quickness on the court. In addition, he was taught to hit heavy topspin shots that angled away from his opponents. By employing a western grip on his forehand, Rafael could hit his topspin shots more effectively without worrying about his shots landing outside the lines.

Though Rafael had an obvious natural talent for tennis, he enjoyed playing soccer even more. His uncle, Miguel Ángel Nadal, was a professional soccer player. Rafael split his time playing soccer, playing tennis, and fishing. By the time he was twelve, he was winning tennis titles in his age group. Since athletics had become all-consuming to Rafael, he was falling behind in his schoolwork. Rafael's father made him decide between playing tennis or soccer. While the Spanish tennis federation was interested in having Rafael join its training program in Barcelona, Rafael's family was against the idea. Although Rafael did train for a short period of time during a couple of summers at the tennis camp in Florida run by Nick Bollettieri, Rafael's uncle continued to serve as his primary coach.

The Road to Excellence

In 2001, Rafael took a chance and joined the professional tennis circuit. While only fifteen years old, he reached the second round of a challenger tournament in Seville, Spain. Rafael pushed himself, and in 2002, he won his first Association of Tennis Professionals (ATP) match in Majorca. Amazingly, Rafael became only the ninth tennis player in the open era to win an ATP match before he turned sixteen. With energy to burn, he moved up in the rankings. In 2003, he finished the year ranked in the top fifty. During the year, he captured two challenger titles and competed in his first Wimbledon. He became the youn-

Career Victories

2004	Orange Warsaw Open
2005	Brazil Open
	Abierto Mexicano Telcel
	Swedish Open
	China Open
	Madrid Masters
2005-07	Rome Masters
2005-08	Monte Carlo Masters
	Godó Tournament
	French Open
2005, 2007	Mercedes Cup
2005, 2008	Canada Masters
2006	Dubai Tennis Championship
2007	Indian Wells Masters
2008	Hamburg Masters
	Queen's Club Championships
	Wimbledon

gest player since Boris Becker in 1984 to reach the third round.

The Emerging Champion

Rafael had a breakout year in 2005. He won eleven titles, including his first French Open. By winning the French Open in his first attempt, he became the first player since Mats Wilander in 1982 to accomplish such a feat. In July, 2005, Rafael became the number-two ranked player in the world. Although the year had many highs, he was disappointed with his performances at both Wimbledon and the U.S. Open. He lost in the second round at Wimbledon and lost in the third round at the U.S. Open.

A foot injury forced Rafael to miss the 2006 Australian Open in January. By February, he was back on the tour. He beat Roger Federer on clay at Monte Carlo, Rome, and the French Open. Rafael captured his second French Open by defeating Federer in a four-set final. He proved how much his game had evolved by advancing to the 2006 Wimbledon final. He lost to Federer on the grass in four sets.

Continuing the Story

By 2007, Rafael had become one of the few tennis players on the circuit who could challenge Federer for the number-one ranking. With a strong work ethic, Rafael had made himself supremely fit. At 6 feet 1 inch and approximately 180 pounds, Rafael

had molded himself into a tough competitor. With his sleeveless shirt and his unique style of shorts that went to his knees, he cut a striking figure on the court. In addition to his brilliant tennis strokes, he became popular with the fans and advertisers alike. While he was almost unbeatable on a clay court, he had to work extremely hard to make his game fit other surfaces.

At the 2007 French Open, Rafael again defeated Federer to capture the title. Rafael seemed always to stand in Federer's way of winning a French Open title, and Federer seemed always to stand in Rafael's way of winning Wimbledon. Federer was once again victorious at Wimbledon in 2007. However, he needed five hard-fought sets to beat Rafael. Rafael was getting closer to equaling Federer on grass. In 2008, he made remarkable strides in his all-court game. He also started his own charity foundation, the Rafa Nadal Foundation; his mother served as president.

While Rafael remained the best clay-court player in the world, he also was winning with more frequency on other court surfaces. He humiliated Federer in straight sets in the finals at the 2008 French Open. With this victory, Rafael had won four consecutive French Opens, making him the only other man besides the great Swedish champion Björn Borg to accomplish the feat. Many assumed Federer would get his revenge at Wimbledon. However, Rafael rose to the occasion and upset Federer at Wimbledon. In what has been called one of the all-time great matches, Rafael captured the Wimbledon title by beating Federer in a five-set match. These two champions played their hearts out on center court, with the final set going to Rafael 9-7. While this victory was an extraordinary highlight for the year, Rafael continued his winning ways by taking the gold medal at the Beijing Summer Olympics in August. On August 18, 2008, Rafael took the number-one ranking from Federer.

Honors, Awards, Milestones

2003	Association of Tennis Professionals Newcomer of the Year
2004	Davis Cup champion (with Spain)
2005	Association of Tennis Professionals Most Improved Player
2006	Laureus World Newcomer of the Year
2008	Gold medal, Olympic men's tennis singles
	Prince of Asturias Awards

Summary

In a relatively short period of time, Rafael Nadal established himself as one of the premier tennis players of his time. After growing up playing almost exclusively on clay courts, he worked hard in order to make himself a true champion on all court surfaces. In addition to his extraordinary natural talent, he proved to be a fierce competitor who refused to give an inch in any match situation. Along with Roger Federer, Rafael was not only a true champion but also a player who was widely respected by fans and other players alike. During the early part of the twenty-first century, Rafael helped to make tennis popular throughout the world.

Jeffry Jensen

Additional Sources

Gregory, Sean. "Court Conquistador: Teen Idol Rafael Nadal Stormed Through the French Open, He Could Be the Game's Next Great Star." *Time* 165 (June 20, 2005).

_____. "A Duel to Fuel Tennis." *Time* 168 (September 4, 2006).

Horn, Geoffrey M. *Rafael Nadal.* Milwaukee, Wis.: Gareth Stevens, 2006.

Klam, Matthew. "The Nemesis (Rafael Nadal)." *Gentlemen's Quarterly* 77 (June, 2007).

Martin, James. "Number One [of a Kind] (Rafael Nadal) (Interview)." *Tennis* 43 (November/December, 2007).

Wertheim, L. Jon. "The Spin Master." *Sports Illustrated* 109 (July 14/July 21, 2008).

Martina Navratilova

Born: October 18, 1956
      Prague, Czechoslovakia (now in Czech
      Republic)
Also known as: Martina Subertova (birth name)

Early Life

Martina Navratilova was born Martina Subertova on October 18, 1956, in Prague, Czechoslovakia (now in the Czech Republic). Her parents divorced when she was three, and her father committed suicide soon afterward. Her mother remarried, and Martina's stepfather and mother both encouraged her participation in sports in general and in tennis in particular. She took the feminine form of her stepfather's name, Navratil.

When Martina was an infant, the family lived in the Riesengebirge Mountains, and she learned to ski as soon as she could walk. When Martina was five, the family moved to Řevnice, a suburb of Prague, and she began to accompany her parents while they played in amateur tennis tournaments. Mirek Navratil, her stepfather, cut down an old racket for Martina to use and began to teach her the game.

The Road to Excellence

Eager to follow her idols, Margaret Court and Billie Jean King, Martina entered her first tennis tournament at the age of eight. Though officials protested that she was too small, she reached the semifinals. At the age of fourteen, Martina won her first national title. She concentrated on sports, participating in hockey, soccer, swimming, and skiing to strengthen her body. By age sixteen, she had won three national women's tennis championships, as well as the national junior title, and became her nation's top-ranked female tennis player. A left-handed player, Martina excelled nearly equally at singles and doubles play.

Martina was fascinated by the possibility of traveling to wonderful places and was thrilled when the Czechoslovakian Tennis Federation allowed her to play an eight-week tour sponsored by the United States Lawn Tennis Association in 1973. She did not win any titles during that tournament, but she went to the finals in the Italian Open and won the junior girls championship at Wimbledon.

The next year Martina played in both the Italian and the German Opens, then returned to the United States for the Virginia Slims circuit. Her performance against tough competition earned her the title of rookie of the year from *Tennis* magazine. However, she was not happy with her game and resolved to work on her weaknesses. She returned home to Řevnice and concentrated on strengthening both her body and her game.

The Emerging Champion

Martina's determination paid off, and she defeated Margaret Court in the Australian Open, though she

Martina Navratilova at Wimbledon in 1975. (Hulton Archive/Getty Images)

lost to Evonne Goolagong. A month later she beat Chris Evert and, later, beat Goolagong. By the end of the year she had won several more titles and led the Czechoslovak team to its first victory in the women's international cup match since 1963.

Martina's career entered a new phase in 1975, the year she turned professional. Her growing reputation resulted in frequent invitations to play in tournaments around the world, especially in the United States. After an increasingly heated battle with the Czechoslovak authorities over her freedom to play when and where she wanted, Martina defected to the United States during the U.S. Open. Choosing between her native country and the freedom to exercise her desire to play tennis led to difficulties for Martina. She reveled in her newfound and unaccustomed freedom, losing concentration on her game. However, soon she was back on track and became the first woman player to top $100,000 for a year after winning the Virginia Slims circuit in 1977.

Martina continued to tally win after win. She came close to winning the calendar-year Grand Slam twice, holding three major championship ti-

Major Championship Victories and Finals

1974, 1985	French Open mixed doubles (with Ivan Molina and Heinz Gunthardt)
1975	French Open finalist
1975, 1982, 1984-88	French Open doubles (with Chris Evert, Anne Smith, Pam Shriver, and Andrea Temesvari)
1976, 1979, 1981-84, 1986	Wimbledon doubles (with Evert, Billie Jean King, and Shriver)
1977, 1978, 1980, 1983-84, 1986-87, 1989, 1990	U.S. Open doubles (with Stove, King, Shriver, Hanna Mandlikova, and Gigi Fernandez)
1977, 1985	Wimbledon doubles finalist (with Betty Stove and Shriver)
1978-79, 1982-87, 1990	Wimbledon
1979	U.S. Open doubles finalist (with King)
1980, 1982-85, 1987-89	Australian doubles (with Betty Nagelsen and Shriver)
1981, 1983, 1985	Australian Open
1981, 1985, 1989, 1991	U.S. Open finalist
1982, 1984	French Open
1983-84, 1986-87	U.S. Open
1985, 1987, 2006	U.S. Open mixed doubles (with Gunthardt, Emilio Sanchez, and Bob Bryan)
1985, 1993, 1995, 2003	Wimbledon mixed doubles (with Paul McNamee, Mark Woodforde, Jonathan Stark, and Leander Paes)
1988-89, 1994	Wimbledon finalist
2003	Australian mixed doubles (with Paes)

Other Notable Victories

1975	On winning Czechoslovakian Federation Cup team
1975, 1981, 1986	U.S. Indoor Championship
1975, 1987	Italian Open doubles (with Evert and Gabriela Sabatini)
1977, 1979, 1981, 1983-86	Virginia Slims Championship
1979, 1981-82	Avon Championship
1980-82	Avon Championship doubles (with King and Shriver)
1981, 1982, 1985	Canadian Open doubles (with Shriver, Candy Reynolds, and Fernandez)
1981, 1984-85	U.S. Indoor Championship doubles (with Shriver)
1982-83	Canadian Open
1982, 1986	On winning U.S. Federation Cup team
1983	On winning U.S. Wightman Cup team

Milestones

Czechoslovakian Federation Cup team (1975)
Ranked number one in the world (1979, 1982-87)
U.S. Federation Cup team (1982-86)
U.S. Wightman Cup team (1983)
Grand Slam doubles (1984)
54 Grand Slam titles

Honors and Awards

1974	Rolex Rookie of the Year
1975	*Tennis* magazine Most Improved Player
1979, 1982-86	International Tennis Federation Player of the Year
1982-84	Women's Sports Foundation Professional Sportswoman of the Year
1983, 1986	Associated Press Female Athlete of the Year
1984	Inducted into Sudafed International Women's Sports Hall of Fame
2000	Inducted into International Tennis Hall of Fame

tles in 1983—Wimbledon, the U.S. Open, and the Australian Open—and three in 1984—Wimbledon, the French Open, and the U.S. Open. Her 1983 single-year record of 86-1 set an unprecedented record.

In 1986, Martina experienced a bittersweet triumph in the Federation Cup, which was played in Prague. An American citizen since 1981, Martina won the hearts of the Czech fans but not of the authorities. Annoyed and insulted by her growing popularity, the Czechoslovak officials finally refused to allow the announcer to use Martina's name.

Between 1983 and 1985, Martina and tennis partner Pam Shriver won 109 consecutive doubles matches, including eighteen Grand Slam doubles. In 1987, she scored a rare triple crown at the U.S. Open: mixed doubles with Emilio Sanchez, women's doubles with Shriver, and the women's singles title.

Continuing the Story

Though Martina was defeated at Wimbledon in 1988, she refused to give up. She came back to win her ninth Wimbledon title in 1990. She continued to play, joining other top female athletes who refused to retire until their late thirties or forties.

Martina's aggressive style extended to aspects of her life other than tennis. She scoffed at the tendency of American women to compromise athletic conditioning and muscle tone for rounded, feminine bodies. Her attitude led to a frank admission of her homosexuality, but Martina refused to allow others' opinions to interfere with winning at tennis.

Martina also changed the shape of sports in other ways. While she was not the first to seek improvement for her mind, body, and spirit, she was such a prominent success that others began to follow her path. Many younger athletes benefited from her willingness to break conventions. She describes her choices in her autobiography, *Martina* (1985). She possessed many talents: Besides her autobiographies, she wrote several successful mystery novels and a book on fitness. She established the Martina Foundation to benefit underprivileged children worldwide. Although not a political activist, she supported the National Center for Lesbian Rights and the Metropolitan Community Church. Furthermore, she founded the Rainbow Endowment as a fund-raising group for gay and lesbian causes.

After retiring from competitive tennis for the first time in 1995, Martina served as a tennis commentator from 1995 to 1999. In 2000, she was inducted into the International Tennis Hall of Fame. She became fitness ambassador for the American Association of Retired Persons.

In 2000, Martina began playing doubles and mixed doubles on the women's tour. With Mariaan de Swardt, she reached the quarterfinals in doubles at the 2000 Wimbledon. In 2003, at forty-seven, she became the oldest player to win a Grand Slam, with the mixed-doubles titles at the Australian Open and Wimbledon. She also won a mixed-doubles Grand Slam title at the 2006 U.S. Open. Her final singles record, 1440-219, is the best in tennis history.

When Martina defected from Czechoslovakia she missed her family and worried that her homeland's communist government would retaliate against them. However, in 2008, her Czech citizenship was restored, and she became a dual citizen. Although she lives in the United States with her life partner, she maintained business interests in Prague.

Summary

Martina Navratilova was a major force in women's tennis, defecting from her native Czechoslovakia to pursue her goal. She won all the major titles in the United States, Europe, and Australia, and equaled or surpassed records set by previous tennis greats. She holds the record for career singles championships.

Mary Johnson, updated by Norbert Brockman

Additional Sources

Blue, Adrianne. *Martina: The Lives and Times of Martina Navratilova.* Secaucus, N.J.: Carol, 1995.

Howard, Johnette. *The Rivals: Chris Evert Versus Martina Navratilova—Their Epic Duels and Extraordinary Friendship.* New York: Broadway Books, 2005.

Navratilova, Martina. *Being Myself.* New York: HarperCollins, 1986.

_____. *The Shape of Your Life.* London: Time Warner, 2006.

Navratilova, Martina, and George Vecsey. *Martina.* New York: Knopf, 1985.

John Newcombe

Born: May 23, 1944
    Sydney, Australia
Also known as: John David Newcombe (full
  name)

Early Life

John David Newcombe was born May 23, 1944, in
Sydney, Australia, the son of George and Lillian
Newcombe. His father was a dentist. Like most outstanding athletes, John took to his sport early; he
began to play tennis when he was only seven years
old.

When John was still a boy, he became excited
when listening on the radio to a Davis Cup match
that pitted Australians Ken Rosewall and Lew Hoad
against Americans Tony Trabert and Vic Seixas.
John decided that he would like to take up the
game in a serious way. An experienced local coach,
Vic Edwards, saw John's talent and guided his initial efforts at serious play. By age ten, John was winning championship tournaments for juniors.

The Road to Excellence

John's game developed rapidly, and he won the
Australian Junior Championship for the first of
three consecutive times in 1961. In 1963, he played
for Australia's Davis Cup team for the first time;
however, he suffered a setback, losing all his
matches. Though not without talent, John lacked
sufficient seasoning to win consistently at the
championship level.

John had the necessary determination to work
on his game for several years, so that he could rise
from the ranks of talented players to attain greatness. He developed an unusual combination of
skills that enabled him to do this. He was a strong
and aggressive player. His game featured a powerful serve, followed by a rush to the net and the use
of volleying to gain the point. He also had a lethal
overhead smash.

Unlike most players whose game stressed power,
though, John was also a keen strategist. He was capable of detecting the slightest weakness in an opponent, at which he would pound away relentlessly.
Against an opponent whose game also stressed

power, John would often vary from his usual pattern and surprise his foe with crosscourt shots characteristic of defensive players such as Ken Rosewall.
John tended to start his match slowly and would
gradually build up the pace of action. He was especially dangerous if an opponent took an early lead.
His record of comebacks in five-set matches was the
best of any player's in the 1960's and 1970's.

The Emerging Champion

Given John's ability and determination, it is not
surprising that his march to the top proved successful. In 1965, he won the Wimbledon doubles title
and in 1967, the Wimbledon singles. In the latter
tournament, in his most difficult match, John
faced Clark Graebner, an outstanding American
amateur. One of the sets of this match lasted 110
minutes. John showed his superb conditioning and
determination by winning that set, 17-15, and,

*John Newcombe kissing the Wimbledon trophy after
winning the tournament in 1970.* (AFP/Getty Images)

Major Championship Victories and Finals

1963, 1966	Australian Championship doubles finalist (with Ken Fletcher)
1964	French Championship doubles finalist (with Tony Roche)
1965-66, 1968-70, 1974	Wimbledon doubles (with Roche)
1965, 1967	Australian Championship doubles (with Roche)
1966	U.S. National Championship finalist
1967	French Championship doubles (with Roche)
	U.S. National Championship
	U.S. National Championship doubles (with Roche)
1967, 1970-71	Wimbledon
1969, 1973	French Open doubles (with Roche and Tom Okker)
1971, 1973	U.S. Open doubles (with Roger Taylor and Owen Davidson)
1971, 1973, 1976	Australian Open doubles (with Roche and Mal Anderson)
1972	U.S. Open doubles finalist (with Davidson)
1973	U.S. Open
1973, 1975	Australian Open
1976	Australian Open finalist

Other Notable Victories

1965	Italian Championship doubles (with Roche)
1968	German Open
1968-70	Professional World Doubles Tournament (with Roche)
1969	Italian Open
	Canadian Open doubles (with Ron Holmberg)
1970	First National Classic doubles (with Roche)
1971	Canadian Open
	Swiss Open
1971, 1973	Italian Open doubles (with Roche and Okker)
1972	U.S. Pro Championship doubles (with Roche)
1974	Japan Open
	WCT Finals

more important, the match. By comparison, John's victory in the final was achieved without difficulty.

Also in 1967, John faced Graebner in another vital match. This time the scene of their confrontation was Forest Hills, and the U.S. National Championship singles title was at stake. John won the first two sets, but Graebner bounced back to take a commanding lead in the third. John was not to be denied, and, showing his unparalleled ability to rally when behind, John closed out Graebner to take the match in straight sets.

In 1968, John turned professional and continued his outstanding record. For the next several years, he was the game's dominant player, and in his first year as a professional, he won more than $174,000. He won the Wimbledon title in both 1970 and 1971. In the latter event, Stan Smith, a serve-and-volley player of great power, had an early lead against John in the final. Once again, John

came from behind to defeat Smith and win the tournament.

Continuing the Story

John's toughest opponents in both his amateur and professional careers were his fellow Australians, including Rosewall and Rod Laver. John's doubles partner, Tony Roche, deprived him of a U.S. title, but John's consolation was that he and Roche were the best doubles team of the late 1960's and early 1970's. In spite of a few major losses, John clearly ranks as best in the world in the period 1968-1971.

John's style of play exacted a heavy toll on his body, and John developed back problems in the early 1970's that drastically reduced his world ranking. He plunged from best in the world to mediocrity, following his elimination in the early rounds of several tournaments.

Despite his impaired physical condition, John retained his determination. He resolved to overcome his problems and regain top ranking. John's efforts met with success in the 1973 U.S. Open. He faced Jan Kodes, the Wimbledon champion, in the final. Kodes at first baffled John with his scrambling recoveries of John's powerhouse shots, and he raced ahead in the match. John's power eventually wore Kodes down, however, and he could offer no defense to John's steady stream of service aces. John was once more U.S. Open champion.

In 1974, John defeated the young sensation Björn Borg in the finals of World Championship of Tennis (WCT). After this victory, John's injuries

Milestones

Australian Davis Cup team (1963-76)
Served as president of the Association of Tennis Professionals

Honors and Awards

1967, 1970-71, 1973, 1975	Ranked number 1 in the world
1978	"Broadcaster of the Year" JAKS Award
1986	Inducted into International Tennis Hall of Fame

proved too much for him, and he was compelled to retire from active play. He became a successful businessman, specializing in selling tennis programs to hotels. He owns a large number of tennis camps and resorts. John also served as Australia's Davis Cup captain.

Summary

John Newcombe seemed similar to most post-World War II players. Strong and talented, John took up the game early and had the advantage of excellent coaching. His game emphasized the serve and volley. Unlike most players of this type, however, John was also a skilled strategist. In his ability to come back from a seemingly lost position, he was without equal. John dominated the game in the late 1960's and early 1970's, until injuries forced his retirement.

Bill Delaney

Additional Sources

Newcombe, John. *Bedside Tennis.* London: Fontana, 1984.

_____. *Newk: Life on and off the Court.* Sydney: Pan Macmillan, 2002.

Newcombe, John, and Clarence Mabry. *The Young Tennis Player.* London: Angus & Robertson, 1981.

Yannick Noah

Born: May 18, 1960
      Sedan, Ardennes, France
Also known as: Yannick Simon Camille Noah
  (full name)

Early Life

Yannick Simon Camille Noah was born on May 18, 1960, in Sedan, France, to athletic parents—a Caucasian French mother, who was a basketball player, and a black father, who was a professional soccer player from Cameroon. When Yannick was two years old, the family relocated to Africa, where Yannick began playing tennis. At the age of eleven, he met Arthur Ashe, the great African American tennis player, who was in Cameroon conducting clinics for African youngsters. Ashe was impressed with Yannick's abilities and arranged for him to return to France to receive quality instruction in a top-rated French Tennis Federation facility.

The Road to Excellence

Yannick grew to be 6 feet 4 inches tall with a slim, powerful, athletic build. He became, after Ashe, the second-best male tennis player of African descent in history. However, the two players were completely different in demeanor and their approaches to the game. Whereas Ashe was quiet, studious, hardworking, and focused, Yannick was flamboyant and fun-loving. Often, he did not take his obligation as a professional athlete seriously. He smoked and drank, liked to party, and sometimes neglected to practice. He did not seem to mind if he won a tournament or not.

After moving back to France, Yannick developed into a top junior player. In 1977, he turned professional and had immediate success. He won some titles, and his rankings began to rise. Like many professional players trained in Europe, Yannick became a "clay-court specialist." Tennis is played on a variety of surfaces—grass, clay, carpet, and several types of "hard-court" materials such as asphalt. Clay is the surface of choice in many European and South American countries, and many players from those regions perform best on clay courts. By contrast, players from the United States rarely play on clay and are traditionally more comfortable on hard courts and other surfaces.

The Emerging Champion

In 1983, Yannick won the singles title at the French Open. This tournament is one of four designated "major" events that collectively make up the tennis

Yannick Noah at the 1983 French Open. (Dominique Faget/AFP/ Getty Images)

world's Grand Slam. The other Grand Slam events are the U.S. Open, the Australian Open, and Wimbledon. The French Open is the only one of the four Grand Slam tournaments played on clay. When Yannick won the event, he not only became the second black male player to win a Grand Slam singles event but also became an instant hero in France. As of 2008, he was the last Frenchman to win the French Open.

As his career progressed, Yannick experienced the ups and downs common to all athletes. His rankings soared to career-high number three in the world in singles and number one in doubles. He won several other titles, including the 1984 French Open men's doubles crown. However, he never won another Grand Slam singles tournament. Moreover, he was often plagued by injuries that kept him from playing competitively for months at a time. Finally, he retired in 1991. He recorded twenty-three singles and sixteen doubles Association of Tennis Professionals (ATP) victories over the course of his career. These numbers are impressive but not spectacular. Nevertheless, Yannick was voted into the International Tennis Hall of Fame in 2005.

Continuing the Story

Retiring from playing tennis did not, however, end Yannick's involvement in the sport. He became the

Association of Tennis Professionals Singles Victories

Year	Tournament
1978	Manila
	Indian Open
1979	Lorraine Open
	ATP Bordeaux, France
1981	Richmond World Championship Tennis
	ATP Nice, France
1982	Indian Wells Masters
	Davidoff Swiss Indoors
	Adidas Open of Toulouse
	Hamburg Masters
	French Open
1985	Rome Masters
	Legg Mason Tennis Classic
	Adidas Open of Toulouse
1986	ATP Forest Hills
	Wembley Championship
1987	Grand Prix of Lyon
	Davidoff Swiss Indoors
1988	Lombardi International
1990	N.S.W. Open/Medibank International

Association of Tennis Professionals Doubles Victories

Year	Tournament	Partner
1981	ATP Nice	Pascal Portes
	Paribas Masters	Ilie Năstase
1982	ATP Nice	Henri Leconte
	Davidoff Swiss Indoors	Leconte
1984	French Open	Leconte
1986	Monte Carlo Masters	Guy Forget
	Rome Masters	Forget
	Davidoff Swiss Indoors	Forget
1987	Grand Prix of Lyon	Forget
	Indian Wells Masters	Forget
	ATP Forest Hills	Forget
	Rome Masters	Forget
	Queen's Club Championships	Forget
1988	Verizon Tennis Challenge	Forget
1990	ATP Nice	Alberto Mancini

coach of both the French men's and the French women's national teams. These squads compete in international competition on an annual basis for the Davis Cup (men) and the Federation Cup (women). Yannick coached the men's team to Davis Cup wins in 1991 and 1996. He then coached the women's team to the Federation Cup in 1997. Such success in both men's and women's tennis is extremely rare for any coach.

In addition to coaching, Yannick enjoyed a dynamic musical career as a reggae and pop singer. He wrote much of his own material, including songs about love, war, politics, and his mixed racial heritage. Yannick issued several recordings in the 1990's and 2000's that were extremely popular in France and also sold well in other countries. Several of his songs have been on the French music charts and have received much airplay on radio stations. Yannick has also played concerts for large and enthusiastic audiences. Many of his young fans are surprised to learn that he was once a great tennis player.

Yannick also enjoyed renewed popularity in the United States, where he maintained a residence, in large part because of the exploits of his son Joakim, who is a basketball player. After leading the University of Florida to National Collegiate Athletic Association championships in 2006 and 2007, Joakim joined the National Basketball Association as a center for the Chicago Bulls.

Summary

Yannick Noah's tennis career was significant because he won several tournaments, and he was a highly ranked player for several years. His win in the 1983 French Open made him the second man of African descent to win a Grand Slam singles title. He was subsequently catapulted to an iconic status in France as one of the few Frenchmen to win that country's premier tennis event.

Roger D. Hardaway

Additional Sources

Fein, Paul. "Noah's Arc: Yannick Noah Discusses Life on the Twentieth Anniversary of His French Open Win." *Tennis Week*, May 2, 2003.

Kaplan, James. "Yannick Noah, with No Strings Attached." *Esquire* 106, no. 3 (September, 1986).

"Noah, Yannick." In *Current Biography Yearbook 1987.* New York: H. W. Wilson Company, 1988.

Jana Novotná

Born: October 2, 1968
    Brno, Czechoslovakia (now in Czech
    Republic)

Early Life

Jana Novotná was born October 2, 1968, in Brno, Czechoslovakia (now in Czech Republic). When Jana was still a youngster, she was absorbed into the Soviet-influenced, state-sponsored tennis program centered in Přerov, in the region of Moravia. Under the guidelines of the program, experienced coaches visited primary schools to select athletically gifted boys and girls. The most talented children began play with wooden rackets while learning fundamentals. Then, they perfected their techniques before progressing to competition at organized national events staged throughout the country. Jana was one of those chosen children, and she was groomed at the youth training center and at the top-level sports center. At each facility, she strengthened her playing skills and gained

Jana Novotná preparing to backhand the ball. (Stan Honda/AFP/Getty Images)

conditioning through a rigorous athletic regimen that included considerable indoor tennis playing, swimming, hiking, skiing, and other vigorous physical exercise.

The Road to Excellence

A seasoned international competitor from the age of fourteen, Jana had grown to a solid, athletic 5 feet 9 inches and was well prepared to turn professional in 1986. During the early years of her professional career, she gained a reputation as a dynamic serve-and-volley player and was better known for her prowess in doubles matches than as a singles player.

However, playing on the International Tennis Federation (ITF) circuit, Jana gained her first triumphs in singles tournaments, winning in Chicago and Italy in 1986. Those represented her only singles victories for several years, as she concentrated on her doubles game. In 1987, the year she joined the Czech Federation Cup team—with which she played from 1987 to 1993 and from 1995 to 1998, helping her team win the tournament in the latter year—she partnered with German Claudia Kohde-Kilsch to win her first significant doubles tournament in Hamburg, Germany. Later that year, she teamed with Frenchwoman Catherine Suire to win doubles titles in Strasbourg, France, and San Diego, California. Over her career, Jana played with doubles partners from around the globe, including Denmark, Puerto Rico, Ukraine, Spain, the United States, the Netherlands, South Africa, Russia, and Canada. She achieved most of her success with Czechs Helena Suková and Martina Hingis and with Spaniard Arantxa Sanchez-Vicario. In 1988, she won a silver medal in doubles tennis at the

Summer Olympics and was poised to make a lasting mark in women's tennis.

The Emerging Champion

In 1989, teaming with Suková, Jana won her first Grand Slam title, taking the women's doubles championship at Wimbledon. With the same partner, she captured six doubles crowns that year on the Women's Tennis Association (WTA) Tour. The following year was even better, as the Novotná-Suková pairing produced nine tour victories, including Grand Slam wins at the Australian Open, French Open, and Wimbledon.

Jana, meanwhile, under the tutorship of fellow Czech Hana Mandlíková, a four-time Grand Slam singles champion, was greatly improving her solo game. In 1991, she reached her first Grand Slam singles final at the Australian Open but lost to Monica Seles in three sets. Two years later, she was ready to try again, reaching the women's singles final at Wimbledon. Facing off against Steffi Graf, Jana played well enough to gain a seemingly insurmountable lead in the third and final set. However, her nerves affected her: She lost five consecutive games and the title to Graf. At the award ceremony, she burst into tears, heartbroken at her failure.

Jana continued to perform well in WTA singles and doubles tournaments and in other venues. She won doubles championships at the 1994 U.S. Open, the 1995 Australian Open, and 1995 Wimbledon with Sanchez-Vicario. She paired with Lindsay Davenport to win the 1997 U.S. Open. She earned a bronze medal in singles and a silver medal in doubles at the 1996 Olympics. However, she did not reach a Grand Slam singles final again until 1997. Once more she failed, losing to Hingis. Jana bounced back to capture the WTA Tour singles championship and ended the year ranked number two in the world in singles.

Continuing the Story

The year 1998 was one of Jana's best. After reaching the finals or semifinals in Grand Slam singles events without success five previous times, she played into the finals at Wimbledon once again. She handily beat Venus Williams in the quarterfinals, topped Hingis in the semifinals, and beat Nathalie Tauziat in straight sets to claim the women's singles championship. At the age of twenty-nine, she became the oldest first-time

Grand Slam Results

1989 Wimbledon doubles (with Helena Suková)
1990 Australian Open doubles (with Suková)
     French Open doubles (with Suková)
     Wimbledon doubles (with Suková)
     U.S. Open doubles finalist (with Suková)
1991 French Open doubles (with Gigi Fernandez)
     Australian Open singles finalist
     Australian Open doubles finalist (with Fernandez)
     Wimbledon doubles finalist (with Fernandez)
     U.S. Open doubles finalist (with Larisa Neiland)
1992 Wimbledon doubles finalist (with Neiland)
     U.S. Open doubles finalist (with Neiland)
1993 Wimbledon singles finalist
     French Open doubles finalist (with Neiland)
     Wimbledon doubles finalist (with Neiland)
1994 U.S. Open doubles (with Arantxa Sanchez-Vicario)
     French Open doubles finalist (with Sanchez-Vicario)
     Wimbledon doubles finalist (with Sanchez-Vicario)
1995 Australian Open doubles (with Sanchez-Vicario)
     Wimbledon doubles (with Sanchez-Vicario)
1996 U.S. Open doubles finalist (with Sanchez-Vicario)
1997 Wimbledon singles finalist
     U.S. Open doubles (with Lindsay Davenport)
1998 Wimbledon singles
     French Open doubles (with Martina Hingis)
     Wimbledon doubles (with Hingis)
     U.S. Open doubles (with Hingis)

Grand Slam singles winner during the open era. That year, she also took doubles titles at Wimbledon, the French Open, and the U.S. Open.

At the end of the 1999 season, Jana retired from professional tennis. She had won a total of one hundred titles, twenty-four in singles and seventy-six in doubles—including twelve Grand Slam doubles championships—on all four surfaces: hard, clay, carpet, and grass. During her twelve-year career, she was ranked the number-one doubles player in the world eleven times and amassed more than $11.2 million in prize money. She compiled a 571-225 record as a singles player and a 697-153 record as a doubles player. One of the few openly lesbian players on the WTA circuit, Jana was inducted into the International Tennis Hall of Fame in 2005. The following year, she gained American citizenship.

Jana, who began living in Highland Beach, Florida, in the mid-1990's, continued to play tennis for charitable events. She appeared in the 2008 Liverpool Tennis Tournament and the 2008 World Team Tennis Smash Hits event, which benefited the Elton John AIDS Foundation and the Atlanta AIDS Partnership Fund.

Summary

One of the best women's singles and doubles players in the world between the late 1980's and late 1990's, Jana Novotná captured one hundred titles during a twelve-year professional career, including thirteen Grand Slam events. Winner of more than $11 million in prize money, the hard-serving Jana triumphed at four Wimbledon, two Australian Open, three French Open, and three U.S. Open doubles championships, and won the 1998 Wimbledon singles title.

Jack Ewing

Additional Sources

Cashmore, Ernest. *Sport Psychology: The Key Concepts*. Champaign, Ill.: Sports, 2002.

Conner, Floyd. *Tennis's Most Wanted: The Top Ten Book of Baseline Blunders, Clay Court Wonders, and Lucky Lobs*. Dulles, Va.: Potomac Books, 2002.

Miller, Toby. *Sportsex*. Philadelphia: Temple University Press, 2002.

Moran, Greg. *Tennis Beyond Big Shots*. Austin, Tex.: Mansion Grove House, 2006.

Alex Olmedo

Born: March 24, 1936
    Arequipa, Peru
Also known as: Luis Alejandro Rodríguez
    Olmedo (full name); Chief

Early Life

Luis Alejandro "Alex" Rodríguez Olmedo was born into an impoverished family on March 24, 1936, in Arequipa, Peru's second-largest city, which is located near the country's southern border. An excellent athlete even as a child, Alex, at the age of nine, borrowed his father's old tennis racket and began to practice tennis by hitting balls for hours each day. By the time he was seventeen, Alex had grown to 6 feet 1 inch, exhibited exceptional agility, and showed great potential in the sport to which he had devoted so much time.

The Road to Excellence

Arequipa offered little in the way of tennis competition for Alex. He desired to head north to the United States to refine his rough athletic skills, but his family was unable to finance such a trip. Luckily for Alex, he had impressed many sports fans with his determination to succeed. Local citizens pooled their money to help Alex realize his dream. In 1954, with the equivalent of $700 in contributions in hand, he boarded a boat and sailed to Havana, Cuba. From Havana, he flew to Miami, Florida. He rode a bus cross-country from Miami to Los Angeles, California.

In Los Angeles, Alex got a day job at a tennis shop. At night, he studied English at the University of Southern California (USC) while working to earn a degree in business. He also found time to play tennis on the Trojans' team. In 1956, Alex—nicknamed "Chief" for his tall and slender physique, his stoic countenance, and a profile reminiscent of ancient Incan leaders—won the National Collegiate Athletic Association (NCAA) singles championship. With a teammate, he also captured the NCAA doubles championship that year. USC was declared ineligible to compete for the championships in 1957, but in 1958, Alex returned to repeat as dual NCAA tennis champion before graduating with his degree.

The Emerging Champion

In 1958, U.S. Davis Cup team captain Perry Jones selected Alex to represent the United States for the major international team event in men's amateur tennis, which pits the world's best national teams against one another. Objections were raised because Alex had been born in Peru. However, because he had lived in the United States for more than three consecutive years and because Peru had no national tennis team, he was approved for the competition.

At the 1958 Davis Cup, Alex dominated with a powerful serve. He beat Italy's Nicola Pietrangeli in a semifinal match. In the finals, he won two singles matches, against Mal Anderson and Ashley Cooper, and teamed with Ham Richardson in a victorious doubles match to lead the United States to the championship against a strong Australian team.

The following year, Alex ascended to the number-one ranking in men's tennis. He began the year 1959 by winning U.S. indoor singles and doubles titles. Then, he captured the Australian Open Tennis Championship, besting Neale Fraser in four sets. Finally, he swept to victory at Wimbledon, beating Australian Rod Laver in straight sets to claim the prestigious singles title. In the process, he became the first Latin American to achieve such a feat. Two weeks prior to the 1959 Davis Cup, Alex was a finalist at the 1959 U.S. Men's Clay Court Championships. In a lackluster performance he lost in

---

Awards and Milestones

1956, 1958	NCAA tennis champion (singles and doubles)
1958-59	Davis Cup team
1959	Ranked number one in the world as an amateur player
	Wimbledon singles champion
	Australian Open singles champion
	U.S. Open runner-up
1987	Inducted into International Tennis Hall of Fame
1997	Inducted into USC Athletic Hall of Fame

the championship match to Fraser, the man he had beaten at the Australian Open. The United States Lawn Tennis Association, suspecting he had thrown the match, threatened to suspend Alex. However, the Peruvian had been practicing on grass to prepare for the Davis Cup and was simply not prepared to play on the clay courts at the U.S. Open. The additional competition tired Alex, and though he won a singles match at the Davis Cup, Australia won the trophy. The media pointed unfairly at Alex as the cause of the U.S. failure to retain the championship.

Continuing the Story

In 1960, Alex turned professional and began touring with other tennis stars, including Pancho Gonzales, Ken Rosewall, Pancho Segura, Lew Hoad, Laver, and Tony Trabert. He also married and fathered four children: Amy—who won the U.S. Public Parks Tennis Championship as a twelve-year-old—Angela, Alex, and David.

In 1965, Alex retired from competition and was hired as the teaching professional at the upscale Beverly Hills Hotel and Bungalows where he continued to teach more than forty years later. During his tenure at the hotel, Alex gave lessons to many celebrities, assisting such entertainers as Katharine Hepburn, Robert Duvall, and Chevy Chase in improving their serves, strengthening their backhands, and solidifying their forehands. His son David became an assistant professional at the same facility.

In 1986, in recognition of his accomplishments, Alex was enshrined in the International Tennis Hall of Fame in Newport, Rhode Island, alongside other tennis greats inducted that year: Billie Jean King, Stan Smith, and Björn Borg. Alex was also inducted into the USC Athletic Hall of Fame.

Summary

The first Latin American to win a singles tennis title at Wimbledon, the hard serving, lightning-quick Peruvian Alex Olmedo shone brightly during a brief, whirlwind amateur career representing the United States. He won NCAA singles and doubles titles twice while at USC and led the U.S. Davis Cup team to victory in 1958. In a single year, 1959, he triumphed in singles and doubles at the U.S. indoor championships, won the men's singles at the Australian Open and at Wimbledon, and was runner-up at the U.S. Open before turning professional.

Jack Ewing

Additional Sources

Barrett, John. *Wimbledon: The Official History of the Championships.* Glasgow, Scotland: HarperCollins, 2001.

Collins, Bud. *The Bud Collins History of Tennis: An Authoritative Encyclopedia and Record Book.* New York: New Chapter Press, 2008.

Fein, Paul. *Tennis Confidential: Today's Greatest Players, Matches, and Controversies.* Dulles, Va.: Potomac Books, 2002.

Fred Perry

Born: May 18, 1909
        Stockport, Cheshire, England
Died: February 2, 1995
        Melbourne, Victoria, Australia
Also known as: Frederick John Perry (full name)

Early Life

Frederick John Perry was born on May 18, 1909, in Stockport, Cheshire, England. His father, S. J. Perry, was a businessman who enjoyed tennis and was responsible for Fred's introduction to the game at the Brentham Garden Suburb Club. Fred was impressed by the number of expensive automobiles parked on the club's premises and once asked his father who owned them. "The tennis players," his father replied.

Fred soon became an avid tennis player. He entered an arrangement with his school friends in which he would play goal for their football practice if, in return, they would feed him returns on the tennis courts so he could practice his shots. The boy spent endless afternoons hitting balls against the backboard to improve his strokes. Long before Fred attracted attention as a tennis player, he became England's champion in table tennis, a sport that may have helped him in some ways.

The Road to Excellence

Fred had one problem as a budding tennis player. He was somewhat handicapped by his continental grip, which allowed him to handle any shot without changing grip. Such a grip, however, in which the hand rests on top of the racket rather than on the side, lacks stability and power of thrust. Fred overcame this by strengthening his wrist until it resembled, as some said, a tree trunk. Before long, his wrist became so mighty and flexible that it was called "the wrist of champions."

By the mid-1920's, Fred had played well enough to reach the doubles final of the Middlesex championships, where he was noticed by a Slazenger company executive.

Known as Pops Summers, this tournament official was impressed by the boy's energy and reaction time. He decided that with Fred's speed and quick reactions, he could be far more successful were he to take the ball on the rise.

Fred quickly agreed with this theory and soon he was bounding toward the net, taking the ball on the rise and blistering it with his tough wrist. Here, his expertise in table tennis stood him well, since it is a game in which the ball is whacked as it rises from the table. Fred worked on his forehand until he was able to deliver it with whiplike power. As a result, he developed one of the finest running forehands ever.

The Emerging Champion

It took a while for members of the British Lawn Tennis Association to recognize the potential in

Englishman Fred Perry, who completed a career Grand Slam in 1935. (Courtesy of International Tennis Hall of Fame)

Major Championship Victories and Finals

1932	Wimbledon doubles finalist (with George Pat Hughes)
	French Championship mixed doubles (with Betty Nuthall)
	U.S. National Championship mixed doubles (with Sarah Palfrey)
1933	French Championship doubles (with Hughes)
1933-34, 1936	U.S. National Championship
1934	Australian Championship
	Australian Championship doubles (with Hughes)
1934-36	Wimbledon
1935	French Championship
	Australian Championship finalist
	Australian Championship doubles finalist (with Hughes)
1935-36	Wimbledon mixed doubles (with Dorothy Round)

Other Notable Victories

1932	British Hardcourt Championship
1933-36	On winning British Davis Cup team
1934	New Zealand Championship
1938, 1940-41	U.S. Pro Championship doubles (with Vincent Richards and Don Budge)
1938, 1941	U.S. Pro Championship
1948-49	Professional World Doubles Tournament (with Budge)

Fred's unorthodox techniques. In 1930, however, the young man played against Bunny Austin in the British final and took the game to match point before finally losing. Two months later at Wimbledon, he reached the Round of 16 in the tournament. Finally, the association decided to send him with the British team as it toured the United States, Argentina, Chile, Brazil, and Uruguay. Fred did not let the team down. He reached the Round of 16 at Forest Hills and won the Argentinian Championship.

The following year, Fred teamed up with Austin to beat the Americans in the round leading to the Davis Cup final. France, however, won the trophy in the end. By 1932, Fred had still not come into his own. He figured out that his backhand was in need of remedy, so he spent endless hours on the practice court. He transformed his backhand until it was equal to his forehand—with the same cocked wrist, the same short, quick strokes. In the next year's Davis Cup play, Fred, with his strengthened backhand, was ready to take on and beat Henri Cochet, the French winner who had beaten him

previously. The match was so strenuous that Fred fainted at the end. Still not physically recovered during the finals, Fred had to draw on all of his experience to win Britain's first Davis Cup victory since 1912.

Fred then went on to win the Wimbledon championship three years in a row and the U.S. National Championship in 1933, 1934, and 1936. In the next three years, he and Austin repeatedly won the highest international team awards. Fred also won the Australian Championship in 1934 and the French Championship in 1935. In fact, over that four-year span, he won everything possible.

Continuing the Story

Fred's personal magnetism lit up the court. He was a debonair champion, always acting the role of the English gentleman—although his gin and tonics never held gin, his pipes no tobacco. He was a showman by nature. His style on the courts had flair—an on-the-go quickness even between points. Often his opponents had to ask the umpire for time between Fred's serves to slow him down. If the rest of Fred's game had matched the quality of his howitzer-like forehand, he would have been more than a compelling player; he would have been unbeatable.

The success he did achieve, however, made him an international celebrity. He married actress Helen Vinson in Hollywood and thought about pursuing a film career. When he finally decided to give up his amateur status in return for the payoffs of professionalism, he signed up for a tour of the United States and Canada with Ellsworth Vines as his opponent.

Eventually, Fred became a commentator for newspaper, radio, and television in the United

Honors, Awards, and Milestones

1931-36	British Davis Cup team
1934-36	Ranked number one in the world
1975	Inducted into National Lawn Tennis Hall of Fame

States, on the European continent, and for the British Broadcasting Corporation (BBC) in England. He then became a successful businessman, like the French champion René Lacoste. Both stars came out with their own lines of tennis clothing, complete with designer emblems. Lacoste's signature was the Lacoste crocodile; Perry's, the laurel wreath.

Summary

In 1934, Fred Perry became the first Englishman to win Wimbledon in a quarter-century. From 1936 until 1976, he was the only player to win Wimbledon three years in succession. The same three years, he also won the U.S. National Championship (now U.S. Open). In fact, from 1933 to 1936, Fred experienced a winning streak that has rarely been matched.

Nan White

Additional Sources

Parsons, John. *The Ultimate Encyclopedia of Tennis: The Definitive Illustrated Guide to World Tennis.* London: Carlton, 2006.

Perry, Fred. *Fred Perry: An Autobiography.* London: Hutchinson, 1984.

Shippey, Kim. "In the Press Box with Tennis Great Fred Perry." *Christian Science Monitor* 87, no. 147 (June 26, 1995): 13.

Torkells, Erik. "Advantage Fred Perry." *Fortune* 146, no. 6 (September 30, 2002): 192.

Mary Pierce

Born: January 15, 1975
      Montreal, Quebec, Canada
Also known as: Mary Caroline Pierce (full name)

Early Life

The daughter of Jim and Yannick Pierce, Mary Caroline Pierce was born on January 15, 1975, in Montreal, Canada. The Pierces later moved to Florida, living in the St. Petersburg area. When Mary was ten years old, she asked her father to teach her to play tennis, quickly demonstrating her skill with a racket. Jim Pierce ambitiously secured coaches, including Australian Davis Cup captain Harry Hopman, and withdrew his daughter from school so she had the opportunity to compete in junior matches. Mary soon advanced to more challenging competition.

The Road to Excellence

In March, 1989, at Hilton Head, South Carolina, Mary, at the age of fourteen, began playing on the professional tennis circuit. At the time, she was the youngest American professional player ever. The elegant, attractive blond quickly gained admiring fans who called her "the Body" because of her sleek, toned physique. Mary's powerful moves on the court earned her victories and respect from her opponents and crowds. Off the court, the photogenic Mary posed for magazine covers and endorsed fashions. She became a sensational teenage tennis star.

Despite his daughter's athletic accomplishments, Mary's father, who considered himself her primary coach, was verbally and physically aggressive, confronting her publicly during games. These dramatic interludes increased existing pressures from which she suffered. Mary reacted to stress by losing self-confidence and becoming panicky during matches, attempting to control her erratic responses to her father's assaults. Most media coverage of Mary's tennis activity profiled her conflicts with her father instead of her performances. In 1990, to appease her father, Mary attained French citizenship so she could play tennis with the French Federation Cup teams. In 1992 and 1996, she played for French Olympic teams.

The Emerging Champion

At the 1993 Virginia Slims championships, Mary defeated Argentine Gabriela Sabatini during the first round, representing the first time that Mary beat a top-ten player. She then won in a quarterfinal match against number-three-ranked Martina Navratilova. During the 1993 French Open, Mary was temporarily relieved of her father's emotional interference. The Women's Tennis Association (WTA) banned him from attending matches for

Mary Pierce serving at the 2006 Acura Classic. (AP/Wide World Photos)

one year after he choked Mary's cousin in the stands. Mary terminated her coaching relationship with her father, and he followed her throughout Europe, threatening to interfere with her tournament play. Mary acquired restraining orders and bodyguards for protection.

In the fall of 1993, Mary underwent intensive training with Nick Bollettieri, who focused on enhancing her fitness through diet and exercise. She mastered techniques to correct her weaknesses, such as improving her ability to achieve complete coverage of the tennis court during matches. Using Bollettieri's strategy, she confidently hit the ball hard and played to her physical abilities instead of responding emotionally to opponents. Mary learned to concentrate and remain calm.

Mary's disciplined approach helped her reach the finals of the 1994 French Open, where she lost to Arantxa Sanchez-Vicario after defeating Steffi Graf in the semifinals. In 1995, Mary won her first Grand Slam title at the Australian Open. She played in the mixed-doubles semifinals at the 1995 U.S. Open and attained her highest individual ranking as the number-three female player that summer. Her play ranked her among the top seven female players in the world each year of the 1990's except 1996. Mary was also a member of the victorious 1997 French Federation Cup team.

Continuing the Story

After heated disagreements, Mary and Bollettieri stopped training together. Despite her international acclaim, Mary struggled for fan acceptance in the United States. She reached three consecutive finals at the Bausch & Lomb Championships held on Amelia Island, Florida. The crowd, however, was not supportive of Mary, cheering for her opponents. Former tennis star Pam Shriver, working as an ESPN tennis analyst, suggested that Mary's aloof and agitated behavior during games

---

Major Championships

1995	Australian Open singles	2000	Family Circle Cup singles
1997	Italian Open singles		French Open singles
	Federation Cup		French Open doubles
1998	Paris Indoors singles	2003	Federation Cup
	Amelia Island singles	2004	Ordina Open
	Amelia Island doubles	2005	Acura Classic
1999	Canadian Open doubles		French Open doubles

---

repelled fans. They disliked how Mary delayed game action by asking for time between points for breaks. Also, even when she was winning, Mary appeared discontented and defensive, alienating others with her depressive bouts.

An erratic player, Mary reached the finals of one tournament only to be swiftly eliminated in the next match. In an attempt to increase her strength, quicken her responses, and improve her consistency to counter powerful teenage competitors, Mary began using creatine, a nutritional supplement that strengthened baseball players such as Mark McGwire. She also underwent laser eye surgery. In July, 1998, Michael de Jongh began coaching her, enhancing her strategy to use her powerful serves—sometimes as fast as 110 miles per hour—and intense forehands to outperform her opponents.

Mary's trainer Mark Verstegen, who operated the International Performance Institute at Bradenton, Florida, oversaw a rigorous 12-hour cross-training workout, incorporating swimming and weightlifting, to prepare Mary physically for Wimbledon and other world-class tournaments. A more muscular Mary rose in rank among international female tennis players from twenty-fifth at the beginning of 1997 to seventh, a rank she retained through 1999. In that year, she played in the Australian Open finals.

In 2000, Mary reconciled with her father, training with him in Florida. Her brother David was her regular coach until 2006. She won the Family Circle Cup in April, 2000, setting a record for losing the fewest games. Mary triumphed in the 2000 French Open, winning her second Grand Slam singles title and her first Grand Slam doubles title. She defeated Conchita Martinez to become the first French woman to win the French Open since Françoise Durr in 1967. She partnered with Martina Hingis to win the French Open doubles crown. In

---

Honors and Awards

1992	France's (rising star) Burgeon Award
1992, 1996	French Olympic team
1997	WTA Comeback Player of the Year Award
	Chase Champion for May

2003, Mary helped France win the Federation Cup.

In 2005, Mary exhibited flashes of her former ability in Grand Slam competitions, losing the French Open to Justine Henin in the championship match and the U.S. Open final to Kim Clijsters. At Wimbledon, Mary teamed with Mahesh Bhupathi to win the mixed-doubles final. Mary capped her 2005 successes by winning the Kremlin Cup in Moscow, making her eligible for the WTA Tour Championships in Los Angeles. Her ranking at the end of the year was fifth, up from twenty-ninth at the year's start. At thirty years of age, Mary was having as strong a year as she had ten years prior. She trained hard over the off-season, and she anticipated improving her level of performance in the coming year. However, Mary's career had always been up and down, great achievements followed closely by crushing setbacks. The year 2006 was one of Mary's worst campaigns.

Foot and groin injuries forced Mary to withdraw from both the French Open and Wimbledon in 2006. After six months of therapy and recuperation, Mary returned to the tour in San Diego, where she lost to Maria Sharapova in the quarterfinals at the Acura Classic. In her next tournament, the U.S. Open, Mary lost in the third round to Na Li of China. In October, 2006, Mary experienced the greatest setback of her career: She ruptured the anterior cruciate ligament in her left knee while competing at Linz, Austria. After successful surgery in December, Mary missed the entire 2007 campaign. However, she was in attendance for the 2007 French Open when an avenue at Roland Garros was named in her honor: Allée Mary Pierce.

Summary

Despite her victories and contributions to women's tennis, including eighteen WTA Tour tournament wins and ten doubles titles, Mary Pierce was better known for withstanding emotional abuse, inner conflicts, and recovering from injuries than for her efforts to succeed at her sport. The mainstream press focused on her volatile family life, and tennis commentators pondered the fate of her professional career. Mary seemed torn, trying to find her role in tennis, in her family, and in the world. Born in Canada, with dual citizenship in France and United States, Mary often seemed to be trying to please her diverse fans, her friends, and her family while playing championship caliber tennis.

Elizabeth D. Schafer, updated by Randy L. Abbott

Additional Sources

Bricker, Charles. "Bad Dad? Pierce's Father Says He Was Trying to Push Her Along." *St. Louis Post-Dispatch*, September 26, 1993, p. 12F.

Gerber, Suzanne. "How a Tennis Star Overcame Her Troubled Past." *Redbook*, September 1, 1995, 52-53.

Jenkins, Sally. "Beauty and Baldy: Mary Pierce, Who Shed Her Cares, and Andre Agassi, Who Shed His Hair, Came up Big Down Under." *Sports Illustrated* 82, no. 5 (February 6, 1995): 46-51.

Wertheim, L. Jon. "Finally, Signs of a Comeback." *Sports Illustrated* 101, no. 10 (September 13, 2004): 63-64.

_____. "Hail Tennis Mary." *Sports Illustrated* 92, no. 25 (June 19, 2000) 48-50.

Bobby Riggs

Born: February 25, 1918
     Los Angeles, California
Died: October 25, 1995
     Leucadia, California
Also known as: Robert Larimore Riggs (full
  name)

Early Life

Robert Larimore "Bobby" Riggs was born in Los
Angeles on February 25, 1918. Bobby was the youngest of seven children, six of whom were boys.

Bobby Riggs at Wimbledon in 1939. (AP/Wide World Photos)

Bobby's father, who had enjoyed sports as a young
man, was a minister in the Church of Christ.
Bobby's competitions with his older brothers and
friends instilled a desire early on to participate in
various sports and excel. With Southern California's year-round dry climate and his family's support, Bobby eventually developed a special interest
in tennis, sparked when his brother John tried out
for the high school team. At the age of twelve, with
a borrowed racket, Bobby looked like a natural on
the court and soon caught the eye of Dr. Esther
Bartosh, a local tennis enthusiast. She
gave Bobby his first formal lessons and
helped him develop the baseline style
of play that paved the way for his future
success.

The Road to Excellence

Bobby's first tournament win came just
a few months after he began formal instruction in the finer points of the game
under Bartosh. Within two years he
was the top player in his age-group in
Southern California. Bobby built a reputation for winning matches by keeping the ball in play until his opponent
made an error. This required great
footwork, agility, and endurance; his
matches often lasted a long time. While
many other players simply served and
volleyed, Bobby's style was unique but
effective. He won the California High
School Championships from 1932
to 1934, the National Boys' Doubles
Championships in 1933, and his first
National Boys' Singles Championships
in 1935.

These successes on the court were
often met by disappointments off the
court. Bobby felt that the tennis establishment in California did not support
him because of his middle-class family
background, his 5-foot-7-inch stature,
and his unorthodox style of play. However, in 1936, at the age of eighteen,

Major Championships

1939	Wimbledon singles	1941	U.S. National singles
	Wimbledon doubles	1945	World Hardcourt men's singles
	Wimbledon mixed doubles	1946	U.S. Professional men's singles
	U.S. National singles	1947	U.S. Professional men's singles
1940	U.S. National mixed doubles	1970	Wimbledon senior men's doubles

Bobby was ranked fourth in the United States in amateur tennis. After enrolling for a semester at the University of Miami, he returned to California to focus on his tennis career. He continued to refine his style of play, which he later referred to as "airtight tennis": playing for high-percentage shots, varying the pace and spin on the ball, and playing intelligently with the score in mind.

The Emerging Champion

In 1937, Bobby was the second-ranked amateur tennis player in the United States. Normally, this would have meant favored treatment by all tennis associations and an automatic spot on the prestigious U.S. Davis Cup team. While he was invited to practice with the team, he was not selected. Bobby's disappointment turned into an even greater determination to prove beyond doubt that he deserved a spot on the 1938 team.

The following three years established a part of his legacy, as he won the deciding match in the 1938 Davis Cup victory over Australia; the 1939 Wimbledon Championships in singles, doubles, and mixed doubles; and the 1939 and 1941 National Singles Championships at Forest Hills, New York. In 1939, he was considered the top-ranked amateur tennis player in the world. His three championships at Wimbledon that year were especially noteworthy because no first-time player had accomplished that before.

Professional tennis players earned their salaries through exhibitions and circuit play, but amateurs like Bobby received only expense money and had few additional incentives to compete. For some time, Bobby felt his confidence and motivation to succeed were enhanced by wagering on himself. During the 1939 Wimbledon championships, he supplemented his expense money with $108,000 in winnings from bets he made on his winning the three titles.

On December 9, 1939, Bobby married Catherine Fischer of Chicago during a tennis tournament. Even though he was employed by the U.S. Advertising Corporation and later, Presbyterian College, his primary and consistent income was generated by his wagers, which he won with steady consistency, until he turned professional in late 1941. World War II interrupted his formal career, though he did play a little while in the Navy. In 1946 and 1947, he returned to competitive tennis to win the U.S. Professional Championships. His trademark style of play carried him until the age of thirty-two, when he began to taper off his competitive play and turned his energies to promoting tennis and baseball events.

Continuing the Story

As Bobby's tennis career declined, so did his marriage to Catherine. In 1952, following their divorce, Bobby married Priscilla Wheeler, whom he later divorced, and turned his sporting interests to golf. Without a lesson, capitalizing on his innate athletic ability and hard work, he became a three-handicap player. Bobby continued to enjoy the challenge of proving himself when something of value was wagered, adding to his reputation as a fierce but fair competitor. A winner of several paddle-tennis titles, Bobby had not gotten the racket sports out of his system and returned to tennis with the advent of open tennis in 1968, when professionals and amateurs competed together in the same tournaments. He captured the 1970 Wimbledon senior doubles title, thirty-one years after winning his first Wimbledon title.

Ever the flamboyant self-promoter, Bobby introduced himself to a new generation in 1973. Feeling that senior men's tennis players were superior to women's tennis players, and deserving of more attention and earnings, Bobby issued an open challenge to all women to play him. Margaret Court Smith was the first to accept his challenge; she lost to Riggs in straight sets. However, on September 20, 1973, before a Houston Astrodome crowd of thirty thousand and a television audience estimated at more than fifty million viewers, Bobby lost the famed "Battle of the Sexes" to Billie Jean King in straight sets. To many observers, this match symbolized significant progress in recognizing women's accomplishments and redefined athletic status.

Summary

In the years following the "Battle of the Sexes," Bobby Riggs added to his legacy as a player the unique role of advancing women's tennis and, consequently, women's opportunities in society. Whether intended or not, whether an example of gamesmanship or hustle, Bobby enjoyed identification with something bigger than just tennis. Likewise, his 1988 diagnosis with prostate cancer, which ultimately claimed his life at the age of seventy-seven, prompted his establishment of the Bobby Riggs Tennis Museum Foundation to promote disease awareness.

P. Graham Hatcher

Additional Sources

Drucker, Joel. "The Battles of the Sexist." *Tennis*, August, 1998, 33-35.

LeCompte, Tom. *The Last Sure Thing: The Life and Times of Bobby Riggs*. Easthampton, Mass.: Skunkworks, 2003.

Leibowitz, Ed. "Dressed to Kill." *Smithsonian* 34, no. 6 (September, 2003): 25-26.

Riggs, Bobby. *Tennis Is My Racket*. New York: Simon & Schuster, 1949.

Riggs, Bobby, and George McGann. *Court Hustler*. New York: New American Library, 1974.

Roberts, Selena. *A Necessary Spectacle: Billie Jean King, Bobby Riggs, and the Tennis Match That Leveled the Game*. New York: Crown Publishers, 2005.

Spencer, Nancy E. "Reading Between the Lines: A Discursive Analysis of the Billie Jean King Versus Bobby Riggs 'Battle of the Sexes.'" *Sociology of Sport Journal* 17, no. 4 (2000): 386-402.

Andy Roddick

Born: August 30, 1982
    Omaha, Nebraska
Also known as: Andrew Stephen Roddick (full
    name); A-Rod

Early Life

Andrew "Andy" Stephen Roddick was the youngest
of three sons born to Blanche and Jerry Roddick,
and he immediately followed in the footsteps of his
two active, older brothers. Not until his family
moved to Boca Raton, Florida, in 1987, did Andy
start playing tennis. The family had a court built in
their backyard for older sons, Lawrence and John,
to improve their game. When Lawrence became
more interested in competitive diving than tennis,
a spot opened on the court for Andy. Modeling his
game after tennis greats Jimmy Connors and Andre Agassi, at the age of ten, Andy signed a contract
with Reebok and began his play in the junior circuit.

The Road to Excellence

Andy faced challenges perfecting his game during
his teenage years because of the significant changes

Andy Roddick in 2001. (AP/Wide World Photos)

in his own height. He grew nine inches between
the ages of fifteen and seventeen. By the time he
reached his final height of 6 feet 2 inches, he had
mastered a booming serve that reached more than
120 miles per hour on a consistent basis. In 1999,
combining his serve with his improved forehand,
Andy was able to capture the Orange Bowl title, a
prestigious international tournament on the junior level.

After winning the Australian Open Junior Championship in 2000, Andy decided to become a professional tennis player with the Association of Tennis Professionals (ATP). He played in nine ATP
events in his first year and finished the year ranked
number 160 on the tour. Andy still competed in as
many junior events as he could and captured the
U.S. Open Juniors and the Sugar Bowl Classic titles. These victories earned him the overall number-one ranking on the junior tennis circuit. In
2001, in a turning point in Andy's career, he defeated Pete Sampras in the Eriksson Open, earning
his first career victory over a top-ten opponent.
Based on his performance in the Eriksson Open,
he earned a spot in the French Open. He won
his opening-round match but was defeated two rounds later. Entering the
French Open, Andy had moved up the
ATP rankings to number twenty-one.

The Emerging Champion

After winning his third professional
event in 2001 at the Legg-Mason Classic, where he broke the 140-miles-per-
hour mark with his serve, Andy became the first teenager since Michael
Chang to be ranked in the ATP's top
twenty. Andy had also become the first
player since Sampras to win three tournaments as a professional before reaching the age of twenty. He finished the
year by advancing to the third round
of the U.S. Open. He was ranked number fourteen in the world.

In 2002, Andy continued to add to
his tennis résumé. He scored wins over

emerging star James Blake in a tournament in Memphis, Tennessee, and over Sampras in Houston, Texas. Andy advanced to the quarterfinals of Wimbledon and lost at the U.S. Open to Sampras, who went on to win the championship. He also helped the American team advance to the Davis Cup semifinals. Searching for an elusive Grand Slam title, Andy appeared poised to win a major tournament in 2003, and he opened the season with a semifinal finish at the Australian Open. After a first-round exit at the French Open, Andy brought in a new coach. He made the semifinals of Wimbledon and won three hard-court titles in tournaments leading up to the 2003 U.S. Open. After a five-set victory in the semifinals of the U.S. Open, Andy beat Juan Carlos Ferrero in the final, capturing his first Grand Slam. After earning the number-one ranking in the world in 2003, Andy finished the following year ranked number two on the tour.

Continuing the Story

Andy's victory at the 2003 U.S. Open left little doubt about his ability to play with the best in the world. However, only a week after gaining the status as the number-one player in the world, Andy lost in the Paris Masters tournament, showing his need for improvement. In 2004, he reached the quarterfinals of the Australian Open, lost in the second round of the French Open, lost in five sets in the Wimbledon finals, and lost in the quarterfinals of the U.S. Open. He represented the United States in the 2004 Olympics, and in 2005, he made the final round of Wimbledon for the second year in a row. Andy continued to play top-level tennis, reaching the finals of the 2006 U.S. Open.

The success that Andy has experienced on the court coupled with his personality have allowed him to become one of the most recognizable faces on the tour. Based on this visibility, Andy gained endorsement contracts with major companies, including Lacoste and Babolat. Finding the ideal balance between on- and off-the-court success allowed Andy to maximize his athletic and business potential from multiple angles.

Summary

With one of the most feared serves in tennis and amazing crowd appeal, Andy Roddick established himself as an elite player. He has a chance to win every time he steps on the court. He emerged as one of the strongest and most passionate tennis players of the 2000's.

Deborah Stroman

Additional Sources

Annacone, Paul. "Paul's Page: Lessons from Andy Roddick." *Tennis* (June, 2008): 60.

Armentrout, David, and Patricia Armentrout. *Andy Roddick.* Vero Beach, Fla.: Rourke, 2005.

Donelson, Tom, and Beth Donelson. *Coming of Age: Andy Roddick's Breakthrough Year.* New York: iUniverse, 2004.

Gallagher, Todd. *Andy Roddick Beat Me with a Frying Pan: Taking the Field with Pro Athletes and Olympic Legends to Answer Sports Fans' Burning Questions.* New York: Three Rivers Press, 2007.

Honors and Awards

2003	Association of Tennis Professionals Player of the Year
	International Tennis Federation World Champion
2004	ESPY Award: Best Male Tennis Player
2005	Arthur Ashe Humanitarian Award

Ken Rosewall

Born: November 2, 1934
Sydney, New South Wales, Australia
Also known as: Kenneth Robert Rosewall (full name); Muscles

Early Life

Kenneth Robert Rosewall was born on November 2, 1934, in Sydney, New South Wales, Australia. He learned to play tennis from his father Robert Rosewall, who was a grocer in Sydney. Ken was a natural left-hander, but his father taught him to play right-handed. His father had learned the game by reading instruction books. He also owned a couple of clay courts behind the Rosewall residence. Ken was a good all-around athlete. He played rugby and cricket in addition to tennis. Robert Rosewall believed that his son could be a champion if he concentrated on tennis and gave up the other sports.

The Road to Excellence

Even though Ken was slight of build and not very tall, he was quick and possessed balance and extraordinary anticipation. In 1953, Harry Hopman, the legendary Australian Davis Cup team captain, chose Ken, at the age of nineteen, to be part of the team. Never a powerful player, Ken relied on precision and focus. He made his first impact on the world of tennis when he was only seventeen and participated in the 1952 U.S. National Championships at Forest Hills, New York. Ken and fellow Australian Lew Hoad both reached the quarterfinals. Ken had beaten America's number-one player, Vic Seixas, in the process. Ken stood only 5 feet 7 inches tall and weighed 135 pounds, but his craftiness and solid strokes always made him a tough opponent.

In 1953, not only did Ken and Hoad help the Australians to win the Davis Cup, but Ken also won his first two major titles by winning the Australian and French championships. He also teamed up with Hoad to capture the Australian, French, Italian, and Wimbledon titles in doubles. Ken was definitely developing into an all-court player and his even temperament was a big plus for his chances at further success. He also worked hard to improve

his volleys and smashes. His ever-increasing amount of doubles play made him stronger in all the strokes necessary to be a champion.

The Emerging Champion

Ken was coming into his own as a world-class tennis player. Hoad, his doubles partner, was also his rival for the major singles titles. They met several times after the first time they played against each other at the age of ten. They were friendly rivals, though their styles of play were very different. Hoad was a power player. In 1956, Hoad beat Ken in the finals at Wimbledon, but Ken got his revenge by turning the tables on Hoad at the U.S. National Championships. The year 1956 was Ken's last as an amateur, and, therefore, he was no longer allowed to compete for the Grand Slam titles. As a professional tennis player, Ken competed against the likes of Pancho Gonzales. In 1957, Ken married Wilma McIver. The first title that he won as a professional was the British Pro Indoor Championships for that year.

Gonzales was the star of the professional ranks, but Ken carved out a place for himself by proving to be just as tenacious as a professional as he had been as an amateur. No tennis player of his era had better ground strokes, and his backhand was considered to be one of the all-time best. In head-to-head matches, Gonzales defeated Ken 50-26, but Ken won more than his share of major professional titles: He won three U.S. Pro Championships. Consistency was one of his major strengths. Ken always gave tennis his best no matter how long the odds were against him.

Honors and Awards

1980 Inducted into International Tennis Hall of Fame
1986 William M. Johnston Award

Milestones

Australian Davis Cup team (1953-56)
Turned professional in 1957
18 Grand Slam victories in career

Major Championship Victories and Finals

1953	French Championship
	French Championship doubles (with Lew Hoad)
1953, 1955	Australian Championship
1953, 1956	Australian Championship doubles (with Hoad)
	Wimbledon doubles (with Hoad)
1954	Wimbledon mixed-doubles finalist (with Margaret Dupont)
	U.S. National Championship mixed-doubles finalist (with Dupont)
1954, 1956, 1970, 1974	Wimbledon finalist
1955	U.S. National Championship finalist
1955, 1968, 1970	Wimbledon doubles finalist (with Neale Fraser and Fred Stolle)
1956	U.S. National Championship
	U.S. National Championship doubles (with Hoad)
	U.S. National Championship mixed doubles (with Dupont)
1968	French Open
	French Open doubles (with Stolle)
1969	U.S. Open doubles (with Stolle)
1970	U.S. Open
1971-72	Australian Open
1972	Australian Open doubles (with Owen Davidson)
1974	U.S. Open finalist

Other Notable Victories

1953	Italian Championship doubles (with Hoad)
1953, 1955-56	On winning Australian Davis Cup team
1957, 1960-63	British Pro Indoor Championship
1957-58, 1960-62, 1966	Professional World Doubles Tournament (with Hoad, Pancho Gonzales, and Frank Sedgman)
1958, 1960-62	French Pro Clay Championship
1960-63, 1968-69	Professional World Singles Tournament
1963-66	French Pro Indoor Championship
1963, 1965, 1971	U.S. Pro Championship
1971	Italian Indoor Championship doubles (with Stolle)
1971-72	WCT Finals
1973	Canadian Open doubles (with Rod Laver)
1982, 1984-85, 1988-89	Grand Masters Championship doubles (with Sedgman, Laver, Mal Anderson, and Davidson)
1982, 1985-89	Grand Masters Championship

Continuing the Story

Ken played the professional circuit from 1957 until 1968, when amateur tournaments were finally opened up to professionals. He then had a chance—once again—to compete in Grand Slam tournaments and possibly win the one title that had eluded him: the singles title at Wimbledon. In his long career, Ken played in the Wimbledon singles final four times. The first final was in 1954 and the last was in 1974, when he lost to Jimmy Connors. He won the doubles title at Wimbledon twice. It is an amazing record of longevity to reach the final twenty years after the first time. Nobody else has been as consistent for as long as Ken.

Two of his most spectacular wins were in 1971 and again in 1972 at the World Championship of Tennis (WCT) finals. Rod Laver was favored both years to walk away as the champion, but in each year, Ken came out the winner. He also won the Australian Open in the same years. Ken was the oldest player to win the Australian title. In 1974, he played for the Pittsburgh Triangles of the World Team Tennis (WTT). In 1979, he played in his last regular tour event and was enshrined in the International Tennis

Hall of Fame the following year. After his retirement from the regular tour, Ken participated in the Legends and Grand Masters tours. Ken also purchased a sports center consulting and design firm, Ken Rosewall and Associates, in Sydney, Australia.

Summary

"Muscles," as Ken Rosewall was affectionately known by his peers, won eighteen Grand Slam tournaments in singles, doubles, and mixed doubles. Ken made the most of his abilities and did it longer than any other male tennis player. Even though he may have looked frail, his strokes were solid. Always a tough competitor, Ken, more times than not, beat opponents who were considered more powerful than he. Ken stands as a champion among champions and a credit to the game that he loved so much.

Jeffry Jensen

Additional Sources

Fein, Paul. *Tennis Confidential: Today's Greatest Players, Matches, and Controversies.* Washington, D.C.: Brassey's, 2002.

Rosewall, Ken. *Ken Rosewall on Tennis.* New York: F. Fell, 1978.

Rowley, Peter, and Ken Rosewall. *Ken Rosewall: Twenty Years at the Top.* New York: Putnam, 1976.

Gabriela Sabatini

Born: May 16, 1970
      Buenos Aires, Argentina
Also known as: Gabriela Beatriz Sabatini (full name)

Early Life

Gabriela Beatriz Sabatini was born on May 16, 1970, in Buenos Aires, Argentina. She is the daughter of Osvaldo, Sr., and Beatriz Sabatini. Gabriela's older brother, Osvaldo, Jr., was born in 1965. Her father was a General Motors executive in Argentina until 1986, when he retired to concentrate fully on Gabriela's tennis career.

Gabriela began playing tennis at the age of seven. When she was twelve years old, tennis coach Patricio Apey saw her play in Brazil at the Banana Bowl junior tournament. He was impressed with her natural talent and believed that with the proper coaching, Gabriela could become a champion tennis player. He did not attempt to rush her development but allowed her natural abilities to blossom under his nurturing.

The Road to Excellence

By the time Gabriela was fourteen, she was the best junior player in the world. In 1984, she won both the French and Italian Open junior titles and was ranked number-one junior player by the International Tennis Federation (ITF). Her coach had brought her onto the world tennis scene, and experts were beginning to predict great things for this attractive teenager from Argentina. Gabriela had grown up in a strict family, and this newfound celebrity status was hard for her to comprehend. She was shy and accustomed to expressing herself only to family members or friends. Gabriela also had trouble expressing herself in any language but Spanish. For the most part, she let her tennis game do the talking for her.

Gabriela entered the 1984 U.S. Open at the age of fourteen. She eventually lost in the third round of the tournament, but in so do-

ing, Gabriela became the youngest player at that time to win a round at the U.S. Open. She won matches because of her topspin ground strokes, and because she was tenacious. What she lacked was a clear strategy. Gabriela was winning because of her raw ability. At the end of 1984, she had a women's ranking of seventy-four.

In January, 1985, Gabriela turned professional. By the end of 1985, her computer ranking had climbed to number eleven. Her most remarkable accomplishments of the year included becoming

Gabriela Sabatini hitting the ball during her U.S. Open finals match, in which she defeated Steffi Graf. (AP/Wide World Photos)

the youngest semifinalist at the French Open and beating three top-ten-ranked women before succumbing to Chris Evert in the final of the Family Circle Magazine Cup. Fans and experts alike were entranced by her graceful game and her stunning good looks.

The Emerging Champion

Gabriela was becoming a tennis star who could draw large tennis crowds merely to see her play. In 1986, her father decided to leave his executive position with General Motors so that he could travel with his daughter and help her cope with life on the road. A new coach was brought in to help Gabriela train. Angel Gimenez, a former Davis-Cup player from Spain, decided that it was time for her to start an aerobic regimen to build up her stamina. The efforts were successful because Gabriela raised her computer ranking to number six by the end of 1987. She teamed with Steffi Graf to capture the 1986 U.S. Clay Court Championship doubles title, and they reached the finals of the French Open doubles in 1986 and 1987. In 1986, Gabriela also became the youngest player ever to reach the semifinals at Wimbledon. Her coach was beginning to talk about her becoming the top-ranked player in the world.

What Gabriela needed to do in order to prove that she could be a great champion was to win a Grand Slam singles title. The talent was there, but again, the lack of an aggressive game plan plus the added pressure of having to compete against the athletic Graf proved to be major barriers. Before 1988, Gabriela and Graf had played eleven times and Graf was victorious every time. The two players were expected to be the new rivalry in women's tennis, replacing the rivalry that has existed between Chris Evert and Martina Navratilova.

Major Championship Victories and Finals

1986-87, 1989	French Open doubles finalist (with Steffi Graf)
1988	U.S. Open finalist
	Wimbledon doubles (with Graf)
1990	U.S. Open
1991	Wimbledon finalist

Other Notable Victories

1985	European Indoor Championship doubles (with Graf)
	Canadian Open doubles (with Zina Garrison)
1986	U.S. Clay Court Championship doubles (with Graf)
1987	Italian Open doubles (with Martina Navratilova)
	Bausch & Lomb Championship doubles (with Graf)
1988	Silver medal, Olympic women's tennis singles
	Lipton International Players Championship doubles (with Graf)
	Canadian Open
1988-89, 1991-92	Italian Open
1988, 1994	Virginia Slims Championship
1989	Lipton International Players Championship
1989, 1991	Bausch & Lomb Championship
1991	*Family Circle* Magazine Cup

Gabriela finally defeated Graf for the first time in the finals of the Virginia Slims of Florida at Boca Raton. She also beat Evert for the first time in the semifinals, a major breakthrough for Gabriela. After these successes, she knew that she could not only compete against, but also defeat the top player. In 1988, Gabriela had an excellent season: She won the Virginia Slims Championship, the Canadian Open, the Wimbledon doubles with Graf, and the Olympic silver medal, and she became the first woman from Argentina to reach a Grand Slam singles final when she did so at the U.S. Open.

Continuing the Story

Gabriela reached the number-three ranking in the world by early 1989. In 1988, Graf had won the Grand Slam by capturing Wimbledon, and the Australian, French, and U.S. Open singles titles. At 5 feet 8 inches and 130 pounds, Gabriela was in fine shape, but her drive to become the number-one player was not producing the desired results. Her family members tried to create the correct emotional atmosphere for her to flourish, but Gabriela seemed to be internalizing her defeats and losing her youthful spirit. She still had some excellent victories during the year,

Honors, Awards, and Milestones

1985	Rolex Rookie of the Year
	Women's International Tennis Association Most Impressive Newcomer
1985-87	Australian Federation Cup team
1987-88	Olympia Award
2006	Inducted into International Tennis Hall of Fame

but the talk of her as a tennis prodigy was starting to seem like misplaced expectations.

Gabriela still attempted to lead a normal life. She loved music, soccer, and video games. Beginning in 1987, she appeared annually in the Lipton/WITA calendars. Gabriela has been described as a Greta Garbo type because of her beauty and her tendency to remain a woman of few words. In 1989, she introduced her own brand of perfume. Tennis was still her life, though, and she did not give up, even if some critics were already writing her off as someone who could not win a Grand Slam singles title.

After the French Open of 1990, Gabriela parted from coach Gimenez. A crafty Brazilian tennis player by the name of Carlos Kirmayr took over the coaching duties. The forty-year-old Kirmayr was known as a very creative player. Gabriela told him that she still wanted to contend for the top spot, so he worked with her to make her tennis game more well-rounded. Gabriela also began working with sports psychologist Jim Loehr, who helped her open up emotionally and bring some fun back into her activities. She finally put the new regime all together at the 1990 U.S. Open, where she defeated Graf in the final to capture her first Grand Slam singles title. The brilliant victory carried over into 1991, and Gabriela was playing with wonderful confidence. She lost a dramatic final to Graf in the 1991 Wimbledon final. She may not have won, but she proved that she could be a force on the grass courts of Wimbledon.

Gabriela won the Italian Open for the fourth time in 1992 and won her second Virginia Slims Championship in 1994. In 1996, Gabriela retired from competitive tennis at the age of twenty-six. After her retirement from tennis, she focused on marketing several fragrances and promoting her own line of clothes, watches, and home linens. In 2006, she was inducted into the International Tennis Hall of Fame.

Summary

Gabriela Sabatini burst onto the tennis scene at an early age and rose quickly to the top echelon of women's tennis. She brought elegance and skill to the game. She also proved to be a great fighter by not giving up on herself when others decided that she could not compete against the likes of Steffi Graf.

Jeffry Jensen

Additional Sources

Harrington, Denis J. "Gabriela Sabatini." In *Top Ten Women Tennis Players.* Springfield, N.J.: Enslow, 1995.

Litsky, Frank. "Off the Court, Sabatini Is Still in Her Prime." *The New York Times,* July 16, 2006, Sec. 8, p. 9.

Mewshaw, Michael. *Ladies of the Court.* New York: Crown, 1993.

Paulson, Amanda. "Tennis Player Gabriela Sabatini." *Christian Science Monitor* 92, no. 197 (August 31, 2000): 19.

Phillips, Caryl. *The Right Set: A Tennis Anthology.* New York: Vintage Books, 1999.

Sabatini, Gabriela. *My Story.* Beverly Hills, Calif.: Great American, 1994.

Pete Sampras

Born: August 12, 1971
      Washington, D.C.

Also known as: Peter Sampras (full name); Petros Sampras (birth name); King of Swing; Pistol Pete

Early Life

Peter Sampras was born Petros Sampras on August 12, 1971, in Washington, D.C., to Soterios Sampras, an aerospace engineer, and Georgia (Vroustrous) Sampras. He was the third of four children. When Pete was a child, the family moved to Rancho Palos Verdes in Southern California.

Before the family moved, Pete had begun hitting tennis balls against the basement wall of his Washington, D.C., home with an old wooden tennis racket. Pete continued his introduction to tennis in California. Pete's parents took him and his sister, Stella, to a public park near their home to play. At the age of six, Pete was already able to run down balls and hit fluid groundstroke returns. On one occasion at the park, passersby were impressed with Pete's prodigious skills. They recommended that he have formal instruction so that his talent could be fully realized.

The Road to Excellence

In 1979, Pete's father took him to the Jack Kramer Tennis Club, which was located near the Sampras's Rancho Palos Verdes home. Dr. Peter Fischer was at the club hitting with a nationally ranked junior player when Pete's father asked him if he would like to coach his son. Fischer was a pediatrician and not a tennis coach, but he knew the game well enough to refer Pete to specialists. He introduced Pete to footwork and volley coaches and to Robert Lansdorp, who had worked with Tracy Austin before she won the 1979 U.S. Open.

Fischer wanted to build Pete's game to be like that of tennis legend Rod Laver. At the age of nine, Pete played in his first ju-

nior tournament; Fischer had him enter junior tournaments that were for older children. Pete was getting beaten most of the time, but he was developing a game that would benefit him in the future. If Pete were to be made in the image of Laver, then he would have to be a serve-and-volley player. When Pete was fourteen, Fischer insisted that he learn to hit his backhand with one hand, not with two as he had been doing. Pete was frustrated during the transitional phase, but he mastered the one-handed backhand eventually. When he was fifteen,

Pete Sampras securing a victory in the fourth round of the 1993 U.S. Open. (Timothy Clary/AFP/Getty Images)

he earned the right to be part of the 1987 boys' Junior Davis Cup team.

The Emerging Champion

As a teenager, Pete grew to 6 feet. With the added height, he was able to generate more speed on his serve. His time as a junior player was solid but not illustrious. In 1987, he and Matt Lucena won the eighteen-and-under International Grass Court Doubles; that was his only title as a junior player. In 1988, he turned professional. Also in that year, his sister, Stella, won the National Collegiate Athletic Association doubles title with Allyson Cooper.

Through the unselfish guidance of Fischer, Pete had realized his dream of becoming a professional player. In 1990, he won his first professional tournament, the U.S. Pro Indoor in Philadelphia, Pennsylvania. In the final, he defeated Andres Gomez, who won the French Open later in the year.

Pete went on to win four titles during the year, the most dramatic of which came at the U.S. Open, one of tennis's four Grand Slam tournaments. Going into the tournament, Pete was seeded twelfth. Without much fanfare, he advanced into a quarterfinal match against three-time champion Ivan Lendl. In a dramatic five-set match, Pete played with a maturity beyond his nineteen years and came away with a win. He did not falter in the semifinals, beating four-time champion John McEnroe. In the final, Pete played an almost flawless match, defeating Andre Agassi in straight sets. With the victory, Pete became the youngest male player to win the tournament; he was also the lowest-seeded player to win the U.S. championship since the tournament became an open competition in 1970. After the victory, Pete acknowledged the contribution Fischer had made to his game.

In December, 1990, Pete won the first Grand Slam Cup, in Munich, Germany, and its top prize of

---

Major Championship Victories and Finals

1990, 1993, 1995-96, 2002	U.S. Open
1992, 2000-01	U.S. Open finalist
1993-95, 1997-2000	Wimbledon
1994, 1997	Australian Open
1995	Australian Open finalist

Other Notable Victories

1990	Grand Slam Cup
1990, 1992	U.S. Pro Indoor Championship
1991	U.S. Hard Courts Championship
1991, 1994, 1996-97, 1999	ATP Tour World Championship
1992, 1995	On victorious U.S. Davis Cup team
1993	*Newsweek* Champion's Cup
1993-94	Lipton International Players' Championships
1994	Italian Open

$2 million. *Tennis* magazine named Pete most improved player of the year for 1990, and his Association of Tennis Professionals (ATP) ranking climbed to number five in the world.

Continuing the Story

In 1991, Pete continued to make steady progress toward becoming a more consistent player. No one doubted his natural skills, but on occasion during a match he could lose concentration. Pete had already severed his close ties with Fischer, but no other adviser had entered his life to fill the void. Pete won four titles in 1991, including the U.S. Hardcourts and the year-end ATP Tour World Championship. However, whereas some tennis players were suited to celebrity as well as competition, Pete became something of an enigma to fans and the press alike. During a match, Pete rarely displayed emotion. Some critics considered him uninteresting. Pete, though, believed that his shot-making, not his personality, should draw attention during a match.

In 1992, former player Tim Gullikson became Pete's coach. Pete matured as a tennis player under Gullikson's tutelage. Blessed with a powerful serve and a precise ground stroke, Pete reached the pinnacle of tennis in 1993 by winning both Wimbledon and the U.S. Open. In April of 1993, he became the number-one ranked player in the world. *Tennis* magazine named him the 1993 player of the year. "The Sweet One," as he was

---

Honors, Awards, and Milestones

1990	*Tennis* magazine Most Improved Player
1993	*Tennis* magazine Player of the Year
1994-99, 2001	ESPY Award: Outstanding Men's Tennis Performer of the Year
1997	USOC Sportsman of the Year
2005	*Tennis* magazine Greatest Player—1965-2005
2007	Inducted into International Tennis Hall of Fame

dubbed by Jim Courier, had taken a giant step toward becoming one of the all-time great tennis champions. In 1994, he continued his domination of Grand Slam tournaments by defeating Todd Martin in the final of the Australian Open and then capturing his second Wimbledon title.

During the 1990's, Pete established himself as one of the all-time great tennis players. In 2000, he won his seventh Wimbledon singles title and his thirteenth Grand Slam singles title. With this victory, he became the all-time leader in Grand Slam singles titles for men. In 2002, he added one more Grand Slam singles title with a four-set victory over Agassi at the U.S. Open. The Australian tennis champion Roy Emerson had held the record with twelve since the 1960's.

In 2000, Pete married Bridgette Wilson, an actress and a former Miss Teen USA. Their first son, Christian, was born in 2002, and their second son, Ryan, was born in 2005. After his retirement from competitive tennis, Pete played a number of exhibitions. In 2007, he was inducted into the International Tennis Hall of Fame.

Summary

Pete Sampras was born with wonderful natural tennis skills. When he played, Pete made spectacular shots seemingly without effort. He will rightly be remembered as one of the great shot-makers of tennis and one of the sport's most respected champions.

Jeffry Jensen

Additional Sources

Boughn, Michael. *Pete Sampras.* Los Angeles: Warwick, 1999.

Miller, Calvin Craig. *Pete Sampras.* Greensboro, N.C.: Morgan Reynolds, 1998.

Sampras, Pete, with Peter Bodo. *A Champion's Mind: Lessons from a Life in Tennis.* New York: Crown, 2008.

Sherrow, Victoria. *Sports Great Pete Sampras.* Springfield, N.J.: Enslow, 1996.

Wushanley, Ying. "Sampras, Peter ('Pete')." *The Scribner Encyclopedia of American Lives Thematic Series: Sports Figures,* edited by Kenneth T. Jackson. 2 vols. New York: Charles Scribner's Sons, 2002.

Arantxa Sanchez-Vicario

Born: December 18, 1971
     Barcelona, Spain
Also known as: Aranzazu Isabel Maria Sanchez-Vicario; the Barcelona Bumblebee

Early Life
Aranzazu "Arantxa" Isabel Maria Sanchez-Vicario was born on December 18, 1971, in Barcelona, Spain. Her father, Emilio Sanchez, was a civil engineer, and her mother, Marisa Vicario, was a teacher

Arantxa Sanchez-Vicario clenching her fist and pumping her arm in celebration after winning a match at the French Open in 1994. (Patrick Kovarik/AFP/Getty Images)

who regularly traveled with Arantxa on the women's tennis tour. Arantxa has three older siblings: Marisa, who became a sports reporter, and Emilio and Javier, who became professional tennis players and achieved success on the men's tour. Arantxa learned to rely on her brothers, especially Emilio, for advice about her game.

Arantxa began playing tennis when she was two years old, after she had accompanied her family to the tennis courts at the Club Real de Tenis in Barcelona, near their apartment. Her mother wanted the children to take up snow skiing, but her father preferred tennis. Along with her older siblings, Arantxa excelled at tennis by combining natural talent and enthusiasm with dedicated practice. When she was a child, her tennis racket was her constant companion.

The Road to Excellence
By the time Arantxa was eleven, she had won several junior titles in Spain, and soon she was competing with, and beating, adults. In 1985, at the age of thirteen, she won the Spanish national women's championship and established her position as the top-ranked female tennis player in her native country.

In 1986, she began playing tennis as a professional on the Women's Tennis Association (WTA) tour. Her game—based on strong ground strokes, consistency, exceptional foot speed, and a courageous spirit—quickly raised her position in the rankings. After her first year on the tour, she received the most impressive newcomer award from the WTA; she had caught the attention of the experts by advancing to the finals of the Argentine Open and by helping to win the women's doubles title at a tournament in Athens, Greece.

The Emerging Champion
By 1988, Arantxa had gained a reputation as one of the top competitors in women's tennis. That year, she won her first professional singles title, the Belgian Open. She also won several doubles titles and reached the quarterfinals

or semifinals in other major tournaments, often upsetting top-ranked players such as Chris Evert, whom she beat in the third round of the 1988 French Open.

Arantxa's success was a result of hard work, physical stamina, concentration, cunning, and a love of the game. Her speed, daring, and tenacity evoked an unusual range of comparisons. The great tennis

Major Championship Victories and Finals

Year	Event
1989,1994,1998	French Open
1990	French Open mixed doubles (with Jorge Lozano)
1991,1995-96	French Open finalist
1992	U.S. Open finalist
	French Open mixed doubles (with Todd Woodbridge)
1992,1995-96	Australian Open doubles (with Helena Sukova, Jana Novotná, and Chandra Rubin)
1993	U.S. Open doubles (with Suková)
	French Open mixed doubles (with Woodbridge)
	Australian Open mixed doubles (with Woodbridge)
1994	U.S. Open
	U.S. Open doubles (with Novotná)
1994-95	Australian Open finalist
1995	Wimbledon doubles (with Novotná)
1995-96	Wimbledon finalist
2000	Australian Open mixed-doubles finalist (with Woodbridge)
2002	Australian Open doubles finalist (with Daniela Hantuchová)
2003	U.S. Open mixed doubles (with Jared Palmer)

Other Notable Victories

Year	Event
1985	Spanish National Amateur Champion
1986	Athens doubles (with Isabel Cueto)
1988	Belgian Open
1989-90,1993	International Championship of Spain
1990	Virginia Slims Newport
1991	Washington, D.C.
1992	Bronze medal, Olympic women's tennis singles
	Silver medal, Olympic women's tennis doubles (with Conchita Martinez)
	Canadian Open
1992-93	Lipton International
1993	Bausch & Lomb Championships
	Citizen Cup
1996	Silver medal, Olympic women's tennis singles
	Family Circle Cup

couturier and benefactor Ted Tinling summed up her game by describing her as "feisty and fiery" and noted that she reminded him of a lion. To others, her speed and agility around the court and her trademark use of a ball-holder at the back of her waist called to mind the image of a rabbit.

These qualities were apparent in 1989, when Arantxa reached the finals of the French Open, a Grand Slam tournament. She was a distinct underdog to the top-ranked Steffi Graf, who seemed unbeatable after winning all four Grand Slam tournaments in the previous year. Arantxa won the first set in a tiebreaker, but the gritty Graf won the second. By never conceding a point to her German rival, Arantxa came back from a 5-3 deficit in the third set to capture her first Grand Slam Championship on the red clay courts of Roland Garros Stadium. She later told reporters that she was nervous as she served for the match, but she had been determined to run down all of Graf's shots. Arantxa became the first Spanish woman to win the French Open; at the age of seventeen years and six months, she was also the youngest woman to win the tournament.

Until that time, she had played professionally as Arantxa Sanchez. After her unexpected triumph in France, she announced that she was becoming Arantxa Sanchez-Vicario in honor of her mother. She explained her stunning victory over the heavily favored Graf by saying that Graf's other opponents had been mentally beaten before they had stepped on the court; Arantxa, however, had never doubted her own ability to win.

Continuing the Story

Arantxa continued to raise the level of her game, winning major tournaments in singles, women's doubles, and mixed doubles. She was a finalist at the French Open in 1991 and at the U.S. Open in 1992, in both cases losing to top-ranked Monica Seles.

Through competition in doubles, she added new dimensions to her game with her volleys and strong serve. Among her many women's doubles titles are the 1993 U.S. Open and 1992 Australian Open with partner Helena Suková. In mixed doubles, she won the French Open in 1990 with Jorge Lozano and in 1992 with Todd Woodbridge, who was also her partner in winning the 1993 Australian Open mixed-doubles title.

Arantxa also represented Spain in various international competitions. She began playing on the Spanish Federation Cup team in 1986; her strong performance helped Spain win the Federation Cup for the first time in 1991 and to recapture the title in 1993. She also played on the Spanish team at the 1988, 1992, 1996, and 2000 Olympic Games. During the 1992 Olympics, which were held in her hometown of Barcelona, she won the bronze medal in singles and the silver medal in doubles with her partner Conchita Martinez. In 1996, Arantxa won a silver medal in singles. Her consistent excellence made her the top female Spanish player since Lili de Alvarez, a Wimbledon finalist of the 1920's.

In 1994, Arantxa enjoyed her greatest success, capturing a second French Open championship and winning both the singles and the doubles titles at the U.S. Open. She won her third French Open in 1998. In Grand Slam competition, she won four Grand Slam singles titles, six Grand Slam women's doubles titles, and four Grand Slam mixed-doubles titles. In 2000, she won her last Grand Slam title by capturing the U.S. Open mixed-doubles title with her partner Jared Palmer. In addition to her Grand Slam titles, Arantxa reached the finals of several Grand Slam tournaments. She was runner-up in singles on eight occasions, in women's doubles on five occasions, and in mixed doubles on four occasions. She was a tenacious competitor who always gave her best on the court, especially in major championships. Over the course of her illustrious career, she won a total of twenty-nine singles titles and sixty-nine doubles titles.

Arantxa was a member of the Spanish team that won the Hopman Cup in 1990 and 2002. In 2000, she married Joan Vehils, but the couple separated the following year. Arantxa retired from competitive tennis in 2002. Although she entered a few doubles events during 2004, she recognized that her competitive tennis career was finished. In 2007, she was inducted into the International Tennis Hall of Fame. She became the first Spanish woman to be so honored.

Summary
Arantxa Sanchez-Vicario's agility and consistency on the court, combined with her tenacity and competitive spirit, left an indelible mark on the game. After she won the 1989 French Open, she remarked that "Paris was the big first stop on my voyage. I can't stop sailing now, I hope." Her determination helped her to remain a major force in women's tennis for almost twenty years.

Karen Gould, updated by Jeffry Jensen

Additional Sources
Higdon, David. "The Glorious Game." *Tennis* 32 (July, 1996).

Mewshaw, Michael. *Ladies of the Court.* New York: Crown, 1993.

Rutledge, Rachel. *The Best of the Best in Tennis.* Brookfield, Conn.: Millbrook Press, 1998.

Sanchez-Vicaro, Arantxa. *Tennis.* New York: Dorling Kindersley, 2000.

Shmerler, Cindy. "Arantxa Sanchez-Vicario." *Tennis* 35 (February, 1999).

Vic Seixas

Born: August 30, 1923
      Philadelphia, Pennsylvania
Also known as: Elias Victor Seixas, Jr. (full name)

Early Life

Elias Victor Seixas, Jr., was born August 30, 1923, in Philadelphia, Pennsylvania. Vic's father, of Portuguese descent, operated a plumbing and heating supply business in Philadelphia.

Although Vic began playing tennis when he was very young, his early life did not resemble that of most sports champions. After graduation as an honor student from high school, in 1942, he enlisted in the Army Air Force. He served from 1942 to 1946 as a test pilot and flight instructor.

After his discharge from the Air Force, he attended the University of North Carolina, majoring in business administration. He played on the school tennis team and won awards for his combination of scholarship and athletic ability. After his graduation, he joined the family business.

The Road to Excellence

Unlike most outstanding athletes, Vic did not display extraordinary ability when he was very young. Although he played tennis both in school and as a pastime throughout his high school and college years, he did not practice the game with single-minded intensity. Further, he did not come under the wing of a first-rate coach who could have guided him toward success.

Vic's rise to the top was sudden and unexpected. He found that his tennis ability rose dramatically after he graduated from college. Taking advantage of the change, Vic began to enter important tournaments and soon established himself as a major presence.

Vic's sudden blossoming, although unusual in its mode, did have an explanation. His quickness and intelligence fitted him for the style of play that came into fashion just after the end of World War II in 1945. During the 1920's, most players tended to remain at the baseline. Long rallies were the order of the day, and the key to success lay in swift and accurate ground strokes.

The new style was different. Pioneered by Jack Kramer, it placed less emphasis on baseline play. Instead, a player rushed the net following service. He attempted to put away his opponent's return with a quick volley. Points were scored more rapidly than before, and the new method proved popular with the fans. Although defenders of the old approach such as Bill Tilden lamented that the skill had gone out of the game, their protests were of no avail. Few players of the immediate postwar period had the ground strokes needed to combat the new technique.

Vic and the new style were made

Vic Seixas. (AP/Wide World Photos)

for each other. He was skilled at volleying, and his knowledge of tennis strategy enabled him to place his shots so that returning them was extremely difficult.

The Emerging Champion

Vic entered Wimbledon in 1950, when he was only twenty-seven. Although he did not win the tournament, he aroused wide attention by defeating the great Australian player John Bromwich in the quarterfinals. Vic made the quarterfinals or semifinals of nearly every tournament he entered that year.

In 1951, Vic's game was even better. He reached the finals of the U.S. National Championship at Forest Hills. There, he suffered a setback. He lost in the finals to the Australian Frank Sedgman, who had unusual strength and won the match by overpowering Vic.

Vic was not one to take defeat lightly. He visited Australia in 1951, in preparation for the Davis Cup. He astonished the Australians by defeating Sedgman to win the New South Wales Championship. However, in the Davis Cup challenge round, he again met defeat at the hands of the powerful Australian.

Vic was never able to establish his superiority over the great Australian players of the early 1950's, who, besides Sedgman, included Ken Rosewall and Lew Hoad. However, he usually gave as good as he got, and his record in many years of Davis Cup play was outstanding.

Continuing the Story

The patterns that emerged at the start of Vic's amateur career continued throughout the early 1950's. As he gained more experience, his skill at volleying and his breakneck rushes of the net made him one of the world's best players.

Vic's chief rival in the United States was Tony Trabert, a younger player who eventually supplanted Vic as the best player in the United States. Vic and Trabert played many close matches, and Vic usually held his own. He won the U.S. National Championship in 1954 and Wimbledon in 1953.

Vic did not let his rivalry for singles honors with Trabert stop him from joining his erstwhile foe as a doubles partner. Both of them were highly intelligent and mastered the intricacies of doubles play without difficulty. During the years of their partnership, they established themselves as the world's best doubles team. Their duels with the Australians were especially notable. Had it not been for Vic and

---

Major Championship Victories and Finals

1951, 1953	U.S. National Championship finalist
1952, 1954	U.S. National Championship doubles (with Mervyn Rose and Tony Trabert)
	Wimbledon doubles finalist (with Eric Sturgess and Trabert)
1953	Wimbledon
	French Championship finalist
	French Championship mixed doubles (with Doris Hart)
1953-56	U.S. National Championship mixed doubles (with Hart)
	Wimbledon mixed doubles (with Hart)
1954	U.S. National Championship
1954-55	French Championship doubles (with Trabert)
1955	Australian Championship doubles (with Trabert)
1956	U.S. National Championship doubles finalist (with Hamilton Richardson)

Other Notable Victories

1948	U.S. Hardcourt Championship doubles (with Ted Schroeder)
1949, 1954	U.S. Clay Court Championship doubles (with Sam Match and Trabert)
1952, 1954, 1957	Pacific Southwest Championship
1953	Italian Championship mixed doubles (with Hart)
1953, 1957	U.S. Clay Court Championship
1954	On winning U.S. Davis Cup team
1955-56	U.S. Indoor Championship doubles (with Trabert and Sam Giammalva)
1976	Grand Masters Championship doubles (with Rex Hartwig)

Honors, Awards, and Milestones

1948	William M. Johnston Award
1951-57	U.S. Davis Cup team
1951, 1954, 1957	Nationally ranked number one
1952, 1964	U.S. Davis Cup team captain
1971	Inducted into National Lawn Tennis Hall of Fame

Tony, the Australians would have been unstoppable on the tennis court in the early 1950's. Instead, Vic's volleying skill, quickness, and intelligence often enabled him to triumph over the physically stronger and more naturally gifted Australians.

Summary

Vic Seixas was one of several outstanding American players in the early 1950's, including Bill Talbert, Budge Patty, and Tony Trabert. He was not a standard-model athlete. He became an outstanding player only after graduation from college and had as a youth played tennis just as a hobby. His quickness and volleying technique secured his rapid rise to the top, and he ranked as one of the world's best players in the early 1950's, in both singles and doubles.

Bill Delaney

Additional Sources

Collins, Bud. *Total Tennis: The Ultimate Tennis Encyclopedia.* Toronto: Sport Media, 2003.

Grimsley, Will. *Tennis: Its History, People, and Events.* Englewood Cliffs, N.J.: Prentice-Hall, 1971.

Seixas, Vic, and Joel H. Cohen. *Prime Time Tennis.* New York: Charles Scribner's Sons, 1983.

Viragh, Helle Sparre, and Jim Schock. *Dynamite Doubles: Play Winning Tennis Today!* Oakland, Calif.: Regent Press, 2004.

Monica Seles

Born: December 2, 1973
  Novi Sad, Yugoslavia (now in Serbia)

Early Life

Monica Seles was born on December 2, 1973, in Novi Sad, Yugoslavia (now in Serbia). Her father, Karolj, worked as a newspaper cartoonist and television director, while her mother, Esther, worked as a computer programmer. Monica has an older brother, Zoltan. Karolj gave Monica her first tennis racket when she was six years old. She played for a few weeks, but then she lost interest.

Monica did not play again until Zoltan won the Yugoslav junior championship two years later. To encourage her not to lose interest, Karolj drew Monica's favorite cartoon characters—Tom and Jerry—on tennis balls. She hit the balls as hard as she could. Her father also put stuffed animals on the tennis court at which Monica could aim.

The Road to Excellence

Monica won the Yugoslav twelve-and-under championship when she was nine years old. In 1984, at ten years old, she won the European twelve-and-under championship, in Paris. In 1985, she was named Yugoslav sportswoman of the year when she was only eleven years old. She was the first individual under the age of eighteen to win this prestigious award. In the same year, she competed in the Orange Bowl twelve-and-under tournament, held in Miami, Florida. While there, she was spotted by the respected tennis coach Nick Bollettieri. Monica won the tournament, and Bollettieri was so impressed with her that he offered her a full scholarship to his tennis academy in Bradenton, Florida.

Monica and her brother moved to Bradenton in 1986. Her parents left their jobs, closed their two Novi Sad homes and their country vacation home, and moved to Bradenton to concentrate on Monica's promising career. Always a perfectionist, Monica began practicing six hours a day. She was deter-

Monica Seles wins the Australian Open in 1996. (AP/Wide World Photos)

mined to be the best. Adjusting to life in Florida was hard for her and her family, but every member of the family was focused on helping Monica succeed, so the cultural shock of living in a new country was only a minor challenge.

Karolj, Zoltan, and Bollettieri all played parts in molding Monica into a complete tennis player. Her father concentrated on drills, while her brother hit with her. Bollettieri handled the strategy. Monica was left-handed, but she hit two-handed shots on both the forehand and the backhand sides, which necessitated quickness to be able to reach wide shots. She also attempted to put the ball away as quickly as possible so as to avoid having to run down shots constantly. The harder Monica hit the ball, the louder she grunted. Grunting became a trademark of her tennis game.

The Emerging Champion

During this time, Monica did not play any junior tournaments at the tennis academy. At first, her unique style of play was kept out of the public eye. That was difficult to do at the academy because of the number of children who were either visiting or part of a tennis program there. The Seles family wanted Monica to have complete privacy, whereas Bollettieri wanted to publicize his star pupil. Monica finally played in her first professional event in 1988. She won her first match in March at the Virginia Slims of Florida, where she upset Helen Kelesi. Monica's best result that year was at a tournament in New Orleans. She reached the semifinals of the tournament by defeating Lori McNeil. Monica may not have won many matches by this point, but she had served notice to the tennis world that she was serious about winning.

Monica turned professional in February, 1989. She was finally ready to compete against the best in the game and not feel overmatched. She believed in hard work and was determined to be a great, not just good, player. In 1989, she made solid strides toward the top of women's tennis. She won her first tournament at the Virginia Slims of Houston, where she defeated Chris Evert in the final. At this tournament, she became the youngest player to reach the final of a Virginia Slims event.

Monica's initial best showing in a Grand Slam tournament was at the French Open, where she reached the semifinals. She took Steffi Graf to a third set before succumbing 6-3 in the final set. In the other Grand Slam events she entered, Wimbledon and the U.S. Open, Monica reached the fourth round. By the end of the year, she had achieved a ranking of number six in the world, and she had grown to a height of 5 feet 9 inches. Monica had to practice even harder so as to adjust her game to her added height.

Continuing the Story

Monica should have entered 1990 confident that she would win a major title eventually, but growing so much made her struggle with her game during the early part of the year. Tension was also growing between Bollettieri and the Seles family. By March, though, Monica's game was in fine form: She defeated Judith Wiesner to capture the Lipton International Players Championship. Soon after the tournament, the Seles family packed up and permanently left the tennis academy. Monica won some important championships during the rest of the year, including the U.S. Hardcourt Championship, the Italian Open, the Virginia Slims Championship, and—most important of all—the French Open. She defeated Graf at the French Open to win her first Grand Slam singles title. Because of her strong play during the year, Monica was named by *Tennis* magazine as the most improved player.

Major Championship Victories and Finals

1990-92	French Open
1991-92	U.S. Open
1991-93, 1996	Australian Open
1992	Wimbledon finalist
1995-96	U.S. Open finalist
1998	French Open finalist

Other Notable Victories

1989	Virginia Slims of Houston
1990	U.S. Hardcourt Championship
	German Open
	Lufthansa Cup
1990-91, 1997	Virginia Slims of Los Angeles
1990-92	Virginia Slims Championship
1990, 2000	Italian Open
1995-98	Canadian Open
1999-2000	Amelia Island
2000	Bronze medal, Olympic women's tennis singles
	Italian Open, Rome
2001	IGA Superthrift Classic
	Kiwi Open
	Brazil Open
	AIG Japan Open
	Shanghai Open
2002	Qatar Total Open
	Spanish Open

Honors, Awards, and Milestones

1985, 1989	Yugoslavian Sportswoman of the Year
1989	Rolex Rookie of the Year
1990	*Tennis* magazine Most Improved Player
1991	Ranked number one in the world
1991-92	WTA Player of the Year
	Associated Press (AP) Female Athlete of the Year
	United Press International (UPI) International Athlete of the Year
1995	*Tennis* magazine Comeback Player of the Year
1995-96, 1998-2000	Federation Cup team
1995, 1998	WTA Tour Comeback Player of the Year
2000	Flo Hyman Award
	ESPY Award: Player of the Decade
2002	Sanex Hero of the Year award
2009	Inducted into International Tennis Hall of Fame

Monica tried her best to adjust to American life. She modeled in such magazines as *Vogue, Seventeen,* and *Elle.* Because she was in the public eye at such a young age, she grew up rapidly. Under the circumstances, she matured in a remarkably graceful manner. Tennis remained the center of her world, though, and she finally advanced to number one in the rankings after winning the 1991 Australian and French Opens.

After Monica captured the first two Grand Slam Championships of the year, she had the possibility to become the first player to win all four Grand Slam titles in a single year since Graf had done so in 1988. However, Monica withdrew at the last minute from Wimbledon and went into seclusion. Numerous rumors circulated about her physical condition, and experts and fans alike were puzzled by her behavior. A statement was finally issued in July, 1991, which said that "shin splints and a slight stress fracture" in her left leg had forced her to bow out of Wimbledon. Monica recovered, and captured her third Grand Slam title of 1991 by defeating Martina Navratilova in the U.S. Open finals.

During the early 1990's, Monica was a dominant force in women's tennis. She won three consecutive French Open singles titles, from 1990 to 1992; three consecutive Australian Open singles titles, from 1991 to 1993; and consecutive U.S. Open singles titles, in 1991 and 1992. In 1993, in Hamburg, Germany, she was stabbed in the back by an irate spectator during the changeover of a tennis match. Not until 1995 did Monica feel physically and psy-

chologically ready to compete again on the court. In 1996, she came back to win the Grand Slam singles title at the Australian Open. She was a finalist at the 1995 and 1996 U.S. Opens and a finalist at the 1998 French Open. Sadly, her father had died only a few weeks before she reached the finals at the French Open.

In 1994, Monica became a U.S. citizen. With her help, the U.S. Federation Cup team won in 1996 and 2000. Monica also won the bronze medal in singles at the 2000 Summer Olympics held in Sydney, Australia. While Monica continued to compete, she was no longer the same dominant player. In 2003, a foot injury forced her to rest. After the 2003 French Open, she never played on the women's tour again. Between 2005 and 2007, she played a few exhibition matches and considered making a comeback. However, her comeback did not materialize. In early 2008, she announced her official retirement. Over the length of her remarkable career, she won fifty-three singles titles—nine of which were Grand Slams titles—and six doubles titles. She also earned almost $15 million in prize money and was later inducted into the International Tennis Hall of Fame.

Summary

In a short time, Monica Seles rose to the top of women's tennis. With her talent and strong work ethic, she became a powerful force in the game. Monica was one of the most important tennis stars of the 1990's.

Jeffry Jensen

Additional Sources

Blue, Rosa, with Corinne J. Naden. *Monica Seles.* Philadelphia: Chelsea House, 2002.

Layden, Joseph. *Return of a Champion: The Monica Seles Story.* New York: St. Martin's Press, 1996.

Rutledge, Rachel. *The Best of the Best in Tennis.* Brookfield, Conn.: Millbrook Press, 1998.

Seles, Monica. *Getting a Grip.* Wayne, N.J.: Avery, 2009.

Seles, Monica, with Nancy Ann Richardson. *Monica: From Fear to Victory.* New York: HarperCollins, 1996.

Maria Sharapova

Born: April 19, 1987
      Nyagan, Russia, Soviet Union (now in
        Russia)
Also known as: Maria Yuryevna Sharapova (full
    name); the Siberian Siren; the Queen of
    Screams

Early Life

Maria Yuryevna Sharapova was introduced to tennis at the age of four, and she immediately fell in love with the sport. Coached by her father Yuri, she practiced constantly, hitting tennis balls at the side of her house. At the age of seven, Maria and her father moved to the United States so she could attend the Nick Bollettieri Tennis Academy in Bradenton, Florida. Because of visa restrictions, her mother was unable to join her for two years.

Maria and her father were forced to live in near-poverty. Yuri worked at a number of low-paying jobs

Maria Sharapova eye to the ball in 2003. (AP/Wide World Photos)

to support Maria's training. Soon, Maria was one of the star pupils at Bollettieri's and began winning junior tournaments. In 2001, she turned professional at the age of fourteen.

The Road to Excellence

In 2002, Maria won her first professional tournament, the International Tennis Federation (ITF) challenger in Gunma, Japan. The ITF provides entry-level competitions to help players qualify for the Women's Tennis Association (WTA) tournaments. Maria won three ITF events and became the youngest player ever to reach the finals of the Australia Junior Open.

In 2003, Maria won her first WTA tournament, the Japan Open, and added another ITF-event victory. She qualified for all four of the WTA major tournaments: the Australian Open, the French Open, the U.S. Open, and Wimbledon. These competitions are collectively referred to as the "Grand Slam" of tennis. While she lost in the early rounds of these tournaments, she showed the drive and ability that soon led her to many world championships.

The public and press became fascinated by Maria not only because of her tennis achievements but also because she was a 6-foot-2-inch blond with exceptionally good looks. In 2003, *YM* magazine, a leading teen publication of the time, named her one of the "coolest girls" in the United States. That same year, she agreed to her first endorsement contract for NEC computers in Japan.

The Emerging Champion

In June, 2004, Maria reached the quarterfinals of the French Open, and later that month, she won both the singles and the doubles championships at Birmingham, England. As the latter were on grass courts, she went to Wimbledon's grass courts encouraged by her chances. In one of the greatest upsets in the history of women's tennis, Maria won at Wimbledon, beating Serena Williams. That year, she went on to win three more WTA events and finished the year as the number-four ranked player in the world. Her five tournament victories were second only to Lindsay Davenport's seven. She was named WTA player of the year and WTA most improved player of the year.

Maria's success and style of play started to draw criticism from other players and members of the press. Maria is a loud and boisterous athlete whose grunts and groans can sometimes be heard all the way to the next court. Some players complained that this threw them off their games, but Maria insisted her game necessitates vociferousness.

Continuing the Story

In 2005, Maria won three WTA events and reached the semifinals of three of the four Grand Slam tournaments. She spent several weeks as the number-one ranked tennis player in the world, the first Russian woman ever to reach that status. Still, her failure to win a Grand Slam event made the year somewhat disappointing for her.

In 2006, Maria reached the semifinals of the Australian Open and Wimbledon. At the U.S. Open, she beat the top two players in the world on her way to winning her second Grand Slam title. She finished the year with a total of five wins and was ranked as the number-two player in the world.

In 2007, Maria won only one event and suffered from nagging injuries. Fully recovered from her injuries, in 2008, Maria won the Australian Open in January, her third Grand Slam victory, and followed that with another win in February at Doha, Qatar, which was her eighteenth career title overall.

Milestone

First Russian woman to be ranked number one (2005)

Honors and Awards

2003	Women's Tennis Association (WTA) Newcomer of the Year
2004	WTA Player of the Year
	WTA Most Improved Player of the Year
2005	Russian Tennis Federation Best Female Player of the Year
	Master of Sports (Russia)
2005, 2007	ESPY Award: Best Female Tennis Player
2007	ESPY Award: Best International Female Athlete
2008	United States Sports Academy Female Athlete of the Month (January)

Maria's on-court success, augmented by off-court talents and interests, made her the wealthiest and most photographed female athlete in the world. She designed her own tennis outfits, and the one she wore at the 2006 U.S. Open, inspired by a dress worn by Audrey Hepburn in *Breakfast at Tiffany's*, particularly impressed the fashion world. Maria appeared in the 2006 *Sports Illustrated* swimsuit issue and is regularly on *People* magazine's list of "the Fifty Most Beautiful People in the World." Her endorsements include Nike, Prince, and Canon.

Summary

Maria Sharapova is the first female athlete to fully combine sex appeal with the drive and talent to be one of best in the world at her sport. Largely because of her success, female athletes can embrace their femininity and be taken seriously as athletes. Furthermore, she has given help to others. She has never forgotten her humble beginnings in Russia and started the Maria Sharapova Foundation for at-risk children. She also acted as ambassador for the Russian city of Sochi in its successful bid to host the 2014 Winter Olympics.

Jerome L. Neapolitan

Grand Slam Victories

2004	Wimbledon
2006	U.S. Open
2008	Australian Open

Other WTA Victories

2003	Bell Challenge
2003-04	Japan Open Tennis Championships
2004	Korea Open Tennis Championships
	WTA Tour Championships
2004-05	DFS Classic
2005	Pan-Pacific Open
2005, 2008	Qatar Total Open
2006	Zurich Open
	Generali Ladies Linz
	Indian Wells Masters
2006-07	Acura Classic
2008	Bausch & Lomb Championships

Additional Sources

Glaser, Jason. *Maria Sharapova.* New York: PowerKids Press, 2008.

Price, S. L. "As Good as They Get." *Sports Illustrated* 105, no. 11 (September 18, 2006): 52.

Savage Jeff. *Maria Sharapova.* Minneapolis: Lerner, 2008.

Wertheim, L. Jon. "Serving Notice." *Sports Illustrated* 108, no. 4 (February 4, 2008): 50.

Pam Shriver

Born: July 4, 1962
     Baltimore, Maryland
Also known as: Pamela Howard Shriver Lazenby
    (full name); Pamela Howard Shriver (birth
    name); Pam Shriver Shapiro

Early Life

Pamela Howard Shriver was born in Baltimore, Maryland, and emerged as a competitive tennis player at a young age. As an unseeded sixteen-year-old, she astonished the tennis world by defeating Martina Navratilova in straight sets during the semifinal match of the 1978 U.S. Open. However, she lost to Chris Evert in straight sets in the final. In her nineteen-year career, that was her only Grand Slam singles final.

In 1978, in Columbus, Ohio, Pam won the first of her twenty-one career singles titles. Pam grew to be 6 feet 1 inch, and with her lanky frame and short haircut, she presented a tomboyish quality on the court. Pam graduated from Mc-Donogh School in Owings Mills, Maryland.

The Road to Excellence

Pam came to prominence during the early 1980's, when tennis peaked in international popularity. Great players, both women and men, captured the imagination of both tennis fans and the occasional viewer. Pam faced some of the modern era's greatest players: Navratilova, Evert, and Steffi Graf.

After Pam's loss at the 1978 U.S. Open, she subsequently lost in the semifinals of eight Grand Slam singles competitions, losing half of them to Navratilova, two to Graf, and one each to Evert and Hana Mandlíková. However, doubles titles, not singles titles, helped Pam earn election to the International Tennis Hall of Fame. With her friend and sometimes singles nemesis Navratilova, Pam was one half of the most successful women's doubles team in tennis history.

The Emerging Champion

During the decades of the 1980's and 1990's, Pam won twenty-one women's doubles titles and one mixed-doubles title at Grand Slam tournaments. She won 112 career doubles titles overall, including seventy-nine with Navratilova. As of 2008, Pam was one of only six women players in the modern era to have won more than one hundred career titles.

With Navratilova as her partner, Pam reached her greatest success. From 1981 through 1988, the pair was named the WTA Tour's doubles team of the year eight consecutive times; they won the WTA Tour Championships title ten times between 1981 and 1992. The talented team won seven Australian

Pam Shriver. (Robert Riger/Getty Images)

Grand Slam Doubles Victories

Year	Tournament	Partner
1982-85, 1987-89	Australian Open	Martina Navratilova
1982-86	Wimbledon	Martina Navratilova
1983-84, 1986-87	U.S. Open	Martina Navratilova
1984-85, 1987-88	French Open	Martina Navratilova
1991	U.S. Open	Natasha Zvereva

Open titles, five Wimbledon titles, five U.S. Open titles, and four French Open titles. In 1984, Pam and Navratilova won all four Grand Slam women's doubles titles. The pair had a record 109-match winning streak between 1983 and 1985. In 1985, Pam briefly held the number-one doubles ranking, until she relinquished it to Navratilova. As a singles player, Pam's highest ranking was third.

Pam also won a gold medal in the Olympics, teaming with Zina Garrison to win the top honors in women's doubles at the 1988 Games in Seoul, South Korea. At the 1991 Pan-American Games in Havana, Cuba, Pam swept all the gold medals: singles, doubles, and mixed doubles.

Continuing the Story

Pam retired from competitive tennis in 1997. However, she remained involved in the sport on many levels. In addition to having been a mentor to Venus Williams, Pam also provided television commentary for ABC, CBS, ESPN, the BBC, and 7 Sport in Australia. Her work as a commentator required her to be on the road fifteen to eighteen weeks per year.

Pam, who once owned a tennis club in Baltimore, started her own company, PHS Ltd., which is involved in charitable activities. Among other ventures, her company arranges and publicizes the annual Chevy Chase Bank Tennis Challenge, a charity event that has been held in Baltimore for many

years. Pam became a minority owner of the Baltimore Orioles, served as president of the USA Tennis Foundation, and was a member of the board of directors for the United States Tennis Association, which owns the U.S. Open. Pam was inducted into the International Tennis Hall of Fame, along with Mats Wilander, in 2002.

Pam has three children and one stepchild and has been married twice. Her first husband, Walt Disney company lawyer Joe Shapiro, died of cancer in 1999, barely a year after their marriage. In 2002, Pam married former James Bond actor George Lazenby. The family moved to Brentwood, California. Furthermore, Pam is a fourth cousin to Maria Shriver, the wife of Arnold Schwarzenegger.

Summary

Pam Shriver teamed with Navratilova for 109 consecutive victories. Twenty of her Grand Slam doubles titles came with Navratilova. Her only Grand Slam singles final was at sixteen. She won twenty-one singles titles and was part of 112 doubles titles, twenty-two in Grand Slams. Pam grew up with tennis, and the sport remained an integral part of her life even after she retired as a player.

Randy L. Abbott

Additional Sources

Shriver, Pam. *Game Plan: Professional Advice—Pam Shriver Answers Your Questions. Tennis,* August, 2004, 26.

Shriver, Pam, Frank DeFord, and Susan B. Adams. *Passing Shots: Pam Shriver on Tour.* New York: McGraw-Hill, 1987.

Honors and Awards

1981-88	WTA Tour Doubles Team of the Year (with Martina Navratilova)
1988	Olympic Games gold medal in women's doubles (with Zina Garrison)
1991	Pan-American Games gold medals in singles, doubles, and mixed doubles
2002	Inducted into International Tennis Hall of Fame

Stan Smith

Born: December 14, 1946
     Pasadena, California
Also known as: Stanley Roger Smith (full name);
    the Steamer

Early Life
Stanley Roger Smith was born in Pasadena, California, on December 14, 1946, the son of a college athletic coach. He developed an early interest in sports, and excelled at both tennis and baseball while attending Pasadena High School. Unlike some champions, Stan did not display extraordinary ability immediately in his chosen sport. Although he was talented, he was also chunky and ungainly. When he practiced at the Los Angeles Tennis Club, most of the outstanding teenage players shunned him.

The Road to Excellence
Stan was undaunted by players who looked down on him. He resolved to make his rivals change their minds and accordingly practiced more tenaciously than anyone else. To overcome his physical awkwardness, he worked out constantly with a jump rope. His efforts soon paid off, and in 1964, he won the National Junior Singles title.

The longtime czar of Los Angeles tennis, Perry Jones, took a liking to Stan and recommended that he team with Bob Lutz, another teenager who, like Stan, was attending the University of Southern California (USC). At USC, Stan's game continued to improve under the instruction of the university's coach, the veteran George Toley.

Several factors made Stan into a championship player. At 6 feet 4 inches in height, he was among the tallest players in the game, which gave him a considerable advantage in gaining power on his serve, one of the fastest in tennis. Because of his strong service, he was nicknamed "the Steamer," after the classic Stanley Steamer motorcar. Stan also possessed a powerful and accurate forehand. During his amateur days, his backhand was less than outstanding; he improved this feature of his game after he turned professional in 1973.

Perhaps even more important than the quality of his shots

Major Championship Victories and Finals

1968, 1974, 1978, 1980	U.S. Open doubles (with Bob Lutz)
1969	U.S. National Championship
1970	Australian Open doubles (with Lutz)
1971	U.S. Open
	Wimbledon finalist
1971, 1974	French Open doubles finalist (with Tom Gorman and Lutz)
1971, 1979	U.S. Open doubles finalist (with Lutz)
1972	Wimbledon
1972, 1974, 1980-81	Wimbledon doubles finalist (with Erik van Dillen and Lutz)

Other Notable Victories

1966	U.S. Hardcourt Championship doubles (with Lutz)
1966-68	U.S. Hardcourt Championship
1966, 1969-70	U.S. Indoor Championship doubles (with Lutz and Arthur Ashe)
1967-68	NCAA Championship doubles (with Lutz)
1968	U.S. Indoor Championship doubles finalist (with Lutz)
	NCAA Championship
	U.S. Clay Court Championship doubles (with Lutz)
1968-72, 1978-79	On winning U.S. Davis Cup team
1969-79	U.S. Indoor Championship
1970	The Masters
1973	WCT Finals
	WCT World Doubles Championship (with Lutz)
1979	Miller Hall of Fame Championship doubles (with Lutz)
	Volvo Tennis Classic doubles (with Lutz)
	European Indoor Open doubles (with Gene Mayer)
1985-86	U.S. Open Invitational doubles (with Lutz)

was his rigid determination. Stan was a "straight arrow" person who concentrated single-mindedly on the task at hand. He was a leading member of the Fellowship of Christian Athletes and, in line with the ideals of that group, never allowed bad habits to interfere with his training.

Stan's personality contrasted sharply with that of his doubles partner, Bob Lutz, who was a happy-go-lucky character who often failed to devote enough time to practice. Lutz had been regarded as a better singles prospect than Stan; however, he never fulfilled his early potential as a singles player. Nevertheless, he and Stan became one of the world's outstanding doubles teams.

Honors, Awards, and Milestones	
1968	William M. Johnston Sportsmanship Award
1968-73, 1975, 1977-79, 1981	U.S. Davis Cup team
1969	Lebair Sportsmanship Award
1969, 1971-73	Nationally ranked number one
1970-72, 1975	Nationally ranked number one in doubles
1972	Ranked number one in the world
1978	ATP-Adidas Sportsmanship Award
1979	ATF Service Award
1987	Inducted into International Tennis Hall of Fame

The Emerging Champion

Stan's careful, almost grim preparation over a number of years paid off in the early 1970's. In 1971, he won the U.S. Open title at Forest Hills, New York. His opponent in the final was the Czech Jan Kodes, who lacked Stan's power but was a player of great finesse. Kodes often defeated power players with his unusual service-return ability. Stan's serve and all-around power proved too much for Kodes, though, and Stan won his first major title.

In 1971, Stan was unable to win the Wimbledon title, although he did reach the final. His opponent was John Newcombe, an Australian whose power was a match for Stan's own. The next year, however, Newcombe was under contract with World Championship of Tennis (WCT), and, under the rules then in effect, was ineligible to compete at Wimbledon.

Stan again reached the finals, and this time his opponent was the Romanian Ilie Nastase, whose personality and technique were the diametric opposite of Stan's. Nastase's game stressed finesse, touch, and variety, in contrast to Stan's power and relentlessness. Stan was unemotional during play and a model of good manners. Ilie was flamboyant and temperamental; his frequent temper tantrums were notorious. In perhaps the best match of his career, Stan dispatched the fiery Romanian.

In addition to his singles titles, Stan compiled an outstanding record in Davis Cup play and in doubles matches. He and his partner Lutz became extremely adept in teamwork. Their careful strategic planning during matches refuted the charges that Stan's game was one-dimensional and unintelligent.

Continuing the Story

In 1973, Stan turned professional. His first year proved successful: He won the WCT finals, one of the most important professional events. To do so, he had to defeat the great Australian players Rod Laver and Ken Rosewall in addition to his fellow American Arthur Ashe. His victory in this tournament was no fluke; during the year, Stan dominated Laver, one of the greatest players of all time. In both 1972 and 1973, Stan was ranked as the world's top player.

Stan's time at the pinnacle was short. After 1973, his game suddenly worsened, and he plunged in the rankings. At various times in the next few years, he developed back and knee problems that sidelined him for long periods. His injuries did not appear to be the initial cause of his decline, though; experts have never been able to agree on the cause of the slump.

Stan's determination again came to the fore. He refused to quit the game and tried repeatedly to return to his former excellence. Although he never again won a major singles title, his efforts once more paid off. He and Lutz continued their outstanding record as a doubles team. They were ranked as one of the best partnerships in the United States as late as 1980. After retiring from competitive tennis, Stan remained close to the game by writing articles for *Tennis Magazine*. In 2000, he served as coach of the U.S. Olympic men's tennis team at the Summer Olympics in Sydney, Australia. He also opened a tennis school in Hilton Head Island, South Carolina, called the Smith Stearns Tennis Academy.

Summary

Stan Smith was a talented, though not extraordinary, tennis player as a teenager. His determination and constant training enabled him to surpass his erstwhile superiors and to develop into the top singles player in the United States during the early 1970's. His career peaked in the period 1971-1973. After these years, he was never again ranked as a great singles player, but he continued to be a top-flight doubles player with his partner since college, Bob Lutz.

Bill Delaney

Additional Sources

Smith, Stan. *Stan Smith's Six Tennis Basics.* New York: Atheneum, 1974.

_____. *Stan Smith's Winning Doubles.* Champaign, Ill.: Human Kinetics, 2002.

Smith, Stan, Larry Sheehan, James McQueen, and Leonard Kamsler. *Stan Smith's Guide to Better Tennis.* London: Hale, 1975.

Bill Tilden

Born: February 10, 1893
    Philadelphia, Pennsylvania
Died: June 5, 1953
    Hollywood, California
Also known as: William Tatem Tilden II (full
    name); Big Bill

Early Life

William Tatem Tilden II was born on February 10, 1893, in Philadelphia, Pennsylvania, the second youngest of five children. Three of the children died during a diphtheria epidemic in 1884; only Bill and his older brother, Herbert, survived. Herbert introduced Bill to tennis, but the boy showed little skill in the early years.

Bill's father, a wealthy businessman, was often away from home, so Bill became close to his mother Linie, who, fearing for his health, had Bill educated at home by private tutors. In 1908, however, Linie contracted Bright's disease, and, with Herbert finishing school and preparing to marry, Bill was sent to Germantown Academy. While attending school there, he lived with a maiden aunt and his cousin. Since Bill never married, these two women remained his "family" for many years.

In 1910, Bill graduated from Germantown Academy and entered the Wharton School of Business at the University of Pennsylvania. He disliked his studies, however, and dropped out for one year after his mother's death in 1911. In 1915, tragedy struck again when both Bill's father and brother died unexpectedly. Too devastated by grief to study, Bill left the University of Pennsylvania in his senior year, deciding to make a career out of tennis.

The Road to Excellence

Bill coached tennis for a year at Germantown Academy and at the University of Pennsylvania before entering competition. He was given a national ranking of seventy and entered the U.S. National Championship matches in 1916, but he lost in the first round. In 1918 and 1919, he reached the final round of competition but lost again. Bill worked hard at building his game, spending many hours on the courts. He mastered a variety of strokes, learning the chops, half volleys, and short lobs that supplemented his already strong forehand and serve.

In 1920, Bill played the reigning Wimbledon titleholder, Gerald L. Patterson of Australia, winning the match with a combination of strokes and an awesome serve, to become the first American to win the men's Wimbledon singles title. That same summer, he won the U.S. National Championship at Forest Hills, defeating Bill Johnston, the number-one ranked U.S. player. Bill became a giant of the game, bringing a virile athletic image to the sport.

Like his contemporaries Babe Ruth in baseball and Jack Dempsey in boxing, Bill caught the public's imagination at home and abroad. Not only was he proficient, but he also had a powerful personal-

Bill Tilden, who was often considered the Babe Ruth of tennis.
(Courtesy of International Tennis Hall of Fame)

Major Championship Victories and Finals

1913-14, 1922-23	U.S. National Championship mixed doubles (with Mary K. Browne and Molla B. Mallory)
1916-17, 1919, 1924	U.S. National Championship mixed-doubles finalist (with F. A. Ballin and Mallory)
1918-1919, 1927	U.S. National Championship finalist
1918, 1921-22, 1923, 1927	U.S. National Championship doubles (with Vincent Richards, Brian Norton, and Francis T. Hunter)
1919, 1926	U.S. National Championship doubles finalist (with Richards and Alfred Chapin)
1920-21, 1930	Wimbledon
1920-25, 1929	U.S. National Championship
1927	Wimbledon doubles (with Hunter)
	French Championship mixed-doubles finalist (with L. de Alvarez)
1927, 1930	French Championship finalist
1930	French Championship mixed-doubles (with Cilly Aussem)

Other Notable Victories

1918, 1922-27	U.S. Clay Court Championship
1919-20, 1926, 1929	U.S. Indoor Championship doubles (with Richards, Frank Anderson, and Hunter)
1920	U.S. Indoor Championship
1920-26	On winning U.S. Davis Cup team
1921-22, 1924	U.S. Indoor Championship mixed doubles (with Mallory and Hazel Wightman)
1930	Italian Championship
	Italian Championship doubles (with Wilbur Coen)
1931, 1935	U.S. Pro Championship
1932	U.S. Pro Championship doubles (with Bruce Barnes)
1934-38	Professional World Doubles Tournament (with Ellsworth Vines and Henri Cochet)

ity, dominating any place he was. He had a natural grace, aided by his physique—tall, broad-shouldered, lean—and nimble footwork. Even in his rare defeats, he was the center of attraction.

The Emerging Champion

Combining intelligence with hard work, Bill mastered the game completely, and it brought him great fame and wealth. He spent money lavishly, traveling widely and entertaining generously. He was often in the company of other celebrities such as movie stars and politicians. In spite of these distractions, Bill continued to play great tennis. He won the U.S. Clay Court Championship singles six

consecutive years, from 1922-1927, the U.S. National Championship doubles five times, the mixed doubles four times, and the U.S. Indoor Championship doubles four times. He took the Wimbledon singles title three times: 1920, 1921, and 1930. Between 1920 and 1930, Bill played on the U.S. Davis Cup team, leading the United States to victory in seven consecutive years.

In 1926, Bill severely injured his knee, and victories became much harder to come by. He and the great French player René Lacoste traded wins between 1926 and 1930. In 1928, one of the most thrilling matches between them occurred in France. The United States Lawn Tennis Association (USLTA) banned Bill only days before the match for violating the player-writer rule, which specified that no amateur player could receive money in connection with the sport. Bill, however, was employed as a tennis columnist. Upon protest by France and by the U.S. ambassador to France, Bill was reinstated. An underdog, since Lacoste had won their previous four meetings, Bill electrified the spectators with his brilliant play, confusing Lacoste's game plan with versatile shots. Bill was at his peak.

Continuing the Story

In 1931, Bill turned professional, forming the Tilden Tennis Tours, Inc., with his former doubles partner Frank Hunter. They made their first appearance at Madison Square Garden in February, pioneering the way for players who preferred "cash to cups." Bill went on to win the U.S. Pro Championship singles title in 1931 and 1935 as well as the doubles in 1932. Although a big draw on tours, he was a poor businessman, running into financial problems through bad investments and careless spending habits. By the end of the 1930's, Bill was almost broke. Still, to most fans, he remained the personification of tennis. His instinctive showmanship was as sharp as ever: He knew the moves and gestures to win over any audience.

After World War II, Bill helped organize the Professional Tennis Players Association and still played well enough to draw crowds, often reaching the quarterfinals in pro tournaments. In the following years, however, Bill came out as a homosexual, and by the 1940's, he was openly defending homosexuality. In November, 1946, he was arrested by the Beverly Hills police on a morals charge. Taken to court, he was found guilty and was sentenced to several months in prison. When Bill came out, he was broken in health and in spirit.

Living in Hollywood from the 1940's until his death, Bill gave lessons on friends' private courts, earning much-needed money. Still enthusiastic about the game, Bill was planning to play in the U.S. Pro Championship that was to be held in Cleveland in June of 1953. He died, however, of an apparent heart attack alone in his apartment the night before his scheduled departure.

Summary

Although Bill Tilden died in relative obscurity, his career was illustrious. His virtuosity, concentration, and "cannonball" serve earned him the admiration of all. In 1949, an Associated Press poll cited him as the top tennis player of the first half-century, giving him 310 votes out of a possible 391; the runner-up received 32 votes. In 1969, a panel of international writers put him at the head of its collective all-time ranking. Few disputed Bill's title as one of the greatest tennis players who ever lived.

S. Carol Berg

Honors, Awards, and Milestones

1920-25	Ranked number one in the world
1920-29	Nationally ranked number one
1920-30	U.S. Davis Cup team
1949	Named the tennis athlete of the first half-century (Associated Press poll)
1959	Inducted into National Lawn Tennis Hall of Fame

Additional Sources

Deford, Frank. *Big Bill Tilden: The Triumphs and the Tragedy.* Rev. ed. Kingston, N.Y.: Total/Sports Illustrated Classics, 2001.

Gurney, A. R. *Big Bill.* New York: Broadway Play, 2004.

Tilden, Bill. *Match Play and the Spin of the Ball.* Edited by Stephen Wallis Merrihew. 2d ed. New York: American Lawn Tennis, 1925.

_____. *My Story: A Champion's Memoirs.* 2d ed. New York: Hellman, Williams & Company, 1948.

Wilner, Barry, and Ken Rappoport. *Harvard Beats Yale 29-29, and Other Great Comebacks from the Annals of Sports.* Lanham, Md.: Taylor Trade, 2008.

Tony Trabert

Born: August 16, 1930
      Cincinnati, Ohio
Also known as: Marion Anthony Trabert (full name)

Early Life

Marion Anthony Trabert was born August 16, 1930, in Cincinnati, Ohio. His father Archibald Taylor was a sales engineer for the General Electric Company. Tony was the youngest of three brothers. Like many famous athletes, Tony became interested in sports at an early age, starting to play tennis when he was only six years old. He continued to play tennis in high school and college, but tennis was not his only sport. He also played on his high school and college basketball teams. He attended Walnut Hills High School and the University of Cincinnati.

The Road to Excellence

There was never any doubt that tennis was Tony's major sport, and in 1951, he won the National Collegiate Athletic Association (NCAA) singles title. An outstanding college player, however, is different from a world-class tennis champion. Several qualities in his game enabled him make the transition to world tennis champion. He was strong and had a powerful serve. His ground strokes were impressive: He hit the ball with unusual force and accuracy. If he was having a good day, few players could stay on the court with him. Interestingly, many American tennis champions have had powerful ground strokes in their play: Don Budge and Ellsworth Vines are the most famous of these. Tony also could hit remarkable recovery shots. He was often able to return shots that seemed sure winners for his opponent.

Tony had another strong point that many aggressive, attacking players lack. A fierce attacking game is difficult to sustain for a long time. Often, attacking players become tired and lose to opponents who can keep the ball in play. This slowdown is especially common in the last rounds of men's tournaments, which usually last five sets. Tony found the answer to this problem. He was superbly conditioned and spent hours on exercise each day of preparation for a tournament. He played five sets with ease, and opponents who waited for the rapid pace of his attack to falter were disappointed.

The Emerging Champion

Tony's attacking game and physical fitness were enough to give him championship potential. To play at the highest level, however, talent is not

Tony Trabert, who won five Grand Slams in the 1950's. (Courtesy of Amateur Athletic Foundation of Los Angeles)

Major Championship Victories and Finals

1950, 1954-55	French Championship doubles (with Bill Talbert and Vic Seixas)
1953, 1955	U.S. National Championship
1954	U.S. National Championship doubles (with Seixas)
	Wimbledon doubles finalist (with Seixas)
1954-55	French Championship
1955	Wimbledon
	Australian Championship doubles (with Seixas)

Other Notable Victories

1950	Italian Championship doubles (with Talbert)
	Pacific Southwest Championship doubles (with Fred Schroeder)
1951	NCAA Championship
1951, 1954-55	U.S. Clay Court Championship doubles (with Hamilton Richardson and Seixas)
1951, 1955	U.S. Clay Court Championship
1954	On winning U.S. Davis Cup team
1954-55	U.S. Indoor Championship doubles (with Talbert and Seixas)
1955	U.S. Indoor Championship
1956	U.S. Pro Championship doubles (with Rex Hartwig)

enough: Skill and knowledge are also required. Tony was fortunate to win the friendship of Bill Talbert, an experienced champion and a master of tennis technique. He worked on building all phases of Tony's game, and with Talbert's help, Tony began to win major championships while he was still in college.

In 1950, Tony won the French Championship doubles title with Talbert, a feat he repeated in 1954 and 1955 with Vic Seixas. Tony became an expert on the strategy of doubles and later wrote a book on the subject.

Tony also became a mainstay of the U.S. Davis Cup team, compiling an excellent record in his five years on the team. Probably his most famous Davis Cup match, however, was a loss. In Melbourne, Australia, in 1953, his opponent was the young Australian Lew Hoad, whose game was an exaggerated version of Tony's. When Hoad was in form, even Tony could not stop him, and Tony lost a close five-set match.

In spite of the loss, Tony's rise to the top continued unabated in the succeeding two years. In 1953, he won the U.S. National Championship singles title at Forest Hills without losing a set in the entire tournament. In 1954, he won the French Championship, a feat few Americans have matched. Most players from the United States perform badly on the hard clay surfaces of the French courts.

Continuing the Story

Tony established himself as the best amateur singles player in the world in 1955. In that year, he again won the French Championship. He also won the U.S. National Championship and Wimbledon, the latter without the loss of a set. These tournaments were three legs of tennis's Grand Slam. The final part of the Grand Slam, the Australian Championship, eluded him; Ken Rosewall defeated him in the semifinals.

Tony thus failed to achieve tennis's supreme feat, an calendar-year Grand Slam. Nevertheless, Tony stood at the top of amateur tennis. He decided to turn professional the following year, 1956. Jack Kramer, the main promoter of professional tennis, signed Tony to a series of matches against the professional champion, Pancho Gonzales. The more experienced Gonzales, who had the fastest service in tennis and an extraordinary will to win, overpowered his challenger. Gonzales won the series of matches, 74-27.

As a professional, Tony did well but was never a real standout. In 1960, he was runner-up to Alex Olmedo for the U.S. Pro Championship singles title. After he retired from active play, Tony became a teaching professional and television commentator. He also served as captain of the U.S. Davis Cup team in the late 1970's.

Summary

Tennis was a popular sport in the United States in the ten years after World War II, and many young athletes tried the game. Most of them featured an

Honors, Awards, and Records

1951-55	U.S. Davis Cup team
1953, 1955	Nationally ranked number one
1970	Inducted into National Lawn Tennis Hall of Fame
1976-80	U.S. Davis Cup team captain

aggressive game, and Tony Trabert was one of the best, if not the best, of the lot. His powerful ground stroke and superb conditioning enabled him to take the giant step from good player to great player. He was the best amateur in the world in 1955, the year he won three major singles championships.

Bill Delaney

Additional Sources

Collins, Bud. *Total Tennis: The Ultimate Tennis Encyclopedia.* Toronto: Sport Media, 2003.

Segura, Melissa. "Tony Trabert, Tennis Champion." *Sports Illustrated* 101, no. 17 (November 1, 2004): 18.

Trabert, Tony, and Gerald Secor Couzens. *Trabert on Tennis: The View from Center Court.* Chicago: Contemporary Books, 1988.

Trabert, Tony, and Jim Hook. *The Serve: Key to Winning Tennis.* New York: Dodd, Mead, 1984.

Trabert, Tony, Ron Witchey, and Don DeNevi. *Tennis Past Fifty.* Champaign, Ill.: Human Kinetics, 2002.

Guillermo Vilas

Born: August 17, 1952
Buenos Aires, Argentina
Also known as: Young Bull of the Pampas

Early Life

Guillermo Vilas was born on August 17, 1952, in Buenos Aires, Argentina. Guillermo's father, José Roque Vilas, was a wealthy lawyer and president of a local tennis club. He encouraged his son to take up the game, and Guillermo began to practice seriously when he was not yet ten years old.

At the age of ten, Guillermo started to take lessons from Felipe Locicero, a local professional. Like many outstanding athletes, Guillermo manifested remarkable early talent. Within one year of commencing his lessons, he was already winning local tournaments, and he soon became the best junior player in Argentina.

Guillermo did not fully commit himself to tennis as a career until the beginning of the 1970's. By the late 1970's, however, he had become a fixture on Argentina's Davis Cup team.

Guillermo Vilas playing in the French Open in 1976. (AFP/Getty Images)

The Road to Excellence

Several factors helped place Guillermo among those with championship potential. He was known as "The Bull" because of his solid physique and power. He had a fast and effective serve and also possessed sharp and accurate ground strokes. Although his power was an asset, he was matched in this regard by several of his contemporaries, such as the American player Jimmy Connors.

What made Guillermo stand out was the topspin he put on his strokes, particularly on his backhand. This spin is difficult to control, but Guillermo was able to manage the feat, at the same time striking the ball with devastating efficiency. A topspin drive under such conditions is difficult to return; mastery of this type of hitting probably was the most essential factor elevating Guillermo to the first rank.

Guillermo developed his skill at topspin by modeling himself on Rod Laver, one of the greatest players of all time. The court conditions of Guillermo's native Argentina also contributed to his stress on the topspin. Most Argentine courts are clay, the comparative slowness of which encourages the development of clever shotmaking and discourages reliance on power alone.

The Emerging Champion

Guillermo seemed to be in an excellent position to do well internationally. When he turned to a full-time professional career at the start of the 1970's, he immediately compiled a fine record. He was unable to win any major tournaments, however, and was frequently criticized for lacking a killer instinct.

Guillermo also had bad luck in that his road to excellence coincided with the peak period of the great Swedish player Björn Borg, the dominant force of the 1970's. Guillermo played many matches against Borg, usually marked by extremely long rallies, as both possessed unusually accurate strokes and were otherwise similar in their styles of play. Although Guillermo gave stiff competition to his great rival, the phlegmatic Swede almost always defeated the mercurial Argentine.

Guillermo refused to be discouraged and continued to perfect his game. His dedication and hard work paid off in 1974, when, in a three-month period, he won fifty-four out of sixty matches. In that year, he was also one of the leading money-winners on the tour.

Although Guillermo seemed destined for the top, he still had not won any of the game's premier tournaments: the U.S. Open, the French Open, the Australian Open, and Wimbledon.

Continuing the Story

Guillermo's battle to reach the top was not over. After his outstanding 1974 season, his game went into a slump. He was once again equal to the challenge and resolved to do whatever was necessary to perfect his game.

Guillermo sought help, turning to Ion Tiriac, an outstanding Romanian player and coach. As a player, Tiriac had never reached the commanding heights and was best known as the doubles partner of Ilie Nastase. As a coach, however, Tiriac was supreme. He advised Guillermo to become more aggressive and instructed him to follow his ground strokes with a move to the net. He put Guillermo through a rigorous exercise program, the result of which was to make him the best-conditioned player on the tour.

Guillermo's work with Tiriac paid off in spectacular fashion. In 1977, Guillermo ran up a streak of fifty-five straight wins. He achieved his first Grand Slam victories the same year, winning both the

French and U.S. Opens. At last, these victories placed him among the world's best. Of this there was no room for doubt, as he had won the U.S. title by a thorough demolition of Jimmy Connors in the finals.

In 1978 and 1979, Guillermo added Australian Opens to his Grand Slam victories. Although he continued to be an outstanding player, never finishing below sixth among the top money-winners in the years from 1974 to 1982, he never matched the position of supremacy he reached during 1977 and early 1978.

Guillermo's struggles with the game's top players, combined with his personality, made him a hero in Latin America. His achievements helped to popularize tennis in that part of the world.

In 1983, Guillermo became embroiled in a controversy about accepting appearance money to play in tournaments. Appearance money is a fee paid to a player to participate in a tournament, whether or not he wins a prize. The criticism deeply affected the temperamental Argentine, and his game steadily declined after 1983. He continued an active role on the circuit throughout the 1980's. In 1993, Guillermo began competing on the Worldwide Senior Tennis Circuit.

Summary

Guillermo Vilas rose to prominence from a region that had not previously produced many topflight

---

Major Championship Victories and Finals

1975, 1978, 1982	French Open finalist
1977	French Open
	U.S. Open
	Australian Open finalist
1978-79	Australian Open

Other Notable Victories

1974	Swiss Championships
	The Masters
	Canadian Open doubles (with Manuel Orantes)
1974, 1976	Canadian Open
1977	South African Open
1978	Swiss Open
	German Open
1980	Italian Open
1982	Monte Carlo Open

Honors, Awards, and Milestones

1970-84	Argentinian Davis Cup team
1974-75, 1977	First in Grand Prix standings
1977	55 consecutive Grand Prix match wins
	57 consecutive match wins on clay
1982	Nationally ranked number one
1991	Inducted into International Tennis Hall of Fame

international tennis players. His mastery of the topspin stroke, learned on the slow clay courts of his native country, gave him a great advantage over his less dexterous rivals. In spite of his talent, he did not attain supreme excellence except for the short period of 1977 and 1978. Nevertheless, he ranks as one of the outstanding players of the 1970's and early 1980's.

Bill Delaney

Additional Sources

Bodo, Peter. "Viva Vilas." *Tennis* 32 (November, 1996): 68-72.

Conner, Floyd. *Tennis's Most Wanted: The Top Ten Book of Baseline Blunders, Clay Court Wonders, and Lucky Lobs.* Washington, D.C.: Brassey's, 2002.

Shifrin, Joshua. *101 Incredible Moments in Tennis: The Good, the Bad, and the Infamous.* College Station, Tex.: Virtualbookworm, 2005.

Virginia Wade

Born: July 10, 1945
       Bournemouth, Dorset, England
Also known as: Sarah Virginia Wade (full name)

Early Life

Sarah Virginia Wade was born on July 10, 1945, at Bournemouth, on England's southern coast. Her parents were Eustace Holland Wade and Joan Barbara Wade. Virginia was the youngest child in the family, with two older brothers and an older sister. She grew up in Durban, South Africa, where her father served as archdeacon of Durban. She attended the Gordon Road Girls' School and Durban High School. She excelled at her schoolwork, particularly mathematics. She also studied piano and became an accomplished pianist.

When she was nine years old, she began playing tennis with a racket that she had found while cleaning a closet. She loved the game immediately and showed a natural talent for the sport. She played as often as possible at the Durban Lawn Tennis Club, which was next to her home. Although she received help from her brothers and sister, along with some additional instruction, her tennis skills were mainly self-taught.

The Road to Excellence

In 1961, when Virginia was fifteen years old, her family returned to England. Although she was disappointed to leave her friends and tennis teammates in South Africa, the move advanced her development as a tennis player. She played in many junior tournaments, participated in a training program in London for promising junior players, and qualified for Wimbledon at the age of sixteen.

Upon graduation from secondary school, Virginia entered the University of Sussex to pursue a degree in mathematics and physics. From 1964 through 1966, Virginia continued to play tennis while attending college. The difficulty of balancing tennis and studies reached a climax in June, 1966, when she took her final exams at the same time that she was competing on Great Britain's Wightman Cup team in its annual match against the United States. Great Britain lost the Wightman Cup, but Virginia earned her B.S. degree.

Once Virginia had completed her formal education, she began playing tennis full time. For two years, in 1966 and 1967, she competed as an amateur on the international tennis circuit. Her record was uneven. She had some important victories in Wightman Cup competition and as British Hardcourt

Virginia Wade following through after hitting a forehand at the 1968 U.S. Open. (Hulton Archive/Getty Images)

champion in 1967 and 1968. At the same time, she did not do as well in some of the Grand Slam tournaments, especially Wimbledon, where British crowds hoped that she might become the champion that England had not had for many years. Overall, she gained important experience that benefited her game.

The Emerging Champion

The late 1960's were significant for tennis and for women's tennis in particular. In 1968, the major events became open to both professional and amateur players. Also, a group of women's tennis players joined together to promote greater equality in prize money for the female professionals.

Virginia was part of this movement and turned professional in 1968. In September, 1968, she won her first Grand Slam tournament at the U.S. Open. By the end of 1968, Virginia was the second-ranked woman tennis player in the world.

Virginia's active career as a professional tennis player extended from the late 1960's through the early 1980's. During this time she was always highly ranked. She won several major tournaments, including the Italian Open in 1971, the Australian Open in 1972, and the British Hardcourt Championship in 1973 and 1974. She was the captain of the British Wightman Cup team from 1973 to 1986. She also played World Team Tennis for the New York Sets.

Virginia brought a great intensity and perfectionism to tennis. She had an excellent serve-and-volley game, well suited for grass courts and hard courts. At times, her performance in tennis matches was uneven because of her mental frustration when the technical execution of her strokes did not meet the high standard of excellence that she set for herself.

The greatest triumph of Virginia Wade's tennis career came when she won the Wimbledon title in 1977. As a British citizen, becoming a Wimbledon champion held special meaning for Virginia. After sixteen years of playing in the tournament she finally became the champion. Her win in the finals over Betty Stove was even more exciting because it was the one hundredth anniversary of the Wimbledon tournament and Queen Elizabeth's Silver Jubilee, celebrating the leader's twenty-five years as British monarch. When Virginia won Wimbledon, Queen Elizabeth II presented her the championship trophy.

Continuing the Story

By the time Virginia won Wimbledon, she had already achieved a full career as a professional tennis

---

Major Championship Victories and Finals

1968	U.S. Open
1969	U.S. National Championship doubles (with Margaret Court)
1970	Wimbledon doubles finalist (with Françoise Durr)
1970, 1972, 1976	U.S. Open doubles finalist (with Rosie Casals, Court, and Olga Morozova)
1972	Australian Open
1973	Australian Open doubles (with Court)
	French Open doubles (with Court)
1973, 1975	U.S. Open doubles (with Court)
1977	Wimbledon
1979	French Open doubles finalist (with Durr)

Other Notable Victories

1967	British Hardcourt Championship doubles (with Ann Jones)
1967-68, 1973-74	British Hardcourt Championship
1968, 1971, 1973, 1983	Italian Open doubles (with Court, Helga Niessen Masthoff, Morozova, and Virginia Ruzici)
1968, 1974-75, 1978	On winning British Wightman Cup team
1971	Italian Open
1976	U.S. Indoor Championship
1977	Colgate Championships doubles (with Durr)
1978	Virginia Slims of Los Angeles doubles (with Betty Stove)

Honors, Awards, and Milestones

1965-85	British Wightman Cup team
1967-83	British Federation Cup team
1973	Member of the British Empire
1973-86	British Wightman Cup team captain
1977	WTA Player of the Year
1982	First woman elected to Wimbledon Committee
1989	Inducted into International Tennis Hall of Fame

player. She continued as an active professional for several more years into the early 1980's. She did not, however, have any more victories as notable as her Wimbledon triumph.

Virginia remained involved with tennis in several ways: playing in ladies' senior competitions, presenting commentaries on tennis for television, and writing two books on tennis: her autobiography, *Courting Triumph* (1978), and *Ladies of the Court* (1984), on women players at Wimbledon.

Virginia received numerous awards and honors for her accomplishments both on and off the tennis court. In 1973, she was made a Member of the British Empire by Queen Elizabeth II. The University of Sussex awarded her an honorary LL.D. in 1985. She was inducted into the International Tennis Hall of Fame in 1989. She continued to pursue a wide variety of interests, including reading and the arts. Beginning in the early 1980's, Virginia worked as a tennis commentator for the BBC and the USA Network.

Summary

Virginia Wade's most memorable win was the 1977 Ladies Championship in Wimbledon's centenary year. Virginia's passion for tennis and her graceful style of play throughout her long professional career contributed much to her sport during an exciting period of growth for women's tennis.

Karen Gould

Additional Sources

Araton, Harvey. "Remember Virginia Wade's Championship? The British Don't Seem To." *The New York Times,* July 8, 2001, Sec. 8, p. 6.

Shifrin, Joshua. *101 Incredible Moments in Tennis: The Good, the Bad, and the Infamous.* College Station, Tex.: Virtualbookworm, 2005.

Wade, Virginia, and Mary Lou Mellace. *Courting Triumph.* New York: Mayflower Books, 1978.

Wade, Virginia, and Jean Rafferty. *Ladies of the Court: A Century of Women at Wimbledon.* New York: Atheneum, 1984.

Hazel Wightman

Born: December 20, 1886
       Healdsburg, California
Died: December 5, 1974
       Chestnut Hill, Massachusetts
Also known as: Hazel Virginia Hotchkiss
    Wightman (full name); Hazel Virginia
    Hotchkiss (birth name); Lady Tennis; Mrs.
    Wightie; Queen Mother of American Tennis

Early Life

Hazel Virginia Hotchkiss, one of the most durable women's tennis champions in the United States, was born in Healdsburg, California, on December 20, 1886. Her father William Hotchkiss had come to California from Kentucky in a covered wagon train when he was two years old. Hazel's mother Emma Groves met William when her family settled on a ranch right next to the Hotchkiss family's land in the Sonoma Valley. After their marriage, William and Emma had five children. Their fourth child, their only daughter, was Hazel.

Hazel was considered a rather delicate child, so her family provided her with many opportunities to develop her strength. She enjoyed the sports her brothers played, and they encouraged her participation. The vigor Hazel grew to possess reflected that of her mother. Hazel's mother showed her indomitable strength even in her sixties, when a car she thought she had parked rolled over her foot. The clear-thinking woman, realizing that the brake had slipped, managed to reach the brake handle and stop the car before she collapsed. A Christian Science practitioner treated her that evening, and by the next morning she was up and about, showing no signs of injury.

The Road to Excellence

By the time Hazel was fourteen, her family had moved to Berkeley, California, where Hazel was introduced to tennis. Her brothers also played the game, so she nearly always had someone to hit with her. When they were not available, Hazel hit against the wall of the house. Hazel and her brothers played on a gravel area in their backyard. Their net was a rope, and in an effort to defend themselves from flying gravel and the erratic bounces of the ball, they became excellent volleyers. This skill later became the earmark of Hazel's success and helped her to revolutionize women's tennis.

Soon after Hazel began to play tennis, she had the opportunity to see the Sutton sisters—Ethel, Violet, Florence, and May—in action. These sisters were renowned as the finest women players in California. Hazel was excited by their performance and eager to compete at their level, but she found their style of play, which relied almost completely

Hazel Wightman, who won a pair of gold medals in tennis at the 1924 Olympic Games in Paris. (Courtesy of Amateur Athletic Foundation of Los Angeles)

Major Championship Victories and Finals

1909-11, 1915	U.S. National Championship doubles (with Edith E. Rotch and Eleanora Sears)
1909-11, 1915, 1918, 1920	U.S. National Championship mixed doubles (with Wallace F. Johnson, Joseph R. Carpenter, Jr., Harry C. Johnson, and Irving C. Wright)
1909-11, 1919	U.S. National Championship
1915	U.S. National Championship finals

Other Notable Victories

1919, 1921-22, 1924, 1927-31, 1933	U.S. Indoor Championship doubles (with Marion Zinderstein Jessup and Sarah Palfrey)
1919, 1927	U.S. Indoor Championship
1923-24, 1926-28	U.S. Indoor Championship mixed doubles (with Burnham N. Dell, Bill Tilden, G. P. Gardner, Jr., and Henry L. Johnson, Jr.)
1924	Gold medal, Olympic doubles (with Helen Wills)
	Gold medal, Olympic mixed doubles (with Richard Norris Williams)
1940-42, 1944, 1946-50, 1952, 1954	U.S. Grass Court Championship-Women's 40 doubles (with Edith Sigourney, Molly T. Fremont-Smith, Jessup, Marjorie G. Buck, and Nell Hopman)

on a backcourt game with only ground strokes, a bit too tame. Hazel preferred to play the more aggressive game that the boys played, which was characterized by volleys as well as ground strokes.

Hazel's primary goal, however, was to beat the Suttons. She soon defeated Violet, Ethel, and Florence, but she was twenty-three years old before she defeated May. The intense rivalry between these two players, both before and after that conquest, provided some of the most exciting tennis in California and is credited with making the game popular for women.

The Emerging Champion

While Hazel developed her tennis skills, she also sewed, played the piano, and graduated from high school and entered the University of California. In 1909, when she had completed her sophomore year in college, Hazel's father took her to Philadelphia to play in her first U.S. National Championship. She had a successful time, winning the women's singles, women's doubles, and the mixed-doubles events. She won the women's doubles with Edith E. Rotch of Boston, with whom she had never played before. She won the mixed doubles with Wallace F. Johnson, a top California player. Hazel

matched this feat in both 1910 and 1911. In the latter year, the weather was so bad that she had to play all three finals matches on the same day.

In 1912, Hazel married George Wightman and settled in the Boston area. During the following seven years, she retired somewhat from tennis to raise three children. She did compete in the 1915 U.S. National Championship and lost to Molla Bjurstedt of Norway, in the finals. In 1919, Hazel returned to win her last U.S. National Championship singles title; that year marked the real beginning of her doubles successes.

Continuing the Story

Hazel was a cheerful, tireless, and gracious player, and her skill at the net made her popular as a doubles partner. Over the years, she played doubles with the finest players, men and women, including Helen Wills and Bill Tilden. In 1923, Hazel donated a cup that was to be awarded to the winner of a team match between women of the United States and Great Britain. The cup, known as the Wightman Cup, was originally meant to parallel the Men's Davis Cup and include many nations, but the idea was not carried through. The Wightman Cup matches, however, have continued with few interruptions since 1923.

Hazel continued to play tennis for the rest of her life, winning forty-five national titles in the sport.

Milestones

U.S. Wightman Cup team captain (1923-24, 1927, 1929, 1931, 1933, 1935, 1937-39, 1946-48)

Presented the USLTA with a sterling vase for international women's team competition (known as the Wightman Cup)

Honors and Awards

1940, 1946	Service Bowl Award
1957	Inducted into National Lawn Tennis Hall of Fame
1960	Marlboro Award
1973	Order of Honorary Commander of the British Empire

She won her last national title in 1954, at the age of sixty-eight. She also won the national squash championship and was runner-up for the national badminton doubles title when she was in her fifties.

Hazel gave as much as she received in tennis. For years she spent hours teaching eager young players all the important aspects of the game. One day she spent an impromptu seven straight hours working with young students, without leaving the court even to eat. She was also a tireless hostess to legions of top tennis players who had come to play in the Boston area. She was deeply respected and appreciated by all in the tennis world and was elected to the International Tennis Hall of Fame at Newport, Rhode Island, in 1957. Hazel died at the age of eighty-seven in Chestnut Hill, Massachusetts, in 1974.

Summary

Hazel Wightman was one of the most respected and durable tennis players in the game's history. She played the game for more than seventy years and won forty-five national championships in the process. Her game was characterized by power and accuracy at the net and by brilliant strategy. A small woman, Hazel brought vigor and determination to the game, but she balanced these qualities with grace and never allowed her opponents to be humiliated regardless of their competitive level. After her retirement, she taught tennis for years and helped to foster some of the game's top women players. She also opened her home to needy players and was known for her capabilities as a hostess. In addition to her accomplishments in tennis, she was also a national champion in squash and badminton. With her passing, tennis and all racquet sports lost a true friend and champion.

Rebecca J. Sankner

Additional Sources

Carter, Tom. *First Lady of Tennis: Hazel Hotchkiss Wightman.* Berkeley, Calif.: Creative Arts, 2001.

Collins, Bud. *Total Tennis: The Ultimate Tennis Encyclopedia.* Toronto: Sport Media, 2003.

Miller, Ernestine G. *Making Her Mark: Firsts and Milestones in Women's Sports.* Chicago: Contemporary Books, 2002.

Sherrow, Victoria, ed. *Encyclopedia of Women and Sports.* Santa Barbara, Calif.: ABC-Clio, 1996.

Wightman, Hazel H. *Better Tennis.* Boston: Houghton Mifflin, 1933.

Woolum, Janet. *Outstanding Women Athletes: Who They Are and How They Influenced Sports in America.* Phoenix, Ariz.: Oryx Press, 1998.

Mats Wilander

Born: August 22, 1964
Växjö, Sweden
Also known as: Mats Arne Wilander (full name)

Early Life
Mats Arne Wilander was born on August 22, 1964, in Växjö, a small industrial city in southern Sweden, to Einar Wilander, a factory foreman, and Karin Wilander, an assembly-line worker. Mats was the youngest of three brothers. At the age of six, he began playing tennis on a makeshift court that his father had fashioned in a factory parking lot. When Mats was not playing against his father, he challenged anyone who passed by, and sometimes his father had to return late at night to force Mats to come home.

In addition to tennis, he also enjoyed playing ice hockey. Mats won his first national tennis tournament as an eleven-year-old playing in the under-twelve division. He also won the under-fourteen and under-sixteen division titles. Mats decided to stop playing ice hockey and concentrate all of his efforts toward improving his tennis game.

The Road to Excellence
Encouraged by his coaches and family but never pressured, Mats continued to make strides as a tennis player. Because of the success of tennis great Björn Borg, an organized tennis program had sprouted in Sweden. In 1981, after turning professional the previous year, Mats joined Team SIAB, which was named for and sponsored by a Swedish construction company. Mats and his teammates traveled together on the professional tennis circuit, and he remained on the team until 1983.

Borg had won his final French Open in 1981. With his retirement from competitive tennis, Sweden did not know from where its next tennis champion would come. Mats entered the 1982 French Open—one of tennis' four Grand Slam tournaments—as an unseeded player. He had foot speed, a solid forehand, and a good two-handed backhand, and he was an unrelenting competitor. He was only seventeen, though, and no one gave him much chance to advance far in the tournament.

Mats proved the experts wrong by beating four top players—Ivan Lendl, Vitas Gerulaitis, Jose-Luis Clerc, and Guillermo Vilas—to win the title. In the final, Mats defeated the powerful former champion Vilas in four grueling sets (1-6, 7-6, 6-0, 6-4). With the victory, Mats became the youngest player to become the French Open champion, a record he held until Michael Chang's victory in 1989. In Sweden, Mats was hailed as the next Borg. Mats, though, did not want to compete with the memory of Borg. He resented the comparison and wanted to be recognized for his own talents.

The Emerging Champion
Because of his fine play in 1982, Mats became the seventh-ranked player in the world. He also was named *Tennis* magazine's Rolex rookie of the year. Mats had made an auspicious entrance into the world of professional tennis.

At 6 feet tall, the right-handed Mats had the potential to become more than a tenacious baseline competitor, and he worked hard to add power to his serve and to become comfortable volleying at the net. In 1983, he won his second Grand Slam title, capturing the Australian Open on the grass courts of Kooyong, near Melbourne. That year, he also reached the final of the French Open, where he lost to Yannick Noah. Mats finished 1983 ranked fourth in the world.

Major Championship Victories and Finals

1982, 1985, 1988	French Open
1983, 1987	French Open finalist
1983-84, 1988	Australian Open
1985	Australian Open finalist
1987	U.S. Open finalist
1988	U.S. Open

Other Notable Victories

1984-85, 1987	On victorious Swedish Davis Cup team
1988	Lipton International Players' Championship

Honors, Awards, and Milestones

1982   Rolex Rookie of the Year
1988   Ranked number one in the world
2002   Inducted into International Tennis Hall of Fame

In 1984, Mats won the Australian Open title again. He also helped Sweden to win the 1984 and 1985 Davis Cup team competitions. He had become a complete tennis player, and he was a threat to win on all court surfaces.

One of the most stabilizing events of Mats's life was when he met his future wife Sonya Mulholland at the 1985 U.S. Open. Sonya was a Manhattan-based model who was born in Zambia but reared in South Africa. Mats had become weary of the constant traveling on the tennis tour, but Sonya helped him to become a more focused and much happier person. On January 3, 1987, Mats and Sonya were married in South Africa.

In 1985, Mats won his second French Open, defeating Lendl in the final. Mats's 1985 world ranking rose one spot to number three, where it remained for 1986 and 1987. In 1987, Mats was runner-up to Lendl at both the French Open and the U.S. Open, but he did help Sweden to once again capture the Davis Cup. Mats had continued to improve his game; with the help of his coach John-Anders Sjogren, he had added new strokes, including a one-handed slice backhand. Mats and Joakim Nystrom won the 1986 Wimbledon doubles title, an indication of how much Mats had improved his play around the net.

In 1988, Mats had his best year. He won three of the four Grand Slam titles, including the Australian, French, and U.S. Opens. At the U.S. Open, Mats outlasted Lendl in a final that was more than four hours long (6-4, 4-6, 6-3, 5-7, 6-4). Mats became the first tennis player to win three Grand Slam titles in a single year since Jimmy Connors in 1974. Lendl had been the number-one ranked player in the world for the previous three years, but with Mats's wonderful string of victories, Mats became the number-one player.

Continuing the Story

Mats had proven that he was a tough competitor in the Grand Slam tournaments. He had fought hard to become the world's top-ranked player, but once he had attained the summit, his motivation began to wane. Always a low-key individual, Mats was content that he had reached number one; he was not as worried about maintaining the ranking. He liked to relax at his home in Greenwich, Connecticut, and he preferred savoring what he had accomplished to fighting hard on the tennis court. Nagging injuries, his father's death, and the birth of a daughter led Mats to look at tennis as something that he enjoys but did not crave, and he retired from competitive tennis in 1991. Mats had earned more than $7 million in prize money and had won thirty-three career titles, including eight Grand Slam titles.

In 1993, Mats came out of retirement, saying that he expected to play tennis for as long as he found competing to be fun. In addition to his family and tennis, Mats loved playing the electric guitar, and he toured Sweden with his group Wilander. He began playing on the Worldwide Senior Tennis Circuit in 1997. He continued to play sparsely throughout the next decade. He and his family moved to Idaho.

Summary
Mats Wilander was one of the fiercest competitors in the history of tennis. Although his tennis game was more suited to clay courts, he adapted his style of play to become a threat on all court surfaces. During his prime years, Mats was always in contention to win a major title.

Jeffry Jensen

Additional Sources
Evans, Richard. *Open Tennis: 1968-1988.* Lexington, Mass.: Stephen Greene Press, 1989.

Fein, Paul. "A Conversation with Mats Wilander." *Scandinavian Review* 90, no. 1 (Summer, 2002): 66.

Shmerler, Cindy. "Mats Wilander: The Former World No. 1 Now Spends Most of His Time Playing Mom to His Four Children, and Loving It." *Tennis* 36 (March, 2000): 18.

Serena Williams

Born: September 26, 1981
Saginaw, Michigan
Also known as: Serena Jameka Ross Evelyn
Williams (full name)

Early Life
The youngest of the five daughters of Richard and
Oracene Williams, Serena Jameka Ross Evelyn Williams was born in Saginaw, Michigan, on September 26, 1981. When Serena was a preschooler her
family moved from Michigan to California, where,
in Compton, her father worked as a neighborhood
tennis coach.

Although Richard Williams had access to dilapi-
dated courts only, he was enthusiastic about tennis.
The son of a Louisiana sharecropper, he was an ambitious man who wanted a good, full life for his family and himself. When Serena and her sister Venus
were quite young, he began teaching them how to
play tennis. He was certain that his daughters,
whom he called "Cinderellas from the ghetto," had
the potential to become tennis champions.

Traditionally, tennis had been the sport of middle-
and upper-class white Americans.
No African Americans had managed to make a major impact
since 1975, when Arthur Ashe
won Wimbledon. The record for
black women in tennis was even
less impressive. No black woman
had won a Grand Slam event
since Althea Gibson won both
the U.S. Open and Wimbledon
in both 1957 and 1958.

The Road to Excellence
Breaking into competitive tennis was not easy for Serena. Her
father recalled that at one Southern California tournament he
heard some people questioning
his daughters' presence at the
competition. He also noted mis-
understandings between black
and white competitors. Richard

Williams had some reservations about allowing the
girls to become involved in what he considered a
sometimes hostile world. However, he decided to
keep his daughters on the tennis circuit, believing
that their talent and skill would triumph over discrimination. In order to enhance the girls' chances
of mastering the game, the Williams family moved
to Florida, where Venus and Serena trained with
Rick Macci at the Macci Tennis Academy.

Serena spent most of her young life working to
become a tennis champion. Her winning technique grew out of talent, discipline, dedication,
good coaching, and a major amount of time in the
gym and on the practice court.

In 1991, the Williams family made the difficult
decision to withdraw the two girls from the junior
competition circuit. In addition to relieving some
of the enormous pressure on the sisters, this move
allowed them to focus on schoolwork and practice.

The Emerging Champion
In 1997, Serena caught the attention of tennis fans
when she defeated five top-ten players faster than

*Serena Williams positioning herself for a strong return during the 2002 French
Open.* (AP/Wide World Photos)

any other professional tennis player in history. Serena, under her father's coaching and management, had earned $348,378 by December of 1998. She was seventeen years old.

In 1999, Serena, who had been known as the younger and less-talented sister of Venus Williams, won a Grand Slam title. The victory was not her first that year. In February, at the Open Gaz de France in Paris, Serena defeated Amelie Mauresmo. In March, Serena overwhelmed Steffi Graf at the Evert Cup in Indian Wells, California.

Serena suffered a minor but unusual setback at the Lipton Championships in Key Biscayne, Florida. She and Venus became the first sisters to meet in the finals of a professional tournament in 115 years. Venus defeated Serena in three sets. For the remainder of the 1999 tour, the sisters planned their schedules to avoid playing each other.

However, on September 10, 1999, Venus and Serena played consecutive semifinal matches at the U.S. Open in New York City. Determined that one of them would win a Grand Slam event, Serena allegedly retreated to the practice courts for some last-minute reinforcement after Venus lost to Martina Hingis. The next day Serena triumphed over Hingis. Her victory made her the first African American woman to win a Grand Slam singles title since Althea Gibson in 1958.

Competing in several major tournaments during any given tour takes a toll on the most talented of athletes. Serena was no exception. In 1999, she pulled out of the Hilton Head Tournament, in South Carolina, citing a knee problem, and she

Major Championships

Year	Event	Year	Event
1998	U.S. Open mixed doubles	2002	Wimbledon doubles
	Wimbledon mixed doubles	(cont.)	U.S. Open singles
1999	U.S. Open singles	2003	Australian Open singles
	U.S. Open doubles		Australian Open doubles
	French Open doubles		Wimbledon singles
	Paris Indoors singles	2005	Australian Open singles
	Grand Slam Cup singles	2007	Australian Open singles
1999, 2001	Indian Wells singles	2008	Wimbledon doubles
2000	Wimbledon doubles		U.S. Open singles
2002	French Open singles	2009	Australian Open singles
	Wimbledon singles		Wimbledon singles
			Wimbledon doubles

skipped Wimbledon because of the flu. Tendinitis in her right shoulder made her unable to compete at Toronto. She also missed the Seat Open in Luxembourg, citing exhaustion.

In 1999, despite her injuries, Serena had a good year. *Forbes* magazine listed both her and Venus among the highest paid black athletes in the United States. Additionally, Serena earned a considerable amount in endorsements: Her clothing contracts totaled about $2.5 million.

Continuing the Story

The year 2000 began on a high note for Serena, who was ranked number four in the tennis world. She defeated Denisa Chladkova to win the Faber Grand Prix. However, she lost to Mary Pierce in the Tennis Master Series-Indian Wells Tournament in California. In April, Serena withdrew from the Family Circle Tournament in Hilton Head out of respect for the National Association for the Advancement of Colored People's boycott of South Carolina for its use of the Confederate flag. A few weeks later she decided against playing in the French Open because of a knee injury. Though she competed at Wimbledon in July, Venus won the tournament. Serena won the Estyle.com Classic, beating Lindsay Davenport, and won the Princess Cup in Tokyo, Japan, in October. In the 2000 Sydney Olympics, Serena won the gold medal in the doubles competition with Venus.

In 2001, Serena and Venus became the fifth women's doubles team to win all four Grand Slam doubles titles. Serena won the Pacific Life Open and made quarterfinals in the

Honors and Awards

1998	WTA Most Impressive Newcomer
	Tennis magazine/Rolex Rookie of the Year
2000	Gold medal, Olympic women's tennis doubles (with Venus Williams)
2002	Women's Tennis Association (WTA) Player of the Year
	International Tennis Federation (ITF) World Champion
	Associated Press Female Athlete of the Year
2003	Laureus Sportswoman of the Year
2004	WTA Comeback Player of the Year
2008	Gold medal, Olympic women's tennis doubles (with Venus Williams)

French Open and Wimbledon. In 2002, she defeated Venus at Wimbledon, ranking her number one in the world, and won her third consecutive Grand Slam singles title at the U.S. Open.

Serena became the fifth woman to complete a career Grand Slam and won her sixth doubles title with Venus at the 2003 Australian Open. A chronic knee injury forced her to withdraw from the Summer Olympics in 2004. In 2005, at the Australian Open, she earned her seventh Grand Slam single title and was ranked number two. She lost to Venus in the Sony Ericsson Open and withdrew from the French Open because of injury. An ankle stress fracture resulted in losses at Wimbledon and the U.S. Open.

In 2006, because of inactivity, Serena fell out of the top 100 rankings. In 2007, after physical and mental recuperation, Serena rose to number seven in the rankings. She won her third Australian Open singles title but lost to Justine Henin at the French Open, Wimbledon, and the U.S. Open. In 2008, Serena and Venus met again, this time in the Wimbledon final. After Serena dominated the early portion of the first set, Venus came back to win both sets. Two months later, Serena and Venus captured the gold medal in doubles at the 2008 Beijing Olympics. Further establishing her return to elite status, Serena captured the 2008 U.S. Open championship with a convincing victory over Jelena Jankovic.

By early 2009, it was clear that Serena was returning to her earlier outstanding form. In January, she won her tenth Grand Slam title by winning her fourth Australian Open singles title, beating Russia's Dinara Safina in straight sets. At the French Open in May, Serena made it to the quarterfinals, in which she was eliminated by another Russian player, Svetlana Kuznetsova, who eventually won the tournament. That loss ended Serena's streak of eighteen-straight wins in Grand Slam matches, but she started a new streak at Wimbledon in June. There she won six more matches before facing her sister, Venus, in a memorable finals battle. Venus was the two-time defending champion, but Serena won to claim her third Wimbledon singles title and eleventh Grand Slam singles title. The win also made Serena and her sister the winners of eight of the last ten Wimbledon tournaments. After taking the singles title, Serena and Venus combined to win their second-straight Wimbledon doubles title and their ninth Grand Slam doubles title overall.

Summary

Serena Williams is noted for her cannonball serve, high-voltage ground stroke, superb volleys, terrific overhead, and astonishing speed. She has compiled a career Grand Slam, winning each of the four major tournaments at least once, and tallied more than thirty tournament victories. Furthermore she has captured multiple doubles championships with her sister Venus; the pair have also won two Olympic gold medals. She and her sister are two of the most dominating tennis players of their generation.

Betty L. Plummer, updated by Sara Vidar

Additional Sources

Aronson, Virginia. *Venus and Serena Williams.* Philadelphia: Chelsea House, 2001.

Beard, Hilary, Venus Williams, and Serena Williams. *Venus and Serena: Serving from the Hip—Ten Rules for Living, Loving, and Winning.* New York: Houghton Mifflin, 2005.

Edmondson, Jacqueline. *Venus and Serena Williams: A Biography.* Westport, Conn.: Greenwood Press, 2005.

Sparling, Ken. *Venus and Serena Williams.* Chicago: Warwick, 2000.

Stewart, Mark. *Venus and Serena Williams: Sisters in Arms.* Brookfield, Conn.: Millbrook Press, 2000.

Venus Williams

Born: June 17, 1980
　　Lynwood, California
Also known as: Venus Ebone Starr Williams (full name)

Early Life

Venus Ebone Starr Williams was born on June 17, 1980, in Lynwood, California. She was the fourth of five daughters born to Richard Williams, co-owner of a security services business, and Oracene "Brandi" Williams, a nurse. Education was important to the Williams family, but Venus's father recognized there was money to be made in tennis. He first taught himself, then his entire family, how to play tennis by reading books and watching videos. Venus began to play at the age of four on public courts in Compton, California, a Los Angeles inner-city neighborhood. Venus and her younger sister, Serena, showed talent very early.

The Road to Excellence

By the age of ten, Venus had won numerous junior tennis competitions, including the Southern Cali-

Venus Williams in 1998. (AP/Wide World Photos)

fornia girls' title in the under-twelve division. The family relocated to Florida, where Venus enrolled in Rick Macci's Tennis Academy. By the age of twelve, Venus had won sixty-three consecutive tournaments and had been featured in *Sports Illustrated*, *Tennis*, and the *New York Times*. In 1991, Venus's father surprised the tennis world when he withdrew Venus and Serena from the junior competition circuit to protect them from undue pressure and to allow them to concentrate on practicing and schoolwork. Critics felt that this was an unwise decision and Venus would not be prepared for professional competition. Ignoring these complaints, her family believed they knew what was best for Venus.

The Emerging Champion

In 1994, at the age of fourteen, Venus entered the professional tennis circuit at the Bank of the West Classic in Oakland, California. She amazed the tennis world by defeating the Women's Tennis Association's (WTA) fifty-ninth-ranked player and by nearly upsetting the number-two-ranked Arantxa Sanchez-Vicario. Over the next three years, the 6-foot-1½ inch prodigy proved to be a powerful player and clocked a 108-miles per hour serve, the ninth-fastest serve recorded on the WTA tour in 1996. In 1997, Venus rose rapidly; she started the season ranked number 211 and jumped to number 64. She had her first win over a top-ten player in the Evert Cup championships and made her first appearance at Wimbledon in England, one of the most prestigious tennis tournaments in the world.

The world was watching Venus, an up-and-coming player, but Venus's father, who also served as her coach and manager, restricted the number of tournaments his daughter entered. He did not want Venus to burn out or neglect her education. An outspoken and candid person, Venus's father was criticized for stating in an interview that racial epithets were directed at Venus during the U.S. Open tournament. Though it was not the first time an African American player or coach had suggested the predominantly white tennis community was not accepting of other races, Venus's father was called a racist for remarks he made regarding white players when defending his daughters. Venus and Serena did not escape controversy and were described by fellow players as distant during and after matches. Venus once responded by saying she came to the courts to play and win.

Major Championships

Year	Event	Year	Event
1998	Grand Slam Cup singles	2001	Ericsson Open singles
	Australian Open mixed doubles		Wimbledon singles
	French Open mixed doubles		U.S. Open singles
	Lipton singles		Australian Open doubles
1999	French Open doubles	2002	Wimbledon doubles
	U.S. Open doubles	2003	Australian Open doubles
	Lipton singles	2005	Wimbledon singles
	Italian Open singles	2007	Wimbledon singles
2000	Wimbledon singles	2008	Wimbledon singles
	Wimbledon doubles		Wimbledon doubles
	U.S. Open singles	2009	Wimbledon doubles

Continuing the Story

In 1998, Venus won her first WTA singles title at the IGA Classic, upgrading her WTA ranking to number twelve. She captured two other tournament titles that year, the Lipton championship and the Grand Slam Cup. During the Swisscom Challenge, Venus set a WTA record by clocking an unprecedented 127-mph serve—a record she later broke with a 129-mph serve. Venus also captured two doubles titles with Serena, and won two mixed-doubles titles, defeating Serena and her partner in the French Open. The Williams sisters met in two singles matches that year, with Venus defeating Serena both times.

In 1999, Venus continued her winning ways by securing six singles and three more doubles titles. The sisters made tennis history in several categories. Venus's win against Serena at the Lipton tournament marked the first time sisters played opposite each other in a WTA title match. Venus's second win at the IGA Classic and Serena's Paris Open victory marked the first time sisters won title matches in the same week. Winning the French Open doubles title made them the first sisters since 1884 to win a Grand Slam title crown together. The sisters, with their beaded, cornrow-braided hairstyles, were called the "beaded wonders."

In 2000, the world was captivated again when Venus won Wimbledon, becoming the first African American woman to win this prestigious tournament since Althea Gibson in 1958. Venus and Serena took home Wimbledon's doubles title as well, becoming the first sisters to accomplish this feat at Wimbledon. Venus also won her first U.S. Open, defeating Serena; the pair became the first sisters to play in a U.S. Open final match. The Williams's success continued at the 2000 Olympics in Sydney, Australia, where the sisters won gold medals in the women's doubles and Venus won the gold medal in the women's singles. Venus received WTA's player of the year and *Sports Illustrated* woman of the year awards for 2000.

In 2001, Venus repeated her wins at both Wimbledon and the U.S. Open; and she signed a deal with Reebok for an estimated forty million dollars, considered, at the time, the most lucrative endorsement contract for a female athlete. While Venus lost to Serena in both Wimbledon and the U.S. Open finals in 2002 and 2003, the sisters won another doubles title at the U.S. Open in 2002. In March, 2002, Venus was ranked number one in the WTA. In 2003, tragedy struck the Williams family when the oldest daughter, Yetunde Price, was shot and killed in Compton, California.

Always encouraged by her parents to pursue her interests, Venus studied interior design and founded V Starr Interiors in 2002

Honors and Awards

1997	WTA Most Impressive Newcomer
	U.S. Olympic Committee Female Athlete of the Month: September
	Tennis magazine Most Improved Female Pro
1998	*Tennis* magazine Most Improved Player
2000	Gold medal, Olympic women's tennis singles
	Gold medal, Olympic women's tennis doubles (with Serena Williams)
2008	Gold medal, Olympic women's tennis doubles (with Serena Williams)

and EleVen, a clothing line, in 2007. Critics said Venus spent too much time away from the game and pointed to her lack of Grand Slam titles in 2003 and 2004; however, Venus reached Grand Slam title matches during this period. In 2005, never one to be counted out, Venus surprised the world when she won her third Wimbledon title as the fourteenth seed, becoming the lowest seeded player to ever win this tournament. In 2007, Venus broke this record when she won Wimbledon as the twenty-third seed. In 2008, she won another Wimbledon title by beating her sister in the final. Later in the year, the sisters captured gold medals at the Summer Olympics. In 2009, the sisters again met in the Wimbledon finals. This time, Serena won. Losing the title to her sister was a disappointment to Venus, but Serena's victory give the sisters a total of eight of the previous ten Wimbledon titles. Afterward, they combined to win their second-straight doubles title.

Summary

Venus Williams is articulate, radiates confidence, supports children's causes, and defends the rights of female athletes. The Williams sisters won prestigious tennis titles, made tennis history, and earned millions of dollars in winnings and endorsements. However, the family kept these successes in perspective and believed the talented Williams children were capable of excelling at anything they chose to do. Venus's successes on and off the tennis court suggest she adopted this attitude.

Felicia Friendly Thomas

Additional Sources

Bolofo, Koto, and Patrick Remy. *Venus Williams.* London: Steidl, 2008.

Bradley, Michael. *Venus Williams.* Tarrytown, N.Y.: Benchmark Books, 2004.

Edmondson, Jacqueline. *Venus and Serena Williams: A Biography.* Westport, Conn.: Greenwood Press, 2005.

Sandler, Michael. *Tennis: Victory for Venus Williams.* New York: Bearport, 2006.

Williams, Venus, Serena Williams, and Hilary Beard. *Venus and Serena: Serving from the Hip, Ten Rules for Living, Loving, and Winning.* Boston: Houghton Mifflin, 2005.

Resources

Bibliography

Golf

Allis, Peter. *The Who's Who of Golf.* Englewood Cliffs, N.J.: Prentice-Hall, 1983.

Apfelbaum, Jim, ed. *The Gigantic Book of Golf Quotations.* New York: Skyhorse, 2007.

Armour, Tommy. *Classic Golf Tips.* Orlando, Fla.: Tribune, 1994.

_____. *How to Play Your Best Golf All the Time.* Rev. ed. New York: Simon and Schuster, 1995.

Baddiel, Sarah. *Golf: The Golden Years—A Pictorial Anthology.* London: Studio Editions, 1989.

Ballesteros, Severiano, with John Andrisani. *Natural Golf.* New York: Atheneum, 1988.

Bamberger, Michael. *The Green Road Home: Adventures and Misadventures as a Caddie on the PGA Tour.* New York: Thunder's Mouth Press, 2006.

Barclay, James A. *Golf in Canada: A History.* Toronto: McClelland & Stewart, 1992.

Barkow, Al. *Best of Golf: Best Golfers, Courses, Moments, and More.* Lincolnwood, Ill.: Publications International, 2002.

Barratt, Michael, and Tony Jacklin. *Golf with Tony Jacklin: Step by Step, a Great Professional Shows an Enthusiastic Amateur How to Play Every Stroke of the Game.* London: A. Baker, 1970.

Barrett, Ted. *The Complete Encyclopedia of Golf.* Chicago: Triumph Books, 2005.

Barrett, Ted, and Michael Hobbs. *The Complete Book of Golf: The Definitive Illustrated Guide to World Golf.* London: Sevenoaks, 1997.

Boros, Julius, and Lealand Gustavson. *Swing Easy, Hit Hard: Tips from a Master of the Classic Golf Swing.* Rev. ed. New York: Lyons & Burford, 2001.

Bowden, Ken. *Teeing Off: Players, Techniques, Characters, and Reflections from a Lifetime Inside the Game.* Chicago: Triumph Books, 2008.

Burnett, Jim. *Tee Times: On the Road with the Ladies Professional Golf Tour.* New York: Scribner, 1997.

Campbell, Malcolm, and Glyn Satterley. *The Scottish Golf Book.* Edinburgh: Lomond Books, 2001.

Carrick, Michael, and Steve Duno. *Caddie Sense: Revelations of a PGA Tour Caddie on Playing the Game of Golf.* New York: St. Martin's Press, 2000.

Casper, Byron. *Billy Casper's Golf Tips.* Edinburgh: Pastime Publications, 2002.

Cherney, Ron, and Michael Arkush. *My Greatest Shot: The Top Players Share Their Defining Golf Moments.* New York: HarperResource, 2004.

Clavin, Thomas. *Sir Walter: Walter Hagen and the Invention of Professional Golf.* New York: Simon & Schuster, 2005.

Clay, Jonathan, and Tom Smith. *My Best Day in Golf: Celebrity Stories of the Game They Love.* Kansas City, Mo.: Andrews McMeel, 2003.

Crosset, Todd. *Outsiders in the Clubhouse: The World of Women's Golf.* Albany: State University of New York Press, 1995.

Curtis, Walter J., Sr. *History's Master Golfers.* Indianapolis: Curtis, 2003.

Elliott, Alan, and John Allan May. *Golf Monthly Illustrated History of Golf.* London: Hamlyn, 1990.

Els, Ernie. *How to Build a Classic Golf Swing.* New York: HarperCollins, 1999.

Els, Ernie, and David Herman. *Ernie Els' Guide to Golf Fitness: Take Strokes off Your Game and Add Yards to Your Drive.* New York: Three Rivers Press, 2000.

Faldo, Nick, and Vivian Saunders. *Golf: The Winning Formula.* New York: Lyons & Burford, 1989.

Fasciana, Guy S., Hale Irwin, and Terry Dill. *Golf's Mental Magic: Four Strategies for Mental Toughness.* Greenville, S.C.: Health and Performance Associates, 2000.

Feherty, D. *David Feherty's Totally Subjective History of the Ryder Cup.* New York: Rugged Land, 2004.

Floyd, Ray, and Larry Dennis. *From Sixty Yards In: How to Master Golf's Short Game.* New York: HarperPerennial, 1992.

Floyd, Ray, and Jaime Diaz. *The Elements of Scoring: A Master's Guide to the Art of Scoring Your Best When You're Not Playing Your Best.* New York: Fireside, 2000.

Frost, Mark. *The Grand Slam.* London: Time Warner, 2005.

_____. *The Greatest Game Ever Played: Harry Vardon, Francis Ouimet, and the Birth of Modern Golf.* New York: Hyperion, 2002.

_____. *The Match: The Day the Game of Golf Changed Forever.* New York: Hyperion, 2007.

Gates, Henry Louis, and Evelyn Brooks Higginbotham, eds. *African American Lives.* New York: Oxford University Press, 2004.

Glenn, Rhonda. *The Illustrated History of Women's Golf.* Dallas, Tex.: Taylor, 1991.

Golf Magazine's Encyclopedia of Golf: The Complete Reference. 2d ed. New York: HarperCollins, 1993.

Grimsley, Will. *Golf: Its History, People, and Events.* Englewood Cliffs, N.J.: Prentice-Hall, 1966.

Harmon, Claude. *The Four Cornerstones of Winning Golf: Butch Harmon Shares the Secrets He's Taught to Greg Norman, Davis Love III, and Tiger Woods.* New York: Fireside, 1998.

Hartman, Robert. *Leonard, Duval, Woods, and Mickelson: Masters of the Millennium—The Next Generation of the PGA Tour.* Champaign, Ill.: Sports, 1999.

Herzog, Brad. *The Sports One Hundred: The One Hundred Most Important People in American Sports History.* New York: Macmillan, 1995.

Hogan, Ben, and Herbert Warren Wind. *Ben Hogan's Five Lessons: The Modern Fundamentals of Golf.* New York: Simon & Schuster, 2006.

Holanda, Raymond. *The Golfer of the Decade on the PGA Tour: From Walter Hagen in the 1920's to Tiger Woods in the 2000's.* New York: IUniverse, 2007.

Hopkins, John, Dave Anderson, and Martin Davis. *The Ryder Cup: Golf's Greatest Event: A Complete History.* Greenwich, Conn.: American Golfer, 2008.

Howell, Audrey. *Harry Vardon: The Revealing Story of a Champion Golfer.* 2d ed. Stroud, Gloucestershire, England: Tempus, 2001.

Hudson, David L. *Women in Golf: The Players, the History, and the Future of the Sport.* Westport, Conn.: Praeger, 2007.

Hutchison, Kay Bailey. *American Heroines: The Spirited Women Who Shaped Our Country.* New York: William Morrow, 2004.

Ireland, Mary Lloyd, and Aurelia Nattiv, eds. *The Female Athlete.* Philadelphia: W. B. Saunders, 2002.

Ironside, Robert, and Harry Douglas. *A History of the Royal Musselburgh Golf Club 1774-1999.* Musselburgh, East Lothian, Scotland: Royal Musselburgh Golf Club, 1999.

Irwin, Hale. *Hale Irwin's Smart Golf: Wisdom and Strategies from the "Thinking Man's Golfer."* New York: Quill, 2001.

Jacklin, Tony, Peter Dobereiner, and Chris Perfect. *Jacklin's Golf Secrets.* London: Hutchinson, 1983.

Jacobsen, Peter, and Jack Sheehan. *Embedded Balls: Adventures on and off the Tour with Golf's Premier Storyteller.* New York: Putnam Adult, 2005.

Jarmin, C. M. *The Ryder Cup: The Definitive History of Playing Golf for Pride and Country.* Chicago: Contemporary Books, 1999.

Kalb, Elliott. *Who's Better, Who's Best in Golf? Mr. Stats Sets the Record Straight on the Top Fifty Golfers of All Time.* New York: McGraw-Hill, 2006.

Kite, Tom. *Fairway to Heaven: My Lessons from Harvey Penick on Golf and Life.* New York: William Morrow, 1997.

Lawrenson, Derek. *The Complete Encyclopedia of Golf.* London: Carlton, 2002.

Lewis, Chris. *The Scorecard Always Lies: A Year Behind the Scenes on the PGA Tour.* New York: Free Press, 2007.

Lopez, Nancy. *The Complete Golfer.* New York: Galahad Books, 2000.

McCord, Robert. *The Golf Book of Days: Fascinating Facts and Stories for Every Day of the Year.* New York: Citadel Press, 2002.

McNew, Monte. *Golf in the Ozarks.* Charleston, S.C.: Arcadia, 2006.

Magee, David. *Endurance: Winning Life's Majors the Phil Mickelson Way.* Hoboken, N.J.: John Wiley & Sons, 2005.

Matthew, Sidney. *Bobby Jones Golf Tips: Secrets of the Master.* Secaucus, N.J.: Citadel Press, 2004.

Mickelson, Phil, with Donald T. Phillps. *One Magical Sunday (But Winning Isn't Everything).* New York: Warner Books, 2005.

Nelson, Byron, and Jon Bradley. *Quotable Byron: Words of Wisdom, Faith, and Success by and About Byron Nelson, Golf's Great Ambassador.* Nashville, Tenn.: TowleHouse, 2002.

Nickerson, Elinor. *Golf: A Women's History.* Jefferson, N.C.: McFarland, 1987.

Norwood, Joe, Marilynn Smith, and Stanley Blicker. *Joe Norwood's Golf-o-Metrics.* 2d ed. Las Vegas, Nev.: Norwood, 1992.

O'Reilly, Jean, and Susan K. Cahn, eds. *Women and Sports in the United States: A Documentary Reader.* Boston: Northeastern University Press, 2007.

Ouimet, Francis. *A Game of Golf.* Boston: Northeastern University Press, 2004.

Palmer, Arnold. *Playing by the Rules: All the Rules of the Game, Complete with Memorable Rulings from Golf's Rich History.* 2d ed. New York: Atria Books, 2004.

Park, Willie, Jr. *The Art of Putting.* 1920. Reprint. Edinburgh: Luath Press, 2007.

Peper, George, and Mary Tiegreen. *The Secret of

Golf: A Century of Groundbreaking, Innovative, and Occasionally Outlandish Ways to Master the World's Most Vexing Game. New York: Workman, 2005.

Player, Gary. *Fit for Golf.* New York: Simon & Schuster, 1995.

Player, Gary, Chris Whales, and Duncan Cruickshank. *The Complete Golfer's Handbook.* Guilford, Conn.: Lyons Press, 2000.

_____. *Gary Player's Top Golf Courses of the World.* London: New Holland, 2007.

Price, Nick, and Lorne Rubenstein. *The Swing: Mastering the Principles of the Game.* New York: Knopf, 1999.

Puett, Barbara, and Jim Apfelbaum. *Golf Etiquette.* Rev. ed. New York: St. Martin's Press, 2003.

Rankin, Judy, and Michael Aronstein. *A Natural Way to Golf Power.* New York: Harper & Row, 1976.

Rankin, Judy, and Peter McCleery. *A Woman's Guide to Better Golf.* Chicago: Contemporary Books, 1995.

Sampson, Curt. *The Eternal Summer: Palmer, Nicklaus, and Hogan in 1960, Golf's Golden Year.* New York: Villard, 2000.

Sanson, Nanette. *Champions of Women's Golf: Celebrating Fifty Years of the LPGA.* Naples, Fla.: Quailmark Books, 2000.

Sheehan, Patty, and Betty Hicks. *Patty Sheehan on Golf.* Dallas, Tex.: Taylor, 1996.

Sherman, Adam. *Golf's Book of Firsts.* Philadelphia: Courage Books, 2002.

Snead, Sam, and Francis J. Pirozzolo. *The Game I Love: Wisdom, Insight, and Instruction from Golf's Greatest Player.* New York: Ballantine Books, 1997.

Sorenstam, Annika. *Golf Annika's Way.* New York: Gotham Books, 2004.

Sounes, Howard. *The Wicked Game: Arnold Palmer, Jack Nicklaus, Tiger Woods, and the Story of Modern Golf.* New York: William Morrow, 2004.

Strange, Curtis, and Kenneth Van Kampen. *Win and Win Again: Techniques for Playing Consistently Great Golf.* Chicago: Contemporary Books, 1990.

Strege, John. *When War Played Through: Golf During World War II.* New York: Gotham Books, 2005.

Stringham, Joan, and Mary Keller. *Famous Female Sports Stars.* Scottsdale, Ariz.: Remedia, 2001.

Vardon, Harry. *The Complete Golfer.* Rev. ed. Trumbull, Conn.: Golf Digest/Tennis, 1986.

Vigeland, Carl A. *Stalking the Shark: Pressure and Passion on the Pro Golf Tour.* New York: W. W. Norton, 1996.

Watson, Tom, and Nick Seitz. *Tom Watson's Strategic Golf.* Turnbull, Conn.: Golf Digest, 1993.

Whitworth, Kathy, and Rhonda Glenn. *Golf for Women.* New York: St. Martin's Press, 1992.

Williams, Jackie. *Playing from the Rough: The Women of the LPGA Hall of Fame.* Las Vegas, Nev.: Women of Diversity Productions, 2000.

Wright, Mickey. *Play Golf the Wright Way.* Dallas, Tex.: Taylor, 1990.

Yocom, Guy. *My Shot: The Very Best Interviews from Golf Digest Magazine.* New York: Stewart, Tabori & Chang, 2007.

Tennis

Antoun, Rob. *Women's Tennis Tactics.* Champaign, Ill.: Human Kinetics, 2007.

Austin, Tracy, and Steve Eubanks. *I Know Absolutely Nothing About Tennis: A Tennis Player's Guide to the Sport's History, Equipment, Apparel, Etiquette, Rules, and Language.* Nashville, Tenn.: Rutledge Hill Press, 1997.

Barrett, John. *Wimbledon: The Official History of the Championships.* Glasgow, Scotland: HarperCollins, 2001.

Buckley, James, and David Fischer. *Greatest Sports Rivalries: Twenty-five of the Most Intense and Historic Battles Ever.* New York: Barnes & Noble, 2005.

Cashmore, Ernest. *Sport Psychology: The Key Concepts.* Champaign, Ill.: Sports, 2002.

Collins, Bud. *The Bud Collins History of Tennis: An Authoritative Encyclopedia and Record Book.* New York: New Chapter Press, 2008.

_____. *Total Tennis: The Ultimate Tennis Encyclopedia.* Kingston, N.Y.: Sport Media, 2003.

Collins, Bud, and Zander Hollander, eds. *Bud Collins' Tennis Encyclopedia.* 3d ed. Detroit: Visible Ink Press, 1997.

Conner, Floyd. *Tennis's Most Wanted: The Top Ten Book of Baseline Blunders, Clay Court Wonders, and Lucky Lobs.* Washington, D.C.: Brassey's, 2002.

Djata, Sundiata A. *Blacks at the Net: Black Achievement in the History of Tennis.* Syracuse, N.Y.: Syracuse University Press, 2006.

Durr, Françoise. *Doubles Strategy: A Creative and Psychological Approach to Tennis.* New York: David McKay, 1978.

Evans, Richard. *The ATP Tour: Ten Years of Superstar Tennis.* New York: Universe, 1999.

_____. *Open Tennis: 1968-1988.* Lexington, Mass.: Stephen Greene Press, 1989.

Fein, Paul. *Tennis Confidential: Today's Greatest Players, Matches, and Controversies.* Washington, D.C.: Brassey's, 2002.

Flink, Steve. *The Greatest Tennis Matches of the Twentieth Century.* Danbury, Conn.: Rutledge Books, 1999.

Grimsley, Will. *Tennis: Its History, People, and Events.* Englewood Cliffs, N.J.: Prentice-Hall, 1971.

Harris, Cecil, and Larryette Kyle-DeBose. *Charging the Net: A History of Blacks in Tennis from Althea Gibson and Arthur Ashe to the Williams Sisters.* Chicago: Ivan R. Dee, 2007.

King, Billie Jean, and Cynthia Starr. *We Have Come a Long Way: The Story of Women's Tennis.* New York: McGraw-Hill, 1988.

Laver, Rodney George, and Bud Collins. *Rod Laver's Tennis Digest.* Chicago: Follett, 1975.

Lendl, Ivan, and George Mendoza. *Hitting Hot: Ivan Lendl's Fourteen Day Tennis Clinic.* New York: Random House, 1986.

Lendl, Ivan, and Eugene L. Scott. *Ivan Lendl's Power Tennis.* New York: Simon & Schuster, 1983.

Lumpkin, Angela. *Women's Tennis: A Historical Documentary of the Players and Their Game.* Albany, N.Y.: Whitston, 1981.

Mangan, J. A., and Roberta J. Park. *From Fair Sex to Feminism: Sport and the Socialization of Women in the Industrial and Post-Industrial Eras.* London: Frank Cass, 1987.

Mewshaw, Michael. *Ladies of the Court.* New York: Crown, 1993.

Miller, Toby. *Sportsex.* Philadelphia: Temple University Press, 2002.

Moore, Bal, and Randy Snow. *Wheelchair Tennis: Myth to Reality.* Dubuque, Iowa: Kendall/Hunt, 1994.

Moran, Greg. *Tennis Beyond Big Shots.* Austin, Tex.: Mansion Grove House, 2006.

Parsons, John. *The Ultimate Encyclopedia of Tennis: The Definitive Illustrated Guide to World Tennis.* London: Carlton, 2006.

Phillips, Caryl. *The Right Set: A Tennis Anthology.* New York: Vintage Books, 1999.

Phillips, Dennis J. *Women Tennis Stars: Biographies and Records of Champions, 1800s to Today.* Jefferson, N.C.: McFarland, 2008.

Rosewall, Ken. *Ken Rosewall on Tennis.* New York: F. Fell, 1978.

Rutledge, Rachel. *The Best of the Best in Tennis.* Brookfield, Conn.: Millbrook Press, 1998.

Sanchez-Vicaro, Arantxa. *Tennis.* New York: Dorling Kindersley, 2000.

Schwabacher, Martin. *Superstars of Women's Tennis.* New York: Chelsea House, 1996.

Seixas, Vic, and Joel H. Cohen. *Prime Time Tennis.* New York: Charles Scribner's Sons, 1983.

Shifrin, Joshua. *One Hundred One Incredible Moments in Tennis: The Good, the Bad, and the Infamous.* College Station, Tex.: Virtualbookworm, 2005.

Shriver, Pam. "Game Plan: Professional Advice—Pam Shriver Answers Your Questions." *Tennis,* August, 2004, 26.

Smith, Stan, Larry Sheehan, James McQueen, and Leonard Kamsler. *Stan Smith's Guide to Better Tennis.* London: Hale, 1975.

Trabert, Tony, and Jim Hook. *The Serve: Key to Winning Tennis.* New York: Dodd, Mead, 1984.

Trabert, Tony, Ron Witchey, and Don DeNevi. *Tennis Past Fifty.* Champaign, Ill.: Human Kinetics, 2002.

Viragh, Helle Sparre, and Jim Schock. *Dynamite Doubles: Play Winning Tennis Today!* Oakland, Calif.: Regent Press, 2004.

Wade, Virginia, and Jean Rafferty. *Ladies of the Court: A Century of Women at Wimbledon.* New York: Atheneum, 1984.

Weinberg, Robert S., and Billie Jean King. *Tennis: Winning the Mental Game.* Oxford, Ohio: Miami University Press, 2002.

Wertheim, L. Jon. *Venus Envy: Power Games, Teenage Vixens, and Million-Dollar Egos on the Women's Tennis Tour.* New York: HarperCollins, 2002.

Golf and Tennis Resources on the World Wide Web

Sports sites on the World Wide Web offer rich sources of information on athletes, teams, leagues, and the various sports themselves. Through careful searching, one can find up-to-date news on almost every sport; schedules; detailed statistics; sports; biographies of athletes; histories of teams, leagues, and individual sports; and much more. Since the previous edition of *Great Athletes* was published in 2001, both the numbers and quality of sports Web sites offering unrestricted access have increased significantly, making it easier than ever before to find information. However, while finding information on the Web has grown easier, evaluating the reliability of the information one finds may be growing harder.

The vast majority of sports Web sites are maintained by fans and bloggers whose objectivity and accuracy can be difficult to judge. Even articles on sites such as Wikipedia may present problems. Wikipedia articles are often detailed, up to date, and accurate, but they are not fully vetted and can be altered at any time by any user. Search engines such as Google and Yahoo! are efficient tools for finding information on athletes quickly, but if they are used carelessly, they may direct users to unreliable sites. For this reason, it is generally wise to begin any Web search with a list of Web sites that are proven to be reliable.

The purpose of this list is to help guide readers to the best Web sources for golf and tennis and to call attention to the variety of sites available online. Preference has been given to sites maintained by professional sports organizations, reputable news services, online magazines, halls of fame, and television networks, as well as other sites that provide accurate and unbiased information.

Most of the sites listed here can be found quickly by entering their names into an online search engine. If that approach does not work, one can simply type a URL (uniform resource locator) into the address line of a Web browser. Note that it is usually unnecessary to enter "http://" and that many sites can be found through more than a single URL. As still more sites are certain to emerge, it is advisable to use text searches to find new sites. Also, look for links to other sites on the pages that you visit.

Every site listed here was inspected and found to be working in January, 2009. Many of these sites offer links to merchandisers, but every effort has been made to avoid sites that serve primarily as sites for vendors and sports handicappers. URLs often change; if a link fails to work, search the name of the Web site with a standard Web search engine such as Google or Yahoo!

General Sites

AllSports
http://www.allsports.com

Black College Sports Review **(magazine)**
http://www.black-sports.com

Broadcast Sports
http://www.broadcastsports.com

Cable News Network (CNN)/Sports Illustrated (SI)
http://sportsillustrated.cnn.com

Canada's Sports Hall of Fame
http://www.cshof.ca

Canadian Broadcasting Corporation (CBC) Sports
http://cbc.ca/sports

CBS SportsLine
http://cbs.sportsline.com

College Sports Information Directors of America (CoSIDA)
http://www.cosida.com

ESPN
http://espn.go.com

Excite: Sports
http://sports.excite.com

Express Sport Live (European Sporting News)
http://www.sportslive.net

FOXSports
http://www.foxsports.com

History of Women in Sports Timeline
http://www.northnet.org/stlawrenceaauw/
    timeline.htm

Home Box Office (HBO) Sports
http://www.hbo.com/realsports

International Association for Sports Information
http://www.iasi.org/home.html

**MaxPreps: America's Source for High School
    Sports**
http://www.maxpreps.com/national/home.aspx

MSNBC Sports
http://nbcsports.msnbc.com

National Collegiate Athletic Association (NCAA)
http://www.ncaa.org

New England Sports Network
http://www.nesn.com

One on One Sports
http://www.1on1sports.com

PioneerPlanet: Sports
http://www.pioneerplanet.com/sports

Real Fans Sports Network
http://www.realfans.com

Rivals
http://www.rivals.com

Sport Science
http://www.exploratorium.edu/sports

The Sporting Life
http://www.sporting-life.com

SportingNews.com
http://www.sportingnews.com

Sports Illustrated **(magazine)**
http://www.pathfinder.com/si

Sports Illustrated for Kids
http://www.sikids.com

Sports Network
http://www.sportsnetwork.com/home.asp

Sports Schedules as You Like 'Em
http://www.cs.rochester.edu/u/ferguson/
    schedules

SportsFan Radio Network
http://www.sportsfanradio.com

SportsFeed (news)
http://www.sportsfeed.com

SportsLine USA
http://www.sportsline.com

Turner Network Television (TNT) Sports
http://tnt.turner.com/sports

USA Network Sports
http://www.usanetwork.com/sports

USA Today-Sports
http://www.usatoday.com

Women's Sports Information
http://www.womenssportsinformation.com

World Wide Web Virtual Library: Sports
http://sportsvl.com

Yahoo! Sports
http://dir.yahoo.com/recreation/sports

Golf

Golf (*Sports Illustrated* and CNN)
http://www.golf.com

The Golf Channel
http://www.thegolfchannel.com

Golf Courses in America
http://www.thegolfcourses.net

GolfCanada.com
http://www.golfcanada.com

GolfWorld in Partnership with ESPN
http://www.golfdigest.com/golfworld

Ladies Professional Golf Association
http://www.lpga.com

Official Site of the Masters Tournament
http://www.masters.com

PGA Tour
http://www.pgatour.com

Professional Golfers' Association (PGA) of America
http://www.pga.com/home

Ryder Cup
http://www.rydercup.com

United States Golf Association
http://www.usga.org

World Golf: Golfing the Globe
http://www.worldgolf.com

Tennis

Association of Tennis Professionals (ATP) Tour
http://www.atptour.com

Australian Open
http://www.australianopen.com

French Open
http://www.frenchopen.org

International Tennis Hall of Fame
http://www.tennisfame.com

NCAA Men's Tennis
http://www.ncaa.com/sports/m-tennis/ncaa-m-tennis-body.html

NCAA Women's Tennis
http://www.ncaa.com/sports/w-tennis/ncaa-w-tennis-body.html

Tennis Canada
http://www.tenniscanada.ca

Tennis Magazine
http://www.tennis.com

United States Tennis Association
http://www.usta.com

U.S. Open
http://www.usopen.org

USA Tennis
http://tennis.teamusa.org

Wimbledon
http://www.wimbledon.org

WTA Tour: Official Site of Women's Professional Tennis
http://www.wtatour.com

Glossary

Golf

albatross. *See* double eagle.

all-American: Nationwide honor awarded yearly to the best high school and college golfers. All-American honors are awarded by a variety of organizations and publications, and their prestige varies.

amateur: Golfer who competes for honors rather than tangible prizes or money and who does not attain professional status. College golfers are amateurs, but many later turn professional.

approach: Shot from the fairway aimed at the green.

apron: Area surrounding the green and bordering the fairway.

back nine: Final nine holes of a standard eighteen-hole golf course.

backswing: Lifting the golf club from the ground to behind the head.

ball-marker: Small indicator, such as a coin, to pinpoint the position of the golf ball on the green so the ball can be removed and later replaced, enabling other golfers within a group to complete their putts on an unobstructed green.

birdie: Finish of a golf hole at 1 stroke under par. *See also* bogey; eagle.

blast: Shot from the bunker, or sand trap, that sprays the ball and sand onto the green.

bogey: Finish of a golf hole at 1 stroke over par. *See also* birdie; double bogey.

break: How a ball rolls on the green after a putt.

British Open: Also known as the Open Championship in the United Kingdom, the oldest major PGA tournament. It is played every July.

bunker: Official term for a concave hazard positioned in a course to increase the difficulty of play. Typically filled with sand, bunkers are often called sand traps.

caddy: Golfer's assistant whose duties are to carry the player's clubs on the course and provide occasional advice on matters such as which clubs to use.

chip shot: Golf shot that reaches the green from a point just outside the green. Slightly longer shots are called pitches.

club: Apparatus used to strike a golf ball. Examples include irons, woods, wedges, and putters. Also called golf club.

course: Golf's field of play. A standard course has eighteen holes, but the sizes and layouts of courses vary greatly.

cup: Also called the hole—the small cylindrical chamber on the green into which players direct their balls.

divot: Small piece of turf dislodged from the ground by a player's swing.

double bogey: Finish of a golf hole at 2 strokes over par. *See also* bogey.

double eagle: Finish of a golf hole at 3 strokes under par. Also called an albatross. *See also* birdie; eagle.

drive: Generally, a long-yardage shot hit for distance and accuracy, as from the tee to any place on the fairway and occasionally to the green.

driving range: Area in which players practice their swings. Driving ranges are often adjacent to golf courses, from which they are usually separated by high chain-link fences.

eagle: Finish of a golf hole at 2 strokes under par. *See also* birdie; double eagle.

fairway: Expansive, well-maintained portion of a golf course situated between a tee and a putting green that does not include water hazards, roughs, or sand traps.

"Fore!": Exclamatory expression that a player about to drive a ball issues to warn other players and spectators to be wary of the possibility that the struck ball may veer off course.

front nine: First nine holes on an eighteen-hole course.

golf: Sport invented in Scotland during the fifteenth century in which players use clubs of various composition to strike a small, round ball across a grass course with the object of placing it in a series of holes. Scores are kept by recording the numbers of strokes players take to complete a course, with honors going to the player with the lowest cumulative score.

golf club. *See* club.

golf pro. *See* pro.

Grand Slam: Collection of the four most prestigious golf tournaments in the world, or the feat of winning them all in the same year. The men's Grand Slam comprises the Masters, U.S. Open, British Open, and Professional Golfers' Association (PGA) Championship. The women's Grand Slam includes the Ladies Professional Golf Association (LPGA) Championship, U.S. Women's Open, Nabisco-Dinah Shore, and du Maurier Classic.

green: Smooth, usually well-manicured portion of a golf course in which a hole is located and where putting is necessary to move the ball. Each standard golf course has eighteen separate greens.

grip: (1) Manner in which a player holds a club. (2) Rubber-coated part of a club at the top of its shaft.

handicap: Numerical rating system used as a means of evening out the range of abilities or skill levels among golfers. A handicap is the number of strokes a player may legitimately deduct from a scorecard after finishing a round or tournament, as compensation for playing against better golfers. A scratch golfer has no handicap.

hazard: Any of various types of obstacles deliberately built into golf courses, such as bunkers and water hazards.

hole: In its narrowest sense, the cup toward which players advance their balls. In a broader sense, a unit of the golf course that includes a tee, fairway, and green, as in a "nine-hole golf course" or "four-par hole." *See also* cup.

hole in one: Feat of hitting a ball into the cup in a single tee shot.

hook: Poorly stroked ball that drifts in a direction crossing the golfer's body—opposite the direction of a slice.

iron: Metal club with a flat face used to strike long, lofted shots. Golfers carry a selection of numbered irons (usually 3 through 9). The striking surface of each is attached to its shaft at a different angle. Irons with higher numbers give the ball more lift than those with lower numbers. *See also* sand wedge; wedge.

Ladies Professional Golf Association (LPGA): Official governing body of women's golf in the United States.

lag: Putt intended to approach a hole but not go in it.

lie: Place where a ball is positioned.

links: Golf course with few trees and near a body of water.

LPGA. *See* Ladies Professional Golf Association.

Masters, The: One of the PGA's four major golf tournaments, played every April at the Augusta National Golf Club in Augusta, Georgia.

match play: Competition in which players form teams and keep score from hole to hole rather than cumulatively.

mulligan: Slang term for a second-chance swing on a shot. The practice is not officially permitted by the rules but frequently practiced in social games. Also known as a do over.

National Collegiate Athletic Association (NCAA): Major governing body of collegiate sports, including golf, in the United States.

out of bounds: Area outside a course's boundaries. A ball hit out of bounds is recorded as a one-stroke penalty against the player.

par: (1) Number of strokes that expert golfers are expected to take to finish a hole or a course in ordinary weather conditions. Par for any given hole is determined by allowing a certain number of strokes from the tee to the green—considering the distance between the two—and allotting 2 strokes for putting. Results of golf matches are typically expressed in strokes over or under par for the entire matches. (2) Verb for scoring par.

PGA. *See* Professional Golfers' Association of America.

PGA Championship: One of golf's four major championships, played each August at an American course.

pin: Metal upright flagstaff that indicates where the hole, or cup, is.

pitch: Shot that positions a ball onto the green from a point just off the green. Shorter shots of this type are called chip shots.

playoff: Period of extended play when a match is tied after regulation play has been completed. In tournaments, playoffs are generally "sudden-death" competitions that end the moment one player falls behind in the score after a hole is completed.

pro: Abbreviation of professional for any professional golf player. Also an experienced golfer hired by a club to provide instruction for its members.

Professional Golfers' Association of America (PGA): Official governing body of golf in the United States, founded in 1916 and headquartered in Palm Beach Gardens, Florida.

putt: Golf stroke made with the ball on the green.

putter: Golf club that is normally used only to move balls to the cup after they reach the green. Putters are generally used in miniature golf.

putting green: Area adjacent to a golf course where golfers can practice putting.

Q-School: Qualifying School—a tournament spread over a week-long period that enables the top thirty golfers to earn the right to participate on either the PGA or LPGA Tour.

reading the green: Setting up a golf putt by closely studying the slope and surface of the green.

rough: Part of a course that borders a fairway; so named because its grass is also to grow tall and thick, making it difficult for players to return the ball to the fairway.

round: Eighteen holes of a golf course or a full game of golf. To play a "round" of golf is to play a game of eighteen holes.

Ryder Cup: Series of men's golf tournaments in which specially assembled teams of top professional players from the United States and various European countries compete. Begun in 1927 by British businessman Samuel Ryder for competition between professional golfers from the United States and Great Britain. Held in every odd-numbered year.

sand trap: Unofficial term for a bunker filled with loose sand.

sand wedge: Club used for hitting a ball out of a sand trap.

scratch golfer: Player who has a handicap of zero and is consequently expected to par the course.

shank: Poor shot struck near the shaft, instead of with the head, of a club.

short game: Shots taken within a chip-shot range of a hole.

skins: Form of match play in which players compete for points for each hole.

slice: Poorly stroked ball that drifts in a direction away from the golfer's body—opposite the direction of a hook.

Solheim Cup: Competition held every other year in which an American team of women professional golfers faces a European team.

stroke: (1) Controlled swing used to hit a ball.

(2) Unit of scoring in golf, one stroke being charged to a player for each shot taken, including penalty strokes.

swing: Movement used to hit a golf ball with a club.

tap-in: Golf ball close the hole that requires only a short putt.

tee: Small elevated cup fitted into the grass on which a golfer places a ball to begin playing a hole. The term is also used for the area where players begin playing a hole.

tee off: To begin play on a hole by driving the ball from a tee.

triple bogey: Finish of a golf hole at 3 strokes over par.

U.S. Open: Grand Slam event that is one of golf's four major championships. Begun in 1895, the tournament is hosted by the United States Golf Association and played each June at shifting venues.

United States Golf Association (USGA): Governing body for golf within the United States and Mexico, founded in 1894.

water hazard: Any body of water, such as a lake, pond, or stream, set within the boundaries of a golf course. The term does not encompass "casual water" that accumulates on a course from rain or other external sources.

wedge: Golf club that provides loft but not length, used for short distances. *See also* iron.

wood: Golf club with a large head used primarily for teeing off.

World Cup: Yearly international four-day tournament in which thirty-two two-person teams compete in stroke play matches.

Tennis

ace: (1) Serve delivered so effectively that the opponent cannot even hit it, thereby scoring a point for the server. (2) Point scored on such a serve. (3) Player noted for powerful serves.

advantage: Juncture in a tennis match when one player needs to score only one point to win.

alley: Designated area that extends the boundary for doubles matches. In a singles match, hitting the ball into the alley is considered out of bounds.

Association of Tennis Professionals (ATP): Governing body for men's professional tennis in the United States.

Australian Open: One of the Grand Slam tennis events, held each January in Melbourne, Australia.

backcourt: Area contained within the service line and the baseline on a court.

backhand: Stroke that originates from the side of the body opposite the racket hand, or forehand side. As the ball is hit, the back of the racket hand is facing the net.

backspin: Backward rotation on a tennis ball imparted by sweeping the racket face down and under the ball at the point of contact.

baseline: Back boundary of a tennis court.

baseline player: Tennis player whose game strategy is to remain mostly at the baseline to hit ground strokes, rarely moving to the net.

clay court: One of four types of playing surfaces used in tennis; made from a clay or a synthetic equivalent, giving the court a burnt orange color. The surface used at the French Open.

cross-court shot: Situation occurring when a ball moves diagonally across the net from one corner of the court to the other.

Davis Cup: Annual international men's tennis tournament between the top sixteen national teams of two to four players each, in both singles and doubles competition. The tournament is played out over the course of a year. Named for American player Dwight Davis.

deuce: Tie score.

double fault: Act of committing two faults in a row while serving from the same court. A server who commits a double fault loses the point.

doubles: Match between two teams of two players each. Mixed doubles matches pit teams each made up of one male and one female player against each other.

drop shot: Light lob over the net that usually forces the opponent to race to the net to hit the ball.

Federation Cup: Davis Cup of women's tennis, started in 1963 by the International Lawn Tennis Federation. Unlike Davis Cup teams, however, Federation Cup teams compete at one location to decide the Cup winner in one week's time. *See also* Davis Cup.

foot fault: Illegal act committed when a server places one or both feet on or over the baseline while making a serve.

forehand: Stroke originating from the same side of the body as the racket hand. As the ball is hit, the palm is facing the net.

French Open: One of the Grand Slam tennis events, played on a clay court and held each May and June at Roland Garros in Paris.

game: Basic unit of play in which sets are divided. During each game, one player or side (in doubles) serves until one side scores at least 4 points and leads by a margin of at least 2 points. A set is won when one side has won at least 6 games and leads by a margin of at least 2 games.

Grand Slam: Four major tennis tournaments; or the feat of winning them all in the same year. They are the same for both men and women: the Australian Open, the French Open, the Wimbledon Championships, and the U.S. Open.

ground stroke: Stroke executed by using the racket to strike the ball after it has bounced on the return. Ground strokes are usually hit from the backcourt area or from just beyond the baseline.

half volley: Stroke made by using the racket to strike the ball the instant it bounces up from the ground on the return.

International Tennis Federation: Governing body of worldwide tennis. "ITF" is the acronym for the French form of the body's name.

kill: Unhittable or unreturnable attacking shot that scores the point for the hitter.

lawn tennis: Original name for tennis; a racket sport played on grass and other surfaces in which a small semi-hard ball is batted between two or four competitors over a waist-high net.

let: Tennis stroke that does not count and must be replayed, as when a serve strikes the net before going over.

lob: High stroke intended to clear an opponent playing near the net.

love: Score of zero.

match: Completed tennis competition consisting of a series of sets.

mixed doubles: Match between two teams consisting of one man and one woman each.

National Collegiate Athletic Association (NCAA): Major governing body for collegiate sports, including tennis, in the United States.

overhead smash: Stroke that is hit from overhead with great force and power. Similar in motion to the serve. An effective put-away shot.

passing shot: Ball that is hit past and outside the reach of an opponent.

point: Score given when a serve or return can not be kept in play or when an opponent double faults.

put-away: Similar to a kill shot, an unhittable or unreturnable shot that scores a point for the hitter in volleyball, tennis, or badminton.

racket: Primary piece of tennis equipment, used to hit the ball. Traditionally made of wood, a racket has a handle at one end and a large open oval loop at the other end over which netting (usually made of nylon) is tightly stretched.

rally: Extended series of returns between opponents.

scoring format: A standard tennis match is scored in the following manner: Enough points wins a game; six (or more) games wins a set; two or three sets wins a match.

serve: Abbreviated form of "service"—the stroke that puts a ball into play.

serve-and-volley player: Tennis player whose game strategy is to rush the net aggressively after serving the ball, anticipating a return volley or put-away.

service court: One of the two rectangular areas marked on each side of the net. When a ball is served, it must land within the service area diametrically opposite the position from which the serve is made. Each service court is bounded by a service sideline on the outside, the service line within the court behind it, the center service line separating it from the adjacent service court, and the net.

service line: Outside boundary of each service court.

set: Score given for winning at least six games by two or more games.

singles: Match between two players.

stroke: Any of several methods of hitting the ball, such as the forehand and the backhand. Also, the controlled swing used to hit the ball.

tennis. Net game played by two teams of one or two players each who use rackets to propel a small ball back and forth across a low net that separates two equal sides of court. The object of the game is to score points by placing the ball within the opponent's half of the court so that it cannot be returned.

tie breaker: Method used to determine a winner when the score of a set is 6 to 6. Players must win sets by a margin of at least two games.

topspin: Forward rotation of a tennis ball imparted by sweeping the racket face up and over the ball at the point of contact.

U.S. Open: One of the four Grand Slam tennis events, held each August and September in Flushing, New York City.

volley: (1) Verb for hitting an airborne ball before it can touch the court. (2) Hitting the ball back and forth in continuous play.

Wimbledon: Oldest and most highly regarded international tennis event in the world. This annual Grand Slam tournament is officially called "The Lawn Tennis Championships" at the All-England Club in Church Road, Wimbledon, England.

Women's Tennis Association (WTA): Governing body for women's professional tennis.

Christopher Rager

Golfers Time Line

Birthdate	Golfer	Birthplace
June 30, 1834	Willie Park, Sr.	Wallyford, near Musselburgh, Scotland
May 9, 1870	Harry Vardon	Grouville, Jersey, Channel Islands
October 21, 1879	Willie Anderson	North Berwick, Scotland
December 21, 1892	Walter Hagen	Rochester, New York
May 8, 1893	Francis D. Ouimet	Brookline, Massachusetts
September 24, 1895	Tommy Armour	Edinburgh, Scotland
April 1, 1901	Johnny Farrell	White Plains, New York
February 27, 1902	Gene Sarazen	Harrison, New York
March 17, 1902	Bobby Jones	Atlanta, Georgia
June 20, 1903	Glenna Collett Vare	New Haven, Connecticut
November 28, 1906	Henry Picard	Plymouth, Massachusetts
May 24, 1910	Jimmy Demaret	Houston, Texas
June 23, 1910	Lawson Little	Newport, Rhode Island
February 4, 1912	Byron Nelson	near Waxahachie, Texas
May 27, 1912	Sam Snead	Ashwood, Virginia
August 13, 1912	Ben Hogan	Stephenville, Texas
August 1, 1914	Lloyd Mangrum	Trenton, Texas
February 13, 1918	Patty Berg	Minneapolis, Minnesota
March 3, 1920	Julius Boros	Fairfield, Connecticut
June 2, 1922	Charlie Sifford	Charlotte, North Carolina
April 14, 1923	Roberto De Vicenzo	Buenos Aires, Argentina
September 7, 1923	Louise Suggs	Atlanta, Georgia
April 13, 1929	Marilynn Smith	Topeka, Kansas
September 10, 1929	Arnold Palmer	Youngstown, Pennsylvania
June 24, 1931	Billy Casper	San Diego, California
March 9, 1934	Marlene Streit	Cereal, Alberta, Canada
February 14, 1935	Mickey Wright	San Diego, California
November 1, 1935	Gary Player	Johannesburg, South Africa
April 4, 1939	JoAnne Carner	Kirkland, Washington
September 27, 1939	Kathy Whitworth	Monahans, Texas
December 1, 1939	Lee Trevino	Dallas, Texas
January 21, 1940	Jack Nicklaus	Columbus, Ohio
September 4, 1942	Ray Floyd	Fort Bragg, North Carolina
July 7, 1944	Tony Jacklin	Scunthorpe, North Lincolnshire, England
January 29, 1945	Donna Caponi	Detroit, Michigan
February 18, 1945	Judy Rankin	St. Louis, Missouri
June 3, 1945	Hale Irwin	Joplin, Missouri
October 13, 1945	Hisako Higuchi	Kawagoe City, Saitama Prefecture, Japan
September 10, 1947	Larry Nelson	Fort Payne, Alabama
June 4, 1948	Sandra Post	Oakville, Ontario, Canada
September 4, 1949	Tom Watson	Kansas City, Missouri
December 9, 1949	Tom Kite	McKinney, Texas
March 24, 1951	Pat Bradley	Westford, Massachusetts

Birthdate	*Golfer*	*Birthplace*
April 2, 1951	Ayako Okamoto	Hiroshima Prefecture, Japan
January 11, 1952	Ben Crenshaw	Austin, Texas
January 30, 1955	Curtis Strange	Norfolk, Virginia
February 10, 1955	Greg Norman	Mount Isa, Queensland, Australia
August 13, 1955	Betsy King	Reading, Pennsylvania
October 27, 1956	Patty Sheehan	Middlebury, Vermont
January 6, 1957	Nancy Lopez	Torrance, California
January 28, 1957	Nick Price	Durban, South Africa
January 30, 1957	Payne Stewart	Springfield, Missouri
April 9, 1957	Seve Ballesteros	Pedreña, Spain
July 18, 1957	Nick Faldo	Welwyn Garden City, Hertfordshire, England
August 27, 1957	Bernhard Langer	Anhausen, West Germany (now Germany)
October 3, 1959	Fred Couples	Seattle, Washington
June 24, 1960	Juli Inkster	Santa Cruz, California
February 22, 1963	Vijay Singh	Lautoka, Fiji
April 13, 1964	Davis Love III	Charlotte, North Carolina
April 28, 1966	John Daly	Carmichael, California
February 3, 1969	Retief Goosen	Pietersburg (now Polokwane), South Africa
October 17, 1969	Ernie Els	Johannesburg, South Africa
May 12, 1970	Jim Furyk	West Chester, Pennsylvania
June 16, 1970	Phil Mickelson	San Diego, California
October 9, 1970	Annika Sorenstam	Bro, near Stockholm, Sweden
August 31, 1971	Pádraig Harrington	Ballyroan, Dublin, Ireland
December 21, 1974	Karrie Webb	Ayr, Queensland, Australia
December 30, 1975	Tiger Woods	Cypress, California
September 28, 1977	Se Ri Pak	Taejon, South Korea
March 6, 1979	Grace Park	Seoul, South Korea
November 15, 1981	Lorena Ochoa	Guadalajara, Mexico
October 11, 1989	Michelle Wie	Honolulu, Hawaii

Tennis Players Time Line

Birthdate	Player	Birthplace
April 15, 1873	Juliette Atkinson	Rahway, New Jersey
December 20, 1886	Hazel Wightman	Healdsburg, California
February 10, 1893	Bill Tilden	Philadelphia, Pennsylvania
August 13, 1898	Jean Borotra	Domaine du Pouy, France
May 24, 1899	Suzanne Lenglen	Compiègne, France
December 14, 1901	Henri Cochet	Lyons, France
July 2, 1904	René Lacoste	Paris, France
October 6, 1905	Helen Wills Moody	Centerville (now Fremont), California
August 26, 1906	Bunny Austin	London, England
May 18, 1909	Fred Perry	Stockport, Cheshire, England
September 28, 1913	Alice Marble	Beckwourth, California
June 13, 1915	Don Budge	Oakland, California
February 25, 1918	Bobby Riggs	Los Angeles, California
March 4, 1918	Margaret Osborne DuPont	Joseph, Oregon
August 1, 1921	Jack Kramer	Las Vegas, Nevada
August 30, 1923	Vic Seixas	Philadelphia, Pennsylvania
August 25, 1927	Althea Gibson	Silver, South Carolina
May 9, 1928	Pancho Gonzales	Los Angeles, California
July 13, 1928	Sven Davidson	Borås, Sweden
September 17, 1934	Maureen Connolly	San Diego, California
November 2, 1934	Ken Rosewall	Sydney, New South Wales, Australia
November 23, 1934	Lew Hoad	Glebe, New South Wales, Australia
March 24, 1936	Alex Olmedo	Arequipa, Peru
November 3, 1936	Roy Emerson	Blackbutt, Queensland, Australia
August 9, 1938	Rod Laver	Rockhampton, Queensland, Australia
August 16, 1939	Tony Trabert	Cincinnati, Ohio
October 11, 1939	María Bueno	São Paulo, Brazil
July 16, 1942	Margaret Court	Albury, New South Wales, Australia
December 25, 1942	Françoise Durr	Algiers, Algeria
July 10, 1943	Arthur Ashe	Richmond, Virginia
November 22, 1943	Billie Jean King	Long Beach, California
May 23, 1944	John Newcombe	Sydney, Australia
July 10, 1945	Virginia Wade	Bournemouth, Dorset, England
December 14, 1946	Stan Smith	Pasadena, California
July 31, 1951	Evonne Goolagong	Griffith, New South Wales, Australia
August 17, 1952	Guillermo Vilas	Buenos Aires, Argentina
September 2, 1952	Jimmy Connors	East St. Louis, Illinois
December 21, 1954	Chris Evert	Fort Lauderdale, Florida
June 6, 1956	Björn Borg	Södertalje, Sweden
October 18, 1956	Martina Navratilova	Prague, Czechoslovakia (now in Czech Republic)

Birthdate	Player	Birthplace
February 16, 1959	John McEnroe	Wiesbaden, West Germany (now in Germany)
March 7, 1960	Ivan Lendl	Ostrava, Czechoslovakia (now in Czech Republic)
May 18, 1960	Yannick Noah	Sedan, Ardennes, France
July 4, 1962	Pam Shriver	Baltimore, Maryland
December 12, 1962	Tracy Austin	Palos Verdes, California
August 22, 1964	Mats Wilander	Växjö, Sweden
January 19, 1966	Stefan Edberg	Västervik, Sweden
November 22, 1967	Boris Becker	Leimen, Germany
October 2, 1968	Jana Novotná	Brno, Czechoslovakia (now in Czech Republic)
June 14, 1969	Steffi Graf	Mannheim, West Germany (now in Germany)
April 29, 1970	Andre Agassi	Las Vegas, Nevada
May 16, 1970	Gabriela Sabatini	Buenos Aires, Argentina
August 17, 1970	Jim Courier	Sanford, Florida
August 12, 1971	Pete Sampras	Washington, D.C.
December 18, 1971	Arantxa Sanchez-Vicario	Barcelona, Spain
February 22, 1972	Michael Chang	Hoboken, New Jersey
December 2, 1973	Monica Seles	Novi Sad, Yugoslavia (now in Serbia)
January 15, 1975	Mary Pierce	Montreal, Quebec, Canada
March 29, 1976	Jennifer Capriati	New York, New York
June 8, 1976	Lindsay Davenport	Palos Verdes, California
August 27, 1976	Carlos Moya	Palma de Majorca, Spain
December 28, 1979	James Blake	Yonkers, New York
June 17, 1980	Venus Williams	Lynwood, California
September 30, 1980	Martina Hingis	Košice, Czechoslovakia (now in Slovakia)
August 8, 1981	Roger Federer	Basel, Switzerland
September 26, 1981	Serena Williams	Saginaw, Michigan
October 15, 1981	Elena Dementieva	Moscow, Russia
June 1, 1982	Justine Henin	Liège, Belgium
August 30, 1982	Andy Roddick	Omaha, Nebraska
June 8, 1983	Kim Clijsters	Bilzen, Belgium
June 3, 1986	Rafael Nadal	Manacor, Majorca, Spain
April 19, 1987	Maria Sharapova	Nyagan, Russia
November 6, 1987	Ana Ivanovic	Belgrade, Yugoslavia (now in Serbia)

All-Time Great Players

World Golf Hall of Fame

Established in Pinehurst, North Carolina, in 1974, the World Golf Hall of Fame later absorbed two older halls of fame and moved its headquarters to St. Augustine, Florida. In contrast to similar institutions for some other sports, the World Golf Hall of Fame does not make retirement from playing a requirement for membership. However, its nominees must record ten victories in approved tournaments, be at least forty years old, and also have been members of the PGA or LPGA Tour for ten years. Membership is also open to other contributors to the game, including promoters, organizers, agents, writers, golf course designers, and celebrity golfers, such as Bing Crosby, Bob Hope, and Dinah Shore.

Only members inducted for their play are listed here. Their years of induction are given in parentheses; dates earlier than 1974 are those of golfers inducted by the halls that the World Golf Hall of Fame absorbed.

Amy Alcott (1999)
Willie Anderson (1975)
Isao Aoki (2004)
Tommy Armour (1976)
John Ball, Jr. (1977)
Seve Ballesteros (1999)
Jim Barnes (1989)
Patty Berg (1951)
Tommy Bolt (2002)
Julius Boros (1982)
Pat Bradley (1991)
James Braid (1976)
Jack Burke, Jr. (2000)
Donna Caponi (2001)
JoAnne Carner (1982)
Joe Carr (2007)
Billy Casper (1978)
Sir Bob Charles (2008)
Harry Cooper (1992)
Henry Cotton (1980)
Ben Crenshaw (2002)
Beth Daniel (2000)
Jimmy Demaret (1983)
Roberto De Vicenzo (1989)
Leo Diegel (2003)
Chick Evans (1975)
Nick Faldo (1998)
Ray Floyd (1989)
Hubert Green (2007)
Ralph Guldahl (1981)
Walter Hagen (1974)
Marlene Bauer Hagge (2002)
Sandra Haynie (1977)
Hisako Higuchi (2003)
Harold Hilton (1978)

Ben Hogan (1974)
Dorothy Campbell Hurd Howe (1978)
Juli Inkster (2000)
Hale Irwin (1992)
Tony Jacklin (2002)
Betty Jameson (1951)
Bobby Jones (1974)
Betsy King (1995)
Tom Kite (2004)
Bernhard Langer (2002)
Lawson Little (1980)
Gene Littler (1990)
Bobby Locke (1977)
Nancy Lopez (1987)
Mark McCormack (2006)
Charles Blair Macdonald (2007)
Lloyd Mangrum (1999)
Carol Mann (1977)
Cary Middlecoff (1986)
Johnny Miller (1998)
Tom Morris, Jr. (1975)
Tom Morris, Sr. (1976)
Kel Nagle (2007)
Byron Nelson (1974)
Larry Nelson (2006)
Jack Nicklaus (1974)
Greg Norman (2001)
Ayako Okamoto (2005)
Francis Ouimet (1974)
Se Ri Pak (2007)
Arnold Palmer (1974)
Willie Park, Sr. (2005)
Henry Picard (2006)
Gary Player (1974)

Nick Price (2003)
Judy Rankin (2000)
Betsy Rawls (1960)
Allan Robertson (2001)
Chi Chi Rodriguez (1992)
Paul Runyan (1990)
Gene Sarazen (1974)
Patty Sheehan (1993)
Denny Shute (2008)
Charlie Sifford (2004)
Vijay Singh (2006)
Horton Smith (1990)
Marilynn Smith (2006)
Sam Snead (1974)
Annika Sorenstam (2003)
Payne Stewart (2001)
Curtis Strange (2007)
Marlene Stewart Streit (2004)
Louise Suggs (1951)
J. H. Taylor (1975)
Carol Semple Thompson (2008)
Peter Thomson (1988)
Jerry Travers (1976)
Walter Travis (1979)
Lee Trevino (1981)
Harry Vardon (1974)
Glenna Collett Vare (1975)
Tom Watson (1988)
Karrie Webb (2005)
Joyce Wethered (1975)
Kathy Whitworth (1975)
Herbert Warren Wind (2008)
Craig Wood (2008)
Mickey Wright (1964)
Babe Didrikson Zaharias (1951)

International Tennis Hall of Fame

Established in 1953 by James Van Alan and sanctioned by the U.S. Tennis Association in 1954, the International Tennis Hall of Fame honors retired players and other contributors to the game of tennis. The organization was known as the National Tennis Hall of Fame until 1976 and is headquartered in Newport, Rhode Island. Players nominated to the hall must have been retired from significant competition for at least five years; nominees are then elected by members of the international tennis media. Of the 211 members elected through 2009, 85 percent have been players. Those players are listed below, with their nationalities and years of induction.

Fred Alexander, United States (1961)
Wilmer Allison, United States (1963)
Manuel Alonso, Spain (1977)
Malcolm Anderson, Australia (2000)
Arthur Ashe, United States (1985)
Juliette Atkinson, United States (1974)
Henry Austin, Great Britain (1997)
Tracy Austin, United States (1992)
Boris Becker, Germany (2003)
Karl Behr, United States (1969)
Pauline Betz, United States (1965)
Björn Borg, Sweden (1987)
Jean Borotra, France (1976)
Lesley Turner Bowrey, Australia (1997)
John Bromwich, Australia (1984)
Norman Brookes, Australia (1977)
Louise Brough, United States (1967)
Mary Kendall Browne, United States (1957)
Jacques Brugnon, France (1976)
Earl Buchholz, Jr., United States (2005)
Don Budge, United States (1964)
María Bueno, Brazil (1964)
May Bundy, United States (1956)
Mabel Cahill, Ireland (1976)
Oliver Campbell, United States (1955)
Rosie Casals, United States (1996)
Malcolm Chace, United States (1961)
Dorothea Chambers, Great Britain (1981)
Michael Chang, United States (2008)
Dorothy Cheney, United States (2004)
Clarence Clark, United States (1983)
Joseph Clark, United States (1955)
William Clothier, United States (1956)
Henri Cochet, France (1976)
Maureen Connolly, United States (1968)
Jimmy Connors, United States (1998)
Ashley Cooper, Australia (1991)

Jim Courier, United States (2005)
Margaret Court, Australia (1979)
Gottfried von Cramm, Germany (1977)
Jack Crawford, Australia (1979)
Sven Davidson, Sweden (2007)
Dwight F. Davis, United States (1956)
Donald Dell, United States (2009)
Lottie Dod, Great Britain (1983)
John Doeg, United States (1962)
Lawrence Doherty, Great Britain (1980)
Reggie Doherty, Great Britain (1980)
Jaroslav Drobny, Czech Republic (1983)
James Dwight, United States (1955)
Margaret Osborne DuPont, United States (1967)
Francoise Durr, France (2003)
Stefan Edberg, Sweden (2004)
Roy Emerson, Australia (1982)
Pierre Etchebaster, France (1978)
Chris Evert, United States (1995)
Bob Falkenburg, United States/Brazil (1974)
Neale Fraser, Australia (1984)
Shirley Fry, United States (1970)
Charles Garland, United States (1969)
Andres Gimeno, Spain (2009)
Pancho Gonzalez, United States (1968)
Bitsy Grant, United States (1972)
Althea Gibson, United States (1971)
Evonne Goolagong, Australia (1988)
Steffi Graf, Germany (2004)
Harold Hackett, United States (1961)
Ellen Hansell, United States (1965)
Darlene Hard, United States (1973)
Doris Hart, United States (1969)
Bob Hewitt, Australia/South Africa (1992)
Lew Hoad, Australia (1980)
Harry Hopman, Australia (1978)

Hazel Wightman Hotchkiss, United States (1957)

Fred Hovey, United States (1974)

Joe Hunt, United States (1966)

Frank Hunter, United States (1961)

Helen Jacobs, United States (1962)

William Johnston, United States (1958)

Ann Jones, Great Britain (1985)

Billie Jean King, United States (1987)

Jan Kodeš, Czechoslovakia (1990)

Karel Koželuh, Czechoslovakia (2006)

Jack Kramer, United States (1968)

Rene Lacoste, France (1976)

William Larned, United States (1956)

Art Larsen, United States (1956)

Rod Laver, Australia (1981)

Ivan Lendl, Czechoslovakia/United States (2001)

Suzanne Lenglen, France (1978)

George Lott, United States (1964)

John McEnroe, United States (1999)

Ken McGregor, Australia (1999)

Kathleen McKane Godfree, Great Britain (1978)

Chuck McKinley, United States (1986)

Maurice McLoughlin, United States (1957)

Frew McMillan, South Africa (1992)

Don McNeill, United States (1965)

Gene Mako, United States (1973)

Molla Mallory, Norway (1958)

Hana Mandlíková, Czechoslovakia/Australia (1994)

Alice Marble, United States (1964)

Alastair Martin, United States (1973)

William McChesney Martin, United States (1982)

Dan Maskell, Great Britain (1996)

Elisabeth Moore, United States (1971)

Angela Mortimer, Great Britain (1993)

Gardnar Mulloy, United States (1972)

Robert Murray, United States (1958)

Ilie Nastase, Romania (1991)

Martina Navratilova, Czechoslovakia/United States (2000)

John Newcombe, Australia (1986)

Yannick Noah, France (2005)

Jana Novotná, Czech Republic (2005)

Hans Nüsslein, Germany (2006)

Betty Nuthall, Great Britain (1977)

Alex Olmedo, Peru/United States (1987)

Rafael Osuna, Mexico (1979)

Sarah Palfrey, United States (1963)

Frank Parker, United States (1966)

Gerald Patterson, Australia (1989)

Budge Patty, United States (1977)

Theodore Pell, United States (1966)

Fred Perry, Great Britain (1975)

Tom Pettitt, Great Britain (1982)

Nicola Pietrangeli, Italy (1986)

Adrian Quist, Australia (1984)

Patrick Rafter, Australia (2006)

Dennis Ralston, United States (1987)

Ernest Renshaw, Great Britain (1983)

William Renshaw, Great Britain (1983)

Vincent Richards, United States (1961)

Nancy Richey, United States (2003)

Bobby Riggs, United States (1967)

Tony Roche, Australia (1986)

Ellen Roosevelt, United States (1975)

Mervyn Rose, Australia (2001)

Ken Rosewall, Australia (1980)

Dorothy Round, Great Britain (1986)

Elizabeth Ryan, United States (1972)

Gabriela Sabatini, Argentina (2006)

Pete Sampras, United States (2007)

Arantxa Sanchez-Vicario, Spain (2007)

Manuel Santana, Spain (1985)

Dick Savitt, United States (1976)

Ted Schroeder, United States (1966)

Eleonora Sears, United States (1968)

Richard Sears, United States (1955)

Frank Sedgman, Australia (1979)

Pancho Segura, Ecuador (1984)

Vic Seixas, United States (1971)

Monica Seles, Yugoslavia (2009)

Frank Shields, United States (1964)

Pam Shriver, United States (2002)

Henry Slocum, United States (1955)

Stan Smith, United States (1987)

Fred Stolle, Australia (1985)

Bill Talbert, United States (1967)

William Tilden, United States (1959)

Lance Tingay, Great Britain (1982)

Bertha Toulmin Townsend, United States (1974)

Tony Trabert, United States (1970)

John Van Ryn, United States (1963)

Guillermo Vilas, Argentina (1991)

Ellsworth Vines, United States (1962)

Virginia Wade, Great Britain (1989)

Marie Wagner, United States (1969)

Maud Wallach Barger, United States (1958)
Holcombe Ward, United States (1956)
Watson Washburn, United States (1965)
Malcolm Whitman, United States (1955)
Mats Wilander, Sweden (2002)
Anthony Wilding, New Zealand (1978)

Richard Williams, United States (1957)
Helen Moody Wills, United States (1969)
Sidney Wood, United States (1964)
Robert Wrenn, United States (1955)
Beals Wright, United States (1956)

Tennis *Magazine's Forty Greatest Tennis Players*

In 2005, *Tennis* magazine celebrated its fortieth anniversary by selecting the forty greatest tennis players of the previous four decades.

1. Pete Sampras, United States
2. Martina Navratilova, Czechoslovakia/ United States
3. Steffi Graf, Germany
4. Chris Evert, United States
5. Björn Borg, Sweden
6. Margaret Court, Australia
7. Jimmy Connors, United States
8. Rod Laver, Australia
9. Billie Jean King, United States
10. Ivan Lendl, Czechoslovakia/United States
11. John McEnroe, United States
12. Andre Agassi, United States
13. Monica Seles, Yugoslavia/United States
14. Stefan Edberg, Sweden
15. Mats Wilander, Sweden
16. John Newcombe, Australia
17. Serena Williams, United States
18. Boris Becker, Germany
19. Roger Federer, Switzerland
20. Ken Rosewall, Australia
21. Roy Emerson, Australia
22. Martina Hingis, Switzerland
23. Evonne Goolagong, Australia
24. Guillermo Vilas, Argentina
25. Venus Williams, United States
26. Jim Courier, United States
27. Arantxa Sánchez Vicario, Spain
28. Ilie Nastase, Romania
29. Lindsay Davenport, United States
30. Arthur Ashe, United States
31. Justine Henin, Belgium
32. Tracy Austin, United States
33. Hana Mandlíková, Czechoslovakia/Australia
34. Lleyton Hewitt, Australia
35. Stan Smith, United States
36. Jennifer Capriati, United States
37. Gustavo Kuerten, Brazil
38. Virginia Wade, United Kingdom
39. Patrick Rafter, Australia
40. Gabriela Sabatini, Argentina

Indexes

Name Index

Country Index